IMMIGRATION LAW AND PROCEDURE
IN A NUTSHELL
SIXTH EDITION

By

DAVID WEISSBRODT

Regents Professor of Law and
Fredrikson & Byron Professor of Law
University of Minnesota Law School

LAURA DANIELSON

Immigration Department Chair,
Fredrikson & Byron P.A., and
Adjunct Professor of Law
University of Minnesota Law School

A Thomson Reuters business

Mat #40775921

COPYRIGHT © 1984, 1989, 1992 WEST PUBLISHING CO.
© West, a Thomson business, 1998
© 2005 David Weissbrodt and Laura Danielson
© 2011 David Weissbrodt and Laura Danielson

Printed in the United States of America

ISBN: 978-0-314-19944-7

PREFACE

This brief text is designed to assist students in obtaining an overview of the material that might be expected to be found in a course on immigration law and procedure.

When the first edition of this Nutshell was written, there did not yet exist a standard casebook on immigration law and it was unclear what substance belonged in a course on immigration law and procedure. At that time only a few law schools considered immigration law worthy of a course. Since then many major law schools have decided to offer immigration law courses and three principal coursebooks have been published: Thomas Alexander Aleinikoff et al., Immigration and Citizenship: Process and Policy (6th ed. 2008); Richard Boswell, Immigration and Nationality Law: Cases and Materials (4th ed. 2010); and Stephen Legomsky and Cristina M. Rodriguez, Immigration and Refugee Law and Policy (5th ed. 2009, 2010 Update). It was gratifying to see that several parts of this Nutshell were reprinted and other views reflected in those coursebooks.

This Nutshell presents the information that a student should want to know about the immigration process as it functions in the United States. With the enactment of new immigration statutes in 1996,

2001, 2002, 2005, and 2010, immigration law and procedures have undergone significant change. In addition to those legislative changes, political upheaval throughout the world has made immigration a far more visible and controversial issue—leading, in turn, to a constantly evolving body of laws, regulations, decisions, and policies. The sixth edition of this text is organized in six parts to reflect these changes and make them as comprehensible and accessible as possible.

The *first* part—chapters 1 through 4—provides a general overview of the history, constitutional source, and institutional structure of immigration law. In addition to tracing the evolution of immigration law and history in the U.S., the first part discusses the increasing recognition of the federal power to regulate immigration and describes the federal agencies and congressional committees responsible for the formulation and implementation of immigration law.

The *second* part—chapters 5 through 7—covers the various standards and application procedures for immigrant, nonimmigrant, and student visas. It should be noted, however, that this Nutshell does not attempt to serve as a manual for practitioners or potential immigrants and should not be considered legal advice.

In part *three*, chapters 8 and 9 explain the grounds for requiring a non-citizen to depart from the United States and the procedures for removal and denial of admission.

In the *fourth* part, chapters 10 and 11 discuss refugee and asylum issues and summarize international law as it relates to immigration.

Because immigration law is ultimately founded upon the relationship between the individual and the state, part *five*—chapters 12 and 13—focuses on citizenship and the rights of non-citizens in the United States.

Part *six*—chapters 14 through 17—identifies several ethical issues which immigration lawyers confront and which may help to clarify for students the nature of the immigration process. Chapters 16 and 17 contain a brief conclusion and a bibliography.

The authors wish to thank several present and former law students who assisted in the preparation of this Nutshell. The students who assisted with the first, second, third, and fourth editions are identified in those respective editions. The authors wish to thank Mila Gumin, Chas Higgins, and Nathaniel Nesbitt for their help in connection with the present sixth edition. Mary Rumsey provided valuable bibliographical assistance—especially on the last chapter. Nicole Gruhot and Janina Urman did excellent secretarial work to make the sixth edition possible.

Benjamin Casper, Eric Cooperstein, Karen P. Ellingson, Michele Garnett McKenzie, and Jennifer Prestholdt generously took time from their busy law practices to review the previous versions of the manuscript and to give much assistance. The authors, of course, must take ultimate responsibility for what remains in this book and what the Nutshell format required to be deleted.

DAVID WEISSBRODT
LAURA DANIELSON

Minneapolis, Minnesota
August 2010

EXPLANATORY NOTES

We have attempted to follow the format of other Nutshell volumes. Accordingly, cases have been cited only where they represent relatively significant landmarks or where they clarify key issues. The text ordinarily contains only the name of the case, the court of decision, and the date. The student will find the full citation in the Table of Authorities, which follows the Outline. Due to limitations of space and format, some cases are omitted where they would have supported statements in the text and one case is often cited where many others would have been usable as authority.

Immigration law is based considerably upon statutes and regulations. Hence, the text contains frequent references to the principal statutes and regulations, but for reasons of space the citations have been abbreviated in the text. Where both a statute and regulation appear relevant, only the statute is cited. The Table of Authorities contains fuller references to cases, statutes, regulations, and other relevant material.

Because the Nutshell format does not admit footnotes, this volume often omits references to secondary material and other sources, even where such citations clearly exist. The bibliography in the last chapter attempts to redress this problem by listing at least most of the principal sources for the use of the serious student who may want to read more.

OUTLINE

Page

Page

Page

TABLE OF CASES

References are to Pages

TABLE OF CASES

TABLE OF OTHER AUTHORITIES

UNITED STATES

UNITED STATES CONSTITUTION

LIII

TABLE OF OTHER AUTHORITIES

UNITED STATES CONSTITUTION

UNITED STATES CODE ANNOTATED
7 U.S.C.A.—Agriculture

8 U.S.C.A.—Aliens and Nationality

18 U.S.C.A.—Crimes and Criminal Procedure

TABLE OF OTHER AUTHORITIES

UNITED STATES CODE ANNOTATED
18 U.S.C.A.—Crimes and Criminal Procedure

21 U.S.C.A.—Food and Drugs

22 U.S.C.A.—Foreign Relations and Intercourse

26 U.S.C.A.—Internal Revenue Code

TABLE OF OTHER AUTHORITIES

TABLE OF OTHER AUTHORITIES

STATUTES AT LARGE

TABLE OF OTHER AUTHORITIES

STATUTES AT LARGE

TABLE OF OTHER AUTHORITIES

STATUTES AT LARGE

POPULAR NAME ACTS

ANTITERRORISM AND EFFECTIVE DEATH PENALTY ACT

HOMELAND SECURITY ACT

IMMIGRATION ACT OF 1990

ILLEGAL IMMIGRATION REFORM AND IMMIGRANT RESPONSIBILITY ACT OF 1996

ILLEGAL IMMIGRATION REFORM AND IMMIGRANT RESPONSIBILITY ACT OF 1996

IMMIGRATION AND NATIONALITY ACT

IMMIGRATION AND NATIONALITY ACT

TABLE OF OTHER AUTHORITIES

IMMIGRATION AND NATIONALITY ACT

TABLE OF OTHER AUTHORITIES

IMMIGRATION AND NATIONALITY ACT

TABLE OF OTHER AUTHORITIES

IMMIGRATION AND NATIONALITY ACT

TABLE OF OTHER AUTHORITIES

IMMIGRATION AND NATIONALITY ACT

TABLE OF OTHER AUTHORITIES

IMMIGRATION AND NATIONALITY ACT

TABLE OF OTHER AUTHORITIES

IMMIGRATION AND NATIONALITY ACT

TABLE OF OTHER AUTHORITIES

IMMIGRATION AND NATIONALITY ACT

IMMIGRATION AND NATIONALITY ACT

TABLE OF OTHER AUTHORITIES

IMMIGRATION AND NATIONALITY ACT

TABLE OF OTHER AUTHORITIES

IMMIGRATION AND NATIONALITY ACT

TABLE OF OTHER AUTHORITIES

IMMIGRATION AND NATIONALITY ACT

TABLE OF OTHER AUTHORITIES

IMMIGRATION AND NATIONALITY ACT

TABLE OF OTHER AUTHORITIES

IMMIGRATION AND NATIONALITY ACT

TABLE OF OTHER AUTHORITIES

IMMIGRATION AND NATIONALITY ACT

TABLE OF OTHER AUTHORITIES

IMMIGRATION AND NATIONALITY ACT

TABLE OF OTHER AUTHORITIES

IMMIGRATION AND NATIONALITY ACT

IMMIGRATION REFORM AND CONTROL ACT

NATIONALITY ACT OF 1940

SELECTIVE SERVICE ACT OF 1940

TABLE OF OTHER AUTHORITIES

MINNESOTA RULES OF PROFESSIONAL CONDUCT

PROPOSED FEDERAL RULES OF CRIMINAL PROCEDURE

CODE OF FEDERAL REGULATIONS

TABLE OF OTHER AUTHORITIES

CODE OF FEDERAL REGULATIONS

TABLE OF OTHER AUTHORITIES

CODE OF FEDERAL REGULATIONS

TABLE OF OTHER AUTHORITIES

CODE OF FEDERAL REGULATIONS

TABLE OF OTHER AUTHORITIES

CODE OF FEDERAL REGULATIONS

TABLE OF OTHER AUTHORITIES

CODE OF FEDERAL REGULATIONS

TABLE OF OTHER AUTHORITIES

CODE OF FEDERAL REGULATIONS

TABLE OF OTHER AUTHORITIES

CODE OF FEDERAL REGULATIONS

TABLE OF OTHER AUTHORITIES

CODE OF FEDERAL REGULATIONS

FEDERAL REGISTER

TABLE OF OTHER AUTHORITIES

FEDERAL REGISTER

EXECUTIVE ORDERS

INTERPRETIVE RELEASE

TABLE OF OTHER AUTHORITIES

INTERPRETIVE RELEASE

OPERATING INSTRUCTIONS

INTERNATIONAL INSTRUMENTS

────────

AFRICAN CHARTER ON HUMAN AND PEOPLE'S RIGHTS

AMERICAN CONVENTION ON HUMAN RIGHTS

CONVENTION ON THE RIGHTS OF THE CHILD

EUROPEAN CONVENTION ON HUMAN RIGHTS

TABLE OF OTHER AUTHORITIES

EUROPEAN CONVENTION ON HUMAN RIGHTS

INTERNATIONAL COVENANT ON CIVIL AND POLITICAL RIGHTS

INTERNATIONAL CONVENTION ON THE PROTECTION OF MIGRANT WORKERS

REFUGEE CONVENTION OF 1951

UNITED NATIONS GENERAL ASSEMBLY RESOLUTION 2312 (XXII)

TABLE OF OTHER AUTHORITIES

UNIVERSAL DECLARATION OF HUMAN RIGHTS

IMMIGRATION LAW AND PROCEDURE

IN A NUTSHELL

SIXTH EDITION

CHAPTER 1

HISTORY OF U.S. IMMIGRA-TION LAW AND POLICY

§ 1-1 COLONIAL IMMIGRATION

Because an immigrant is defined by *Black's Law Dictionary* as one who leaves a country to settle permanently in another to live, one tends to think of United States immigration as dating from the nation's inception. Most anthropologists, however, believe that the first newcomers to the region that is now the United States entered from Asia over tens of thousands of years ago across the land bridge where the Bering Strait now lies and from South America. These peoples first settled the western regions, and distinct cultural groups lived in areas spanning to the Atlantic Ocean before any European explorers or later settlers arrived.

Much later, in settling the English colonies, immigrants arrived freely and were at first welcomed by other Europeans already settled. Immigration was limited principally by the cost of travel, disease, and conflict with indigenous inhabitants. By 1640, the population of the colonies had reached approximately 25,000. Population records can only suggest the rate of new arrivals because no immigration records were kept.

The newcomers to the colonies in the years before the American Revolution came from many places and for diverse reasons. Most Europeans—English, French, German, Dutch, Spanish, and Portuguese—came for economic reasons or to avoid religious persecution in their homelands.

Unfortunately, some of these immigrants began to encounter that same hostility and persecution in the colonies. The Quakers set themselves apart in Pennsylvania and the Scotch–Irish Presbyterians moved west to settle the Mississippi frontier when they received a cold reception in the East. Others, like the French Huguenots, assimilated more easily. Some religious restrictions were adopted by individual colonies attempting to exclude Quakers and Catholics or to subject them to discriminatory taxes. The colonial restrictions were somewhat effective in discouraging certain immigrants.

Others came involuntarily as punishment or under servitude. Slaves from Africa were forcibly brought. Children were kidnapped from English slums and Ireland to be sold for American labor. English judges were empowered to send both vagrants and felons to the colonies as punishment. These groups also met with disfavor and colonial restrictions; colonies began legislating to exclude ''paupers'' and ''criminals'' as early as 1639. Those restrictions excluding ''public charges'' embraced not only people sent by English courts but also the poor and the diseased who came voluntarily. Southern colonies especially tried to restrict criminals, because that region received the greatest influx of the 50,000 sent under penal sanction during the fifty years before the Revolution.

These restrictions illustrate the hostility felt toward newcomers by colonists who had just arrived themselves. Although aimed primarily at those banished from England and at public charges who would be added to relief rolls, these restrictions were also a product of religious and national rivalries imported from Europe. Despite these attempts, the colonies were generally unable to check the influx of migrants, for they lacked both legal authority and a centralized administrative structure. In addition, immigration was still favored to the extent that the colonies needed more people for labor and security. To outsiders, the New World held great promise. Accordingly, by the start of the American Revolution in 1776, the population of the colonies stood at about 2,500,000, or 100 times the 1640 figure.

The colonial immigration restrictions may have influenced the later legislation of the United States on this subject. In fashioning its laws, the federal government eventually excluded the same general classes of immigrants as did the colonies. The federal legislation also used certain colonial sanctions on immigrants, such as head taxes on individuals and deportation of undesirable persons.

§ 1–2 EARLY U.S. IMMIGRATION POLICY

Although colonial attitudes continued after the American Revolution, extensive federal legislation dealing with immigration was not enacted for some time, primarily for two reasons. First, for almost 100 years, it was unclear whether the federal government was even intended by the Constitution to have power to regulate immigration. Second, the United States officially favored unrestricted immigration for about the same period of time after the nation's birth.

The locus of power over the subject of immigration was not definitively identified in any early proclamation of the new government. Under the Articles of Confederation of 1781, each state apparently determined its own immigration policy, but there was confusion over the status of prior colonial enactments. The United States Constitution, adopted in 1789, granted Congress broad power to regulate foreign commerce in Article I, § 8, but it was not clear whether foreign commerce included immigration. Not until 1875 did the U.S. Supreme Court in *Henderson v. City of New York*, 92 U.S. 259 (1875) declare state restrictions on immigration to be unconstitutional, as an infringement on the federal power over foreign commerce.

During this long period of uncertainty, Congress did not generally attempt to invoke its power to regulate immigration, but principally passed a series of acts regulating naturalization and a few other nonrestrictive pieces of legislation. Congress adopted the first such law in 1790, liberally granting citizenship to immigrants. Subsequent legislation, however, required increasingly longer periods of residency as well as the renunciation of former allegiances and titles of nobility. In 1798 Congress authorized the President to expel "dangerous" aliens in the Alien Friends Act and the Alien Enemies Act, but the Alien Friends Act expired without extension after two years. A new Naturalization Act in 1802 reestablished the provisions of a 1795 act, creating a five-year residency requirement for citizenship. In addition, the "passenger acts" of 1819, 1847, 1848, and 1855 set certain minimum space and provisions standards for overseas vessels. Further, in 1808, Congress enacted a law forbidding the importation of slaves.

Apart from piecemeal legislation, the first 100 years of the nation's existence can be characterized as a period of unrestricted immigration. The spacious frontier and the need for labor primarily motivated this unrestrictive policy. No official immigration records were kept until 1820, but it is estimated that 250,000 immigrants arrived in the United States between 1790 and 1820. From 1820 to 1880, while the issue of power over immigration was being debated, over 10 million people arrived.

Discontent with the open immigration policy increased with the rate of immigration and with change in the immigrant demographic. Between 1820 and 1880, political conditions and economic devastation brought over 2.8 million Irish immigrants to the United States. German Catholic immigrants came in large numbers during the European depressions of the 1840s. In a predominantly Protestant country, the Catholic Irish and Germans were not well accepted. The anti-Catholicism that had prevailed in colonial days resurfaced. Several groups and overlapping political parties, including social reformers, Protestant evangelicals, the Nativists, the Order of the Star–Spangled Banner, and the Know–Nothing Party, campaigned for legislation halting immigration and prohibiting even naturalized immigrants from participating in the nation's political process. These groups were somewhat successful at the state level, but failed at the federal level because the Irish and Germans constituted a large voting bloc. Politicians at the national level actively sought the vote of these and other newly arrived groups. Hence, federal policy, and apparently the majority of the nation, continued to favor immigration.

Eventually, the Civil War drowned the protests of groups like the Know–Nothings. The need for labor in both the North and South was magnified during the war years; an 1864 Act even facilitated immigration by validating contracts pledging future wages in payment for overseas passage.

§ 1–3 RESTRICTION BEGINS: EXCLUDING THE UNWANTED

After the Civil War, federal law began to reflect the growing desire to restrict the immigration of certain groups. The Facilitating Act of 1864 was repealed in 1868, and in 1875 Congress passed the first restrictive statute. That statute, borrowing from earlier colonial legislation, barred convicts and prostitutes from admission. These limits were the first of many "quality control" exclusions based on the nature of the immigrants themselves. The list of unacceptable types of immigrants continued to grow in subsequent enactments.

The 1875 Act also attempted to solve the new problem faced by the western states. Westward expansion demanded huge numbers of laborers for work in the mines and on the railroads. Imported Chinese labor had been used since about 1850, and tension between the Chinese workers and the settlers of European descent ran high. Chinese labor depressed wage scales and some Chinese women were being imported as prostitutes. The Chinese did not assimilate and the European groups were not willing to tolerate the cultural differences. In response, Congress adopted a law outlawing so-called "coolie labor" contracts and immigration for lewd and immoral purposes. Many Chinese, however, continued to immigrate voluntarily or were routed through Canada. Hence, in 1882 Congress took stronger action in the Chinese Exclusion Act, the nation's first racist, restrictive immigration law, and one of several acts in the 1880s aimed at stemming the tide of Chinese immigration. The Act suspended all immigration of Chinese laborers for ten years and forbade any court to admit Chinese to citizenship. The Act was extended in 1902 and later made permanent. Not until 1943 was it finally repealed so that Chinese immigrants could become citizens.

By the 1880s, Congress finally decided that immigration was appropriate for federal control. The Act of 1882 may be considered the first general federal immigration act. It continued to base restrictions on quality controls; in addition to the 1875 exclusions of "convicts" and "prostitutes," it barred "lunatics," "idiots," and those "likely to become public charges." For the first time, the Act also imposed a head tax on every arriving immigrant. The tax served the express function of raising revenues to defray administrative expenses. Congress did not want the poor of other nations to be added to the government relief rolls; the tax served the underlying function of deterring the immigration of people unable to pay. In several subsequent statutes, the head tax was raised from fifty cents to two dollars, making the barrier relatively substantial at that time.

Despite these limits, over 5.2 million immigrant aliens arrived in the 1880s. Immigration came to be seen as a threat to the U.S. economy, and Congress began expanding the list of "undesirable classes," hoping both to upgrade the type of immigrants and to limit overall entry. An 1891 act added the "diseased," "paupers," and "polygamists" to the list of excludable persons. It also forbade advertising in foreign countries that encouraged immigration to America. In addition, immigrants were required to take medical examinations to determine whether they were "diseased." A few years later, special boards of inquiry were established to decide other questions of admissibility under the "quality" restrictions. The 1891 law established the Bureau of Immigration, the forerunner of the Immigration and Naturalization Service (INS) (now the U.S. Citizenship and Immigration Services, the U.S. Immigration and Customs Enforcement, and the U.S. Customs and Border Protection). The Bureau was responsible for inspecting entrants at the twenty-four ports of entry to the U.S.

Immigration did abate somewhat in the 1890s, totaling 3.6 million—a reduction of over 1.5 million from the previous decade. There was a sharp increase in immigration, however, at the turn of the century, and Congress tried to stem the flow by excluding more classes of immigrants. In 1903, a new law excluded epileptics, the "insane," "beggars," and "anarchists." In 1907 the "feebleminded," the tubercular, and those persons with a mental or physical defect that "may affect" their ability to earn a living were added to the list. During this period, Japanese immigration was restricted by a 1907 agreement negotiated between the United States and Japan. Although the cumulative list was long, these quality controls were not easily enforced. Moreover, at that time the Bureau of Immigration and Naturalization (renamed by the 1907 Immigration Act) had only 1,200 employees in the U.S. to process arriving immigrants and enforce the entry restrictions. Nonetheless, almost 8.8 million immigrants were admitted by the Bureau in the first decade of the 1900s.

More than the huge numbers concerned Congress, however. Once again, the type of person immigrating was changing. In the 1880s, 72% of immigrants to the U.S. came from northern and western Europe. In contrast, during the 1900–10 decade, 71% came from countries in southern or eastern Europe. These "new immigrants" were Italians, Slavs, and Jews, who were often considered "inferior" by the predominantly Anglo–Saxon population. Much like the Chinese who preceded them by several decades, the "new immigrants" were slow to assimilate, living together in urban ethnic neighborhoods. The Anglo–Saxons feared that their predominance was threatened and pressured Congress for more restrictive measures.

Because the earlier "quality control" exclusions did little to stem the flow of immigrants, those groups favoring restrictions on immigration began to advocate literacy as an entrance requirement. In 1907, after several failed attempts to pass a literacy bill, Congress established a joint congressional-presidential commission to study the impact of immigration on the United States. In 1911 the Commission published its findings. It concluded that twentieth century immigration to the U.S. was significantly different from earlier immigration and that the new immigration was dominated by the so-called "inferior" and "less desirable" groups. As a result, the Commission concluded that the United States no longer benefited from a liberal immigration policy and should impose further entry restrictions. The Commission recommended a literacy test as one such restriction.

In 1917, over President Wilson's veto, Congress responded. The 1917 Act was clearly aimed at restricting the immigration of specific nationalities. One important purpose of the 1917 Act was to limit immigration from southern and eastern Europe, which was accomplished by barring people unable to read. Because the new immigrants were largely illiterate, the impact of literacy tests limited that region's immigration more than any other. The Act also increased the head tax to eight dollars, raising yet another obstacle.

In addition, Congress addressed the growing concern over foreign "anarchists" in the 1917 Act. This group had been excluded by an earlier law of 1903 that was enacted in response to President McKinley's assassination. In 1917, Congress apparently channeled the anti-immigrant mood prevalent during World War I. This sentiment led to the subsequent enactment of the Anarchist Act of 1918, which more specifically defined "anarchists."

The last major exclusion of the 1917 Act prohibited all immigration of Asians from countries within specified latitudes and longitudes. Many similar racist exclusions were proposed in Congress that year, and the Asiatic Barred Zone survived as an undebated amendment to the 1917 Act. Congressional attempts to prevent blacks from immigrating to the U.S. were defeated, however, due in large part to intensive lobbying by the NAACP.

The literacy entrance requirement and the anxiety surrounding World War I about the ability to assimilate foreign born persons built into an Americanization movement. Beginning in 1919, many states established Americanization programs to ensure that immigrants would learn English. Industry joined the movement, establishing similar programs for workers. By 1923, the Bureau of Immigration and Naturalization reported 252,808 immigrants in 6,632 programs across the country.

§ 1–4 THE QUOTA LAWS

World War I naturally limited immigration by making shipping less available, but after the war, immigration began to grow again. The U.S. favored an isolationist policy and wanted to protect its own labor force from the anticipated postwar flood of European refugees. Dissatisfied with its latest set of quality exclusions, Congress implemented numerical controls. Enacted first as a temporary measure, the 1921 Quota Law marked a major shift in the U.S. approach to immigration control. The law limited immigration from each nation to 3% of the number of foreign-born persons of that nationality residing in the U.S. as of the 1910 census. The total quota was 357,000, but because fewer foreign-born persons from the South and East of Europe lived in the U.S. in 1910, that region's total quota was 45,000 less than that from the North and West of Europe. The effect of the quota allotments was to restrict immigration from the disfavored regions; the northern and western countries of Europe did not even fill their quotas under this law. Fortunately for the restricted group, Congress established certain "non-quota" exceptions. For example, the law permitted a person to be admitted to the United States as an immigrant if the individual had lived in the Western Hemisphere for one year (later changed to five years). Hence, by temporarily living in a Western Hemisphere country (such as Canada, Chile, or Mexico) some could avoid the quotas.

In 1924, Congress further restricted immigration by reducing the immigration quota from 3% of foreign-born persons under the 1910 census to 2% of the foreign-born under the 1890 census. This change cut the total quota to 164,667 and made the southern and eastern quotas proportionately even smaller than before. Again, people from those regions had to use the non-quota provisions to enter the U.S. Although under the 1924 Act only Western Hemisphere natives were not subject to the quota, Europeans and others used another provision exempting spouses of U.S. citizens from the quotas.

Despite the restrictive 1924 Act, immigration from the southern and eastern countries of Europe equaled entries from the northern and western countries, defeating the restrictive purposes of Congress. The quota and quality restrictions resulted in increased surreptitious border crossing. Moreover, although Europe was the targeted region, immigration from the Western Hemisphere began to climb in the 1920s, presenting border control problems. In response, the Bureau created the Border Patrol in 1924, hiring forty-five men to guard the country's 8,000 miles of land and sea borders. Total immigration in the years 1924–29 reached 1.5 million.

In 1929, as provided by the 1924 Act, a new quota took effect. The "national origins formula" used the ethnic background of the entire U.S. population, rather than the first generation immigrant population, as its base for calculating national quotas. Because the U.S. population was still predominantly Anglo–Saxon, the national origins quota restricted the newer immigrant groups more severely than the foreign-born formula of the previous quota laws. The national origins quota allotted 85% of the total quota of 150,000 to countries from the North and West of Europe, while the South and East received only 15% of that total quota.

The effect of the national origins formula, however, cannot accurately be measured. Soon after it took effect, the U.S. economy collapsed. The Great Depression limited immigration; only one-half million immigrated to the U.S. during the 1930s. In 1932, at the height of the Great Depression, emigration far exceeded legal immigration. Only 35,576 entered the country in that year, while over 100,000 left. The potential for immigration increased during those years, however, with the growth of highways and increased airplane traffic. By 1938, there were 186 ports of entry into the U.S. On June 14, 1940, the INS was transferred from the Department of Labor to the Department of Justice.

One of the most tragic consequences of the restrictive U.S. immigration policy fell upon refugees trying to flee Europe before World War II. In 1939, Congress defeated a bill that would have accommodated 20,000 children fleeing from Nazi Germany—despite the availability of willing sponsor families—because the number of children would have exceeded the quota allocated to German nationals. In 1940 the State Department did permit consuls outside Germany to issue visas to German refugees when the German quota was unfilled, but this and other measures were inadequate to help the vast majority of victims of Nazi persecution.

World War II brought an economic upswing, and immigration increased in response, bringing the total of entrants in the 1940s to one million. The United States again needed labor from abroad and negotiated with Mexico for a temporary worker program to satisfy the country's wartime employment needs. Congress also repealed the ban on Chinese immigration, largely due to the wartime alliance of the United States with China. Congress established a small quota for Chinese immigrants and also permitted Chinese immigrants to be naturalized as U.S. citizens.

As the United States became painfully aware of the Nazi atrocities and the fate of the refugees it had refused, there was a short period of liberalization of the strict quota laws. President Truman issued a directive in

1945, admitting 40,000 war refugees. Under the War Brides Act of 1945 and the Fiancées Act of 1946, about 123,000 spouses, children, and fiancées of WW II military personnel were admitted to the U.S. The Displaced Persons Act of 1948 admitted 400,000 war refugees from Austria, Germany, and Italy to the U.S., but these admissions "mortgaged" their countries' quotas, sometimes limiting or closing off all immigration from a country for several years thereafter.

By the late 1940s the work of the INS had burgeoned. In 1949, the U.S. had 416 ports of entry by land, sea, and air at which the INS annually made about 90 million inspections of immigrants, nonimmigrants, and returning citizens for compliance with entry requirements. The Border Patrol force remained stable at about 1,100, yet its total apprehensions of deportable aliens tripled in three years from 100,000 in 1946 to 300,000 in 1949.

In contrast to its liberalizing post-war legislation, Congress acted soon after to restrict yet another group. Anti–Communism rose after WW II and particularly during the war in Korea. As a result, national security legislation received high priority in Congress. The Internal Security Act of 1950 amended the 1918 Anarchists Act. The exclusions, however, were expressly directed this time at Communists; the Act broadly defined the excluded group, barring anyone "likely to" engage in "subversive activity."

At the same time, however, Congress continued to liberalize refugee admissions. In 1953 Congress passed the Refugee Relief Act, which admitted an additional 214,000 refugees. Although designed primarily to facilitate the admission of refugees fleeing from Eastern European countries dominated by the Soviet Union, the Act also included provisions to prevent the admission of undesirable aliens. Similar measures were passed in 1956 and 1957 to assist the entry of Hungarians and others fleeing from Communism as well as persons fleeing from countries in the Middle East. The 1960 Refugee Fair Share Law established a temporary admission and assistance program for those World War II refugees and displaced persons who remained in camps under the mandate of the United Nations High Commissioner for Refugees.

§ 1–5 THE 1952 ACT AND LATER AMENDMENTS

The Immigration and Nationality Act of 1952 (INA) consolidated previous piecemeal immigration laws into one coordinated statute. As amended, the 1952 Act provided the foundation for immigration law in effect today.

The 1952 Act retained, over President Truman's veto, the controversial national origins quota. The 1952 quota was calculated differently from the original national origins quota and established a 150,000 person limit on immigration from the Eastern Hemisphere. Congress exempted the Asia–Pacific Triangle from this quota, because so few people from that region lived in the U.S. as a consequence of the Barred Zone law of 1917; the quota would have been grossly inequitable in that respect. Instead, a modest quota of 2,000 was established for that area. Congress also retained the detailed "quality control" exclusions found in earlier legislation and added several new ones. Within the quota system, four types of entrance preferences were established. First preference was given to those entrants with skills or experience needed by the U.S. economy. Those persons with close family relations to U.S. citizens or permanent residents received lower preferences. This ordering was changed by amendment in 1965, but it should be noted that spouses, children, and parents of U.S. citizens were not and are still not subject to the quota or preference system. For that reason, they are called "immediate relatives."

Several aspects of the 1952 Act drew heavy criticism. The national origins quota, based on the 1920 census, was a blatant form of racial and ethnic discrimination. Also, despite some increased procedural safeguards for non-citizens, the 1952 Act did not provide them procedural due process.

The 1952 Act presented the INS with new and complex laws to enforce, yet Congress did not supply the Service with increased personnel or appropriations to perform its new work. Moreover, the early 1950s saw a large increase in apprehensions of deportable non-citizens aimed at the expulsion of Mexicans from the U.S. The Border Patrol, still about 1,000 strong, apprehended 800,000 deportable non-citizens in 1952; in 1954, that number increased to one million. Because of "Operation Wetback," 90% of those apprehended came from Mexico. It is believed that this expulsion included U.S. citizens of Mexican descent who were not given an opportunity to prove their claim to citizenship.

During the 1950s, Congress made several minor revisions in the 1952 Act, and over 2.5 million people immigrated to the U.S. The number of people entering the U.S. increased again in the 1960s, reflecting the growing availability of all means of travel. To facilitate the necessary inspections, in 1963 the INS consolidated duties at the ports of entry with several agencies. Hence, one officer performed the duties of the INS, Customs, U.S.

Public Health Service, and the Bureau of Plant Quarantine at the Mexican border. This joint approach eased the workload somewhat, for in 1964 the INS made 178 million inspections, almost twice the 1949 figure, yet total INS personnel had only increased from 6,900 to 7,058. In 1966, 200 million persons—immigrants, nonimmigrants, and returning citizens—were inspected at over 400 ports of entry. Total immigration for the 1960s was 3.3 million.

The criticized national origins formula was not abolished until 1965 when President Johnson successfully urged enactment of former President Kennedy's program of immigration reform. The 1965 amendments replaced the national origins formula with a limit of 20,000 on each country in the Eastern Hemisphere and an overall limit of 170,000 for that hemisphere. The law established a quota of 120,000 for the Western Hemisphere, without preferences or country limits—to take effect in 1968.

The 1965 amendments abolished the old four-preference system and established in its place a seven-preference system for close relatives and those immigrants with needed occupational skills from the Eastern Hemisphere. Again, spouses of U.S. citizens were permitted to immigrate without reference to the quota or preference system. Under the preference system, unmarried adult children of U.S. citizens received highest preference; second preference was granted to spouses and unmarried children of permanent residents. The preference for immigrants of "exceptional ability" and those in "the professions" was changed from first to third. Other relatives of citizens and permanent residents received the fourth and fifth preferences. Sixth preference was given to needed workers. Seventh preference was allocated to refugees.

The abolition of the national origins formula was in large part the result of a pervasive attitudinal change. Anti–Catholic, -Asian, and -Semitic sentiment decreased as the civil rights movement stimulated an increased tolerance of racial and ethnic differences. Unfortunately, there remained strong prejudice against certain immigrant groups. After World War II, the proportion of Spanish-speaking immigrants increased, and much prejudice was directed toward these newcomers from Mexico as well as Central and South America. Although the 1952 Act did not place a numerical limit on immigration from these areas, Congress included the Western Hemisphere quota of 120,000 in the 1965 amendments as a compromise for abolishing the national origins system. As a result, it created a steadily growing backlog of Latin American applicants forced to wait several years for a visa.

In 1976, a new law was passed which applied the Eastern Hemisphere preference system to the Western Hemisphere. Hence, both hemispheres were subject to the 20,000 per country limit and the seven preference system. The law, however, did retain separate annual limits—120,000 for the Western and 170,000 for the Eastern Hemisphere—and a special 600 person ceiling for colonies and dependencies.

A 1978 amendment established a world-wide quota of 290,000 and applied the same per country limits and seven preference system to both hemispheres. This worldwide ceiling eliminated the hemisphere consideration and allowed visas to go where the need was greatest. The 20,000 per country limit, however, was a serious restraint on immigration from a few countries such as Mexico.

Meanwhile, the INS staff became increasingly overworked. The number of deportable non-citizens, which fell in the 1950s, climbed rapidly in the 1960s and 1970s, as did the number of total entries. In 1972, one half million deportable non-citizens were apprehended. By 1977, that annual figure had doubled. The Border Patrol had grown to a force of 2,400, still too few to guard the borders. The Immigration Service estimated that, between undetected border crossings and violations of legal entry conditions, millions of undocumented non-citizens were living in the U.S. in 1974. In 1973, 250 million persons were inspected at about 1,000 ports of entry. By 1979, 274 million were inspected annually, and the Border Patrol apprehended one million deportable non-citizens. That year, the INS employed almost 11,000 personnel under a 300 million dollar budget.

In March 1980, Congress dealt again with the issue of refugees. The 1980 Refugee Act broadened the definition of refugees to accord with the international definition in the Convention and Protocol relating to the Status of Refugees. Further, the Refugee Act set an annual maximum of 50,000 refugees through the year 1982, but permitted the Administration, in consultation with Congress, to set the number of refugees to be admitted each year after 1982. The initial numerical limits in the Refugee Act were undermined, however, by the deluge of Cuban refugees soon after its enactment. More than 100,000 Cubans arrived in the U.S. in the spring of 1980—mostly via the port of Mariel, Cuba. Eventually, the Carter Administration concluded that the influx of "Mariel" Cubans was not within the contemplation of the Refugee Act and asked for special legislation to deal with the problem. The 1980 Act reduced the worldwide immigrant quota from 290,000 to 270,000 to partially offset the separate allocation for refugees.

In 1981 Congress adopted another series of amendments to the immigration law, which eliminated the permanent exclusion of non-citizens five years after deportation. Also, a person convicted of a single minor marijuana offense could obtain a waiver of excludability. There were a number of other amendments concerning foreign medical graduates, congressional reporting requirements as to visas issued, exchange visitors, and treaty investors. But these minor changes did not address the national perception that the U.S. had lost control of its borders and required a much more thorough revision of immigration law.

Congress enacted the Immigration Marriage Fraud Amendments in 1986 to deter immigration-related marriage fraud. The 1986 Fraud Amendments imposed a two-year conditional residency requirement on non-citizen spouses and children before they could obtain permanent resident status on the basis of a "qualifying marriage" to a U.S. citizen or permanent resident alien. To obtain permanent status, couples were required to file a petition and, in some cases, be interviewed by the INS to verify that the couple had not entered into the marriage solely to procure immigration benefits and had not divorced during the conditional period. In 1990 Congress amended those provisions to permit waivers for cases of battered spouses or children as well as other hardships. See § 5–2.1(c), *infra*, for further discussion of the conditional residence provisions.

The 1986 Fraud Amendments also imposed criminal penalties for immigration-related marriage fraud of not more than five years and/or not more than $250,000 in fines. In addition, the 1986 Fraud Amendments explicitly made marriage fraud an additional ground for deportation as well as a perpetual bar to future immigration. Furthermore, the Fraud Amendments restricted adjustment to permanent residence status based on a marriage undertaken while a non-citizen is in removal proceedings. INA § 245(e). *See* § 5–2.1(c), *infra*.

§ 1–6   THE 1986 IMMIGRATION REFORM AND CONTROL ACT (IRCA)

In 1980 the United States Census Bureau counted 2,047,000 undocumented non-citizens in the country. Based on the Bureau of Census' experience in miscounting other segments of the population, the Bureau had estimated that there were 5,965,000 undocumented persons in the country on census day April 1, 1980. As the INS attempted to confront these problems with inadequate resources, it was criticized for inefficient internal operations, misconduct, and a general inability to control the flow of undocumented immigration.

Thirty-four years had passed since the enactment of the last major immigration reform when Congress finally adopted in 1986 the Immigration Reform and Control Act (IRCA). IRCA was not easily adopted, after unsuccessful attempts in three previous congressional sessions. It represented a political compromise between four interests—(1) those people seeking to deter illegal immigration by discouraging unauthorized employment in the U.S.; (2) those seeking a one-time amnesty for non-citizens who, for years, had been locked out as illegal immigrants; (3) those who wanted to insure continued access to low-cost agricultural labor without elaborate federal regulation; and (4) those who wished to insure that penalizing employers for illegally hiring undocumented workers would not encourage discriminatory employment practices. Ultimately, the Act that was adopted focused almost exclusively on illegal immigration. The Act was a partial response to the 1981 recommendations of the Select Committee on Immigration and Refugee Policy chaired by (Rev.) Theodore M. Hesbergh, then President of the University of Notre Dame. IRCA dealt with the major problem of undocumented workers by imposing sanctions on employers, and at the same time legalizing the status of undocumented entrants who had arrived prior to January 1, 1982. Because Congress was concerned that employer sanctions would result in discrimination in the workplace, IRCA included provisions prohibiting discrimination on the basis of national origin or citizenship status. IRCA also provided the INS with significant new resources to enforce the immigration laws. Furthermore, in response to the demand for foreign agricultural labor, IRCA created a program that granted temporary and permanent resident status to qualified agricultural workers. Despite these major provisions and a number of less important ones, IRCA did not substantially restructure the immigration law as it pertains to immigration quotas or the requirements for admission.

The employer sanction provisions of the Act penalized a "person or other entity" who hired, recruited, or referred for a fee for employment in the United States a non-citizen, knowing that person was unauthorized, or who employed any individual without complying with the Act's employment verification system. Employers would also be sanctioned, if after lawfully hiring a non-citizen, the employer continued to employ the worker knowing that he or she had since become unauthorized. Those sanctions, however, did not apply to employees hired, recruited, or referred before November 6, 1986. Violating employers were subject to civil fines, injunctions, and criminal penalties. In a reversal of previous law, the felony of "harboring an illegal alien" was made applicable to circumstances involving employment. IRCA explicitly preempted all state criminal statutes concerning the employment of undocumented non-citizens, leaving unaffected only areas such as licensing or laws regarding "fitness to do business." Interestingly, to this day there are no direct sanctions against non-citizens who illegally accept employment other than the threat of removal and penalties for document fraud. *See* chapter 14, *infra*.

A significant obstacle to earlier immigration reform was the concern that employer sanctions would result in widespread discrimination against persons who looked or sounded "foreign." IRCA attempted to resolve this potential problem by prohibiting employment discrimination on the basis of national origin or citizenship status. IRCA stated that it is an unfair immigration-related employment practice for a person or other entity employing four or more persons to discriminate against any individual who is authorized to work in the U.S., with respect to employment or discharge, on the basis of the individual's national origin or citizenship status. Employers were concerned about their inability to verify an employee's identity, authorization, and national origin without appearing to discriminate in their hiring practices. President Reagan addressed this concern by announcing that these anti-discrimination provisions would be interpreted to require actual discriminatory intent and not simply a disparate impact resulting from employment practices.

The implementation of the employer sanction provisions of IRCA received mixed reviews. Surveys taken by the General Accounting Office in the three years following IRCA's passage offered inconsistent evidence as to whether employers were aware of and complying with their obligations under the new law. *See* INA § 274A(j)(1). While one survey reported that the vast majority of responding employers had learned of their obligations under the new law, others reported that a large percentage or even a majority believed that the INS had not adequately informed employers of their obligations and that most businesses did not understand their responsibilities. Social service agencies responded that about nine percent of their clients had unjustly lost their jobs because their employers were inadequately informed of the law.

IRCA's anti-discrimination provisions did not succeed in eradicating concern about discrimination in the workplace. The majority of respondents believed that IRCA had already resulted in discrimination against workers with a foreign appearance. Reports indicated that discrimination against Hispanics and Asians was particularly severe.

§ 1–6.1 Amnesty for Undocumented Non–Citizens

Another major goal of IRCA was improvement of enforcement and services. The Act increased border patrol and other enforcement activities to deter unlawful entry of aliens and increased the service activities of the INS to adjudicate applications more quickly. To facilitate these goals, the Act increased appropriations for the INS and the Executive Office for Immigration Review (EOIR).

In exchange for the increased enforcement provisions of IRCA, Congress offered a broad amnesty for many undocumented non-citizens already present in the country. The one-time, limited amnesty program allowed qualified non-citizens who met its strict deadlines to obtain permanent resident status. To qualify, non-citizens were required to show that they had entered the United States before January 1, 1982, and had resided unlawfully and continuously in the United States from that date until the date they applied for amnesty. Non-citizens who entered with a valid nonimmigrant status that later expired could also qualify for amnesty by showing that their unlawful status was known to the U.S. government. Applicants were specifically required to (1) have been physically present in the U.S. since November 1986, except for "brief, casual, and innocent" absences; (2) meet most of the requirements of immigrant admissibility to the United States; (3) have not been convicted of any felony or of three or more misdemeanors committed in the United States; (4) have not assisted in any form of persecution; and (5) register for the draft, if required to do so.

Non-citizens who met these requirements and filed an application between May 5, 1987, and May 4, 1988, were granted temporary residence. After eighteen months of temporary residence, the non-citizens had one year in which to apply for adjustment to permanent resident status or they would become undocumented once again. To adjust to permanent resident status, applicants were again required to meet the criteria for permanent residence and also meet minimal English and civics requirements.

Realizing that many undocumented non-citizens would be reluctant to bring their unlawful presence to the attention of the INS by applying for amnesty, IRCA mandated procedures to ensure strict confidentiality. The Act allowed voluntary organizations to receive applications and forward them to the INS. Whether a non-citizen applied through such an organization or directly to the INS, access to information in the applications was restricted to INS officers with no deportation responsibilities and the INS could only use the information to make a determination on the application or impose penalties for false statements.

Despite these precautions, response to the amnesty program was less enthusiastic than expected. The INS originally estimated that between two and four million applications would be filed, but when the program ended, only 1.4 million people had applied for amnesty. After a slow initial response, the INS sought innovative means to encourage non-citizens to apply for amnesty, such as inserting 80,000 amnesty program reminders into tortilla packages in Texas. The INS also sent letters to those people who were granted temporary residence, asking them to encourage and help their friends, relatives, and neighbors to apply for amnesty. Significant barriers to participating in the program remained, however, including a high application fee, problems with obtaining the required documentation, and the non-citizens' fear of the INS. A proposal to extend the application deadline passed the House of Representatives but died in the Senate, due to fears that an extension would send the message that the U.S. could not enforce its immigration laws. The program thus ended as planned on May 4, 1988.

Another concern in adopting IRCA was the potential adverse financial impact on the states. For this reason, IRCA included extensive provisions disqualifying newly legalized non-citizens (except Cuban/Haitian entrants) from receiving most federal public welfare assistance for five years. Appropriations were also included to compensate state and local governments for other public assistance and medical benefits conferred upon people granted amnesty, as well as for the costs of incarcerating undocumented non-citizens and "Mariel" Cubans.

In addition, IRCA established a separate program for granting temporary and permanent status to qualified agricultural workers. This program was the result of agribusiness pressure for greater availability of such farm workers.

§ 1–6.2 Visa Lottery Programs

Beginning in 1986, Congress began to act on growing constituent concern over the difficulty of immigration from European countries, most notably, Ireland and Italy. This situation was generally thought to have arisen with the repeal of the Western Hemisphere quota in 1965 accompanied by a steady increase in immigration from Asia, Africa, and the Middle East. In § 314 of IRCA and in § 3 of P.L. 100–658 (the Immigration Amendments of 1988), Congress created what came to be known as the NP–5 and the OP–1 programs respectively.

The NP–5 program created a "first-come, first-served" worldwide mail registration program benefiting persons from thirty-six countries whose immigrant visa availability was adversely affected by the unification of the worldwide quota system in 1965. This program, in effect, "gave away" 30,000 immigrant visas, between fiscal years 1987 and 1988, to earliest-registered applicants and their immediate families, requiring them only to meet the nationality, health, and morals qualifications of immigration laws. This program was extended to cover 30,000 more NP–5 registrants over fiscal years 1989 and 1990.

The OP–1 program was a pure lottery based on a one-time registration program without the facets of early or multiple filings that were characteristic of the NP–5 program. It benefited natives of 162 countries that used less than 25% of their maximum quota entitlement in fiscal year 1988.

The significance of these programs was their underlying policy of expanding immigration to countries other than the Eastern Hemisphere sources which had increasingly benefited from U.S. immigration during the preceding decades.

§ 1–7 THE IMMIGRATION ACT OF 1990

In 1990, Congress passed a series of amendments to the Immigration and Nationality Act, collectively referred to as the Immigration Act of 1990 ("1990 Act" also known as "IMMACT 90"). Like the INA of 1952, the 1965 Amendments, and IRCA, IMMACT 90 was a landmark in immigration legislation. IMMACT 90 primarily reformed the rules pertaining to the *legal* entry of foreign nationals. It augmented the regulations enacted by IRCA (*see* § 1–6, *supra*), which focused primarily on illegal immigration. IMMACT 90 was followed by the Immigration Technical Amendments Act of 1991, which modified some of the provisions in the 1990 Act and clarified certain aspects of the new quota system. The framework established by these two acts remains largely intact today and their provisions are treated in their proper context throughout this book. This section presents a synopsis of the most prominent changes made by the 1990 Act and the Technical Amendments.

§ 1–7.1 Overall Increase in Worldwide Immigration

The most visible feature of IMMACT 90 was the increase by approximately 35% in the numerical limitation system, or overall immigration allowed. IMMACT 90 established an annual limit for worldwide immigration of 700,000 for three years, after which it decreased to 675,000. Because other provisions of the 1990 Act allowed immigration of groups not counted in the 700,000, and a separate law permitted as many as 125,000 refugees to be legally admitted, the actual worldwide immigration limit was closer to 800,000.

The groups benefiting from this increase illustrate congressional priorities, and reflect a moderately optimistic belief in the country's capacity to absorb new immigrants. The 1990 Act increased the allocation for both family-related and employee-related immigration. In addition, the new law created a separate basis by which "diversity" immigrants, that is, nationals of countries with relatively low numbers of immigrants since 1965, could gain entry. The 1990 Act eliminated the nonpreference category that had been unavailable due to excessive demand since late 1976. All-in-all, of the 700,000 annual allotment, 465,000 visas were made available to family-sponsored immigrants, 140,000 for employment-based immigrants, and 55,000 for diversity immigrants.

a. Family–Sponsored Immigration

Beginning October 1, 1991, all family-sponsored immigration was limited to approximately 480,000 annually for two years, after which the yearly limit dropped to 465,000. The relatively large percentage of the overall limit allocated to family-related immigration reflected the continued commitment to family unity as a primary goal of immigration policy. The 1990 Act did not dramatically increase the total number of family-sponsored immigrants, however. Immediate relatives (*i.e.*, spouses, minor children, and parents) of U.S. citizens, who were not counted under the previous quota system, are now deducted from the total allocation for family-sponsored immigrants, although there is still no limit on immigration by immediate relatives. The 1990 Act did guarantee admission of at least 226,000 other relatives of U.S. citizens and permanent residents, an increase of approximately 65,000 over the former quota. *See* § 5–3.1(a), *infra*.

b. Employment–Related Immigration

Responding to fears concerning the U.S. work force's ability to compete in the global economy, the 1990 Act significantly changed the allowances for employment-related immigration. The 1990 law replaced the previous third and sixth preferences (which distinguished between professional and skilled employees) with five new classifications that allowed for a total of 140,000 immigrants per year. The first employment-based preference category allocated 28.6% of the total employment-based quota (currently 40,000) for "priority workers," that is, non-citizens with an extraordinary potential for contribution to their fields. This category includes noted professors, researchers, and multinational executives, as well as individuals who have attained widespread acclaim.

The second employment-based preference category allocated another 28.6% of the employment-based quota for professionals with advanced degrees or persons with exceptional ability in science, the arts, or business. Hence, the new second preference largely covered the old third preference for professionals. The new third employment-based preference class allotted 28.6% for skilled workers or professionals with baccalaureate degrees, as well as other unskilled workers. The new category combined the balance of the old third preference with the old sixth preference that included "other unskilled workers." Within this category, the number of unskilled workers was limited to 10,000 per year. The fourth employment-related category allocated 10,000 places for certain religious workers and employees of the U.S. mission in Hong Kong.

The "Employment Creation" fifth preference encouraged the immigration of non-citizens who invest at least $1 million in a business that benefits the U.S. economy and employs at least ten U.S. citizen workers or current permanent residents. Up to 10,000 investors may be admitted each year under this preference. Any unused portion of this allotment "spills up" to the first preference category and unused first-preference places "spill down" to the second and third categories. Investors are granted a conditional permanent residence for two years, after which they can petition for the condition's removal. This provision was criticized for allowing wealthy foreign nationals to "buy their way in." Its supporters contended, however, that the previous law curtailed foreign investment by impeding a company's principal investor from obtaining residence in the U.S. The employment creation program was temporarily halted in 1997, due to concerns about fraudulent investment schemes. The program was reinstated in 1998 with new regulations intended to prevent such fraud. In an effort to increase the popularity of the Employment Creation category, the U.S. Citizenship and Immigration Services (CIS) created the immigrant investor pilot program. The pilot program sets aside 3,000 of the fifth preference visas for immigrants who make investments in economically depressed areas preapproved by the CIS as Regional Centers. In exchange for investing in areas of economic need, immigrant investors only need to invest $500,000, indirectly create 10 U.S. jobs, and are not required to directly manage the business enterprise. While the fifth preference category has never reached its numerical limit, its popularity has steadily increased since its inception. *See* § 5–3.1(b), *infra*.

The new employment-based preference system places a high priority on educational attainment, or excellence in a profession. To illustrate: most employment-based immigrants must have an outstanding offer of employment and labor certification, but these requirements are waived for applicants with extraordinary ability (first preference class). Multinational managers and executives are also exempted from the certification requirement. Because employers have often been unwilling to wait for labor certification to employ low-skilled workers, and because of the low allocation of 10,000 visas, the 1990 Act offered limited opportunities for individuals without skills or formal education.

The 1990 Act did not substantially change the Labor Department's certification process which requires showing that no qualified U.S. workers are available to work in the position sought. One minor revision required that notice of filing for labor certification be given to the union representative of the affected employees in the potential place of employment. The Act also replaced the Schedule A (list of occupations with shortages) and Schedule B (list of occupations with surpluses) with a pilot program in which the Labor Department was to determine whether labor shortages or surpluses exist in ten occupations. The pilot program, however, has expired and the Schedules A & B prevailed.

(1) DIVERSITY VISAS

Because the families of immigrants who arrived in the U.S. two or more generations ago no longer qualified for family-related visas (*see* § 1–2, *supra*), several of the countries which figured most prominently in this nation's early immigration history were considered "under-represented." Section 132 of the 1990 Act established a mail-in lottery to address the problem of under-representation by allocating 40,000 "diversity" visas (55,000 beginning in 1994) to nationals from "adversely affected" countries. Of the visas made available in this category, 40% were designated for natives of Ireland—a preference later dropped by the Technical Amendments. Significantly, this allotment formalized a method by which foreign nationals could immigrate without a close relative to sponsor them and without a job for which there is a labor shortage. Because "winners" would be selected on a random basis from millions of applications, the diversity visa became an unpredictable way for a foreign national to gain entry.

(2) INHABITANTS OF HONG KONG

Motivated by the then impending return of Hong Kong to the People's Republic of China, the 1990 Act allowed for separate means of aiding Hong Kong residents who wanted to immigrate to the U.S. The provision increased the allocation for immigration from Hong Kong to 10,000 (from 5,000) for the first three years of the Act, after which the level rose to 20,000. Other provisions benefited employees of certain U.S. businesses in Hong Kong, and employees of the U.S. mission there. In addition, the new law extended visas issued to Hong Kong residents until January 1, 2002, allowing them five years after the colony's return to China to decide whether to immigrate.

(3) REFUGEES AND TEMPORARY PROTECTED STATUS

The 1990 Act altered the process of attaining permanent residence for refugees. Refugees and asylees may apply for permanent residence one year after being admitted to the United States or after being granted asylum in the United States. The 1990 Act increased the number of refugees who may become permanent residents to 10,000 annually (from 5,000); moreover, refugees who had previously qualified were granted permanent residence by a special provision. The 1990 law also offered "Temporary Protected Status" (TPS) to aliens prevented from returning to their home countries because of war, disaster, or other unstable circumstances. The Technical Amendments extended this status to stateless residents of designated countries. The Attorney General was authorized to determine which countries are "protected." The Homeland Security Act of 2002 transferred the authority to determine protected status to the Secretary of Homeland Security and transferred responsibility for administering the program to U.S. Citizenship and Immigration Services. Countries are designated for TPS for a limited period of time, which can be renewed. El Salvador received designated TPS status from the statute itself; this designation expired in 1994 but was reinstated in 2001. Other countries have also been given TPS designation, including Bosnia–Herzegovina (1992), Kuwait (1991), Lebanon (1991), Liberia (1991), Somalia (1991), Rwanda (1994), Burundi (1997), Montserrat (1997), Sierra Leone (1997), Sudan (1997), Kosovo Province (Yugoslavia) (1998), Guinea–Bissau (1999), Honduras (1999), Nicaragua (1999), Angola (2000), and Haiti (2010); most of these designations have since expired.

Similar to TPS, the President, based on his constitutional powers to conduct foreign relations, may grant Deferred Enforced Departure for non-citizens from designated countries. DED is a temporary, administrative stay of removal and not a change of immigration status.

§ 1–7.2   Nonimmigrant Provisions

The 1990 Act modified some of the INA's provisions pertaining to non-citizens who seek entry for a temporary period of time or for a limited purpose. The 1990 law added four categories of nonimmigrants to the previous fourteen. Hence, the 1990 Act defined eighteen nonimmigrant categories, identified as A through R. The visa waiver pilot program benefiting foreign travelers, previously applicable to eight countries, was extended to any country designated by the Attorney General and Secretary of State. The 1990 law also modified visa categories for crewmembers (D), traders (E), temporary workers (H), and intracompany transferees (L).

The nonimmigrant categories added in 1990 are category O for nonimmigrants who have documented extraordinary ability in the arts, sciences, education, business, or athletics and seek entry to work within their field of expertise; category P for athletes, entertainers, and members of performance groups who seek entry to perform within their discipline; category Q for international cultural exchange programs and participants; and category R for persons within certain religious occupations.

§ 1–7.3 Naturalization

Until the 1990 Act, federal district courts had the ultimate responsibility to grant naturalization upon a recommendation by the INS and to administer the oath of allegiance to new U.S. citizens. Under the 1990 Act, the INS made the actual determination on naturalization and the district director administered the oath. The Immigration Technical Amendments Act of 1991, however, left the naturalization decision with the INS, but returned most oaths of allegiance to the federal district court. The courts were considered more conveniently located for the administration of oaths and better able to handle the problems of changing names which often occur with acquisition of U.S. citizenship.

The 1990 Act also provided that a non-citizen denied naturalization by the INS may seek *de novo* judicial review. In addition, the 1990 Act effectively overruled three Supreme Court determinations denying naturalization to Philippine veterans of World War II (see *INS v. Hibi*, 414 U.S. 5 (1973); *United States v. Mendoza*, 464 U.S. 154 (1984); *INS v. Pangilinan*, 486 U.S. 875 (1988)), thus naturalizing Filipinos who performed honorably in World War II.

§ 1–7.4 Grounds for Exclusion

Prior to the 1990 Act, there were more than thirty-four separate grounds for exclusion, many of which had complex rules and subdivisions. Some of these provisions were considered obsolete. For example, as a result of the McCarran–Walter Act of 1952, individuals could be excluded for beliefs or party membership, rather than specific acts. The 1990 Act attempted to simplify the rules but did not significantly narrow the grounds for exclusion.

a. *Health–Related Exclusion*

The health-related provisions were modified to exclude only persons with communicable diseases that threatened public health. This determination would be made by the Secretary of Health and Human Services. Moreover, the 1990 Act attempted to bring the health-related grounds for exclusion up to date with modern medical knowledge and procedure. A meaningful illustration of the 1990 Act's reforms was the elimination of the exclusion of gay men and lesbians. Further, the waiver for close relatives was expanded, thus diminishing the number of family-sponsored immigrants excluded for health reasons.

b. *Crime–Related Exclusion*

The substantive rules of criminal exclusion were not significantly modified by the 1990 Act. For persons under eighteen years of age, minor criminal conduct was not considered a ground for exclusion, provided the individual was convicted at least five years prior to his or her application for admission. One significant revision reduced the number of discretionary waivers by requiring the criminal conviction to have occurred at least fifteen years prior to application.

c. *Security as a Ground of Exclusion*

The 1990 Act barred any person who had engaged in terrorist activities, adding this ground of exclusion to espionage, sabotage, or violent overthrow of the U.S. government. Further, the Secretary of State was authorized to bar any non-citizen who would adversely affect the foreign policy of the United States. Critics of these provisions contended that the new law placed too much discretion in the Secretary of State. Moreover, they feared that the term "terrorism" would be construed broadly or for political reasons. Subsequent extensions of the terrorism ground (*see* § 1–10, *infra*) tend to support this concern.

d. *Communists*

The 1990 Act limited the exclusion of members of the Communist or another totalitarian party. This exclusion would no longer be applicable to nonimmigrants, and involuntary membership was excused. In addition, membership was excused if it was terminated at least two years prior to application (five years if the country was still controlled by a totalitarian dictatorship, *e.g.*, China). Again, a discretionary waiver is permitted for close relatives or if the waiver is in the public interest.

e. *Exclusion for Misrepresentation*

The 1990 Act retained the exclusion for misrepresentation (extended by the Immigration Marriage Fraud Act) with two modifications. First, the waiver for close relatives was expanded by changing the term "child" to "son or daughter," which included adult married children. Second, if the misrepresentation occurred more than ten years prior to the application, waiver was permitted. Unfortunately, a ten year bar is still excessive for many people.

§ 1–7.5 Grounds for Deportation

a. Marriage Fraud

The 1990 Act substantially modified three provisions of the 1986 Immigration Marriage Fraud Act. First, and most significantly, the new law recognizes marriages entered into while deportation or exclusion proceedings are pending. The law, however, required "clear and convincing evidence" that the marriage was undertaken in good faith and not for the purposes of evading immigration laws. Second, when a marriage is terminated within two years of the conditional grant of residence, the non-citizen spouse can petition for removal of the condition, regardless of who initiated the divorce. Third, discretionary waiver of the conditional residence requirement was made available if the non-citizen spouse or his or her child is the victim of battery or abuse.

b. National Security Concerns

The 1990 Act eliminated the provision for deporting members of the Communist party or other "subversive" organizations. Like the related ground of exclusion, the Act prescribed deportation for non-citizens who have engaged in terrorist activity or who would pose a threat to national security. Again, the Secretary of State has considerable discretion in determining whether an individual threatens foreign relations.

§ 1–8 THE VIOLENT CRIME CONTROL AND LAW ENFORCEMENT ACT OF 1994

In 1994, Congress authorized the Violent Crime Control and Law Enforcement Act of 1994 (108 Stat. 1796). The Violent Crime Control Act established a "criminal

alien tracking center," added harsher penalties for passport and visa offenses, increased Border Patrol funding,
and authorized faster removal procedures for aliens denied asylum and certain criminal aliens. The Act also
created the State Criminal Alien Assistance Program
that allows states and local governments to apply for
federal funds to cover expenses for incarcerating non-
citizens. Between 1997 and 2005, the federal government
distributed $4.1 billion to states in SCAAP funding.
Lastly, the Act added the S-nonimmigrant visa (or
"snitch" visa) for individuals supplying information
about a criminal or terrorist enterprise. *See* INA
§ 101(a)(15)(S).

§ 1–9   THE ACTS OF 1996
(AEDPA AND IIRIRA)

Congress responded to perceived anti-immigration sentiment in the 1990s with three new acts, each of which
was signed by President Bill Clinton in 1996. The first of
these acts was the Antiterrorism and Effective Death
Penalty Act (AEDPA), which became law on April 24,
1996. The second was the Personal Responsibility and
Work Opportunity Reconciliation Act (Welfare Act),
which became law on August 22, 1996. The third was the
Illegal Immigration Reform and Immigrant Responsibility Act (IIRIRA), which became law on September 30,
1996. While the Welfare Act removed many federal services for non-citizens, AEDPA and IIRIRA focused on
enforcement of immigration laws by, for example, increasing Border Patrol staffing, adding new grounds of
inadmissibility and removal, modifying the procedures
for exclusion and removal of non-citizens, and limiting
judicial review of immigration decisions. The AEDPA and

IIRIRA also increased the number of criminal acts for which a non-citizen could be removed and eliminated nearly all forms of relief for non-citizens with criminal convictions. One result of the 1996 statute was a dramatic increase in naturalizations, as long-time U.S. residents felt that their security was threatened by the denial of federal benefits and the new grounds for removal.

§ 1–9.1 Major Provisions of the 1996 Acts

Although both AEDPA and IIRIRA were examples of a similar immigration policy direction, IIRIRA, which was signed latest, went further and replaced many of AEDPA's provisions. For example, while AEDPA restricted judicial review of immigration decisions, IIRIRA restricted judicial review even further, barring review of decisions to deny admission to non-citizens and of most discretionary actions by the INS. IIRIRA also barred judicial review of removal orders based on an "aggravated felony" conviction. *See* § 9–4.3, *infra*.

One of the most significant changes made by IIRIRA modified the previous distinction between exclusion and deportation. Before IIRIRA, non-citizens who entered the U.S., even if they had avoided inspection, were subject to deportation proceedings. Persons who had not entered the U.S., including non-citizens who were paroled into the U.S., were subject to exclusion proceedings. After IIRIRA, all non-citizens who have not been inspected and admitted to the U.S. are subject to the grounds of inadmissibility. The grounds of inadmissibility were also expanded beyond the former grounds of exclusion to include unlawful presence in the United States. Non-citizens who have been lawfully admitted to the United States are subject to the grounds of removability. In addition, IIRIRA eliminated the procedural differences between exclusion and deportation proceedings, and provided that there would be only one "removal proceeding" for excluding or deporting non-citizens. Certain inadmissible non-citizens may, however, be subject to "expedited removal" proceedings and can be removed without a hearing unless they indicate intent to apply for asylum. *See* § 9–2.6, *infra.*

Both AEDPA and IIRIRA enlarged the definition of "aggravated felony." AEDPA added felonies such as those relating to gambling and passport fraud. IIRIRA expanded the definition further to include, for example, certain convictions imposing sentences of one year or more, even if the sentence was suspended. Formerly, aggravated felonies included crimes with sentences of five years or more. In addition to broadening the definition of aggravated felony, IIRIRA made aggravated felons ineligible for nearly all forms of relief from removal and barred review of the removal decision. Also, because AEDPA and IIRIRA provided for mandatory detention of aliens subject to removal for aggravated felonies, many more aliens have had to be detained. IIRIRA further provided for increasing detention space.

IIRIRA consolidated several earlier forms of relief from removal into a new provision called cancellation of removal. This type of relief is available to permanent residents and some "nonpermanent" residents (including undocumented non-citizens) who meet durational residency requirements and other criteria. *See* § 9–3.1(b), *infra.*

IIRIRA also stiffened the requirement for affidavits of support for immigrants entering on the basis of their relationship to U.S. citizens or permanent residents. A sponsor must have an income equal to or greater than

125% of the federal poverty standard and must agree in the affidavit to provide support for the immigrant. In addition, the sponsor must reimburse the government if the non-citizen receives means-tested public benefits within ten years of admission, unless he or she has naturalized. IIRIRA further added a ground of removability for any non-citizen who becomes a "public charge" within five years of admission.

Like the affidavit of support requirement, the 1996 Welfare Act reflected Congress' concern that immigrants were placing an increasing burden on the federal budget. The Welfare Act made most non-citizens, including permanent residents, ineligible for federal benefits such as food stamps and Supplemental Security Income (SSI). Immigrants who entered the country after August 22, 1996, were ineligible for all means-tested public benefits for a period of five years. The Welfare Act also authorized the states to deny benefits to certain classes of non-citizens. *See* § 13–4.4, *infra*.

§ 1–9.2 Judicial Response to the 1996 Acts

Judicial decisions since 1996 have limited the impact of some provisions of IIRIRA, particularly those provisions related to judicial review. Considering IIRIRA's limitations on judicial review, the Supreme Court in *Reno v. American–Arab Anti–Discrimination Committee*, 525 U.S. 471 (1999), narrowly construed a provision of the Act that attempted to bar review of the INS' decision to "commence proceedings, adjudicate cases, or execute removal orders." The Court found, however, that since the immigration authorities' power to commence proceedings is unreviewable, non-citizens have no claim against the government for selective enforcement of immigration laws. In *INS v. St. Cyr*, 533 U.S. 289 (2001), the Court found that the bars on judicial review do not prevent removable non-citizens from challenging their removal in *habeas corpus* proceedings. For further developments, *see* § 1–10.8, *infra*. In another decision favorable to removable non-citizens, the Court held in *Zadvydas v. Davis*, 533 U.S. 678 (2001) that immigration authorities may not hold a non-citizen in detention indefinitely following a removal order when that person cannot be returned to his or her home country. The Supreme Court has affirmed, however, that due process does not entitle a non-citizen to release pending removal proceedings. *Demore v. Kim*, 538 U.S. 510 (2003).

§ 1–9.3 Immigration Legislation, 1996–2002

For a time after 1996, Congress appeared to soften its anti-immigration stance somewhat. Recognizing the devastating effect the Welfare Act had on some impoverished residents, Congress in 1998 reinstated federal benefits for most permanent residents who were receiving them before passage of the Act. Congress also enacted several measures to make it easier for certain immigrants to obtain U.S. citizenship, including the Child Citizenship Act of 2000 (114 Stat. 1631) and the Hmong Veterans Naturalization Act of 2000 (114 Stat. 316). *See* § 12–2.2(c), *infra*. The Nicaraguan and Central American Relief Act of 1997 (NACARA) allowed certain nationals of Cuba and Nicaragua to adjust to permanent resident status despite having entered the U.S. illegally; that act also provided special forms of relief from removal for persons from some Central American and Eastern European countries.

The economic boom of the late 1990s increased the demand for foreign labor, and in response Congress passed two acts, the American Competitiveness and

Workforce Improvement Act of 1998 (112 Stat. 2681) and the American Competitiveness in the Twenty–First Century Act (114 Stat. 1251), which temporarily increased the number of H–1B visas for professional workers. The latter act imposed a fee on employers that would be used to fund technology training programs to reduce dependence on foreign labor.

Other laws passed during this period created new nonimmigrant classifications. The Victims of Trafficking and Violence Protection Act of 2000 (114 Stat. 1464) added the T category for victims of trafficking in persons. The Violence Against Women Act of 2000 (114 Stat. 1518) created the U category for persons who have suffered physical or mental abuse. That act also made it easier for persons who had been abused by a U.S. citizen spouse or parent to obtain citizenship or permanent residence.

A few laws passed during the late 1990s reflected concerns that the INS was effectively unable to process the growing number of immigration and naturalization petitions. The Child Status Protection Act of 2002 (114 Stat. 927) allowed children to retain their priority as minor children if they married or reached the age of twenty-one while waiting for immigration processing. The Legal Immigration and Family Equity (LIFE) Act (114 Stat. 2762) expanded the K visa (for spouses and accompanying children, in addition to fiancé(e)s, of U.S. citizens) and created the V visa (for spouses and children of permanent residents) to allow applicants to live and work in the U.S. while waiting for their immigrant petitions to be processed.

§ 1–10 IMMIGRATION LAW AS A CONSEQUENCE OF SEPTEMBER 11, 2001

The September 11, 2001, attacks resulted in significant changes in immigration law and policy. Congress passed several acts intended to improve national security, including the USA PATRIOT Act (115 Stat. 272), the Enhanced Border Security and Visa Entry Reform Act (116 Stat. 543), the Homeland Security Act (116 Stat. 2135), and the REAL ID Act (119 Stat. 231). One of the most dramatic consequences of these measures was the elimination of the INS and the transfer of immigration functions to the Department of Homeland Security in 2003. Other provisions of these acts broadened the class of people who can be excluded or removed for terrorist activity, mandated increased screening of applicants for admission, called for new data systems to track non-citizens in the U.S., and modified the forms of judicial review available for removal decisions.

Agencies involved in immigration responded to the perceived security threat by formulating rules that imposed special registration requirements on nonimmigrants from certain, mainly Arab or Muslim, countries; allowed the detention of persons suspected of terrorist connections; and permitted removal hearings for such persons to be conducted in secrecy. Immigration authorities have also selectively targeted non-citizens from Muslim and Arab backgrounds for enforcement of existing immigration laws.

In the years following September 11, the government increased its efforts to prosecute, remove, and prevent further immigration of undocumented non-citizens. The federal government sought to enhance border security by increasing the number of border patrol officers, expanding the use of "expedited removals," and building fences along the southern border. These efforts led to a rise in non-citizen detentions and the increased involvement of local law enforcement in implementing federal immigration laws. In addition, in the absence of comprehensive immigration reform, many state and local governments attempted to enact their own immigration policies. *See* § 2–2.5, *infra*.

§ 1–10.1   Department of Homeland Security

In November 2002, Congress passed the Homeland Security Act (116 Stat. 2135), which abolished the Immigration and Naturalization Service and transferred most immigration functions to the Department of Homeland Security (DHS). As suggested by the Commission on Immigration Reform some years earlier (*see* § 1–7.6, *supra*), the INS' service and enforcement functions were separated in this reorganization. These functions have been divided among three bureaus within the DHS: the U.S. Citizenship and Immigration Services (CIS), which adjudicates immigrant and nonimmigrant petitions, naturalization petitions, asylum applications, and other matters; the U.S. Customs and Border Protection (CBP), which includes the Border Patrol and immigration inspections at ports of entry; and the U.S. Immigration and Customs Enforcement (ICE), which enforces immigration laws in the interior of the U.S.

§ 1–10.2   Restrictions on Immigration

The USA PATRIOT Act (115 Stat. 272) and the REAL ID Act (119 Stat. 231) broadened the definition of "terrorist" as used in the grounds for inadmissibility and removal. Under these acts, anyone who endorses or provides material support to a terrorist organization, is a member of such an organization, or who actually participates in terrorist activities, is inadmissible or removable. *See* INA § 212(a)(3)(B).

To identify possible terrorists, U.S. consulates are required to check visa applicants' names against "lookout lists" prior to issuing a visa. This practice has increased processing time for many non-citizens seeking admission to the U.S. and caused some people to be denied admission because they were incorrectly identified as terrorists.

§ 1–10.3 Monitoring of Non–Citizens in the U.S.

After September 11, the INS was criticized for its inability to track non-citizens in the U.S. or to identify persons who might pose a threat to national security. In 2002, the INS initiated the National Security Entry–Exit Registration System ("NSEERS") that required nonimmigrants from twenty-five countries to register at INS district offices and report periodically as to their whereabouts and activities in the U.S. *See* § 8–2.2(c), *infra*. DHS scaled back the NSEERS in 2003 but retained the authority to fully reinstate the program if necessary. Along with NSEERS, the DHS and the State Department implemented the Student and Exchange Visitor Information System (SEVIS), a new database system, to track foreign students. *See* § 7–2, *infra*. Immigration authorities also began to enforce change of address reporting requirements that had been part of the INA since 1952 but were rarely publicized or enforced.

In order to better track the entry and exit of non-citizens, the Department of Homeland Security (DHS) enhanced the Visitor and Immigrant Status Indicator

Technology (US–VISIT) system. A 2008 rule issued by the DHS mandates, with limited exceptions, that all non-citizens entering the United States comply with US–VISIT procedures. US–VISIT requires non-citizens to provide biometric data in the form of a photograph and finger prints at visa offices and ports of entry. DHS uses the biometric data to check against criminal and terrorist watch lists and to ensure that the individual entering the United States is the same person who received a visa. DHS is developing expansions of US–VISIT to monitor the exits of non-citizens from the United States as well.

The USA PATRIOT ACT and the Enhanced Border Security and Visa Entry Reform Act of 2002 called for improved sharing and coordination of information and the development of comprehensive database systems. The Terrorist Screening Center (TSC) is one such example. Created in 2003, the TSC maintains the government's Terrorist Screening Database and provides access for local, state, and federal agencies to a single source of identifying information for persons suspected to be involved in terrorism.

§ 1–10.4 Post–September 11 Investigations and Detentions of Suspected Terrorists

In 2001 and 2002, the U.S. government carried out extensive investigations that targeted thousands of non-citizens, primarily from Arab and Muslim backgrounds. The Department of Justice interviewed approximately 8,000 non-citizens from Muslim and Arab backgrounds in an attempt to find people with information about terrorist activities. Some non-citizens suspected of ties to terrorism were detained for weeks or months without formal charges. Ultimately, none of the detainees were found to have terrorist connections, but the vast majority was removed because of immigration violations. Immigration officials refused to release information about people held in these "special interest" cases, and the Executive Office for Immigration Review authorized their removal hearings to be closed to the public. In addition, non-citizens from Muslim and Arab backgrounds were frequently singled out for enforcement of routine immigration violations. These practices were challenged in several cases, with mixed results. *See, e.g.*, *Center for Nat'l Sec. Studies v. Department of Justice*, 331 F.3d 918 (D.C.Cir.2003) (reversed order releasing information about special interest detainees); *Detroit Free Press v. Ashcroft*, 303 F.3d 681 (6th Cir.2002) (ordering removal hearings opened to the public); *North Jersey Media Group, Inc. v. Ashcroft*, 308 F.3d 198 (3d Cir.2002) (upholding closure of removal hearings). In 2009, an inmate challenged the detention program claiming that it violated equal protection demands of the Constitution. The Supreme Court determined that the adverse effect of the detention policy on Arab Muslims was not discriminatory and that the arrests and detentions were justified by national security interests. *Ashcroft v. Iqbal*, 129 S.Ct. 1937 (2009).

§ 1–10.5 Further Efforts to Prevent Undocumented Immigration

The federal government undertook a variety of efforts to prevent undocumented immigration during the first decade of the twenty-first century. These policies aimed to deter immigration through increased criminal prosecutions, enhanced border security, and improved citizenship verification systems.

Criminal prosecution of non-citizens for immigration violations increased dramatically in the 2000s, and immigration offenses rose to account for a significant number of all federal criminal convictions. The majority of these prosecutions were for charges of improper entry or reentry of a removed alien. Criminally prosecuting undocumented non-citizens for these immigration violations represented a shift in policy; previously, apprehended non-citizens were processed almost exclusively through civil removal hearings. A prominent component of this policy shift was Operation Streamline, a "zero tolerance" immigration enforcement strategy that quickly prosecuted non-citizens for misdemeanor violations and sentenced offenders for up to six months in jail, followed by removal. Operation Streamline replaced the Department of Homeland Security's earlier "catch and release" program that allowed suspected immigration offenders out of detention to await their removal hearings.

To demonstrate their intensified focus on combating illegal immigration, federal authorities staged high profile raids of businesses suspected of employing large numbers of undocumented workers. For example, in 2008, the Immigration and Customs Enforcement agency arrested more than 300 undocumented non-citizens working at a meat plant in Postville, Iowa. Within four days, more than 260 of these non-citizens pled guilty and were convicted of aggravated identity theft for using social security numbers on work documents that belonged to other people; they were sentenced to five months in prison before being subject to removal. In 2009, the Supreme Court ruled that the identity theft statute used by prosecutors in the Postville raid was inapplicable unless the defendant knowingly used the identification of another person. *Flores–Figueroa v. United States*, 129 S.Ct. 1886 (2009). Unfortunately for those convicted at Postville, the Supreme Court's decision came after their sentences and removals were completed.

The government also attempted to stem undocumented immigration by increasing its patrol of the United States–Mexico border. The Department of Homeland Security increased the number of Border Patrol agents from approximately 9,000 agents in 2001 to nearly 18,-000 agents in 2008. In 2006, President George W. Bush deployed 6,000 National Guard Troops to the southern border to augment border security efforts. In addition to increased agents along the border, the U.S. Customs and Border Protection agency began using new surveillance technologies such as remote video surveillance camera systems, ground based sensors, "virtual fences," and remote piloted Predator drones to detect unauthorized immigration.

The construction of fences along the southern border became a controversial component of the government's border security strategy. The Secure Fence Act of 2006 (Pub. L. 109–367) authorized the Department of Homeland Security to install reinforced fences and physical barriers along the southwest border. In response, DHS began construction of 670 miles of fencing in targeted border areas. Critics of the fences argue that it is ineffective in preventing illegal crossings, reroutes unauthorized immigrants into more dangerous crossing areas, and causes environmental harm to sensitive wildlife habitats.

Beginning in 2004, the federal government expanded its use of "expedited removals" to process and remove non-citizens apprehended at the border more efficiently. During an expedited removal, a DHS officer determines a non-citizen's removability, not an immigration judge.

The IIRIRA vested authority in the Attorney General (now Secretary of Homeland Security) to use the expedited removal process for any non-citizen who attempts to gain admission without proper documentation or through fraud. Initially, expedited removals were used only at ports of entry. In 2004, DHS expanded the application of expedited removals to all non-citizens apprehended within 100 miles of the U.S. border who lack proper documentation or commit fraud and have been present in the country for less than 14 days. The number of expedited removals more than doubled from 2004 to 2007. In 2007, expedited removals accounted for one-third of all non-citizen removals.

Many argue that the expanded use of expedited removals has been detrimental to asylum seekers. Studies found that during expedited removals, officers often failed to conduct complete asylum interviews, non-citizens who expressed fear of return were removed without being allowed to petition for asylum, and many non-citizens were not informed of their right to apply for asylum.

Another way authorities attempted to deter unauthorized immigration was by improving employment verification systems to reduce employment opportunities for undocumented workers. Federal law requires employers to report the name and social security numbers of their employees. In 2007, the Department of Homeland Security issued a rule requiring employers whose reports contain employee names that do not match the given social security numbers to resolve the inaccuracies within 90 days or face criminal penalties. A California District Court, however, entered a preliminary injunction to prevent the DHS from implementing the "no match" program based on a significant potential for errors in the verification system and possible discrimination against lawful employees. *AFL–CIO v. Chertoff*, 552 F.Supp.2d 999 (N.D.Cal.2007). In 2009, the Obama Administration announced that it was rescinding the "no-match" final rule. *See* § 3–3.6, *infra*.

In 2008, President George W. Bush issued an executive order requiring all federal contractors to verify the eligibility of their employees by using the Federal Electronic Verification System (E–Verify). Additionally, many states mandate the use of E–Verify for various employment sectors. E–Verify allows employers to check the names and social security numbers of their employees against Social Security Administration and DHS records electronically and within seconds. The use of E–Verify raises accuracy concerns, however, because of the potential for data entry errors and delayed entries regarding status changes. Fearing that these inaccuracies could lead to employment discrimination, Illinois passed a law in 2007 prohibiting employers within the state from using E–Verify. DHS sued the state to prevent the law's implementation and Illinois agreed not to enforce the statute until the lawsuit is resolved. Another major criticism of E–Verify is that the system is not designed to detect identity fraud. Some have proposed reforming the E–Verify system by requiring biometric social security cards, green cards, and immigration work authorization cards to ensure accuracy in employment verification.

The success of these increased efforts by the government to prevent undocumented immigration is difficult to measure. The number of non-citizen apprehensions declined from 1,676,000 in 2000 to 724,000 in 2008, the lowest level of apprehension since 1976. Nearly all of these apprehensions (97 percent in 2008) occurred along the southwest border and were of Mexican nationals (91 percent in 2008). It is unclear whether the decrease in apprehensions was the result of increased deterrence or because declines in the U.S. economy and labor markets lessened the motivation for unauthorized immigration. Still, despite government efforts, the number of unauthorized non-citizens residing in the United States increased from 2000 to 2008 from an estimated 8.5 million to 11.6 million. Non-citizens from Mexico comprise the largest group (61 percent in 2008) of these unauthorized immigrants.

§ 1–10.6 Increased Detentions

As a result of increased immigration enforcement, detentions of non-citizens rose dramatically during the first decade of the twenty-first century. In 2001 there were 95,214 immigration detentions; by 2007 the detention population increased to 311,169. While the number of detainees increased over this period, the average length of detention decreased from 89 days in 2001 to 30 days in 2008.

Immigration and Customs Enforcement (ICE) oversees immigrant detention at eight ICE operated facilities, six private facilities, and over 300 state and local facilities. The treatment of non-citizens at these facilities has been the subject of significant criticism. In *Orantes–Hernandez v. Gonzales*, 504 F.Supp.2d 825 (C.D. Cal. 2007), the court found non-citizens' access to counsel was hindered by inconvenient meeting hours, lack of privacy in lawyer–client meetings, and restrictions on telephone use. Furthermore, detainees are frequently moved from one detention center to another, making it difficult for detainees' lawyers and family members to locate them.

Detainee medical treatment has also been called into question. Between 2003 and 2009, 90 non-citizens died in detention facilities while many others suffered from inadequate medical attention. The Department of Immigration Health Services is charged with providing medical care for detainees, but in 2008 nearly 30 percent of DIHS positions went unfilled. Lack of oversight is also a concern; unlike standards for criminal inmates, standards for detainee treatment are not legally enforceable.

In response to these criticisms, ICE revised its National Detention Standards in 2008 making improvements to its legal and medical access standards. The new standards establish a Detention Facilities Inspection Group to monitor compliance. ICE and DIHS are also developing a new medical records system and treatment authorization process.

§ 1–10.7   State and Local Involvement

As part of its efforts to control undocumented immigration, the federal government expanded the role of state and local officials in enforcing immigration regulations. In 2002, the Department of Justice's Office of Legal Council (OLC) issued an Opinion declaring that state police may arrest a non-citizen solely on the basis of civil deportability. The OLC's determination reversed a 1996 Opinion that concluded that state police could only enforce provisions of the INA that related to criminal violations. Additionally, ICE developed the Agreements of Cooperation in Communities to Enhance Safety and Security (ACCESS) program to allow state and local law enforcement personnel to carry out immigration functions authorized by § 287(g) of the INA. Under the § 287(g) agreements, state and local officers can search, arrest, detain, and interrogate suspected immigration violators. *See* § 2–2.3, *infra*. Critics of the § 287(g) agreements fear that enforcement of immigration law by local police will lead to increased discrimination and racial profiling and discourage both documented and undocumented non-citizens from cooperating with local officials.

With the federal government's inability to enact comprehensive immigration reform, state and local legislatures became increasingly active in attempting to regulate immigration. In 2007, 1,562 pieces of legislation were introduced in all 50 states aimed at deterring undocumented immigration; 240 of the bills passed in 41 states. The number of immigration bills introduced in 2007 represented a five-fold increase from 2005. Many of these laws attempted to tighten citizenship verification and eligibility for employment, state benefits, and state licenses. *See* § 2–2.5, *infra*.

Cities and towns also enacted numerous immigration laws, representing both sides of the immigration debate. In 2006, the town of Hazleton, Pennsylvania, received much attention for enacting ordinances requiring apartment dwellers to prove their citizenship or resident status and prohibiting the employment or harboring of "illegal aliens." A federal district court declared both of Hazleton's ordinances unconstitutional on a variety of grounds. *Lozano v. City of Hazleton*, 496 F.Supp.2d 477 (M.D. Pa. 2007). In contrast to Hazleton's efforts to restrict undocumented immigration, cities such as Seattle, Washington, passed so-called "sanctuary laws" prohibiting city employees from "inquiring into the immigration status of any person." Another sanctuary city, New Haven, Connecticut, began issuing undocumented non-citizens city identification cards to ensure undocumented residents access to municipal services. *See* § 2–2.5, *infra*.

§ 1–10.8   The REAL ID Act and Judicial Review

In 2005, Congress enacted the REAL ID Act (119 Stat. 231) primarily to improve security standards for state issued drivers' licenses, but the act also modified the forms of judicial review available for removal decisions. In response to the Supreme Court's decision in *INS v. St. Cyr*, 533 U.S. 289 (2001), the REAL ID Act attempts to eliminate habeas corpus review for removal decisions by designating the courts of appeals as the "sole and executive means" for judicial review of a removal orders. INA § 242(a)(5). The act allows for judicial review at the district court level only when removal decisions raise "constitutional claims or questions of law." *See* § 2–2.1, *infra*.

§ 1–11   MORAL AND POLICY ISSUES OF IMMIGRATION

Immigration transforms the demographic profile of the U.S. population, particularly in large cities. Fears of overcrowding, unemployment, scarcity of resources, and of cultural fragmentation make the politics of immigration extremely complex. Immigration law is the principal means by which the country not only determines who will gain access to the limited resources and opportunities in the U.S., but also what will be the national and cultural identity of the U.S.

The argument in favor of free immigration—that is, an "open-door" policy of admission—asserts that fears are greatly exaggerated that the U.S. national and cultural identity will be destroyed by immigration. The United

States functions best as a heterogeneous, diverse population, and is expansive enough to absorb many new immigrants. Contrary to fears about job security, immigration is a necessary ingredient in plans for future U.S. economic growth and an enlarged workforce. In fact, even the influx of unskilled workers—often the group most feared for the potential to sap the country's social programs and resources—aid U.S. economic growth by filling jobs that many U.S. citizens and permanent residents do not want.

There is a moral component to the argument in favor of free immigration as well. Given the U.S. tradition as a country of immigrants, it is difficult to comprehend how current citizens—almost all of whom have benefited from immigration—can claim any right to exclude future immigrants. Also, family reunification is at the core of much of our immigration policy and is based upon a fundamental respect for the right to be with one's loved ones. Moreover, immigration law is only as effective as its enforcement. Weak enforcement and illegal immigration mock the actual numerical limits. Some scholars argue that the U.S. should adopt an immigration policy commensurate with the country's capacity for enforcement, or at least, legally recognize the actual number of non-citizens who enter the U.S.

The arguments against free immigration—that is, for maintaining a restrictive immigration policy—have figured prominently in the history of U.S. immigration law. These reasons are often based upon a fear that increased immigration will compromise the U.S. standard of living. It is argued that the very reason immigrants have historically been attracted to the United States—*i.e.*, the "American Dream"—is weakened if the country becomes overcrowded.

Specifically, the arguments against more lenient immigration are as follows: First, xenophobia plays a strong role in persons who seek to protect the cultural identity of the U.S.; the English-only movement is one example. Second, individuals who oppose freer immigration argue that there are finite resources and jobs; accordingly, U.S. citizens and lawful permanent residents should not have to compete with immigrants for them. Third, advocates of a restrictive immigration policy argue that there must be limits somewhere—certainly, the U.S. cannot allow the whole world to come here. Once the need for some limits is recognized, the U.S. ought to structure those limits in a realistic and pragmatic way that will be most advantageous to the future of the U.S. Fourth, some scholars argue that the U.S. should commit its resources to helping needy countries so that potential immigrants will be encouraged to remain in their developing countries. This perspective contends that immigration is a drain on other countries' human resources. All countries would benefit if these potential immigrants remained in their country of origin.

The tension throughout the debate comes from the fact that the U.S. is largely a nation of immigrants who did not inherit this land by divine right, but rather, by an open immigration policy and by taking the land from the indigenous inhabitants. It appears to be an act of selfishness, if not moral ingratitude, to bar future groups seeking to immigrate. In addition, U.S. citizens like to believe that this nation helps the world's needy, sharing the plentiful resources that the U.S. enjoys. U.S. immigration policy turns on this moral inquiry: what is the U.S. obligation to those people in need of a better place to live, and where should the lines be drawn?

Some political forces have played upon the nation's fears that open borders will exacerbate domestic problems such as crime, drugs, urban violence, unemployment, and homelessness. They remain unconvinced that freer immigration is a pragmatically or morally persuasive policy. Fears that foreign nationals will seek admission to the United States have influenced immigration policy for more than a century. Although this concern has come to the forefront of national attention since September 11, 2001, the attempt to keep out so-called dangerous elements—whether anarchists, Communists, or terrorists—has been a constant theme of immigration regulation.

Most immigration legislation has represented a compromise between these competing viewpoints. The 1990 Immigration Act, the 1996 acts, and legislation of the late 1990s all attempt to strike a balance between encouraging immigration of persons with family connections to the U.S. and individuals with skills that are needed in the U.S. economy, on the one hand, and preventing immigration of those people who would pose a financial burden or threaten the security of the nation, on the other. Since September 11, 2001, the balance seems to have shifted in favor of preserving national security at the expense of free immigration, raising new questions about the right to exclude others and the treatment of non-citizens within the U.S.

CHAPTER 2

THE SOURCE AND SCOPE OF THE FEDERAL POWER TO REGULATE IMMIGRATION AND NATURALIZATION

The broad power of the federal government to regulate the admission, removal, and naturalization of non-citizens has its roots in the early history of the United States. Modern statutes, Supreme Court decisions, and federal agency regulations attest to the plenary nature of this power. This chapter examines the source of federal power over immigration, the limits such federal power imposes on state attempts to regulate non-citizens, and the allocation of this power among the three branches of the federal government—Congress, the courts, and executive agencies.

§ 2–1 THE SOURCE OF THE FEDERAL POWER

Throughout the history of the United States the Supreme Court has upheld all manner of federal statutes regulating immigration. By contrast, Supreme Court decisions preclude states from passing legislation that directly impinges on this area of federal dominion. The Supreme Court's basis for action is clear when the area regulated is naturalization. Article 1, § 8, clause 4, of the United States Constitution specifically grants Congress the power to establish a "uniform Rule of Naturalization." By expressly allocating this power to Congress, the Constitution prevents the confusion that would result if individual states could bestow citizenship. The Constitution does not, however, explicitly provide that the power to deny admission or remove non-citizens rests with the federal government as opposed to state governments. Hence, in the early immigration cases the Supreme Court faced the problem of identifying the source of the federal government's exclusive and plenary power over immigration. Later cases considered the plenary power to be an aspect of an inherent sovereign power, although there have been recent challenges to that view. Some scholars have argued that the plenary power Congress enjoys is susceptible to abuse, often at the expense of fundamental human rights. These critics argue that Congress' current plenary power over immigration is an outdated manifestation of repression arising from racism, past wars, and post-September 11 fears.

§ 2–1.1 The Commerce Clause

In the earliest cases, the Court looked to the federal power over foreign commerce. The Commerce Clause in Article I, § 8, clause 3, of the United States Constitution provides Congress with the power "to regulate Commerce with foreign Nations, and among the several States." The Supreme Court in the *Passenger Cases* (*Smith v. Turner*, 48 U.S. 283 (1849)) invoked the Commerce Clause to ban the levy of fees upon foreigners wishing to disembark at state ports. The Court invalidated state immigration fees even though Congress had yet to implement any relevant federal regulations. The Court reasoned that Congress exclusively controlled foreign affairs and foreign commerce even when that power had not been exercised. In the *Head Money Cases*, 112 U.S.

580 (1884), the Court upheld a federally imposed tax on foreign immigrants, again with direct citation to the commerce power of Congress. As congressional action began to reach beyond taxation to other forms of regulation, however, the Court sought a broader ground for decision.

§ 2–1.2 Other Constitutional Provisions

Early cases also cite other specific constitutional provisions to support the inference that the federal government possesses complete power over international relations, arguably including immigration matters. In addition to citing the foreign commerce power, the Supreme Court in *Nishimura Ekiu v. United States*, 142 U.S. 651 (1892) cites the power to establish a uniform rule of naturalization; the power to declare war, and to provide and maintain armies and navies; and the power to make all laws necessary and proper. The *Fong Yue Ting v. United States*, 149 U.S. 698 (1893) case adds the power to define and punish piracies, felonies committed on the high seas, and offenses against the law of nations; as well as the presidential power to make treaties, to appoint ambassadors, and to select other public ministers and consuls.

The Migration and Importation Clause in Article I, § 9, clause 1, of the Constitution has also been considered a potential grant of power to Congress. This clause provides: "The Migration or Importation of such Persons as any of the States now existing shall think proper to admit, shall not be prohibited by the Congress prior to the year one thousand eight hundred and eight . . . ." The specific limit on congressional power before 1808 could be construed to imply that after 1808, Congress would have power over migration and importation. The prevailing interpretation, however, is that this clause was simply intended to bar any attempts by Congress to stop the slave trade before 1808.

The War Power, found in Article I, § 8, clause 11, could be cited as a potential source of federal control over immigration. The War Power gives Congress the authority to "declare war." The War Power authorized the exclusion and expulsion of enemy aliens. In the Alien and Sedition Acts, for example, Congress granted this power to the President. The Supreme Court upheld the constitutionality of such provisions in *Ludecke v. Watkins*, 335 U.S. 160 (1948), but it is difficult to stretch this rationale to cover the myriad of immigration provisions not apparently related to national security.

The Naturalization Clause in Article I, § 8, clause 4, has served as an argument for federal control over immigration, although the dissent in the *Passenger Cases* rejected it. *Passenger Cases*, 48 U.S. 283 (1849). As mentioned earlier, the Naturalization Clause's granting of power to "establish an uniform Rule of Naturalization" concerns decisions about citizenship rather than immigration generally.

Another way of looking at the possible constitutional provisions that provide specific federal power is to view them as indicative of an original intent to give the federal government power over all immigration. Under this view, the Commerce, War, and Naturalization Clauses together imply a federal right to regulate non-citizens. Later cases clarified, however, that such constitutional provisions are not the source of an implied right of the federal government to regulate non-citizens, but only show that the federal government is the national government and therefore the keeper of the inherent sovereign power to regulate international affairs.

§ 2–1.3 National Sovereignty

The Court eventually found the source of the federal power to regulate immigration in a combination of international and constitutional legal principles. *The Chinese Exclusion Case* (*Chae Chan Ping v. United States*, 130 U.S. 581 (1889)) was the first case to hold that the federal power to exclude non-citizens is an incident of national sovereignty. The Court reasoned that every national government has the inherent authority to protect the national public interest. Immigration is a matter of vital national concern. Furthermore, it is the role of the federal government to oversee matters of national concern, while it is the province of the states to govern local matters. Therefore, the Court found that the inherent sovereign power to regulate immigration clearly resides in the federal government. Subsequent cases reinforced national sovereignty as the source of federal power to control immigration and consistently reasserted the plenary and unqualified scope of this power. *Fong Yue Ting v. United States*, 149 U.S. 698 (1893) explicitly held that the power to expel or deport (now "remove") non-citizens rests upon the same ground as the exclusion power and is equally "absolute and unqualified."

§ 2–1.4 Delegated Versus Inherent Power

In *United States v. Curtiss–Wright Export Corp.*, 299 U.S. 304 (1936), the Court clearly distinguished between powers delegated to the federal government in the Constitution and inherent sovereign powers. Delegated powers over internal affairs were carved from the general mass of legislative powers previously governed by the states. States never possessed international powers, however, and the inherent sovereign powers were transferred from Great Britain to the *union* of states when the U.S. declared its independence. These powers were thus vested in the national government before the Constitution was written and exist without regard to any constitutional grant. It has been suggested that the apparently limitless scope of federal authority over immigration results from this undefined and indefinable source. The Supreme Court has upheld every exercise of this power and has consistently termed it "plenary and unqualified."

Other theorists suggest sources of federal immigration power that lie somewhere between the explicitly delegated powers of the Constitution and the inherent powers. The "Rule of Necessity," for instance, suggests that because federal power over immigration is *necessary* to the successful operation of the Constitution, this power may be interpolated into the Constitution.

Structural arguments have also been used to justify the exclusive federal immigration power. These arguments draw an inference of power from the structure of the Constitution as a whole, rather than from individual clauses. The Constitution's primary goal is to create a system of government for the nation, and a process through which its citizens establish the rules governing people within the territory. Under this premise, two structural arguments emerge.

First, the power to regulate immigration is essential to a nation's self-preservation. To be a sovereign nation, a people must have control over its territory. Without such control, a nation would be unable to govern itself and its borders effectively, and as a result, would be subject to the sovereignty of other nations. The power to regulate immigration is therefore inherent in the Constitution's creation of a sovereign nation.

Second, the power to regulate immigration is essential to the process of national "self-definition." Through the governmental process, a nation's citizens determine the values espoused by the nation, and hence, formulate the nation's identity. By determining who will comprise the nation and participate in creating the nation's identity, immigration laws constitute the process of self-definition itself. Decisions about who may enter a country say much about a nation. Although the process of national self-definition may be characterized as racist, discriminatory against outsiders, and otherwise unjust, it is an essential characteristic of a sovereign nation. These theories of self-preservation and self-definition mandate broad federal powers over immigration.

In addition, scholars have cited the constitutionally "implied" power of the executive over foreign affairs to authorize federal control over immigration. In *The Chinese Exclusion Case* (*Chae Chan Ping v. United States*), 130 U.S. 581 (1889)) (*see* § 2–1.3, *supra*), Justice Field stated that the Foreign Affairs Power is the foundation for all federal control over immigration. Moreover, this power has been cited as a basis for invalidating state statutes that attempt to regulate immigration. *See also*, *Chy Lung v. Freeman*, 92 U.S. 275 (1875).

Today the source of the federal government's power to control international affairs generally, and immigration in particular, is typically accepted. For example, during the Iranian hostage ordeal of 1979–81, the D.C. Circuit upheld the Attorney General's authority to order all Iranian students in the United States to report to INS offices and demonstrate the lawfulness of their presence in the country. *Narenji v. Civiletti*, 617 F.2d 745 (D.C. Cir.1979). Similarly, in 2001, Congress authorized the President to "use all necessary and appropriate force ... in preventing future acts of international terrorism against the United States." 50 U.S.C.A. § 1541. Many cases refer to these powers as constitutional when, in fact, the powers are drawn from a more ancient foundation. The practically unlimited scope of the federal power over non-citizens may possibly be traced back to the undefined nature of its source.

§ 2–2 THE SCOPE OF THE FEDERAL POWER

§ 2–2.1 Plenary Congressional Power

To date there have been no successful challenges to federal legislation that refuses admission to classes of non-citizens or removes resident aliens. Federal immigration power thus appears limitless. Indeed, the Supreme Court has stated: "[O]ver no conceivable subject is the legislative power of Congress more complete." *Fiallo v. Bell*, 430 U.S. 787 (1977); *Kleindienst v. Mandel*, 408 U.S. 753 (1972); *Oceanic Steam Nav. Co. v. Stranahan*, 214 U.S. 320 (1909). Extreme judicial deference bears witness to the truth of this statement.

Both the Constitution and the U.N. Charter have been dismissed as grounds for opposing federal immigration power. The federal courts and immigration authorities have without much consideration rejected assertions in *Hitai v. INS*, 343 F.2d 466 (2d Cir.1965), *Vlissidis v. Anadell*, 262 F.2d 398 (7th Cir.1959), and *Matter of Laurenzano*, 13 I. & N. Dec. 636, Interim Decision (BIA) 2065 (BIA 1970) that the immigration quota system is inconsistent with the U.N. Charter. The Supreme Court has upheld the constitutionality of federal statutes that detain non-citizens for the brief period necessary for their removal proceedings (*Demore v. Kim*, 538 U.S. 510 (2003)) and that exclude non-citizens on the basis of race (*The Chinese Exclusion Case*, 130 U.S. 581 (1889)) and political belief (*Kleindienst v. Mandel*, 408 U.S. 753 (1972)). Moreover, excluded non-citizens have no constitutional right to a hearing. *Shaughnessy v. United States ex rel. Mezei*, 345 U.S. 206 (1953). *Mezei* also determined that excludable non-citizens can be indefinitely detained if their country of origin refuses to accept them. The Supreme Court in *Zadvydas v. Davis*, 533 U.S. 678 (2001), however, distinguished between excludable non-citizens and non-citizens already within the country and found that non-citizens within the United States are entitled to constitutional protections against indefinite detention. For a discussion on the constitutionality of indefinite detention of resident aliens and excludable (now "inadmissible") non-citizens, see § 9–5, *infra*.

Even where the First Amendment and Equal Protection rights of U.S. citizens were jeopardized, in *Mandel,* the Supreme Court refused to look behind the Executive's negative exercise of discretion on the basis of a "facially legitimate and bona fide reason" in refusing entry to a Belgian Communist. First Amendment rights of U.S. citizens were arguably jeopardized again in 2001, when the Attorney General closed "special interest" removal hearings to the public and press. In *Detroit Free Press v. Ashcroft*, 303 F.3d 681 (6th Cir.2002), the court held that non-substantive immigration laws do not require special deference to the government and that closure violated the First Amendment right of access. The Third Circuit disagreed and in *North Jersey Media*

Group, Inc. v. Ashcroft, 308 F.3d 198 (3d Cir.2002), the court deferred to the Attorney General's judgment and held that no First Amendment right of access to removal hearings existed—allowing the hearings to remain closed. In 2003, the Supreme Court denied certiorari to *North Jersey Media Group, Inc.* One district court found non-citizens have First Amendment rights not to be deported (now "removed") for political activity. The U.S. Court of Appeals reversed for lack of standing and ripeness in *American–Arab   Anti–Discrimination   Committee   v. Thornburgh*, 940 F.2d 445 (9th Cir.1991), but later affirmed an injunction against deportation of the non-citizens. *American–Arab Anti–Discrimination Committee v. Reno*, 119 F.3d 1367 (9th Cir.1997). In 1999, the Supreme Court vacated the judgment of the Ninth Circuit, holding that INA § 242(g) deprives the federal courts of jurisdiction over claims of selective enforcement of immigration laws by the Attorney General. The Supreme Court, however, has not reached a conclusion regarding whether there are First Amendment protections for non-citizens at deportation hearings. *Reno v. American–Arab Anti–Discrimination Committee*, 525 U.S. 471 (1999). *See* § 13–4.5, *infra*.

Federal courts have sustained the detention of non-citizens convicted of aggravated felonies without the opportunity for a pre-detention hearing under the Fifth and Eighth Amendments. Courts have also rejected other Fifth Amendment Due Process and Equal Protection claims. The Fifth Circuit, in response to an Equal Protection challenge to the Nicaraguan Adjustment and Central American Relief Act, held that "[d]ue process does not require Congress to grant aliens from all nations the same chances for admission to or remaining within the United States." *Rodriguez–Silva v. INS*, 242 F.3d 243

(5th Cir.2001). The Supreme Court also rejected a Fifth Amendment claim by refusing to reach the issue of whether the Equal Protection principles inherent in the Due Process Clause of the Fifth Amendment protected a class of undocumented Haitians detained without parole. Instead, the Court ruled that the non-citizens' claims were to be judged under nondiscriminatory federal statutes and regulations. *Jean v. Nelson*, 472 U.S. 846 (1985). In *Fernandez–Roque v. Smith*, 734 F.2d 576 (11th Cir.1984), the Eleventh Circuit held that Cuban nationals found excludable had no constitutionally-based liberty interest in challenging denial or revocation of parole. In *Garcia–Mir v. Meese*, 781 F.2d 1450 (11th Cir.1986), the same court further held that unadmitted "Mariel" Cuban parolees did not have any other Due Process liberty interest entitling them to parole revocation hearings, nor were they entitled to such hearings on the basis of international law. *See* 8 C.F.R. § 212.12 for parole determinations and revocations respecting "Mariel" Cubans. Similarly, deportation (now "removal") orders are consistently upheld despite a myriad of conceivable constitutional challenges. Courts inclined to limit Due Process restrictions have cited *Mathews v. Diaz*, 426 U.S. 67 (1976) ("In the exercise of its broad power over naturalization and immigration, Congress regularly makes rules that would be unacceptable if applied to citizens.").

Although the authority of Congress to regulate immigration is extensive, the Constitution does afford protections to non-citizens within the United States. Justice Murphy explained in his concurrence to the Supreme Court's decision in *Bridges v. Wixon*, 326 U.S. 135 (1945) that once non-citizens enter into the United States they become "invested with the rights guaranteed by the Constitution." For example, the Court observed in *Zad-*

vydas v. Davis, 533 U.S. 678 (2001) that "a statute permitting the indefinite detention of an alien would raise a serious constitutional problem." The Court avoided the anticipated constitutional issue by reading an implicit limitation into the statute at issue. Accordingly, the Court interpreted 8 U.S.C. § 1231(a) to provide that after a presumptively reasonable six month detention, continued detention is authorized only if removal is reasonably foreseeable. Justice Scalia's opinion for seven justices in *Clark v. Martinez*, 543 U.S. 371 (2005) reaffirmed that courts, while still respecting the plenary power of Congress, may avoid potential constitutional conflicts and read limitations into immigration statutes to respect the rights of non-citizens. Following the Supreme Court's example in *Zadvydas*, the Ninth Circuit held that it is "constitutionally doubtful" that Congress may authorize the detention of a non-citizen for 30 months without providing a removal hearing. *Tijani v. Willis*, 430 F.3d 1241 (9th Cir.2005). The Ninth Circuit also extended *Zadvydas* protections against indefinite detention to arriving non-citizens whose removal is not reasonably foreseeable. *Nadarajah v. Gonzales*, 443 F.3d 1069 (9th Cir.2006).

In *McNary v. Haitian Refugee Center*, 498 U.S. 479 (1991), the Supreme Court held that challenges to the constitutionality of the practices, procedures, and policies of the INS were proper subjects for judicial review. In that case Congress had required non-citizens to seek judicial review of individual denials of special agricultural worker (SAW) status only in the context of exclusion or deportation. Since the Haitian Refugee Center was not challenging an individual determination but the entire process, because of the presumption in favor of review of administrative actions, and because constitutional issues were at stake, the court found jurisdiction. In 1992, the U.S. Court of Appeals held in *Haitian Refugee Center v. Baker*, 949 F.2d 1109 (11th Cir.1991) that non-citizens, who were detained on the high seas and, therefore, had never presented themselves at a U.S. border, had no right to judicial review of INS decisions under the Administrative Procedure Act. Moreover, the court held that these non-citizens had no individual right of action, unless they qualified for refugee status. Further, the court held that the refugee center and their attorneys had no First Amendment claim for gaining access to those detained non-citizens. The Supreme Court denied certiorari over the objections of Justice Blackmun, who complained that this challenge to the U.S. procedures for determining whether a group faces political persecution should not go unheard by the Court. In *Sale v. Haitian Centers Council, Inc.*, 509 U.S. 155 (1993), the Court upheld summary return of Haitians intercepted on the high seas without considering their asylum claims. The interdiction agreement ceased to exist in 1994, when Haitian President Aristide withdrew his government's consent. *See* § 9–1.1(a)(2), *infra*.

Courts continue to review the practices, procedures, and policies of immigration authorities even though Congress has attempted to restrict judicial review. For example, INA § 242(g) provides that no court shall have jurisdiction to hear a claim "arising from the decision or action by the Attorney General to commence proceedings, adjudicate cases, or execute removal orders...." The Supreme Court followed this directive in *Reno v. American–Arab Anti–Discrimination Committee*, 525 U.S. 471 (1999), but in 2001, the Court warned that a "strong presumption in favor of judicial review of administrative action" exists and the INS must overcome "the long-

standing rule requiring a clear and unambiguous statement of congressional intent to repeal habeas jurisdiction." *INS v. St. Cyr*, 533 U.S. 289 (2001). *See* §§ 2–3.2,
9–4.3 *infra*.

In 2005, Congress tried to provide such a clear and
unambiguous statement with the REAL ID Act, seeking
to eliminate habeas jurisdiction of removal orders. *See*
INA § 242(a)(5). The Act, however, allows for judicial
review of factual and discretionary decisions that prompt
constitutional claims or questions of law. *See* INA
§ 242(a)(2)(D). Courts have taken divergent approaches
in determining which immigration decisions raise "questions of law." For example, the Second Circuit in *Chen v.
Gonzales*, 162 Fed.Appx. 37 (2d Cir.2006) refused to
review the decision of an immigration judge that a petitioner's untimely application for asylum was not excused.
The court held that to be a "question of law," the issue
must be more than a "quarrel" over the fact-finding and
discretionary determinations of immigration authorities.
In contrast, the Ninth Circuit in *Ramadan v. Gonzales*,
479 F.3d 646 (9th Cir.2007) asserted that it could review
an immigration official's decision regarding whether an
untimely asylum application was excusable because "the
application of law to fact" constitutes a question of law
under the court's jurisdiction.

Federal legislative decisions removing or refusing admission to non-citizens are subject to a very limited scope
of judicial scrutiny. Cases sustaining the broad authority
of Congress over immigration have relied upon *Fiallo v.
Bell*, 430 U.S. 787 (1977). Thus far, the courts have
largely resisted prodding by scholars and litigants to
encourage the courts to scrutinize federal power over this
subject matter.

§ 2–2.2 Permissible and Impermissible State Regulations

States may not usurp the federal power over immigration. State attempts to regulate concurrently in a field already occupied by a federal statute have been struck down under the doctrine of preemption. In *Hines v. Davidowitz*, 312 U.S. 52 (1941), for example, the Court held that the Federal Alien Registration Act preempted Pennsylvania alien registration provisions. Under the preemption doctrine, federal law in a specific area may even preclude consistent state regulations.

The courts will also invalidate state statutes that conflict with federal policy. This ground has been coupled with the Equal Protection Clause to invalidate state discrimination against non-citizens. In the nineteenth and early twentieth centuries, the Supreme Court allowed states to pass laws discriminating against non-citizens. In 1915, however, the case of *Truax v. Raich*, 239 U.S. 33 (1915) reversed this trend. *Truax* rested on the dual ground of equal protection and exclusive federal control over immigration. The Court overturned an Arizona statute restricting non-citizen employment. Besides being a denial of equal protection, the statute ran contrary to the implied intent of Congress that non-citizens allowed into the country under federal immigration laws would be free to pursue a livelihood. Similarly, the Court rejected state laws restricting fishing rights of non-citizens denied naturalization in *Takahashi v. Fish and Game Commission*, 334 U.S. 410 (1948), and length of residency requirements for non-citizens seeking welfare in *Graham v. Richardson*, 403 U.S. 365 (1971). In each of these cases, the Court perceived a conflict between the burdensome state regulation and the decision by federal authorities to grant residency privileges to the affected non-citizens. This approach forced the Court to strike down the state laws because "[t]o permit state legislatures to adopt divergent laws on the subject of citizenship requirements would appear to contravene this explicit constitutional requirement [Art. I, § 8, cl. 4] of uniformity." *Graham v. Richardson*, 403 U.S. 365 (1971).

In a somewhat different vein, the Court in *Nyquist v. Mauclet*, 432 U.S. 1 (1977) invalidated a New York law that made commencing naturalization procedures a prerequisite to receiving financial assistance for higher education. Although the *Mauclet* case relied heavily on the Equal Protection Clause for its outcome, the Court noted that encouraging naturalization is an illegitimate purpose for discrimination in light of federal dominion over that field. It seems then that even where state statutes do not directly conflict with federal policy covering the same subject, the state statute may still be struck down if it meddles in immigration policy.

The mere existence of the federal immigration power does not, however, automatically preclude state regulations affecting non-citizens. The Supreme Court so held in *De Canas v. Bica*, 424 U.S. 351 (1976). In *De Canas* the Court upheld a California statute prohibiting an employer from knowingly employing a non-citizen who is not entitled to lawful residence in the U.S. if such employment would have an adverse effect on lawful resident workers. Writing for the majority, Justice Blackmun stated, "[T]he Court has never held that every state enactment which in any way deals with aliens is a regulation of immigration and thus per se preempted by this constitutional immigration power, whether latent or exercised."

In finding that the Immigration and Nationality Act (INA) did not preempt the California statute, the Court noted that the nature of the subject matter does not compel a conclusion of exclusive federal control. Furthermore, the INA does not show a congressional intent to occupy the field totally. The Court distinguished previous preemption cases in the immigration field on four grounds. First, the California statute did not cover ground specifically addressed by the INA. (Such a federal statute, however, was adopted in 1986.) Second, Congress seemed at that time to authorize concurrent state legislation in the area regulated by the state law. Third, the federal interest is not as predominant in a "situation in which state law is fashioned to remedy local problems, and operates only on local employers and only with respect to individuals whom the federal government has already declared cannot work in this country." Fourth, the previous cases overturned statutes that "imposed burdens on aliens lawfully within the country that created conflicts with various federal laws." *De Canas* indicates that states may fill gaps in the federal regulatory scheme governing non-citizens so long as the state regulations do not run afoul of federal policy. For example, Georgia's law restricting issuance of driver's licenses to "illegal aliens" was upheld because it "mirrored federal objectives and furthered a legitimate state goal." *John Doe No. 1 v. Georgia Dep't of Pub. Safety*, 147 F.Supp.2d 1369 (N.D.Ga.2001) (quoting *Plyler v. Doe*, 457 U.S. 202 (1982)).

State immigration regulations must also be consistent with the Equal Protection Clause. In *Plyler v. Doe*, 457

U.S. 202 (1982), the Supreme Court struck down a Texas statute that denied access to public education for undocumented children. The Court held that denying educational opportunities and imposing a lifetime hardship on an isolated group of children who have little control over their undocumented status was an affront to the goals of the Equal Protection Clause. The *Plyler* decision is careful to point out that while undocumented children may receive protection as a "suspect class," this treatment does not apply to adult undocumented aliens because "their presence in this country in violation of federal law is not a 'constitutional irrelevancy.' " The Equal Protection Clause, however, does apply to lawful permanent residents. In *Graham v. Richardson*, 403 U.S. 365 (1971), the Supreme Court affirmed that the word "person" in the Fourteenth Amendment encompasses lawfully admitted resident aliens and that state laws affecting this "discrete and insular" minority of residents are subject to strict judicial scrutiny.

§ 2–2.3 Local Enforcement of Federal Immigration Law and "Sanctuary" Policies

Lower courts have upheld state and local enforcement of the criminal provisions of federal immigration law. *Gonzales v. City of Peoria*, 722 F.2d 468 (9th Cir.1983), *overruled on other grounds (standing) by Hodgers–Durgin v. De La Vina*, 199 F.3d 1037 (9th Cir.1999). In addition, courts have determined that federal statutes do not preempt state laws authorizing police to arrest noncitizens for violations of federal immigration law. *United States v. Vasquez–Alvarez*, 176 F.3d 1294 (10th Cir.1999) (holding that 8 U.S.C.A § 1252c does not "displace the preexisting general authority of state or local police officers to investigate and make arrests for violations of federal law, including immigration law"). Disputes remain, however, concerning the authority and role of state and local authorities in enforcing the civil provisions of federal immigration policy.

Seeking to clarify the scope of the Ninth Circuit's decision in *Gonzales v. City of Peoria*, 722 F.2d 468 (9th Cir.1983), the Office of Legal Counsel (OLC) of the Department of Justice stated in a 1996 opinion that state and local authorities may not detain a non-citizen "solely on the suspicion of civil deportability." The opinion explains that the civil provisions of the INA represent a "pervasive and preemptive regulatory scheme" that precludes local enforcement of federal civil immigration laws. In 2002, the OLC reversed its 1996 opinion and asserted that state and local officers possess the "inherent power" to arrest non-citizens for both criminal and civil immigration violations. The 2002 opinion determined that federal law did not preempt state and local authorities from making arrests based on civil deportability; rather, the opinion concludes, federal immigration regulation "accepts state arrest authority as a given." While OLC opinions are not controlling for judicial decisions or binding on state and local governments, they do represent the interpretation of statutes and case law by the Department of Justice and inform the actions of the department.

The OLC's 2002 opinion relies on a pair of Tenth Circuit decisions to justify its conclusion that state and local authorities may make arrests for civil immigration violations. In the first case, *United States v. Salinas–Calderon*, 728 F.2d 1298 (10th Cir.1984), a state trooper pulled over a truck for erratic driving and was informed by a passenger that six men inside the vehicle were in the country without authorization. The Tenth Circuit found that the officer had probable cause to arrest the non-citizens without a warrant given that state troopers have "general investigatory authority to inquire into possible immigration violations." The *Salinas–Calderon* decision, however, did not differentiate between criminal and civil immigration regulations. Furthermore, the Tenth Circuit's ruling concerned the possible suppression of evidence from the arrest against the driver of the truck and not the validity of the charges against the six undocumented non-citizens.

In the second case on which the OLC relied for its 2002 opinion, *United States v. Vasquez–Alvarez*, 176 F.3d 1294 (10th Cir.1999), the Tenth Circuit again did not distinguish between criminal and civil immigration violations. The court upheld an arrest by an Oklahoma police officer of a previously removed non-citizen for selling illegal drugs. The officer was unaware of the non-citizen's status as a previously removed alien at the time of the arrest. The Tenth Circuit found that the Oklahoma law authorizing state officers to make arrests for federal crimes included the authority to make arrests for federal immigration violations. It is unclear whether this holding applies to civil immigration violations because the non-citizen was charged with the criminal violation of reentry of a previously removed alien. The decision in *Salinas–Calderon*, like the decision in *Vasquez–Alvarez*, could be interpreted as supporting the position of the 2002 OLC opinion, but it is not dispositive.

The federal government cannot compel state and local officials to enforce federal immigration law. Federal statutes, however, can authorize willing state and local officials to carry out federal immigration laws in designated circumstances. Under 8 U.S.C. § 1103(a)(8), the Attorney General may recruit state and local law enforcement to perform immigration duties in the event of an actual or imminent "mass influx of aliens." Federal law also provides express permission for state and local officials to arrest and detain individuals who (1) are illegally present in the United States and (2) have been previously convicted of a felony and deported (now "removed") from the country. 8 U.S.C. § 1252c. Congress intended § 1252c to solicit the aid of state and local police in capturing non-citizens in violation of INA § 276 that prohibits reentry of a removed alien. The statute requires state and local police to confirm the illegal status of a non-citizen with federal authorities before making an arrest.

INA § 287(g), added by IIRIRA in 1996, allows state and local police to receive expanded authority to enforce federal immigration policy by entering into agreements with the Attorney General (now Secretary of Homeland Security). With these § 287(g) agreements, state and local authorities become "qualified to perform a function of an immigration officer in relation to the investigation, apprehension, and detention" of non-citizens suspected of immigration violations. INA § 287(g)(1). The § 287(g) agreements, also known as memorandums of understanding (MOU), between the federal government and state and local authorities vary in particulars but generally stipulate that the Immigration and Customs Enforcement (ICE) agency will train state and local officers, local enforcement will be conducted under the supervision of ICE, and state and local officers will be treated as federal employees under the Federal Tort Claims Act. The MOUs must also specify the powers and responsibilities of the state and local officers and the duration of the agreement. Since 2003, many state and local governments across the country have entered into MOUs with the federal government pursuant to § 287(g).

The 2002 OLC opinion and the prevalence of § 287(g) agreements are troubling to many. Critics argue that enforcement of federal immigration laws by state and local agencies leads to increased racial profiling of individuals based on their foreign appearance. In addition, studies show that non-citizens are less willing to report crimes and cooperate with state and local officers because of their fear that the police will enforce federal immigration laws. Others worry that state and local enforcement agencies lack the resources and expertise to administer federal immigration law properly.

These concerns have led numerous cities and states to establish "sanctuary" laws. The term "sanctuary" as it relates to modern immigration policy dates back to the 1980s when it referred to the policy of a number of churches and synagogues that offered assistance to individuals from Central America who were denied opportunity for asylum. State and local governments enact "sanctuary" measures through local ordinances, executive orders, and administrative policies to limit government employees from investigating an individual's immigration status. A Detroit, Michigan, statute, for example, prohibits city officials from asking the immigration status of people not suspected of crimes. New York City has a similar policy that limits the extent to which city officials can gather information regarding immigration status and limits what can be disclosed to federal officials. Alaska and Oregon both passed legislation that prevents state agencies from using resources to make immigration inquiries.

Sanctuary policies, however, do not allow local officials to impede federal immigration investigations or refuse to cooperate with federal immigration authorities. Sections of Illegal Immigration Reform and Immigrant Responsibility Act (IIRIRA), 110 Stat. 3009, and the Personal Responsibility and Work Opportunity Act ("Welfare Reform Act"), 110 Stat. 2105, state that local laws may not prohibit government employees and agencies from exchanging information with federal immigration officials. New York City challenged these provisions from IIRIRA and the Welfare Reform Act on Tenth Amendment grounds in *City of New York v. United States*, 179 F.3d 29 (2d Cir. 1999) but was unsuccessful. The Second Circuit ruled that the federal statutes preempted an executive order prohibiting New York City officials from voluntarily providing the immigration status of non-citizens to federal authorities. There was no Tenth Amendment violation because IIRIRA and the Welfare Reform Act did not "compel states and local governments to enact or administer any federal regulatory program."

§ 2–2.4 Local Laws Affecting International Relations

The Supreme Court has upheld state probate laws that incidentally and indirectly affect foreign nationals. *Clark v. Allen*, 331 U.S. 503 (1947) called into question a state statute that conditioned a nonresident alien's right to inherit property upon the existence of a reciprocal right of U.S. citizens to inherit property in the non-citizen's nation. The statute's opponents claimed it was an incursion into an area of exclusive federal control. The Court labeled that claim "far fetched" and held that such laws are valid unless they conflict with a federal law or statute.

Of course, if states use their probate laws to implement foreign policy, they enter a forbidden field. Hence, in *Zschernig v. Miller*, 389 U.S. 429 (1968) the Court struck down an Oregon statute requiring non-citizens entitled to inherit property to show that their government would allow the receipt of such property without confiscation. The provision necessarily mandated judicial inquiry into the current status of political rights in foreign countries. Such inquiries are the exclusive responsibility of the federal government. A state may not cross the line between incidental and direct effects on either immigration or foreign policy. *See, e.g., Crosby v. National Foreign Trade Council*, 530 U.S. 363 (2000) (holding that federal sanctions and a Burma Executive Order preempted a Massachusetts' law that limited the purchase of goods or services from companies that did business with Burma).

California has similarly attempted to cross the line into immigration and foreign policy. For example, the U.S. District Court for California's Central District held in *League of United Latin American Citizens v. Wilson*, 908 F.Supp. 755 (C.D.Cal.1995) that California's Proposition 187 inappropriately usurped federal authority in purporting to deny primary/secondary education and federally funded benefits to undocumented non-citizens. The court said that federal law preempts Proposition 187's requirement that state agents discover, report, and initiate the removal of non-citizens who are unlawfully present according to state-created criteria. The District Court, however, found that California could limit post-secondary education, state-funded benefits, and even some cooperative state-federal benefits to lawful U.S. residents. Congress eliminated these areas of state regulation left open by the court when it enacted the Personal Responsibility and Work Opportunity Reconciliation Act. The three areas that California could limit were now either preempted or invalid. *League of United Latin American Citizens v. Wilson*, 997 F.Supp. 1244 (C.D.Cal.1997).

§ 2–2.5 Local Enforcement of Local Immigration Laws

While some localities have sought to make it easier for undocumented immigrants to live in society through "sanctuary" policies, other localities have enacted ordinances that impose burdens on undocumented immigrants to deter their presence. The increased proliferation of local laws targeting undocumented non-citizens has prompted litigation throughout the country. Based on the Supreme Court's analysis in *DeCanas v. Bica*, 424 U.S. 351 (1976), federal immigration law preempts these local immigration ordinances if states and cities go too far in seeking to restrict the employment, housing, and benefits of non-citizens. Hazleton, Pennsylvania, for example, passed an ordinance entitled the Illegal Immigration and Reform Act that imposed fines on landlords renting to undocumented immigrants, and suspended or removed the licenses of businesses that hired undocumented workers. Hazleton's local immigration law, however, was struck down in *Lozano v. Hazleton*, 496 F.Supp.2d 477 (M.D. Pa.2007). The federal Immigration Reform and Control Act (IRCA) contains an express preemption clause for state or local laws that create civil or criminal sanctions for immigration offenses. The district court in Pennsylvania held that while the IRCA allows for states or localities to impose punishments through licensing for violations of federal immigration law, states and localities cannot use licensing sanctions to punish violations of non-federal immigration laws, which the Hazleton ordinance attempted to do.

The district court also held that the landlord provisions of Hazleton's IIRA conflicted with federal immigration policy. For example, the Hazleton ordinance denied housing to certain classes of non-citizens that are permitted to work in the United States, such as immigrants who have completed an asylum application, immigrants who have filed an application for adjustment of status to lawful permanent resident, and immigrants who have filed an application for suspension of deportation. In addition, the district court held that provisions of the Hazleton law violated due process because the law did not provide sufficient notice to individuals facing eviction or provide access to appropriate judicial procedures.

In *Villas at Parkside Partners v. City of Farmers Branch*, 496 F.Supp.2d 757 (N.D. Tex. 2007), a federal district court in Texas also held a local ordinance that restricted renting to non-citizens preempted by federal law. The district court issued a permanent injunction blocking the ordinance, which required owners and property managers to obtain "evidence of citizenship or eligible immigration status" of those seeking to rent an apartment. The court found that the city's ordinance created potential conflicts for landlords because its requirements for "eligible immigration status" relied on U.S. Department of Housing and Urban Development (HUD) regulations that are not consistent and coextensive with federal immigration standards. The HUD regulations define eligibility for federal housing subsidies but are not meant to determine a person's immigration status. Under the ordinance, a landlord would have faced criminal sanctions for renting apartments to certain non-citizens, such as foreign students, who are in the country legally but do not qualify for HUD subsidies.

In 2010, Arizona passed a far-reaching immigration law aimed at dramatically expanding the power of local law enforcement officials to curtail undocumented immigration. The law authorizes local and state police to detain and conduct status checks of individuals they suspect are undocumented immigrants. The law also makes it a criminal misdemeanor for immigrants not to carry documentation of their citizenship or residency status. A provision of the law allows local citizens to sue local governments and agencies to enforce state and federal immigration laws. Many, including President Obama, condemned the Arizona law for invading federal authority as well as encouraging harassment and racial profiling of Hispanics.

§ 2–2.6 The Role of the States and Localities in the Federal E–Verify Program

The E–Verify program, formerly the Basic Pilot Program, is an Internet-based system in which employers can learn about their employees' employment eligibility status utilizing data from the Social Security Administration (SSA) and the Department of Homeland Security (DHS). States and cities have enacted legislation mandating the use of E–Verify by local employers with varying degrees of success. The Hazleton, Pennsylvania, ordinance, discussed above, required participation in the Basic Pilot Program under certain circumstances. In *Lozano v. Hazleton*, 496 F.Supp.2d 477 (M.D. Pa. 2007), the district court held that because federal law did not mandate the use of this program and considered it "voluntary" and "experimental," there was a conflict between the local ordinance and federal immigration law. The court also was troubled by the severely limited appeals process available to employees under the Hazleton ordinance, noting that federal law allows for individuals to contest a finding by E–Verify that they are undocumented workers.

Several states have passed laws mandating the use of E–Verify by state agencies and contractors, including California, Colorado, Minnesota, Mississippi, Missouri, and Rhode Island. In 2007, Oklahoma also passed a law requiring that public employers participate in the E–Verify program. The United States Chamber of Commerce filed suit against the state on the grounds that the Immigration Reform and Control Act (IRCA) preempted the state law. *Chamber of Commerce v. Henry*, 2008 WL 2329164 (W.D. Okla.2008). The district court granted a preliminary injunction to prevent the implementation of the Oklahoma law based on the court's ruling that the statute imposes a civil penalty by increasing the tax rates of employers who do not comply with the E–Verify program. The court held that IRCA preempts efforts by states to regulate immigration by imposing civil or criminal sanctions.

In *Arizona Contractors Association, Inc. v. Candelaria*, 534 F.Supp.2d 1036 (D. Ariz.2008), however, a district court held that an Arizona statute mandating that employers use E–Verify was not preempted by federal law and that the state law did not conflict with federal immigration policies. The court held that there is no evidence of congressional intent to prevent states from mandating the use of E–Verify and that federal policy encourages the program's use. Hence, the court found no conflict between the Arizona law requiring the use of E–Verify and federal policy that, at the time of the court's decision, made such use merely voluntary. The Arizona law satisfied due process, the court concluded, by mandating a full evidentiary hearing in the Superior Court of Arizona before an employer could be sanctioned for employing undocumented non-citizens.

Perhaps the factor distinguishing the Oklahoma and Arizona statutes is the form of penalties employers face if they do not comply with E–Verify. While Oklahoma imposed increased taxation on non-compliant employers, the Arizona law allows for the possible suspension or revocation of business licenses. IRCA states that federal immigration law shall "preempt any State or local law imposing civil or criminal sanctions (*other than through licensing and similar laws*) upon those who employ, or recruit or refer for a fee for employment, unauthorized aliens." 8 U.S.C. § 1324a(h)(2) (emphasis added). The decisions in *Henry* and *Candelaria* indicate that the constitutionality of state E–Verify mandates will depend on the language of each state's statute and the penalties it imposes.

While some states have mandated the use of E–Verify, Illinois attempted to prohibit the use of the program by all employers within the state. The Illinois Right to Privacy in the Workplace Act sought to prevent employers from using E–Verify until studies indicated that the system is ninety-nine percent accurate. The federal government filed a lawsuit seeking to enjoin the enforcement of this Illinois statute. The federal government argued that Congress mandated that E–Verify be available for all employers in all fifty states, and that the Illinois law is thus preempted under the Supremacy

Clause. In 2009, a district court sided with the federal government and granted a permanent injunction against Illinois from implementing the statute.

§ 2–2.7 Local Immigration Policy Through Driver's License Regulations

States have used their authority to issue driver's licenses to play a role in immigration policy. Often states have used their authority to deny undocumented immigrants the opportunity to obtain a driver's license. A small minority of states have granted undocumented non-citizens driver's licenses in order to better protect public safety. Proponents of issuing driver's licenses to undocumented non-citizens argue that it increases the number of licensed drivers on the road, reduces the number of uninsured drivers, reduces the number of "hit and run" accidents, and increases the trust and communication between immigrants and law enforcement officers. Furthermore, some argue that granting driver's licenses to undocumented migrants will help state and local police by bringing more people into the largest law enforcement databases in the country. Others argue, however, that minimal requirements for driver's licenses pose a threat to national security.

Despite the public safety benefits of providing undocumented non-citizens with driver's licenses, over the past two decades there has been a move among states to restrict this practice. While undocumented non-citizens have tried to challenge these restrictions in class action lawsuits, they have been mostly unsuccessful. A district court in *John Doe No. 1 v. Georgia Dep't of Pub. Safety*, 147 F.Supp.2d 1369 (N.D. Ga. 2001), for example, found no federal preemption of a Georgia law that deprived undocumented non-citizens the chance to obtain a driver's license. The statute mirrored federal immigration objectives by denying benefits to non-citizens present in the country illegally. The court also held that Georgia had a legitimate state interest in limiting the issuance of driver's licenses to citizens and legal residents in order to deter illegal immigration.

Congress attempted to influence state requirements for driver's licenses through the enactment of the REAL ID Act of 2005. Under the act, states that issue driver's licenses to undocumented non-citizens risk having their state driver's licenses declared unacceptable as a form of identification for federal purposes, including air transportation. States have until 2013 to fully implement all of the REAL ID Act's requirements before the act's consequences take effect. The impact of the REAL ID Act, however, is still uncertain as many states have passed legislation refusing to implement the requirements of the act.

§ 2–2.8 Local Immigration Policy Regarding Access to Education

With its ruling in *Plyler v. Doe*, 457 U.S. 202 (1982), the Supreme Court established that states cannot deny elementary and secondary public education to undocumented school-age children. *See* § 13–4.3, *infra*. A federal district court used the *Plyer* decision to invalidate the sections of California's Proposition 187 that sought to deny access of undocumented children to public schools in California. *League of United Latin American Citizens v. Wilson*, 908 F.Supp. 755 (C.D. Cal. 1995).

The right of an undocumented non-citizen to public education, however, may not extend to higher education. In *Equal Access Education v. Merten*, 305 F.Supp.2d 585

(E.D. Va. 2004), controversy arose when the Virginia Attorney General issued a memorandum to all Virginia public universities and colleges, stating that "illegal and undocumented aliens should not be admitted into our public colleges and universities at all...." The memorandum also instructed school officials to report suspicions that a university student is unlawfully present in the country to federal immigration officials. The federal district court upheld the state's policy, finding that there is "no Supremacy Clause bar to a state admissions policy that denies admission to illegal aliens, provided that in doing so, the institutions implementing the policy adopt federal immigration standards." The court also held that Congress has not manifested its intent to preempt state laws or policies that deal with immigrant access to post-secondary education. The denial of access to undocumented non-citizens to public universities and colleges is not universal among states. California and Texas, for instance, offer in-state tuition benefits for undocumented non-citizens who can prove residency within the state.

§ 2–2.9　Local Control Over Access to Benefits

The 1996 Personal Responsibility and Work Opportunity Act ("Welfare Act"), 110 Stat. 2105, gave states the authority to determine a person's eligibility for public benefits in which states play a role in funding. As a result, states differ in the benefits they offer and in their eligibility requirements for non-citizens. In *Aliessa v. Novello*, 754 N.E.2d 1085 (N.Y.2001), New York argued the Welfare Act granted the state authority to deny state Medicaid benefits to the plaintiffs based on their status as legal aliens. The New York Court of Appeals held, however, that the New York statute was unconstitutional based on the Supreme Court's analysis in *Graham v.*

Richardson, 403 U.S. 365 (1971). The court found that the Welfare Act's delegation of authority that allowed states to distinguish between certain categories of legal immigrants in administering benefits violated the constitutional obligation of Congress to establish a uniform, national system for regulating immigration. Since this provision of the Welfare Act was not a valid federal delegation of authority and aliens are considered a "discrete and insular" minority, the court subjected the New York law to strict scrutiny. The New York court concluded that the statute violated the Equal Protection Clause because it denied benefits based on citizenship status.

The Tenth Circuit considered the same question presented in *Aliessa* and reached the opposite conclusion. In *Soskin v. Reinertson*, 353 F.3d 1242 (2004), the Tenth Circuit upheld a Colorado law that removed the Medicaid benefits of "legal" non-citizens who did not meet the state's requirements of a "qualified alien." The Tenth Circuit reasoned that the Welfare Act created two separate welfare systems, one for citizens and one for non-citizens. States, based on the Welfare Act, have the discretion to decide which types of non-citizens qualify for benefits, subject only to a rational-basis review under the Equal Protection Clause. The Colorado classification system survived a rational-basis review, the court found, because it aligned with federal policy in its definition of a "qualified alien." The Tenth Circuit's decision relied on the Supreme Court's precedent in *Mathews v. Diaz*, 426 U.S. 67 (1976) that Congress may discriminate between different classes of non-citizens.

As the contrasting New York and Tenth Circuit decisions of *Aliessa* and *Soskin* illustrate, the limits on the authority of states to determine what benefits should be given to certain classes of immigrants are still unclear.

It is clear that the scope of federal immigration power is not so broad as to preclude all state statutes touching the field. While state statutes may be preempted, the *De Canas* case holds that the unexercised federal power over immigration is not by itself a bar to state regulations which single out non-citizens. State statutes that do not discriminate against foreign residents should be analyzed under the preemption doctrine to determine if they conflict with congressional intent or govern an area already exclusively covered by federal law.

Somewhat related issues of federalism were raised by Arizona and California in seeking federal reimbursement for state expenditures incurred by reason of the federal government's failure to control immigration. The U.S. Court of Appeals in *Arizona v. United States,* 104 F.3d 1095 (9th Cir.1997) and *California v. United States*, 104 F.3d 1086 (9th Cir.1997) held that the states' claims presented non-justiciable political questions and should be dismissed. The U.S. Supreme Court denied review. The federalism issue also arose in *City of New York v. United States*, 179 F.3d 29 (2d Cir.1999) when the City challenged two federal statutes that preempted an executive order prohibiting City officials from voluntarily providing the immigration status of non-citizens to federal authorities. The court held that the federal statutes forbidding the restriction of information to the authorities did not violate the Tenth Amendment because they did not "compel states and local governments to enact or administer any federal regulatory program."

§ 2–3 THE FUNCTIONS OF THE THREE BRANCHES OF THE FEDERAL GOVERNMENT IN REGULATING IMMIGRATION

§ 2–3.1 The Legislature

The plenary and unqualified power of the federal government to regulate immigration, naturalization, and related foreign policy belongs to Congress. The possible international consequences of decisions in this area have made the federal judiciary extremely reluctant to substitute its judgment for the legislature's. Justice Jackson articulated the Court's position in *Harisiades v. Shaughnessy*, 342 U.S. 580 (1952): "[A]ny policy towards aliens is vitally and intricately interwoven with contemporaneous policies in regard to the conduct of foreign relations, the war power, and the maintenance of a republican form of government. Such matters are so exclusively entrusted to the political branches of government as to be largely immune from judicial inquiry or interference." Subsequent decisions echo this sentiment. Since the judiciary poses no obstacle, Congress has been historically free to "exclude aliens altogether or prescribe the terms and conditions upon which they may enter and stay in this country." *Lapina v. Williams*, 232 U.S. 78 (1914). For example, Congress exercised its plenary authority in the Illegal Immigration Reform and Immigrant Responsibility Act of 1996 (IIRIRA) that facilitated the removal of non-citizens. IIRIRA appears to show that the legislative branch wields the full measure of the federal plenary power over immigration. In light of two 2001 Supreme Court decisions, some scholars have questioned whether the plenary power may have its limits, but in each case the Court recognized the potential for legislative plenary power.

In *Nguyen v. INS*, 533 U.S. 53 (2001), the Court upheld INA § 309(a)'s distinction between illegitimate children of U.S. citizen fathers and mothers, but rather than using a weak rational basis review, the Court applied the same intermediate scrutiny standard it would apply for ordinary gender-based classifications. This approach appears to be a step toward limiting the plenary power doctrine, but the Court noted that it did not need to address the "wide deference accorded to Congress in the exercise of its immigration and naturalization power" because it held that no equal protection violation had occurred. Similarly, in *Zadvydas v. Davis*, 533 U.S. 678 (2001), the Court described the legislature's plenary power as being "subject to important constitutional limitations." The Court, however, decided the case on statutory grounds and held that a reasonable time limitation on post-removal detention must be inferred because "a statute permitting indefinite detention would raise a serious constitutional problem."

§ 2–3.2   The Judiciary

Historically, the Supreme Court has taken a virtual "hands off" approach to immigration law, but it has stopped short of abdicating all responsibility. The Court has reserved a narrow ground for review that is worth examining for hints of a possible future trend of limitation on Congress's plenary power.

a.   Decisions Relating to Exclusion (Now "Inadmissibility")

Non-citizens who are outside the national boundaries of the United States have no constitutional rights and as a practical matter have absolutely no basis for challenging their exclusion (now "inadmissibility") from this country. Although the Supreme Court has not quite deemed exclusion cases non-justiciable under the political question doctrine, the extreme degree of deference the Court has given to legislative determinations on this issue makes the ground of review so narrow as to be practically nonexistent. Indeed, earlier cases show a complete "hands off" attitude by the courts. Later cases refer to a narrow ground of review.

Fiallo v. Bell, 430 U.S. 787 (1977) illustrates the Court's ginger approach to exclusion (now "inadmissibility") cases. A federal statute governing immigration preferences made it more difficult for illegitimate children and fathers to be reunited in this country than illegitimate children and mothers. *See* § 5–2.1, *infra*. U.S. citizens and resident aliens disadvantaged by the statute challenged it on equal protection grounds. In a footnote, Justice Blackmun, for the majority, explicitly rejected the government's contention that admission of non-citizens is not an appropriate subject for review by stating, "[O]ur cases reflect acceptance of limited judicial responsibility under the Constitution even with respect to the power of Congress to regulate the admission and exclusion of aliens. . . ." Having once established the reviewability of this type of case, however, Blackmun applied a standard of review that is, as dissenter Justice Marshall noted, "toothless." The Court acknowledged that the statute discriminates on the basis of sex and that the fathers have no opportunity to prove a close relationship in order to overcome the statutory presumption. Blackmun flatly stated, "[T]he decision nonetheless remains one solely for the responsibility of the Congress and wholly outside the power of this Court to control." After the Court's decision, Congress did resolve the problem raised in this case by providing that illegitimate children can obtain the same immigration benefits from the natural father as from the natural mother, "if the father has or had a bona fide parent-child relationship." INA § 101(b)(1)(D).

Federal courts have since reserved a narrow ground of review in a few exclusion (now "inadmissibility") cases: *Hill v. INS*, 714 F.2d 1470 (9th Cir.1983) (although the power of Congress is plenary, exclusion of homosexuals is improper without a medical certificate of psychopathic personality, sexual deviation, or mental defect); *Allende v. Shultz*, 845 F.2d 1111 (1st Cir.1988) (government impermissibly denied visa to widow of former Chilean president invited to speak in U.S. on the basis of general harm to foreign policy created by her presence); *Abourezk v. Reagan*, 785 F.2d 1043 (D.C. Cir.1986) (when noncitizen is a member of Communist or anarchist organization, government may exclude non-citizen based on projected engagement in activities prejudicial to public interest, only if reason for threat to public interest is independent of membership in proscribed organization); and *Harvard Law School Forum v. Shultz*, 633 F.Supp. 525 (D.Mass., *vacated without opinion* 852 F.2d 563 1st Cir.1986) (Law School forum entitled to preliminary injunction prohibiting Secretary of State from refusing travel permission to a Palestine Liberation Organization member without a "facially legitimate and bona fide reason" for the INS decision). These court decisions presaged legislative actions in 1990 that removed restrictions on the immigration of homosexuals and eased issuance of nonimmigrant visas to members of the Communist Party and other controversial visitors. In 2008, the Ninth Circuit held that a visa denial for the spouse of a

U.S. citizen is subject to review to ensure that the denial was for a "facially legitimate and bona fide reason." *Bustamante v. Mukasey*, 531 F.3d 1059 (9th Cir.2008).

b. Resident Alien Cases

Resident aliens possess recognized constitutional rights. When pitted against the federal power to regulate immigration, however, these rights provide little protection. Deportation proceedings (now "removal proceedings") must observe procedural due process. *Japanese Immigrant Case*, 189 U.S. 86 (1903). The Court does not, however, examine the adequacy of the fair hearing Congress prescribes. *Id*. Although in early deportation cases the Court refused to recognize substantive Due Process guarantees, recent cases indicate this practice may change. In *Galvan v. Press*, 347 U.S. 522 (1954) the Court at least looked at the congressional classification making Communists deportable and found "it was not so baseless as to be violative of due process and therefore beyond the power of Congress." Similarly, in *Mathews v. Diaz*, 426 U.S. 67 (1976) the Court implicitly applied equal protection analysis to a federal statute that discriminated between two classes of non-citizens. The Court upheld the classification as rational. Instead of declaring a harsh provision unconstitutional, the Second Circuit in *Francis v. INS*, 532 F.2d 268 (2d Cir.1976) construed INA § 212(c) very broadly to give relief to non-citizens who had lived in the United States for at least seven years. Despite Congress enacting IIRIRA and repealing the statute that provided this discretionary relief, the case still shows the court's willingness to recognize non-citizens' rights. The Supreme Court followed suit in *INS v. St. Cyr*, 533 U.S. 289 (2001) by declaring that INA § 212(c) relief remains available for non-citizens who entered plea agreements at a time when the relief would have been available. *See* § 9–3.1(c), *infra*.

On the heels of *St. Cyr*, the Supreme Court decided *Zadvydas v. Davis*, 533 U.S. 678 (2001) and once again hinted at a willingness to recognize substantive due process guarantees. The INS ordered Zadvydas deported, but Germany, the Dominican Republic, and Lithuania refused to accept him in 1994, 1996, and 1998, respectively. Zadvydas challenged his continued detention. By reading the INA in light of the Constitution's demands, the Court held that the statute implicitly limits post-removal detention to a reasonable length of time and thus avoided constitutional concerns about indefinite detention. The Court narrowed this holding in *Demore v. Kim*, 538 U.S. 510 (2003). Based on the fact that Zadvydas faced "potentially permanent" detention, while Kim's detention had a "definite termination point," the Court rejected a due process challenge to the mandatory detention provision and held that Congress may detain Kim and non-citizens such as him "for the brief period necessary for their removal proceedings." *Demore v. Kim, supra*. Despite this narrowing holding, the Court did not revert back to its "hands off" approach. In *Clark v. Martinez*, 543 U.S. 371 (2005), the Supreme Court applied the holding from *Zadvydas* that allows the government to detain non-citizens only as long as "reasonably necessary" to non-citizens ordered removed who are inadmissible and non-citizens ordered removed based on the determination that they pose a risk to the community or are a flight risk.

Congress explicitly stated in INA § 236(e) that the Attorney General's discretionary judgment "shall not be subject to judicial review," but the Court cited *INS v. St.*

Cyr, 533 U.S. 289 (2001) and held that this language did not show a "particularly clear" statement that Congress intended to preclude *habeas* review. For a discussion on judicial review of removal orders, see § 9–4.3, *infra*. Although these cases provide no direct precedent for questioning the plenary authority of Congress over immigration matters, they do suggest that congressional power in this area may some day fail to support an arbitrary act or classification.

In fact, the Supreme Court has more than once expressed in dicta regret in not being able to afford some measure of protection to resident aliens. For example, in *Galvan v. Press*, 347 U.S. 522 (1954), Justice Frankfurter remarked:

> [C]onsidering what it means to deport an alien who legally became a part of the American community, and the extent to which, since he is a "person" an alien has the same protection for his life, liberty and property under the Due Process Clause as is afforded to a citizen, deportation without permitting the alien to prove that he was unaware of the Communist Party's advocacy of violence strikes one with a sense of harsh incongruity. If due process bars Congress from enactments which shock the sense of fair play—which is the essence of due process—one is entitled to ask whether it is not beyond the power of Congress to deport an alien who was duped into joining the Communist Party, particularly when his conduct antedated the enactment of the legislation under which his deportation is sought. And this is because deportation may ... deprive a man "of all that makes life worth living."

The weight of authority backing the government's plenary power to deport was too great to push aside with the mere invocation of "fair play," however, and the Court held due process was satisfied in this case. These judicial rumblings may yet produce results.

Congress attempted to clarify the role of judicial review in deportation (now "removal") cases in the REAL ID Act of 2005. The language of the act bars habeas review and makes petition to the courts of appeals the sole and exclusive means for review of removal orders. Courts of appeals may review "constitutional claims or questions of law" that arise from such immigration decisions. *See* 2–2.1, *infra*.

Deportation (now "removal") is not a criminal penalty. Therefore, deportation orders cannot be challenged as a violation of the *ex post facto* clause when past conduct, that was not illegal when committed, is the basis for a deportation order (*Mahler v. Eby*, 264 U.S. 32 (1924); *Harisiades v. Shaughnessy*, 342 U.S. 580 (1952)). For the same reason denial of bail (*Carlson v. Landon*, 342 U.S. 524 (1952)), double jeopardy (*United States v. Ramirez–Aguilar*, 455 F.2d 486 (9th Cir.1972)), speedy trial (*Argiz v. U.S. Immigration*, 704 F.2d 384 (7th Cir.1983)), and cruel and unusual punishment (*Fong Yue Ting v. United States*, 149 U.S. 698 (1893)) challenges are of no use. Similarly, IIRIRA's repeal of § 212(c) discretionary waivers of deportation does not have an impermissible retroactive effect on non-citizens convicted at trial of aggravated felonies prior to the repeal. *Rankine v. Reno*, 319 F.3d 93 (2d Cir.2003). The Supreme Court held that the repeal does not apply retroactively for those non-citizens who pleaded guilty since plea agreements involve a *quid pro quo* between a criminal defendant and the government. *INS v. St. Cyr*, 533 U.S. 289 (2001). *See* § 9–3.1(c), *infra*.

c. Naturalization Cases

The Fourteenth Amendment "contemplates two sources of citizenship, and two only, birth and naturalization. Citizenship by naturalization can only be acquired by naturalization under the authority and in the forms of law." *United States v. Wong Kim Ark*, 169 U.S. 649 (1898). As with exclusion and deportation (now "inadmissibility" and "removal"), the Supreme Court has accorded great deference to the naturalization guidelines set by Congress. In *United States v. Ginsberg*, 243 U.S. 472 (1917) the Court stated, "An alien who seeks political rights as a member of this nation can rightfully obtain them only upon the terms and conditions specified by Congress. Courts are without authority to sanction changes or modifications; their duty is rigidly to enforce the legislative will...." In cases involving classifications in the naturalization process, the Court has given a near absolute presumption of validity to distinctions drawn by Congress. For example, the Supreme Court has twice upheld INA § 309(a) despite the fact that the acquisition of citizen provision "imposes a set of requirements on the children of citizen fathers born abroad and out of wedlock to a non-citizen mother that are not imposed under like circumstances when the citizen parent is the mother." *Nguyen v. INS*, 533 U.S. 53 (2001). *See also Miller v. Albright*, 523 U.S. 420 (1998). These cases applied an intermediate level of scrutiny, but would have "assessed the implications ... of wide deference accorded to Congress ... [i]f INA § 309(a) did not withstand conventional equal protection scrutiny." *Nguyen v. INS*, 533 U.S. 53 (2001).

As discussed above, the legislative branch guides all phases of immigration, including the regulation of foreign residents and naturalization. In most cases the judiciary has refused to second-guess federal legislation, although the courts retain the power of review. *See* chapter 4, *infra.*

d. Asylum Cases

The Supreme Court has also deferred to Congress on issues involving asylum. The problem has been reconciling the nation's commitments under the Protocol relating to the Status of Refugees with Congress' expressions of substantive and procedural rights under the Refugee Act of 1980. In *INS v. Cardoza–Fonseca*, 480 U.S. 421 (1987) the Supreme Court used its power of review to determine the standard to be applied in granting asylum. Specifically, the Court held that refugees seeking asylum pursuant to § 208(a) (now § 208(b)) of the INA must show only a "well-founded fear of persecution" in their country of origin, and not a "clear probability" of persecution, as was required for withholding of deportation under § 243(h) (now § 241(b)(3)) of the INA. *See* § 10–2.3, *infra.* The Court had earlier decided in *INS v. Stevic*, 467 U.S. 407 (1984) that the "well-founded fear" standard did not govern § 243(h) (now § 241(b)(3)) applications for withholding of deportation.

In rejecting the "clear probability" test, Justice Stevens made it clear that the Court was within its boundaries. He wrote:

> [C]ourts must respect the interpretation of the agency to which Congress has delegated the responsibility for administering the statutory program. . . . But our task today is much narrower, and is well within the province of the judiciary. We do not attempt to set forth a detailed description of how the well-founded fear test should be applied. Instead, we merely hold that the

Immigration Judge and the BIA were incorrect in holding that the two standards are identical.

Therefore, while generally deferring to Congress, the Court will take an indirect role in shaping immigration policy by ruling on issues of statutory interpretation, including whether INS (now Department of Homeland Security) regulations are consistent with the intent of legislation.

Critics have also charged that persons seeking asylum are victims of discrimination on the basis of their nationality. In particular, persons from El Salvador and Guatemala have alleged that they have not been given fair adjudications of their asylum claims. In a significant settlement, the Department of Justice agreed to re-adjudicate up to 150,000 asylum claims; further, all Salvadorans who had arrived to this country by September 19, 1990, and Guatemalans who had arrived by October 1, 1990, were for a period of time protected from deportation (now "removal") and received work authorization. *American Baptist Churches v. Thornburgh*, 760 F.Supp. 796 (N.D.Cal.1991). It is estimated that as many as half a million people might have been affected by the settlement. Congress extended the protection from removal for certain Salvadorans and Guatemalans in the Nicaraguan Adjustment and Central American Relief Act by allowing them to apply for cancellation or suspension of removal. Similarly, Congress passed the Haitian Refugee Immigration Fairness Act of 1998, which prevents the deportation of some 48,000 Haitians who fled persecution in Haiti in the early 1990s.

§ 2–3.3 The Executive

As in other areas of the law, the function of executive agencies in the field of immigration is to enforce the legislation passed by Congress. The structure of the federal executive agencies that administer and enforce the immigration laws is discussed in chapter 3, *infra*. Once Congress determines which classes of non-citizens will be denied admission or removed, the executive decides who fits within each class. Since the executive has no inherent power over immigration, it must stay within the grant of authority defined by the statute. Any unauthorized executive decisions are illegal and the courts may overturn them. *Mahler v. Eby*, 264 U.S. 32 (1924).

Congress need not give the agencies detailed direction. The courts have not hesitated to uphold broad delegations of power to the enforcement agency. *Jay v. Boyd*, 351 U.S. 345 (1956). In general, Congress need only delineate basic policy. Agencies then have relatively free rein in creating procedures to implement, administer, and enforce the immigration laws. Congress may also make the executive decisions final, thereby precluding review by the courts of agency factual findings. IIRIRA, for example, stripped the courts of jurisdiction to review any individual determination which arose from or is related to summary removal under INA § 235(b)(1). INA § 242(a)(2)(A)(i). The courts are also precluded from reviewing any decision by the Attorney General to invoke the summary removal provisions. INA § 242(a)(2)(A)(ii). The application of summary removal to individual non-citizens, including the determination of a non-citizen's credible fear, is not subject to judicial review. INA § 242(a)(2)(A)(iii). In addition, IIRIRA bars judicial review of procedures and policies adopted by the Attorney General to implement the summary removal provisions of INA § 235(b)(1). INA § 242(a)(2)(A)(iv). Courts have interpreted these limitations on judicial review narrowly. *See* § 9–4.3, *infra*.

In 1983, an issue surfaced concerning the division of power between the executive and legislative branches that pertained to deportation procedures. Congress had reserved the power of one house of Congress to veto any individual decision by the INS to suspend deportation (now "cancel removal"). See § 9–3, *infra*, for a discussion of cancellation of removal. An East Indian from Kenya, who was to be deported after the House of Representatives exercised this veto, challenged the congressional action as a violation of constitutional separation of powers. The Supreme Court held in the landmark decision of *INS v. Chadha*, 462 U.S. 919 (1983) that such legislative veto provisions violated the constitutional requirement that, before becoming law, all bills must pass both the House and the Senate, and be presented to and signed by the President.

Finally, Congress may not give the executive the power to impose punishment for crimes. The courts alone may exercise this power and the procedures must comply with the constitutional requirements for all criminal prosecutions. Deportation (now "removal") is not considered criminal punishment, however, even when triggered by illegal acts.

CHAPTER 3

ADMINISTRATIVE STRUCTURE OF IMMIGRATION LAW

There are five major departments of the executive branch of the federal government involved in the immigration process: the Department of Homeland Security, the Department of State, the Department of Justice, the Department of Labor, the Department of Health and Human Services, and the Social Security Administration. Congress has a role in the immigration process as discussed in chapter 4, *infra*.

In November 2002, Congress passed the Homeland Security Act, 116 Stat. 2135, which abolished the Immigration and Naturalization Service and transferred most immigration functions to the Department of Homeland Security. This chapter describes immigration administration after the Homeland Security Act (HSA).

§ 3–1 THE DEPARTMENT OF HOMELAND SECURITY

Under the Homeland Security Act, most of the immigration functions originally delegated to the Attorney General by the Immigration and Nationality Act (*see* INA § 103(a)) were transferred to the Secretary of Homeland Security. The functions of enforcing immigration law and administering immigration and citizenship benefits are now principally handled by three subdivisions of the

Department of Homeland Security: the U.S. Citizenship and Immigration Services, the U.S. Immigration and Customs Enforcement, and the U.S. Customs and Border Protection.

§ 3–1.1 The U.S. Citizenship and Immigration Services

The U.S. Citizenship and Immigration Services (CIS) reviews petitions for immigration, adjustment of status, and naturalization, as well as asylum and refugee applications. The Director of the CIS reports directly to the Deputy Secretary of Homeland Security.

In 2007, CIS redesigned its operating structure. CIS is divided now into four regions with headquarters in Burlington, Vermont (Northeast Region); Dallas, Texas (Central Region); Laguna Niguel, California (Western Region); and Orlando, Florida (Southeast Region). These regions are further subdivided into 26 management districts that oversee 82 field offices located throughout the United States. These field offices provide the in-person services that immigration matters may require. CIS also operates four Region Service Centers that process designated immigrant, nonimmigrant, and asylum applications based on each center's jurisdiction. Applicants mail their appropriate forms directly to the service centers. In 2003, the CIS created the National Benefits Center (NBC) to complete all pre-interview processing of forms and to process Legal Immigration and Family Equity (LIFE) Act and other benefit claims. Applicants submit forms to the NBC by mailing the appropriate materials to CIS "lockbox" locations for initial processing. CIS maintains 29 overseas offices that provide a variety of services, particularly the processing of immigrant applications, inter-country adoption, and military naturalizations.

Immigration officers have broad discretion in deciding whether an application is complete, accurate, credible, and in compliance with statutory and regulatory requirements. A division called the Administrative Appeals Office, located in Washington, D.C., handles administrative appeals from certain decisions of lower adjudicatory officers. CIS is monitored by the Ombudsman Office, an independent office within the Department of Homeland Security that assists individuals and employers in resolving problems with CIS and issues reports and recommendations to improve CIS's services.

§ 3–1.2   The U.S. Immigration and Customs Enforcement

The U.S. Immigration and Customs Enforcement (ICE) agency is responsible for enforcement of immigration laws. It is divided into five operational divisions for immigration investigations, detention and removal, Federal Protective Service, international affairs, and intelligence. The immigration investigations program seeks to identify and remove non-citizens who are in the United States in violation of the law. The detention and removal program supervises the detention of non-citizens, represents the government in immigration proceedings, and executes the removal of non-citizens who have received a final removal order. The intelligence program provides information to aid in policy-making and day-to-day immigration operations.

ICE is a subdivision of the Directorate of Border and Transportation Security, one of the four directorates within the Department of Homeland Security. The Directorate of Border and Transportation Security also includes the U.S. Customs and Border Protection, the Transportation Security Administration, the Federal Protective Service, the Federal Law Enforcement Training Center, and the Office for Domestic Preparedness.

In 1996, IIRIRA gave the Attorney General (now the Secretary of Homeland Security) the authority to enter into agreements with states and subdivisions of states to implement the administration and enforcement of federal immigration laws. INA § 103(a). With the appropriate agreements, for example, states can receive federal funds to construct and rehabilitate space for detention and confinement. *Id.* The Secretary may also enter into agreements with law enforcement agencies at the state and local levels to enforce immigration laws. *Id.*

ICE is responsible for the detention and removal of non-citizens. ICE operates eight detention centers and uses more than 300 state and local facilities under intergovernmental service agreements for detention purposes. In 2008, ICE was responsible for an average daily detention population of 31,345 persons, an increase of approximately 45 percent from 2002. In an effort to reform its treatment of detainees, ICE enacted performance-based national detention standards for all detainee facilities and created a Detention Facilities Inspection Group to enforce compliance.

ICE service counsels present the government's case for the removal of a non-citizen before immigration judges and file any necessary appeals to the Board of Immigration Appeals. If a final removal order is issued, ICE supervises the removal of the non-citizen. The removal process may include working with foreign governments to secure travel documents and clearance, securing transportation for non-citizens, and ensuring the actual depar-ture of non-citizens who are ordered removed.

The Office of Investigations within ICE is the largest investigative unit of the DHS. The office conducts inves-tigations into human smuggling and trafficking opera-tions, immigration fraud, and employer compliance with immigration regulations. ICE officials have played key roles in staging worksite raids and dismantling criminal smuggling networks.

In 2003, ICE established the first of its Fugitive Opera-tion Teams to locate, arrest, and remove non-citizens who have failed to leave the United States after receiving a final order of removal, deportation, or exclusion. In its first year, the fugitive operations program made 1,900 arrests; in 2006 the number of arrests reached 15,462 and increased to 34,155 arrests in 2008. Although origi-nally designed to capture violent offenders, arrests of non-citizens with criminal records comprised only nine percent of the total arrests made by operation teams in 2007.

§ 3–1.3   The U.S. Customs and Border Protection

While ICE is primarily concerned with enforcement of immigration laws within the United States, the U.S. Customs and Border Protection (CBP), a section of the Department of Homeland Security, focuses on preventing illegal entries while facilitating trade into the United States. CBP performs customs and agricultural inspec-tions, as well as immigration inspections. CBP's immi-gration inspectors work at ports of entry, including bor-der crossings and airports, to prevent the unauthorized entry of non-citizens. *See* chapter 6, *infra*. CBP also conducts inspections of travelers at preclearance stations in Canada and the Caribbean. CBP inspects and admits over 400 million people annually into the United States. Like ICE, CBP is a subdivision of the Directorate of Border and Transportation Security.

The U.S. Border Patrol is a division of the CBP and is responsible for patrolling the United States' borders with Mexico and Canada and coastal waters around Florida, in order to prevent illegal entries and intercept undocumented immigrants. Since 2001, the number of Border Patrol agents has nearly doubled and is expected to continue increasing.

§ 3–1.4   Asylum Adjudication

In 1990, the INS issued regulations creating a new system for processing asylum applications and authorizing the installation of a documentation center to collect and disseminate information on worldwide human rights conditions. Under this system, which now falls within CIS, a corps of asylum officers reports directly to the Refugee, Asylum, and International Operations Directorate in Washington, D.C., rather than to district offices. The asylum officers are trained in international relations and international law, and receive briefings about human rights from the documentation center. 8 C.F.R. § 208.1(b).

Asylum officers adjudicate affirmative applications for asylum, *i.e.*, applications filed by non-citizens who are not yet subject to removal proceedings. (Affirmative applications should be distinguished from defensive applications, which are filed with the immigration judge by non-citizens in removal proceedings). Non-citizens seeking asylum submit an application to a Regional Service Center, which then forwards the application to the appropriate asylum office. After a nonadversarial interview and an examination of supporting documents, the asylum officer determines whether the applicant has established a valid claim for asylum. The asylum officer may grant asylum, or, if the applicant appears to be removable, refer the application to an immigration judge for adjudication in removal proceedings. 8 C.F.R. § 208.14(b)(2). See chapter 10, *infra*, for a more complete discussion of asylum procedures.

§ 3–2 THE DEPARTMENT OF STATE

For most non-citizens the immigration process begins abroad in the over 200 U.S. consulates and embassies that are a part of the Department of State. To obtain the visa necessary to travel to this country, non-citizens must file an application at the U.S. consulate in their country of last residence. A common example is the B–2 tourist visa, which is obtained abroad. A person who wishes to enter the U.S. as an immediate relative or fiancé(e) of a U.S. citizen, or under almost all employment-sponsored temporary visa statuses, must first have a petition filed by the sponsoring relative or employer for such classification with the U.S. Citizenship and Immigration Services in the United States. A U.S. citizen or permanent resident residing abroad may in some circumstances submit family petitions at immigration offices abroad. If the CIS grants the petition, it notifies the U.S. embassy or consulate in the non-citizen's country of last residence, and the visa is sought by the non-citizen following a separate application process.

Consular officers screen visa applications and grant or deny visas according to standards established by the Secretary for Homeland Security. HSA § 428(b)(1).

These decisions are subject to very limited review. The Secretary of State or the Secretary of Homeland Security may direct a consular officer to refuse a visa if warranted by the U.S. foreign policy or security interests. *See* HSA §§ 428(b), (c). The Secretary of Homeland Security, however, may not overturn a consular officer's decision to deny a visa. HSA § 428(b).

The Department of State conducts a highly discretionary informal review system in which each visa refusal is reviewed by the principal consular officer, or a specifically designated alternate. 22 C.F.R. § 41.121(c). If the consular officer does not agree with the refusal, that officer must refer the case to the Department of State or assume responsibility by reversing the refusal. *Id.* The Visa Office of the Department of State may request a report and issue an advisory opinion. 22 C.F.R. § 41.121(d). Although technically only binding as to legal questions, the Visa Office advisory opinion is usually followed. As another means of review, the Homeland Security Act authorizes the Secretary of Homeland Security to place Department of Homeland Security employees in embassies and consulates, to provide advice and training to consular officers, to participate in terrorist lookout committees, or to provide input on visa applications. HSA § 428(e).

Consular decisions denying visas to non-citizens not yet present in the United States are generally held to be neither administratively nor judicially reviewable. *See, e.g., Saavedra Bruno v. Albright,* 20 F.Supp.2d 51 (D.D.C.1998); *Li Hing of Hong Kong, Inc. v. Levin,* 800 F.2d 970 (9th Cir.1986); *Ventura–Escamilla v. INS,* 647 F.2d 28 (9th Cir.1981). Several courts, however, have asserted a narrow ground of review in visa denial cases.

For example, courts may exercise a narrow form of judicial review in cases in which a visa denial affects the constitutional rights of U.S. citizens. In *Allende v. Shultz*, 605 F.Supp. 1220 (D.Mass.1985), the court found that U.S. citizens claiming that the denial of a visa for the Chilean speaker violated their First Amendment rights of free speech and association were entitled to judicial review because "[t]he exercise of judicial review, though necessarily limited in scope, is particularly appropriate in cases ... which involve fundamental rights of U.S. citizens." Further, the Ninth Circuit in *Bustamante v. Mukasey*, 531 F.3d 1059 (9th Cir.2008) upheld judicial review for cases in which U.S. citizens allege that their constitutional rights were violated by the denial of a visa to a non-citizen. In *Bustamante*, the court agreed that a U.S. citizen wife "has a protected liberty interest in her marriage that gives rise to a right to constitutionally adequate procedures in the adjudication of her husband's visa application." In such an instance, the court will apply a highly constrained review based on the Supreme Court's decision in *Kleindienst v. Mandel*, 408 U.S. 753 (1972) to determine whether the consular official denied the visa for a "factually legitimate and bona fide reason." *See* § 2–2.1, *infra*.

Even receipt of a visa, however, does not ensure admission to the United States. The CBP officer at the U.S. border or port of entry (referred to as an "inspector") may disagree with the consular officer and refuse admission. If the non-citizen indicates an intent to apply for asylum, the inspector must hold the individual for a credible fear determination. *See* chapter 10, *infra*. Otherwise, the inspector will either give the non-citizen an opportunity to withdraw the application for admission, or, if the non-citizen has given false information, subject the non-citizen to "expedited removal." To avoid making these determinations at the port of entry, border security officials often examine non-citizens either in their country of departure or on the high seas, in "preinspection" or "interdiction" programs.

The Department of State's role extends beyond issuing visas. The Department of State supervises embassy adjudications of citizenship questions when a person outside the U.S. claims to be a U.S. citizen. It issues advisory opinions on refugee and asylum petitions, and supervises consular actions in other matters that might affect the relationship of the U.S. government with other countries. The Department of State also provides consular services for U.S. citizens abroad, such as for persons with lost passports or a need for other documents, as well as for U.S. citizens arrested in foreign countries.

The Department of State is also responsible for cultural and educational exchange programs, sending U.S. citizens to other countries, and encouraging thousands of foreign nationals to visit the U.S. The Fulbright program is one example of an exchange arrangement overseen by the Department of State. The Department of State promulgates all of the regulations concerning exchange visitor programs, including employment-related provisions. See § 7–10, *infra*, for more information on exchange programs.

§ 3–3 THE DEPARTMENT OF JUSTICE

Until 2003, the Department of Justice was responsible for most immigration functions. The Immigration and Naturalization Service (INS), an agency of the Department of Justice, handled immigration and citizenship services and enforced immigration laws. These functions have now been transferred to the Department of Homeland Security. The Department of Justice has, however, retained authority over the Executive Office for Immigration Review.

In 1983, the Department of Justice removed immigration judges from the INS and placed them under the direct supervision of the Associate Attorney General in the newly created Executive Office for Immigration Review. *See* 8 C.F.R. § 3. The Homeland Security Act of 2002 placed the EOIR under the control of the Attorney General. HSA § 1102. The EOIR is charged with interpreting and administering federal immigration laws and maintains three components: the Office of the Chief Immigration Judge is responsible for managing the immigration courts; the Board of Immigration Appeals conducts appellate reviews of the decisions of immigration judges; and the Office of the Chief Administrative Hearing Officer focuses on employment cases related to immigration. The EOIR is an administrative body, not a court under Article I or III of the Constitution.

§ 3–3.1 The Office of the Chief Immigration Judge

The Office of the Chief Immigration Judge oversees the more than 50 immigration courts and 200 immigration judges across the United States. Immigration judges preside primarily over removal hearings. Under the Criminal Alien Program, immigration judges may conduct on-site removal hearings in detention and correctional facilities. They may also participate in other adjudications such as proceedings to rescind adjustments of status under INA § 246, hearings to withdraw approval of schools for attendance by nonimmigrant students, 8

C.F.R. § 214.4, and challenges brought by aliens ordered to remain in the country under the provisions of 8 C.F.R. §§ 215, 215.4, 215.5. Decisions made by immigration judges are final unless appealed to the Board of Immigration Appeals. 8 C.F.R. §§ 3.36, 3.37.

Until 1983, immigration judges were a part of the INS. These judges were senior immigration officers who held hearings in addition to their enforcement responsibilities. Concerns about the neutrality of judges with enforcement responsibilities prompted due process challenges to these hearings. In 1950, the Supreme Court ruled that the Administrative Procedure Act (APA) demands a separation of functions between immigration judges and enforcement officials. *Wong Yang Sung v. McGrath*, 339 U.S. 33 (1950). Shortly thereafter, Congress passed a provision exempting immigration adjudications from the APA separation-of-functions requirements. Under the INA, Congress again expressly provided that immigration judges could also serve as enforcement officials. INA § 242(b). The act, however, did prohibit an immigration judge from presiding over a case on which he or she had previously acted as prosecutor or investigator. *Id.* The Supreme Court found no due process violation under these new provisions. *Marcello v. Bonds*, 349 U.S. 302 (1955).

While due process arguments failed, the desire for professionalism within the INS and the need for more predictable, rational adjudication resulted in changes. Beginning in 1956, the INS required immigration judges to have law degrees. In 1962, the INS began to employ a staff of trial attorneys to present the government's case; it became standard practice for a trial attorney (now "Service Counsel" under the authority of ICE) or other

INS officer to appear in almost every deportation and exclusion proceeding (now "removal proceeding"). In 2006, the EOIR developed new measures to improve the quality of the immigration courts. These measures included new examinations and performance evaluations for immigration judges and BIA members as well as producing the *Immigration Court Practice Manual* to create a more uniform system of practice in the courts.

§ 3–3.2 The Board of Immigration Appeals

Unlike the immigration courts, the Board of Immigration Appeals (BIA) was never a part of the INS and has always been directly accountable to the Attorney General. In fact, the BIA was not created by the INA, but pursuant to regulations promulgated by the Attorney General. For many years, the Board consisted of five permanent members appointed by the Attorney General. During the 1990s, as its workload increased, the Board was expanded to twenty-three members. For many years, the Board heard all appeals in three-member panels. Due to a mounting backlog of cases, a 1999 rule allowed individual members to affirm immigration judges' decisions in certain circumstances. A 2002 rule enacted to streamline the BIA reduced the size of the Board to eleven members and made single-member review the standard for nearly all cases. Additionally, the single board member may affirm without opinion if he or she determines the case fits within the guidelines listed in 8 C.F.R. § 1003.1(a)(7). Affirmance without opinion caused problems in the federal court system, because many more cases have been appealed beyond the BIA and the federal courts then have difficulty determining the basis for the decision below. Reforms in 2006 increased the number of BIA members to 15 and sought to decrease the number of affirmances without opinions. Affirmances without opinions dropped significantly as a result of these reforms to comprise less than 10 percent of decisions. Review by three-member panels is reserved for cases posing complex or novel legal questions. *En banc* review is also available for particularly important cases. Recent regulations also mandate more three-member panel reviews and precedent decisions. 8 C.F.R. § 1003.

Most appeals to the Board are from immigration judges' decisions on removal. *See* 8 C.F.R. § 242.21; 8 C.F.R. § 1003.1(b)(1), (2). The Board also hears appeals from other decisions of immigration judges, for example, relating to bonds, parole, or detention of non-citizens; the imposition of fines and penalties on carriers; and rescission of adjustment of status. The Board also reviews certain immigration adjudications, including determinations made on immigrant visa petitions based on family relationship. 8 C.F.R. § 1003.1(b). The Attorney General may review certain decisions of the Board. 8 C.F.R. § 1003.1(h).

The Administrative Appeals Office of the CIS (*see* § 3–1.1, *supra*) also has limited authority to hear appeals from immigration judge decisions. Hence, a practitioner is advised to consult the regulations to determine which route of appeal—the BIA or AAO—is appropriate. *See* 8 C.F.R. §§ 1003.1(b), 103.3.

§ 3–3.3 The Office of the Chief Administrative Hearing Officer

The Immigration Reform and Control Act of 1986 (IRCA) created the Office of Chief Administrative Hearing Officer (OCAHO) to deal with employment discrimination. The office hears allegations of employer violations—particularly the employment of non-citizens who do not have work authorization and employer discrimination on the basis of national origin or citizenship status. Additionally, IRCA created the Office of Special Counsel for Immigration–Related Unfair Employment Practices (OSC) to investigate and bring charges under the employer sanctions provisions of the statute. OSC is part of the Civil Rights Division of the Department of Justice.

§ 3–4   THE DEPARTMENT OF LABOR

Most non-citizens wishing to immigrate to the U.S. based upon an offer of permanent employment by a U.S. employer must first obtain certification from the Department of Labor that the employment cannot be performed by a qualified, willing U.S. worker and that it will not adversely affect U.S. wages or working conditions. The labor certification program is a stark reminder that one Congressional aim in controlling immigration is to protect the U.S. labor force. Under the 1990 Act, labor certification is required for immigrants in the second employment-related preference class (members of the professions holding advanced degrees and aliens of exceptional ability), the third preference class (skilled workers, professionals, and other workers), and for H–2 nonimmigrant visas. The Department of Labor will grant certification if it determines that there are insufficient qualified and willing U.S. workers available where the non-citizen will be employed and that the non-citizen's employment will not have an adverse impact on wages or working conditions of similarly employed U.S. workers. INA § 212(a)(14). Employers seeking labor certifications must adhere to Program Electronic Review Management (PERM) procedures that the Department of Labor instituted in 2005 to streamline the labor certification process. Under PERM, employers must try to recruit qualified U.S. workers and keep records of their efforts. After concluding their search for qualified U.S. workers, employers must file a Form ETA 9089 labor certification application to the Department of Labor. Based on the submitted Form ETA 9089, the Department of Labor will determine whether to grant a labor certification. The Department of Labor may also decide to audit an employer to ensure the employer followed PERM requirements in its employee recruitment process. Denials may be appealed by the prospective employer to the Board of Alien Labor Certification Appeals (BALCA), an appellate process that can last two years. For a further discussion of the procedure to obtain a labor certificate, see § 5–5.1, *infra.*

The Wage and Hour Division of the Department of Labor is responsible for ensuring employer compliance with employment standards for non-citizen workers, particularly non-citizens with H–1B, H–2A, and H–2B visas. The Wage and Hour Division also assists ICE and CIS in preventing employers from employing undocumented workers.

§ 3–5 THE DEPARTMENT OF HEALTH AND HUMAN SERVICES

The Department of Health and Human Services also plays a role in the administration of immigration law. The Department's Public Health Service certifies doctors abroad and in the various CIS districts to give medical exams before permanent residence is granted. These doctors play a significant role in the immigrant process by determining whether an individual's physical or mental condition is within the grounds for inadmissibility.

The Refugee Act of 1980 authorized federal assistance in the resettlement of refugees. As a result, the Office of Refugee Resettlement (ORR) was formed as part of the Department of Health and Human Services. The ORR implements programs to provide foster care services for unaccompanied refugee minors, aid victims of human trafficking, and resettle refugees in "preferred communities" with special support services.

§ 3-6 THE SOCIAL SECURITY ADMINISTRATION

The Social Security Administration (SSA) plays a role in the immigration process through its regulation of social security taxes and benefits. Immigrants and non-citizens who work in the United States are required to have social security numbers and pay social security taxes. Employers are required to report wages annually for their employees to the SSA using a Form W–2. When an employee's social security number on a Form W–2 does not match SSA records, the SSA issues a notice, known as a "no-match" letter, to both the employee and the employer. In 2007, the Department of Homeland Security (DHS) issued final rule "Safe–Harbor Procedures for Employers who Receive a No–Match Letter" requiring employers who receive SSA "no-match" letters to complete an inquiry into social security number inaccuracies within 90 days. Employers who failed to resolve these inaccuracies would be subject to criminal penalties. Citing discrepancies within the SSA verification system and the possibility of discrimination against lawful immigrant employees, a California District Court issued a preliminary injunction against the DHS and SSA from implementing the "Safe Harbor" rule. AFL–CIO v. Chertoff, 552 F.Supp.2d 999 (N.D.Cal. 2007). In 2009, the DHS rescinded the "Safe Harbor" rule. Nonetheless, individuals whose Form W–2 does not match SSA records may need to take steps to resolve the discrepancies. This process will usually involve contacting a local Social Security office.

The SSA is also involved in the E–Verify program. Before hiring a prospective employee, employers use the on-line E–Verify system to check the information on a person's Form I–9 against SSA records. For certain areas of employment, the federal government and many states require employers to use the E–Verify system. *See* § 2–2.6, *infra*.

CHAPTER 4

THE CONGRESSIONAL ROLE IN THE IMMIGRATION PROCESS

§ 4–1 INTRODUCTION

Members of the U.S. Senate and House of Representatives are important actors in the formation of immigration law and policy. They draft and approve legislation that, with Presidential signature, becomes the foundation of U.S. immigration law. Congress performs other vital immigration functions as well. In cases of extreme hardship, private legislation may be passed providing lawful permanent residence or even citizenship to an individual. Senators and Representatives are available to take up the case of a non-citizen who may be having administrative problems with immigration authorities. Both houses of Congress hold oversight hearings in which they examine the internal workings of the immigration agencies. Furthermore, particularly in the area of refugees, the executive branch must regularly consult with Congress.

This chapter will address each of these congressional immigration activities. While all of them are important, private legislation receives the most extensive treatment, primarily because of the distinctive technical rules governing that process.

127

§ 4–2 LEGISLATION

The most obvious responsibility of Congress in the immigration arena is considering public legislation. Congress took virtually no action in this regard until passing its first general immigration statute in 1882. Over the next 70 years, Congress passed a variety of restrictive immigration laws. In large part these laws were aimed at excluding Asians, criminals, and the diseased from the U.S.

In 1952 Congress passed, over President Truman's veto, the Immigration and Nationality Act of 1952 (also known as the Walter–McCarran Act). This legislation consolidated and revised many earlier immigration statutes. To this day the Walter–McCarran Act remains the foundation of U.S. immigration law.

Congress has passed much significant immigration legislation since then. Major reforms have occurred in 1965, 1980, 1986 (the Immigration Reform and Control Act), in 1990 (the Immigration Act of 1990), in 1996 (the Illegal Immigration Reform and Immigrant Responsibility Act), and most recently, 2002 (the Homeland Security Act). The Immigration Reform and Control Act of 1986 offers an example of congressional action to establish an amnesty program for some of the hundreds of thousands of undocumented non-citizens in the U.S., to impose criminal sanctions on employers of non-citizens not eligible for legalization, and to provide for stricter border control in the future.

The 1990 Act was an example of an attempt by Congress to update family immigration quotas in light of increasing demand, modernize grounds of inadmissibility, toughen laws related to non-citizen criminal offenses, and to create a more globally competitive workforce while trying to protect the U.S. labor market. The 1996 Act manifests the capacity of Congress to make radical changes in immigration legislation, especially in enforcement, grounds for inadmissibility and removal, restrictions of benefits for non-citizens, and procedures for seeking asylum. The 2002 Act demonstrates the power of Congress to alter the structure of immigration agencies, as it dismantled the Immigration and Naturalization Service (INS) and created U.S. Citizenship and Immigration Services (handling immigration benefits), U.S. Immigration and Customs Enforcement (handling interior enforcement), and U.S. Customs and Border Protection (handling border enforcement). Congress placed these restructured immigration agencies within the newly formed Department of Homeland Security. *See* § 3–1, *infra*.

§ 4–3 PRIVATE LEGISLATION

§ 4–3.1 The Theory

Private legislation provides another way for Congress to contribute in the immigration area. Private legislation, through a private bill, may be introduced specifically to benefit an individual non-citizen or a group of non-citizens. In effect, through this process, a non-citizen is asking that he or she be exempted from the general immigration laws. In conjunction with this request, Congress acts as a tribunal of last resort—primarily through the House and Senate Subcommittees on immigration. Congress is generally hesitant to provide exceptions to immigration laws, however, unless individual circumstances are compelling enough to outweigh concerns about undermining those laws. Former House Subcommittee Chairman Mazzoli, in introducing the House procedures and policy for private bills in the 99th Congress, spoke to this practice. "Since the Subcommittee acts as a court of equity in deciding whether to grant special relief in private immigration cases, it must reserve affirmative action to those of extraordinary merit and posing heavy hardship."

The constitutional rationale for private bills has never been adequately developed. Some members of Congress view this process as one in which individuals are able to use the First Amendment to petition for a redress of grievances. Complaints that private bills violate the separation of powers were rejected in *Paramino Lumber Co. v. Marshall*, 309 U.S. 370 (1940), in which the Supreme Court found that such measures did not intrude into judicial matters.

§ 4–3.2 The History of Private Legislation

Private immigration bills have traditionally served a number of useful purposes. As mentioned already, they are a way for Congress to provide some flexibility in situations where the strict application of immigration law would produce harsh or unjust results. Also, a number of private bills pertaining to similarly situated noncitizens may lead to legislation amending the immigration law from which hardship is emanating. For example, a private bill was introduced on behalf of a grandmother who faced removal because her daughter died before the completion of her application for permanent residence. The law, as it stood, forced most applicants to abandon their applications if their sponsor died before completion of the process. Members of Congress felt that this result was unfair and the private bill led to the Family Sponsor Immigration Act of 2001. President Bush signed the bill into law in 2002, allowing specified family members to assume the role of sponsor if the original sponsor dies before the application process is completed.

The transformation from private bill exceptions to immigration law is justified on the theory that:

It is unfair and improper to extend the benefit of legislative relief solely to a few selected individuals who are in a position to reach the Congress for redress of their grievances. It is felt that that humanitarian approach should be extended to an entire defined class of aliens rather than to selected individuals.

House Report No. 1199, 85th Congress, 1st Session.

While keeping these benefits in mind, it is important to understand that very few privately introduced immigration bills ever gain congressional approval. For example, in the 77th Congress (1941–42), 22 of 430 private immigration bills were passed, in the 98th Congress (1983–84) 33 of 454 bills were passed, and in the 104th Congress (1995–96), that number was 2 of 27. Given these statistics, one may question the feasibility of a private bill for most non-citizens seeking relief from removal (formerly ''deportation'') or other benefits. Despite the low likelihood of success, there has continued to be requests for private bills as a result of the severe hardships caused by the 1996 Illegal Immigration Reform and Immigrant Responsibility Act (IIRIRA). The 105th Congress (1997–98) had 67 private immigration bills introduced, but passed only 9. The number of private bills introduced nearly doubled for the 106th Congress (1999–2000), but only 19 of 121 bills passed. Strikingly, the 107th Congress (2001–02) passed only 1 of 85 private bills and the 109th Congress (2005–06) rejected all 73 private bills.

Traditionally, however, the introduction of these bills was almost as important as their passage, as the mere introduction of a private immigration bill would automatically halt deportation activity during the bill's pendency. *See United States ex rel. Knauff v. McGrath*, 181 F.2d 839 (2d Cir.1950). After the introduction of a private bill, the House or Senate Judiciary Committee would request a report from the Immigration Service on the individual who was the subject of the bill. According to its operating instructions, the Service would generally authorize a stay of deportation when it received a committee's report request. If a bill was introduced early in a session of Congress, it could effectively gain the applicant a stay of deportation for the remainder of the session (up to two years). Also, it was not uncommon for a Representative or Senator to reintroduce an expired private bill at the beginning of the next Congress, thereby continuing the stay of deportation.

As the effectiveness of these tactics in delaying removal became apparent, private legislation grew in popularity. By the 90th Congress (1967–68), 7,293 private immigration bills were introduced; 218 were enacted. Because of this volume, 4,896 of these private bills were still pending at the end of that Congress. These numbers led the House of Representatives to tighten considerably the requirements for the introduction and consideration of private bills. Most significantly, the new House requirements restricted the requests for Immigration Service reports that effectively stayed deportation to cases involving extreme hardship. An earlier decision, *Roumeliotis v. INS*, 304 F.2d 453 (7th Cir.1962), established that there was no right to a stay of deportation without such a request for a report from the Immigration Service.

For a time, the Senate refused to follow the House of Representatives' lead, but in 1981, the Senate approved rules similar to those enacted by the House of Representatives. These rules were a significant factor in greatly reducing the number of private bills.

§ 4–3.3   How Private Legislation Works Today

The process begins when a Senator or Representative is persuaded to offer a private bill on behalf of a non-citizen. Both Senate and House rules indicate that the introduction of a private bill should be a last resort undertaken only after a non-citizen has exhausted all other immigration procedures. The bill is introduced on the floor of the House of Representatives or Senate and is then referred to the applicable Judiciary Committee. From there it is referred to either the House Subcommittee on Immigration, Citizenship, Refugees, Border Security, and International Law or the Senate Subcommittee on Immigration, Refugees, and Border Security. At this stage the author of the bill normally provides the respective Subcommittee with information on the non-citizen's case and requests that the Subcommittee order a report from the Department of Homeland Security (DHS), which would stay the non-citizen's removal. The Senate and House Subcommittees evaluate the private bill based on the hardship suffered by the non-citizen and the precedents established by passage of past private laws.

If the Subcommittee approves the private bill, it will then return to the Senate or House Judiciary Committee. Favorable consideration at the Committee level will send the private bill to the Senate or House floor. The private bill will then be placed on the Private Calendar and considered on the first or third Tuesday of the month. After an affirmative vote, which almost always occurs after Committee and Subcommittee approval, the bill will be referred to the other house of Congress for its review. Normally, this step involves referral to the Judiciary Committee and Subcommittee of the other house. An exception to this procedure occurs if both houses take action on a similar or identical bill concurrently, in which case the bill's approval may be expedited. After the Senate and House both approve a private bill, it is sent to the President for signing. The extensive screening and investigation done by Congress on each of these bills usually assures presidential approval.

As this overview demonstrates, the action taken by the Subcommittees is the key to a private immigration bill's passage. Meeting the requirements of the Subcommittees and gaining their approval will often ensure favorable consideration by subsequent actors. It is important, therefore, to explore what the Subcommittees seek in a private bill.

§ 4–4 MEMBERS OF CONGRESS AS OMBUDSMEN

Senators and Representatives are often asked to help ensure that the various government agencies are responsive to the needs and requests of the public. Members of Congress typically have staff working solely on helping their constituents in dealing with bureaucratic procedures and/or obstacles. In essence, members of Congress are the liaisons between their constituents and government agencies, and often act as advocates for their constituents' interests. Politically, casework service for constituents is often vital to the Congressperson's reelection.

Casework in the immigration area often involves the interests of a U.S. citizen who has filed a petition on behalf of a non-citizen relative or prospective employee. A complaint to a Senator or Representative that one of the immigration bureaus is giving inadequate treatment to a citizen's petition will normally lead to communication from the member of Congress or the congressional staff to immigration officials. Such communication is occasionally helpful in relieving excessive delays and ensuring that the immigration bureau is enforcing immigration laws in accordance with congressional intent. Members of Congress may, and often do, request a status report on a DHS petition, or request DHS review of a particular case. Sometimes, the Congressperson will also write a letter in support of a non-citizen, either to the DHS directly or to a U.S. embassy abroad. To ensure that a letter of support is warranted, however, the Congressperson will often require extensive information on the status of the non-citizen. A Senator or Representative will also be reluctant to take action that might place a non-citizen applying for an immigration benefit ahead of other deserving applicants, and the DHS will nearly always refuse to give preferential treatment.

Finally, another important aspect of the casework process is its function in educating a legislator about the bureaucratic workings of the DHS. Consistent problems in particular areas may lead to congressional hearings and investigations. The result of such hearings and investigations may be legislation that solves the problem.

§ 4–5 CONGRESSIONAL OVERSIGHT OF THE DHS

The oversight function of Congress is related to and sometimes a direct result of the constituent casework done by Senators and Representatives. Under the Legislative Reorganization Act of 1946, oversight is intended to ensure that the various administrative agencies execute laws in the manner prescribed by Congress. The oversight task is shared by the standing committees and applicable subcommittees. With the creation of the Department of Homeland Security, Congress reorganized the committee and subcommittee oversight tasks. The House of Representatives created the Select Committee on Homeland Security to oversee the DHS, and the Senate gave the duty of DHS oversight to the Government Affairs Committee. While House and Senate immigration subcommittees do not have DHS oversight authority, they still retain legislative jurisdiction over immigration matters.

There are three principal aspects of oversight: investigations, hearings, and reporting requirements. Pursuant to the Legislative Reorganization Act of 1946, Congress investigates how well the laws are being executed and whether administrators are performing effectively. Congress can conduct investigations by holding oversight hearings, commissioning independent studies, and conducting interviews. Congress may also send inquiry letters to agencies but specific agency investigations are not frequently undertaken.

The focal point of oversight is the hearing process. Congress holds annual hearings to determine the necessary appropriations for the DHS. At that time committee members are able to question DHS and Department of Justice officials about the operation of their programs. Congress also holds hearings when it considers new immigration legislation. These hearings provide an excellent opportunity for members of Congress to question immigration experts about the potential consequences of the pending legislation and also to receive information from groups that would be affected. Hearings also provide Congress with the ability to investigate the effects of recently enacted legislation. For example, Congress used the hearing process to monitor the transition of the INS to the DHS.

The oversight process also involves reporting. Legislation often requires the President or the Secretary of Homeland Security to report to Congress on the progress of certain immigration programs. For example, § 402 of the Immigration Reform and Control Act of 1986 required annual Presidential reports to Congress on the implementation of § 274A of the Immigration and Nationality Act (relating to unlawful employment of noncitizens) during the first three years after its implementation. This requirement was meant to facilitate congressional oversight of the newly established employee verification system.

§ 4–6 EXECUTIVE CONSULTATION WITH CONGRESS

§ 4–6.1 Refugees

The President and Congress have attempted to deal with problems involving refugees several times after refugee issues initially arose as a consequence of World War II and the Holocaust. In 1948, Congress adopted the Displaced Persons Act that allowed for the admission into the U.S. of some 400,000 non-citizens. Congress has passed several other measures facilitating refugee admission, most notably the Refugee Act of 1980.

Despite these congressional responses, many other refugees have made requests for relief. Two notable examples were the demands of Hungarians and Cubans in 1956 and 1960, respectively. The Attorney General paroled these groups to the United States, pursuant to INA § 212(d)(5)(A). This provision gave the Attorney General discretion to parole into the United States temporarily for emergency reasons or for reasons deemed strictly in the public interest, any non-citizen applying for admission. As a matter of practice, the Attorney General regularly consults the relevant congressional committees about the use of the parole provision—particularly where large groups are involved. Under IIRIRA, the amended version of INA § 212(d)(5)(A) requires the Attorney General's (now Secretary of Homeland Security's) discretion to be used on a "case-by-case basis for urgent humanitarian reasons or significant public benefit."

Wary of the use of parole, particularly as far as it bypassed legislative participation, Congress created a seventh preference category for refugees to immigrate as part of the Immigration and Nationality Act Amendments of 1965. This preference category, however, was only open to non-citizens fleeing persecution from a Communist-dominated country or from a country in the Middle East. Six percent of the Eastern Hemisphere immigration quota could be filled by such refugees. In 1976 this preference was also opened to Western Hemisphere refugees, and in 1978 the refugee quota was set at a flat 17,400 non-citizens per year.

Despite the new refugee preference category, the parole power was used extensively in the late 1960s and 1970s. The primary beneficiaries were hundreds of thousands of Cubans and Southeast Asians. Recognizing that the seventh preference provision was inadequate to meet refugee demand, Congress passed the Refugee Act of

1980. That legislation, codified at INA § 207, repealed the seventh preference provision and required extensive presidential consultation with Congress in order to set yearly refugee quotas. Specifically, a cabinet-level representative of the President must review the refugee situation with members of the House and Senate Judiciary Committees. The administration must provide the Committee members:

(1) A description of the nature of the refugee situation.

(2) A description of the number and allocation of the refugees to be admitted and an analysis of conditions within the countries from which they come.

(3) A description of the proposed plans for their movement and resettlement and the estimated cost of their movement and resettlement.

(4) An analysis of the anticipated social, economic, and demographic impact of their admission to the United States.

(5) A description of the extent to which other countries will admit and assist in the resettlement of such refugees.

(6) An analysis of the impact of the participation of the United States in the resettlement of such refugees on the foreign policy interests of the United States.

(7) Such additional information as may be appropriate or requested by such members.

For fiscal years 1980–82, the Refugee Act authorized a 50,000 refugee quota unless the President determined after congressional consultation that a larger number was justified by humanitarian concerns or was otherwise in the national interest. INA § 207(a)(1). Since 1982, the refugee quota has been determined entirely through presidential-congressional consultation. The refugee ceiling remained at 70,000 from 2003 to 2007 before increasing to 80,000 in 2008; these quota levels are significantly lower than the quota levels set during the 1990s. *See* § 10–1, *infra*, for regional allocations of the refugee admissions ceiling. In the event of an "unforeseen emergency refugee situation," the President may still, after appropriate congressional consultation, expand the admissible number of refugees if such action is justified by "grave humanitarian concerns or is otherwise in the national interest." INA § 207(b). For example, President George H.W. Bush expanded the original ceilings of 72,-500 for 1988 and 94,000 for 1989, by 15,000 and 22,500 respectively, to help accommodate refugees from Eastern Europe and the Soviet Union.

While the Refugee Act of 1980 has provided a more realistic framework for congressional involvement in the refugee area, it has experienced problems. Soon after its passage in 1980, the Mariel boatlift brought over 125,000 Cubans to the U.S. During the same period thousands of Haitian boat people came to this country. The Carter Administration eventually again resorted to the parole process to handle this influx, later asking for special authorizing legislation from Congress. Section 202 of the Immigration Reform and Control Act of 1986 provided eligibility for permanent resident status for certain Cuban and Haitian entrants who had continuously resided in the United States since before January 1, 1982.

§ 4–6.2 Cancellation of Removal (Formerly "Suspension of Deportation")

Until the mid–1980s, Congress was also a key actor in suspension of deportation proceedings. Pursuant to INA

§ 244, the Attorney General had the discretion to suspend deportation of a non-citizen and adjust his or her status to that of a non-citizen lawfully admitted for permanent residence in situations where the non-citizen is of good moral character, has been continuously present in the U.S. for a requisite period, and where deportation would cause extreme hardship. The Attorney General was required to report to Congress on the first day of each calendar month during congressional sessions with a complete and detailed statement of the facts and pertinent provisions of law in each suspension of deportation case.

Before *INS v. Chadha*, 462 U.S. 919 (1983), Congress was authorized to revoke the suspension of deportation through either a resolution or concurrent resolution, depending on the statutory section used for suspension of deportation by the Attorney General. Congress had until the end of the succeeding legislative session to take such action. In *Chadha*, the Supreme Court found this legislative veto provision to be unconstitutional as a violation of the separation of powers doctrine. The legislative veto provision violated the Constitution because it did not require action by both houses of Congress or presentment of the action for consideration by the President. In the aftermath of *Chadha*, the Immigration and Technical Corrections Act of 1988 repealed the statute that provided a possible congressional veto for suspension of deportation decisions (''cancellation of removal''). *See also* § 9–3.1, *infra*.

CHAPTER 5

IMMIGRANTS

§ 5–1 INTRODUCTION

Non-citizens lawfully admitted to the United States fall into one of three categories: (1) persons who seek admission for a limited period of time and usually for a limited purpose (known as "nonimmigrants"), (2) persons who want to become permanent residents of the U.S. (known as "immigrants"), and (3) refugees. The Immigration and Nationality Act (INA) defines the classifications by which non-citizens may be admitted into the U.S. The INA also provides separate grounds for barring admission (grounds of "inadmissibility") and grounds for removing non-citizens who have been admitted, along with the associated procedures for seeking admission and removal.

Non-citizens desiring to be admitted to the United States are presumed to be seeking permanent residence and therefore must qualify for one of the immigrant classifications or demonstrate that they are nonimmigrants. INA § 101(a)(15). The primary classes of persons seeking permanent residence are family-sponsored, employment-based, diversity immigrants, and refugees. Refugees are discussed in chapter 10, *infra*. There is no limit to the number of people who may immigrate as immediate relatives (spouses, parents, or children) of U.S. citizens. INA § 201(b). All other immigrant classifications are subject to numerical limitations.

In order to qualify for permanent residence, applicants must ordinarily demonstrate that they have the intent to live indefinitely in the United States. Immigrants in the numerically-limited classes must obtain a visa number, issued by the State Department, for which there may be a long wait due to quotas.

§ 5–2   IMMIGRANTS NOT SUBJECT TO NUMERICAL LIMITATIONS

§ 5–2.1   Immediate Relatives of U.S. Citizens

A non-citizen may immigrate as an immediate relative of a U.S. citizen if the person is a child, spouse, or parent of the citizen. INA § 201(b). There is no limit to the number of immediate relatives who can immigrate each year, but immigration by immediate relatives reduces the annual quota for other family-sponsored immigration categories. INA § 201(c). The admittance of immediate relatives has increased significantly in recent decades, from nearly 80,000 in 1970 to over 480,000 in 2008.

a.   Children

To qualify as a "child" of a U.S. citizen, the person must be unmarried and under twenty-one years of age. The INA definition of "child" encompasses stepchildren and adopted children as well as biological children. INA § 101(b)(1). Children may obtain immediate relative status through either parent if they are born in wedlock. Children born out of wedlock can qualify for permanent residence through their natural mother, or through their natural father if they are legitimated before the age of eighteen or the father "has or had a bona fide parent-child relationship with the [child]." INA § 101(b)(1)(D). Stepchildren are considered immediate relatives if they were less than eighteen years of age at the time of the marriage creating the relationship, regardless of the age at which they seek to immigrate.

The INA treats children born out of wedlock differently depending on whether they claim immigration benefits through their mother or father. The Supreme Court has repeatedly upheld the constitutionality of such gender discrimination in analogous cases related to citizenship, most recently in *Nguyen v. INS*, 533 U.S. 53 (2001), affirming the government's broad power to expel or exclude non-citizens. The Act also distinguishes children who have been legitimated from those who have not. The term "legitimated" applies to any child born out of wedlock who has been accorded legal rights identical to a child born in wedlock. *See De Los Santos v. INS*, 690 F.2d 56 (2d Cir.1982).

The INA distinguishes between two types of adoptive relationships. The first is when a child is adopted while under the age of sixteen and has been in the legal custody of the adopting parents for two or more years. INA § 101(b)(1)(E). Such children are considered "adopted," for the purpose of obtaining immigration benefits. The second is when both parents have died, disappeared, or abandoned the child, or if the sole or surviving parent is incapable of providing proper care and has in writing irrevocably released the child for emigration and adoption. INA § 101(b)(1)(F). These children are called "orphans." To immigrate as an immediate relative, an orphan must be adopted or be coming to the United States to be adopted by a U.S. citizen and spouse jointly, or by an unmarried U.S. citizen at least twenty-five years of age. Adopted children may immigrate at any age, provided that the residence requirement is satisfied and the adoption is completed before they turn sixteen, but orphans may only immigrate while under the age of sixteen. Sixteen-or seventeen-year old children may, however, qualify for orphan or adopted child status if their sibling has been adopted. INA § 101(b)(1)(E)–(F). Adoption of orphans grew steadily in the 1990s, but leveled off in the following decade: in 1991, approximately 8,000 orphans were adopted overseas; since 2001, that number has remained around 20,000. The majority of adoptions during this period have been from China, Guatemala, and Russia.

The Intercountry Adoption Act of 2000 (114 Stat. 825) added another definition of "child" that pertains only to orphans adopted from countries that are parties to the Hague Convention on Intercountry Adoptions. *See* INA § 101(b)(1)(G). The Convention establishes procedures for adoptions between ratifying countries in order to protect the rights of children and parents and ensure that each adoption is in the child's best interest. Parents wishing to adopt children from Convention countries must obtain approval from the U.S. State Department and the central adoption authority in the country where the adoption is to take place.

b. Parents

A parent who has any of the relationships described under the definition of "child" meets the statutory definition of a "parent," INA § 101(b)(2), provided the sponsoring citizen son or daughter is at least twenty-one years old. INA § 201(b). When an adopted child or orphan obtains citizenship after being adopted by U.S. citizen parents, the child's natural parents are barred from claiming any rights to immigrate on the basis of the child's citizenship. INA § 101(b)(1)(E)–(G).

c. Spouses

In order to immigrate as the spouse of a U.S. citizen, the non-citizen must have a "valid and subsisting marriage" with that citizen. The validity of the marriage is generally determined by the laws of the country where the marriage took place. The INA defines the term "spouse" in the negative by identifying who cannot qualify as a spouse. INA § 101(a)(35). A spousal relationship cannot be created through a proxy marriage unless the marriage has been consummated. Marriages adverse to public policy, health, and morals, such as incestuous or polygamous marriages, cannot create the necessary relationship. The Court of Appeals in *Adams v. Howerton*, 673 F.2d 1036 (9th Cir.1982) denied immediate relative classification to a homosexual spouse. The court reasoned that Congress did not intend for homosexual marriages to confer spousal status under INA § 201(b). Additionally, in the Defense of Marriage Act, 110 Stat. 2419 (1996), Congress affirmed that administrative agencies must interpret the word "marriage" in congressional acts and regulations as "a legal union between one man and one woman," and the word "spouse" as "a person of the opposite sex who is a husband or wife."

Sham marriages, that is, marriages entered into for the purpose of conferring an immigration benefit, do not provide the requisite relationship, regardless of their validity in the country where the marriage took place. Immigration authorities formerly denied spousal petitions if they determined that the parties "did not intend to establish a life together at the time they were married" (*Bark v. INS*, 511 F.2d 1200 (9th Cir.1975)) or that the marriage was "factually dead" or nonviable at the time of petitioning. The Court of Appeals in *Dabaghian*

v. Civiletti, 607 F.2d 868 (9th Cir.1979), however, rejected the "factually dead" test and held that if the marriage
is not a sham or fraudulent from its inception, it is valid
for adjustment of status purposes until legally dissolved.
Subsequent separation of the spouses alone, therefore,
should not be the sole basis for denying a spousal petition.

The Immigration Marriage Fraud Amendments of
1986 attempted to deter immigration-related marriage
fraud. The Fraud Amendments impose a two-year conditional residency requirement on non-citizen spouses and
their "sons and daughters" before they may obtain permanent resident status on the basis of a "qualifying
marriage" to a U.S. citizen or permanent resident alien,
if the marriage is less than two years old at the time of
obtaining such status. To remove the conditional status,
the couple must file a petition within the last ninety days
of the conditional status period. An immigration officer
will either remove the condition based on the couple's
documentation, or interview the couple to ascertain that
(a) the "qualifying marriage" was not entered into "for
the purpose of procuring an alien's admission as an
immigrant;" (b) the marriage has not been judicially
annulled or terminated, other than through the death of
a spouse; or (c) a fee or other consideration other than
attorney's fees was not given for the filing of the alien's
petition. INA § 216.

As part of the petition to remove conditional resident
status, the couple must provide evidence that their marriage was bona fide, such as leases or property records
showing joint tenancy or ownership of property, joint
financial accounts (if applicable), birth certificates of
children born to the couple, and any other similar docu-

mentation. Since the focus of the inquiry is on the couple's intent at the time of the marriage, however, such evidence does not preclude a finding that the marriage was fraudulent. In *Nikrodhanondha v. Reno*, 202 F.3d 922 (7th Cir.2000), the court found that the petitioning couple's marriage was a sham, even though they had two children together, because they gave conflicting testimony regarding their courtship, they only lived together for three months, and they maintained separate finances. It should be noted, however, that maintaining separate finances is acceptable if there is other evidence that the marriage is bona fide.

If the immigration officer makes a favorable determination, conditional status is removed and lawful permanent resident status granted. If the officer makes an unfavorable determination, the conditional resident status is terminated. The non-citizen spouse and children are then subject to removal.

Immigration authorities must also terminate the non-citizen spouse's conditional resident status if the couple fails to file the petition or to appear at the interview, unless the non-citizen qualifies for a waiver. INA § 216(c). One way a non-citizen may qualify for a waiver is to show that extreme hardship would result if he or she were removed. INA § 216(c)(4). To obtain a waiver on this ground, conditional residents must prove that the hardship they face is extreme in comparison to the hardship normally inherent to removal and that it is based on factors that arose after they became conditional permanent residents. 8 C.F.R. § 216.5(e)(1). Non-citizens may find it easier to obtain a waiver on one of the other two grounds provided by § 216. If the marriage has been terminated (other than through the death of the spouse), non-citizens may obtain a waiver by proving that they entered the marriage in good faith and were not at fault for failing to file a joint petition to have the conditional status removed. INA § 216(c)(4)(B). Regardless of the present status of the marriage, a waiver is available if a good faith marriage resulted in the battery of or "extreme cruelty" to the non-citizen spouse or the couple's child, again assuming the non-citizen was not at fault for failing to file the required petition or appear for a personal interview. INA § 216(c)(4)(C). Congress added this provision as part of the Violence Against Women Act (see § 5.5–1(c), infra), so that non-citizens would not have to remain in abusive relationships in order to maintain their immigration status. Immigration regulations, which were intended to prevent fraudulent abuse claims, state that non-citizens should support the waiver petition with evidence such as police reports or professional evaluations. 56 Fed.Reg. 22635–01. Immigration authorities must nonetheless consider any credible evidence of abuse presented by petitioners. INA § 216(c)(4).

Under statute, non-citizens who marry while in removal proceedings may not obtain immediate relative or preference status by reason of that marriage until they have resided outside the United States for two years following the marriage date. INA § 204(g). A common exception to this foreign residency requirement applies if the non-citizen establishes by "clear and convincing evidence" that the marriage was undertaken in good faith and not for the purpose of evading immigration laws, and further, that no fee was paid in consideration of the petition. INA § 245(e). The Marriage Fraud Amendments impose criminal penalties for immigration-related marriage fraud of not more than five years and/or not more than $250,000 in fines, and make marriage fraud an additional ground for removal as well as a perpetual bar to permanent residence. INA § 275(c).

§ 5–3 IMMIGRANTS SUBJECT TO NUMERICAL LIMITATIONS

Prior to the 1990 Act, immigrants were divided into six preference and one nonpreference categories. Persons in the nonpreference category were only allowed to immigrate if the annual immigration quota was not filled by persons in the preference categories. Because the quota for the preference categories had been filled since 1978, the 1990 Act eliminated the nonpreference category altogether. 1990 Act § 162, *amending* INA § 203.

The 1990 Act increased worldwide immigration levels to 700,000 per year for three years, after which the limit decreased to 675,000 annually. Immigrants subject to numerical limitation are divided into three categories: family-sponsored, employment-based, and diversity immigrants. INA § 201(a). The State Department issues a "visa number" to each immigrant in these categories according to the annual limits. In the past, some visa numbers were also available to persons outside these categories, such as the spouses and children of formerly undocumented aliens who benefited from IRCA's amnesty program and certain employees of U.S. businesses operating in Hong Kong. 1990 Act §§ 112, 124, *amending* INA § 203.

Immigration in the family-sponsored and employment-based categories is also subject to per-country numerical caps; the 1990 Act created a series of calculations necessary to determine these limits. *See* INA § 202. Generally, the per-country ceiling is at least 25,000, and does not count immigration by immediate relatives. In an attempt to ease the backlog of second preference admissions (spouses and minor children of permanent resident aliens), particularly from Mexico, the 1990 Act exempted 75% of the second preference limitation from the per-country limits. In addition, if the quota for employment-based immigration exceeds the demand in that category in any calendar quarter, any remaining openings may be filled without regard to the per-country limits. INA § 202(a)(5).

With few exceptions, immigrants are "charged" against the immigration quota of the country in which they were born, even if they have become citizens of another country. INA § 202(b). One exception to this policy is where an immigrant's accompanying spouse and children were born in a different country than the primary immigrant and would have to wait longer for a visa number as a result; in this circumstance the spouse and children are "cross-charged" to the primary immigrant's country of birth. Exceptions to the chargeability rule are also made for children born in the United States (e.g., children of diplomats), and for children born in a country where neither of their parents were born or have a residence; in both cases, the children are charged to their parent's country of citizenship.

In general, immigrants within each preference category are issued visa numbers in the order in which their applications are received. Some countries with high immigration rates may become "oversubscribed" if the number of otherwise qualified applicants in a particular category exceeds the number of people who can immigrate within the per-country limits. To prevent an oversubscribed country's immigration quota being entirely filled by immigrants in one preference category, the State Department prorates that country's visa numbers so that the number of people allowed to immigrate in each category is proportional to the worldwide level of immigration in that category. This proration may result in a longer wait for immigrants in some popular categories. The State Department publishes a monthly bulletin that summarizes the availability of visa numbers, and lists any countries that are oversubscribed.

§ 5–3.1 Preference Categories

Prior to the 1990 Act, immigrants subject to numerical limitations were divided into six preference categories. The 1990 Act separated family-sponsored immigrants from employment-based immigrants and created new, though often only slightly modified, categories for each. The annual limit on family-sponsored immigrants is at least 226,000, while the limit on the employment-based categories is 140,000.

In an effort to avoid separation of nuclear families seeking to immigrate, the law provides that if the spouse or child of a family-sponsored, employment-based, or diversity immigrant cannot otherwise immigrate, the spouse or child is admitted in the same preference category, with the same priority, as the principal immigrant. To obtain this derivative status the spouse or child must be "accompanying" or "following to join" the principal immigrant. INA § 203(d). A spouse or child acquired after the principal immigrant obtains permanent resident status is not given this derivative status and must apply under the second preference family-sponsored class, discussed below.

a. Family–Sponsored Preferences

The 1990 Act authorized the immigration of up to 480,000 immediate relatives and persons in family-sponsored preference categories each year. The quota for the numerically-limited family-sponsored preference categories is calculated by subtracting the number of immediate relatives who immigrated in the previous fiscal year from the total allocation of 480,000 and adding the number of unused employment-based visa numbers. INA § 201(c). Regardless of the actual result of this computation, the Act mandates that the family-sponsored immigration quota must be at least 226,000. Due to high levels of immigration by immediate relatives, the quota only rarely exceeds the statutory minimum. Since immigration by immediate relatives is unlimited, the overall number of persons immigrating on the basis of family relationships each year is usually far more than 480,000.

The four numerically-limited family-sponsored preference categories are as follows:

First Preference—Unmarried sons and daughters of U.S. citizens—23,400 plus any unused visa numbers from the other family-sponsored preference classes.

Second Preference—Spouses, children, and unmarried sons and daughters of lawful permanent resident aliens—114,200, plus any visa numbers in excess of 226,-000. Separate numerical limits exist for:

    A.   Spouses and children—77% of the visa numbers issued under this preference, or about 87,900;

    B.   Unmarried sons and daughters (at least twenty-one years old)—23% of the visa numbers issued under this preference, or about 26,300.

Third Preference—Married sons and daughters of U.S. citizens—23,400 plus any unused visa numbers from the first and second family-sponsored preference categories.

Fourth Preference—Brothers and sisters of U.S. citizens, if the citizen is at least twenty-one years old—65,000 plus any unused visa numbers from the first, second, and third family-sponsored preference categories.

The term "sons and daughters" is used in the preference categories to refer to children of U.S. citizens or lawful permanent residents who are married or over the age of twenty-one. As defined in the Act, "children" refers only to unmarried persons under the age of twenty-one. INA § 101(b). The term "unmarried" used in the first and second preference classes is defined as the marital state of the immigrant at the time of immigration, regardless of any previous marriage. INA § 101(a)(39). The term "brothers and sisters" used in the fourth family-sponsored class is undefined, but may be derived from the defined term "children" from common "parents."

b.   Employment–Related Preferences

The 1990 Act dramatically increased the quota for employment-based immigration, from 54,000 to 140,000, plus any unfilled spots in the family-preference categories (which are highly unlikely). The American Competitiveness in the Twenty–First Century Act of 2000 further increased this allocation by "recapturing" employment-based visa numbers that were not used in fiscal years 1999 and 2000. 114 Stat. 1254. Beginning in fiscal year 2001, these "recaptured" numbers were to be added to the quota for the first three employment-based preference categories each year until they were all used. The REAL ID Act of 2005 created a similar recapturing program for 50,000 employment-based visa numbers that went unused from 2001 through 2004.

Backlogs in the employment-based visa processing system have become a source of frustration for many visa applicants. The sources of the processing backlog date back to July of 2007 when visa applications increased dramatically in anticipation of an increase in visa processing fees.

Employment-based immigrants must qualify for one of the following five preference categories:

First Preference—Priority Workers—28.6% of the total worldwide level (40,000 at present) plus any unused visa numbers from the fourth and fifth employment-related preference categories. INA § 203(b)(1). Priority workers consist of:

A. Persons of "extraordinary ability" in the sciences, arts, education, business, or athletics;

B. Outstanding professors and researchers;

C. Certain multinational executives and managers.

"Extraordinary ability" is defined as a "level of expertise indicating that the individual is one of that small percentage who have risen to the very top of the field of endeavor." 56 Fed.Reg. 60897–01. The 1990 Act requires that the immigrant's extraordinary ability be reflected through "sustained national or international acclaim" and extensive documentation of the person's contribution to his or her field. INA § 203(b)(1). Likewise, to be considered an "outstanding" professor or researcher, an immigrant must be internationally recognized in his or her field, as shown by published works, awards, or other achievements. 8 C.F.R. § 204.5(i). To qualify as a multinational executive or manager, an immigrant must have been employed for at least one year in an executive or managerial capacity at an overseas office of a company that has an affiliated office in the United States. Persons in the "extraordinary ability" category may file their own immigration petitions, but professors, researchers, executives, and managers must be sponsored by an employer.

Second Preference—Professionals holding advanced degrees, or persons of exceptional ability in the sciences, arts, or business—28.6% of the total worldwide level (40,000 at present) plus any unused visa numbers from the first preference category. An "advanced degree" is any academic or professional degree above the baccalaureate. A baccalaureate degree plus five years' progressive work experience can be substituted for a master's degree, but if the immigrant's profession customarily requires a doctorate, he or she must have that degree. 8 C.F.R. § 204.5(k)(2). The term "exceptional ability" means a degree of expertise significantly above that ordinarily encountered in the arts, sciences, or business. For example, an average musician is not included, but one with national recognition is. *Cf. Lee v. INS*, 407 F.2d 1110 (9th Cir.1969). The possession of a degree, diploma, certificate, or license to practice a particular profession is not, by itself, sufficient evidence of exceptional ability. INA § 203(b)(2).

In most cases, a non-citizen seeking admission to the U.S. under this preference category must have proof of a job offer. This requirement may be waived, however, when the immigrant's employment is in the national interest. Physicians who agree to work for at least five years in areas with a shortage of health care professionals are entitled to national interest waivers if a federal or state agency attests that their work will be in the public interest. INA § 203(b)(2)(B)(ii). In the case of *In re New*

York State Department of Transportation, 22 I. & N. Dec. 215, Interim Decision 3363 (BIA 1998), the Board of Immigration Appeals established a three-part test to determine what other circumstances warrant the issuance of a national interest waiver. To be entitled to such a waiver, the immigrant must work in an area of "substantial intrinsic importance," his or her employment must provide a benefit that is national in scope, and the immigrant must be capable of serving the national interest to a greater degree than would a qualified U.S. worker.

Third Preference—Skilled workers in short supply, professionals holding baccalaureate degrees, and other workers in short supply—28.6% of the total worldwide level (40,000 at present) plus any unused visa numbers from the first and second employment-related preference categories. No more than 10,000 "other workers" may immigrate each year.

The term "professionals," used in the second and third preference categories, includes architects, engineers, lawyers, physicians, surgeons, and teachers. INA § 101(a)(32). Workers in other occupations that require at least a baccalaureate degree are also considered professionals. 8 C.F.R. § 204.5(*l*)(2). "Skilled worker" means one who is capable of performing a job which requires at least two years of training or experience. 8 C.F.R. § 204.5(*l*)(2).

Fourth Preference—Certain Special Immigrants— 7.1% of the total worldwide level (10,000 at present). This category includes the special immigrants detailed in § 5–4, *infra*. Principally, this preference category is comprised of religious workers, former employees of the U.S. government and international organizations, and juveniles who are dependent on a U.S. court or state agency. The numerical allotment for special immigrants is expected to be sufficient for the next several years. INA § 101(a)(27)(C)–(M).

Fifth Preference—Employment Creation—7.1% of the total worldwide level (10,000 at present). This preference category is comprised of investors who will create at least ten U.S. jobs by investing in a new commercial enterprise benefiting the U.S. economy. The minimum required investment is $1 million, though it may be reduced to $500,000 if the investment is in a rural area or an area of high unemployment. If the commercial enterprise is located in an area of low unemployment, the U.S. Citizenship and Immigration Services (CIS) may raise the required investment to $3 million, but it has not yet done so. To avoid fraud, investors are accorded only conditional permanent resident status for two years, after which the CIS reviews the investment.

The requirement of creating at least ten jobs deterred many investors. In an effort to increase immigration through investment, Congress established the Immigrant Investor Pilot Program in 1992, that sets aside 3,000 of the 10,000 EB–5 visas for immigrants who invest $500,000 in a CIS-designated "Regional Center." 8 C.F.R. § 204.6(m). To achieve official designation as a "Regional Center," a business must demonstrate, among other things, that it will promote domestic economic growth and create jobs. Unlike the traditional EB–5 visa, the immigrant's investment must only indirectly create ten or more new jobs and the immigrant investor need not directly manage the business. An immigrant investor is granted conditional status for the first 21 months, after which permanent residence will be granted if the immigrant can demonstrate that the investment was made and ten jobs were created. The pilot program has proven to be popular and President Obama extended the program through September 2012.

Since the employment creation category was instituted in 1990, the number of immigrant investors has never reached the annual limit. The number of immigrants in this category peaked in 1997 at approximately 1,400. In December of that year, concern about possible fraud prompted the INS to halt processing of these petitions temporarily. The Service was particularly concerned about partnerships that allowed a prospective immigrant to make small payments towards the required investment during the conditional status period and pay the balance after the condition was removed. Some such partnerships offered the immigrant a guaranteed return on the investment, or offered to buy back the immigrant's shares as soon as the balance came due. The INS resumed processing of fifth-preference petitions in mid–1998 after issuing four administrative decisions clarifying the requirements for this preference category. These decisions held in part that the investment must involve a degree of risk which is absent from schemes involving a guaranteed return or buy-back option, and that the immigrant must have a comprehensive business plan and document the source of his or her funds. *See In re Hsiung*, 22 I. & N. Dec. 201, Interim Decision (BIA) 3361 (BIA 1998); *In re Ho*, 19 I. & N. Dec. 582, Interim Decision (BIA) 3051 (BIA 1988); *In re Soffici*, 22 I. & N. Dec. 158, Interim Decision (BIA) 3359 (BIA 1998)*; In re Izummi*, 22 I. & N. Dec. 169, Interim Decision (BIA) 3360 (BIA 1998). After the BIA issued these decisions, the number of people seeking to immigrate as investors dropped significantly, to only 200 in 1999 and 2000. In recent years, however, the number of admissions has climbed, reaching 1,360 in 2008; 248 of these admissions were through the pilot program.

c. Diversity Immigrants

The 1990 Act attempted to restore the flexibility that the nonpreference categories were intended to create under the INA, while at the same time, reverse the drastic reductions in immigration from certain, mostly European, countries. The 1986 Immigration Reform and Control Act established the NP–5 pilot lottery program, through which persons from "adversely affected" countries, that is, countries contributing disproportionately few immigrants, could become permanent residents. Approximately 1.3 million people applied for 10,000 diversity immigrant openings. In 1988, Congress increased the allotment from 10,000 over two years, to 20,000—again in an effort to assist the admission of immigrants from "under represented" countries.

The 1990 Act established a permanent diversity immigration program, which began in 1995 (now known as the DV–1 program). 55,000 diversity immigrants were selected by lottery each year. INA § 201(e). Under the Nicaraguan Adjustment and Central American Relief Act (NACARA) passed in 1997, however, 5,000 of the 55,000 diversity visas are reserved for the NACARA program. 111 Stat. 2199. Therefore, since 2000, only 50,000 diversity visas have been available yearly. The program uses a complicated formula to categorize countries as either "low-admission" or "high-admission," based on immigration rates during the past five years. Nationals of high-admission countries are not eligible for the lottery. Another formula is used to designate geographic regions as high-admission or low-admission. Countries in low-admission regions (currently Europe and Africa) receive a greater percentage of the diversity immigration allotment than countries in high-admission regions. To qualify for the diversity program, an applicant must have attained a high school education or its equivalent, or have at least two years of work experience in an occupation which requires at least two years of training or experience. Lottery "winners" are selected by random drawing from petitions received during a designated annual application period; those selected must obtain immigrant status by the end of the fiscal year. The Department of State selects more than 50,000 winners each year, on the assumption that not everyone who is selected will complete the application process. Because more people are selected than are ultimately approved, it is vital that applicants take steps to acquire immigrant status as soon as eligible. The lottery is a highly uncertain way to obtain permanent residence: for the 2009 lottery, more than 9.1 million people applied for this program.

d. *Inhabitants of Hong Kong and Other Special Groups*

The 1990 Act and subsequent amendments made special provisions for specific groups of immigrants. For example, anticipating increased immigration from Hong Kong following that territory's return to the People's Republic of China in 1997, the 1990 Act provided that the per-country immigration limit for Hong Kong would be the same as that for an independent country (approximately 20,000). 1990 Act § 103. The Act further provided that immigrant visas issued to Hong Kong residents would remain valid until January 1, 2002, so that visa holders could decide after 1997 whether to immigrate or stay. Although the latter provision has lapsed, the treatment of Hong Kong as an independent country with regard to immigration limits remains in effect. Similarly, Northern Ireland is treated as a separate foreign state for purposes of the diversity immigrant program. INA § 203(c)(1)(F).

§ 5-4 SPECIAL IMMIGRANTS

"Special immigrants" are resident aliens returning from temporary trips abroad; former U.S. citizens; certain religious workers, their spouses, and their children; employees of the U.S. government abroad with fifteen or more years of service; certain employees of the Panama Canal Company or Canal Zone government, their spouses, and their children; certain officers and employees of international organizations, their spouses, and their children; graduates of foreign medical schools who are fully licensed to practice in a state and have been practicing in such a state since January 1978 or earlier, their spouse, and their children; certain non-citizens declared dependent on a juvenile court in the U.S. and deemed eligible for foster care; non-citizens with qualifying periods of service in the U.S. armed forces; and some foreign-language broadcasters. INA § 101(a)(27). In 2008 and 2009, Congress authorized special immigrant visas for Iraqi and Afghan nationals who worked on behalf of the U.S. government in their respective governments. The statutes allow for 5,000 annual special immigrant visas for Iraqi nationals through 2012 and 1,500 annual special immigrant visas for Afghan nationals through 2013.

Until the 1990 Act, special immigrants were not subject to numerical limitations. After 1990, however, only resident aliens returning from temporary trips abroad and former U.S. citizens remained free from numerical limits. INA §§ 201(b)(1), 203(b)(4). The remaining special immigrant visas are limited to 10,000 per year, and the majority of these visas are used annually. The special immigrant group is the subject of frequent legislative modifications, so the possible inclusion or exclusion of any particular individual must regularly be checked against the statutory language.

Commuter aliens, or "green card commuters," are an interesting group included in the special immigrant category. Commuter aliens are non-citizens who reside in Mexico or Canada, but who are admitted into the U.S. as immigrants on a daily or seasonal basis for employment. These individuals are placed under the special immigrant category of resident aliens returning from temporary trips abroad. The great majority of these workers commute from Mexico. 8 C.F.R. § 211.5.

§ 5–5 PROCEDURAL REQUIREMENTS

§ 5–5.1 Petitions and Certification

Before individuals in family-sponsored or employment-based categories can immigrate to the U.S., a petition must be filed on their behalf and approved by the United States Citizenship and Immigration Services. INA §§ 203(f), 204. For immediate relatives and family-sponsored immigrants, the petition is filed by the U.S. citizen or resident alien who claims the requisite relation to the prospective immigrant using Form I–130 or, for adopted orphans, Form I–600. For employment-based immigrants, this petition is usually filed by the immigrant's intended employer. In some circumstances, however, the immigrant is allowed to file the petition. *See* § 5–5.1(b), *infra*.

All petitions are made under oath (INA § 204(a)(1)) and the burden of proof is always on the applicant. INA § 291. Petitions may be voluntarily withdrawn at any time. Approval of a petition may be revoked if there is a change in either party's status, such as death, divorce, or loss of the job offer, prior to final decision on an application for permanent residency. 8 C.F.R. § 205.1.

a. Family–Sponsored Immigration Petitions

The process of applying for family-sponsored immigration begins when the prospective immigrant's relative submits Form I–130. 8 C.F.R. § 204.1(e)(1). For example, the citizen-wife of a non-citizen might submit Form I–130 on behalf of her husband. All petitioners living within the United States must submit the Form I–130. A Form I–485 Adjustment of Status may be filed concurrently with the Form I–130. The petition must be accompanied by proof of the petitioner's U.S. citizenship or permanent resident status and by documents which prove the petitioner's relationship to the non-citizen (*e.g.*, a marriage certificate in the case of a spouse). 8 C.F.R. § 204.1(f).

The 1986 Immigration Marriage Fraud Amendments attempted to eliminate benefits gained as a result of a prior sham marriage. A permanent resident who immigrated through marriage to a prior spouse is prohibited from petitioning on behalf of a new non-citizen spouse for five years after attaining permanent resident status. This condition is eliminated if the marriage was terminated because the prior spouse died or the permanent resident can meet the burden of proving that the prior marriage was not fraudulent. INA § 204(a)(2).

A spouse or child accompanying an immigrant in one of the numerically limited preference categories is granted the same preference as the primary immigrant. INA § 203(d). Therefore, the sponsoring relative is only required to file one petition for family members immigrating together. This derivative status does not apply, however, to immediate relatives. The sponsoring U.S. citizen must file a separate petition for each immediate relative. 8 C.F.R. § 204.2(a)(4).

U.S. citizens seeking to adopt an orphan overseas may obtain advance processing of their petition by filing Form I–600A. This form is used to determine the petitioners' suitability as adoptive parents and must include a home study conducted by an authorized or licensed public adoption agency. 8 C.F.R. § 204.3(c). The petitioners must also submit proof of citizenship and marital status, if they are currently or ever have been married. Once the petitioners have identified an orphan they wish to adopt, they must complete the petition by submitting Form I–600 along with proof that the child is an orphan and has been legally adopted in his or her country of origin.

b. *Employment–Based Immigration Petitions*

Immigrants seeking admission as persons of "extraordinary ability," or through the fourth and fifth employment-based preference categories may file their own petitions. INA § 204(a)(1)(E), (G), (H). Immigrants of exceptional ability who qualify for a national interest waiver may also self-petition. 8 C.F.R. § 204.5(k)(1). For all other employment-based immigrants, the employer must submit a Form I–140 petition to either the Nebraska or Texas Service Center, depending on where the immigrant will be employed. 8 C.F.R. § 204.5(b)– (c).

Petitions for second-or third-preference immigrants must include an approved labor certification, unless the immigrant qualifies for a national interest waiver. 8 C.F.R. § 204.5(k)(4). A second employment-related preference petition must also include documents that prove the beneficiary's qualifications, such as diplomas and licenses or records of national or international recognition, including any recognized prizes or awards received. 8 C.F.R. § 204.5(k)(3).

The Permanent Foreign Labor Certification (PERM) program replaced the previous labor certification process for all applications filed after March 28, 2005. 20 C.F.R. § 656.17(d). Any application filed before that date may be re-filed under the PERM procedure, and if done correctly, will maintain the original priority date. PERM replaced a labor certification system that produced delays of up to three years, and streamlined the certification process by relying on employer attestations and reducing the amount of documents employers must submit to the Department of Labor (DOL). Employers, however, must maintain detailed employment records for auditing by the DOL, which is commonplace. PERM seeks to resolve labor certification applications within six months of filing and meets this goal in the majority of cases—a significant improvement from the previous system, although backlogs remain.

Under PERM, the DOL will only issue a labor certification if it determines that: (a) there are not sufficient qualified workers available at the place where the immigrant will be employed; and (b) that employment of the immigrant will not adversely affect wages or working conditions of similarly employed U.S. workers. INA § 212(a)(5). An employer applies for labor certification by filing Form ETA 9089, which is typically submitted electronically. The employer must describe the job, qualifications, wages, the proposed immigrant's work experience, and unsuccessful domestic recruitment efforts.

PERM requires the employer to attest to its unsuccessful attempts to recruit a U.S. worker for the job. The employer need not submit documented evidence, but must retain all supporting documentation for five years from the date of filing. 20 C.F.R. § 656.10(f). The employer must have placed a job order with the State Workforce Agency (SWA), advertised the job to the public and to its other employees through newspaper and other postings, describing the job with particularity, offering the prevailing wage rate, working conditions, and requirements for the occupation in the region of intended employment. For professional occupations, the employer must take at least two additional recruitment steps, such as attending job fairs, posting on a website, or conducting on-campus recruiting. The employer must also have offered wages and employment terms and conditions as favorable as those offered to the prospective immigrant. 20 C.F.R. § 656.17. To determine the wage, the employer must request a prevailing wage determination from the SWA. 20 C.F.R. § 656.40. The employer may appeal the SWA's prevailing wage determination to the Certifying Officer (CO) of the Department of Labor. 20 C.F.R. § 656.41. Furthermore, the employer must document that all U.S. applicants for the job were rejected solely for lawful, job-related reasons. 20 C.F.R. § 656.17(g).

After it receives the employer's application for labor certification, the CO decides whether to grant the labor certification, request more information, audit the employer, or deny the application, based on whether the employer has complied with the procedures and whether there is a qualified and available United States worker. 20 C.F.R. § 656.24(b). If the CO grants labor certification, the employer is mailed the approved application and a Final Determination form, which allows the employer to file necessary documents with DHS. 20 C.F.R. § 656.24(d). The employer has 180 days to file an approved permanent labor certification in support of a Form I–140 petition with DHS or the labor certification will expire. 20 C.F.R. § 656.30(b).

If the CO denies the request, the employer will be notified of the reasons and has 30 days to request review before the Board of Alien Labor Certification Appeals. 20 C.F.R. § 656.24(e). If the administrative appeal is unsuccessful, judicial review in federal district court is available under the Administrative Procedure Act.

PERM removed much of the Certifying Officer's discretion in determining what is required for the "basic job" by implementing a new system called O*NET, which provides the standard experience and educational requirements for labor certification positions. 20 C.F.R. § 656.17(h). The employer cannot demand more experience than what O*NET provides for the position. 20 C.F.R. § 656.17(i). O*NET has led to controversy, as some employers have wished to require higher qualifications. For example, under O*NET, a biomedical engineer position may not require more than a bachelor's degree and two to four years of experience, even for a senior position. If the employer raises the requirements, the employer must be prepared for an audit or to provide documentation demonstrating that the heightened requirements are supported by business necessity. Additionally, a foreign language requirement can only be included if a large majority of the employer's customers cannot communicate effectively in English. 20 C.F.R. § 656.17(h). For household domestic workers, live-in requirements are acceptable only if the employer can demonstrate that the requirement is essential to perform the job duties. 20 C.F.R. § 656.17(j)(2).

Labor certification will be denied if a non-citizen is self-employed or if the employer's application for certification does not clearly show that the job opportunity has been and is still open to any qualified U.S. worker. 20 C.F.R. § 656. If the immigrant has an ownership interest or familial relationship with the employer, the employer must still demonstrate the existence of a bona fide job opportunity available to all U.S. workers. 20 C.F.R. § 656.17(*l*). In *Hall v. McLaughlin*, 864 F.2d 868 (D.C. Cir.1989), the U.S. Court of Appeals held that no genuine employment relationship exists where the intending immigrant and the corporation were inseparable and the immigrant was indispensable. The court followed a two-part test for determining whether a genuine employment relationship exists. First, the court considered whether the arrangement was a "sham" and inquired whether the corporation was established for the sole purpose of obtaining labor certification for the immigrant. Second, the court considered the "inseparability" question: "Whether the corporation, even if legitimately established, relies so heavily on the pervasive presence and personal attributes of the alien that it would be unlikely to continue in operation without him." The court reasoned that if the immigrant is inseparable from the corporation, the corporation will not truly consider hiring a U.S. worker.

The position for which the employer seeks labor certification must also be permanent in nature. There is, however, no guarantee that immigrants seeking admission under the second or third employment-based preference categories will not later change occupations and compete with U.S. workers. In *Yui Sing Tse v. INS*, 596 F.2d 831 (9th Cir.1979), labor certification was upheld despite evidence of the immigrant's intent to change his occupation eventually. The American Competitiveness in the Twenty–First Century Act permits immigrants to change jobs while waiting for approval of an employment-based application to adjust to permanent residence status if they are in the U.S., their application has been pending for more than 180 days, and the new job is in a same or similar occupational classification. 114 Stat. 1254.

The employer must document the entire process, including all recruitment efforts, as the Certifying Officer (CO) may issue an audit, whether for quality control purposes, suspicion about the application, or through random selection. 20 C.F.R. § 656.20(a). In the case of an audit, the employer has thirty days to provide all required documentation or the application is denied and considered unreviewable.

If the employer fails to comply substantially with the certification procedures, the CO may order supervised recruitment for pending or future applications. 20 C.F.R. § 656.21. Supervised recruitment requires the employer to obtain approval from the CO for all advertisements and refer all applicants to the CO. If the employer rejects any applicant, the employer must provide to the CO the names, addresses, and resumes of all rejected applicants and explain with specificity why the applicants were neither qualified nor able to acquire the skills on the job within a reasonable amount of time.

If the CO learns that an employer or agent is involved in possible fraud or willful misrepresentation, the matter is referred to the Department of Justice and the Department of Homeland Security. 20 C.F.R. § 656.31(b). The application is suspended during investigation. Any employer, attorney, or agent that commits fraud or willful misrepresentation during the certification process will be barred from submitting any permanent labor certifications for six years and risks possible criminal penalties. 20 C.F.R. § 656.31(f). Additionally, employers may not substitute a different non-citizen employee after filing an application and barter or sale of an application or approved certification is prohibited. 20 C.F.R. § 656.12.

For a very few occupations, listed in 20 C.F.R. § 656.5, Schedule A, there is an abbreviated labor certification process. This list includes only physical therapists, professional nurses, and persons of "exceptional ability in the sciences or arts." The "exceptional ability" group under schedule A is similar to the first preference category, for which no labor certification or employer petition is required; consequently, most persons who might qualify for inclusion in this group would likely pursue a first-preference classification instead. If the immigrant's occupation is included in Schedule A, the employer need only document that appropriate wages are being offered, that other employees had notice of the job opportunity, and that the immigrant is qualified for the designated profession. 20 C.F.R. § 656.15. Schedule A labor certification determinations are filed directly with the CIS, and decisions by the CIS are final and may not be appealed. 20 C.F.R. § 656.15(e). If denied, the employer may re-file under the normal procedures, unless the employee is a physical therapist or professional nurse, in which case the employer may not re-file the application. 20 C.F.R. § 656.15(g). Sheepherders are in a category to themselves, but undergo substantially the same process as Schedule A filings. 20 C.F.R. § 656.16.

An employer seeking to employ a college or university teacher may use either the standard process or special handling. 20 C.F.R. § 656.18. For these professions, the INA provides that a labor certification can be issued if there is no *equally* qualified U.S. worker. INA § 212(a)(5)(A).

PERM eliminated the previous Schedule B occupations, for which no labor certification was available.

c. *Self–Petitioning*

Although most people cannot immigrate unless a sponsoring relative or employer petitions for them, a few individuals may file their own petitions. Self-petitioning is available to persons of extraordinary ability in the first employment preference category; immigrants in the second employment preference category who qualify for a national interest waiver; special immigrants and investors; applicants for the diversity lottery program; widows or widowers of U.S. citizens; certain Amerasian children; and battered spouses or children of U.S. citizens or permanent resident aliens. *See* INA §§ 204(a)(1), 204(f).

In some cases, Congress has made self-petitioning available to persons who would be considered immediate relatives when their citizen relative cannot or will not file a petition. For example, widows or widowers of U.S. citizens who could have qualified for permanent residence but for the death of their spouse may self-petition if they apply within two years of being widowed. Section 204(f) allows certain children fathered by U.S. citizens in

Southeast Asia before 1982 to petition for permanent residence, whether or not they have contact with, or even know, their citizen fathers.

The self-petitioning provisions for battered spouses and children serve a slightly different purpose. Congress enacted the provisions in the Violence Against Women Acts of 1994 and 2000 (VAWA) to enable victims of domestic violence to leave abusive relationships without jeopardizing their immigration status. 114 Stat. 1518. To qualify, the petitioner must be a person of good moral character residing in the U.S. and must have lived in the U.S. with the abusive spouse or parent at some time. If petitioning as the spouse of a U.S. citizen or lawful permanent resident, he or she must show that the marriage was entered in good faith and that either the petitioner or the petitioner's child was subject to extreme cruelty by the citizen or permanent resident. INA § 204(a)(1)(A)–(B). A child must show that he or she suffered extreme cruelty at the hands of a U.S. citizen or lawful permanent resident parent.

Section 204 formerly required that a self-petitioning spouse remain married to the citizen or lawful permanent resident at the time of filing the petition. Congress amended this provision in the Violence Against Women Act of 2000, so that a battered spouse may self-petition if within the last two years the abuser died or lost citizenship or residence status because of domestic violence, or if the marriage was terminated because of the abuse. INA § 204(a)(1)(a)(iii). The Violence Against Women Act of 2000 also eliminated a requirement that the battered spouse prove that removal from the U.S. would result in extreme hardship. 114 Stat. 1519. The self-petitioner must provide evidence of the battery, such as police reports, photos, or affidavits. 8 C.F.R. § 204.2. Immigration authorities are required to consider any credible evidence in support of the petition, but they have discretion as to what is considered credible. INA § 204(a)(1)(H).

d. *Affidavit of Support*

The petitioner's responsibilities in the immigration process do not end after the immigration petition is approved. INA § 212 requires all family-sponsored immigrants and some employment-based immigrants to obtain an affidavit of support from their petitioner as evidence that the immigrant will not become a public charge. INA § 212(a)(4). By signing the affidavit, the petitioner (or sponsor) contracts with the U.S. government to provide financial support to the immigrant if needed until the immigrant has worked in the U.S. for forty qualifying quarters (usually ten years), or until the beneficiary acquires U.S. citizenship. INA § 213A. The sponsor must be domiciled in the United States and must have an income equal to at least 125% of the federal poverty guideline. The income requirement may be satisfied by proof of significant assets (equal to five times the difference between the sponsor's salary and the income requirement) held by the sponsor or the immigrant. If the sponsor cannot meet the income requirement, he or she may obtain a co-sponsor who has sufficient income. The affidavit of support is submitted in the final stages of the application process and must be accompanied by the sponsor's tax returns for the past three years.

e. *Priority Dates*

The date on which a petition is filed by or on behalf of an immigrant becomes that person's priority date as soon as the petition is approved. 22 C.F.R. § 42.53(a). In the case of family-based immigrants, this is the date on which the sponsoring relative files an I–130 petition, or when a self-petitioning immigrant files an I–360 petition. 8 C.F.R. § 204.1(c). For employment-based petitions that require labor certification, the priority date is the date that a labor certification request is accepted for processing by the Department of Labor; when no labor certification is required, the priority date is the date that the employer or immigrant files an I–140 or I–360 petition. 8 C.F.R. § 204.5(d).

Employment-based and family-sponsored immigrants are issued visa numbers in chronological order according to the immigrant's priority date and country of origin. Depending on the immigrant's preference category, he or she could be able to immigrate immediately, or could have to wait ten or more years for the priority date to become current. Residents of oversubscribed countries may have to wait even longer.

An applicant retains his or her priority date even if he or she changes preference categories due to changing marital status, turning twenty-one years old, or the naturalization of the sponsoring relative. 8 C.F.R. § 204.2(i). This rule has created problems for immigrants who changed to a less-favorable preference category while their applications were pending. To remedy this situation, Congress enacted the Child Status Protection Act of 2002. 116 Stat. 927. This Act provides that children of U.S. citizens who marry or turn twenty-one while waiting for their application to be processed will remain in the immediate relative preference category.

§ 5–5.2 Processing for Immigrants Outside the U.S.

After approval of the preference petition, the next step of the application process begins for an immigrant who resides outside the United States. Approved petitions are sent to the National Visa Center (NVC) in New Hampshire. The NVC handles the rest of the application processing except for the final interview with the applicant, which is conducted at the consulate. This section describes the standard procedure for NVC processing, which is updated regularly on the travel.state.gov website.

When a petition has been approved and a visa number is available immediately, the NVC sends a packet of instructions to the applicant. If no visa number is available because the applicant's priority date is not yet current, the NVC notifies the applicant that his or her name has been placed on a waiting list. When a visa number is available, the applicant must submit a biographical information form (Form DS–230 Parts I and II) to the NVC with the application fee. 22 C.F.R. § 42.63. The applicant must also assemble and submit relevant documents including, for example, a birth certificate; marriage certificate; police clearances from any country where the applicant has lived for more than a year since attaining the age of sixteen; and prison or military records. 22 C.F.R. § 42.65. As the required documents vary among countries, the NVC provides all specific requirements online, at the travel.state.gov website. At the same time, the applicant's sponsor must complete the Affidavit of Support (*see* § 5–5.1(d), *supra*) and send it to the NVC.

The NVC will first ascertain if all documents have been properly submitted; if they have not, the NVC will send the applicant a notice of the inadequacies and the applicant or agent has 60 days to provide further documentation. The application is considered minimally qualified if the Form DS–230, the I–864 Affidavit of Support, and the police certificates have been received. Once the applicant is deemed at least minimally qualified, the NVC will schedule an interview with the relevant consulate, forward all of the applicant's submitted documents to the consulate, and notify the parties involved (the applicant, sponsor, and/or agent) of the interview location and date.

Immigration officials will check the information contained in an immigrant's application against the security databases and watch lists of several government agencies. The security procedures for immigrant applicants is similar to the security procedures for nonimmigrants detailed in § 6–1, *infra*. In addition to a background and security check, immigrant applicants must pass a medical examination.

A consular officer conducts a personal interview, and if all is in order, has the applicant sign the formal application under oath. The consul then rules on the application. The authority to determine the eligibility of an applicant belongs exclusively to the consul. INA §§ 104(a), 221(a). The principal consular officer must review any denial of an immigration application, but there is no formal review available after that decision. 22 C.F.R. § 42.81. The consulate must inform the applicant of the provision of law or regulation upon which it bases a denial. 22 C.F.R. § 42.81(b). The Department of State may also review a denial but, other than in matters of interpretation of law, its opinion to the consul is only advisory. 22 C.F.R. § 42.81(d). The applicant has one year to overcome the objection on which the refusal was based or else the entire application process must be started anew. 22 C.F.R. § 42.81(e). The burden of proof is always on the applicant to establish eligibility. INA § 291.

The doctrine of consular non-reviewability prevents courts from applying judicial review to visa denials (*Saavedra Bruno v. Albright*, 197 F.3d 1153 (D.C. Cir. 1999)), but this doctrine is subject to a narrow exception. Courts may review the denial of visas that implicate the constitutional rights of U.S. citizens. *Kleindienst v. Mandel*, 408 U.S. 753 (1972). The standard of review of a consular officer's decision to deny a visa is limited to examining whether the denial was for a "facially legitimate and bona fide" reason. *Id.* Courts may not "look behind" the consular officer's decision and reassess the merits of the denial unless there is a well supported allegation of bad faith. For a further discussion concerning judicial review of visa denials see § 6–1, *infra*.

§ 5–5.3   Visa Issuance and Admission

If the consul rules in favor of the applicant, the consul issues an immigrant visa. INA § 101(a)(16). The visa consists of an envelope containing Form OF–155A, which shows the consul's approval, the applicant's completed Form OF–230, and any documents necessary in determining the applicant's identity, classification, and eligibility. 22 C.F.R. § 42.73(b). The visa allows the individual to enter the U.S. as an immigrant and is valid for a period of six months (3 years for an adopted child) and may not be extended beyond that time. 22 C.F.R. § 42.72(a), (b). A new immigrant visa, however, may be issued to immigrants not subject to numerical limitations if they are unable, for reasons beyond their control, to travel to the U.S. during the six-month period, provided they remain qualified for the visa. 22 C.F.R. § 42.74. An immigrant subject to numerical limitations may receive a replacement visa if the immigrant was unable to travel to the U.S. during the six-month period, but only if the replacement visa is issued in the same fiscal year as the original visa and the immigrant's number was not returned to the Department of State for reissuance. 22 C.F.R. § 42.74(b).

Once the immigrant actually arrives in the U.S., an immigration officer at the border briefly examines the immigrant's eligibility for permanent residence. If the inspecting immigration officer finds the immigrant to be inadmissible, the officer may commence removal of the immigrant, in spite of the visa. INA § 221(h). In that case, the immigrant may be temporarily detained, either aboard the vessel of arrival or in the U.S. while further determination is made. 8 C.F.R. § 235.3. If the immigration officer finds the visa to be in order and the immigrant to be admissible, the visa is retained by the CIS as a permanent record of admission. INA § 221(e). The immigrant is then issued a Form I–551 (green card) and becomes a permanent resident alien. "Green cards" (which are no longer green) must be renewed every ten years.

§ 5–5.4　Permanent Resident Procedures for Immigrants Already Inside the U.S.

Individuals who want to immigrate are ordinarily expected to remain outside the United States until an immigrant visa is available. Nonetheless, many people are admitted to this country as nonimmigrants and then apply to adjust status to permanent residence. *See* INA § 245. In recent years, adjustments of status have accounted for around one-half to two-thirds of all persons granted permanent residence. The procedures for the underlying immigrant petitions and labor certificates are precisely the same for immigrants in or outside the U.S. Persons in numerically-limited preference categories must obtain a visa number, even though they are already in the U.S. and do not need an immigrant visa, because they are counted against the worldwide immigration quotas. The wait to obtain a visa number is the same whether an applicant adjusts status or immigrates from outside the United States; processing of adjustment of status applications, however, typically takes considerably longer than consular processing of immigration applications. Immediate relatives and persons who are in a preference category that is "current" may file an application for adjustment of status immediately upon approval (or in most cases, filing) of any underlying petition at the CIS Chicago Lockbox. 8 C.F.R. § 245.2(a). Otherwise, they must wait for their priority date to become current. Adjustment of status is generally only available to people who entered the U.S. lawfully and have maintained lawful nonimmigrant status. INA § 245(i) allowed persons who entered the country without inspection or fell out of status to adjust status on payment of a one thousand dollar fine. This provision applies only to immigration petitions or labor certifications filed before April 30, 2001, and it has not yet been renewed by Congress. Adjustment of status is discussed further in the last section of chapter 6, *infra*.

The Legal Immigration Family Equity (LIFE) Act, enacted in 2000, has made it possible for certain family-based immigrants to enter or remain in the United States while their immigration petitions are pending, alleviating some of the difficulties these individuals face as a result of the high demand for admission to the U.S. The Act provides that spouses of U.S. citizens and their accompanying minor children may enter the United

States on a K nonimmigrant visa after filing an immigration petition. INA § 101(a)(15)(K). *See* § 6–13, *infra*.

The LIFE Act also permits spouses and children of legal permanent residents who filed petitions prior to December 21, 2000, and have been waiting for a visa number for at least three years to enter the country on a V nonimmigrant visa and to work until their priority date becomes current. INA § 101(a)(15)(V). *See* § 6–24, *infra*.

CHAPTER 6

NONIMMIGRANT VISITORS AND TEMPORARY WORKERS

Nonimmigrants constitute the largest group of people admitted to the United States each year. For example, in fiscal year 2008, 39,381,928 nonimmigrants entered the United States. The vast majority of them were tourists (29.4 million) or temporary business visitors (5.6 million). Despite a short-term decline in the number of nonimmigrants after September 11, 2001, there has been a long-term increase in nonimmigrant entrants: the number of visitors in 1998 was 24.8 million; in 1990, 17.5 million; and in 1985, 6.6 million. Nonimmigrants are divided into twenty-three status categories plus one special purpose category for NATO personnel, which will not be considered further. A nonimmigrant's status category determines what activities he or she may engage in while in the U.S.; the most significant differences relate to whether the individual may pursue employment or attend school. The main categories are given letter designations corresponding fairly closely with the alphabetical and numerical subdivisions of their enabling legislation, INA § 101(a)(15) and 8 C.F.R. § 214.2.

§ 6–1 NONIMMIGRANT VISA PROCESSING

Nonimmigrants from most countries need a visa to enter the United States. The exceptions to this rule are

Canadian nationals, temporary visitors from countries in the Visa Waiver Program, and Mexican nationals with Border Crossing Cards. *See* § 6–4, *infra.* To obtain a visa, most nonimmigrants submit applications to a U.S. consulate and then undergo an in-person interview with a consular officer. Most employment-based and student applications require some type of preapproval by a different agency or entity before visas can be applied for. *See* 6–10, *infra* for the employment-based visa process and *see* 7–2, *infra* for the student visa process. The Department of State (DOS) is moving towards a completely electronic visa processing system. Beginning in 2006, visa applicants began electronically filing the nonimmigrant supplemental information Form DS–156. The DOS hopes to replace the Form DS–156 and other visa application forms with a new Form DS–160. The Form DS–160 will be an on-line application that will collect the application fee, schedule the nonimmigrant's visa interview, and use the information entered by the nonimmigrant to initiate his or her background check.

During a visa interview, the consular officer ensures that the information contained in the visa application is correct and questions the nonimmigrant to make certain that there are no grounds for inadmissibility. Most consulates prohibit lawyers from attending visa interviews. For several visa categories, nonimmigrants must demonstrate that they have a residence in a foreign country which they have no intention of abandoning. Consular officers may request that applicants produce evidence that substantiates their ties and intent to return to their country of residency. INA § 222(d). Most nonimmigrants must pay a substantial visa processing fee to the U.S. Consulate.

Immigration officials submit the personal information of visa applicants to several security watch lists. The Consular Lookout and Support System (CLASS) is one database in which consular officials check the names of visa applicants against records complied by the FBI and other law enforcement agencies. Consular officials also can access the Consular Consolidated Database that stores records of previous visa determinations. Other watch lists include the records kept by the Terrorist Screening Center, the TIPOFF database, the National Automated Immigration Lookout System, the Nonimmigrant Information System, and the Terrorist Threat Integration Center.

In addition to screening visa applicants against watch lists, the DOS and the Department of Homeland Security (DHS) have issued guidelines to consular officials to determine if an applicant requires extra scrutiny. These guidelines are not public, but possible factors may include an applicant's country of birth, educational and employment background, and military training. If a nonimmigrant falls into a category of applicant that requires further review, the consular officials must request a Security Advisory Opinion (SAO) from the DOS. Nonimmigrants applying for temporary employment-based or student visas in fields involving sensitive information or technology often will require an SAO. In issuing an SAO, the DOS will coordinate with other government agencies to ensure the applicant does not pose a threat to the United States. Once the process has been initiated, consular officials cannot grant a visa until the DOS issues an SAO. Although the DOS has worked to improve its processing time, SAO procedures can result in significant delays for applicants who require such a review. The DOS issued over 280,000 SOAs in 2008.

If the information in the visa application is correct and the consular officer has no concerns during the interview or the applicant's background, the consular officer will issue a visa to the nonimmigrant. The visa is embedded into the nonimmigrant's passport and contains a visa number, the place of issue, the date of issue, the expiration date, the visa classification, a photograph, and biometric data. The visa also indicates the number of entries into the United States for which it is valid; if the visa is valid for multiple entries, the visa will be marked with the letter "m."

Consular officers have the discretion to grant or deny visas and base their decisions on regulations promulgated by the Department of Homeland Security (DHS) and the Department of State (DOS). The INA states that a nonimmigrant is "presumed to be an immigrant until he establishes to the satisfaction of the consular officer . . . that he is entitled to a nonimmigrant status." INA § 214(b). The burden is thus on visa applicants to show that they are admissible under one of the nonimmigrant classifications listed in INA § 101(a)(15). A consular official may find a nonimmigrant applicant inadmissible for a number of reasons, including that the applicant poses a security or health risk to U.S. citizens, that the applicant does not intend to stay in the U.S. temporarily, or that the applicant's past actions disqualify him or her from a nonimmigrant category.

The visa determinations of consular officers are for the most part final and non-reviewable. Consular officers act under the authority of the DOS; however, INA § 104(a)(1) explicitly prohibits the Secretary of State from challenging the decisions of consular officers to grant or deny visas. The DOS has an internal review system in which a supervising consular officer reviews samples of visa issuances and denials to ensure uniform and correct application of visa policies. 71 Fed.Reg. 37494. If a supervising consular officer believes a visa has been denied based on a misapplication of policy, he or she may issue a visa under his or her own authority. The DOS's Visa Office may also request a report concerning the visa application of a specific individual or group of nonimmigrants. The DOS may then issue an advisory opinion to the consular officer to help guide his or her visa determinations. While advisory opinions from the DOS are binding on consular officers regarding interpretations of law, the DOS opinions are not binding concerning the application of law to facts. 22 C.F.R. § 41.121(d).

The Homeland Security Act, 116 Stat. 2187, vested the DHS with the authority to determine guidelines for the issuance of visas and to place DHS officials at consulates to assist consular officers. In addition, DHS officials may veto a consular officer's issuance of a visa if the DHS believes that the visa applicant poses a security threat. DHS officials, however, may not grant visas to applicants who have been denied by consular officers. In practice, the DHS has only placed officials in selected "high-risk" consulates.

Nonimmigrants do not have a right to judicial review of consular decisions and therefore cannot generally seek judicial review of their visa denials. *Saavedra Bruno v. Albright*, 197 F.3d 1153 (D.C. Cir.1999). Courts will, however, allow review of a consular officer's visa denial if the denial implicates the constitutional rights of U.S. citizens. In these cases, U.S. citizens must bring the challenge and courts will examine the consular officer's decision to ensure that the visa was denied for a "facially legitimate and bona fide reason." *Kleindienst v. Mandel*, 408 U.S. 753 (1972). This form of judicial review is very narrow; the Supreme Court has stated that when a consular officer acts on the basis of facially legitimate and bona fide reason, courts should "neither look behind the exercise of that discretion, nor test it by balancing its justifications against the First Amendment interests" of U.S. citizens. *Id.* Accordingly, U.S. citizens must show that a consular officer acted in bad faith in denying a visa in order for a court to overturn the officer's decisions. *American Academy of Religion v. Napolitano*, 573 F.3d 115 (2d Cir. 2009); *Bustamante v. Mukasey*, 531 F.3d 1059 (9th Cir. 2008).

Although review of visa determinations is limited, nonimmigrants may reapply for a visa after an initial denial. The most common cause for refusals of nonimmigrant visas is the inability of applicants to persuade consular officers that they have no intent to abandon their country of residence. *See* INA § 214(b). The burden is on nonimmigrants to prove that they have ties to their country that are strong enough to compel them to leave the United States at the end of their visa authorization.

Visa denials based on national security concerns are more difficult for nonimmigrants to overcome. When nonimmigrants are denied visas because their names appear on a government watch list or because their personal information in government databases troubles consular officials, the nonimmigrants will not be notified of the reason for their denial. Consular officials will not reveal whether a nonimmigrant's name appears on a watch list or what information about the nonimmigrant the officials find suspect. Consequently, applicants may be denied visas based on their presence on a watch list, but, if their presence on the list is a mistake, they may not have access to information needed to remedy the error. The Second Circuit has ruled, however, that before a nonimmigrant is denied a visa based on INA § 212(a)(3)(B) for knowingly providing material support for a terrorist organization, the consular officer must confront the applicant with the allegation of supporting terrorism and afford the nonimmigrant the opportunity to refute that allegation. *American Academy of Religion v. Napolitano*, 573 F.3d 115 (2d Cir. 2009). The Second Circuit's holding applied to a case in which the denial of a nonimmigrant visa implicated the rights of U.S. citizens, and the reach of the court's decision is unclear. Also unclear is whether the DOS and DHS will modify its policies based on the court's ruling, as visa denials without explanations are common.

Nonimmigrants who do not qualify for a visa may in some instances apply for a visa waiver. INA § 212(d)(1) grants the Secretary of Homeland Security the discretion to waive nonimmigrant requirements and issue a temporary visa if he or she determines that it is in the national interest to do so. The Secretary may not grant a visa waiver, however, if the applicant was denied for security reasons based on INA § 212(a)(3).

A visa does not guarantee nonimmigrants admission into the United States. Customs and Border Patrol (CBP) agents at ports of entry make independent determinations of a nonimmigrant's admissibility. INA § 221(h). Nonimmigrants are required to fill out a Form I–94 as part of their CBP inspection. A nonimmigrant's authorized length of stay is determined by CBP policy or regulations rather than the expiration date on his or her visa. A visa is nothing more than permission to enter the country. Hence, nonimmigrants whose visas expire while they are present in the United States are not in violation of the law so long as they have not extended their stay past the date on their Form I–94.

§ 6–2 NONIMMIGRANT CATEGORIES

The twenty-three main categories of nonimmigrants are as follows: A, career diplomats; B, temporary visitors for business and pleasure; C, aliens in transit; D, crew-members; E, treaty traders, investors, and temporary Australian workers; F, students; G, international organization representatives; H, temporary workers; I, foreign media representatives; J, exchange program visitors; K, fiancé(e)s or spouses (and their children) of U.S. citizens; L, intracompany transferees; M, students in non-academic institutions; N, parents and children of special immigrants; O, aliens with extraordinary abilities; P, entertainers and athletes; Q, cultural exchange program participants; R, religious workers; S, aliens coming to the United States to provide information for a criminal investigation; T, victims of human trafficking; TN, for NAFTA professionals; U, victims of domestic abuse or crime; and V, spouses and children of permanent residents who filed an immigration petition more than three years ago. Only four of the nonimmigrant categories, H–1B, H–2B, T–1, and U–1 are subject to numerical limitations. Each of the twenty-three categories is treated in greater depth below.

§ 6–3 DIPLOMATIC PERSONNEL

A–1 status is granted to ambassadors, public ministers, career diplomatic or consular officers, and members of their immediate families. Other foreign government employees and officials and their family members have A–2 status. The A–3 category is for personal employees, attendants, and servants of persons with A–1 or A–2 status. 22 C.F.R. §§ 41.12, 41.21. Persons with A–1 or A–2 status retain that status as long as their official position is recognized by the Secretary of State. A–3 status is valid for three years and may be extended in increments of not more than two years. 8 C.F.R. § 214.2(a). Family members of a person with A–1 or A–2 status may engage in employment in the United States if their country of nationality grants reciprocal privileges to dependents of U.S. officials stationed in that country. 8 C.F.R. § 214.2(a).

§ 6–4 TEMPORARY VISITORS

Most nonimmigrants entering the U.S. each year are visitors for pleasure, who are granted B–2 status. Business travelers are the next-largest group of nonimmigrants; they are granted B–1 status. B–1 and B–2 visitors are usually admitted for three to six months and may extend their stay in six-month increments, generally up to a maximum of one year. 8 C.F.R. § 214.2(b).

The B–1 and B–2 categories are often used for visitors who do not clearly qualify for another nonimmigrant status. For example, in addition to tourists, the B–2 category includes prospective F–1 students coming to the U.S. to select a school and visitors entering the U.S. for medical treatment. 22 C.F.R. § 41.31. Persons who intend to enroll in a school in the U.S. are advised to declare this intention when they apply for the B–2 visa or they may not be permitted to change to F–1 status later. 67 Fed.Reg. 18065–01. B–1 status may also be available to persons other than spouses (*e.g.*, elderly parents or cohabiting partners) who come to the U.S. to live with a nonimmigrant admitted under another status category. 78 Interp.Rel. 1175. INA § 101(a)(15)(B) explicitly excludes persons who are coming to the U.S. to perform skilled or unskilled labor from the B–1 and B–2 statuses. Current regulations do, however, allow persons with B–1 status to supervise but not perform construction work. Foreign workers may also be granted B–1 status to install or repair equipment purchased overseas, but only if the purchase contract specifically requires the seller to provide this service. 78 Interp.Rel. 937.

It can be difficult to distinguish conducting business, which is permitted under B–1 status, from engaging in employment, which is not permitted. State Department regulations for the issuance of B–1 visas state that "business" includes attending conventions, engaging in consultations, and carrying out other commercial activities. 22 C.F.R. § 41.31. In *Matter of Hira*, 11 I. & N. Dec. 824, Interim Decision (BIA) 1647 (BIA 1966), the Board of Immigration Appeals established three criteria for B–1 eligibility: (1) business visitors must maintain a residence in a foreign country, (2) they must accrue any profits outside the U.S., and (3) each visit must be temporary, even if the business activity is ongoing. In practice, if there is any doubt as to whether a visitor is coming to the United States for business or employment, Customs and Border Protection (CBP) will deny entry on B–1 status.

Most temporary visitors must present a valid passport and a B–1 or B–2 visa to enter the United States. INA § 212(a)(7)(B). The State Department requires visitors seeking such a visa to demonstrate that they will leave the U.S. at the end of their intended stay, that they have permission to enter another foreign country at that time, and that they have sufficient funds for the purpose of their visit. 21 C.F.R. § 41.31.

Some visitors are exempt from the visa requirement. Canadian nationals do not need a visa to enter the United States. Citizens of Mexico can obtain a combination Border Crossing Card/B–1/B–2 visa, valid for ten years, that allows entry to the U.S. when presented with a valid passport. 22 C.F.R. § 41.32. In 1998, the State Department began issuing new Border Crossing Cards (or "laser visas") with machine-readable biometric identifiers, such as fingerprints. The old Border Crossing Cards expired in 2002. Holders of the Border Crossing Card (BCC) may make visits of up to thirty days within twenty-five miles of the U.S.–Mexico border (seventy-five miles in Arizona); for longer stays or travel outside the twenty-five-mile zone, Mexicans must pay a small fee for a Form I–94 (entry/departure) authorizing their stay. Previously, Canadian and Mexican nationals did not need a passport to enter the United States; however, the Western Hemisphere Travel Initiative (WHTI) now requires all nationals of Canada and Mexico (and Bermuda) to show a valid passport when entering the United States by air. 71 Fed.Reg. 68412. Substantially the same requirements apply for land and sea entries, although Mexican nationals only need to present a valid BCC when entering by land or sea. 73 Fed.Reg. 18384–01.

The Visa Waiver Program, initiated on a trial basis in 1986 and made permanent in 2000, allows citizens of designated countries to enter the U.S. for business or pleasure without a visa. INA § 217. In 1999, more than 50% of the temporary visitors to the U.S. were admitted under this program. Visitors admitted under the Visa Waiver Program may remain in the U.S. no longer than ninety days and are prohibited from adjusting their status to that of immigrant (except as immediate relatives) or to that of any other nonimmigrant classification. INA §§ 245(c), 248(a)(4). Such visitors also waive any right to review or appeal an immigration officer's admissibility determination, or to contest, other than on the basis of an application for asylum, any action for removal. INA § 217(b). To qualify for the program, a country must offer reciprocal privileges to U.S. citizens, must have a low rate of nonimmigrant visa refusals, must not represent a security risk, and must issue machine-readable passports. INA § 217. If the passport was issued after October 2006, it must also contain an integrated chip with information from the passport's data page and a digital picture. The Secretary of Homeland Security reviews each country's eligibility for the program every two years. The Secretary may also terminate a country's eligibility on an emergency basis in case of war, social unrest, or economic collapse. In 2002, for example, Argentina was removed from the program due to a serious economic crisis. 67 Fed.Reg. 7943–01. In 2009, the visa waiver program included thirty-five countries: Andorra, Australia, Austria, Belgium, Brunei, Czech Republic, Denmark, Estonia, Finland, France, Germany, Hungary, Iceland, Ireland, Italy, Japan, Latvia, Liechtenstein, Lithuania, Luxembourg, Malta, Monaco, the Netherlands, New Zealand, Norway, Portugal, San Marino, Singapore, Slovakia, Slovenia, South Korea, Spain, Sweden, Switzerland, and the United Kingdom.

In 2009, DHS implemented a new Electronic System for Travel Authorization (ESTA), which requires all visitors from countries participating in the Visa Waiver

Program to apply electronically for authorization before traveling to the United States. Once approved through ESTA, visitors receive an application number that they must present when entering the United States. ESTA authorizations are generally valid for two years. 73 Fed. Reg. 32440–01.

§ 6–5   VISITORS IN TRANSIT

Foreign nationals in "immediate and continuous transit" through the United States are granted C–1 status, under which they may remain in the country for a maximum of twenty-nine days. INA § 101(a)(15)(C); 8 C.F.R. § 214.2(c). C–2 status is for persons who have a right of transit to the United Nations. Foreign officials in transit through the U.S. are granted C–3 status. 8 C.F.R. § 214.2(c). Persons granted C status may not extend their stay or change status to another nonimmigrant classification. 8 C.F.R. §§ 214.1(c), 248.2(b). No employment is permitted under this visa class. 8 C.F.R. § 214.1(e).

In 2003, the Secretary of Homeland Security and the Secretary of State suspended the "transit without visa" program because of "credible intelligence concerning a specific threat." 68 Fed.Reg. 46926–01. The program had allowed most travelers in transit through the United States to enter without a visa if they continued their journey within eight hours or on the next available transport. DHS has announced its intention to terminate the program and establish a new program allowing in-transit travelers that will incorporate higher security measures.

§ 6–6   CREW MEMBERS

The D nonimmigrant classification permits crew members serving in a capacity required for normal operation on board a vessel to enter the U.S. for up to twenty-nine days for shore leave or to change vessels. D–1 status is granted to employees remaining with their vessel; employees who intend to work on another vessel are granted D–2 status. 8 C.F.R. § 252.1. Persons in D status are prohibited, with few exceptions, from engaging in longshore work in the ports or coastal waters of the U.S. Crew members are not allowed to change to another nonimmigrant status or to adjust to immigrant status, even through marriage to a U.S. citizen. INA § 248.

Each crew member must apply for an individual crew visa. In 2004, the Department of State—citing security concerns—eliminated "crew list" visas, which allowed crew members to obtain D status as a group. 69 Fed.Reg. 43515–01.

Immigration inspectors will not admit crew members who arrive in the U.S. intending to work for an employer that is currently involved in a strike or lockout, unless they have worked for that employer during the year preceding the labor dispute. 8 C.F.R. § 214.2(d). Such crew members may, however, be paroled into the U.S. if the Secretary for Homeland Security determines that it is necessary for national security.

§ 6–7   TREATY WORKERS

Foreign nationals (and their family members) who come to the United States to carry on trade or develop an enterprise in which they have invested are granted E status. These nonimmigrants are entitled to enter the

U.S. pursuant to a treaty of commerce existing between the U.S. and the country of which they are nationals. Unlike nonimmigrants seeking visas for other employment classifications, treaty traders and investors are not required to file a petition with the U.S. Citizenship and Immigration Services (CIS) before application is made at the U.S. consulate abroad. Additionally, pursuant to a treaty agreement with Australia, a temporary work visa (E–3) is now available solely for Australian citizens.

E–1 (treaty trader) status is granted to persons entering the U.S. to engage in substantial trade in goods or services, including trade in services or technology, on their own behalf or as employees of a treaty trader. INA § 101(a)(15)(E). To qualify for E–1 status, employees must be executives or managers or possess essential skills. 8 C.F.R. § 214.2(e). "Substantial trade" refers to a continuous flow of trade between the U.S. and the treaty country involving numerous transactions. The monetary value of individual items is a relevant factor in determining whether trade is substantial, but greater weight is given to the number of transactions. More than 50% of the trade must be between the U.S. and the treaty country.

E–2 (treaty investor) status is granted to individuals coming to the U.S. temporarily to direct or develop a bona fide enterprise in which they have made substantial investment. INA § 101(a)(15)(E). "Investment" means placing capital at risk. *Nice v. Turnage*, 752 F.2d 431 (9th Cir.1985) established that immigration authorities could deny E–2 status when a petitioner fails to prove that he or she was the source of funds used to make the investment. While the employment creation preference category for *immigrants* requires a minimum investment of one million dollars, there is no minimum dollar amount requirement for treaty investors. Rather, the investment must be substantial in relation to the total cost of purchasing or creating the type of enterprise involved and it must be sufficient to ensure the investor's commitment to developing the enterprise. 8 C.F.R. § 214.2(e). *See also Matter of Walsh and Pollard*, 20 I. & N. Dec. 60, Interim Decision (BIA) 3111 (BIA 1988). E–2 status is generally denied if the expected return on the investment will provide a living only for the investor and his or her family.

E–1 or E–2 status is granted to both the principal trader or investor and his or her spouse and children. Until recently, only the principal nonimmigrant was permitted to engage in employment and that was limited to the activity for which the status was granted. In 2002, Congress passed legislation that allows spouses of treaty traders and investors to obtain work authorization. 115 Stat. 2402. Treaty traders and investors are initially admitted for a period of two years and may extend their stay in two-year increments as long as they continue working in the same capacity. 8 C.F.R. § 214.2(e).

As a result of the Australia–United States Free Trade Agreement, Congress created the E–3 visa in the REAL ID Act of 2005. 119 Stat. 231. The E–3 visa functions similarly to an H–1B visa, but is only available for Australian citizens. INA § 212(t)(1). With a job offer, an Australian citizen may enter the United States to work for a period of two years if an employer attests that it has posted notice of the job, is offering the prevailing wage, and that granting the job to an Australian citizen will not adversely affect U.S. workers. Unlike the H–1B visa, however, the E–3 visa may be renewed indefinitely.

The E–3 visa has a high independent quota of 10,500, separate from the 65,000 H1–B annual cap. INA § 214(g)(11). While the nonimmigrant must be a citizen of Australia, the children and spouse of the nonimmigrant do not need to be Australian citizens and the spouse is entitled to an E–3D (dependent) visa and work authorization. Further, the dependents' visas do not count against the quota. INA § 214(g)(11)(C).

§ 6–8 ACADEMIC STUDENTS

F–1 status allows a student to temporarily enter the U.S. solely to pursue a full course of study at an established academic high school, college, university, seminary, conservatory, or language school. Spouses and children of F–1 students are granted F–2 status. INA § 101(a)(15)(F). IIRIRA bars individuals in F–1 status from attending a public secondary school for an aggregate period of more than twelve months and requires that students reimburse the local school authorities for any period of attendance at a public school. INA § 214(m). As a result, individuals who wish to study at secondary schools for longer than twelve months must attend private institutions.

F–1 status is valid for the time necessary to complete the course of study and any attendant practical training, as determined by the institution the student is attending, plus sixty days. 8 C.F.R. § 214.2(f)(5). Schools may authorize extensions of status for students who are unable to complete their program in the time initially specified because of compelling academic or medical reasons. 8 C.F.R. § 214.2(f)(7). Students with F–1 status may engage in part-time employment on campus and may work off-campus with authorization. 8 C.F.R. § 214.2(f)(9).

See chapter 7, *infra*, for a more complete discussion of student visas.

§ 6–9   INTERNATIONAL ORGANIZATION REPRESENTATIVES

This class of visas is subdivided into five separate groups. G–1 is for principal representatives of governments, recognized *de jure* by the U.S., to an international organization, their staff, and their family members. G–2 covers other accredited representatives of foreign governments to international organizations, their staff, and their family members. G–3 includes non-citizens who would qualify for G–1 or G–2, except that their government is not recognized *de jure* by the U.S.; G–3 also includes their family members. G–4 visas are for officers and employees of international organizations and their family members, and G–5 is for the attendants, servants, and personal employees of G–1, G–2, G–3, and G–4 visa holders, as well as members of their immediate families. INA § 101(a)(15)(G). Except for the G–5 category, persons with G status retain that status as long as their official position is recognized by the Secretary of State. G–5 status is valid for three years and may be extended in increments of not more than two years. 8 C.F.R. § 214.2(g).

Dependents of officials with G–1 or G–3 status may seek employment authorization if permitted under a formal bilateral agreement or an informal arrangement between the U.S. and their country of origin; dependents of G–4 nonimmigrants are also permitted to seek employment authorization and no agreement is required. 8 C.F.R. § 214.2(g)(5).

The Immigration Reform and Control Act of 1986 authorized certain G–4 nonimmigrants who had resided and been physically present in the U.S. for specified periods of time to adjust to special immigrant status. This provision applies to unmarried sons and daughters of officers or employees of international organizations, retired employees of international organizations and their spouses, and surviving spouses of deceased employees of such organizations. INA § 101(a)(27)(I). The 1986 Act affords nonimmigrant status under the N-visa category to certain parents and children of these special immigrants. INA § 101(a)(15)(N). *See* § 6–14, *infra*.

§ 6–10   TEMPORARY WORKERS

The H status category is designed principally to help employers meet an immediate and temporary need for labor. This category is divided into six classes: H–1B for workers in "specialty occupations," H–1C for registered nurses, H–2A for temporary agricultural workers, H–2B for temporary workers in other occupations, H–3 for trainees, and H–4 for the spouses and children of persons in the other H classes.

Prior to the 1990 Act, the H–1B category consisted of professionals and persons of exceptional ability in the sciences and arts. Under the 1990 Act, however, the H–1B classification was redefined to include persons working in "specialty occupations" and artists were relegated to the O and P categories. A job is in a specialty occupation if it requires theoretical and practical application of a highly specialized body of knowledge. In addition, to satisfy credential requirements, a person seeking H–1B status must either:

(1) obtain a state license to practice in the occupation, if such a license is required to practice;

(2) have attained a bachelor's or higher degree in the specific specialty; or

(3) have attained experience in the specialty equivalent to the completion of the bachelor's degree, as well as positions of expertise which demonstrate specialty.

The 1990 Act's allowance of experience as a substitute for a formal degree ended an earlier trend within the INS which discouraged such equivalencies. Compare *Matter of Portugues do Atlantico Information Bureau, Inc.*, 19 I. & N. Dec. 194, Interim Decision (BIA) 2982 (BIA 1984) with 8 C.F.R. § 214.2.

The 1990 Act for the first time subjected H–1B admissions to a numerical limit of 65,000 annually. By 1997, this number had proved insufficient to meet the demand for temporary workers, particularly in high-tech fields. The demand for temporary workers was largely due to a shortage of U.S. workers trained in information technology and engineering, skills that were in high demand during the 1990s. To rectify this situation, Congress imposed a fee of $1,500 ($750 for employers with less than twenty-five employees) on employers petitioning for H–1B workers, to fund technology training programs. INA § 214(c)(9). The demand proved so great that Congress raised the annual limitation on H–1B admissions in both 1998 and 2000. The limitation reached 195,000 for fiscal year 2003, but was reduced to the original limitation of 65,000 for fiscal year 2004 even though that cap was reached by February 2004. For fiscal years 2008 and 2009, the cap was reached on the very first day of filing. DHS accepts applications for the first five business days before randomly selecting for H–1B visas in order to reduce the problems associated with the rush of filing on the first day. 8 C.F.R. § 214.2(h)(8)(ii)(B).

The H–1B Visa Reform Act of 2004 added the H–1B Advanced Degree Exemption, which creates 20,000 additional H–1B visas for foreign workers with a Master's degree or higher from a U.S. institution. 118 Stat. 2809. This cap was also reached on the first day of fiscal year 2009. Employers may no longer file petitions for the same nonimmigrant under both the normal H–1B visa and the H–1B Master's Degree Exemption. 73 Fed.Reg. 15389–01. If the nonimmigrant is eligible for the Master's Degree Exemption, the employer should file under that exemption first; any applicants not selected for the 20,000 cap will then be added to the pool for the normal H–1B selection. The H–1B Visa Reform Act also exempted nonimmigrants who will be employed by institutions of higher education or nonprofit organizations from the H–1B statutory cap. INA § 214(g)(5).

Citizens of Chile and Singapore are eligible for a separate H–1B admission, labeled the H–1B1. Every year 6,800 visas of the 65,000 are set aside: 1,400 for nationals of Chile and 5,400 for nationals of Singapore. Unused H–1B1 visas are made available for H–1B applicants. H–1B1 visas allow for "temporary entry," meaning that H–1B1 visa applicants must demonstrate that they have no intent to establish permanent residency in the United States.

Labor organizations and other groups have expressed concerns regarding H–1B status, chiefly that nonimmigrants take jobs away from U.S. workers, that the availability of foreign workers depresses wages in the U.S., and that nonimmigrants are vulnerable to exploitation by employers who control their immigration status. The

1990 Act addressed the first two concerns by requiring employers petitioning for an H–1B worker to file a Labor Condition Application with the Secretary of Labor. INA § 212(n). The application consists of assertions by the employer that the wages to be paid equal or exceed the prevailing average for the occupation or the employer (whichever is higher), that the position's working conditions will not have an adverse effect on similarly situated U.S. workers, and that no labor dispute or lockout exists at the place of employment. A copy of this application must be conspicuously posted at the principal place of work for ten business days. A complaint procedure exists to permit adversely affected parties to challenge these assertions. Civil penalties, backpay awards, and debarment from filing other immigration petitions may be assessed for successful complaints. In addition, employers must pay a $500 fee, which funds CIS efforts to combat fraud. INA § 286(v).

The 1998 American Competitiveness and Workforce Improvement Act provided for increased scrutiny of employers deemed "H–1B–dependent," meaning that more than 15% of their workforce is made up of nonimmigrants with this status. Such employers had to attest in each labor condition application that the nonimmigrant sought will not displace a U.S. worker within the employer's business and that the employer will not place the nonimmigrant in a position with another employer that would displace a U.S. worker. INA § 212(n). H–1B applications filed by H–1B–dependent employers are subject to more regulation than other employers' applications.

Congress addressed the issue of exploitation of nonimmigrant workers in the American Competitiveness in the Twenty–First Century Act by providing for increased portability of H–1B status. Nonimmigrant workers previously in H–1B status may now change jobs as soon as their new employer files an H–1B petition, rather than waiting for the petition to be approved. INA § 214(n). The nonimmigrant must not have engaged in any unauthorized work and must apply for the change of jobs while still in H–1B status. This measure was intended to reduce the ability of a single employer to control a nonimmigrant's legal status. An H–1B extension or transfer petition is not subject to any cap.

H–1B status is granted initially for three years and may be extended to a maximum of six years. After six years in the U.S., persons with H–1B status must spend one full year outside the country before they can be readmitted with H or L status. 8 C.F.R. § 214.2(h)(13). An H–1B nonimmigrant involved in Department of Defense research may receive an extension of five years, not to exceed ten total years spent in the United States. The limitation on admission does not apply, however, to nonimmigrants engaged in seasonal work, intermittent work of less than six months per year, or people who did not reside in the United States for more than six months yearly. 8 C.F.R. § 214.2(h)(13)(v). Nor does it apply to nonimmigrants that reside abroad and regularly commute to the United States for part-time employment. The six-year limitation may also be extended in one-year increments when the nonimmigrant's request for labor certification or application for employment-based immigration has been pending for more than 365 days. 114 Stat. 1251. Once the employment-based petition has been approved, the H1B can be extended for three year increments if the adjustment of status application has not yet been approved.

Often, individuals in H status (and other nonimmigrant categories) wish to immigrate to the U.S. Because most nonimmigrant statuses require an intention to return to one's home country (sometimes referred to as "nonimmigrant intent"), many nonimmigrants have had either to hide their intent, or postpone their plans. The 1990 Act recognized the propriety of "dual intent" for persons with H–1 or L status. 1990 Act §§ 205(b), (e). First, the Act removed the requirement that persons seeking H–1 status have a foreign residence which they have no intent to abandon. 1990 Act § 205(e); see also INA § 101(a)(15)(H)(i). Second, persons seeking H–1 or L status are exempted from the presumption of immigrant intent that usually accompanies the application process. 1990 Act § 205(b)(1); INA § 214(b). Third, the Act explicitly allows H–1 and L nonimmigrants to seek permanent resident status, without affecting the terms of the H visa. 1990 Act § 205(b)(2); INA § 214(h).

In the Nursing Relief for Disadvantaged Areas Act of 1999 (113 Stat. 1312), Congress created the H–1C nonimmigrant classification for registered nurses coming to the U.S. to work temporarily at hospitals in areas with a shortage of nurses. Congress reauthorized The Nursing Relief Act in 2006 and provided for the admission of 500 nurses per year through 2009, and it is likely that this allocation will be continued. Nurses admitted to this class may remain in the U.S. for a maximum of three years, which cannot be extended. 8 C.F.R. § 214.2(h)(13). To qualify for this status, nurses must have received nursing education in the United States or possess a full nursing license from the country where they received their education; must possess a nursing license from a U.S. state or territory, or pass a nursing examination; and must be eligible for licensure in the state where they intend to practice. 8 C.F.R. § 214.2(h)(3). Nurses who meet the requirements for H–1B, H–2B, or H–3 status can seek admission in one of those categories, but most nurses will not possess the specialized qualifications required for those statuses.

The H–2 classification covers anyone coming to the U.S. temporarily for work of a temporary nature and includes seasonal workers of all types. The Immigration Reform and Control Act of 1986 (IRCA) created an "H–2A" nonimmigrant classification for temporary agricultural workers. Perishable crop growers complained that the procedures for obtaining H–2 workers were too slow and unpredictable for their industry. They feared that, because of their dependence upon undocumented alien workers, implementation of the employer sanction provisions of IRCA would put an end to some of their operations. In response, IRCA provided for expedited procedures for approving grower requests for foreign agricultural workers and for review of denied applications. The employer, however, must still first make an effort to recruit domestic workers. INA § 218. H–2A status is valid for the duration of the approved petition, and an agricultural worker may obtain an extension to work in another temporary agricultural position. Persons with H–2A status may not remain in the U.S. longer than three years. 8 C.F.R. § 214.2(h)(5).

The H–2B category is specifically for nonimmigrants entering temporarily to fill *temporary*, nonagricultural positions. *Matter of Artee Corporation*, 18 I. & N. Dec. 366, Interim Decision (BIA) 2934 (BIA 1982) held that the test of whether a position is temporary is based on the need of the petitioning employer, not on the nature of the underlying job. The standard from *Matter of Artee*

Corporation is now codified in 8 C.F.R. § 214.2(h)(6)(ii). Consequently, a temporary staffing service that has a permanent need for persons with a particular skill cannot petition for H–2B workers to fill its clients' short-term openings. H–2B temporary workers are limited to 66,000 per fiscal year. INA §§ 214(g)(1)(B), (g)(2). The employer must attain a temporary labor certification which is an abbreviated form of the procedure described at § 5–5.1(b), *supra*. H–2B status is valid for the duration of the approved petition, to a maximum of three years. 8 C.F.R. § 214.2(h)(13).

H–3 status covers trainees coming to the U.S. for up to two years to receive training not available in the nonimmigrant's own country, except for graduate medical training and training programs designed to provide employment. H–3 visas include persons coming to the U.S. to receive training in the education of children with physical, mental, or emotional disabilities. 56 Fed.Reg. 50349–02.

H–4 status is granted to the spouse and children of nonimmigrants with H–1, H–2, or H–3 status. H–4 status holders may not accept employment in the U.S. unless they are specifically included in the employer's petition. INA § 101(a)(15)(H); 8 C.F.R. § 214.2(h).

§ 6–11   INFORMATION MEDIA REPRESENTATIVES

The single class I status category includes any representative of foreign press, radio, film, television, or other media provided that U.S. citizens are granted reciprocal privileges by the media representative's government. Spouses and children of the representative are granted the same status as the representative. I status is valid for the duration of employment, but I status holders must obtain authorization to change employers or work in a different medium. INA § 101(a)(15)(I); 8 C.F.R. § 214.2(i).

§ 6–12 EXCHANGE VISITORS

J–1 status is granted to individuals accepted to participate in exchange visitor programs designated by the U.S. Department of State. INA § 101(a)(15)(J); 22 C.F.R. § 41.62(a)(1). J–1 nonimmigrants cover a wide range that includes distinguished scholars, teachers, professors, business trainees, high school students, nannies, and camp counselors participating in qualified exchange programs. J–1 visitors' spouses and children receive J–2 status. Both J–1 and J–2 status holders may work in the United States, subject to significant restrictions.

Certain exchange visitors must reside in their own country for two years after completion of their program before they are eligible to apply for permanent resident status or for H or L nonimmigrant status. INA § 212(e).

See chapter 7, *infra*, for a more complete discussion of J–1 status.

§ 6–13 FIANCÉ(E)S AND SPOUSES OF U.S. CITIZENS

For many years, the K status was used only to permit foreign citizens to come to the United States to marry U.S. citizens. In the LIFE Act of 2000 (114 Stat. 2762), Congress extended this nonimmigrant status to allow the non-citizen spouses, fiancé(e)s, and children of U.S. citizens to live in the U.S. while waiting for a petition for permanent residence to be approved. There are four types of K visas: a K–1 allows the fiancé(e) of a U.S. citizen to enter for the purpose of marriage, a K–3 allows the spouse of a U.S. citizen to enter to promote family unity, and the K–2 and K–4 are for the minor children of the fiancé(e) or spouse, respectively. INA § 101(a)(15)(K). All of the K status categories permit employment, but K–1 and K–3 nonimmigrants must first apply to CIS to gain employment authorization. 8 C.F.R. § 274a.12. K status holders may not change to another nonimmigrant classification. INA § 248.

For a fiancé(e) to obtain a K visa to enter the U.S., the U.S. citizen must first file a petition, Form I–129F, with the CIS in the region where the citizen resides. 8 C.F.R. § 214.2(k). The approved petition is forwarded to the U.S. consulate where the fiancé(e) applies for the visa. Before the visa is approved, the applicant must submit to a medical examination. 22 C.F.R. § 41.108. This is the only nonimmigrant visa for which a medical examination is required. The requirement is imposed in the expectation that the nonimmigrant will become a permanent resident following the marriage. The fiancé(e) is granted K–1 status; any accompanying children receive K–2 status. If the marriage does not occur within ninety days, the non-citizen must depart the U.S. INA § 214(d).

The Immigration Marriage Fraud Amendments of 1986 sought to prevent marriage fraud with respect to K nonimmigrants by requiring the alien fiancé(e) and the U.S. citizen to "have previously met in person within two years before the date of filing the petition, [and] have a bona fide intention to marry...." INA § 214(d). The personal meeting requirement may be waived in rare circumstances, such as if the U.S. citizen demonstrates that the requirements would cause extreme hardship or would violate "strict and long-established customs of the fiancé(e)s culture." 8 C.F.R. § 214.2(k). The Fraud Amendments also prohibit adjustment to permanent resident status of K nonimmigrants prior to their marriage, when they become eligible for immediate relative status. INA § 245(d).

Before the non-citizen spouse of a U.S. citizen can obtain K status, the citizen must file an I–130 immigrant petition. INA § 214(d). The non-citizen may then apply for a K visa to enter the U.S. Non-citizen spouses are granted K–3 status; their minor children are granted K–4 status. 8 C.F.R. § 214.2(k). Both statuses are valid for two years and may be extended if the immigrant petition is still pending. If the immigrant petition is denied or the couple divorces before it is approved, the non-citizen spouse must leave the United States within thirty days.

§ 6–14 INTRACOMPANY TRANSFEREES

The L status was intended to enable multinational corporations to transfer high-level or essential employees from overseas offices to aid or initiate business operations in the U.S. The employer must first submit a petition, Form I–129L, to the Regional Service Center in the region where the transferee will be employed. 8 C.F.R. § 214.2(*l*)(2). The employer must maintain offices abroad and in the United States for the duration of the period for which the petition is sought. The offices may have a parent-subsidiary relationship or may be affiliates owned by the same parent company, provided that at least 50% of each entity is owned and controlled by the same shareholders. To qualify, an L–1 beneficiary must have been employed by the firm abroad for at least one year out of the last three and must either hold a managerial or executive position, or have specialized knowledge of the company's product or procedures. INA § 101(a)(15)(L). *Karmali v. INS*, 707 F.2d 408 (9th Cir. 1983) denied a petition for entry into the US as an intracompany transferee because Karmali did not meet the requirement of one-year continuous employment abroad prior to seeking entry into the U.S.

L status is usually granted for three years and may be extended to a maximum of five years for persons with specialized knowledge or seven years for managers and executives. Transferees who have been in the U.S. for the maximum period must remain outside the country for one year before applying to return in H or L status. 8 C.F.R. § 214.2(*l*). Employers may file a blanket petition for intended employees rather than filing individual petitions. Moreover, the L status holder may possess dual intent to seek permanent residency while maintaining nonimmigrant status. *See* § 6–8, *supra*. Spouses of transferees are granted L–2 status and can apply for employment authorization. INA § 214(c)(2)(E).

§ 6–15   VOCATIONAL STUDENTS

M–1 status is for vocational or nonacademic students who enter the U.S. temporarily to pursue a full course of study at an established or recognized vocational or other nonacademic institution. INA § 101(a)(15)(M). The spouse and children of an M–1 student are granted M–2 status. Both statuses are normally granted for the period of time necessary to complete the course of study plus thirty days, or for one year, whichever is less, and are renewable. 8 C.F.R. § 214.2(m). M–2 status holders may not accept employment during their stay in the U.S. In some circumstances, temporary employment for practical training may be authorized for M–1 students after completion of studies.

See chapter 7, *infra*, for a more complete discussion of student visas.

§ 6–16 RELATIVES OF EMPLOYEES OF INTERNATIONAL ORGANIZATIONS

The Immigration Reform and Control Act of 1986 created the N status for certain relatives of international organization employees. INA § 101(a)(15)(N). Officers or employees of international organizations who meet certain residence requirements may become permanent residents of the United States under INA § 101(a)(27). The children of these "special immigrants" are eligible for N-nonimmigrant status. Children of some international organization employees may also qualify for special immigrant status. In that case, their parents are entitled to N-nonimmigrant status so long as the child is unmarried and under the age of twenty-one.

§ 6–17 PERSONS WITH EXTRAORDINARY ABILITY

Nonimmigrant O status is available to individuals who have extraordinary ability in the sciences, arts, education, business, or athletics, or have an extensively documented record of extraordinary achievement in motion pictures or television, if they are seeking entry to the U.S. to work in their area of expertise. Extraordinary ability must be demonstrated by sustained national or international acclaim, although a somewhat lesser standard applies to artists. O–1 status holders are also allowed to have dual (nonimmigrant and immigrant) intent.

Persons seeking entry solely to accompany and assist the artistic or athletic performance of an O–1 status-holder are granted O–2 status. Those seeking an O–2 visa must be an integral part of the performance and have a foreign residence with no intent to abandon it. 8 C.F.R. § 214.2(o).

Spouses and children of persons with O–1 or O–2 status are granted O–3 status, provided they are accompanying or following to join the principal nonimmigrant.

Individuals seeking either O–1 or O–2 status must have a petition filed on their behalf by a U.S. employer or agent. 8 C.F.R. § 214.2(o)(2). The petitioning employer must obtain an advisory opinion attesting to the individual's extraordinary ability from a labor organization or peer group in the nonimmigrant's field of expertise, if one exists. INA § 214(c)(3); 8 C.F.R. § 214.2(o)(5). O visas are valid for the duration of the event for which the individual is admitted, up to three years, and extensions may be granted in one-year increments with no limitation.

§ 6–18 INTERNATIONALLY RECOGNIZED ATHLETES AND ARTISTS

The P nonimmigrant category provides for the admission of athletes and certain artists. P–1 status covers athletes coming to the U.S. to perform or compete at an internationally recognized level and members of internationally recognized entertainment groups. The majority of the members of entertainment groups must have had a sustained and substantial relationship with the group for at least one year and must be integral to the group's performance. The P–2 classification applies to artists and entertainers coming to the U.S. under reciprocal exchange programs. P–3 status is granted to individual artists or entertainers and groups coming to the U.S. to perform, teach, or coach in a culturally unique program. Spouses and children of P nonimmigrants are granted P–4 status. INA § 101(a)(15)(P). Essential support personnel can also obtain P–1, P–2, or P–3 status, but must file a separate petition. 8 C.F.R. § 214.2(p).

As with the O category, persons seeking P status must be the beneficiaries of a petition filed by a U.S. employer or agent, or in the case of the P–2 and P–3 categories, by the organization sponsoring the program. Consultation with a labor organization or peer group is required for P–1 or P–3 petitions. INA § 214(c)(4). P status is valid for the duration of the competition, event, or performance for which the beneficiary is admitted, not to exceed one year. Individual athletes may enter for an initial period of up to five years, which may then be extended for another five years. Other persons with P status can obtain extensions in one-year increments to complete the activity for which they were admitted. 8 C.F.R. § 214.2(p)(14).

§ 6–19 CULTURAL VISITORS

The 1990 Act established Q nonimmigrant visas for participants in international cultural exchange programs. These exchange programs provide opportunities for foreign citizens to engage in training or employment through which they can share their culture with the American public. 8 C.F.R. § 214.2(q). Examples of such programs include organizations that provide entertainment with a cultural component, from the Walt Disney Company to traveling circuses, and educational establishments such as language camps. Q–1 status is granted to persons coming to the U.S. temporarily to engage in such programs. These nonimmigrants are admitted for up to fifteen months and they must have a foreign residence which they do not intend to abandon. 8 C.F.R. § 214.2(q).

The Irish Peace Process Cultural and Training Act of 1998, 112 Stat. 3013, later known as the "Walsh Visa Program," created a temporary cultural exchange program for disadvantaged young people from Northern Ireland and certain northern counties in the Republic of Ireland. Nonimmigrants admitted under the program were granted Q–2 status. The program expired in 2008.

§ 6–20 RELIGIOUS WORKERS

The 1990 Act also created the R status for qualified religious workers. To qualify, the nonimmigrant must have been a member for at least two years of a religious denomination that has nonprofit status in the U.S. The nonimmigrant must be coming to the U.S. for the purpose of acting as a minister of that religious denomination, working for the organization in a professional capacity, or working for an organization affiliated with the religious organization in a religious vocation. INA § 101(a)(15)(R). Religious workers are admitted with R–1 status for an initial period of three years, which may be extended for a further two years. 8 C.F.R. § 214.2(r). The religious worker's spouse and children are admitted with R–2 status.

§ 6–21   WITNESSES AND INFORMANTS

S nonimmigrant visas are available for non-citizens who have critical reliable information necessary for the successful prosecution of a criminal organization or enterprise or a terrorist organization. S–5 status is granted to persons who have information useful to criminal prosecutions, while persons with counterterrorism information receive S–6 status. 8 C.F.R. § 214.2(t). S-nonimmigrant status is granted only at the request of the federal or state law enforcement agency or court that needs the information. Individuals granted this status are admitted to the United States for no more than three years and must report quarterly to the requesting law enforcement agency as to their whereabouts. S-nonimmigrants may not change to any other non-immigrant classification.

§ 6–22   VICTIMS OF TRAFFICKING IN PERSONS

The Victims of Trafficking and Violence Protection Act of 2000 (114 Stat. 1464) created the T nonimmigrant status for victims of trafficking in persons. Congress enacted this measure primarily to prevent the exploitation of women and girls in the sex trade, finding that they are often lured into the trade with promises of good jobs and transported to foreign countries where they do not have support systems. Victims of "a severe form of trafficking" (meaning sex trafficking or slavery) may obtain T status if removal from the United States would pose a severe hardship for them and they agree to assist law enforcement officers in investigating or prosecuting such trafficking. INA § 101(a)(15)(T). If necessary to avoid hardship, the victim's spouse and children, as well as parents (if the victim is under twenty-one years of age), may also obtain T status. The T status category is subdivided into T–1 for victims, T–2 for spouses, T–3 for children, and T–4 for parents. The T–1 subcategory is one of the few numerically limited nonimmigrant statuses: only 5,000 people may be admitted to this status per year. 8 C.F.R. § 214.11(m). There is no limit to the number of family members who may be granted derivative status. This status is valid for three years and may not be renewed, although the status holder may apply for adjustment to permanent residence at the end of the T status period. Persons with T status are authorized to engage in employment.

§ 6–23 VICTIMS OF CRIMINAL ACTIVITY

The Victims of Trafficking and Violence Protection Act also created the U nonimmigrant class to assist victims of criminal activity. Congress intended this provision to facilitate the prosecution of domestic violence and other crimes by enabling the victims of such crimes to acquire a lawful nonimmigrant status. Individuals who have been the victim of domestic violence, rape, prostitution, female genital mutilation, or other listed crimes may obtain U status if they are willing to assist law enforcement officials in the prosecution of those crimes. INA § 101(a)(15)(U); 8 C.F.R. § 214.14(b). The criminal activity must have occurred within the United States or have violated a U.S. federal law that provides for extraterritorial jurisdiction. U status may also be granted to the spouse, child, or parent of a victim, if necessary to avoid hardship. 8 C.F.R. § 214.14(f). Only 10,000 people may be admitted to U status each year; as with the T status, this limitation applies only to the principal nonimmigrant and not to family members. 8 C.F.R. § 214.14(d).

§ 6–24 SPOUSES AND CHILDREN OF LAWFUL PERMANENT RESIDENTS

The Legal Immigration Family Equity (LIFE) Act of 2000 created a new V nonimmigrant status for a limited number of relatives of lawful permanent residents who are waiting for an immigration petition to be approved. 114 Stat. 2763. A spouse or child who was the beneficiary of an immigrant petition filed before December 21, 2000, and who has been waiting more than three years to receive an immigrant visa or adjust status may apply for the V status. INA § 101(a)(15)(E). This status allows the nonimmigrant to enter or remain in the United States for up to two years and permits employment. 8 C.F.R. § 214.15. If the nonimmigrant's immigrant petition or application to adjust to permanent resident status is denied or the nonimmigrant and permanent resident divorce, the person with V status will have thirty days to leave the United States. The V status is no longer available for spouses because, as of August 2008, CIS was processing applications for permanent residents sponsoring spouses received by October 2003. It is applicable to minor children, however, since as of August 2008, CIS was still processing applications from 1999 or earlier.

§ 6–25   CANADIAN AND MEXICAN BUSINESS TRAVELERS AND THEIR FAMILIES

The North American Free Trade Agreement, ratified in 1994, establishes special provisions for the temporary admission of Canadian and Mexican business visitors, traders and investors, intra-company transferees, professionals, and their families wishing to enter the United States. U.S. citizens traveling to Canada and Mexico receive reciprocal rights of entry. The agreement, and the occupational schedules which have been promulgated to implement it, facilitate entry by expediting the admission of particular occupational groups. The legislation created a new TN status for "NAFTA professionals." Their spouses and children are eligible for TD status, which allows for studying but not work authorization. The requirements for TN applicants are somewhat similar to those for the H–1B category, but only applicants in certain listed specialty occupations qualify. Canadian citizens may, however, obtain TN status at any port of entry to the U.S. simply by showing proof of citizenship and documentation of their intended professional activity and qualifications. No prior petition or labor certification is required and there is no limit to the number of Canadians who may be admitted to TN status. Mexican citizens, once required to obtain labor certification and limited to an annual cap of 5,500, are now free of those limitations and may enter the United States in TN status by applying directly to a U.S. Consulate for a visa. *See* 69 Fed. Reg. 11287–01. A TN visa will be issued upon adjudication of the nonimmigrant visa application (the electronic Form DS–156, *see* § 6–24 *infra*), proof of citizenship, and evidence of an offer of employment and minimum education or work experience. TN status is granted for up to three years at a time and can be renewed indefinitely, but TN beneficiaries must have the intent to return to their home countries. 8 C.F.R. § 214.6(b).

§ 6–26 PROCEDURAL REQUIRE-MENTS FOR NONIMMI-GRANT VISAS

Persons seeking a visa to enter the U.S. as nonimmigrants must apply using the specific procedures for the particular visa sought. Those procedures may be broadly divided into three categories: (1) Applications which require no preliminary petition or approvals (visas A, B, C, D, E, G, and I); (2) applications which require proof of acceptance in an authorized program (visas F, J, and M); and (3) applications which require approved petitions that provide the basis for the non-citizen's presence in the U.S. (visas H, K, L, O, P, Q, R, and V). A fourth category of applications (visas S and T), which will not be treated in detail here, requires endorsement by a law enforcement agency. Applications for S visas may be filed only by the requesting law enforcement agency. Applications for T status are filed by the nonimmigrant while in the United States.

Legislation passed in 2000 created a premium processing system for certain employment-based visa petitions. *See* INA § 286(u); 66 Fed.Reg. 29682–01. For a fee of $1,000, the CIS will adjudicate a visa petition within fifteen calendar days. Premium processing is currently available for E, H, L, O, P, Q–1, R–1, and TN status. Petitions for spouses or children of the primary beneficiary are also given premium processing with no additional fee, if filed concurrently with the primary nonimmigrant's petition.

For the first category of visas, where no preliminary approval is needed, applicants must submit Form DS–156. In 2004, the State Department announced an electronic bar-coded DS–156 available on its website, and the DS–156 can now be completed online at evisaforms.state.gov. In addition to Form DS–156, all male applicants between the ages of sixteen and forty-five must complete a supplementary information form, DS–157. The consular officer has the discretion to accept applications from individuals who do not reside in the consular district, but are physically present there. 22 C.F.R. § 41.101. In such cases, the consular officer may examine the applicant's reasons for not applying to the consulate where he or she resides. Personal interviews are now mandatory for virtually all applicants. 22 C.F.R. § 41.102. The consular officer may also require additional documents to verify the applicant's purpose in requesting the visa. Supporting documents will usually concern the person's eligibility to enter the U.S. and intention to depart at the end of the intended stay. 22 C.F.R. § 41.105. Intention to depart from the U.S. is typically established by proof of ties to one's home country such as a job, residence, and family. Provided there are no complicating issues, the machine-readable visa is issued shortly after the interview and is imbedded in the nonimmigrant's passport, along with a photograph (and eventually a fingerprint). 22 C.F.R. § 41.113.

For the second category of visa (F, J, or M visas), the applicant must also present an acceptance form from the school or program. For the student (F and M) visa, SEVIS Form I–20 is executed by an accredited school where the student will study. 22 C.F.R. § 41.61; 8 C.F.R. § 214.2(f)(1). Exchange visitors must present Form DS–2019, executed by the program sponsor, indicating the applicant's participation in an approved program. 22 C.F.R. § 41.62. If the consulate is satisfied that the applicant has sufficient funds to cover expenses while in the U.S., intends to return to his or her home country, and has the necessary knowledge of the English language, a visa will be granted. 22 C.F.R. §§ 41.61, 41.62. The Department of State has implemented a computerized system that allows schools to issue these documents and communicate with consular officers electronically. The SEVIS system is also designed to improve monitoring of students in the U.S. For example, an exchange visitor's acceptance documentation must be verified by a consular official's review of SEVIS and notification of issuance of a J visa must be entered into the SEVIS database. 22 C.F.R. § 41.62(a)(5).

The third category of visas (H, K, L, O, P, Q, R, and V) requires that the applicant be a beneficiary of a petition, usually Form I–129, approved by the CIS. In most cases, the applicant's prospective employer or program sponsor (in the case of Q visas) submits the petition. Certain employers of L visa applicants may file a blanket petition rather than separate, individual petitions. For a K visa, the applicant's intended U.S. spouse files the petition. Applicants for the K–3 and V visas must have an immigrant petition (Form I–130) filed on their behalf by their lawful permanent resident parent or spouse. Once the underlying petition is approved, the beneficiary may apply for a visa to enter the United States. If the consular officer finds the supporting documents in order and the applicant eligible in all other respects, the visa will be granted.

The consular officer may require additional proof of the applicant's eligibility for any visa if the officer is not satisfied with the initial application or knows or has reason to believe that the applicant is ineligible for such visa. If the added proof is still deemed insufficient after review, the consulate may deny the visa application, informing the applicant of the grounds for refusal. 22 C.F.R. § 41.121. The Department of State cannot overrule the consulate's decision so long as the decision was based on the application of law to facts. INA §§ 104A, 221(a). Although there is generally no judicial review available, several courts have reserved a narrow ground of review in visa denial cases to ensure that the constitutional rights of U.S. citizens are not denied unless there is a "facially legitimate and bona fide" reason. *See, e.g., American Academy of Religion v. Napolitano*, 573 F.3d 115 (2d Cir.2009); *Abourezk v. Reagan*, 785 F.2d 1043 (D.C. Cir.1986); *Allende v. Shultz*, 605 F.Supp. 1220 (D.Mass.1985). *See also* § 3–1, *supra*.

Upon entry to the U.S., anyone holding a nonimmigrant visa will be subject to inspection by an immigration officer and will receive a Form I–94 indicating the length and terms of their stay. Persons admitted through the visa waiver program receive Form I–94W. Canadian citizens and Mexican citizens making short visits with a border crossing card are exempt from the Form I–94 requirement.

In the wake of the attacks on September 11, 2001, the admission and monitoring of nonimmigrants in the U.S. came under close scrutiny. In response to security concerns, Congress passed three statutes that affect nonimmigrants: the USA PATRIOT Act (115 Stat. 272), the Enhanced Border Security and Visa Entry Reform Act (116 Stat. 543), and the Homeland Security Act (116 Stat. 2135). The measures mandated by these Acts include implementation of an entry-exit tracking system called for in the IIRIRA; the integration of immigration data systems; a requirement that the State Department issue only machine-readable visas by October 2004, and that persons seeking entry under the visa waiver program carry machine-readable passports by that date; and enhanced screening of nonimmigrant visa applicants who are nationals of countries that have been designated as state sponsors of international terrorism. The Homeland Security Act gives the U.S. Immigration and Customs Enforcement authority to make further regulations governing nonimmigrant visas.

The Department of State and the INS (now U.S. Immigration and Customs Enforcement) also implemented regulatory changes to increase national security. One such change was the introduction of the supplementary information form DS–157, discussed earlier in this section. The State Department has also limited the ability of nonimmigrants to obtain automatic revalidation of expired visas following trips to Mexico and Canada. 67 Fed.Reg. 10322–01.

Under a rule implemented in September 2002, some nonimmigrants were subject to special registration requirements under the National Security Entry–Exit Registration System (NSEERS). *See* 8 C.F.R. § 264.1(f); 67 Fed.Reg. 52584–01. Persons subject to the requirements were fingerprinted and photographed upon arrival and sometimes required to appear at an ICE office to provide additional documentation that the nonimmigrant had complied with conditions of his or her visa status such as proof of residence, employment, or registration and matriculation at an educational institution. 8 C.F.R. § 264.1(f)(3). The special registration requirements originally applied to male nonimmigrants born on or before November 15, 1986, from twenty-five designated countries.

The US–VISIT (Visitor and Immigration Status Indicator Technology) program has replaced NSEERS registration. 80 Interp.Rel. 690. Under US–VISIT, almost all nonimmigrant visas holders are required to provide a digital finger scan and have their picture taken when entering the country. 69 Fed.Reg. 468–01. In 2009, a DHS rule expanded the application of US–VISIT to virtually all non-citizens, including lawful permanent residents. 73 Fed.Reg. 77473. US–VISIT biometric entry procedures are in place in most airports, seaports, and land ports of entry. DHS plans to expand a pilot program requiring biometric exit procedures at certain airports to all air and sea ports of departures. 73 Fed.Reg. 22065–01. The proposed rule would require all commercial air carriers and cruise lines to collect fingerprints of all exiting international visitors and transmit them to DHS within twenty-four hours of leaving the United States. DHS is also seeking to enhance security measures by replacing all two-fingerprint scanners with ten-fingerprint scanners.

§ 6–27　CHANGING NONIMMIGRANT CLASSIFICATION

INA § 248 permits most nonimmigrants in the U.S. to change classifications, so long as they have maintained lawful nonimmigrant status. Persons admitted under the visa waiver program and nonimmigrants in the C, D, K, and S statuses are barred from changing nonimmigrant classification, as are J-visa holders who are subject to the two-year foreign residence requirement. INA § 248. Nonimmigrants wishing to change classifications usually submit an application to the CIS with any evidence required for the status they are seeking. 8 C.F.R. § 248.3. If the new status requires an employer's petition, the employer must submit Form I–129 on behalf of the nonimmigrant. Nonimmigrants may also change classifications by leaving the U.S. and applying for a new nonimmigrant visa at a consulate.

Changing nonimmigrant classifications may extend the duration of the nonimmigrant's stay or his or her ability to work in the U.S. It does not automatically grant the nonimmigrant permission to leave and re-enter the U.S.: unless exempt from visa requirements, individuals who have changed status will still need to apply for a visa to re-enter the U.S. in their new status if they leave the country. Further, nonimmigrants who overstayed a previous status may have to return to their home country to obtain a new visa, and may be barred from re-entering the U.S. *See* § 8–1.2(d), *infra*.

Immigration authorities may view an attempt to change nonimmigrant classifications soon after arriving in the U.S. as evidence that a nonimmigrant misrepresented his or her intent at the time of admission. Such a misrepresentation would make the person inadmissible under INA § 212(a)(6). In *Lun Kwai Tsui v. Attorney General*, 445 F.Supp. 832 (D.D.C.1978), the court found that the INS properly denied the plaintiffs' applications to change to student status because the rapid series of events following their entry into the U.S. as tourists showed that they had misrepresented their intent.

§ 6–28   ADJUSTMENT OF STATUS
TO IMMIGRANT

Generally, all nonimmigrants who are in the U.S. may apply to have their status adjusted to permanent residence status, with the exception of crew member (D) visa holders, J visa holders with the two-year home residence requirement, and most beneficiaries of the visa waiver program. INA § 245. Nonimmigrants other than immediate relatives of U.S. citizens are ineligible to adjust to permanent residence status if they have accepted unauthorized employment or have otherwise failed to maintain lawful immigration status since entering the United States. INA § 245(c). Section 245(k) of the Immigration and Nationality Act limits the restriction of INA § 245(c) by allowing adjustment of status if the nonimmigrant is lawfully present in the United States on the date of filing for adjustment of status through employment and has not failed to maintain lawful status continuously, engaged in unauthorized employment, or otherwise violated the terms and conditions of his or her admission for an aggregate period exceeding 180 days. INA § 245(k). Further restrictions apply to persons who seek to adjust status on the basis of a marriage entered while in removal proceedings. INA § 245(e).

Immigration authorities usually treat an application to adjust to permanent residence status as evidence of immigrant intent, which could prevent a nonimmigrant from extending certain nonimmigrant statuses. For this reason, it is advisable to change to a nonimmigrant status that allows dual intent before applying to adjust to permanent residence.

See § 5–5.4, *supra*, for further information on adjustment of status.

CHAPTER 7

NONIMMIGRANT STUDENTS

§ 7–1 INTRODUCTION

International students make up a significant, and growing, percentage of students in U.S. colleges and universities. In 2000, nearly 700,000 foreign students were admitted into the U.S.; in 2008, foreign student admissions reached over 900,000. These students contribute billions of dollars to the U.S. economy each year. Three nonimmigrant classifications are available to individuals who come to the U.S. to study: the F–1 status for academic students, the M–1 status for vocational or nonacademic students, and the J–1 status for exchange visitors. The focus of this chapter is the F–1 status, which is the one most commonly sought by students.

To qualify for F–1 status, students must be entering the U.S. temporarily and solely to pursue a full course of study in an academic program. Unlike many other nonimmigrants, persons with F–1 status frequently remain in the United States for a number of years. The regulations for F status, at 8 C.F.R. § 214.2(f), address some of the issues which are likely to arise during a student's stay in the United States. Regulations governing the M–1 and J–1 classifications are similar to those governing the F–1 classification. Some of the key differences between the classifications are described in section 7–9, *infra*.

In 2002, Congress created a new status for "border commuter" students. INA § 101(a)(15)(F), (M). This status allows students who reside in Canada or Mexico to enter the United States in order to attend school full-time or part-time. Previously, part-time students were not eligible for F or M status, but ports of entry would admit such students on B visitor visas. The INS ordered ports to stop this practice in June 2002, abruptly terminating many students' studies. In response to public outcry, immigration officers temporarily granted humanitarian parole to students so that they could complete their current term. The Border Commuter Student Act of 2002, 116 Stat. 1923, regularized border commuter status by creating the F–3 and M–3 visa classifications. The requirements for border commuter student status are similar to those for other F or M students, except that such students are granted entry only for their current term and may not engage in employment in the U.S. 8 C.F.R. § 214.2(f)(18), (m)(18).

It should be noted that nonimmigrants in other classifications are also permitted to study in the U.S., although this objective cannot be their primary purpose for entry. For example, spouses and children of temporary workers with H status are permitted to study full-or part-time without changing to F–1 status. 8 C.F.R. § 248.3. Such students will not, however, be able to take advantage of the limited employment opportunities available to those with F–1 status. In addition, many nonimmigrants, including tourists and temporary workers, may engage in part-time studies incidental to the activity for which they were granted status. Nonimmigrants, however, who are admitted under a B–1 (business) or B–2 (tourist) visa, violate their status if they enroll in a course of study. 8 C.F.R. § 214.2(b). Nonimmigrants with a B–1 or B–2 visa must obtain an F–1 or M–1 visa if they wish to enroll in a course of study.

§ 7–2 COMING TO THE
U.S. AS A STUDENT

The first step for a student who wants to study in the U.S. is to gain admission to a school that has received approval to admit foreign students. Schools that can admit F–1 students include colleges and universities, seminaries, conservatories, academic high schools, private elementary schools, and language schools. Community colleges can accept F–1 students or M–1 students depending on the program of study. Vocational schools accept M–1 students. 8 C.F.R. § 214.3. The U.S. Citizenship and Immigration Services (CIS) approves schools to admit foreign students. Each approved school appoints a Designated School Official (DSO), who handles most of the administrative aspects of the F–1 and M–1 programs. The DSO provides immigration officials with information about admitted students through the Student and Exchange Visitor Information System ("SEVIS"). In the wake of September 11, 2001, the U.S. PATRIOT Act mandated the use of SEVIS and the U.S. Immigration and Customs Enforcement (ICE) uses the system to monitor foreign students while they are in the United States. Apart from monitoring students through SEVIS, immigration officials have very little involvement with foreign student programs. Foreign students must pay a SEVIS fee along with their visa application, the amount of which varies depending on the student visa classification.

In 2009, ICE began replacing SEVIS with the web-based SEVIS II system. Foreign students enter SEVIS II by creating user accounts on the system's website. In creating a user account, a student receives an immigration identification number and creates an electronic signature in order to authenticate electronic forms. A foreign student then may complete and submit the visa application on the SEVIS II website. Government officials access a foreign student's SEVIS II account to document decisions concerning visa issuances, entry into the U.S., changes in status, and employment authorizations. SEVIS II allows a foreign student to monitor the visa status through the user accounts.

To prevent fraudulent visa applications, immigration regulations require all prospective students to apply in writing to the school they wish to attend. Schools may accept only those students whose qualifications meet their admission standards. 8 C.F.R. § 214.3. After accepting a student, the institution completes a Certificate of Eligibility for Nonimmigrant (F–1) Student Status in the student's SEVIS II account. The student then may apply for an F–1 visa by completing a visa application. The student must next interview at a United States consulate in the student's home country. Students should be prepared to present persuasive evidence that they are maintaining a residence abroad to which they intend to return on completion of their studies in the United States. They must also provide documentation showing that they have sufficient funds available to support themselves during their entire course of study. Moreover, students must demonstrate that they have sufficient English skills for the course in which they are enrolled, or that they will be taking preparatory English classes in the U.S. 22 C.F.R. § 41.61.

Students pursuing studies in certain sensitive high-technology fields, particularly students at the graduate or post-graduate level, may face heightened scrutiny when they apply for a student visa. In response to concerns that the U.S. is training potential terrorists, the George W. Bush administration initiated special screening procedures for F, M, and J students studying in fields where they would have access to sensitive, but unclassified information. In addition, students from countries designated as state sponsors of terrorism face heightened scrutiny when applying for student visas and have, in many cases, been denied. *See*, § 6–1, *supra* for further discussion of the nonimmigrant security screening process.

Once a visa is issued, the student may travel to the United States. Students may enter the U.S. up to thirty days before their studies commence. 8 C.F.R. § 214.2(f)(5). At the port of entry, students present their passport with the F–1 visa stamp for inspection. Students may also be required to present evidence of financial support and to verify their intent to attend the school that issued the I–20. The inspecting officer will issue a Form I–94 and enter the student's admission number into his or her SEVIS II account. SEVIS II notifies the school that the student has been admitted to the United States.

§ 7–3 FAMILY OF THE STUDENT

Spouses and children of students are granted F–2 status. Spouses and children may accompany students to the United States or they may follow later. If family members are accompanying the student, they do not need an I–20 A–B of their own to apply for an F–2 visa, because they are included on the student's I–20 A–B. If the family members are following, they must present an original Form I–20 issued in the name of each F–2 dependent by the school that admitted the F–1 student. 8

C.F.R. § 214.2(f)(3). The F–2 spouse and children of an F–1 student may not, under any circumstances, accept employment unless they change to a different non-immigrant classification. 8 C.F.R. § 214.2(f)(15). Children of F–1 students may enroll in elementary and secondary schools without a change in status. *Id.*

§ 7–4 DURATION OF STATUS

Students and their family members are generally admitted for the student's "duration of status." "Duration of status" is defined as the period during which the student is pursuing a full course of study in any educational program or is receiving authorized practical training, plus sixty days within which to depart from the United States. 8 C.F.R. § 214.2(f)(5). An F–1 student who continues from one educational level to another, from one educational program to another, and/or from one school to another, remains in status as long as the proper procedures are followed. 8 C.F.R. § 214.2(f)(5). There are a number of requirements for maintaining status. The consequences of failing to adhere to these requirements can include removal, inability to change to another nonimmigrant status or to permanent resident status, and inadmissibility. See § 7–8, *infra.*

§ 7–4.1 Full Course of Study

Students must be pursuing a full course of study that leads to a specific educational or professional objective. The conditions necessary to satisfy the full course of study requirement vary depending on the academic program involved. For postgraduate or postdoctoral study, or studies at a conservatory or religious seminary, a full course of study is a program certified as such by the school's DSO. An undergraduate student must generally take twelve semester or quarter hours per term, unless fewer hours are required for the student to complete the course of study at that institution in the current term. A primary or high school student must take at least the minimum number of hours per week required by the school for normal progress toward graduation. 8 C.F.R. § 214.2(f)(6)(i).

Students may take fewer than the required number of hours for a full course of study only if allowed to do so by their DSO because of English language difficulties; unfamiliarity with U.S. teaching methods; improper course level placement; or illness. 8 C.F.R. § 214.2(f)(5)–(6). School officials generally exercise discretion in allowing students to take a reduced course load.

§ 7–4.2 Deadline for Completion of Studies

When a school issues an I–20 to a student, it must state when the student is expected to complete the course of study. In estimating the completion date, schools may add a one-year grace period to the time normally required for a particular course. Students who are unable to complete their degree objectives by this date must apply to the school for an extension of stay. 8 C.F.R. § 214.2(f)(7). After the estimated completion date has passed, a DSO may only grant an extension to a student who has maintained student status and whose inability to complete by the date on the I–20 is caused by "compelling academic or medical reasons." 8 C.F.R. § 214.2(f)(7)(iii). Circumstances that justify an extension include a change of college major, unexpected research difficulties, and documented illnesses. Delays caused by academic problems (academic probation, suspension) are not acceptable reasons for extension. Students who fail to complete their course on time and are ineligible for an extension are considered out of status and must apply for reinstatement to continue their studies (see § 7–9, *infra*). Schools must notify immigration authorities of an extension by submitting Form I–538 and must give the student a new Form I–20 showing the adjusted completion date.

Following completion of their studies, and any optional post-completion practical training (see § 7–6, *infra*), students have sixty days in which to depart from the U.S. 8 C.F.R. § 214.2(f)(5).

§ 7–4.3 Transferring or Changing Educational Levels

Students who wish to transfer schools must notify their current school of their intent to transfer and must complete a new Form I–20 in their SEVIS II account. Students remain in status so long as the transfer is properly executed and they continue to make progress towards their educational objectives. Students who have failed to pursue a full course of study at the school they are currently authorized to attend are not eligible to transfer unless they apply to the USCIS for and are granted reinstatement to student status. 8 C.F.R. § 214.2(f)(8).

Students who have completed a course and wish to continue their studies at a higher educational level, whether at the same or a different institution, also follow the transfer procedure outlined above.

§ 7–4.4 Vacations and Other Interruptions

F–1 students are considered to be in status during summer vacation if they are eligible and intend to register for the upcoming term. Students at schools that operate on the trimester or quarter system may take any term as a vacation, so long as they take only one vacation term per year, are eligible and intend to register for the next term, and have completed the equivalent of a full academic year before taking the vacation. With the approval of the DSO, students may remain in status if they are forced to interrupt or reduce their course of study because of illness or other medical condition, provided they return to a full course of study upon recovery. 8 C.F.R. § 214.2(f)(5).

§ 7–4.5 Student and Exchange Visitor Information System ("SEVIS")

Because of their numbers and the length of time they remain in the U.S., it is very difficult for immigration authorities to monitor foreign students. While schools are required to maintain records on all foreign students, until recently there was no central repository for most of this information. The 1993 bombing of the World Trade Center raised serious concerns about the activities of foreign students in the U.S. because one of the perpetrators had been a foreign student. In 1996, Congress mandated the creation of a computerized system to track students. IIRIRA § 641. The INS subsequently initiated a pilot test of such a system, which was underway when the September 11, 2001, attacks occurred. At least one of the hijackers involved in those attacks entered the U.S. as a student, and two others had applied for student status. Consequently, the USA PATRIOT Act required all schools that admit foreign students to begin using the system, now known as "SEVIS." 67 Fed.Reg. 34862. The Homeland Security Act made the U.S. Immigration and Customs Enforcement (ICE) responsible for SEVIS, which ICE maintains through its Student and Exchange Visitor Program (SEVP).

SEVIS and SEVIS II were designed to facilitate tracking of students, both for security purposes and to help students maintain status. Under SEVIS, schools were required to enter information into the Internet-based system about each F–1 or M–1 student they enroll, including the student's name, date of birth, citizenship, current enrollment status, current address, and expected completion date. In order to improve the accuracy of student records, SEVIS II makes students responsible for entering their biographical information into the system and keeping their records current. Schools must report in SEVIS II employment authorizations, disciplinary actions taken as a result of a criminal conviction, and any failure of a student to maintain status.

§ 7–5 EMPLOYMENT

Subject to some restrictions, F–1 students may seek employment while they are studying. An F–1 student may work on-campus up to 20 hours per week while school is in session and while enrolled as a full-time student. After completing nine months in F–1 status, students may also seek authorization from the CIS to work off-campus to alleviate an unanticipated economic hardship or for practical training. Foreign students who gain employment in the U.S. will need to obtain a Social Security Number.

§ 7–5.1 On–Campus Employment

An F–1 student pursuing a full course of study is permitted to engage in on-campus employment so long as the employment will not displace a United States resident. Students may not work more than twenty hours per week while school is in session, but they may work full time during school breaks. "On campus" includes employment with commercial firms which provide services for students on campus, such as book stores or food service companies. 8 C.F.R. § 214.2(f)(9). On campus employment does not include employment with commercial firms which do not provide direct student services, such as a company constructing a school building.

On campus employment also includes work for off-campus organizations that are affiliated with the school through its established curriculum or a contractually funded research program. This arrangement was designed to permit graduate students to conduct research at off-campus locations under the supervision of their professors. Immigration regulations specify that such employment must be an integral part of the student's educational program and be commensurate with the level of study. 8 C.F.R. § 214.2(f)(9).

On-campus employment pursuant to the terms of a scholarship, fellowship, or assistantship is permitted and is deemed a part of the academic program of a student otherwise taking a full course of study. Hence, students assigned teaching or research responsibilities pursuant to the terms of a scholarship or fellowship may carry a reduced course load. Note, however, that the student's total employment may never exceed 20 hours per week while school is in session.

§ 7–5.2 Off–Campus Employment

F–1 students must obtain permission from CIS to engage in off-campus employment, unless the employment is pursuant to a curricular practical training program (see § 7–6, *infra*.). CIS may grant a student an off-campus employment authorization based on severe economic hardship. The employment authorization may be granted in one year intervals up to the expected date of completion of the student's current course of study. 8 C.F.R. § 214.2(f)(9). To be eligible, students must demonstrate that they need to work because of "severe economic hardship caused by unforeseen circumstances beyond the student's control." The rules define the unforeseen circumstances as follows: (1) loss of financial aid or on-campus employment without fault on the part of the student; (2) substantial fluctuations in the value of currency or exchange rate; (3) inordinate increases in tuition or living costs; (4) unexpected changes in the financial condition of the student's source of support; or (5) medical bills or other substantial and unexpected expenses. 8 C.F.R. § 214.2(f)(9).

The rules also require that students: (1) have completed one full academic year (nine months) in F–1 status; (2) be in good academic standing and carrying a full course of study; (3) obtain a recommendation from their DSO in favor of work authorization; (4) obtain an employment authorization document from CIS; and (5) work no more than twenty hours per week when school is in session (full-time work is permissible during vacation periods). 8 C.F.R. § 214.2(f)(9).

Immigration regulations allow the Director of CIS to temporarily suspend the normal restrictions on employment in emergency circumstances. 8 C.F.R. § 214.2(f)(9)(ii). This rule was implemented to benefit students from certain Asian countries that were severely impacted by the 1998 economic crisis in that region. Students from those countries who were enrolled in U.S.

schools during the crisis were permitted to work an unrestricted number of hours on-or off-campus, and could take a reduced course load. 75 Interp.Rel. 954.

F–1 students are also permitted to work for recognized international organizations. Students may apply to CIS for authorization for such employment by presenting a current I–20 and written certification from the international organization. 8 C.F.R. § 214.2(f)(9)(iii).

§ 7–6 PRACTICAL TRAINING

Practical training is an authorized period of temporary employment which allows students to obtain work experience related to their course of study. A student who is engaged in authorized practical training remains in status for the duration of the training. There are two types of practical training available: curricular and optional. "Curricular practical training" refers to employment required as part of a course of study. "Optional practical training" refers to employment related to, but not required for, a course of study.

Practical training is available to F–1 students who have been lawfully enrolled on a full-time basis and have completed a full academic term. 8 C.F.R. § 214.2(f)(10). Exceptions to the completed academic term requirement are provided for students enrolled in graduate studies which require immediate participation in curricular practical training. 8 C.F.R. § 214.2(f)(10).

§ 7–6.1 Curricular Practical Training

Curricular practical training is undertaken while a student is studying and includes internships, alternate work/study programs, or other work experience. 8 C.F.R. § 214.2(f)(10). A DSO may authorize curricular practical training for a foreign student if the training is an integral part of an established curriculum and the sponsoring employer agrees that the training will serve an academic purpose.

The school may authorize employment for the student if satisfied that the work qualifies as curricular practical training. DSOs must report the curricular practical training authorization in SEVIS and immigration officials receive notice of the training authorization through this process. All other types of off-campus employment require independent authorization from immigration officials. In practice, many DSOs interpret the concept of "internship" liberally to permit foreign students an opportunity to gain work experience. A student who receives one year or more of full-time curricular practical training is ineligible for optional practical training. Consequently, curricular practical training is usually authorized for less than one year. Both on-campus and off-campus employment count towards the one-year limit.

§ 7–6.2 Optional Practical Training

Students may apply for 12 months of optional practical training directly related to their major area of study. 8 C.F.R. § 214.2(f)(10). Unlike curricular practical training, optional practical training can be authorized only by CIS, upon recommendation of the school. Students may take practical training during the school year (up to twenty hours per week), over their annual vacation, while writing a thesis, or after completing their studies, but they must complete all optional practical training no later than fourteen months after finishing their studies. 8 C.F.R. § 214.2(f)(10). Students may receive up to twelve months of optional practical training and may receive an additional twelve months if they advance to a higher educational level. Students in the fields of science, technology, engineering, and mathematics are eligible for seventeen months of optional practical training if they and their employers fulfill certain requirements under 8 C.F.R. § 214.2(f)(10).

Students who wish to undertake optional practical training after completing their studies must apply for an Employment Authorization Document (EAD) no sooner than 120 days before commencing employment and no later than sixty days after graduation (student status ends sixty days after graduation if the student is not then engaged in optional practical training). 70 Interp.Rel. 727. The application for an EAD must include a recommendation from the student's DSO. Students may not accept employment until they have been issued an Employment Authorization Document. 8 C.F.R. § 214.2 (f)(11).

§ 7–7 CHANGE TO OR FROM F– 1 NON–IMMIGRANT STATUS

Generally, nonimmigrants may change their status to that of an F–1 student if they qualify as students and have a valid I–20A–B Certificate of Eligibility for Nonimmigrant (F–1) Student Status from the school they wish to attend.

A special situation is presented by a change from B–2 visitor for pleasure to F–1 student. Because the B–2 visitor visa is believed to be easier to acquire than the F–1 visa, immigration authorities are skeptical of applications for change from visitor status to student status B particularly during the first 60 days after arrival. Such an application may create the impression that the individual planned all along to study in the United States, and thus obtained the B–2 visa through misrepresentation. Prospective students may legitimately travel to the U.S. on a B–2 visa, however, in order to select a school or to complete an admissions process that requires a personal visit. Students who have not yet received an I–20 authorization from their school may also be permitted to travel to the U.S. on a B–2 visa if their circumstances demand an immediate departure. In these situations, the student should notify the consular officer of his or her intent and the consular officer should mark the B–2 visa "prospective student." If the B–2 visa is not marked in this way, the holder will not be permitted to change to F–1 status later. 67 Fed.Reg. 18065. Consular officers may require prospective students to show that they would eventually be eligible for F–1 status by producing the supporting documentation required of any applicant for an F–1 visa, including proof of financial resources and of the bona fide intent to return home on completion of studies. Prospective students admitted to the U.S. on a B–2 visa may not begin their course of study until a change to F–1 or M–1 status is approved, which can present a significant problem, as the adjudication period can take many months. 67 Fed.Reg. 18062.

F–1 nonimmigrant students may qualify to obtain a work-related H–1B visa after completing their studies in F–1 status. While exchange visitors with J status are sometimes subject to a two-year foreign residency requirement, there is no such requirement for F–1 students. Students applying for H–1B classification must demonstrate that they are qualified to work in a specialty occupation. An employer seeking to hire a student must file a Labor Condition application with the Department of Labor and must petition to CIS for the student's change of classification before the student's status expires. Students who cannot change classifications immediately because the annual cap on H–1B visas has been reached (see § 6–8, *supra*) may have their student status extended, but may not work until an H–1B visa is available. 64 Fed.Reg. 32146. Some students use the change to H–1B status as an intermediary step towards obtaining permanent residence.

F–1 nonimmigrant students may qualify to adjust directly to permanent resident status through either a relative or an employer. If a student's spouse, adult child, or parent is a U.S. citizen, the student may be eligible to acquire permanent residence as an immediate relative. Students may not marry solely to obtain immigration benefits, however (*see* INA § 275(c)), and recently married students who obtain permanent residence through marriage will have conditional status for two years. INA § 216. For more information on visas for immediate relatives of U.S. citizens see § 5–2.1, *supra*. Other relationships to United States citizens and to permanent residents may qualify the student to adjust status in a family-sponsored preference category, subject to numerical limitations and waiting periods. *See* § 5–3.1(a), *supra*.

Due to the waiting periods for the employment-based preference categories, it is extremely difficult for students to adjust to permanent residence status directly, without first obtaining H–1B status. Students seeking permanent resident status through an employer would most likely want to apply for the second employment-related preference category, for professionals with advanced degrees or exceptional ability in science, art, or business, or the third preference category, for professionals with baccalaureate degrees, skilled workers, and other workers. Both of these preference categories require the employer to obtain labor certification showing that there is no U.S. citizen or resident available who can fill the position. *See* § 5–3.1(b), *supra*.

§ 7–8　VIOLATION OF STUDENT STATUS: CONSEQUENCES AND RISKS

§ 7–8.1　Reinstatement to Student Status

In some circumstances, immigration officials will reinstate the status of students who have remained in the U.S. after their status has expired or have otherwise violated the conditions of F–1 status. Reinstatement is only allowed if the student:

(1) makes a written request for reinstatement, accompanied by a properly completed I–20A–B from the school the student is attending or intends to attend;

(2) has not been out of status for more than 5 months at the time of filing the request for reinstatement or demonstrates that the failure to file within the 5 month period was the result of exceptional circumstances and that the student filed the request for reinstatement as promptly as possible under these exceptional circumstances;

(3) can establish that the violation of status resulted from circumstances beyond the student's control or that failure to reinstate the student would result in extreme hardship to the student;

(4) is currently pursuing or intends to pursue a full course of study;

(5) has not engaged in unauthorized employment;

(6) provides documentary proof of funding to continue in school and maintain full-time status; and

(7) is not removable on any ground (other than her/his violation of student status). 8 C.F.R. § 214.2(f)(16).

The requirement of not engaging in unauthorized employment can be a particularly difficult barrier to reinstatement, because students are only permitted to work while in status. A student who continues to work after losing status is engaging in unauthorized employment and may therefore be unable to obtain reinstatement. The district director's decision to disallow reinstatement is not subject to review, except pursuant to a declaratory judgment action in a U.S. district court.

§ 7–8.2 Re-entry Upon Violation of the Student Status

F–1 students should carefully protect their status, because violations can affect a student's ability to travel to and from the United States in the future.

Unless an F–1 student can obtain reinstatement after losing status, his or her entry visa is subject to automatic cancellation. The student will then need to leave the United States to obtain a new visa for re-entry, usually in his or her country of nationality. INA § 222(g)(2)(A).

Furthermore, since April 1997, students who remain in the U.S. for 180 days or more after the USCIS determines that they are out of status (*e.g.*, after CIS denies reinstatement) are barred from re-entering the U.S. for a period of three years. INA § 212(a)(9)(B)(i)(I). Students who remain in the U.S. for one year or more after being adjudged out of status will not be allowed to re-enter the

U.S. for 10 years. INA § 212(a)(9)(B)(i)(II). *See* § 8–1.2(d), *infra*.

§ 7–8.3 Adjustment to Permanent Resident Status

Anyone who has failed to maintain legal status continuously since entry into the United States is ineligible to adjust to permanent resident status. 8 C.F.R. § 245.1(b). The only exceptions to this rule are if the person is an immediate relative as defined in INA § 201(b), or is a special immigrant described in INA § 101(a)(27)(H), (I) or (J), or if the failure was for technical reasons for which the nonimmigrant was not at fault. A student's departure and subsequent re-entry will not eliminate this bar to adjustment of status. 8 C.F.R. § 245.1(c).

This provision does not prevent any individual from leaving the United States and returning on an immigrant visa obtained from a U.S. consulate abroad, if the individual is not subject to the three-and ten-year bars for unlawful presence. The application process may require many months of consular procedures before the visa interview is granted.

§ 7–8.4 Inadmissibility

Included in the Immigration Marriage Fraud Amendments of 1986 was an amendment to INA § 212(a) which increased the sanctions applicable to students who fraudulently or willfully violate the terms of their student status. This amendment provided that any person who fraudulently or willfully misrepresents a material fact in order to procure any benefit conferred by the Immigration and Nationality Act is ineligible to receive a visa and will be denied admission into the United States. Before the 1986 amendment, the language of this provision applied only to individuals who obtained a visa or other documentation or sought to enter the United States through the use of fraud or willful misrepresentation. The prior provision did not include as a ground for inadmissibility or denial of a visa the use of fraud to obtain "other benefit[s] provided under this Chapter." This broad inadmissibility provision could prevent a student from re-entering the United States, either as an immigrant or as a nonimmigrant, if that student misrepresented a material fact in order to qualify for immigration benefits such as permission to be employed or permission to take less than a full course of study.

§ 7–9 M–1 STUDENTS

Students who come to the United States to study at a vocational or nonacademic institution (other than a language training program) are granted M–1 status. The regulations for admission as an M–1 student are similar to those for F–1 students, but M–1 students face more limitations on their activities in the U.S. than do F–1 students. While F–1 students are admitted for duration of status, M–1 students are admitted for the length of their course of studies plus thirty days, or for one year, whichever is less. They may, however, extend their stay up to three years if needed to complete a course of study. 8 C.F.R. § 214.2(m)(10). M–1 students are not permitted to engage in employment while studying. They are allowed one month of practical training for every four months of study, to a maximum of six months, but only if equivalent training is not available in their country of origin. M–1 students can transfer schools only during their first six months of study and they may not change their educational objective. Nor are they permitted to change to F–1 status. 8 C.F.R. § 248.1. The M status is not to be used as a means of obtaining employment in the U.S.; hence, M–1 students are not allowed to change to H status in order to work in their field of study. They may change to H status only to work in another field. 8 C.F.R. § 248.1.

§ 7–10   J–1 EXCHANGE STUDENTS

J–1 status is granted to individuals who come to the United States under the sponsorship of an exchange program approved by the Department of State. A few such programs are specifically aimed at students and scholars, including scholarship programs for college and university students (such as the Fulbright program) and secondary school exchange programs. Just as designated school officials have great authority over the status of F–1 and M–1 students, exchange program sponsors are largely responsible for the status of J–1 students.

To be admitted to J–1 status as a college or university student, the nonimmigrant must satisfy one of four criteria: (1) either the student or the program must be funded by the U.S. government, the government of the student's home country, or an international organization; (2) the program must be carried out pursuant to an agreement between the United States and a foreign government; (3) the program must be carried out pursuant to an agreement between a U.S. university and either a foreign university or foreign government; or (4) the student must be supported substantially from a source other than personal or family funds. 22 C.F.R. § 62.23. J–1 status has some advantages over the F–1 status, in that spouses and children of J–1 students are permitted to work in the United States, and the students themselves are allowed a longer period of practical training than are F–1 students.

The primary disadvantage of J–1 status is that certain J–1 students are required to live outside the United States for two years after completing their course of study. The foreign residence requirement applies to J–1 holders who: (1) participated in a program which received financing from the U.S. government or from their own government; (2) are nationals or residents of countries designated by the U.S. Department of State as clearly requiring the services of persons engaged in the visitor's field of specialized knowledge or skill (such specializations are published in the form of a skills list); or (3) obtained J status in order to receive graduate medical training in the United States. INA § 212(e).

J–1 status is also available to foreign students between the ages of fifteen and eighteen-and-a-half who participate in secondary school exchange programs. Such programs allow students to stay with a host family in the United States and study at a U.S. school for up to one year. Secondary exchange students are only permitted to engage in sporadic employment, such as babysitting or yard work. 22 C.F.R. § 62.25.

Exchange visitors may remain in the U.S. for the duration of the exchange program (as defined by the program sponsor), plus thirty days. J–1 status holders may work for the program sponsor or another designated employer, within the guidelines of the approved exchange program. Spouses or children of J–1 students, who have J–2 status, may obtain permission to work, but only for their own support or to pay for recreational activities and not for the support of the J–1 recipient. 8 C.F.R. § 214.2(j)(1).

Exchange visitors who have received graduate medical training are ineligible to change their status to that of any other nonimmigrant classification. Other persons with J status who are subject to the two-year foreign residency requirement may not change their visa to any other nonimmigrant visa except A (for foreign diplomats), G (for designated principal resident representatives of foreign governments), T (for victims of trafficking), or U (for victims of criminal activity) before complying with the requirement. INA § 248. Exchange visitors, however, are able to re-enter the U.S. in certain nonimmigrant statuses such as O–1 or B–1 before completing their two-year foreign residency requirement. Exchange visitors may seek waivers of the foreign residency requirement through the U.S. State Department in cases where (1) a U.S. government agency states that a waiver would be in the national interest; (2) the requirement will pose an exceptional hardship to a U.S. citizen or permanent resident spouse, parent, or child of the status holder; (3) the status holder fears persecution on account of nationality, race, religion, political opinion, or membership in a particular social group; or (4) where the status holder's home country does not object to the grant of a waiver. INA § 212(e). Medical graduates are not entitled to a waiver through the fourth category.

CHAPTER 8

GROUNDS FOR INADMISSIBILITY AND REMOVAL

As discussed in the preceding chapters, non-citizens who wish to come to the United States must satisfy the specific eligibility criteria for one of the immigrant preference categories or nonimmigrant classifications. Having satisfied these criteria, however, non-citizens may still be denied admission to the United States if any of the grounds for "inadmissibility" apply to them. Further, non-citizens who have been lawfully admitted to the U.S. may be forced to leave based on one of the many grounds for "removal" (commonly called "deportation"). This chapter describes the grounds for inadmissibility and removal.

Most non-citizens within the United States who are charged with either inadmissibility or removability have the right to remain in the U.S. for a "removal hearing." Non-citizens who are deemed inadmissible when attempting to enter the U.S. are subject to "expedited removal" and can be removed without a hearing unless they have a credible claim to asylum. These proceedings, and forms of relief from removal, are described in chapter 9, *infra*.

Grounds for inadmissibility and removal apply only to non-citizens. U.S. citizens cannot be barred from entering the United States or forced to leave the country against their will. Removal proceedings may only be commenced against a naturalized citizen after the successful completion of denaturalization proceedings to remove the individual's U.S. citizenship. *See* § 12–3, *infra.*

§ 8–1   INADMISSIBILITY

§ 8–1.1   The Meaning of "Admission"

Grounds of inadmissibility apply only to non-citizens seeking admission to the United States. The phrase "seeking admission" encompasses more than attempting to obtain a visa or cross a border. Admission means lawful entry into the U.S. after inspection and authorization by an immigration officer. INA § 101(a)(13). Non-citizens are deemed applicants for admission when they arrive at a port of entry to the United States and also when they are present in the U.S. but have not been lawfully admitted. INA § 235(a). Consequently, non-citizens who have lived in the U.S. for many years can be considered "inadmissible" if they evaded inspection when they entered the country. See INA § 212(a)(6). In practice, however, such individuals are generally considered removable for being present in the U.S. in violation of the law. INA § 237(a)(1).

Nonimmigrants applying to adjust to permanent resident status are also considered to be seeking admission and are therefore subject to the grounds of inadmissibility. INA § 245. Consequently, persons lawfully admitted to the U.S. as nonimmigrants could become inadmissible for permanent residence based on acts committed while in the U.S. and could be subject to removal if they apply to adjust status. See INA § 237(a)(1). Because the grounds for inadmissibility and removal are different, the same individuals might not be removable if they remain nonimmigrants.

Admissibility is also an issue for individuals seeking naturalization as U.S. citizens, because one of the requirements for naturalization is that the applicant was lawfully admitted to permanent residence. INA § 316. If the U.S. Citizenship and Immigration Services determines that an applicant for naturalization was inadmissible at the time he or she became a permanent resident, it may not only deny citizenship but may also initiate removal proceedings. Frequently, a person's inadmissibility or removability only comes to the attention of immigration authorities when he or she applies for one of these immigration benefits.

Non-citizen crew members and persons who are paroled into the U.S. for humanitarian reasons, although lawfully present in the country, are not considered admitted. INA § 101(a)(13)(B). Non-citizens paroled into the U.S. are considered "arriving aliens." 8 C.F.R. § 1.1(q). The consequence of being considered an "arriving alien" as opposed to being considered admitted is that certain parolees may be subject to inadmissibility rather than removal. The distinction (between inadmissible and removable) to some extent perpetuates certain differences between deportation and exclusion that were eliminated by the Illegal Immigration Reform and Immigrant Responsibility Act (IIRIRA) of 1996. *See* § 8–1.1(a), *infra*. For example, several constitutional rights applicable to admitted non-citizens may not be available to certain parolees.

a. Admission vs. Entry

Before enactment of the Illegal Immigration Reform and Immigrant Responsibility Act (IIRIRA) in 1996, the event that determined a person's status with respect to removal was not admission, but "entry." Entry refers to physically crossing into United States territory, free from restraint. Entry may be achieved after being inspected and authorized by an immigration officer, or by evading inspection, but physical presence as a result of parole does not constitute entry. *See, e.g., Matter of Pierre*, 14 I. & N. Dec. 467, Interim Decision (BIA) 2238 (BIA 1973). Under pre-IIRIRA law, individuals who had not yet entered the U.S. were subject to "exclusion" hearings. Those persons who had entered the country, with inspection or without, were subject to "deportation" hearings and were entitled to rights not available in exclusion hearings. Pre–IIRIRA law recognized that some persons may have remained in the U.S. after having entered and thus were entitled to the greater procedural rights offered in a deportation hearing. It was not always easy, however, to determine whether an individual had successfully evaded inspection and thus become free of restraint. *See, e.g., Matter of G–*, 20 I. & N. Dec. 764, Interim Decision (BIA) 3215 (BIA 1993). Also, basing the distinction between deportation and exclusion on entry actually encouraged non-citizens to evade inspection, so that they would obtain the greater rights available in deportation proceedings. The IIRIRA removed this rather perverse incentive by changing the focus from entry to admission and consolidating the removal procedures, but it retained separate grounds for exclusion (inadmissibility) and deportation (removal).

The IIRIRA revised INA § 101(a)(13) by repealing the old definition of "entry" and replacing it with the new definition of "admission," leaving unresolved the precise meaning of "entry" where it still remains in the statute. *See, e.g.*, INA §§ 212(a)(3) (entering to engage in terrorist activity), 212(a)(5)(A)(I) (entering to perform labor), INA § 237(a)(1)(A) (inadmissibility at entry), and § 237 (a)(1)(E)(i) (smuggling aliens within five years of entry). The criminal provisions of the INA also continue to make entry an essential element of various offenses.

b. Re–Entry of Permanent Residents

The question of whether permanent residents returning to the U.S. after traveling abroad should be subject to grounds of inadmissibility has been disputed for many years. In *United States ex rel. Volpe v. Smith*, 289 U.S. 422 (1933), the Supreme Court upheld the exclusion of a non-citizen who, after twenty-four years of residence in the U.S. following a lawful entry, was held to be inadmissible on his return from a brief visit to Cuba. The Court's restrictive view concluded that "entry" included any coming of a non-citizen from a foreign country whether such coming was the person's first entry or not. The Court in *Rosenberg v. Fleuti*, 374 U.S. 449 (1963) departed from this rigid application, recognizing that a person does not make an "entry" upon his return to the United States where he had no intent to leave, or did not in fact leave the country voluntarily. Hence, permanent residents would not be subject to the conditions of an entry after making a brief, innocent, and casual trip outside the United States.

In its new definition of "admission," the BIA and several federal circuits have held that IIRIRA did not reincorporate the *Fleuti* doctrine. Now, permanent residents will not be regarded as seeking admission (and thus are not subject to the grounds of inadmissibility) unless they (1) have abandoned or relinquished their permanent resident status; (2) have been absent from the United States for a continuous period in excess of

180 days; (3) have engaged in illegal activity after their departure from the U.S.; (4) have departed from the U.S. while in removal or extradition proceedings; (5) have committed a criminal or related offense identified in section 212(a)(2) (including "crimes of moral turpitude," drug trafficking, or prostitution); or (6) are attempting to enter at a place other than a designated port of entry or have not been admitted to the U.S. after inspection and authorization by an immigration officer. INA § 101(a)(13)(C).

Although this definition made it clear that permanent residents are automatically admitted to the U.S. if none of these circumstances apply, it initially appeared to leave open the question of whether the converse is true: must permanent residents who fall within one of the listed categories be considered applicants for admission after any departure from the U.S.? Review by the BIA and federal courts seem to say yes. In the case of *In re Collado–Munoz*, 21 I. & N. Dec. 1061, Interim Decision (BIA) 3333 (BIA 1997), the Board of Immigration Appeals held that the new definition of admission had entirely replaced the *Fleuti* doctrine and that permanent residents who fall within these categories would be subject to the grounds of inadmissibility even if they made only a brief, casual, and innocent visit outside the U.S. In *Tineo v. Ashcroft*, 350 F.3d 382 (3d Cir.2003), a lawful permanent resident briefly left the United States to visit the Dominican Republic and upon his return he was charged with being inadmissible for convictions of various offenses in the United States. Based on its own interpretation and deference to the BIA, the court agreed that the IIRIRA rejected the *Fleuti* exception for "innocent, casual, and brief" departures. The First and Ninth

Circuits have followed the BIA interpretation in *Collado–Munoz* as did the Third Circuit decision in *Tineo*. *De Vega v. Gonzales*, 503 F.3d 45 (1st Cir. 2007); *Camins v. Gonzales*, 500 F.3d 872 (9th Cir.2007). Some relatively minor crimes that are grounds for either removal or inadmissibility might not come to the attention of immigration authorities until a permanent resident returns to the U.S. after traveling abroad, at which time he or she could be denied entry. Permanent residents who have criminal records should therefore exercise caution in making any trip abroad, seeking new immigration benefits, or applying for citizenship.

§ 8–1.2 Grounds of Inadmissibility

At least in theory, immigration law requires a higher standard of personal conduct for individuals who wish to be admitted to the United States than for persons who have already been properly admitted and have committed some offense for which they may be subject to removal. Individuals who have been admitted and lived in the United States ordinarily have jobs, family, friends, and other significant ties to this country—ties which should not be disrupted without a showing of very unacceptable conduct. Persons seeking admission can be subject to more stringent requirements because they usually do not have such ties. In practice, however, some of the grounds for removal, especially the "aggravated felony" grounds (*see* § 8–2.2(b), *infra*), are more stringent than the grounds of inadmissibility. It is possible for a non-citizen who is a lawful resident in the United States to be removed for committing a relatively minor crime that would not be an absolute bar to admission. *See* § 8–1.2(b)(2), *infra*.

The grounds of inadmissibility are listed in INA § 212. When a non-citizen applies for a visa to travel to the U.S., the consular officer ordinarily considers whether any of these grounds apply, but a finding that none do is not conclusive. Immigration officers make an independent determination of a non-citizen's admissibility when he or she arrives at a port of entry.

Before the 1990 Act, the INA listed thirty-four classes of inadmissibility (formerly "exclusion"). The 1990 Act updated what was previously considered an unnecessarily complex classification scheme. Until the 1990 changes, even the most archaic classes remained intact; *e.g.*, inadmissibility of "paupers, professional beggars, or vagrants" as one class and homosexuals as another. The 1990 Act eliminated both classes. Congress has made additional updates to this section, most notably in the USA PATRIOT Act of 2001, which extended the inadmissibility grounds related to terrorism and made persons who have engaged in money laundering inadmissible. Section 212(a) now contains ten general categories of inadmissibility grounds: health-related grounds; criminal and related grounds; security and related grounds; public charge proscription; labor certification requirements and qualifications for certain immigrants; illegal entrants and immigration violators proscription; documentation requirements; ineligibility for citizenship; previous unlawful presence; and miscellaneous.

Many of the grounds of inadmissibility can be waived in individual cases. For example, INA § 212(d)(3) allows the Secretary of Homeland Security to waive any of the grounds, except for a few security-related provisions, for nonimmigrants applying for a visa or seeking admission. Waivers for immigrants are more limited.

a. Health–Related Grounds

Section 212(a) begins with grounds of inadmissibility based on physical or mental health. Individuals who have a "communicable disease of public health significance" are inadmissible, as are those persons with a "physical or mental disorder and behavior associated with the disorder that may pose . . . a threat to the property, safety, or welfare of the alien or others." INA § 212(a)(1)(A). Moreover, a drug addict or abuser is inadmissible under this section. INA § 212(a)(1)(A)(iv). Individuals seeking admission as immigrants, including those adjusting status in the U.S., are inadmissible unless they can document that they have received certain vaccines. INA § 212(a)(1)(A)(ii).

The communicable diseases that constitute grounds of inadmissibility include tuberculosis; leprosy; syphilis and other, less common, sexually-transmitted diseases; and Human Immunodeficiency Virus (HIV). 42 C.F.R. § 34.2. The admittance of persons with HIV has been controversial. Congress originally declared people testing HIV-positive inadmissible under an appropriations bill rider in 1987. The 1990 Act, however, referred only to "communicable diseases of public health significance" and did not explicitly mention HIV or AIDS. In response, the Department of Health and Human Services (HHS) promulgated proposed regulations that restricted this class to diseases whose public health significance resulted from their contagious nature. Because AIDS/HIV cannot be spread through casual contact, it was initially removed from the list of grounds of inadmissibility. The HHS proposal generated considerable criticism, and Congress, in response, amended § 212(a) to make inadmissible any non-citizen "who is determined to have a communicable disease of public health significance, which shall include infection with the etiologic agent for acquired immune deficiency syndrome.'' In 2008, Congress repealed this amendment to § 212(a) and allowed immigration officials to admit individuals with HIV/AIDS.

INA § 212(g) provides for a waiver of inadmissibility for any non-citizen who has communicable disease of public health significance, including HIV, and who is the spouse, parent, unmarried son or daughter, or the minor unmarried lawfully adopted child of a U.S. citizen or permanent resident. This waiver is also available for persons who are granted permanent residence after being battered by a U.S. citizen or permanent resident spouse or parent. In addition, the vaccination requirement for persons seeking permanent residence may be waived if a doctor certifies that vaccination would be medically inappropriate, if the immigrant objects on religious grounds, or, in the case of adopted children under the age of eleven, if the adopting parent agrees to have the child vaccinated in the U.S.

b. Criminal and Related Grounds

INA § 212(a)(2) lists the criminal grounds of inadmissibility. Any person is inadmissible who (1) was convicted of or admits to committing a ''crime of moral turpitude'' or a controlled substance violation, (2) was convicted of two or more offenses of any type and received aggregate sentences of five or more years, (3) trafficked or assisted in the trafficking of controlled substances, or knowingly benefited from a spouse or parent's trafficking activities, (4) is coming to the U.S. to engage in prostitution or commercialized vice, (5) previously departed the U.S. as a condition of receiving immunity from prosecution for a serious crime committed in the U.S., (6) engaged in severe violations of religious freedoms as an official in a foreign government, (7) has engaged in trafficking in persons or knowingly benefited from a spouse or parent's trafficking, or (8) has engaged in money laundering or is coming to the U.S. to launder money.

(1) CRIMES OF MORAL TURPITUDE

Although the term has been used in immigration law since 1891, possibly the most difficult criminal ground to define is the "crime of moral turpitude." "Moral turpitude" is not defined by statute. The courts generally agree that crimes of moral turpitude include crimes of violence and crimes "commonly thought of as involving baseness, vileness or depravity," and that they are defined, at least in part, by reference to current moral standards. *Jordan v. De George*, 341 U.S. 223 (1951). This definition, however, is nearly as vague and open-ended as "moral turpitude." Nonetheless, the Supreme Court in *Jordan* held that the use of the term "moral turpitude" did not render the INA unconstitutionally vague because "the language conveys sufficiently definite warning as to the proscribed conduct when measured by common understanding and practices."

Some of the specific crimes that have been found to involve moral turpitude include murder, rape, robbery, kidnapping, voluntary manslaughter, theft, spousal abuse, any crime involving fraud (such as passing bad checks), and some aggravated DUI offenses. *See In re Torres–Varela*, 23 I. & N. Dec. 78, Interim Decision (BIA) 3449 (BIA 2001). Many of these crimes involve a specific "evil" intent, but this is not a requirement; for example, spousal abuse often does not involve any different intent than simple assault, but is considered a crime of moral turpitude because of the relationship between the abuser and the victim. *See In re Tran*, 21 I. & N. Dec. 291, Interim Decision (BIA) 3271 (BIA 1996). Nor does the determination depend on the seriousness of the crime; possession of stolen property, for example, may involve moral turpitude even if the value of the property is trivial, if the state law includes an intent requirement. *See Michel v. INS*, 206 F.3d 253 (2d Cir.2000) (noncitizen deemed inadmissible after conviction for possessing stolen bus transfers).

In determining whether a crime involves moral turpitude, the court may look only at the statute under which an individual was charged, and not at the person's actual conduct. If the statute is divisible and contains some offenses that involve moral turpitude and some that do not, the court may look to the record of conviction to determine with which offense the person was charged. It is worth noting, however, that § 212(a)(2) does not require that an applicant for admission have been convicted of a crime; simply admitting to acts that would constitute a crime of moral turpitude is enough to make a person inadmissible.

(2) EXCEPTIONS AND WAIVERS OF THE CRIMINAL GROUNDS

The ground of inadmissibility for moral turpitude does not apply if the person seeking admission committed the crime before the age of eighteen and at least five years have passed since the end of any confinement, or if the maximum possible penalty for the crime was less than one year and the person was actually sentenced for no longer than six months. INA § 212(a)(2)(A). A noncitizen convicted of two or more offenses for which the total sentence is at least five years will, however, still be inadmissible. INA § 212(a)(2)(B).

In addition, inadmissibility may be waived for persons who have committed crimes of moral turpitude or a single controlled substance violation involving possession of thirty grams or less of marijuana, persons who have multiple convictions for certain crimes, individuals engaged in prostitution, and those who received immunity from prosecution. Such individuals may qualify for a waiver if (1) the crime was committed more than fifteen years before the application for admission or if it was a prostitution offense, the perpetrator has been rehabilitated, and a waiver would not be contrary to national security; (2) the individual is the spouse, parent, son, or daughter of a U.S. citizen or permanent resident and denying admission would cause extreme hardship to the citizen or permanent resident; or (3) the individual is seeking permanent residence after being battered by a U.S. citizen or permanent resident spouse or parent. INA § 212(h). No waiver is available, however, if the crime was murder or involved torture. These waivers are discretionary and the decision to grant or deny them is non-reviewable. Persons admitted by a 212(h) waiver may apply to adjust for lawful permanent resident status.

Waivers of the criminal grounds of inadmissibility are not available to lawful permanent residents who commit an aggravated felony after being admitted to permanent residence, or permanent residents who have continuously resided in the U.S. for fewer than seven years before the commencement of removal proceedings. INA § 212(h). As a result, a permanent resident who commits an "aggravated felony" (*see* § 8–2.2(b), *infra.*) and subsequently leaves the United States, whether removed or not, will be denied admission, but a nonimmigrant in similar circumstances might be able to obtain a waiver. In *Lara–Ruiz v. INS*, 241 F.3d 934 (7th Cir.2001), the court held that the unfavorable treatment of lawful permanent residents under this provision does not violate equal protection because Congress could have had a rational basis for considering permanent residents who commit crimes a greater threat to the country than nonimmigrant criminals. Other federal courts and the BIA have similarly held that the difference in treatment in INA § 212(h) is rationally related to a legitimate government purpose. *See, e.g., Jankowski–Burczyk v. INS,* 291 F.3d 172 (2d Cir.2002); *In re Michel,* 21 I. & N. Dec. 1101, Interim Decision (BIA) 3335 (BIA 1998). Some courts, however, have found that the difference in treatment in INA § 212(h) violates the Equal Protection Clause. *See Roman v. Ashcroft,* 181 F.Supp.2d 808 (N.D. Ohio 2002); *Song v. INS,* 82 F.Supp.2d 1121 (C.D. Cal.2000).

c. Security and Related Grounds

The national security grounds of inadmissibility have historically reflected popular fears of threats to the United States. A 1903 Immigration Act, 32 Stat. 1213, passed after the assassination of President McKinley, excluded anarchists and others who advocate the forceful overthrow of the U.S. government. In the 1950s, Congress added provisions excluding Communists and members of a number of other "subversive" organizations. *See* INA § 212(a)(3). Since the 1990s, the primary security concern has been terrorism. The 1990 Act rendered inadmissible persons believed to have committed terrorist attacks and those suspected of seeking admission to the U.S. to engage in terrorism. The AEDPA and IIRIRA, passed in the wake of the 1993 attack on the World Trade Center and the Oklahoma City bombing, expanded the terrorist ground by excluding all representatives or members of terrorist organizations designated by the

Secretary of State. The USA PATRIOT Act and the REAL ID Act, passed in response to the September 11, 2001, attacks, further extended this ground by broadening the definition of terrorist organizations and adding to the list of inadmissible non-citizens those who use positions of prominence to endorse terrorism, representatives of groups that support terrorist organizations, and spouses or children of persons inadmissible on terrorism grounds. *See* INA § 212(a)(3)(B). The PATRIOT Act further enabled immigration authorities to detain any non-citizen suspected of terrorist activity and keep that person in detention until finally removed or cleared of the charge. *See* INA § 236A(a)(1).

The current terrorism grounds make inadmissible any person who (1) has engaged in terrorist activities; (2) is deemed by a consular officer, the Attorney General, or the Secretary of Homeland Security as engaged or likely to engage in terrorism; (3) has incited terrorist activity (4) is a representative or spokesperson of a terrorist group or a group that endorses terrorism; (5) is a member of a terrorist group; (6) endorses terrorism or persuades others to support terrorism; (7) has received militarily-type training from a terrorist organization; or (8) is the spouse or child of a non-citizen who is inadmissible on terrorist grounds, unless the spouse or child did not know about the terrorist activity or has renounced it. INA § 212(a)(3)(B)(i). The Act also excludes anyone who has been associated with a terrorist organization and intends to endanger the welfare, safety, or security of the U.S. INA § 212(a)(3)(F). "Terrorist activities" defined by the statute include hijacking or sabotaging a conveyance, holding people hostage, committing an assassination, or using any kind of weapon to harm people or property, other than for purely personal gain. INA

§ 212(a)(3)(B)(iii). "Engaging in terrorist activities" includes preparing, planning, or committing such activities; soliciting funds or providing material support; and soliciting individuals to participate in such acts. INA § 212(a)(3)(B)(iv). "Terrorist organizations" include those designated by the Secretary of State, as well as any group of two or more people, whether designated as a terrorist organization or not, that engages in terrorist activities. INA § 212(a)(3)(B)(vi). Membership in or support of a terrorist organization may not render noncitizens inadmissible if they can demonstrate by clear and convincing evidence that they did not know, and should not reasonably have known, that the organization they belonged to or supported was a terrorist organization.

To identify possible terrorists, U.S. consulates are instructed to check names of visa applicants against "lookout" lists prior to issuing a visa. If an applicant's name matches a name on one of the lookout lists, U.S. State Department approval is required before the consulate can issue a visa. State Department approval is also required for any applicant holding a passport from a country designated as a state sponsor of terrorism (currently Cuba, Iran, Sudan, and Syria), and for applicants working in certain high-technology fields. The Homeland Security Act authorized the U.S. Immigration and Customs Enforcement (ICE) to place staff in U.S. consulates to help in compiling lookout lists and to train the consular staff who issue visas to identify possible terrorists.

In addition to the terrorism grounds, INA § 212(a)(3) makes inadmissible anyone who is believed to be seeking entry to the U.S. to engage in espionage, violent opposition to the U.S. government, or any other unlawful activity; persons whose activities in the U.S. would be adverse to foreign policy, unless they are foreign government officials or candidates for office in a foreign government; and members of the Communist party and other totalitarian parties. Also inadmissible are people who assisted in persecutions carried out by the Nazi government, as well as anyone else who has participated in genocide. Individuals who have commissioned acts of torture, participated in extrajudicial killings, or recruited child soldiers are also barred.

The inadmissibility grounds related to foreign policy and membership in "subversive" groups have been subject to several judicial challenges. The Supreme Court upheld these provisions against a First Amendment challenge in *Kleindienst v. Mandel*, 408 U.S. 753 (1972). The Court reasoned that non-citizens have no constitutional right to be admitted into the United States, and U.S. citizens have no right to insist that non-citizens be admitted to the country so that ideas may be exchanged. Essentially, Congress's plenary power to control immigration supersedes a citizen's right to receive information under the First Amendment. The D.C. Circuit held in *Abourezk v. Reagan*, 785 F.2d 1043 (D.C. Cir.1986) that the government's decision that an anarchist or a Communist party member is inadmissible must be based on projected engagement in activities prejudicial to the public interest, and such perception must be independent of the fact of membership alone in an organization. The current version of the INA provides that no one may be excluded under the foreign policy ground solely for past beliefs, statements, or associations, if such beliefs, statements, or associations would be lawful in the United States. INA § 212(a)(3)(C).

Inadmissibility on the basis of Communist or other totalitarian party membership may be waived where the membership was involuntary or was solely to obtain employment, food rations, or other necessities, where membership was terminated more than two years ago (five years if the totalitarian party still governs the noncitizen's country), or to assure family unity if the individual has a close relative who is a U.S. citizen or permanent resident. INA § 212(a)(3)(D). There are no other waivers specific to the national security grounds.

d. Inadmissibility for Violations of Immigration Law or Procedure

Several of the inadmissibility grounds in § 212(a) are related to the enforcement of other immigration laws and procedures. Non-citizens who enter the U.S. without being admitted or paroled, those who stay beyond the expiration of their nonimmigrant status, and those who have been removed from the U.S. may all be inadmissible for varying periods.

(1) ILLEGAL ENTRANTS AND IMMIGRATION VIOLATORS

Any non-citizen who is present in the U.S. without being admitted or paroled, or who arrives in the United States at a place other than a designated port of entry is inadmissible. INA § 212(a)(6)(A)(i). This ground applies only to persons in the United States, not to those applying for admission from overseas. In addition to being inadmissible, those persons are subject to civil penalties for illegal entry of $50 to $250 for each entry or attempted entry. The fine doubles for a person who has previously been subjected to a civil penalty under this section. INA § 275(b). The only exemption from this ground is for victims of domestic violence who can demonstrate a connection between the abuse they have suffered and their illegal entry. INA § 212(a)(6)(A)(ii).

A number of other immigration violations are grounds of inadmissibility under section 212(a)(6). Individuals who are ordered removed *in absentia* for failing, without reasonable cause, to attend a removal proceeding are inadmissible for ten years after their departure or removal. INA § 212(a)(9). See § 9–2.1, *infra*, for more information on *in absentia* removal orders. Persons who made a material misrepresentation of fact in the application process or falsely claimed U.S. citizenship in order to obtain immigration or other government benefits are inadmissible. INA § 212(a)(6)(C). Non-citizens who are stowaways; who have encouraged, induced, assisted, abetted, or aided the illegal entry of other non-citizens; or who violated the terms of F–1 student visa status are also inadmissible. Violators of F–1 status are inadmissible until they have been outside the U.S. for a continuous period of five years after the date of violation. INA § 212(a)(6)(D), (E), (G).

Some waivers and exceptions apply to these grounds. Immigration authorities may waive inadmissibility for visa and admission misrepresentation, INA § 212(a)(6)(C)(i), if an immigrant's exclusion would result in extreme hardship to a U.S. citizen or permanent resident spouse or parent. INA § 212(i). The smuggling ground (assisting the illegal entry of others) may be waived for returning permanent residents or non-citizens seeking admission as permanent residents if they only assisted a spouse, parent, son, or daughter to enter illegally. INA § 212(d)(11). Although not waivable, the inadmissibility ground for false citizenship claims does not apply to persons who obtained permanent residence before the age of sixteen, have a natural or adopted parent who is a U.S. citizen, and reasonably believed that they were also citizens. INA § 212(a)(6)(C).

(2) Previous Removal and Unlawful Presence

INA § 212(a)(9)(A) describes the inadmissibility grounds related to previous removal from the United States. While § 212(a)(6)(A) applies to persons within the U.S., this section applies to persons applying for a visa at a consulate or seeking admission at a port of entry. Non-citizens who received a removal order after expedited removal proceedings are inadmissible for a period of five years. Persons who were removed after any other removal proceeding, or who left the U.S. while in removal proceedings, are inadmissible for a period of ten years. Those who return to the U.S. and are removed for a second or subsequent time are inadmissible for twenty years. Any non-citizen who is removed after committing an aggravated felony is permanently inadmissible. Non-citizens may avoid this ground of inadmissibility by obtaining the Secretary of Homeland Security's consent to their admission prior to re-entering the United States from a foreign country. INA § 212(a)(9)(A).

Since 1996, non-citizens who depart the U.S. after extended periods of unlawful presence are also inadmissible. Before enactment of IIRIRA, individuals who departed the country before the INS initiated removal proceedings against them could seek readmission by applying for a new visa in their country of origin. IIRIRA ended this method of avoiding removal. Now, a non-citizen who has been unlawfully present in the U.S. for a period of more than 180 days but less than one year and voluntarily leaves before removal proceedings are initiated is inadmissible for three years. INA § 212(a)(9)(B)(i)(I). A non-citizen who has been unlawfully present for one year or more is barred from admission into the U.S. for ten years. INA § 212 (a)(9)(B)(i)(II). The ten-year bar applies regardless of whether the individual's departure is voluntary. Further, anyone who has previously been removed and enters or attempts to enter the U.S. without being admitted becomes permanently inadmissible. INA § 212(a)(9)(C). An entry or attempted entry after being removed can also trigger criminal penalties under INA § 276. Unlawful presence is not generally cumulative; for example, two separate four-month periods of unlawful presence will not constitute grounds of inadmissibility.

Persons who remain in the U.S. unlawfully for fewer than 180 days do not entirely escape sanction. INA § 222(g) denies readmission to nonimmigrants who stay beyond the expiration of their status as noted on the I–94 entry-departure card unless they apply for a new nonimmigrant visa in their country of origin. Also, non-citizens are less likely to receive a new visa if they overstayed their previously-permitted period of stay.

The INA defines "unlawful presence" as being present in the U.S. without being admitted or paroled, or being present after the non-citizen's nonimmigrant status expires (referred to as an "overstay"). INA § 212 (a)(9)(B)(ii). To date, no regulations have been issued to clarify when unlawful presence begins, but the INS addressed this issue in several memos. *See* 74 Interp.Rel. 562. Unlawful presence is triggered when immigration authorities commence removal proceedings or when either ICE or an immigration judge determines that an individual has violated the terms of nonimmigrant status. Without such a determination, a violation of status other than an overstay will not trigger unlawful presence. Most non-citizens in removal proceedings continue to accumulate unlawful presence, such that if they are compelled to leave the United States the admission bar still applies, even if they are granted voluntary departure.

Some exceptions apply to this ground of inadmissibility. Minors, applicants for asylum, persons protected by family unity, certain battered women and children, and victims of trafficking do not accumulate unlawful presence. INA § 212(a)(9)(B)(iii). (The family unity program grants protected status to spouses and unmarried children under twenty-one years of age of certain lawful permanent residents, if they have resided in the U.S. since 1988 or earlier.) Further, the three-and ten-year bars may be waived for an immigrant who is a spouse, son, or daughter of a U.S. citizen or permanent resident if excluding the immigrant would cause extreme hardship to the citizen or permanent resident spouse or parent. INA § 212 (a)(9)(B)(v). The permanent bar for those attempting to enter unlawfully after prior removal may be waived for battered women and children and for any person whose last departure from the U.S. was more than ten years ago. INA § 212(a)(9)(C).

Until April 2001, INA § 245(i) permitted some persons who entered the U.S. without inspection or overstayed a lawful status to adjust to permanent resident status upon the payment of $1,000, if an immigrant visa was available and no other bar applied. INA § 245(i). After being extended twice, this provision expired on April 30, 2001, and despite several proposals for another extension, has not been renewed as of this writing. Some individuals are, however, still allowed to adjust status under this provision if they filed an application before it expired in 2001.

e. The Public Charge Ground

Any non-citizen who is believed likely to become a public charge is inadmissible at the time of application. INA § 212(a)(4)(A). Factors that immigration and consular officers must consider in determining whether a noncitizen is likely to become a public charge include age, health, family status, education, assets, resources, and financial status. INA § 212 (a)(4)(B).

Immediate relatives of U.S. citizens, immigrants under family-based preferences, and a select group of employment-based immigrants are inadmissible without an affidavit of support. INA § 212 (a)(4)(C), (D). A sponsor must have an annual income equal to or greater than 125% of the federal poverty guidelines and must agree in the affidavit to provide support for the immigrant and his or her family for ten years or until the immigrant becomes a U.S. citizen. The affidavit is a legally binding contract. *See* § 5–5.1(d), *supra*.

f. Other Grounds of Inadmissibility

(1) LABOR CERTIFICATION

The INA lists the criteria for labor certification, without which most non-citizens immigrating under § 203(b) would be inadmissible. INA § 212(a)(5). This ground of inadmissibility has resulted in a process, administered by the U.S. Department of Labor and the State Employment Services, known as labor certification. Prospective employers must obtain labor certification before petitioning for an immigrant by demonstrating to the satisfaction of the Department of Labor that there are not sufficient qualified, willing U.S. workers to serve in a position for which an immigrant is qualified and is willing to perform. *See* 5–5.1(b), *supra.*

(2) DOCUMENTATION REQUIREMENTS

Section 212(a)(7) spells out the documentation requirements for non-citizens seeking admission. An unexcused failure to possess the required travel documents renders a non-citizen inadmissible. Immigrants must have a valid passport, travel document, or other document establishing identity and nationality, as well as a valid immigrant visa, border crossing card, or other valid entry document. Nonimmigrants must have a passport valid for six months beyond the date of admission and a valid nonimmigrant visa, unless they are entering under the visa waiver program or the requirements are waived by another provision. INA § 212(a)(7).

(3) PERSONS INELIGIBLE FOR CITIZENSHIP

INA § 212(a)(8) renders inadmissible any immigrant who is "permanently ineligible to citizenship" and any person who departed from or remained outside the United States in order to avoid military training or service during a period of war. As defined in INA § 101(a)(19), the phrase "ineligible to citizenship" refers to ineligibility for citizenship due to violation of Selective Service laws or any section of the INA. Since commission of an "aggravated felony" is a permanent bar to obtaining citizenship (*see* § 8–2.2(b), *infra*), this section could be read to exclude anyone who has committed an aggravated felony. The Board of Immigration Appeals, however, interpreted the phrase in this context as referring only to ineligibility for citizenship due to draft evasion. *In re Kanga*, 22 I. & N. Dec. 1206, Interim Decision (BIA)

3424 (BIA 2000). The Board reasoned that, since Congress has passed a series of laws making various aggravated felonies grounds for removal, if it intended to make the same crimes grounds of inadmissibility, it would have done so explicitly.

(4) MISCELLANEOUS

The "miscellaneous" grounds of inadmissibility listed in INA § 212(a)(10) include entering the U.S. to practice polygamy, being an international child abductor, and voting unlawfully. The same section makes former U.S. citizens who renounced citizenship to avoid taxation inadmissible. INA § 212(a)(10). The provision excluding persons who voted unlawfully was added by the IIRIRA in 1996. Congress amended this provision in the Child Citizenship Act of 2000 to provide an exemption for persons who obtained permanent residence before the age of sixteen as the natural or adopted child of a U.S. citizen and who reasonably believed when they voted that they were citizens.

g. Section 212(d)(3) Waivers

INA § 212(d)(3) grants the Secretary of the Department of Homeland Security broad discretion to admit otherwise inadmissible non-citizens. The only grounds of inadmissibility that cannot be waived based on § 212(d)(3) are related to terrorism under §§ 212(a)(3)(i)–(iii) or participation in genocide under § 212(a)(3)(E). A waiver under § 212(d)(3) must be tied to a non-immigrant visa such as a tourist or student visa. Although nearly all inadmissible non-immigrants qualify for § 212(d)(3) waiver, the decision to grant such a waiver is highly discretionary. To determine whether to grant a § 212(d)(3) waiver, immigration officials will evaluate (1) the risk of harm to society if the applicant is admitted; (2) the seriousness of the applicant's previous immigration or criminal law violations; and (3) the applicant's purpose in entering the U.S. *Matter of Hranka*, 16 I. & N. Dec. 491, Interim Decision 2644 (BIA 1978).

§ 8–2   REMOVAL

Removal is the expulsion of a non-citizen who has already been admitted to the United States. In general, non-citizens may be removed because they were inadmissible at the time of entry, because they have violated a condition of their status in the U.S., or because they have committed other prohibited acts. The Immigration and Nationality Act lists six major categories of persons subject to removal. These categories cover non-citizens who (1) were inadmissible at time of entry or adjustment of status or have violated status, (2) have committed certain criminal offenses, (3) have failed to register or have falsified documents, (4) have engaged in terrorism or otherwise threatened national security or U.S. foreign policy, (5) have become a public charge, or (6) unlawfully voted. These categories are further subdivided, so there are many more specific grounds for removal. The 1990 Act reduced the number of grounds for removal in an attempt to make the list comprehensible and more current. Subsequent amendments, such as the Technical Amendments Act of 1991, the Antiterrorism and Effective Death Penalty Act of 1996 (AEDPA), and IIRIRA, expanded the list once again, particularly the crime-related grounds. Before examining these grounds in detail, some general aspects of removal will be examined.

§ 8–2.1   General Considerations

In theory at least, removal is not a criminal punishment, but is a civil proceeding designed primarily to rid the United States of statutorily defined undesirables. The courts have long recognized the plenary power of Congress to expel and remove non-citizens. That Congress allows non-citizens to enter the United States "is a matter of permission and tolerance. The government's power to terminate hospitality has been asserted by this court since the question first arose." *Harisiades v. Shaughnessy*, 342 U.S. 580 (1952).

Even though the courts do not consider removal a criminal punishment, they recognize that it is a severe penalty. Most non-citizens have voluntarily chosen to come to the United States and removal forces them to leave their homes, jobs, friends, and in some cases, families. Indeed, removal may result "in loss of both property and life; or all that makes life worth living." *Ng Fung Ho v. White*, 259 U.S. 276 (1922). Further, persons who have been removed are barred for a minimum of ten years from entering the United States unless they obtain special permission. INA § 212(a)(9). Because the consequences of removal are drastic, the student of immigration law should become familiar with the many and varied aspects of removal.

Several specific classes of non-citizens are exempt from the removal statutes, including ambassadors, public ministers, accredited career diplomats, consular officers, and the members of their families. Employees of international organizations such as the United Nations are also exempt from removal statutes. INA § 102. All other non-citizens, including lawful permanent residents, may be removed.

Removing a non-citizen often results in the "de facto" removal of the individual's U.S. citizen children. The Third Circuit rejected the claim that removal denies a non-citizen's children the right, as U.S. citizens, to continue to reside in the United States. Removal of a child's parents will merely postpone, but not bar, the child's residence in the United States, if he or she should later choose to live in this country. The court reasoned that Congress did not intend to give such children the ability to confer immigration benefits on their parents. *Acosta v. Gaffney*, 558 F.2d 1153 (3d Cir.1977).

Unlike most statutes regulating conduct, the INA frequently applies retroactively. ICE may remove non-citizens for conduct which was not a ground for removal at the time they committed the act. For example, a Nazi who legally entered the United States in 1965 may be removed under the provisions of a 1978 amendment to the act, despite residing in the United States for a number of years. Removal for acts which were not grounds for removal when committed does not violate the constitutional prohibition against *ex post facto* laws. *Mahler v. Eby*, 264 U.S. 32 (1924). The INA also does not contain a general statute of limitations, although there are particular statutes of limitation contained within the classes of persons subject to removal. For example, non-citizens who become dependent on government benefits are removable only if they become a public charge within five years of entry into the United States. INA § 237(a)(5). Accordingly, ICE may remove a non-citizen (A) who becomes a public charge four years after entry, but not a non-citizen (B) who becomes a public charge five and a half years after entry. Because there is no general statute of limitations, however, ICE can remove the non-citizen (A)—*at any time*—even if he or she ceases to be a public charge.

§ 8–2.2   Grounds for Removal

a.   Inadmissibility at Entry and Status Violations

The first class of removal grounds applies to non-citizens who were inadmissible when they entered the United States or adjusted status and those who have violated conditions of their admission. INA § 237(a)(1). Section 237(a)(1)(A) allows ICE to remove anyone who should not have been granted admission because of the inadmissibility or exclusion grounds in effect at the time that person entered the country. This concept has profound implications. Individuals who have committed no offenses since being admitted can still be removed on the basis of their actions prior to entry.

Non-citizens who are present in the U.S. in violation of the INA or any other law of the U.S. are removable. INA § 237(a)(1)(B). Non-citizens who violate or fail to comply with any terms imposed at entry are also subject to removal, as are those who fail to maintain the nonimmigrant or immigrant status in which they were admitted. INA § 237(a)(1)(C). Violations of status that could constitute grounds for removal include overstaying the time limit of a nonimmigrant visa or accepting employment without the requisite authorization. Individuals accorded permanent resident status on a conditional basis under INA § 216 (referring to spouses of U.S. citizens) or § 216A (investors) become removable if they fail to have their status converted from conditional to unconditional. INA § 237(a)(1)(D). A non-citizen who knowingly encourages, aids, or abets another non-citizen to enter the United States illegally may be removed; this provision may, however, be waived if the person who illegally entered the United States was the non-citizen's spouse, parent, son, or daughter, and such a waiver would serve humanitarian purposes, assure family unity, or would be in the public interest. INA § 237(a)(1)(E).

Non-citizens may also be removed for gaining admission to the U.S. by committing marriage fraud, defined as marrying a United States citizen solely to obtain immigration benefits. INA § 237(a)(1)(G). Marriage fraud is presumed if a non-citizen gains admission based on a marriage contracted less than two years before the date of admission and the marriage is terminated or annulled within two years after the non-citizen is admitted to the United States. The non-citizen can only overcome this presumption by demonstrating that the marriage was *bona fide*. *See* § 5–2.1(c), *supra*. ICE also has authority to determine whether any previous marriage was fraudulent and if so, to remove the non-citizen.

The INA also permits a waiver for a non-citizen found inadmissible at the time of admission for misrepresentation, if the non-citizen possesses an otherwise valid immigrant visa and the non-citizen is the spouse, parent, son, or daughter of a U.S. citizen. INA § 237(a)(1)(H). A waiver is also available for victims of domestic abuse.

b.   Criminal Grounds

In fiscal year 2008, there were nearly 100,000 removals based on criminal grounds, accounting for 27% of all formal removals. Drug crimes and immigration violations were the most common charges. Removal for criminal conduct applies only after a conviction. The conviction must be final; hence, a non-citizen may not be removed while a direct appeal is pending. Given the wide variation in statutes among the states, the federal courts struggled for some time to create a uniform definition of "conviction" for immigration purposes.

In *Matter of Ozkok*, 19 I. & N. Dec. 546, Interim Decision (BIA) 3044 (BIA 1988), the court stated that there must be three elements present to find a conviction for immigration purposes: (1) a judge or jury has found the person guilty or the person has entered a plea of guilty or nolo contendre or has admitted sufficient facts to warrant a finding of guilty; (2) the judge has ordered some form of punishment, penalty, or restraint on the person's liberty; and (3) a judgment or adjudication of guilt may be entered without any further proceedings to determine the person's guilt or innocence if he or she violates the terms of probation or fails to comply with the requirements of the court's order.

IIRIRA's amendments to the INA altered *Ozkok* by codifying only the first two prongs of the *Ozkok* test. The INA thus currently defines conviction as "a formal judgment of guilt of the alien entered by a court or, if adjudication of guilt has been withheld, where (i) a judge or jury has found the alien guilty or the alien has entered a plea of guilty or nolo contendre or has admitted sufficient facts to warrant a finding of guilt, and (ii) the judge has ordered some form of punishment, penalty, or restraint on the alien's liberty." INA § 101(a)(48)(A). This new definition applies retroactively to offenses committed before enactment of the IIRIRA. *In re Punu*, 22 I. & N. Dec. 224, Interim Decision (BIA) 3364 (BIA 1998).

Because of the considerable expansion of these grounds since 1986, virtually any criminal activity other than the most petty offenses and misdemeanors can have serious adverse consequences to non-citizens and their family members. The criminal grounds for removal are listed in INA § 237(a)(2).

(1) CRIMES OF MORAL TURPITUDE

Non-citizens are subject to removal if convicted within five years of admission to the U.S. of a crime of moral turpitude carrying a possible sentence of one year or more, or if convicted at any time of two or more crimes of moral turpitude "not arising out of a single scheme of criminal misconduct," regardless of the sentence imposed. INA § 237(a)(2)(A). The difficulties of defining moral turpitude are discussed in § 8–1.2(b), *supra*. Unlike the inadmissibility grounds, which apply even if an individual merely admits to committing a crime of moral turpitude, the removal grounds apply only after a conviction.

Problems have arisen, however, because many "crimes of moral turpitude" are relatively minor offenses for which the punishment can be ameliorated by state rehabilitative statutes. For example, some state courts will expunge a conviction after the offender successfully completes a period of probation; other courts may defer judgment so that a conviction is never entered unless the offender violates certain conditions. In the first case, a non-citizen offender could potentially be removed at any time during or after the probationary period, because a conviction had been entered, while in the second case removal proceedings could only be instituted if the noncitizen failed to comply with court-ordered conditions, because only then would a conviction occur.

The BIA held in the case of *In re Roldan–Santoyo*, 22 I. & N. Dec. 512, Interim Decision (BIA) 3377 (BIA 1999) that because of the new definition of conviction, expungement under a state rehabilitative statute does not cancel a conviction for immigration purposes. The Board reasoned that giving effect to the various state rehabilitation statutes would conflict with Congress' desire for a uniform immigration standard. The Ninth Circuit subsequently reversed this decision as applied to first-time drug offenses, finding that it conflicted with the Federal First Offender Act. *Lujan–Armendariz v. INS*, 222 F.3d 728 (9th Cir.2000). Then the BIA held that a judgment vacated through a mechanism other than a rehabilitative statute would not be considered a conviction for immigration purposes. *In re Rodriguez–Ruiz*, 22 I. & N. Dec. 1378, Interim Decision (BIA) 3436 (BIA 2000). The BIA addressed this issue again in the case of *In re Pickering*, 23 I. & N. Dec. 621, Interim Decision 3493 (BIA 2003) and held that a non-citizen would not have a conviction within INA § 101(a)(48) if the court vacates the conviction based on a defect in the conviction or proceedings, but because the Canadian court quashed the conviction solely for immigration procedures, the non-citizen had a conviction. The BIA has also held a judgment deeming someone a youthful offender or juvenile delinquent is not a conviction. *In re Devison–Charles*, 22 I. & N. Dec. 1362, Interim Decision 3435 (BIA 2000). Consequently, a few avenues remain open by which non-citizens could avoid being deported for minor crimes.

(2) AGGRAVATED FELONIES

Section 237(a)(2)(iii) authorizes the removal of any non-citizen who has been convicted of an "aggravated felony" at any time after entry. When first introduced in 1988 as a ground for removal, "aggravated felony" referred to murder, drug trafficking and trafficking in firearms. 102 Stat. 4141. The list of aggravated felonies has since been expanded several times, most notably in 1996 in the AEDPA and IIRIRA. In addition to the original offenses, the definition of "aggravated felony" now includes rape, sexual abuse of a minor, money laundering, crimes of violence for which the term of imprisonment is at least one year, theft, burglary, kidnapping, child pornography, RICO offenses, running a prostitution business or transporting people for the purpose of prostitution, fraud offenses where the loss exceeds $10,000, forgery, obstruction of justice, and other crimes. INA § 101(a)(43). The term aggravated felony is fully retroactive and applies regardless of when the conviction was entered. *Id*. As with crimes of moral turpitude, these offenses run the gamut from very serious crimes to relatively minor ones.

In determining whether a particular crime is an aggravated felony, federal law, not state law, controls. A crime categorized as a misdemeanor under state law constitutes an aggravated felony if it falls within the INA definition. *See, e.g., In re Small*, 23 I. & N. Dec. 448, Interim Decision (BIA) 3476 (BIA 2002) (holding that misdemeanor sexual abuse of a minor is an aggravated felony). Further, INA § 101(a)(48) states that the suspension of a sentence does not change the classification of a crime as an aggravated felony. In *United States v. Pacheco*, 225 F.3d 148 (2d Cir.2000), the Court of Appeals found that a misdemeanor theft charge for which the defendant received a one-year suspended sentence constituted an aggravated felony for immigration purposes. Pacheco had stolen a ten-dollar video game. He also had a misdemeanor conviction for domestic assault, constituting an independent ground for removal.

Although included as one of the original aggravated felonies, drug trafficking has been the subject of some controversy in recent years, in part because the definition of that crime includes the relatively common offense of possession. *See* 18 U.S.C.A. § 924(c); 21 U.S.C.A. § 801 *et seq.* In the case of *In re K.V.D.*, 22 I. & N. Dec. 1163, Interim Decision (BIA) 3422 (BIA 1999), the BIA held that state law misdemeanor drug convictions would be considered aggravated felonies if the analogous federal crime was a felony. The Board subsequently overruled this decision and decided instead to defer to the federal circuit courts of appeal as to whether a particular state crime constitutes a felony drug trafficking offense. *In re Yanez–Garcia*, 23 I. & N. Dec. 390, Interim Decision (BIA) 3473 (BIA 2002).

Like drug trafficking, the "crime of violence" provision can encompass some relatively minor crimes. In a well-publicized example, removal proceedings were initiated against a permanent resident who had lived in the U.S. since infancy after the INS discovered that she once received a one-year suspended sentence for pulling another woman's hair. Only an executive pardon saved her from removal. 77 Interp.Rel. 1012. For some time, DUI offenses were also treated as crimes of violence. In the case of *In re Puente*, 22 I. & N. Dec. 1006, Interim Decision (BIA) 3412 (BIA 1999), the Board held that driving under the influence would be considered an aggravated felony when punishable by a sentence of one year or more. After four of the circuit courts disagreed, the BIA reconsidered this decision and decided that DUI convictions are not crimes of violence. *In re Ramos*, 23 I. & N. Dec. 336, Interim Decision (BIA) 3468 (BIA 2002). In *Leocal v. Ashcroft*, 540 U.S. 1176 (2004), the Supreme

Court ruled unanimously that a DUI conviction does not constitute a crime of violence.

The consequences of being convicted of an "aggravated felony" are severe. In addition to being subject to removal, non-citizens removed for having been convicted of such offenses are permanently barred from re-entering the U.S. and may be sentenced to up to twenty years in prison if they re-enter illegally. INA §§ 212(a)(9)(i)(A), 276(b). A person convicted of an aggravated felony cannot establish good moral character and is thus permanently barred from naturalizing as a U.S. citizen through residence. See INA §§ 101(f)(8), 316(a). Persons convicted of aggravated felonies are subject to mandatory detention, can be placed in expedited removal proceedings, and are ineligible for most forms of relief from removal. INA §§ 236, 238, 240A, 240B. In addition, removal orders based on an aggravated felony are not subject to judicial review, although federal courts do have jurisdiction to determine whether a particular offense is an aggravated felony and to review constitutional claims and questions of law. INA § 242(a)(2)(C)–(D); *see also Flores–Miramontes v. INS*, 212 F.3d 1133 (9th Cir.2000).

(3) OTHER CRIMINAL GROUNDS

Other sections of the INA allow removal for conviction of specific crimes. INA § 237(a)(2)(A)(iv) provides for the removal of any non-citizen convicted of a crime related to high speed flight from an immigration checkpoint. ICE may remove a non-citizen convicted of violating any law or regulation relating to a controlled substance, such as narcotic drugs and marijuana. INA § 237(a)(2)(B). *Cf.* § 1–5, *supra*. Moreover, any non-citizen who at any time after admission abuses or becomes addicted to drugs is subject to removal. INA § 237(a)(2)(B)(ii). Unlike the general moral turpitude category, a non-citizen need not be sentenced in order to be removed for narcotics offenses. Likewise, a non-citizen convicted of practically any firearms violation is removable. INA § 237(a)(2)(C). Non-citizens convicted of violating the Selective Service Act, espionage statutes, or certain other statutes dealing with the national defense are subject to removal if immigration authorities designate the non-citizen as an undesirable. INA § 237(a)(2)(D).

(4) Avoiding the Immigration Consequences of Crimes

Because of the serious, sometimes unanticipated consequences of criminal conduct for non-citizens and their families, lawyers representing non-citizens accused of a crime, prosecutors, and judges have several special considerations to keep in mind. First, if the non-citizen is accused of a crime of moral turpitude, or an "aggravated felony," the lawyer will want to consider pleading the non-citizen to a lesser offense that does not involve moral turpitude, has a maximum sentence of less than one year, and/or is not classified as an aggravated felony for immigration. "Misdemeanor" is not an immigration concept and many state misdemeanors are aggravated felonies under immigration law. Some prosecutors and judges are not aware of the severe consequences of criminal convictions for non-citizens who may, in some cases, be the sole support of U.S. citizen or permanent resident family members. In many cases, the rehabilitative and punitive purposes of prosecuting and sentencing can be achieved through imposing a stronger sentence for a lesser level crime without causing collateral unwanted immigration consequences.

Second, the INA also specifies that the moral turpitude or aggravated felony provisions do not apply to non-citizens who have been granted a full and unconditional pardon by the President or the governor of the state of conviction. INA § 237(a)(2)(A)(vi). Hence, as a last resort, the lawyer may attempt to obtain a full pardon for the non-citizen. A pardon has no effect, however, on the other criminal grounds such as firearm or drug offenses. *See, e.g., In re Suh*, 23 I. & N. Dec. 626, Interim Decision (BIA) 3494 (BIA 2003) (holding that a pardon did not waive removability for a conviction of domestic violence under INA § 237(a)(2)(E)(i) because a pardon waives only INA § 237(a)(2)(A)(vi) grounds of removal and no implicit waivers may be read into the statute). The statute does not provide for an automatic stay of removal upon filing a pardon application, so attorneys should apply for such a stay before applying for a pardon for their clients.

c.   *Registration Requirements*

Under INA § 265, all non-citizens who remain in the United States for longer than thirty days, including permanent residents, are required to report any change of address to immigration authorities within ten days. Failure to satisfy this requirement, or any other registration requirement, constitutes grounds for removal. INA § 237(a)(3)(A). Although part of the INA since 1952, this provision was rarely enforced. After the terrorist of attacks of September 11, 2001, however, tracking non-citizens in the U.S. became a matter of great public concern. Consequently, in 2002 the Justice Department announced that it would begin enforcing the change of address requirement and would impose special registration requirements on nonimmigrants who are considered security risks. 67 Fed.Reg. 52584–01. The Department of Homeland Security replaced the special registration requirements enacted after September 11, 2001, with the US–VISIT program in 2003. *See* § 6–24, *supra*.

d. National Security Grounds

ICE also may initiate removal proceedings against non-citizens for engaging in acts that threaten national security or U.S. foreign policy after their entry into the United States. Since there is no statute of limitations in the INA, the non-citizen may be removed any time after the prohibited act is committed. The national security removal grounds parallel the grounds of inadmissibility. Like the inadmissibility grounds, the removal grounds have changed as national security concerns have changed. Prior to 1990, the statute classified as removable "subversives," such as anarchists, Communists, and persons advocating the overthrow of the United States government.

The 1990 Act and subsequent amendments revised these provisions to shift the focus from subversive activity to terrorism. The current law permits removal of any non-citizen who violates U.S. espionage law, engages in criminal activity that endangers public safety or national security, or engages in any activity whose purpose is to overthrow the U.S. government by force or unlawful means. INA § 237(a)(4)(A). A non-citizen who has engaged, is engaged, or at any time after admission engages in terrorist activity, as defined in section 212(a)(3), also is subject to removal. INA § 237(a)(4)(B). Since this section relies on the definition of terrorism contained in section 212(a)(3), the changes made to that definition by the USA PATRIOT Act and REAL ID Act affect removal as well as inadmissibility. The Secretary of State has the discretion to recommend for removal a non-citizen whose presence he or she believes will have serious adverse consequences for U.S. foreign policy. INA § 237(a)(4)(C).

In addition, a 1978 amendment to the INA, updated in the 1990 Act, permits ICE to remove non-citizens who participated in Nazi activities or other acts of genocide. According to the Act, any non-citizen who "ordered, incited, assisted, or otherwise participated in the persecution of any person because of race, religion, national origin, or political opinion" may be removed. INA §§ 237(a)(4)(D), 212(a)(3)(E). This provision was unsuccessfully challenged as an unconstitutional bill of attainder and *ex post facto* law. The Second Circuit in *Linnas v. INS*, 790 F.2d 1024 (2d Cir.1986) held that the provision is not a bill of attainder because removal is not punishment. Linnas, who was found to be chief of a Nazi concentration camp, was ordered removed to the Soviet Union, even though he was convicted *in absentia* in the Soviet Union and sentenced to death there for his war crimes. Linnas' argument that his removal would be unlawful extradition was likewise unsuccessful.

e. *Other Removal Grounds*

The INA also provides for the removal of certain other statutorily defined undesirables. Non-citizens convicted of a crime of domestic violence, stalking, child abuse, child neglect, child abandonment, or of a violation of a protective order relating to domestic violence are removable. INA § 237(a)(2)(E). ICE may also remove a non-citizen who knowingly or recklessly prepares, files, or assists another in preparing or filing a false application or document for immigration benefits. INA § 237(a)(3)(C)(i). A waiver is available for a first violation by a permanent resident who committed a document fraud offense solely to assist or support a spouse or child.

INA § 237(a)(3)(C)(ii). IIRIRA also added new grounds for removal and criminal penalties for non-citizens who falsely claim citizenship. INA § 237(a)(3)(D). Non-citizens who within five years of admission become "public charges" by applying for certain government benefits can be removed unless they can show that the need for such benefits arose after their admission. INA § 237(a)(5). Further, IIRIRA amendments provide for removal of those non-citizens who have voted unlawfully. INA § 237(a)(6). As with the similar ground of inadmissibility, the unlawful voting ground is waived in the case of anyone who has a U.S. citizen parent, became a lawful permanent resident while under the age of sixteen, and reasonably believed that he or she was also a citizen.

CHAPTER 9

REMOVAL PROCEEDINGS AND RELIEF FROM REMOVAL

The preceding chapter described the various grounds of inadmissibility and removal. This chapter discusses the methods used to identify inadmissible and removable non-citizens, the removal proceeding, and various forms of relief from removal.

Two agencies within the Department of Homeland Security, the U.S. Immigration and Customs Enforcement (ICE) and the U.S. Customs and Border Protection (CBP), have significant roles in enforcing immigration laws. Like all law enforcement agencies, ICE can and does exercise a great deal of prosecutorial discretion. They exercise this discretion in deciding where to focus investigative resources, whether to initiate removal proceedings against a particular individual, whether to detain a person after initiating removal proceedings (when detention is not mandatory), and whether to support or oppose a non-citizen's request for relief from removal. Under INA § 242(g), added by the IIRIRA, decisions to "commence proceedings, adjudicate cases, or execute removal orders" are unreviewable.

Immigration authorities' exercise of discretion was challenged in *Reno v. American–Arab Anti–Discrimination Committee*, 525 U.S. 471 (1999) by a group of non-citizens who claimed they had been singled out for removal because of their membership in a politically unpopular group, the People's Front for the Liberation of Palestine. A District Court initially enjoined the deportation of the plaintiffs, finding that they had been subject to selective prosecution. The Ninth Circuit upheld the decision. The Supreme Court reversed, however, on the basis that § 242(g), enacted while the appeal was pending, precluded judicial review of the INS' decision to commence proceedings.

Subsequent to that decision, the Immigration Commissioner published guidelines describing the factors that could warrant a favorable exercise of discretion (*i.e.*, not to initiate proceedings against an individual). *See* 77 Interp.Rel. 1673. These factors include lawful permanent resident status; a lengthy residence in the U.S.; the (relatively minor) nature of any criminal conduct; humanitarian concerns such as family ties in the U.S. and medical conditions affecting the non-citizen or his or her family; lack of previous immigration violations; the likelihood of ultimately removing the individual; the person's eligibility for other relief; and public opinion regarding the case, although this factor does not alone justify favorable exercise of discretion. These guidelines do not, however, create any enforceable legal rights in non-citizens.

§ 9–1 INVESTIGATION AND APPREHENSION

ICE and CBP use a variety of techniques to investigate potentially removable non-citizens who are inside or seeking to enter the United States. While ICE is primarily concerned with enforcement of immigration laws within the United States, CBP focuses on preventing illegal entries. The agencies' current enforcement priorities are deterring illegal entries, locating and removing non-citizens who have committed crimes, penalizing employers who hire non-citizens without work authorization, prosecuting document fraud schemes, breaking up alien smuggling operations, and stopping terrorism. To achieve these goals, CBP inspects vehicles, persons, and belongings at the border and at certain fixed check-points both inside the border and in other countries. ICE uses roving patrols inside the U.S. to identify and detain suspected illegal entrants, audits and searches businesses alleged to unlawfully employ non-citizens, works with other law enforcement agencies to identify criminal non-citizens, and acts on information obtained through informants. This section examines the scope of the power of ICE and CBP to investigate and apprehend non-citizens.

§ 9–1.1 Immigration Service Powers Prior to Arrest

The INA provides that any immigration officer may, without a warrant:

(1) Interrogate any alien or person believed to be an alien as to his or her right to be or remain in the United States;

(2) Arrest any alien who in the officer's presence or view is entering or attempting to enter the United States in violation of any law or if the officer has reason to believe the alien is in the United States in violation of any law and is likely to escape if not arrested;

(3) Board and search any vehicle to look for illegal aliens within a reasonable distance from the border. INA § 287(a).

Immigration officers must take non-citizens arrested without a warrant before an examining officer "without unnecessary delay." INA § 287(a). The Code of Federal Regulations defines a reasonable distance from the border to be "100 air miles from any external boundary of the United States." 8 C.F.R. § 287.1(a)(2). The statute appears to confer broad investigatory powers on immigration officials. The Supreme Court has held that evidence obtained in violation of the Fourth Amendment may be used in removal proceedings. Using a balancing test, the Court decided that the likely costs of excluding unlawfully obtained evidence outweigh the likely social benefits. Excluding such evidence would hinder the deliberately simple removal hearing system, would possibly suppress large amounts of information that had been obtained lawfully, and would "compel the courts to release from custody persons who would then immediately resume their commission of a crime through their continuing, unlawful presence in this country." In the Court's view, the social benefits from excluding such evidence would be minor because exclusion would have little deterrent effect on future Fourth Amendment violations by immigration officials. *INS v. Lopez–Mendoza*, 468 U.S. 1032 (1984).

a. *Outside the Territorial Bounds of the United States*

Ordinarily, the United States only has legal authority over persons and property contained within its territorial bounds, including its territorial waters. There are a few exceptions to this rule in the immigration context, including "pre-inspection" of non-citizens traveling to the U.S. from foreign ports, interdiction of undocumented migrants on the high seas, and cooperation with foreign law enforcement officials to investigate and prosecute alien smugglers and other human traffickers.

(1) Pre-Inspection

Congress has authorized the Secretary of Homeland Security, with the consent of the Secretary of State, to detail immigration officers for duty in foreign countries. INA § 103(a). Under that authority, CBP operates pre-boarding inspection offices in Aruba, the Bahamas, Bermuda, Canada, and Ireland, to inspect non-citizens before their departure to the United States. Pre-inspection occurs only when the vessel proceeds directly to this country and eliminates the need for inspection at the border.

(2) Interdiction

For several decades, U.S. law enforcement officials, primarily the Coast Guard, have been trying to prevent the entry of undocumented migrants by interdicting vessels in territorial waters and on the high seas. Those efforts gained attention in the early 1980s following the Mariel boatlift from Cuba and a mass exodus from Haiti. In 1981 the President of the United States, pursuant to an agreement with Haiti, issued Executive Order 12324, which gave the Coast Guard the authority to stop and board vessels coming from either the U.S. or Haiti. The Coast Guard would briefly interview the passengers and forcibly repatriate any who did not have an apparent claim for refugee status. In *Haitian Refugee Center v. Gracey*, 809 F.2d 794 (D.C. Cir.1987), the court upheld the interdiction agreement, finding that it did not violate due process because non-citizens have no right to enter the U.S.

Nonetheless, Haitians continued coming to the U.S. During fall-winter of 1991–92, more than 16,000 Haitians were intercepted on the high seas and taken to the U.S. Naval Base at Guantánamo Bay in eastern Cuba. They were questioned as to whether they had prima facie claims to asylum status. Except for a very brief period the Haitians had no access to lawyers. They also had no right to appeal. The interdiction and interview procedures were challenged in federal court and the challenge was initially sustained. The Eleventh Circuit, however, held in *Haitian Refugee Center v. Baker*, 953 F.2d 1498 (11th Cir.1992) that the Administrative Procedure Act does not give non-citizens who were detained on the high seas and, thus, had never presented themselves at a U.S. border, a right to judicial review of immigration decisions. Moreover, the court concluded that these individuals had no private right of action, unless they qualified for refugee status. Further, the court stated that the Refugee Center and the Haitians' attorneys had no First Amendment claim for gaining access to the detainees. The Supreme Court denied certiorari. Ultimately, 35% of the Haitians were found to have prima facie claims and were transported to the U.S. for adjudication of their asylum cases. Almost all of the others were returned to Haiti.

In May 1992, George H.W. Bush ordered the Coast Guard to return any Haitians leaving their country in boats without an inquiry as to whether they qualified for asylum. The U.N. High Commissioner for Refugees and the Haitian Refugee Center challenged this measure as a violation of the U.S. government's obligations under the Protocol relating to the Status of Refugees. In *Sale v. Haitian Centers Council, Inc.*, 509 U.S. 155 (1993), the Court again upheld the President's executive order that authorized summary return of Haitians intercepted on the high seas without considering asylum claims. The court did not find any violation of Article 33 of the U.N. Protocol relating to the Status of Refugees or INA § 243(h) (now INA § 241(b)(3)), both of which prohibit the return of refugees to territories where their lives or freedom would be threatened. On April 4, 1994, Haitian President Aristide withdrew his government's agreement to stopping Haitian boats on the high seas and President Clinton ordered that Haitians would no longer be subject to interdiction without individualized inquiry as to whether they qualify for refugee or asylum status.

In 1995, after years of sporadic discussions, the U.S. and Cuba entered an agreement allowing the U.S. government to interdict Cuban vessels and repatriate undocumented migrants from that country. Although such traffic has slowed since 1994, Cubans, Haitians, and others continue to try to reach the U.S. from the sea. In recent years, the Coast Guard has interdicted an increasing number of Ecuadorian and Chinese migrants. Ecuadorians travel by sea to Mexico and then try to enter the U.S. over land. Chinese migrants often travel by sea to Guam and then use fraudulent documents to obtain air passage to the U.S., or travel by air to South America and then by sea to the U.S. In addition to interdiction, the U.S. is now engaged in efforts to stop the smuggling rings that transport many of these migrants.

(3) ALIEN SMUGGLING

Smuggling of undocumented migrants is an international business believed to generate billions of dollars in annual revenues. Several smuggling disasters have attracted global attention. In 1993, a cargo ship carrying hundreds of undocumented Chinese migrants ran aground off the coast of New York; several of the passengers died trying to swim to shore. In January 2000, three Chinese migrants were found dead in a sealed container on board an ocean freighter docked in Seattle. In Britain that same year, fifty-eight Chinese migrants died of suffocation in the back of a freight truck found in Dover port. The Chinese are not the only people engaging in this traffic, however: Mexican smuggling operations regularly bring Mexican and Central American migrants across the U.S. border, and other smuggling rings transport people from the Middle East and the former Soviet bloc to Western Europe. In an effort to address this problem, in December 2000, 79 countries signed the United Nations Protocol Against Smuggling Migrants. The Protocol, which entered into force in January 2004, provides for cooperative efforts among State parties, including exchange of information and interdiction of vessels suspected of smuggling migrants. The United States has signed and ratified the protocol.

The United States also attempted to address the problem of human smuggling by enacting the Trafficking Victims Protection Act of 2000. The Act called for the President to "establish and carry out international initiatives to enhance economic opportunity for potential victims of trafficking," to increase public awareness, and to "establish and carry out programs of border interdiction outside the United States." 22 U.S.C.A. § 7104. As a result, government agencies have responded with various initiatives and programs to combat smuggling. For example, ICE partnered with the Office of Intelligence within the DOJ to form special units that investigate and dismantle human smuggling operations. ICE also trains foreign law enforcement officials in smuggling prevention.

b. At the Border

CBP has the authority to stop all vehicles and persons at the border or its functional equivalent. *See* INA § 235. The Inspections Division of CBP determines the admissibility of non-citizens arriving at designated ports of entry, while the Border Patrol works to prevent non-citizens from entering the U.S. through locations other than the authorized ports of entry and to apprehend non-citizens who have entered illegally. The Border Patrol accounts for approximately 95 percent of all apprehensions made by immigration authorities each year. Most of these occur near the U.S.-Mexico border, which has been increasingly patrolled since the enactment of Operation Gatekeeper in 1994. Operation Gatekeeper increased resources and manpower on the Southwest border, and focused on patrolling strategic areas to funnel illegal immigrants to specific points of entry. The Border Patrol continued to increase its efforts along the Southwest border throughout the 2000s by doubling its number of agents, utilizing new surveillance technologies, and constructing border fences. *See* § 1–10.5, *infra*. The effectiveness of the Border Patrol's efforts is debatable. Studies show that unauthorized immigration increased steadily from 1989 through 2005 with the number of undocumented migrants living in the United States rising from 2.5 million to over 11 million during that period. Unauthorized immigration has leveled off since 2005. In addition, the increased patrol has forced non-citizens to take dangerous paths when crossing into the United States and an increasingly high number of migrants have died in crossing attempts.

Immigration officers may board and search any vehicle, including boats and aircraft, which they believe contains non-citizens. These searches may be legally conducted without a search warrant and can occur at the border or in the territorial waters of the United States. INA §§ 235, 287.

When non-citizens arrive at the border, CBP is authorized to inspect them to determine whether they may be admitted into the United States. INA § 235(a). A visa is usually essential for admission but it does not guarantee admission. After the inspection, which is extremely brief in most cases, the examining officer decides whether to admit the non-citizen. If the examining immigration officer determines that a non-citizen is not clearly and beyond doubt entitled to be admitted and the non-citizen has not requested asylum, the officer may summarily order the non-citizen's removal. INA § 235(b)(1)(A). If a person's admissibility is questionable, the officer may detain him or her for secondary inspection or defer inspection and parole the individual into the U.S. Inadmissible non-citizens may be allowed to withdraw their application for admission during inspection and thus escape the consequences of removal. Non-citizens removed upon their arrival are barred from entering the United States for five years. INA § 212(a)(9)(A). Most inadmissible non-citizens are given the option of withdrawal, unless they have presented false documents or have misrepresented a material fact in order to obtain a visa or gain admission to the U.S., in which case they will be removed. INA § 235(a)(4).

If a non-citizen appears inadmissible, the officer may temporarily detain him or her for further inquiry. This procedure is customarily referred to as secondary inspection. Although secondary inspection involves an interrogation, the Fifth Circuit held in *United States v. Henry*,

611 F.2d 983 (5th Cir.1979) that no *Miranda*-type warning is necessary unless the questioning becomes custodial in nature. Applicants for admission have no right to counsel during inspection unless taken into custody on criminal charges. 8 C.F.R. § 292.5(b).

As a result of changes enacted by IIRIRA, immigration officers are authorized to remove many inadmissible noncitizens through a special process known as expedited removal. *See* § 9–2.3, *infra*. For example, if an inspections officer suspects that an individual is inadmissible on national security grounds, the officer may order that person removed without further inquiry, subject only to review by the Secretary of Homeland Security. INA § 235(c).

The immigration officer also may elect to release a non-citizen on parole pending further investigation, unless the non-citizen is inadmissible on criminal or national security grounds. *See* INA § 212(d)(5). Inspectors grant parole chiefly as a matter of practicality, because time constraints often prevent them from making a thorough investigation at the border. Immigration officers can also parole non-citizens who might be able to overcome inadmissibility, so that they can gather additional evidence or seek a waiver of the grounds of inadmissibility. These cases are referred to an appropriate official, such as a CIS district director, for consideration. 8 C.F.R. § 235.2. Non-citizens who enter on parole have not been admitted, and may be subject to expedited removal proceedings if ultimately deemed inadmissible. The Board of Immigration Appeals held in *Matter of Castellon*, 17 I. & N. Dec. 616, Interim Decision (BIA) 2847 (BIA 1981) that parole is purely discretionary and no administrative review of the decision is possible, although judicial review may lie in a district court for a declaratory judgment or in a court of appeal for *habeas corpus* action.

c.   *100 Miles Inside the Border*

(1) INVESTIGATORY STOPS FOR IDENTIFICATION

While CBP can search any person or vehicle at the border, its powers within the United States are more limited. INA § 287(a) authorizes immigration officers to board vehicles within a "reasonable distance" from the border solely to search for non-citizens. The Code of Federal Regulations defines a reasonable distance from the border to be "100 air miles from any external boundary of the United States." 8 C.F.R. § 287.1(a)(2). Despite this seemingly broad statutory authority, the Supreme Court has held that this power is limited by the Fourth Amendment in the context of criminal prosecutions. In *Almeida–Sanchez v. United States*, 413 U.S. 266 (1973), the Supreme Court held that a warrantless search of an automobile made by a roving patrol without probable cause or consent violated the non-citizen's right to be free from unreasonable searches and seizures. The Court has, however, upheld the right of Border Patrol officers to make brief investigatory stops using either roving patrols or fixed checkpoints.

In its Fourth Amendment jurisprudence, the Supreme Court seeks to balance the government's interest in law enforcement against the intrusion into the individual's privacy. In the immigration context, the Court has consistently found that the government has a strong interest in preventing the illegal entry of non-citizens and that such entries cannot be entirely halted at the border. It has also found the intrusion caused by a brief investigatory stop to be modest. *United States v. Brignoni–Ponce*, 422 U.S. 873 (1975). Hence, it has held that a roving patrol stopping a vehicle and questioning the occupants about their citizenship and immigration status does not violate the Fourth Amendment so long as the officer has a reasonable suspicion, based on the "totality of circumstances," that the particular vehicle may contain noncitizens who entered the U.S. illegally. *United States v. Arvizu*, 534 U.S. 266 (2002). A suspicion is reasonable if it is based on articulable facts that, viewed in the light of the officer's experience, give rise to an inference that criminal activity may be afoot, even if each individual fact viewed separately could have an innocent explanation. *Id.* Factors relevant to the existence of a reasonable suspicion include proximity to the border, traffic patterns, previous experience with undocumented non-citizens travelling in the area, the driver's behavior, the appearance of the vehicle, and the officer's experience in recognizing the characteristic appearance of foreign nationals. *United States v. Brignoni–Ponce*, 422 U.S. 873 (1975).

In addition, Border Patrol officers can make routine investigatory stops at reasonably located fixed checkpoints even in the absence of any suspicion that the vehicle contains illegal aliens. The Court in *United States v. Martinez–Fuerte*, 428 U.S. 543 (1976) reasoned that the intrusion on Fourth Amendment rights involved in such a stop is less severe than that caused by roving patrols since motorists are given advance warning of the stop which involves only the briefest detention—usually less than a minute. At such stops, most drivers are typically waived through, while a small percentage are stopped for further questioning regarding their citizenship and immigration status. The Court held that vehicles may not be searched at such stops without either the consent of the driver or probable cause to believe that the vehicle contains undocumented non-citizens. *United States v. Ortiz*, 422 U.S. 891 (1975). When conducting the search, immigration officers may inspect only those areas of the car where a person could reasonably hide. In other words, the officer may not, as the Supreme Court observed in *United States v. Ross*, 456 U.S. 798 (1982), open and search small pieces of luggage or other small containers and compartments to look for non-citizens. Border Patrol officers may also search for narcotics in the course of an immigration stop, but the Fifth Circuit has held that they may not prolong the search beyond the time needed to determine whether any immigration violations have occurred unless the officers have an individualized suspicion of wrongdoing. *United States v. Portillo–Aguirre*, 311 F.3d 647 (5th Cir.2002).

The mechanisms used by the Border Patrol inside the border include fixed checkpoints on major highways, roving patrols, video cameras, and electronic sensors on unpatrolled roads. These efforts are primarily focused on areas near the U.S.-Mexico border. The focus on entries from Mexico has raised the question of whether and to what extent a person's Hispanic appearance may be used to justify an investigatory stop. In *Brignoni–Ponce*, the Court held that ethnic appearance could not alone create a reasonable suspicion of illegal activity. In dicta, however, the Court stated that ethnic appearance could justify a traffic stop when combined with other suspicious circumstances, as there was a significant probability that any particular individual of Hispanic appearance was a non-citizen. Twenty-five years later, noting that Hispanic persons had become a majority in many border areas, the Ninth Circuit held that ethnic appearance could no longer be considered a relevant factor. *United States v.*

Montero–Camargo, 208 F.3d 1122 (9th Cir.2000). The court found that a characteristic shared by a substantial percentage of the population could not be the basis for a particularized suspicion of wrongdoing.

(2) Temporary Detention for Questioning

One step between an investigatory stop for identification and an actual arrest is the forcible detention of a suspected non-citizen for interrogation. While the person questioned during an investigatory stop is free to leave, a person forcibly detained is not, even though he or she is not technically under arrest. *Yam Sang Kwai v. INS*, 411 F.2d 683 (D.C. Cir.1969). Immigration officers may forcibly detain persons temporarily when the circumstances warrant a reasonable suspicion that they are illegally in the United States. The First Circuit rationalized in *Navia–Duran v. INS*, 568 F.2d 803 (1st Cir.1977) that, since a forcible detention falls short of an actual arrest, no *Miranda*-type warning is necessary before questioning a forcibly detained non-citizen. Other circuits endorse this view. Courts will consider, however, the voluntariness of any statement given by the non-citizen in the absence of a *Miranda*-type warning. If immigration officials coerce the non-citizen, his or her right to due process, as guaranteed by the Fifth Amendment, may be violated. The court, as in *Navia–Duran*, may suppress any evidence obtained through coercion during the removal hearing.

d. *Interior of the United States*

With the exception of areas within 100 miles of the external boundaries of the United States, CBP and ICE may not make investigatory stops using roving patrols or fixed check-points. They may, however, briefly detain non-citizens for interrogation. As with detentions made near the border, immigration authorities must have a reasonable belief that individuals are illegally present in this country before detaining them for interrogation. INA § 287(a).

(1) ENFORCING RESTRICTIONS ON EMPLOYMENT

ICE's investigative efforts include searching businesses believed to employ unauthorized non-citizen workers. In the past, the target of these searches was the workers themselves. After 1986, IRCA instituted civil and criminal penalties for employers, and immigration authorities shifted their focus to them, in particular employers who commit human rights abuses or may be part of alien smuggling rings. ICE, however, continues to search out and arrest undocumented workers employed at various businesses and increased its use of workplace raids to apprehend undocumented workers during the George W. Bush administration. *See* § 1–10.5, *infra*. The federal courts typically apply a relaxed Fourth Amendment standard to such searches. *See, e.g., International Molders' and Allied Workers' Local Union No. 164 v. Nelson*, 799 F.2d 547 (9th Cir.1986). In *INS v. Delgado*, 466 U.S. 210 (1984), the Supreme Court held that a factory search did not constitute a ''seizure'' of the workers, and thus did not violate their Fourth Amendment rights, where they were free to move about the factory during the search. For a discussion on labor law, see § 13–4.7, *infra*.

(2) ''SPECIAL CIRCUMSTANCES''

Special circumstances may enlarge immigration officials' authority. The D.C. Circuit upheld the Attorney General's authority, during the Iranian hostage crisis, to order nonimmigrant Iranian students to report to INS district offices and to demonstrate their lawful status.

Narenji v. Civiletti, 481 F.Supp. 1132 (D.D.C.1979). Following the September 11, 2001, attacks, the INS detained more than 700 non-citizens of Middle Eastern background on immigration violations. Citing national security concerns, the Service refused to release the names of the persons held, most of whom had committed only minor immigration offenses. As of this writing, immigration officials still have not stated how many were eventually removed. A court order requiring the Service to make this information public was reversed on appeal. *See Center for Nat. Sec. Studies v. Dept. of Justice*, 331 F.3d 918 (D.C.Cir.2003).

Civil lawsuits by plaintiffs challenging the lawfulness of their post-September 11 detentions have had mixed success. In *Ashcroft v. Iqbal*, 129 S.Ct. 1937 (2009), the Supreme Court dismissed a detainee's lawsuit by ruling that the detainee's factual pleadings, even if taken as true, still did not establish that the Attorney General and Director of the FBI violated his constitutional rights by detaining him. Courts, however, have allowed detainee lawsuits to proceed that allege that detainees suffered verbal and physical abuse while in detention. *Turkmen v. Ashcroft*, 2006 WL 1662663 (E.D.N.Y.2006). In one instance, the government settled a lawsuit for $300,000 with a former detainee who claimed that he was routinely beaten by detention officers, subjected to repeated strip and body cavity searches, denied adequate nutrition and personal hygiene supplies, and kept in solitary confinement for the whole of his eleven-month detention. *Elmaghraby v. Ashcroft*, 2005 WL 2375202 (E.D.N.Y. 2005).

At the same time as the INS detentions, the Attorney General's Anti–Terrorism Task Force interviewed some 5,000 students, tourists, and visitors from mostly Middle

Eastern countries, seeking information about terrorist activities. Although immigration violations were not the focus of these interviews, interviewers were instructed to notify immigration authorities if they suspected that any interviewee was in violation of status. 78 Interp.Rel. 1816. Additionally, under the National Security Entry/Exit Registration System (NSEERS), male non-citizens from twenty-five designated countries were required to register with immigration officials following the September 11, 2001. Of the 82,000 non-citizens who registered under the program, more than 13,000 became subject to removal proceedings based on previous immigration violations. While the government ended the registration portion of NSEERS in 2003, it retains the authority to reinstate the program.

(3) Delegation to Local Law Enforcement

Local law enforcement officials have in the past participated in immigration enforcement activities. In *Gonzales v. City of Peoria*, 722 F.2d 468 (9th Cir.1983), the court found that the federal power over immigration does not necessarily preclude local enforcement of some provisions of the INA. State and local law agencies usually enforce immigration laws indirectly, however, by reporting persons who are suspected of violating immigration laws to immigration authorities.

A few provisions of the INA allow local law enforcement agencies to participate more directly in immigration enforcement. Section 103(a)(8) allows the Secretary of Homeland Security to delegate any immigration powers he or she deems necessary to local law enforcement in the event of a "mass influx of aliens." Section 103(c) authorizes the Secretary (formerly the Attorney General) to enter cooperative agreements with state and local agencies to enforce immigration laws. INA § 287(g)(1) further authorizes the Secretary to enter written agreements with any state or local officer or employee qualified to perform the functions of an immigration officer.

Although § 287(g)(1) was added to the INA in 1996 as part of the IIRIRA, it was not implemented until 2002. As part of its efforts to combat terrorism and undocumented immigration, ICE began entering into § 287(g) agreements with state and local officials that allow state and local law enforcement officers to perform immigration functions. Participating officers, supervised by immigration officials, can interrogate persons suspected of immigration violations, prepare Notices to Appear (which initiate removal proceedings) for signature by authorized immigration officials, and assist in pre- or post-arrest processing of non-citizens. 79 Interp.Rel. 1120. Many local communities have passed ordinances prohibiting cooperation with federal immigration authorities because they feel assistance would undermine their ability to fight crime and enforce state or local laws in immigrant communities.

§ 9–1.2   Arrests

a.   Arrests Without a Warrant

The INA empowers an immigration officer to arrest, without a warrant, "any alien in the United States, if he has reason to believe that the alien so arrested is in the United States in violation of any such law or regulation and is likely to escape before a warrant can be obtained for his arrest...." INA § 287(a)(2). The Tenth Circuit in *Roa–Rodriguez v. United States*, 410 F.2d 1206 (10th Cir.1969) has limited this authority by holding that a belief that an individual intends to violate his or her

entry conditions is insufficient for an arrest. The arresting officer must base the belief on something more than
mere suspicion. After an arrest made without a warrant,
immigration officials must follow specific administrative
procedures. Once arrested, the non-citizen is taken before a different immigration officer for questioning unless no other officer is readily available. 8 C.F.R. § 287.3.
If the examining officer determines that a prima facie
case exists for removing the non-citizen, he or she refers
the case to an immigration judge, orders the individual's
expedited removal, or takes other applicable action. 8
C.F.R. § 287.3.

Even though removal is a severe result, courts have
concluded that removal proceedings are civil and not
criminal in nature and hence, uniformly agree that a
Miranda warning at the time of the arrest for removal is
not required. After ICE makes the decision to proceed
with removal (except in the case of non-citizens subject
to the expedited removal provision), 8 C.F.R. § 287.3
requires arresting officers to advise non-citizens of (1)
the reason for the arrest, (2) their right to counsel at no
expense to the government and the availability of any
free legal service programs, and (3) their right to remain
silent. While not technically a *Miranda* warning, in essence, arresting officers are required to advise non-citizens of their rights as defined by the Court in *Miranda v.
Arizona*, 384 U.S. 436 (1966). Although the statute requires officers to give the warning only after they decide
to proceed with removal, the court may scrutinize any
statements given by non-citizens before the warning to
determine whether the statements were made voluntarily. In addition, non-citizens must be informed within
forty-eight hours whether they will be detained further
or released on bond or recognizance and whether a

Notice to Appear and warrant of arrest will be issued. 8 C.F.R. § 287.3.

Immediately after the September 11, 2001, attacks, the INS published an interim rule permitting immigration officials to hold non-citizens in custody without charges for a "reasonable period of time" during emergency situations. 66 Fed.Reg. 48334–01. The Service stated that extra time was required to obtain necessary information from other law enforcement agencies. The USA PATRIOT Act subsequently authorized detention of suspected terrorists for up to seven days without charges. *See* INA § 236A. Reports have been issued, however, including a July 2003 report by the Department of Justice Inspector General, regarding abuses in the implementation of the PATRIOT Act. Complaints have ranged from beatings to verbal abuse of those detained.

b. *Arrests With a Warrant*

If ICE issues a warrant for arrest, it simultaneously issues a Notice to Appear before the immigration court to contest the removal. Once issued, ICE must serve the warrant within a reasonable period of time. *See United States v. Weaver*, 384 F.2d 879 (4th Cir.1967). Should ICE determine that a non-citizen is not subject to removal, any officer authorized to issue an arrest warrant may cancel it.

The Code of Federal Regulations also requires arresting officers to inform non-citizens at the time of their arrest of the reason for the arrest and to advise them of their rights. 8 C.F.R. § 287.8(c). Non-citizens who are not advised of these rights or fail to understand them may move to suppress evidence obtained because of the lack of warning. *Navia–Duran v. INS*, 568 F.2d 803 (1st Cir.1977).

c. Release on Bond or Personal Recognizance

ICE has discretion to release non-citizens it has taken into custody, unless they are subject to removal on criminal grounds or have been certified as suspected terrorists. Detention is mandatory for suspected terrorists and persons removable on certain grounds related to criminal conduct. INA §§ 236, 236A. Where detention is not mandatory, ICE may (1) continue to detain the arrested non-citizen pending removal proceedings; (2) release the non-citizen upon bond in the amount of not less than $1500 with security approved by the Secretary of Homeland Security and containing such conditions as the Secretary may prescribe; or (3) release the non-citizen on conditional parole. INA § 236(a). The INA also authorizes ICE to revoke the bond or parole at any time and rearrest the non-citizen under the original warrant. INA § 236(b).

Traditionally, as the Board observed in *Matter of Patel*, 15 I. & N. Dec. 666, Interim Decision (BIA) 2491 (BIA 1976), non-criminal aliens were granted release on personal recognizance unless immigration authorities suspected that they would not appear for subsequent hearings. This practice became known as "catch and release." The factors considered relevant by the Board in *Patel* to determine whether a non-citizen is a bail risk include prior arrests in this country, convictions in the person's native country, illegal entry into the United States, participation in subversive activities, employment status, and the presence of relatives in the United States. In 2006, the Department of Homeland Security announced the end of "catch and release" practices as part of its

Secure Borders Initiative. Rather than releasing non-criminal aliens on their own recognizance, immigration authorities began detaining nearly all apprehended non-citizens until their removal hearings. Bail or parole decisions are not subject to review by a federal court. INA § 236(e).

INA § 236(c) mandates detention until the removal hearing of any non-citizen convicted of an aggravated felony. The Ninth Circuit held, in *Kim v. Ziglar*, 276 F.3d 523 (9th Cir.2002), that this statute violates the constitutional right of due process when applied to permanent residents because it does not allow individual hearings to determine whether a particular person presents a flight risk. The Supreme Court upheld the statute, however, finding that detention for "the brief period necessary for . . . removal proceedings" is an appropriate way to ensure that removable non-citizens will appear for their removal hearings and will not commit additional crimes before being removed. *Demore v. Kim*, 538 U.S. 510 (2003). ICE has begun experimenting with alternatives to traditional detention. For example, it initiated the Electronic Monitoring Program to use ankle bracelets to monitor non-citizens awaiting their hearing.

d. *Decision Not to Continue Removal Proceedings*

In some cases, ICE may decide not to continue removal proceedings after taking an individual into custody. ICE must make this decision before jurisdiction vests with the immigration judge. 8 C.F.R. § 239.2. ICE must also inform the individual of such a decision in writing. Having exercised its prosecutorial discretion in this manner, ICE should not reinitiate proceedings against the individual unless new facts come to light or there is a change in circumstances. *See* 77 Interp.Rel. 1673.

§ 9–2   REMOVAL HEARING

In general, persons who are subject to removal after being lawfully admitted and non-citizens who are present in the U.S. without having been admitted are entitled to a removal hearing. Non-citizens denied admission at a port of entry are not entitled to a removal hearing and are removed immediately unless they request asylum. *See* chapter 10, *infra*.

§ 9–2.1   Notice to Appear

The removal process officially commences when a Notice to Appear is filed with an immigration court. ICE officials, as well as CBP and CIS officials in certain circumstances, have the authority to issue a Notice to Appear. An official must make a prima facie showing of removability when issuing a Notice to Appear. *Abel v. United States*, 362 U.S. 217 (1960).

The INA lists the specific requirements for a Notice to Appear. It must state the nature of the proceeding, the legal authority under which the proceeding is conducted, the act or conduct alleged to be in violation of the law, the charges against the non-citizen, and the statutory provisions alleged to have been violated. INA § 239(a)(1). In addition, the Notice to Appear states that further proceedings will be held and notifies the non-citizen of the need to keep the government apprised of his or her address and the consequences of failing to do so. INA § 239(a)(1). The Notice must inform the non-citizen of his or her right to counsel and must include a list of free legal service programs available in the locale. The Court of Appeals in *Montilla v. INS*, 926 F.2d 162 (2d Cir.1991) held that a failure to give the alien notice of these rights may result in a new hearing.

Before filing the Notice with the immigration court, immigration officials must serve it on the non-citizen. Immigration officials may either deliver the notice by personal service or by registered mail to the non-citizen or the non-citizen's "counsel of record." INA § 239(a)(1). In practice, notice is usually served by mail. The INA requires all non-citizens to notify immigration authorities within ten days of any change of address. *See* § 8–2.2(c), *supra.* In the past, this requirement was not strictly enforced. In one case, the BIA held that mailing a Notice to Appear to a non-citizen's last known address was not effective service of process where the non-citizen had failed to report an address change and the INS knew that the Notice had not reached the intended recipient. *In re G–Y–R–*, 23 I. & N. Dec. 181, Interim Decision (BIA) 3458 (BIA 2001). After that decision, the INS began to enforce the reporting requirement more strictly and notice of the requirement is now given on most immigration forms. Consequently, mail to a non-citizen's last known address should in the future serve as sufficient service of process.

After receiving a Notice to Appear, the non-citizen must immediately give ICE his or her current address and telephone number in order to receive written notice of scheduled proceedings. INA § 239(a)(1). A non-citizen who fails to appear at a scheduled hearing will be ordered removed *in absentia* if ICE establishes by "clear, unequivocal, and convincing evidence" that the individual is removable and that ICE either provided written notice of the proceeding or was not required to do so because the non-citizen did not provide a current address. INA § 240(b)(5). A person ordered removed *in absentia* after receiving oral notice of the proceedings in a language he or she understood is ineligible for most forms of discretionary relief for ten years, unless the failure to appear was due to exceptional circumstances. INA § 240(b)(7). If the failure to appear was due to exceptional circumstances, the non-citizen may move within 180 days to reopen proceedings. Non-citizens who did not receive written notice of the hearing at their address of record or did not appear because they were in custody at the time of the hearing may move to reopen at any time. INA § 240(b)(5). The Board of Immigration Appeals endorsed the fairness of this procedure in *Matter of S-*, 7 I. & N. Dec. 529, Interim Decision (BIA) 890 (1957).

Sections 239 and 240 outline the basic requirements for the proceedings: (1) non-citizens must be given proper notice; (2) they may choose to be represented by counsel; (3) they shall have the opportunity to offer evidence in their behalf and examine evidence against them; (4) a decision to remove must be based upon "reasonable, substantial, and probative evidence." INA §§ 239(a), 240(b)(4)(A), 240 (b)(4)(B), 240(c)(3).

§ 9–2.2 Participants in the Removal Hearing

Of course, the most obvious party to the proceedings is the non-citizen, whose rights will be discussed in a following subsection. The removal hearing also involves an immigration judge, the service counsel, the non-citizen's counsel, an interpreter if necessary, and often witnesses.

a. *Immigration Judge*

In the past, the immigration judge was called an "inquiry officer," and served as investigator, prosecutor, and judge. The judicial function was separated from the investigation and prosecution functions in a 1983 reorganization. Immigration judges and the Board of Immigration

Appeals are part of the Executive Office for Immigration Review (EOIR), an office within the Department of Justice. *See* § 3–2.2, *supra.*

Immigration judges are selected by the Attorney General. The judges may conduct specified classes of proceedings, including removal hearings. INA § 101(b)(4). The INA authorizes the immigration judge to "conduct proceedings for deciding the inadmissibility or deportability [removability] of the alien, ... [to] administer oaths, receive evidence, interrogate, examine, and cross-examine the alien and any witnesses, and ... [to] decide whether an alien is removable from the United States." INA § 240. The INA allows the immigration judge to serve as both prosecutor and judge, although in practice the judge acts as a prosecutor rarely and only when the non-citizen concedes removability. The Ninth Circuit in *LeTourneur v. INS*, 538 F.2d 1368 (9th Cir.1976) has, however, held that the dual role of the immigration judge is consistent with due process.

In addition, the Code of Federal Regulations provides the immigration judge with the authority to consider claims for discretionary relief and to determine the country of removal. 8 C.F.R. §§ 1240.11, 1240.10(f). As a presiding officer in a removal hearing, the immigration judge has the authority to hear motions for postponements, to rule on the admissibility of evidence, to order the taking of depositions if a witness is not readily available and his or her testimony is essential, and to issue subpoenas. 8 C.F.R. §§ 1240.6, 1240.7, 1003.35(a), 1003.35(b). The immigration judge may not, however, exercise authority in matters exclusively under the control of the Department of Homeland Security, even if the immigration judge would otherwise have such authority, including, but not limited to, waivers of inadmissibility, Notices to Appear, and extensions of temporary stay. Finally, if the immigration judge considers him- or herself unqualified to conduct the hearing, he or she may withdraw pursuant to the provisions of 8 C.F.R. § 1240.1(b). According to the Fifth Circuit in *Marcello v. Ahrens*, 212 F.2d 830 (5th Cir.1954), one such circumstance calling for withdrawal occurs when the immigration judge performed an investigatory function in the case. The immigration judge may have performed this function if he or she was former service counsel. The non-citizen must request the judge to withdraw if he or she is unqualified or biased and if the judge refuses, the ruling may be questioned on appeal.

b. Service Counsel

ICE assigns a service counsel, who acts as "prosecutor" for the government, to the case. 8 C.F.R. § 1240.2(b). The service counsel has the authority "to present evidence, and to interrogate, examine and cross-examine the alien or other witness in the proceedings." 8 C.F.R. § 1240.2(a). The service counsel need not be a lawyer. The Board of Immigration Appeals in *Matter of Reyes–Gomez*, 14 I. & N. Dec. 258, Interim Decision (BIA) 2179 (BIA 1973) concluded that using a lay-person as service counsel does not violate due process. The service counsel may appeal a decision of the immigration judge and may move for reconsideration. 8 C.F.R. § 1240.2(a).

c. Counsel for the Non–Citizen

The INA provides that non-citizens "shall have the privilege of being represented, at no expense to the Government, by counsel of the [non-citizen's] choosing who is authorized to practice in such proceedings.'' INA § 240(b)(4). Non-citizens are informed of this right, and of the availability of pro bono legal services, several times during the removal process, including at the time of arrest, when served with the Notice to Appear, and at the outset of the removal hearing. Removal hearings may not be scheduled until at least ten days after a Notice to Appear is filed, to allow the non-citizen to obtain counsel. INA § 239(b)(1). (In practice, there is usually a much longer wait for a hearing.) The Code of Federal Regulations allows the following persons to represent non-citizens in removal proceedings: (1) attorneys who are members in good standing of the highest court of any state; (2) under certain conditions, law students and law graduates not yet admitted to the bar; (3) reputable individuals of good moral character; (4) representatives of accredited organizations recognized by the Board of Immigration Appeals; and (5) accredited officials of the government to which the non-citizen owes allegiance. 8 C.F.R. §§ 1.1(f), 292.1(1)–(5).

d. *Interpreter*

Although there is no statutory requirement for them to do so, immigration authorities will generally provide an interpreter to any non-citizen who requests one. According to the Seventh Circuit in *Niarchos v. INS*, 393 F.2d 509 (7th Cir.1968), a removal hearing conducted without the assistance of an interpreter, in a language the non-citizen does not understand, may violate due process. An interpreter in a removal case is sworn to interpret and translate accurately. 8 C.F.R. § 1240.5. Courts have held that a non-citizen's due process right to a full and fair hearing is violated if an interpreter provides an inaccurate translation, but the non-citizen has the burden of proving the interpreter's incompetence. *United States ex rel. Catalano v. Shaughnessy*, 197 F.2d 65 (2d Cir.1952). Non-citizens must show that the faulty translation prevented them from presenting relevant evidence and caused immigration officials to find that their testimony was not credible. *Perez–Lastor v. INS*, 208 F.3d 773 (9th Cir.2000). The interpreter usually interprets only direct questions or statements to the non-citizen and the non-citizen's responses; accordingly, the non-citizen may not understand additional testimony, arguments of counsel, and other matters arising in the hearing.

§ 9–2.3 The Non–Citizen's Rights During the Removal Hearing

In 1903, the Supreme Court considered the due process rights of non-citizens during removal proceedings in the *Japanese Immigrant Case*, 189 U.S. 86 (1903). That case established that non-citizens have the right to notice of charges and an opportunity to be heard. Those rights are now codified in INA § 239 *et seq.*

The INA also provides that non-citizens "shall have a reasonable opportunity to examine the evidence against [them], to present evidence in [their] own behalf, and to cross-examine witnesses presented by the Government." INA § 240(b)(4)(B). Non-citizens may present any evidence that is material and relevant either to the issue of removability or discretionary relief, including oral testimony and written depositions. If an essential witness is unavailable to testify, the non-citizen may request the immigration judge to order a deposition or may apply for a subpoena to compel the presence of a witness at the hearing. The request for a subpoena must state what the requester expects to prove by the testimony, and must affirmatively show that a diligent effort was made to produce the witness without the subpoena. 8 C.F.R. § 287.4(a)(2). The right to cross-examine includes the right to examine government witnesses whose testimony was submitted via an affidavit, but, as the Sixth Circuit concluded in *Weinbrand v. Prentis*, 4 F.2d 778 (6th Cir.1925), non-citizens must request an opportunity for cross-examination at the time the witnesses' testimony is introduced.

Non-citizens have the right to be present at and participate in their own removal hearing. As noted in § 9–2.1, *supra*, however, non-citizens who do not provide their current address to ICE or who fail to appear for a hearing after receiving written notice may be ordered removed *in absentia*. At the hearing, the non-citizen may choose either to testify or remain silent. The Supreme Court in *Hyun v. Landon*, 350 U.S. 984 (1956), however, affirmed the right of the immigration judge to draw unfavorable inferences from the non-citizen's silence. *See also Cabral–Avila v. INS*, 589 F.2d 957 (9th Cir.1978) (same holding). If necessary, the immigration judge can compel the non-citizen to testify. According to the Seventh Circuit in *Laqui v. INS*, 422 F.2d 807 (7th Cir. 1970), non-citizens in removal hearings may claim the Fifth Amendment privilege against self-incrimination only if their alleged actions constitute a crime.

Immigration judges and the Board of Immigration Appeals consider themselves unable to address the constitutionality of the statutes and regulations that they administer. They do, however, rule on questions of due process concerning the conduct of proceedings, and apply a fundamental fairness standard. At least one circuit court has ruled that non-citizens who do not raise a procedural due process claim before the BIA, waive the claim on federal review. *See Barron v. Ashcroft*, 358 F.3d 674 (9th Cir.2004).

§ 9–2.4   The Hearing

a.   Conduct of the Hearing

Removal hearings are open to the public unless the immigration judge closes the hearing in order to protect witnesses, the non-citizen, or the public interest. 8 C.F.R. § 1003.27. Closure is also authorized in cases that involve domestic abuse. In September 2001, the Chief Immigration Judge directed all immigration judges to close proceedings to the public in "special interest cases." 78 Interp.Rel. 1816. "Special interest cases" are primarily those involving non-citizens suspected of having ties to terrorism. The two Circuit Courts that have considered the issue have split on whether the First Amendment guarantees public access to such hearings. *See Detroit Free Press v. Ashcroft*, 303 F.3d 681 (6th Cir.2002); *North Jersey Media Group, Inc. v. Ashcroft*, 308 F.3d 198 (3d Cir.2002). While these cases were pending, the EOIR promulgated an interim rule permitting immigration judges to issue protective orders sealing evidence that implicates national security and to close proceedings that involve such evidence. 67 Fed.Reg. 36799–01. Non-citizens may review sealed evidence but may not reveal it outside the court on penalty of losing their right to discretionary relief.

At the outset of the hearing, the immigration judge must advise the non-citizen of his or her rights during the hearing and inquire as to whether he or she waives any of those rights, place the non-citizen under oath, read and explain the allegations of the Notice to Appear, enter the notice as an exhibit in the official record, and ask the non-citizen to plead to the allegations in the Notice to Appear. 8 C.F.R. § 1240.10(a). In a procedure analogous to pleading in the criminal context, the non-citizen must either admit or deny the allegations of the Notice to Appear. If the non-citizen admits the allegations and concedes removability, as frequently occurs, the immigration judge accepts the plea and the hearing moves forward to determine issues of discretionary relief. 8 C.F.R. § 1240.10(c). Alternatively, if the non-citizen denies the allegations, the immigration judge requests ICE to assign a service counsel and continues with both sides presenting evidence. 8 C.F.R. § 1240.10(d). Most immigration judges handle these preliminary matters at a "Master Calendar Hearing," at which they schedule a later, separate hearing on the merits of the case for those cases in which there is a tenable argument that the non-citizen is not removable or is entitled to some form of relief.

b. *Evidence*

Both the service counsel and the non-citizen are allowed to present evidence at the removal hearing. The rules of evidence applicable to criminal proceedings, however, do not apply to removal hearings. The Supreme Court in *Bilokumsky v. Tod*, 263 U.S. 149 (1923), noted that a failure to abide by judicial rules of evidence does not render a removal hearing unfair. Evidence during a removal hearing is controlled by the Code of Federal Regulations; any type of evidence is admissible so long as it is material and relevant to the issues before the hearing. 8 C.F.R. § 1240.7(a). The regulation allows hearsay evidence if it meets the test of relevance. Courts have held that hearsay evidence must also be reliable. In *Ezeagwuna v. Ashcroft*, 325 F.3d 396 (3d Cir.2003), the court found that an asylum denial based on an untrustworthy and multiple hearsay letter violated the due process rights of a non-citizen. In *Cunanan v. INS*, 856 F.2d 1373 (9th Cir.1988), the Ninth Circuit refused to admit into evidence an affidavit from the non-citizen's spouse indicating that her marriage was fraudulent. The court stated that admission of the affidavit would violate Due Process because the INS did not introduce the spouse as a witness and did not inform the non-citizen about her statement until the hearing date. Evidence may take the form of depositions and affidavits. If authenticated, tangible evidence is admissible. Either party may call witnesses to testify, and such testimony will be taken under oath or affirmation administered by the immigration judge.

c. *Ancillary Matters*

(1) ADDITIONAL CHARGES

In most cases, the Notice to Appear states all of the charges against the non-citizen. The Ninth Circuit concluded in *Madrona Banez v. Boyd*, 236 F.2d 934 (9th Cir.1956), that incorrect statements or errors in the Notice to Appear do not, however, render it invalid, if the service counsel establishes the correct information at the hearing. During the hearing, the service counsel may lodge additional charges for removal. 8 C.F.R. § 1240.10(e). The additional charges must be submitted in writing and the immigration judge must read and explain them to the non-citizen. Again, the judge must inform the non-citizen that he or she has a right to retain counsel and a right to request additional time to meet the charges. 8 C.F.R. § 1240.10(e). The Second Circuit in *United States ex rel. Catalano v. Shaughnessy*,

197 F.2d 65 (2d Cir.1952) upheld the procedure of lodging additional charges as consistent with due process.

(2) DESIGNATION OF COUNTRY AND APPLICATION FOR DISCRETIONARY RELIEF

During the hearing, the immigration judge must provide the non-citizen with an opportunity to designate a country to which he or she will be sent in the event removal is ordered. INA § 241(b)(2). This designation does not constitute an admission of removability. The immigration judge may, however, disregard the non-citizen's designation and name as an alternative country of removal any country of which the non-citizen is a subject or national in the event that the designated country does not accept the non-citizen. INA § 241(b)(2). The same section of the Immigration and Nationality Act sets up a system for determining more alternates if needed. Moreover, the Secretary of Homeland Security may disallow a country if he or she determines that removal there would be prejudicial to the interests of the United States. In *Jama v. INS*, 329 F.3d 630 (8th Cir. 2003), the court allowed Jama to be removed to Somalia even though the country had no functioning government to accept him. The Supreme Court upheld the Eighth Circuit's decision, but attempts to remove Jama to Somalia were unsuccessful and he eventually immigrated to Canada.

Non-citizens who believe that they are eligible for some form of discretionary relief must apply for it during the hearing. 8 C.F.R. § 1240.11. (The types of discretionary relief available will be more fully discussed in "Relief From Removal" § 9–4, *infra*.) Like the designation of a destination country, an application for discretionary relief is not construed as an admission of removability. The immigration judge must inform non-citizens of their apparent eligibility to apply for asylum, cancellation of removal, adjustment of status, or registry, and must allow them an opportunity to apply. The judge is not required to inform non-citizens about other types of available relief.

(3) THE DECISION

(i) Burden of Proof. The removal decision must be based on reasonable, substantial, and probative evidence. INA § 240(c)(3)(A). ICE has the burden of establishing by clear and convincing evidence that a non-citizen who has been lawfully admitted to the U.S. is removable. INA § 240(c)(3)(A). This standard is slightly less stringent than the standard announced by the Supreme Court in *Woodby v. INS*, 385 U.S. 276 (1966). In *Woodby*, the Court required proof by "clear, unequivocal, and convincing evidence." The Second Circuit held in *United States ex rel. Bishop v. Watkins*, 159 F.2d 505 (2d Cir.1947) that initially, the government has the burden of proving that the non-citizen is, indeed, a non-citizen. The burden then shifts to the non-citizen to prove, by clear and convincing evidence, that he or she is lawfully present in the U.S. pursuant to a prior admission. INA §§ 240(c)(2), 291. If lawful presence is established, the burden shifts back to ICE to prove that the non-citizen is removable.

Arriving non-citizens who are in proceedings upon arrival, or revocation or expiration of parole, must prove that they are clearly and beyond a doubt entitled to be admitted into the U.S. and are not inadmissible as charged. 8 C.F.R. § 1240.8(b). Non-citizens present in the United States without being admitted or paroled face the same burden once immigration authorities prove they are non-citizens, unless they demonstrate by clear and convincing evidence that they are lawfully in the United States pursuant to a prior admission. 8 C.F.R. § 1240.8(c).

(ii) Rendering the Decision. The decision of the immigration judge may be either written or oral and must include a finding as to inadmissibility or removability. A formal enumeration of findings is not required. 8 C.F.R. § 1240.12(a). The decision must direct either the non-citizen's removal, the termination of the proceedings, or the granting of discretionary relief. The decision may be in the alternative. 8 C.F.R. § 1240.12(c). If the decision is written, a copy must be served on the non-citizen and the service counsel. Oral decisions, however, must be made with both parties present. 8 C.F.R. § 1240.13. The decision is final unless there is an appeal. 8 C.F.R. § 1240.14. The non-citizen may appeal any decision to the Board of Immigration Appeals (except there shall be no appeal from an order of removal entered *in absentia*), but must do so within thirty days of the decision. 8 C.F.R. § 1240.15.

§ 9–2.5   The Removal Hearing for Inadmissible Non–Citizens

Although the IIRIRA consolidated the former exclusion and deportation hearings into a single removal hearing, significant differences remain between the treatment of inadmissible non-citizens and those who have been lawfully admitted. As noted above, persons charged with inadmissibility have the burden of proving their entitlement to admission beyond a reasonable doubt. Further, they are not eligible for some forms of discretionary relief.

The chief difference, however, concerns a procedure known as expedited removal, which applies to any non-citizen attempting to enter the U.S. who lacks either the documents required for admission, presents false documents, or misrepresents a material fact to obtain a visa or gain admission to the U.S. INA § 235(b)(1); 8 C.F.R. § 235.3. The same statute allows immigration authorities to impose expedited removal on non-citizens who have been present in the U.S. for less than two years after entering without inspection. Immigration officials used their expedited removal authority to remove Haitians who arrived to the United States by boat in 2002. After this incident, immigration officials issued a rule requiring the expedited removal of non-citizens who arrive to the United States by sea, have not been admitted or paroled, and have been present in the country for less than two years. 67 Fed.Reg. 68924.

In 2004, the Department of Homeland Security (DHS) greatly expanded its use of expedited removal procedures. In that year, DHS announced that it would use expedited removal for non-citizens apprehended within 100 miles of U.S. borders if they could not establish that they had been present in the U.S. for fourteen days prior to their apprehension. 69 Fed.Reg. 48877. Since this change in policy, the number of expedited removals per year has doubled and expedited removals now account for more than a third of all removals.

Under expedited removal procedures, an immigration officer may order such persons removed without further hearing or review, unless they indicate an intent to apply for asylum and have a credible fear of persecution. INA § 235(b)(1). A similar procedure applies to persons deemed inadmissible on security grounds. INA § 235(c). Expedited removal decisions may only be challenged in *habeas corpus* proceedings, in which review is limited to determining whether the petitioner (1) is an alien, (2) was ordered removed under INA § 235(b)(1), (3) can prove by a preponderance of the evidence that he or she is a lawful permanent resident, and (4) is entitled to further inquiry as to his or her status as a refugee or asylee. INA § 242(e)(2).

IIRIRA, by effectively barring judicial review of expedited removal, gave individual immigration officers tremendous unreviewed discretion to remove non-citizens and prevent them from reentering the United States for five years. The 1996 Act states that no court has jurisdiction to review (1) a decision to invoke the expedited removal provision, or (2) the application of expedited removal to specific individuals, including the determination regarding the non-citizens' "credible fear of persecution" (*see* chapter 10, *infra*), or (3) procedures and policies adopted by immigration authorities to implement the expedited removal provisions. INA § 242(a)(2)(A).

The Supreme Court has long held that persons arriving at the borders of the United States are not entitled to the due process rights afforded those individuals within the country. *See Shaughnessy v. United States ex rel. Mezei*, 345 U.S. 206 (1953). Whatever process Congress accords such persons is considered sufficient. The Court did, however, create an exception to this rule for permanent residents returning from a short trip abroad, finding that their connection to the U.S. entitles them to due process protections such as notice and a right to counsel. *Landon v. Plasencia*, 459 U.S. 21 (1982).

§ 9–2.6 Expedited Removal for Aggravated Felonies

The INA gives the Attorney General the authority to provide for special expedited removal proceedings for aggravated felons. INA § 238(a)(1). These special proceedings are to take place at the federal, state, or local correctional facility where the felon is incarcerated. INA § 238(a)(1). The initiation and completion of removal proceedings, as well as subsequent administrative appeals should be completed "to the extent possible" before the aggravated felon's release from prison. INA § 238(a)(3). The intention of allowing special expedited proceedings for aggravated felons is to have the entire removal process occur while the non-citizen is serving his or her sentence.

In addition to providing for removal hearings in correctional facilities, the INA establishes two special procedures for removing "aggravated felons." INA § 238(b) authorizes ICE to issue an administrative order of removal for any felon who is not a permanent resident. No formal hearing is required, but ICE must give the non-citizen notice and an opportunity to inspect the evidence and rebut the charges. Once an administrative removal order has been issued, the non-citizen has fourteen calendar days to apply for judicial review. INA § 238(b). The second special procedure is judicial removal. INA § 238(c) allows district court judges to enter a removal order during the sentencing phase of a felony trial. The U.S. attorney prosecuting the case must obtain the consent of ICE and notify the non-citizen before requesting such an order. INA § 238(c). The provisions for judicial removal are rarely, if ever, used.

§ 9–3   RELIEF FROM REMOVAL

§ 9–3.1   Discretionary Relief

Non-citizens in removal proceedings may apply for one or more of the available types of discretionary relief, if applicable. If granted, discretionary relief eliminates or postpones the execution of the order of removal, and in some cases even confers lawful permanent residence. Some of the forms of relief discussed in this section (*e.g.*, asylum, registry, and adjustment of status) are also available outside of removal proceedings, but are considered here only as they apply to non-citizens in removal proceedings.

Non-citizens must generally apply for discretionary relief during the removal hearing. *See* 8 C.F.R. § 1240.11. Non-citizens may apply for discretionary relief after the hearing by moving to reopen proceedings, but such a motion will only be granted if the circumstances which form the basis of the relief arose after the removal hearing. 8 C.F.R. § 1003.23(b)(v)(3). Hence, a non-citizen who believes he or she is eligible for any type of discretionary relief must apply during the removal hearing or risk being denied the opportunity to apply.

In determining whether to grant the requested relief, the immigration judge undertakes a two-step process. First, the judge determines whether the non-citizen is eligible for the particular form of relief. The non-citizen has the burden of proving that he or she meets the statutory requirements. 8 C.F.R. § 1240.8(d). Then, if the non-citizen has established eligibility, the judge has discretion to decide whether or not to grant the requested relief. The Supreme Court held in *United States ex rel. Hintopoulos v. Shaughnessy*, 353 U.S. 72 (1957), that an immigration judge may, in the exercise of discretion, deny relief even when the non-citizen satisfies the basic criteria for eligibility.

IIRIRA specifically bars judicial review of most discretionary decisions to grant or deny relief. INA

§ 242(a)(2)(B)(i). Nonetheless, courts have permitted review of such decisions in some circumstances. *See* § 9–4.3(a), *infra*.

a. Voluntary Departure

ICE officials may permit removable non-citizens to depart voluntarily from the United States at their own expense in lieu of facing removal proceedings. INA § 240B(a)(1); 8 C.F.R. § 1240.25. This form of relief is commonly called "administrative voluntary departure." In addition, immigration judges may permit a non-citizen to depart voluntarily at the non-citizen's own expense after the conclusion of or during removal proceedings. INA § 240B(a), (b). An immigration judge may only grant voluntary departure during proceedings if the non-citizen admits removability. 8 C.F.R. § 1240.26. Certain non-citizens are ineligible for voluntary departure, including those found removable under aggravated felony or terrorism grounds, and those who were previously permitted voluntary departure after being found inadmissible for being present without admission or parole. INA §§ 240B(a)(1), 240B(b)(1)(C), 240B(c).

Both versions of the voluntary departure, *i.e.*, voluntary departure in lieu of or prior to the completion of removal proceedings (INA § 240B(a)), and at the conclusion of removal proceedings (INA § 240B(b)), are strictly limited in time. A non-citizen who is granted permission to depart voluntarily in lieu of being subject to removal proceedings or during such proceedings must depart within 120 days (INA § 240B(a)(4)) and may be asked to post a bond. INA § 240B(a)(3). A non-citizen who is granted voluntary departure at the conclusion of removal proceedings must depart within sixty days (INA § 240B(b)(2)) and must post a bond. INA § 240B(b)(3).

Failure to depart, under either form of voluntary departure, results in a civil penalty, future inadmissibility for ten years, and ineligibility for several other forms of discretionary relief.

Voluntary departure is one of the most sought-after types of relief, especially when the non-citizen concedes removability. Voluntary departure avoids the stigma of removal, enables non-citizens to select their destinations, and most importantly, facilitates the possibility of return to the United States. A non-citizen granted voluntary departure is not considered removed and, consequently, is not subject to the ten-year bar on re-entry after removal. *See* § 8–1.2(d)(2), *supra*. (The bar is twenty years for persons convicted of a second immigration offense and is permanent for persons convicted of an aggravated felony.) The non-citizen will, however, still be subject to the three- or ten-year bars for unlawful presence accumulated prior to the grant of voluntary departure, but surprisingly, a person who has been present in the U.S. for between 180 days and one year and is granted voluntary departure at the commencement of removal proceedings is not subject to the three-year bar. *See* INA § 212(a)(9)(B).

In order to be eligible for voluntary departure in lieu of or during removal proceedings, the non-citizen must prove that he or she meets the statutory requirements. *Hibbert v. INS*, 554 F.2d 17 (2d Cir.1977). First, the non-citizen must demonstrate the ability to pay his or her own departure expenses. The government may, however, grant voluntary departure under § 240B(a) and pay the non-citizen's expenses if it is deemed to be in the best interest of the United States. INA § 240B(a). Second, the INA provides that no individual who is removable under aggravated felony or terrorism grounds shall be entitled to voluntary departure in lieu of removal proceedings or before the completion of removal proceedings. INA § 240B(a)(1).

The eligibility requirements for voluntary departure at the conclusion of removal proceedings are more extensive. To be entitled to voluntary departure at the conclusion of removal proceedings the non-citizen (1) must have been physically present in the U.S. for at least one year immediately before the date the notice to appear was served; (2) must have been a person of good moral character for the previous five-year period; (3) must not have been removable under aggravated felony or national security (including terrorism) grounds; and (4) must show by clear and convincing evidence that he or she has the means to depart and intends to do so. INA § 240B(b)(1).

Good moral character is a prerequisite for several forms of relief from removal. The INA defines "good moral character" in the negative, by listing actions that preclude a finding of good moral character. *See* INA § 101(f). These actions include being a habitual drunkard, being convicted of certain crimes, deriving one's income primarily from illegal gambling, and giving false testimony to receive immigration benefits. See § 12–2.2(b)(4), *infra*, for further discussion.

If the non-citizen meets the statutory requirements, he or she is eligible for voluntary departure. The final decision, however, lies with the immigration judge and is discretionary. A decision to deny relief is not subject to judicial review. INA §§ 240B(f), 242(a)(2)(B)(I). Further, the Secretary of Homeland Security may issue regulations that further limit eligibility for voluntary departure, and no court may review any such regulation. INA § 240B(e).

b. *Cancellation of Removal*

IIRIRA consolidated several earlier forms of relief from removal into one single form: cancellation of removal. INA § 240A. There are two types of cancellation of removal, one of which is available only to permanent residents, while the other is available to both permanent and "nonpermanent" residents. The first type is available to any removable non-citizen who (1) has been lawfully admitted for permanent residence for not less than five years, (2) has resided in the U.S. continuously for seven years after having been admitted in any status, and (3) has not been convicted of any "aggravated felony". INA § 240A(a). This provision roughly corresponds to a pre-IIRIRA form of relief known as "212(c) relief." While IIRIRA removed some previous bars to this form of relief, it also significantly expanded the definition of "aggravated felony" which now disqualifies a broader range of non-citizens. *See* INA § 101(a)(43). As with most forms of relief, cancellation of removal is granted or denied at the discretion of the immigration judge.

The second type of cancellation of removal corresponds with the pre-IIRIRA "suspension of deportation." INA § 240A(b) allows immigration authorities to cancel a non-citizen's removal and adjust his or her status to that of a lawful permanent resident. Although this section refers to "nonpermanent" residents, it also applies to lawful permanent residents who do not meet the requirements of § 240A(a) and to undocumented non-citizens who satisfy the residency requirements. According to the Ninth Circuit in *Fong v. INS*, 308 F.2d 191 (9th Cir. 1962), the sole purpose of cancellation of removal is to ameliorate the harsh consequences of removal for those non-citizens who have been present in the United States for long periods of time.

To be eligible for cancellation of removal under § 240A(b), the non-citizen must (1) have been physically present in the United States for a continuous period of not less than 10 years, (2) have been a person of good moral character, (3) have not been convicted of any of the crimes or document offenses that would make him or her inadmissible or removable, and (4) not be subject to any of the security grounds of inadmissibility or removability. Further, the non-citizen must show that his or her removal would result in exceptional and extremely unusual hardship to his or her citizen or lawful permanent resident spouse, parent, or child. INA § 240A(b)(1).

Congress has waived or reduced some of the requirements for cancellation of removal for persons who have been abused by a citizen or permanent resident spouse or parent. For such individuals, the physical presence requirement is reduced to three years. The non-citizen may qualify by showing that removal would cause hardship to him- or herself, instead of showing hardship to a spouse, parent, or child. The hardship requirement is the slightly lower standard of "extreme hardship," rather than "exceptional and extremely unusual hardship." INA § 240A(b).

The INA sets forth general eligibility rules that apply to both prongs of cancellation. INA § 240A(c). Non-citizens are ineligible for cancellation of removal if they are inadmissible or otherwise removable on national security grounds, fail to depart under a grant of voluntary departure, or are ordered removed after failing to appear at a removal proceedings. *See* INA § 240A(c)(1)–(6).

Again, non-citizens applying for cancellation of removal bear the burden of proving statutory eligibility. 8 C.F.R. § 1240.8(d).

INA § 240A(d) defines continuous physical presence for cancellation of removal. An absence of more than 90 days or aggregate absence of more than 180 days interrupts continuous presence. INA § 240A(d)(2). Continuous residence or continuous physical presence ends when the non-citizen commits an offense that makes him or her removable, or when he or she is served with a Notice to Appear, whichever is earlier. INA § 240A(d)(1). In contrast, permanent resident status only ends when a final removal order is entered against the non-citizen. 8 C.F.R. § 1.1. In the case of battered spouses and children, an absence in excess of the 90/180 day limits will not interrupt continuous presence if the non-citizen can show that the absence was related to the battery or cruelty.

To qualify for cancellation of removal under § 240A(b), the non-citizen must show that his or her removal would cause "exceptional and extremely unusual hardship" to a citizen or permanent resident spouse, child, or parent. INA § 240(b)(1)(D). Considering a precursor to § 240, the Supreme Court held that hardship to other relatives does not satisfy this requirement, even if the non-citizen's relationship to that relative is the "functional equivalent" of a parent-child relationship. *INS v. Hector*, 479 U.S. 85 (1986). A hardship claim must be supported by affidavit or other evidentiary material. The "exceptional and extremely unusual" hardship standard is very difficult to satisfy. The BIA has held that the claimed hardship must be substantially different from that normally expected from the removal of a non-citizen with close family in the United States. *In re Monreal–Aguina-ga*, 23 I. & N. Dec. 56, Interim Decision (BIA) 3447 (BIA 2001). In the case of *In re Andazola–Rivas*, 23 I. & N. Dec. 319, Interim Decision (BIA) 3467 (BIA 2002), the BIA found that the financial and educational detriment to a non-citizen's two citizen children did not meet this standard, even though the non-citizen's status as a single mother and her lack of family in the country to which she would be removed made her case unusual. In contrast, the BIA granted cancellation of removal in *Matter of Gonzalez Recinas*, 23 I. & N. Dec. 467, Interim Decision 3479 (BIA 2002) for a single mother of six children, four of whom were U.S. citizens who had lived their entire lives in the U.S. The BIA explained that the complete dependency of the four U.S. children on their mother's support, the inability of the children to speak Spanish, the mother's lack of family in Mexico, and the lawful presence of the mother's family in the U.S. made the burden of removal exceptional and an extremely unusual hardship. The BIA noted that its decision to grant cancellation of removal in this case represented the "outer limit" of the exceptional and extremely unusual hardship standard.

The immigration courts exercise considerable discretion in determining what constitutes an exceptional and extremely unusual hardship. *INS v. Jong Ha Wang*, 450 U.S. 139 (1981). The IIRIRA made this discretion unreviewable. INA § 242(a)(2)(B). The immigration court's discretion allows it to deny a non-citizen's motion to reopen a case for the purpose of requesting cancellation of removal, even if the non-citizen can show that intervening circumstances have given rise to prima facie eligibility for relief. *INS v. Rios–Pineda*, 471 U.S. 444 (1985); *INS v. Abudu*, 485 U.S. 94 (1988). In *Rios–Pineda,* the only change in circumstances was the passage of enough time for the petitioner to meet the seven-year residence requirement. The Court reasoned that the immigration courts can "legitimately avoid creating a further incentive for stalling by refusing to reopen [cancellation of removal] proceedings for those who became eligible for such [cancellation] only because of the passage of time while their meritless appeals dragged on." INA § 240A now stops the accumulation of time in residence when a Notice to Appear is served. INA § 240A(d).

When an immigration judge grants adjustment to permanent resident status based on cancellation of removal, the non-citizen is admitted to the United States as a permanent resident as of the date of the cancellation of removal or adjustment of status. INA § 240A(b)(3). The number of adjustments to permanent resident status based on such cancellations is limited to 4,000 per year. *Id.* The annual limitation upon adjustments evoked considerable debate when in February 1997, seven months before the end of the fiscal year, the INS had almost reached the 4,000 annual cap on adjustments. The Office of the Chief Immigration Judge instructed immigration judges to reserve decisions in any case in which cancellation applications might otherwise be granted until a resolution could be reached within the Department of Justice. The demand for cancellation of removal was reduced in 1997 when the President signed the Nicaraguan Adjustment and Central American Relief Act (NACARA) which removed certain Cubans and Nicaraguans from the statutory cap, along with some Salvadorans, Guatemalans, and Eastern Europeans.

Current regulations authorize judges to reserve decisions on requests for cancellation made after the annual cap has been reached. *See* 8 C.F.R. § 1240.21(c). The immigration judge may deny cancellation of removal if the applicant does not meet the statutory requirements or if the applicant instead qualifies for asylum or adjustment of status. Otherwise, the judge must decide whether to grant the application or deny it as a matter of discretion, but may not release the decision until the start of the next fiscal year, when additional grants are available.

c.   Section 212(c) Relief

Before the AEDPA and IIRIRA amendments, INA § 212(c) granted relief to lawful permanent residents who had resided in the U.S. for at least seven years. This form of relief was available even to those who had committed crimes that made them removable. Many permanent residents who committed crimes entered plea bargains with the expectation that they could use this provision to avoid removal. With IIRIRA, this statute was repealed even for those whose convictions predated IIRIRA. In *INS v. St. Cyr*, 533 U.S. 289 (2001), the Court ordered the INS to allow persons who entered plea agreements prior to April 1997, to apply for § 212(c) relief. The Court found that Congress had not clearly indicated an intent for the AEDPA amendments to apply retroactively to removal proceedings commenced before that statute's enactment. Further, the Court found that applying the new rules to persons who entered plea agreements while § 212(c) was still in effect could create a constitutional problem by attaching unexpected consequences to criminal conduct.

The circuit courts have since limited the applicability of *St. Cyr*. In *Chambers v. Reno*, 307 F.3d 284 (4th Cir.2002), the Fourth Circuit found that a non-citizen who was deported after being convicted of armed robbery at trial while § 212(c) was still in effect was not entitled to this form of relief because he had not relied on the availability of relief in deciding to go to trial rather than to plead guilty. Applying similar reasoning, the Ninth Circuit in *United States v. Velasco–Medina*, 305 F.3d 839 (9th Cir.2002), found that a non-citizen who had been ordered removed several years after pleading guilty to burglary was not entitled to § 212(c) relief because he was not removable at the time he pleaded guilty. Velasco–Medina only became removable after IIRIRA changed the definition of aggravated felony to include his crime. Since he was not removable at the time of his guilty plea, the court found that he had not relied on the availability of relief in pleading guilty.

Under 8 C.F.R. § 1003 (*see* 69 Fed.Reg. 73437), lawful permanent residents with at least seven years residence in the United States who pleaded guilty to crimes before April 1, 1997, may apply for § 212(c) relief. Relief is barred, however, if the non-citizen is subject to removal on national security grounds, is unlawfully present in the United States after a previous immigration violation, was convicted of a firearms offense, or served five or more years for an aggravated felony offense. The rule gave non-citizens with a final removal order 180 days after publication (Dec. 13, 2004) of the final rule to apply for relief.

d.   *Adjustment of Status*

Still another type of discretionary relief for which most eligible non-citizens may apply during removal proceedings is adjustment of status. Adjustment relieves persons who are eligible for permanent residence from the hardship and expense of going abroad and enduring the long wait for an immigrant petition to be processed. The INA permits immigration authorities to adjust an eligible non-citizen's status to that of a lawful permanent resident if an immigrant visa is immediately available to him or her at the time his or her application is filed. INA § 245(a).

Two provisions of the INA substantially limit the availability of adjustment of status as a means of avoiding removal. With the exception of those married to U.S. citizens or victims of domestic violence, § 245(c) requires non-citizens applying for adjustment of status to have maintained legal immigration status since admission to the U.S. and to be in status on the date of filing the application. Consequently, most non-citizens who accept unauthorized employment prior to filing an application for adjustment of status are statutorily ineligible to adjust their status. INA § 245(c). Section 245(k), however, exempts non-citizens adjusting status with an employment-based immigration petition from this requirement if they have not accumulated more than 180 days of unauthorized presence. Section 245(e) makes a non-citizen seeking an immigrant visa on the basis of a marriage entered into during removal proceedings ineligible for adjustment of status unless he or she can show the marriage was entered in good faith. INA § 245(e).

In order to be eligible for adjustment of status, non-citizens must show that they meet the statutory requirements. First, they must show that they have been inspected and admitted into the United States. Hence, according to the BIA in *Matter of Woo*, 11 I. & N. Dec. 706, Interim Decision (BIA) 1613 (BIA 1966), non-citizens who enter illegally or on the basis of a willfully false claim of United States citizenship may not adjust their status. Second, applicants must show that they are eligible for a permanent resident visa. Since non-citizens applying for adjustment of status are considered to be seeking admission, they must not be inadmissible under any of the categories of INA § 212(a). Third, and most importantly, each applicant must show that there is an immigrant visa immediately available to him or her at the time the application is filed. INA § 245(a). After IIRIRA, adjustment of status is one of the remedies unavailable for ten years to those non-citizens who fail to comply with the terms of their voluntary departure orders. INA §§ 240(b)(7), 240B(D).

Non-citizens who have stayed in the U.S. after the expiration of their immigration status ("overstays") and persons who entered without being admitted have limited options to adjust status. Overstays still may adjust status if they have a U.S. citizen spouse. Both overstays and undocumented individuals were previously able, however, upon the payment of $1,000, to apply for the adjustment of status to that of a lawful permanent resident, if an immigrant visa was available and no other bar applied. INA § 245(i). Section 245(i), which allowed overstays and entrants without inspection to avoid inadmissibility bars, expired on April 30, 2001, and has not yet been renewed by Congress. Those non-citizens who had an immigration petition filed on or before the date the provision expired are, however, still eligible to adjust status under § 245(i).

e. *Asylum*

Unlike cancellation of removal or adjustment of status, asylum does not guarantee a non-citizen permanent residence in the United States. *See* chapter 10, *infra*. Asylum is the granting of indefinite status, and the right to work in the United States for the period of time that the non-citizen is entitled to asylee status. According to the INA, "any alien physically present in the United States or who arrives in the United States, irrespective of such alien's status, may apply for asylum. . . ." INA § 208(a). Hence, a non-citizen may apply for asylum as a form of discretionary relief during a removal hearing, and may be granted asylum so long as he or she meets the requirements of refugee status. The INA defines "refugee" to mean "any person who is outside any country of such person's nationality . . . and who is unable or unwilling to return to, and is unable or unwilling to avail himself or herself of the protection of, that country because of persecution or a well-founded fear of persecution on account of race, religion, nationality, membership in a particular social group, or political opinion. . . ." INA § 101(a)(42)(A). Asylum is not available, however, to persons who have participated in persecution of others, those who have committed particularly serious crimes, and those who present a danger to the United States. INA § 208(b)(2).

Non-citizens must apply for asylum within one year of entering the United States, unless they can demonstrate the existence of changed circumstances that materially affect their eligibility for asylum or extraordinary circumstances relating to the delay in filing the application. INA § 208(a)(2). The non-citizen and the service counsel present evidence relating to the request for asylum. If the immigration judge grants the requested asylum, the non-citizen is admitted indefinitely. The non-citizen's asylum status may be terminated, however, if circumstances change such that he or she is no longer a "refugee" under the provisions of the INA. INA § 208(c)(2).

See § 10–2.4, *infra* (discussing asylum procedure, termination, and eligibility to adjust status).

f. Stay of Removal

Non-citizens may apply for a stay of a final order of removal by submitting Form I–246 to the CIS office in their district. Such a stay is temporary and is granted at the discretion of the CIS district director. Since the mere filing of a motion to reopen does not automatically stay removal, the regulations authorize non-citizens to couple a motion to reopen with a request for a stay to permit a decision on the motion. 8 C.F.R. § 1003.6. Although a stay of removal is commonly used in connection with a motion to reopen or reconsider, or when a non-citizen is appealing an order of removal to a federal court, non-citizens under removal orders may also move for a stay pending an application for permanent residence and in other exceptional circumstances. A pending application for immigration status, however, does not entitle a non-citizen to a stay of removal; instead, the stay remains a discretionary matter. *Armstrong v. INS*, 445 F.2d 1395 (9th Cir.1971). If granted, the CIS district director may impose such conditions as he or she decides are appropriate and must set a specific time limit for the stay. An application for a stay does not relieve the applicant from strict compliance with an outstanding order of removal. *Id.* The district director's decision on the application is not appealable, although the non-citizen may renew the application before the BIA. *Id.*

g. Parole

When a non-citizen seeking admission to the U.S. is not clearly qualified for admission, the inspecting immigration officer may elect to release the non-citizen on parole pending further investigation. 8 C.F.R. § 235.2. Immigration authorities may also grant parole for humanitarian reasons or reasons of public interest. INA § 212(d)(5). Parole allows a non-citizen to travel within the United States while remaining entitled in most cases to the same procedural rights in removal proceedings as a person who is just arriving at a U.S. border. A person who is paroled into the country is not officially "admitted" and is generally not entitled to the greater procedural rights in a later removal proceeding of a person who has been inspected and accepted.

In the past, parole was sometimes granted to groups of non-citizens *en masse*, as an alternative to asylum or as a relief analogous to temporary protected status. IIRIRA ended this practice by requiring each parole decision to be rendered on a case-by-case basis. INA § 212(d)(5)(A).

The concept of parole has been extended to include "advance parole" where a non-citizen in the U.S. who wishes to leave, but who will not possess a status entitling him or her to re-admission, may be issued advance parole before departing, thus ensuring a successful return to the U.S. Advance parole is most commonly granted to persons with pending applications for adjustment of status. Advance parole does not remove any applicable grounds of inadmissibility apart from the lack of a valid immigration visa. Consequently, a non-citizen who departs from the U.S. after committing a crime that constitutes a ground of inadmissibility, or who has accumulated more than 180 days of unlawful presence in the U.S., may still be detained at the border as an inadmissible non-citizen. *See Balogun v. Attorney General*, 304 F.3d 1303 (11th Cir.2002). To overcome this problem, the non-citizen must apply for a visa at a consulate outside the

United States and request a waiver of inadmissibility. 72 Interp.Rel. 1842. Any pending adjustment of status application, however, may be invalidated.

h. Registry

Registry is available to non-citizens who entered the United States prior to January 1, 1972. Registry creates a record of lawful admission for permanent residence when such a record is not otherwise available (usually because the non-citizen entered the U.S. without inspection). INA § 249. In addition to proving that he or she entered prior to the specified date, the non-citizen must also show that he or she has been a continuous resident of the United States, is a person of good moral character, and is otherwise eligible for citizenship. *Id.* The sole and limited purpose of registry is to ameliorate the harsh consequences of removal for those persons who have been long-term residents of the United States. AEDPA amended § 249(d) to make a non-citizen "who has engaged, is engaged, or at any time after admission engages in any terrorist activity" ineligible for registry. INA § 249(d). Further, according to IIRIRA, non-citizens who have failed to appear at their removal hearings or to comply with their voluntary departure orders are ineligible for registry for ten years. INA §§ 240(b)(7), 240(B)(D).

§ 9–3.2 Other Forms of Relief

a. Restriction on Removal

A form of relief related to asylum is the relief identified by INA § 241(b)(3)(A) as "restriction on removal." Unlike asylum, which is granted only at the CIS' discretion, restriction on removal *must* be granted to anyone who qualifies for it. *Matter of McMullen*, 17 I. & N. Dec. 542, Interim Decision (BIA) 2831 (BIA 1980). The INA provides that a non-citizen may not be removed to a country if his or her "life or freedom would be threatened in that country because of the alien's race, religion, nationality, membership in a particular social group, or political opinion." INA § 241(b)(3)(A). This relief was previously known as "withholding of deportation" and immigration officials and lawyers often continue to use the phrase "withholding of removal" for this relief.

Although the criteria for restriction on removal are similar to the grounds for asylum, there are a few significant differences between the two forms of relief. Most importantly, restriction on removal is non-discretionary. Another difference is that restriction on removal only prevents removal to the country where the non-citizen would be in danger and does not prevent removal to a third country. *See also* § 10–2.1, *infra*. In practice, however, non-citizens who are granted restriction on removal are almost never removed from the U.S. The Supreme Court held in *INS v. Stevic*, 467 U.S. 407 (1984) that a non-citizen seeking to avoid removal pursuant to this section of the INA must establish a clear probability of persecution. This is a higher standard of proof than the "well-founded" fear required to claim asylum. Asylum leads within one year to permanent residence; restriction on removal, however, only grants the non-citizen temporary residence in the United States and only for so long as the non-citizen's life or freedom is threatened. An application for asylum is automatically construed as a concurrent application for restriction on removal; if the request for asylum is denied, the immigration judge must consider whether the applicant is instead entitled to restriction on removal. 8 C.F.R. § 208.3(b).

Certain non-citizens are ineligible for the relief of "restriction on removal": those applicants who (1) assisted in Nazi persecution or engaged in genocide; (2) assisted in the persecution of an individual because of the individual's race, religion, nationality, membership in a particular social group, or political opinion; (3) are a danger to the community of the U.S., having been convicted by a final judgment of a particularly serious crime; (4) committed a serious nonpolitical crime before entering the U.S.; or (5) otherwise represent a threat to the national security. INA § 241(b)(3)(B).

The BIA previously held that a non-citizen under exclusion proceedings could not apply for restriction on removal because he or she was not "within the United States" as required by the previous wording of the Act. *Matter of Cenatice*, 16 I. & N. Dec. 162, Interim Decision (BIA) 2571 (BIA 1977). INA § 241(b)(3) now allows arriving aliens to apply for restriction on removal as a relief from removal for inadmissibility.

b. *Temporary Protected Status (TPS)*

INA § 244 authorizes the Secretary of Homeland Security to provide temporary protection to nationals of countries experiencing civil upheaval or natural disasters. The Secretary may designate a country for TPS in case of ongoing war or armed conflict, natural disaster, or other extraordinary conditions that prevent the safe return of that country's nationals. INA § 244(b)(1). Nationals of a designated country must then apply to the CIS individually for TPS. If an individual in removal proceedings is eligible for TPS, the immigration judge will close the case and direct the individual to apply for TPS. If the CIS grants the relief, this status protects such individuals from removal until the Secretary of Homeland Security ends that country's designation.

Unlike asylum, TPS does not lead to lawful permanent residence. It does, however, confer lawful nonimmigrant status on individuals to whom it is granted. Persons granted TPS may change to another nonimmigrant classification or adjust to permanent residence status if they qualify on some other ground (such as marriage to a U.S. citizen). See §§ 10–2.4, 10–2.5, *infra*, for further discussion.

c. Other

There are a few other forms of relief available. Many are discussed elsewhere in this Nutshell. For a discussion on the Convention Against Torture, see §§ 10–2.2, 14–3.4, *infra*. NACARA relief is discussed in § 10–2.6, *infra*. The LIFE Act of 2000, providing relief to further family unity and creating the V nonimmigrant visa is discussed in §§ 5–5.4, 6–22, *supra*. Relief may also be sought through private legislation. See § 4–3, *supra*. Other forms of relief that may be available include amnesty, deferred action, and deferred enforced departure.

§ 9–3.3 Estoppel

Although not a form of relief, estoppel may be used in the context of removal. Occasionally, the conduct of the United States government is a substantial cause of a non-citizen's removability, such as when a non-citizen relies on false information given by a government employee. In these cases the courts have been quite reluctant to estop the government from removing the non-citizen. Despite opportunities to do so, however, the

Supreme Court has not completely ruled out the doctrine of estoppel in removal cases. In holding that a lengthy delay on the part of the INS in processing the non-citizen's adjustment of status application falls short of affirmative misconduct in *INS v. Miranda*, 459 U.S. 14 (1982), the Court was not required to reach the question of whether affirmative misconduct in a particular case would estop the government from enforcing the immigration laws.

Similarly, in most cases where the estoppel issue has been addressed by a lower court the decision has turned on whether affirmative misconduct occurred. The courts usually have held that there was no affirmative misconduct and therefore no estoppel was appropriate. *See Moosa v. INS*, 171 F.3d 994 (5th Cir.1999). A few lower courts, however, have held the government was estopped from removing a non-citizen as a result of the government's affirmative misconduct. In *McLeod v. Peterson*, 283 F.2d 180 (3d Cir.1960), the non-citizen would have complied with the continuous presence requirement for cancellation of removal had the INS not erroneously informed him that he was ineligible for nonquota status and advised him that his voluntary departure from the United States would aid his wife in making the necessary application for his legal re-entry. The Third Circuit ignored the non-citizen's departure and held that he had complied with the requirement of five years presence. In *Corniel–Rodriguez v. INS*, 532 F.2d 301 (2d Cir.1976), U.S. consular officers in the Dominican Republic violated 22 C.F.R. § 42.122(d), by failing to warn a non-citizen who was issued a visa as the unmarried minor child of a special immigrant that she would forfeit her exemption from the labor certification requirement for entry if she married before admission to the United States. This violation of a regulation by the consular officers precluded removal of the non-citizen despite her marriage three days before her departure from the Dominican Republic.

The estoppel doctrine also has been addressed in immigration cases outside the removal context. *See, e.g.*, *Montana v. Kennedy*, 366 U.S. 308 (1961) (refusal of a U.S. consular officer to issue a passport to a pregnant U.S. citizen to enable her to re-enter the U.S., at a time when the U.S. did not require passports for citizens to return to the U.S., was not misconduct such that the government was estopped from denying the child's U.S. citizenship when born abroad); *INS v. Hibi*, 414 U.S. 5 (1973) (the government's failure after World War II to publicize fully the statutory right of Filipino servicemen to apply for naturalization and to provide a naturalization representative in the Philippines at all times during the period of eligibility did not rise to the level of affirmative misconduct); *INS v. Pangilinan*, 486 U.S. 875 (1988) (Supreme Court rejected applicability of estoppel doctrine to claims about the same situation in the Philippines as in *Hibi*); *Podea v. Acheson*, 179 F.2d 306 (2d Cir.1950) (individual born in the U.S. did not lose his U.S. citizenship by serving in a foreign army and swearing allegiance to a foreign sovereign after an erroneous State Department ruling that the alien had already lost his U.S. citizenship because of certain prior acts).

§ 9–4 APPEALS

The INA provides for administrative appeals from decisions of an immigration judge, and, in limited cases, for judicial review of administrative orders. The IIRIRA significantly restricted both the circumstances in which judicial review is available and the scope of such review.

§ 9–4.1   Motion to Reopen or Reconsider

A non-citizen may move to reopen or to reconsider the decision of the immigration judge by submitting Form I–328 or the judge may do so on his or her own motion. 8 C.F.R. § 1003.23(b)(ii). A motion to reopen is based on the existence of material facts that were not available at the time of the removal hearing. INA § 240(c)(7). The motion must state the new facts and provide evidence to support them. 8 C.F.R. § 1003.23. A motion to reconsider is based on errors of law or fact in the removal order. INA § 240(c)(6).

Non-citizens have thirty days after a final administrative order of removal to file a motion to reconsider. INA § 240(c)(6). The deadline for filing a motion to reopen is ninety days after a final administrative order of removal. INA § 240(c)(7). There is no time limit on filing a motion to reopen if the motion is based on a request for asylum due to changed country conditions or if the basis of the motion is to apply for relief as a battered spouse or child. INA § 240(c)(7).

A motion to reopen for the purpose of providing the non-citizen an opportunity to apply for discretionary relief that was available during the hearing will be denied unless the non-citizen's right to make the application was not fully explained at the time of the hearing. 8 C.F.R. § 1003.23. The immigration judge may also deny the motion if the non-citizen has not established a prima facie case for the underlying substantive relief sought. *INS v. Abudu*, 485 U.S. 94 (1988). Likewise, in regard to a belated application for asylum, the judge may hold that the non-citizen has not reasonably explained his or her failure to apply for asylum prior to completion of the initial removal proceedings, as required by 8 C.F.R.

§ 208.4. *Abudu*. Furthermore, in cases requesting discretionary relief (asylum, cancellation of removal, and adjustment of status, but not withholding of removal), the judge may ignore the above concerns and simply decide that even if the application were properly asserted, the non-citizen is not entitled to the discretionary relief. *Id.* The appropriate standard of review of such denials on any of these grounds is abuse of discretion. The Court in *Abudu* stressed that motions to reopen are disfavored in removal proceedings because "[g]ranting such motions too freely will permit endless delay of deportation by aliens creative and fertile enough to continuously produce new and material facts sufficient to establish a prima facie case." *Id.*

Filing a motion to reconsider or reopen will not automatically stay the execution of a pending removal order. The non-citizen must therefore request a stay of removal when filing such a motion.

§ 9–4.2 Administrative Appeals

An appeal taken from a removal hearing is heard by the Board of Immigration Appeals (BIA). 8 C.F.R. § 1003.1(b)(2). The BIA is supervised by the Department of Justice and its members are appointed by the Attorney General. 8 C.F.R. § 1003.1(a)(1). The BIA has jurisdiction over appeals from immigration judges' decisions concerning discretionary relief; administrative fines; petitions for immigrant status; bond, parole, or detention of non-citizens; rescission of an adjustment of status; asylum; and Temporary Protected Status. 8 C.F.R. § 1003.1(b).

For many years, the BIA heard all cases in three-member panels. Although the size of the board was incrementally increased from twelve positions in 1995 to twenty-three in 2002, it faced an increasing backlog of cases. A 1999 rule attempted to reduce this backlog by permitting individual Board members to affirm immigration judges' rulings summarily in certain circumstances. 64 Fed.Reg. 56135–01. In 2002, Attorney General John Ashcroft reduced the Board to eleven members and restructured the appeals process in an attempt to eliminate the backlog. 67 Fed.Reg. 54878–01. The 2002 rule made single-member review the standard operating procedure, with panel review reserved for cases that present novel or complex issues. Further reforms in 2006 increased the number of board numbers to 15 and sought to decrease the number of affirmances without opinions. Proposed regulations would also require more three-member panel reviews. *En banc* review is available for cases of particular importance. 8 C.F.R. § 3.1(a)(5). *See also* § 3–3.2, *supra* (discussing affirmance without opinion).

The powers conferred on the Board by the Attorney General include the right to dismiss summarily any appeal from removal proceedings if the party fails to substantiate the basis for the appeal. 8 C.F.R. § 1003.1(d)(2). The Board may also dispose of a case by remanding it to the immigration judge for additional factual development, or in rare cases, by referring the case to the Attorney General for a decision. 8 C.F.R. § 1003.1(d), (h). Any decision made by the Board is administratively final, although non-citizens may seek judicial review in some circumstances (*see* § 9–4.3, *infra*). 8 C.F.R. § 1003.1(d)(2). The Board bases its decisions on the record of the removal hearing, briefs submitted by counsel, and oral argument. 8 C.F.R. §§ 1003.1(e), 1003.3(c), 1003.5. Oral arguments are heard only if requested by the petitioner. 8 C.F.R. § 1003.1(e). The BIA formerly reviewed both issues of fact and law *de novo*, but the 2002 rule that reorganized the Board also provided that immigration judges' findings of fact could only be reversed if clearly erroneous. 67 Fed.Reg. 54878–01.

Execution of a removal order is automatically stayed during any appeal to the BIA. 8 C.F.R. § 1003.6. To prevent abuse of this provision, INS regulations provide for sanctions against attorneys who file frivolous appeals. 8 C.F.R. § 1003.1(d)(iii).

§ 9–4.3 Judicial Review of Removal Orders

The INA authorizes the courts to take jurisdiction over certain decisions appealed from the BIA. *See* INA § 242. While the IIRIRA severely restricted the availability and scope of judicial review, the courts have interpreted these restrictions narrowly, thus retaining some power to review removal decisions.

a. *Limitations on Judicial Review*

The IIRIRA eliminated review of many immigration decisions, including denials of discretionary relief, removal orders based on criminal offenses, and custody determinations. INA § 242. The circuit courts have, however, engaged in limited review of some "unreviewable" removal decisions for the purpose of determining whether they have jurisdiction. *See, e.g.*, *Guerrero–Perez v. INS*, 242 F.3d 727 (7th Cir.2001). For example, although the court is barred from reviewing a removal order based on an aggravated felony conviction, it may independently determine whether the underlying crime was an aggravated felony.

The IIRIRA also prohibited judicial review of any decision by the Attorney General to "commence proceedings, adjudicate cases, or execute removal orders." INA § 242(g). The Supreme Court construed § 242(g) narrowly as prohibiting review only of those three discretionary actions. *Reno v. American–Arab Anti–Discrimination Committee*, 525 U.S. 471 (1999). Section 242(g) would not, therefore, preclude review of other decisions during the removal process, such as the decision to open an investigation, reschedule a hearing, or refuse reconsideration of an order.

In addition to limiting the availability of judicial review, the IIRIRA limited the scope of such review. The court of appeals must decide the petition on the basis of the administrative record and may not take any new evidence. INA § 242(b)(4)(A). Further, administrative findings of fact are conclusive unless any reasonable adjudicator would be compelled to conclude otherwise. INA § 242(b)(4)(B). Immigration court decisions denying asylum or finding a non-citizen inadmissible are also conclusive unless manifestly contrary to law. INA § 242(b)(4)(C), (D).

b. Habeas Corpus Proceedings

Prior to 1996, the INA specifically granted non-citizens held in custody the right to challenge their removal through *habeas corpus* proceedings. INA § 106(a)(10). The AEDPA repealed this provision. Then the IIRIRA added INA § 242(b)(9), described as a "zipper clause," which states that no judicial review of removal decisions is available except as provided under § 242. These amendments called into question the continuing availability of *habeas corpus* for non-citizens. In *INS v. St. Cyr*, 533 U.S. 289 (2001), the Supreme Court found that non-citizens subject to removal were still entitled to bring a *habeas corpus* action under 28 U.S.C.A. § 2241.

The Court found that Congress had not indicated a clear intent to eliminate all *habeas* jurisdiction. *Id.* Further, the Court determined that a reading of the INA that precluded *habeas corpus* review would raise a constitutional issue in the case of criminal non-citizens, who have no other means to challenge their removal. *Id.* Congress responded to the Supreme Court's decision in *St. Cyr* through the REAL ID Act, 119 Stat. 231. The REAL ID Act explicitly eliminated *habeas* jurisdiction but preserved judicial review of removal decisions in the courts of appeals as a substitute for *habeas corpus* review. *See* INA § 242(a)(5).

Prior to the REAL ID Act, *habeas corpus* review was limited to claims of constitutional or statutory error and a non-citizen could not use such proceedings to challenge the immigration judge's exercise of discretion. *Gutierrez–Chavez v. INS*, 298 F.3d 824 (9th Cir.2002). Under the scheme established by the REAL ID Act, courts of appeals may review the decisions of immigration officials that raise "constitutional claims or questions of law." INA § 242(a)(2)(D). Courts have interpreted the REAL ID Act as allowing for the review of the same types of issues that courts traditionally considered in *habeas corpus* proceedings. *Chen v. Gonzales*, 162 Fed.Appx. 37 (2d Cir.2006). Accordingly, under INA § 242(a) courts of appeals may review removal decisions for errors of law and erroneous application or interpretation of statutes. *Id.*

The REAL ID Act preserved *habeas corpus* review for inadmissible non-citizens, and *habeas corpus* is the only available means for inadmissible non-citizens to challenge a removal order. The scope of such proceedings is limited to determining whether the petitioner is an alien, whether the petitioner was subject to expedited removal, and whether he or she is a permanent resident, refugee, or asylee. INA § 242(e). The non-citizen may not use *habeas corpus* to challenge CBP's finding that he or she is inadmissible. *Brumme v. INS*, 275 F.3d 443 (5th Cir.2001).

c. *Procedural Requirements*

Appeals may only be taken from a final order of removal. INA § 242(a)(1). Further, the INA authorizes judicial review only after the non-citizen has exhausted all available administrative remedies. INA § 242(d)(1). A federal court may review a final administrative order of removal only if another federal court has not decided the validity of the administrative order, unless the petition for review presents grounds that could not have been presented in the earlier proceeding or the remedy provided in that proceeding was inadequate or ineffective to test the validity of the administrative order. INA § 242(d)(2).

The INA sets forth specific requirements for granting a petition for review. Non-citizens have thirty days after an administratively final order of removal to file a petition for review with the Court of Appeals for the circuit in which the removal hearing was conducted. INA § 242(b)(1). In *Foti v. INS*, 375 U.S. 217 (1963), the Supreme Court noted that a fundamental purpose behind the petition procedure is to prevent delaying tactics by those subject to removal. The petition does not automatically stay removal. INA § 242(b)(3)(b). On a petition for review, the court may consider both the finding of removability and the denial of any motion to reopen.

Certain immigration decisions made outside the context of removal proceedings are not subject to review. *See Cheng Fan Kwok v. INS*, 392 U.S. 206 (1968). Kwok sought review of an INS district director's denial of relief from removal, but the Court found that it lacked jurisdiction because the director's decision was made after Kwok had been ordered removed in proceedings.

Judicial review is available, however, to challenge the constitutionality of immigration procedures other than removal hearings. *INS v. Chadha*, 462 U.S. 919 (1983). Chadha, a non-citizen who had been ordered removed, challenged the House of Representatives' authority to veto an immigration judge's suspension of deportation (now a form of cancellation of removal). Congress argued that the one-House veto authorized by the INA was not a removal proceeding and that the Court of Appeals therefore lacked jurisdiction to review its constitutionality. The Court interpreted the term "final order" to encompass all matters "on which the validity of the final order is contingent, rather than only those determinations actually made at the hearing." Because Chadha's removal was contingent upon the validity of the challenged veto and because Chadha was directly attacking the removal order, the Court of Appeals had jurisdiction.

In *Mohammadi–Motlagh v. INS*, 727 F.2d 1450 (9th Cir.1984), the Ninth Circuit confirmed that the *Chadha* decision did not signify a retreat from the narrow construction of § 242 (former INA § 106) adopted in *Cheng Fan Kwok*. The Court of Appeals in *Mohammadi–Motlagh* found no jurisdiction to review the denial of the non-citizen's request for a school transfer because, in contrast to the purely legal question presented in *Chadha*, the non-citizen's challenge of the district director's decision raised factual questions as to whether discretion was properly exercised.

Courts may permit an exception to the requirement of exhausting all administrative remedies if an administrative appeal would be futile because the BIA is absolutely bound by immigration regulations and could not help but render the same decision as the immigration court. *See Bak v. INS*, 682 F.2d 441 (3d Cir.1982). The plaintiffs in *Bak* sought review of an immigration judge's decision not to reopen proceedings and permit them to apply for asylum. They did not appeal the decision to the BIA, claiming that it would be bound by immigration regulations to reach the same decision. In their case, the court found that the BIA had discretion to overturn the judge's decision and denied the appeal. Another potential exception to the exhaustion requirement is an allegation of "a wholesale, carefully orchestrated program of constitutional violations." *Haitian Refugee Ctr. v. Smith*, 676 F.2d 1023 (5th Cir.1982). In *Haitian Refugee Center,* 4,000 Haitians claimed they had been denied due process and equal protection by accelerated removal procedures instituted to achieve the mass removal of Haitian nationals seeking political asylum in the United States. The Fifth Circuit decided that a pattern or scheme by immigration officials to violate the constitutional rights of non-citizens is independently reviewable in the district court under its federal question jurisdiction. The court, however, stressed the uniqueness of the case in warning that its holding was not to be construed as permitting a constitutional challenge in the district court based on a procedural ruling in a removal case with which a non-citizen is dissatisfied.

§ 9–5   POST–REMOVAL DETENTION

When a non-citizen is ordered removed, the INA provides that immigration officials "must" remove the individual from the United States within a ninety-day removal period. The removal period begins when the removal order becomes administratively final, when a reviewing court confirms the order, or when the non-citizen is released from detention after serving a criminal sentence. INA § 212(a). Persons who have been ordered removed are required by statute to comply with CBP efforts to achieve their repatriation and can be subject to criminal penalties for willful failure to do so. INA § 243(b). If ICE is not able to remove a non-citizen within ninety days, it may grant the non-citizen supervised release. INA § 241(a)(3).

In some cases, it may be nearly impossible to effect a non-citizen's removal. Some countries do not accept the return of their nationals from the United States. Other countries may delay issuing or refuse to issue required travel documents. Some removable non-citizens are stateless, and as a consequence no country will accept them. In such cases, a non-citizen could theoretically remain in detention indefinitely. The Supreme Court, in *Zadvydas v. Davis*, 533 U.S. 678 (2001), found that indefinitely detaining non-citizens who had entered the United States would potentially violate their due process rights. To avoid the constitutional problem, the Court read into the INA a presumptive six-month limit on detention, after which non-citizens must be released if their removal does not appear likely in the reasonably foreseeable future. *Zadvydas v. Davis*, *supra*. In *Clark v. Martinez*, 543 U.S. 371 (2005), the Supreme Court held that the presumptive six-month limit on detention established in *Zadvydas* applies to the detentions of removable criminal aliens and inadmissible non-citizens.

After *Zadvydas* and *Clark*, the Attorney General promulgated regulations requiring immigration officials to grant a hearing to any removable or inadmissible non-citizen who has been detained for six months or more. Such non-citizens are entitled to supervised release unless they have a highly contagious disease, their release would be adverse to U.S. foreign policy, they were removed on national security grounds or present a threat to national security, or they are determined to be especially dangerous. 8 C.F.R. § 241.4. In these hearings, the non-citizens have the burden of showing that they have complied with efforts to execute the removal order and that there is no significant likelihood of removal in the reasonably foreseeable future. 8 C.F.R. § 241.13.

CHAPTER 10

REFUGEES AND ASYLUM

The United States has a long-standing commitment to the protection of victims or potential victims of serious human rights violations who have fled their country. Refugee or asylum status, along with occasional lotteries (*see* chapters 1 and 5, *supra*), constitute the only significant avenues for immigrating to the United States for individuals without family ties or without employment or investment opportunities in the U.S. The United States will only grant individuals refugee or asylum status if they have suffered past persecution or have a well-founded fear of persecution in their home countries. To be eligible for either refugee or asylum status, the applicant must qualify as a refugee, under the definition in INA § 101(a)(42). Although the refugee and asylee must satisfy the same basic requirements, the refugee applicant applies from abroad, whereas the asylum applicant seeks relief while present in the United States or at its border. Refugee and asylum status differ in several other aspects, as discussed below.

§ 10–1 REFUGEES

The President has authority under INA § 207 to admit as refugees those non-citizens who are outside the United States and who qualify for refugee status. The President may, after consultation with Congress and before the beginning of the fiscal year, set a worldwide refugee admission ceiling for the year at such number as the President determines is "justified by humanitarian concerns or is otherwise in the national interest." INA § 207(a)(2). The President must also allocate this number among refugees from regions of the world that are of special humanitarian concern to the United States. In the event of an "unforeseen emergency refugee situation," the President may, after appropriate consultation with the relevant congressional committees, expand the admissible number of refugees if such action is justified by "grave humanitarian concerns or is otherwise in the national interest." INA § 207(b).

For example, President George W. Bush set the annual refugee admission ceiling at 70,000 for most of his presidency. For fiscal year 2008, President Bush set the refugee admission ceiling at 80,000 to account for an expected increase in Iraqi, Bhutanese, and Iranian refugees. Though President Bush set the fiscal year 2008 number at 80,000, only 60,108 refugees were actually admitted. Since September 11, 2001, the number of admitted refugees has failed to approach the number set by the admissions quota due to changes in refugee processing that provide stricter security screening and other impediments. For 2009, President Obama allocated the total number regionally as follows: Africa (16,000); East Asia, including Amerasians (25,000); Europe and Central Asia (3,000); Latin America and the Caribbean (5,500); Near East and South Asia (39,500); and an unallocated reserve of 5,000. The regional allocations do not reflect the distribution of refugees throughout the world, but instead show U.S. foreign policy interests. Also, unused allocations may be transferred to regions where needed.

An applicant for refugee status, like an asylum applicant, must meet the definition of a refugee contained in INA § 101(a)(42). Among other requirements, the applicant must possess a "well-founded fear of persecution on account of race, religion, nationality, membership in a particular social group, or political opinion." While numerical limitations apply to refugee applicants, such limitations do not exist for asylum applicants. In addition, beneficiaries of the Lautenberg amendment codified in P.L. 101–167 (Nov. 21, 1989)—Soviet Jews, Soviet Evangelical Christians, Ukrainian Catholics, Ukrainian Orthodox, and most Indochinese (Vietnamese, Lao, and Khmer)—needed only assert a fear of persecution and show a credible basis for concern about the possibility of such persecution. Most courts have held that this reduced admission standard applies only to affected refugee, and not asylum, applicants. *See, e.g., Tsupylo v. INS*, 182 F.3d 922 (7th Cir.1999).

In addition to meeting the statutory definition of refugee, a non-citizen must be of special humanitarian concern to the United States, must not have firmly resettled in any other country, and must be admissible under most of the provisions of INA § 212(a). *See* chapter 5, *supra*. Refugees are not subject to admissibility criteria relating to labor certification, foreign medical graduates, public charges, and valid entry documents and visas. INA § 207(c)(3). The Attorney General may waive certain other inadmissibility provisions for humanitarian purposes, to assure family unity, or when it is otherwise in the public interest. INA § 207(c)(3).

Each refugee, however, must be sponsored by a "responsible person or organization." *See* 8 C.F.R. § 207.2(d). Relatives, churches, community organizations, and other voluntary agencies often fill this role. The sponsor must also guarantee transportation for the applicant from his or her present abode to "the place of resettlement in the United States."

To apply for refugee status, non-citizens must complete Form I–590 (Registration for Classification as a Refugee). Applicants fourteen years of age or older also must submit Form G–325 (Biographical Information) and Form FD–258 (Applicant Card). 8 C.F.R. § 207.2. Applicants must file these completed forms, along with supplementary statements and documentary evidence, at a CIS office outside the United States. An asylum officer will then interview the applicant to determine eligibility, and the applicant must "submit to a medical examination." 8 C.F.R. § 207.2(b), (c).

Waiting lists are maintained for each designated refugee group of special humanitarian concern. The filing date of an applicant's approvable application determines his or her position on the waiting list. The Secretary of Homeland Security may, however, adopt appropriate criteria for selecting refugees and assigning priorities for each designated group based on considerations of family reunification, close association with the United States, compelling humanitarian concerns, and public interest factors. 8 C.F.R. § 207.5.

If "an officer in charge outside of the United States" approves the I–590 application, the refugee must enter the United States within four months of the date of approval. 8 C.F.R. § 207.4. Spouses and children (unmarried and under the age of twenty-one on the date such parent applied for refugee status) accompanying or following to join a refugee may be admitted if not otherwise entitled to admission, and if they have not participated in the persecution of others. Spouses and children are charged against the numerical limitation under which the refugee's entry was charged. INA § 207(c)(2). An applicant may not appeal the denial of his or her application. 8 C.F.R. § 207.4.

Upon arrival and inspection in the United States, the refugee is authorized to accept employment incident to status as a refugee. The refugee is not required to apply for an Employment Authorization Document (Form I–765), as refugees are a protected class, automatically entitled to work.

After one year in the United States, the refugee is eligible to apply for adjustment of status to lawful permanent residence. INA § 209(a)(1)(B). Whereas asylum status may be terminated if conditions improve in the asylee's home country, making asylum unnecessary, refugee status is not conditional in this respect. INA §§ 207(c)(4), 208(c)(2). Applicants for the benefits of INA § 209(a) must now mail Form I–485 directly to a designated service center rather than submitting it to a local office. Under this Direct Mail procedure, "the service center will evaluate each application and determine whether an interview is necessary. Immigration officials may decide to adjudicate an application without an interview in cases where the evaluation does not indicate questions concerning the applicant's eligibility for adjustment of status." 63 Fed.Reg. 30105–01. Subsequently, applicants will be notified to appear at an Application Support Center (ASC) or other designated location to be fingerprinted.

Although INA § 209(a) provides for the adjustment of status of non-citizens *admitted* to the United States under INA § 207, a non-citizen may be removed from the

United States through removal proceedings if it is subsequently determined that the non-citizen was not in fact a refugee within the meaning of § 101(a)(42) at the time he or she was admitted. INA §§ 207(c)(4), 209(a). If the non-citizen is found to be eligible for adjustment of status, permanent resident status will be granted and made effective as of the date the non-citizen arrived in the United States. INA § 209(a)(2). While there is an annual numerical limitation of 10,000 on adjustment of status for asylees, there is no numerical limitation on adjustment of status for refugees. INA § 209(b). *See* O.I. 209.3K. Despite the lack of a numerical limit, the process has become quite lengthy.

The Office of Refugee Resettlement (ORR) within the Department of Health and Human Services coordinates with other government and non-profit agencies to provide employment, educational, housing, and cultural resources for refugees arriving in the United States. For example, the ORR funds the Refugee Cash Assistance and Refugee Medical Assistance programs that provide financial and medical aid to refugees who do not qualify for welfare and Medicaid services. The ORR is also responsible for the care and placement of unaccompanied immigrant and refugee children.

In 2007, the U.S. government launched an inter-agency effort to resettle a large number of Iraqi refugees displaced by the Iraq War. United States Citizenship and Immigration Service (CIS) deployed additional officers to the Middle East to interview and process Iraqi refugees in Iraq, Jordan, Syria, Egypt, Turkey, and Lebanon. In the first two years of the program, CIS interviewed more than 35,000 applicants and resettled more than 19,000 Iraqi refugees in the United States.

§ 10–2 ASYLUM

Non-citizens who are present in the United States or who arrive at its border may be granted asylum if they qualify as refugees. INA § 208(b)(1). A refugee is defined in INA § 101(a)(42)(A) as "any person who is outside any country of such person's nationality or ... any country in which such person last habitually resided, and who is unable or unwilling to return to, and is unable or unwilling to avail himself or herself of the protection of that country because of persecution or a well-founded fear of persecution on account of race, religion, nationality, membership in a particular social group, or political opinion." In 1996, IIRIRA augmented the definition of refugee to include those non-citizens who face "forced abortion or involuntary sterilization, or persecution for failure or refusal to undergo such procedure or for other resistance to a coercive population control program" as persecution on account of political opinion. INA § 101(a)(42). Asylum can provide relief from removal and a grant of asylum may lead to permanent residence.

A non-citizen may apply for asylum or analogous relief in at least three different contexts: (a) upon arrival at the frontier or the airport; (b) after arrival, ordinarily within one year; and (c) during the removal process as a defense to removal, again, ordinarily if within one year of admission.

(a) A non-citizen who arrives at the U.S. border is deemed an applicant for admission. INA § 235(a)(1). The non-citizen is inspected for admission. If deemed inadmissible under INA § 212(a)(6)(C) or § 212(a)(7), the inspector orders the non-citizen removed unless the non-citizen indicates an intention to apply for asylum. INA § 235(b)(1)(A). The inspector also has the authority to allow inadmissible non-citizens to withdraw their application for admission. *See* 8 C.F.R. § 235.4.

Claims for asylum presented at the border are referred to an asylum officer for a summary determination as to whether the non-citizen has a "credible fear" of persecution. *See* INA § 235(b)(1)(B). Credible fear is defined as a "significant possibility" that the non-citizen "could establish eligibility for asylum under INA § 208," considering the "credibility of the statements made by the alien in support of the alien's claim" and "such other facts as are known to the officer." INA § 235(b)(1)(B)(v). If the asylum officer determines the non-citizen does not have a credible fear of persecution, the officer must order the non-citizen to be removed from the United States. INA § 235(b)(1)(B)(iii). The non-citizen, subject to regulations provided by the Secretary of Homeland Security, has an opportunity to request prompt review by an immigration judge. To the extent possible, review must be concluded within twenty-four hours. At the latest, review must be completed within seven days of the asylum officer's determination. The non-citizen must be detained during these proceedings. INA § 235(b)(1)(B)(iii)(IV). There is no other administrative review unless the non-citizen testifies under oath to have been lawfully admitted as a permanent resident, a refugee, or an asylee. INA § 235(b)(1)(C). If the asylum officer finds credible fear at the initial interview, the non-citizen is placed in removal proceedings by the filing of a Notice to Appear, and subsequently is permitted to file an application for asylum with the Immigration Judge. The asylum seeker ordinarily is detained during the pendency of removal proceedings, although detention is not mandatory and practice varies depending on jurisdiction. *See* § 10–2.4(b), *infra*.

(b) If a non-citizen has been admitted to the United States, has effected entry without inspection, or has his or her lawful nonimmigrant status expire, he or she may file an asylum application (Form I–589, see application process discussed § 10–2.4, *infra*) within one year of last arrival in the U.S. and may be considered for work authorization 180 days after filing an asylum application if the application remains pending. Non-citizens may be permitted to file an application for asylum more than one year after admission if they demonstrate that they qualify for an exception to the filing deadline as enumerated in § 208 of the INA or 8 C.F.R. § 208.4.

(c) If a non-citizen who lacks an immigration status or a person whose nonimmigrant visa has expired applies for asylum, immigration authorities will become aware that the non-citizen is out of immigration status and if asylum is not granted, removal proceedings will be initiated to force the non-citizen to depart the United States. The application for asylum is considered "referred" to an immigration judge for further consideration. In light of the small percentage of applicants actually granted asylum affirmatively (for fiscal years 2000 (14.5%); 2001 (13%); and 2002 (11.9%)) individuals should consider carefully whether they wish to apply for asylum because if their application is rejected, they will be subject to removal proceedings. If the U.S. Immigration and Customs Enforcement (ICE) has initiated removal proceedings against a non-citizen, the non-citizen may apply for asylum as a defense to removal if the application is submitted within one year of his or her latest entry to the United States.

§ 10–2.1 "Restriction on Removal" (Formerly "Withholding of Deportation")

The provisions of INA § 241(b)(3)(A) governing "restriction on removal" are closely connected to those of INA § 208(a) governing asylum. This relief was previously known as "withholding of deportation" under old INA § 243(h) and immigration lawyers sometimes continue to use the phrase "withholding of deportation" for this relief. The Nutshell uses these phrases interchangeably. *See* § 9–3.2(a), *supra*.

Section 241(b)(3) provides that, with certain exceptions, a non-citizen may not be removed to a country where the non-citizen's "life or freedom would be threatened ... because of the alien's race, religion, nationality, membership in a particular social group, or political opinion." A non-citizen will most often apply for asylum as relief in removal proceedings along with a request for restriction on removal under INA § 241(b)(3). Moreover, an application for asylum is also considered as an application for restriction on removal. 8 C.F.R. § 208.3(b).

While similar in many aspects, asylum as a defense to removal and restriction on removal have significant differences. Restriction on removal does not grant the successful applicant an opportunity to apply for permanent resident status, to petition to bring family members to the United States, or to obtain a refugee travel document. A person granted restriction on removal is permitted to remain in the United States and to annually apply for an Employment Authorization Document. It is important to remember that persons granted restriction on removal *are ordered removed* from the United States, and only removal to a particular country is prohibited. Therefore, persons granted restriction still may be removed to a third country if such country is willing to accept the individual. The applicable standard of proof is also higher for restriction on removal applicants as discussed in § 10–2.3, *infra*. In addition, asylum is a discretionary matter, whereas INA § 241(b)(3) relief (old § 243(h)) is mandatory if the applicant is qualified. A non-citizen, therefore, having established a clear probability of persecution, must be granted restriction on removal to the country of persecution, but may be denied asylum at the discretion of an immigration judge.

A CIS asylum officer or district director may, following a further interview, terminate removal restriction on removal due to changed country conditions, fraud, or commission of an act which is grounds for denial under § 241(b)(3)(B). 8 C.F.R. § 208.24. Even though country conditions may change, it is extremely rare for immigration authorities to devote limited resources to the initiation of proceedings to terminate withholding of removal.

§ 10–2.2   Convention Against Torture

In 1994, the United States ratified the Convention Against Torture and Other Cruel, Inhuman or Degrading Treatment of Punishment. Article 3 of the Convention provides that no country shall "expel, return (refouler) or extradite" a person to another country if there are "substantial grounds for believing that he would be in danger of being subjected to torture." The Federal Regulations incorporate the definition of torture contained in Article 1 of the Convention Against Torture, but the United States' definition of torture is different than the CAT definition. *See* 8 C.F.R. § 208.18. In 1998, Congress passed the Foreign Affairs Reform and Restructuring Act (FARRA) to ensure compliance with the Convention.

To constitute torture, an act must (1) cause severe physical or mental pain or suffering; (2) be intentionally inflicted; (3) be inflicted for a proscribed purpose; (4) be inflicted by or at the instigation of, or with the consent or acquiescence of, a public official who has custody or physical control of the victim; and (5) cannot arise from lawful sanctions. *See* 8 C.F.R. § 208.18(a); *In re J–E–*, 23 I. & N. Dec. 291, Interim Decision (BIA) 3466 (BIA 2002). That the individual is likely to be subject to indiscriminate human rights violations or generalized violence is insufficient to require relief under the regulations.

Pursuant to FARRA, the INS adopted implementing regulations that became effective on March 22, 1999. 64 Fed.Reg. 8478–01. The regulations provide a new form of restriction on removal and create a new protection called deferral of removal. To qualify for either of these forms of relief, non-citizens must file an asylum application (Form I–589) and answer question 7 of part C ("Do you fear being subjected to torture in your home country?") in the affirmative. An immigration judge then determines whether the non-citizen has established that he or she "is more likely than not to be tortured in the country of removal." 8 C.F.R. § 208.16(c)(4). The non-citizen need not show that he or she faces torture on account of race, religion, nationality, membership of a particular social group, or political opinion. The "more likely than not" burden is a higher standard to be met than the asylum standard of "well-founded fear." The torture, however, must be by government officials or by private actors with government acquiescence. *See, e.g., In re M–B–A–*, 23 I. & N. Dec. 474, Interim Decision (BIA) 3480 (BIA 2002) (holding that a Nigerian woman failed to meet her more likely than not standard because she provided little current or historical evidence on the enforcement of a Nigerian decree that criminalized her drug behavior in the United States).

If the burden is met, relief is mandatory. The immigration judge will grant the new CAT form of restriction on removal if the non-citizen meets his or her burden of proof and is not subject to the bars of INA § 241(b)(3)(B). If the non-citizen is subject to the bars, such as being a persecutor of others or security threat, the judge will grant deferral of removal under 8 C.F.R. § 208.17. Deferral of removal is more easily terminated in that it only requires a motion to schedule a hearing, whereas termination of restriction on removal requires a motion to reopen. *See* 8 C.F.R. §§ 208.17(d)(1), 208.24(e). As with withholding of removal, CAT relief allows removal to a third country. Both forms of relief are available as affirmative claims to asylum officers and defensive claims to immigration judges, but neither give the successful applicant the beneficial immigration status that asylum provides. Moreover, receiving deferral of removal relief does not guarantee release from detention. Decisions on a non-citizen's release are governed by part 241 of the Code of Federal Regulations. 8 C.F.R. § 208.17(c). These regulations are relatively strict since they ordinarily apply to non-citizens ordered removed. This strictness could lead to a large percentage of non-citizens who are detained even though granted CAT relief.

The Board of Immigration Appeals has considered the CAT regulations on several occasions. For example, in the case of *In re S–V–*, www.uncr.org/reworld/pdfid/3ae6b 7660.pdf, the Board defined the Torture Convention's requirements as providing narrower relief than offered by the BIA in *Kasinga*, see § 10–2.3(b), *infra*. The BIA in

Kasinga held that a fear of persecution by non-state actors that the government was unable to control was sufficient for an asylum applicant to show a risk of persecution. The Board distinguished that asylum case by deciding that CAT relief requires the individual face a specific risk of being tortured by the government, or "at the instigation of or with the consent or acquiescence of" the government. The BIA defined acquiescence as "willfully accepting."

The federal courts have jurisdiction to review CAT claims. *See Saint Fort v. Ashcroft*, 329 F.3d 191 (1st Cir.2003). For example, the Ninth Circuit disagreed with the BIA's *In re S–V–* definition of "acquiescence" and held that Congress intended to "require only 'awareness,' and not to require 'actual knowledge' or 'willful acceptance' in the definition of acquiescence." *Zheng v. Ashcroft*, 332 F.3d 1186 (9th Cir.2003). The Second and Sixth Circuits have also adopted the Ninth Circuit's definition of "acquiescence." *Khouzam v. Ashcroft*, 361 F.3d 161 (2d Cir.2004); *Amir v. Gonzales*, 467 F.3d 921 (6th Cir.2006).

§ 10–2.3   Burden and Standard of Proof in Asylum Cases

a.   *Well–Founded Fear of Persecution*

The burden of establishing eligibility as an asylee is on the applicant. 8 C.F.R. § 208.13. Applicants must show that they have a well-founded fear of persecution in their home country on account of race, religion, nationality, membership in a particular social group, or political opinion. Applicants may sustain their burden of proof either by showing that they suffered past persecution or by demonstrating a "well-founded fear of future persecution" upon return to their country of nationality or country of last habitual residence. 8 C.F.R. § 208.13(b).

Applicants can show past persecution by establishing that they have suffered persecution in the past on account of race, religion, nationality, membership in a particular social group, or political opinion and are "unable or unwilling to return to, or avail [themselves] of the protection of that country owing to such persecution." 8 C.F.R. § 208.13(b)(1). Similarly, applicants may establish "well-founded fear" by establishing that they have a fear of persecution on account of the aforementioned five grounds, there is a "reasonable possibility of suffering such persecution," and they are unable or unwilling to return to or receive protection from that country because of such fear. 8 C.F.R. § 208.13(b)(2).

An applicant's petition for asylum must satisfy both a subjective and an objective component. Subjectively, the applicant must show that his or her fear is genuine. The objective component requires a showing by credible and specific evidence in the record of facts that would support a reasonable fear of persecution. *Arriaga–Barrientos v. INS*, 937 F.2d 411 (9th Cir.1991). In *Arriaga–Barrientos,* the court held that "acts of violence against a petitioner's friends or family members may establish a well-founded fear, notwithstanding an utter lack of persecution against the petitioner herself." Similarly, the Ninth Circuit remanded *Hernandez–Perez v. Ashcroft*, 55 Fed. Appx. 426 (9th Cir.2003) to the BIA to reconsider "the harms suffered by Mr. Hernandez–Perez's family." If the applicant can establish that there is a "pattern or practice" of persecution in his or her country on account of race, religion, nationality, membership in a particular social group, or political opinion, and that his or her fear of persecution upon return is reasonable because the persecuted group of persons is similarly situated to the applicant, the applicant need not provide evidence that he or she will be individually singled out for persecution. 8 C.F.R. § 208.13(b)(2)(iii).

If the applicant is found to have established past persecution, it is presumed that he or she has a well-founded fear of persecution. This presumption can be rebutted if the government establishes by a preponderance of evidence that conditions in the country have changed to an extent that it is no longer more likely than not that the applicant would face persecution. The government may sustain its burden of establishing changed circumstances by proving "a fundamental change in circumstances such that the applicant no longer has a well-founded fear of persecution." 8 C.F.R. § 208.13(b)(1)(i)(A). In addition to establishing changed circumstances, the government may rebut the presumption by establishing that the applicant can avoid future persecution by relocating to another part of the applicant's country of nationality, and that it would be reasonable to expect the applicant to do so. 8 C.F.R. § 208.13(b)(1)(i)(B).

If the government successfully rebuts the presumption of a well-founded fear of future persecution, a non-citizen may still be granted asylum by demonstrating compelling reasons for being unwilling or unable to return to his or her country arising out of the severity of the past persecution. *See* 8 C.F.R. § 208.13(b)(1)(iii)(A); *see also Matter of Chen*, 20 I. & N. Dec. 16, Interim Decision (BIA) 3104 (BIA 1989). Also, the applicant may be granted asylum if he or she establishes that there is a reasonable possibility that he or she may suffer other serious harm upon removal to that country. 8 C.F.R. § 208.13(b)(1)(iii)(A)–(B).

The requirement of a "well-founded fear" has not been clearly defined. The applicable standards are clearly different in the context of asylum applications and restriction on removal applications. As the Supreme Court cases discussed below demonstrate, restriction on removal applications require a higher standard of proof.

In *INS v. Stevic*, 467 U.S. 407 (1984) and *INS v. Cardoza–Fonseca*, 480 U.S. 421 (1987) the Supreme Court established the standard of proof which the adjudicator must apply in considering asylum applications and examined the procedures available for review if such applications are denied. Stevic was a Yugoslav citizen who was ordered removed from the United States. While his motion to reopen his removal was pending before an immigration judge, he applied for asylum. The immigration judge denied the reopening and his appeal to the Board of Immigration Appeals was dismissed. The Board noted that "[a] motion to reopen based on a ... claim of persecution must contain prima facie evidence there is a clear probability of persecution to be directed at the individual." The Board concluded that Stevic had failed to prove that he would be singled out for persecution if he returned to Yugoslavia.

Stevic sought review by the U.S. Court of Appeals of the Board's denial of his motion to reopen the removal proceedings on the asylum matter; this appeal was consolidated with his appeal from the denial of his *habeas corpus* petition in the federal district court concerning an earlier motion to seek withholding of deportation on the basis of INA § 243(h) (now "restriction on removal" under INA § 241(b)(3)).

The Second Circuit held that when the United States acceded to the Protocol relating to the Status of Refugees in 1968, and later adopted the Refugee Act of 1980, it intended to establish a more generous standard in evaluating asylum claims than the " 'clear probability' that an individual will be singled out for persecution" approach used by the Board of Immigration Appeals. The Court of Appeals indicated that the same burden of proof should apply to both the withholding procedure and to affirmative applications for asylum.

The Supreme Court granted certiorari and concluded from an analysis of legislative history and statutory language that the applicant must show a clear probability of persecution in order to obtain withholding of deportation under INA § 243(h) (now "restriction on removal" under INA § 241(b)(3)). The Court defined the clear probability of persecution standard as inquiring whether it is more likely than not that the applicant would be subject to persecution. The Supreme Court suggested that a different standard might be applicable to an asylum application.

In *INS v. Cardoza–Fonseca*, 480 U.S. 421 (1987) the Supreme Court directly addressed the standard of proof applicable to applications for asylum under § 208(a). Cardoza–Fonseca was a Nicaraguan citizen who overstayed her nonimmigrant visa. When the INS commenced removal proceedings, Cardoza–Fonseca requested restriction on removal pursuant to INA § 243(h) and asylum pursuant to § 208(a). To support her asylum claim, she attempted to show a "well-founded fear of persecution" upon her return to Nicaragua with evidence that her brother had been tortured and imprisoned because of his political activities in Nicaragua. Cardoza–

Fonseca claimed that she, too, would be tortured if forced to return, because the Sandinista government knew she had fled Nicaragua with her brother and would want to interrogate her about her brother's whereabouts. Because of the status of her brother, the Nicaraguan government would become aware of her own political opposition to the Sandinistas.

At the removal hearing, the immigration judge applied the "more likely than not" standard of proof to Cardoza–Fonseca's asylum claim. The judge held that she was not entitled to asylum because she had failed to establish "a clear probability of persecution." The Board of Immigration Appeals (BIA) affirmed the decision. The Ninth Circuit reversed, holding that the § 208(a) "well-founded fear" standard is more generous than the § 243(h) (now § 241(b)(3)) clear probability standard in that § 208(a) requires only a showing of past persecution or "good reason" to fear future persecution. The Court of Appeals remanded the case to the BIA, to be evaluated under this standard.

The Supreme Court affirmed the judgment of the Court of Appeals, holding that the § 243(h) (now § 241(b)(3)) clear probability standard does not govern asylum applications under § 208(a), and that "the reference to 'fear' in the § 208(a) standard obviously makes the eligibility determination turn to some extent on the subjective mental state of the alien." The Court, however, declined to give concrete meaning to the phrase "well-founded fear," leaving this task to the process of case-by-case adjudication. After the Supreme Court's ruling in *Cardoza–Fonseca*, the BIA held that an applicant for asylum has a well-founded fear of persecution if a reasonable person in the applicant's position would fear persecution. *Matter of Mogharrabi*, 19 I. & N. Dec. 439, Interim Decision 3028 (BIA 1987). The BIA also concluded that a reasonable person may fear persecution even when the likelihood of persecution is less than clearly probable. *Id.*

If the asylum applicant has satisfied the § 243(h) (now § 241(b)(3)) clear probability standard as to withholding of removal, the applicant has *a fortiori* satisfied the more generous "well-founded fear" standard governing asylum claims. *Hernandez–Ortiz v. INS*, 777 F.2d 509 (9th Cir. 1985). In *Hernandez–Ortiz,* the non-citizen's evidence of threats or acts of violence against members of her family in El Salvador showed a clear probability that her life would be threatened by return to El Salvador, and that the threat of persecution was related to her political opinion. Having established a clear probability of persecution, the non-citizen had *a fortiori* established a well-founded fear of persecution, thereby entitling her to asylum status. In such cases, if the applicant is statutorily and discretionarily eligible for asylum, asylum status will be granted; if the applicant is statutorily or discretionarily barred from asylum, withholding will be granted.

b. *Basis for Asylum*

As mentioned above, in order to establish a claim for asylum, the applicant must show that he or she has a well-founded fear of persecution in his or her home country on account of one or more of the five grounds: (1) race, (2) religion, (3) nationality, (4) membership in a particular social group, or (5) political opinion.

In a 1992 case, the Supreme Court held that a guerrilla organization's coercion to join its organization does not necessarily constitute persecution on account of political opinion for the purposes of INA §§ 101(a)(42), 208. *INS v. Elias–Zacarias*, 502 U.S. 478 (1992). In that case, Jairo Jonathan Elias–Zacarias testified during removal proceedings that he would be subject to persecution if he was returned to his native Guatemala. He described how guerrillas had forced their way into his home and requested that Elias–Zacarias and his parents join their organization. They refused and the guerrillas promised to return. Elias–Zacarias testified that he believed joining the organization would subject him to retaliation by the government.

In his opinion for six members of the Court, Justice Scalia reviewed the applicable standards for granting asylum under INA § 208(a). First, he noted that the fear of persecution had to be such that a reasonable factfinder would conclude that it existed. He reasoned that the political opinion in question was not that of the applicant, but rather, that of the guerrilla organization (the persecutor). In response, Elias–Zacarias had argued that failure to join the guerrillas was itself tantamount to expressing a political opinion, but the Court was not persuaded and held that Elias–Zacarias had failed to show evidence that compelled reversal of the BIA decision.

In a dissenting opinion for three members of the Court, Justice Stevens stated that "[a] political opinion can be expressed negatively as well as affirmatively," and that in these circumstances, expression led to a reasonable fear of persecution. For a period after this Supreme Court decision, it was unclear whether the "forcible recruitment" and imputed political opinion theory could still prevail with the proper evidence. Indeed, it now appears that the doctrine of imputed political opinion is still viable. For example, the Board granted asylum to a Sri Lankan national who was kidnapped by the Tamil Tigers and forced to work in their camp. *In re S–P–*, 21 I. & N. Dec. 486, Interim Decision (BIA) 3287 (BIA 1996). When the Tiger's camp was raided by the Sri Lankan Army, the soldiers accused the applicant of being a Tamil Tiger, imprisoned him, and ill-treated him during inter-rogations. The Board reasoned that in the context of general civil unrest, "it is not easy to evaluate whether the applicant's harm was inflicted because of imputed political views rather than a desire to obtain intelligence information." The difficulty of determining motive in such situations should not, however, "diminish the pro-tections of asylum for persons who have been punished because of their actual or imputed political views, as opposed to their criminal or violent conduct."

In *Cordon–Garcia v. INS*, 204 F.3d 985 (9th Cir.2000), the Ninth Circuit ruled that imputed political opinion could be found where "one party to a conflict insists to the victim that the victim is aligned with the other side." Petitioner was a Guatemalan national who taught litera-cy classes at a government-funded agency. Guerillas kid-napped her and tried to dissuade her from working for the government because literacy made it more difficult to "reach" the people. Petitioner then received protection from the government until she left the country. The guerillas, however, killed her father and uncle in an attempt to locate her. The Ninth Circuit reversed the BIA's denial of petitioner's asylum claim and stated that a "presumed affiliation" was the equivalent of an oppos-ing political opinion, "whether or not she actually holds such an opinion." The court remanded petitioner's case for credibility determinations, advising the BIA to grant her asylum claim if her testimony is found to be credible. The Ninth Circuit has since faced similar imputed political opinion asylum claims. Several applicants have sought relief claiming a well-founded fear of future persecution based on past persecution on account of an imputed political opinion. *See, e.g., Agbuya v. INS*, 241 F.3d 1224 (9th Cir.2001); *Mendoza v. INS*, 13 Fed.Appx. 515 (9th Cir.2001). The Ninth Circuit has ruled that such applicants must show that: (1) they were victims of persecution, (2) they hold a political opinion or have had one imputed to them, (3) their political opinion was known to or imputed by their persecutors, and (4) the persecution was on account of their actual or imputed political opinion.

Although courts have accepted the imputed political claim, they have been slow to accept other imputed claims. For example, the Third Circuit reviewed the BIA's dismissal of a claim of persecution on account of imputed membership in a social group (homosexuals). *Amanfi v. Ashcroft*, 328 F.3d 719 (3d Cir.2003). The BIA had summarily dismissed the claim because it deemed such an extension "to be without legal precedent." The Third Circuit acknowledged that no other circuit had considered this issue, but held that persecution on account of membership in a social group "includes what the persecutor perceives to be the applicant's membership." In July 2010, the United Kingdom held that a homosexual from Iran qualified for asylum. *HJ and HT v. Secretary of State for the Home Department*, [2010] 3 W.L.R. 386 (U.K. Sup.Ct.2010).

Situations in which persecutors may have mixed motives present difficult cases for courts. Presently, for an asylum claim to succeed, the applicant had to show that he or she was persecuted "on account of" one of the five enumerated grounds. The Ninth Circuit, however, ruled that one of the five grounds need only be a motive and not the sole motive for persecution. *See Navas v. INS*, 217 F.3d 646 (9th Cir.2000). Nonetheless, a motive must still be proved. In *Quinonez–Colop v. INS*, 61 Fed. Appx. 474 (9th Cir.2003), a Guatemalan native was denied asylum because "there was no basis for concluding that the guerillas were interested in persecuting the applicant because his political beliefs were antithetical to theirs." Similarly, in *Lukwago v. Ashcroft*, 329 F.3d 157 (3d Cir.2003), the petitioner was abducted by the Lord's Resistance Army in Uganda, but the court found substantial evidence that he was not targeted for persecution based on his age (social group).

In order to clarify the applicant's burden of proof, the REAL ID Act of 2005 revised INA § 208(b)(1)(B) to state, "the applicant must establish that race, nationality, membership in a particular social group, or political opinion was or will be *at least one central reason* for persecuting the applicant." (emphasis added). Subsequently, the BIA has held that under the revised version of INA § 208, "the protected ground cannot play a minor role in the alien's past mistreatment or fears of future mistreatment," and "cannot be incidental, tangential, superficial, or subordinate to another reason for harm." *Matter of J–B–N– & S–M–*, 24 I. & N. Dec. 208, Interim Decision 3569 (BIA 2007).

In re Kasinga, 21 I. & N. Dec. 357, Interim Decision (BIA) 3278 (BIA 1996) held that the practice of female genital mutilation (FGM) can form the basis for a grant of asylum. Kasinga, a 19–year old native of Togo, feared that she would be subjected to FGM and forced marriage upon her return to her country. The BIA stated the "applicant's testimony in *Kasinga* established that she had a well-founded fear of persecution on account of her membership in a 'particular social group,' *i.e.*, young women of the Tchamba–Kunsuntu Tribe who have not suffered FGM and who oppose the practice." In *Abankwah v. INS*, 185 F.3d 18 (2d Cir.1999), the Second Circuit reaffirmed *Kasinga* by stating that "FGM involves the infliction of grave harm" and constitutes persecution under INA § 208.

The BIA has held that domestic violence constitutes "persecution," and that victims of domestic abuse may apply for asylum. In order to qualify for asylum, a victim of domestic violence must still identify with a particular social group and establish a nexus between the abuse and a statutorily protected ground. *See Matter of R–A–*, 22 I. & N. Dec. 906, Interim Decision 3403 (BIA 2001). For example, in *Matter of S–A–*, 22 I. & N. Dec. 1328, Interim Decision 3433 (BIA 2000), the BIA granted asylum to a Moroccan woman whose father physically abused her because of her liberal Muslim views.

§ 10–2.4　Basic Asylum Application Procedures

Asylum is not considered a right. Rather it is granted at the discretion of the asylum officer or immigration judge in the district where the non-citizen resides or enters the United States. 8 C.F.R. § 208.14. The Refugee Act of 1980 established the basic standard for granting asylum in INA § 208. IIRIRA, codified in 1996, provided additional restrictive rules regarding timing, eligibility for judicial review, and procedures for filing an asylum claim.

a. Jurisdiction and Judicial Review

Asylum officers in the CIS have initial jurisdiction over an asylum application filed by non-citizens physically present in the U.S. who are not in removal proceedings. 8 C.F.R. § 208.2. Asylum officers receive special training in international human rights law, non-adversarial interview techniques, and other relevant national and international refugee laws and principles. 8 C.F.R. § 208.1(b). The Director of International Affairs in cooperation with the Department of State compiles and disseminates to asylum officers information concerning the persecution of persons in other countries, as well as other information relevant to asylum determinations. *Id.*

Immigration judges have jurisdiction over all non-citizens in removal proceedings, including applicants for asylum. Asylum seekers may be placed in removal proceedings in a number of ways: they may be referred to an immigration judge if their affirmative asylum application is not approved by the Asylum Office; they may be arrested at the port of entry, establish credible fear of return, and subsequently be placed in removal proceedings; or they may be arrested by immigration officials for other immigration status violations. Once a Notice to Appear is filed with the immigration court, jurisdiction over the individual rests with the immigration judge, and any claim for asylum or related relief will be adjudicated by the immigration judge.

The decision of the immigration judge is subject to both a BIA appeal and judicial review. The BIA administrative appeals process was streamlined in September 2002 in an attempt to eliminate the backlog and delayed adjudication of appeals, and to increase Board efficiency, including reallocating resources to difficult or controversial legal cases. The Department of Justice sought to achieve these goals by implementing several procedural changes. Each case is now subject to a five-member screening panel that will conduct an initial review. This review will usually result in one member of the panel adjudicating the case without oral arguments. This method replaces three-member panels, which are now reserved for cases requiring "searching appellate review" and must qualify under one of six categories. *See* 67 Fed.Reg. 54878–01; 8 C.F.R. § 1003.1. Additionally, the non-citizen must file a notice to appeal within 30 days. Briefs are filed simultaneously if the non-citizen is detained, otherwise the reply brief must be filed within 21 days. The screening panel then has 90 days to decide the case or qualify it for review by a three-member panel. This panel would then have 180 days to issue its opinion. Other procedural changes to streamline the BIA include priority to cases involving detained non-citizens, summary dismissal of an appeal brought for an improper purpose, elimination of *de novo* review unless the immigration judge's findings are clearly erroneous, and reduction of the Board from 23 to 15 members. *See* § 3–3.2, *supra*.

Courts use a "substantial evidence" standard for reviewing asylum or withholding of removal. Before applying the substantial evidence standard, the court must first determine whether it reviews the immigration judge's or BIA's decision. The process generally followed is that if the BIA conducts a *de novo* review of the record and makes an independent determination, the court will review the BIA's decision. *See de Leon–Barrios v. INS*, 116 F.3d 391 (9th Cir.1997). If the BIA reviews the immigration judge's decision for an abuse of discretion and simply adopts the immigration judge's findings and reasoning, the court will review the immigration judge's decision to determine if it was supported by substantial evidence. *Id.*; *see also Ochave v. INS*, 254 F.3d 859 (9th Cir.2001). Courts must also take note of several INA § 242 provisions that may deprive them of jurisdiction. For example, the Ninth Circuit in *Alvarez–Santos v. INS*, 332 F.3d 1245 (9th Cir.2003) considered whether INA § 242(a)(2)(c) stripped the court of jurisdiction to review the BIA's decision to deny asylum and remove a criminal non-citizen. The court held that the provision did not deprive courts of jurisdiction to review the appeal. The REAL ID Act of 2005 modified INA § 242 so that only courts of appeals have jurisdiction to review orders of removal. See discussion on judicial review of removal orders at § 9–4.3, *supra*.

The courts of appeals use a substantial evidence standard to review BIA decisions. The substantial evidence standard is slightly stricter than the clear error standard. With the clear error standard, the standard of review used by appellate courts in reviewing trial court decisions, the appellate court must uphold the trial court's factual findings unless it is "clearly erroneous." In applying the substantial evidence standard, the appellate court must uphold the BIA's determination "if supported by reasonable, substantial, and probative evidence on the record considered as a whole." *INS v. Elias–Zacarias*, 502 U.S. 478 (1992). This standard requires the appellate court to uphold the findings "unless the evidence not only supports, but compels, contrary findings."

b. *The Application Process*

Persons seeking asylum must file an application for asylum (Form I–589) together with any additional supporting evidence in accordance with the instructions on the form. 8 C.F.R. § 208.3. The Secretary of Homeland Security may also require applicants to submit finger-prints and a photograph. INA § 208(d)(1). Applicants must further demonstrate that they are filing an applica-tion within one year of the date of arrival in the United States. INA § 208(a)(2)(B). A non-citizen may not apply for asylum if a previous asylum application was denied by an immigration judge or the BIA. INA § 208 (a)(2)(C). These conditions may be waived if the non-citizen proves "either the existence of changed circumstances which materially affect the applicant's eligibility for asylum or extraordinary circumstances relating to the delay in fil-ing the application." INA § 208(a)(2)(D). Examples of changed or extraordinary circumstances are listed in 8 C.F.R. § 208.4.

Provided the non-citizen is not in removal proceedings, he or she files the application materials with the CIS Service Center, which then forwards them to the Asylum Office having jurisdiction over the applicant's place of residence. Following an interview with an asylum officer, the asylum officer may approve the application for asy-lum in the exercise of discretion to an applicant who qualifies as a refugee under INA § 101(a)(42) and whose identity has been checked pursuant to INA § 208(d)(5)(i). Generally the asylum officer issues a "rec-ommended approval" of the application, pending the successful completion of the required background check. Asylum applicants whose applications have not yet been pending 150 days may apply for an Employment Authori-zation Document (EAD) upon issuance of the recom-mended approval. If the applicant is cleared, an "asylum approval" is issued, together with Form I–94 (entry/de-parture) as evidence of the asylum status. Once asylum is approved, the asylee is authorized to accept employment incident to status, without need for an EAD; may petition to bring immediate family members not physically present in the U.S. at the time of the asylum approval; and may apply for a refugee travel document to permit foreign travel.

If the asylum officer determines that the asylum application cannot be granted and if the applicant appears to be inadmissible or removable under INA §§ 212(a) or 237(a), the asylum officer must refer the application to an immigration judge, together with the appropriate charging documents, for adjudication in removal proceedings. 8 C.F.R. § 208.14(c)(1). The decision by an asylum officer to approve or deny asylum and refer the asylum application to the immigration judge must be communicated in writing to the applicant. 8 C.F.R. § 208.19. The regulations do not require an asylum officer to state reasons for referrals, although formal written assessments are maintained by the asylum office and are available to the applicant through the Freedom of Information Act (FOIA). There is no right to appeal a decision of an asylum officer, but the application can be renewed *de novo* in removal proceedings. If the asylum officer finds the application unmeritorious and the non-citizen is still maintaining valid immigrant, nonimmigrant, or Temporary Protected Status at the time the application is decided, the asylum officer will deny the application for asylum rather than refer the matter to an immigration judge. 8 C.F.R. § 208.14(c)(2). There is no provision for appeal at this stage.

In considering the asylum application, the asylum officer is expected to interview each applicant for asylum in a non-adversarial manner and—unless the applicant requests otherwise—separate and apart from the general public. 8 C.F.R. § 208.9. The applicant may have counsel and may present witnesses, affidavits of witnesses, and other evidence. In making a determination, the asylum officer may rely on information provided by the State Department and the Office of International Affairs, as well as other "credible" sources, such as international organizations, private voluntary agencies, news organizations, or academic institutions. 8 C.F.R. § 208.12.

Prior to the 1990 regulations, comments from the Bureau of Human Rights and Humanitarian Affairs (BHRHA) of the Department of State were required. Courts, however, were critical of the weight given to BHRHA opinions. The Second Circuit affirmed the admissibility of the State Department's opinions on the degree of persecution that exists in the country of prospective deportation. *Zamora v. INS*, 534 F.2d 1055 (2d Cir.1976). The advisory opinions are admissible provided the State Department reveals, so far as possible, the basis for its views and does not attempt to apply such knowledge to the particular case. Under the current regulations, comment from the Department of State (usually the Bureau of Democracy, Human Rights and Labor) is optional. 8 C.F.R. § 208.12.

Travel during the application process is severely limited. The most severe restriction has been detention of asylum seekers. Arriving asylum seekers are subject to mandatory detention until they have established a credible fear of persecution. See § 10–2, supra. Once an asylum seeker has established a credible fear of persecution, they may be released on parole. Parole guidelines, contained in agency memoranda, allow for release on parole of asylum seekers who demonstrate credible fear of persecution, establish their identity, establish community or family ties in the United States, do not pose a danger to the community, and are not otherwise barred from asylum. Whether an asylum seeker will be released on parole depends on many other factors, including the practices and bed space available at the particular port of entry. In other cases, blanket denials of parole have been issued. For example, in 2003, Operation Liberty Shield detained arriving asylum applicants from thirty-four countries thought to have active terrorist groups. Despite international standards against such arbitrary detention, the United States continues to detain specified groups of asylum applicants upon arrival. *See* § 11–4.2, *infra*. According to Human Rights First, more than 6,000 new asylum seekers were subject to mandatory detention upon their arrival in the United States during fiscal years 2007 and 2008.

Asylum applicants who are not detained still face restrictions on their freedom to travel. An applicant is required to file change of address information within ten days of any move. An applicant who leaves the United States without first obtaining advance parole is presumed to have abandoned his or her application for asylum or withholding of removal. 8 C.F.R. § 208.8. If an applicant misses an immigration court hearing date, an *in absentia* order of removal will be issued and exceptions to the order are issued only in extreme circumstances, such as the applicant was hospitalized at the time. Moreover, an unexcused failure to appear for a scheduled interview without prior authorization may result in the dismissal of the application or a waiver of the right to an interview. 8 C.F.R. § 208.10.

c. Bars to Asylum

Asylum will be denied as a matter of statutory eligibility if the applicant (1) fails to qualify as a refugee; (2)

participated in the persecution of any other person on account of race, religion, nationality, membership in a particular social group, or political opinion; (3) constitutes a danger to the community of the United States, having been convicted by a final judgment of a particularly serious crime; (4) has committed a serious non-political crime outside the United States prior to arrival in the United States or there are serious reasons for believing the applicant has committed such a crime; (5) is regarded as a danger to the security of the United States; (6) is inadmissible or removable on terrorist activity grounds; or (7) has been firmly resettled in another country prior to arriving in the United States. INA § 208(b). Also, the 1996 Act added that "an alien who has been convicted of an aggravated felony shall be considered to have been convicted of a particularly serious crime," disqualifying the applicant from asylum. INA §§ 208(b)(2)(A)(ii), 208(b)(2)(B)(i). IIRIRA considerably expanded the definition of aggravated felony. *See* INA § 101(a)(43). Despite aggravated felons being ineligible for asylum, they are still eligible for restriction on removal if convicted of an aggravated felony for which the noncitizen has been sentenced to an aggregate term of imprisonment of less than five years and for deferral of removal under the Convention Against Torture. INA § 241(b)(3)(B); 8 C.F.R. § 208.17; *see also Saint Fort v. Ashcroft*, 329 F.3d 191 (1st Cir.2003). *See* § 10–2.2, *infra.*

In the case of Elian Gonzalez—a six year old boy whose mother had died during their journey in a small boat from Cuba to the United States—the INS was compelled to decide whether a child was independently eligible to apply for asylum. In *Gonzalez v. Reno*, the Eleventh Circuit stated that, as a matter of statutory interpretation, the statutory language of "any alien" in

INA § 208(a) means that children are clearly eligible to apply for asylum. *See Gonzalez v. Reno*, 212 F.3d 1338 (11th Cir.2000). Initially, the INS received the application for asylum filed in the name of Elian Gonzalez through his great uncle in Florida. The Eleventh Circuit ruled that although children are eligible to apply for asylum, it was reasonable for the INS to determine that the petitioner lacked the capacity to apply since his father in Cuba opposed the asylum application. In affirming the denial of an asylum hearing, the court stated that "the only proper adult to represent a six-year-old child is the child's parent," and that the INS had made a sound policy choice to which the court owed deference.

In re Q–T–M–T–, 21 I. & N. Dec. 639, Interim Decision (BIA) 3300 (BIA 1996) dealt with a Vietnamese man convicted of illegal sale of firearms prior to the date on which the IIRIRA amendments expanding the definition of aggravated felony became effective. For this transitional period shortly after the IIRIRA amendments, the BIA stated that a non-citizen convicted of an aggravated felony who has been sentenced to less than five years' imprisonment is subject to a rebuttable presumption that he or she has been convicted of a particularly serious crime. Such a conviction bars the non-citizen's eligibility for restriction on removal under INA § 241(b)(3). The appropriate standard to evaluate whether the non-citizen has overcome the presumption that he or she has committed a particularly serious crime is "whether there is any unusual aspect of the alien's criminal conduct that convincingly evidences that the crime cannot rationally be deemed 'particularly serious' in light of treaty obligation under the Protocol [relating to the Status of Refugees]." In the *Q–T–M–T–* case, the nature and circumstances of the respondent's convictions for illicit trafficking in firearms fulfilled the definitions of both "aggravated felony" under INA § 101(a)(43)(C) and also "particularly serious crime" under the Protocol, such that the non-citizen was disqualified from relief from removal.

The Board has attempted to retreat from its position in *Q–T–M–T–* on two occasions. The *Q–T–M–T–* holding was considerably narrowed by *In re L–S–*, 22 I. & N. Dec. 645, Interim Decision (BIA) 3386 (BIA 1999), where the Board dealt with a Laotian man who was convicted of bringing an illegal alien into the United States and was sentenced to approximately three and one-half years. The Board stated that although the *per se* rule (that any aggravated felony disqualifies the applicant from asylum status because such a felony constitutes a "particularly serious crime") applies in the context of asylum applications, it found no grounds to apply the same rule in the context of restriction on removal proceedings. The Board reasoned that because restriction on removal does not necessarily lead to permanent residency, allowing a noncitizen to apply for restriction on removal will "preserve the balance between upholding our international obligations under the Protocol and protecting the safety of the public." The BIA stated two different rules for applying the *per se* "particularly serious crime" rule to asylum and withholding of removal. While "any alien convicted of an aggravated felony is considered to have been convicted of a particularly serious crime" in the context of asylum, the same rule applies only if the individual "was sentenced to a term of imprisonment of five years or more" in the context of withholding of removal. The Board adopted the "seriousness standard," which included factors such as "the nature of the conviction, the circumstances and underlying facts of the conviction, the type of sentence imposed, and most importantly, whether the type and circumstances of the crime indicate that the respondent is a danger to the community."

The Board also departed from its position in *Q–T–M–T–* when it decided *In re S–S–*, 22 I. & N. Dec. 458, Interim Decision (BIA) 3374 (BIA 1999), but this decision was later overruled. The BIA originally held that a case-by case determination is required to decide whether an aggravated felony is a particularly serious crime when the sentence is less than five years. This approach was rejected by the Attorney General and the Board returned to its rebuttable presumption approach. *See In re Y–L–*, 23 I. & N. Dec. 270, Interim Decision (BIA) 3464 (BIA 2002) (holding that aggravated felonies of unlawful trafficking in controlled substances are presumed to be "particularly serious crimes").

Also on the list of circumstances that make applicants ineligible for asylum are the commission of serious non-political crimes, persecution of others on one of the five grounds for refugee status, and terrorist activity. The Board of Immigration Appeals in *Matter of McMullen*, 19 I. & N. Dec. 90, Interim Decision 2967 (BIA 1984) concluded that the non-citizen's effective membership in the Provisional Irish Republican Army, a "clandestine, terrorist organization" engaged in the persecution of individuals opposed to the organization and its terrorist activities, constituted persecution of others on account of political opinion, making the applicant ineligible for asylum. The Board also found that the organization's random bombing of civilian targets during the period of the applicant's active membership provided "serious reasons for considering that the alien has committed a serious non-political crime outside the United States." The Board held that a crime is non-political if the crime is grossly out of proportion to the political objective or if it involves acts of an atrocious nature.

In 2002 the BIA decided *In re U–H–*, 23 I. & N. Dec. 355, Interim Decision (BIA) 3469 (BIA 2002) involving a member of the Mujahedin-e Khalq, a group designated as a foreign terrorist organization. The Board found that "§ 412 of the USA Patriot Act did not change the standard for determining whether there is reasonable ground to believe an applicant has engaged, or will engage, in terrorist activity" and held that respondent was statutorily ineligible for asylum because this standard was not met. Section 412 imposed mandatory detention for noncitizens whom the Attorney General (now Secretary of Homeland Security) has reasonable grounds to believe are engaged in terrorist activity or are a danger to national security.

INA § 212 defines "engaged in terrorist activity" to include providing material support to a terrorist organization. INA § 212(a)(3)(B)(iv). The INA provides no exception for those individuals who provide material support to terrorist organizations under duress or coercion. For example, villagers living in areas controlled by rebel or paramilitary groups and forced to pay a "tax" to the guerrillas provide material support to a terrorist organization under INA § 212. The villagers thus jeopardize their eligibility for refugee admission or asylum by paying the "tax." Beginning in 2006, the DOS and DHS began granting waivers for refugees and asylum seekers who provided material support to specific terrorist organizations under duress. The DOS and the DHS waived the material support provision for refugees and asylum seekers who gave support under duress to the following groups: Arakan Liberation Party; Chin National Front; Chin National League for Democracy; Cuban Alzados; Karen National Union; Karenni National Progressive Party; Kayan New Land Party; National Liberation Army of Colombia; Revolutionary Armed Forces of Colombia; and Tibetan Mustangs. These waivers did not apply to refugees or asylum seekers who were members of these organizations. The Consolidated Appropriations Act of 2008 replaced the waiver provisions for these specific groups with a general waiver procedure. The Secretary of State or the Secretary of Homeland Security, in consultation with the other and the Attorney General, may waive the terrorism-related grounds for inadmissibility with respect to any alien. Refugee and asylum supporters, however, continue to advocate for a change to INA § 212 that allows for a specific waiver of the material support provision for all refugees who provide support under duress.

In addition to statutory ineligibility, asylum may be denied as a matter of discretion by either the asylum officer or the immigration judge with jurisdiction over the case. *See INS v. Aguirre–Aguirre*, 526 U.S. 415 (1999) (holding that even if asylum eligibility is established, the decision whether to grant asylum is in the Attorney General's discretion). A common basis for discretionary denial of asylum, even though statutory eligibility has been proved, involves cases where the noncitizen has fraudulently or grossly circumvented U.S. legal procedures to enter the U.S. and make an asylum claim. *See, e.g., Matter of Salim*, 18 I. & N. Dec. 311, Interim Decision (BIA) 2922 (BIA 1982) (holding that while the non-citizen established the requisite probability of persecution in Afghanistan, he was to be denied asylum as a matter of discretion because he arrived in the United States with a fraudulently obtained passport). In *Matter of Pula*, 19 I. & N. Dec. 467, Interim Decision (BIA) 3033 (BIA 1987), however, the Board did not find the applicant's use of false documents to enter the U.S. such a disqualifying factor as to justify denial of asylum as an exercise of discretion. The negative factor of fraud had to be weighed against such positive factors as fear of persecution, lack of knowledge about procedures for seeking refugee status, family ties in the U.S., etc. These factors are to be considered only when an adverse factor might "overcome the presumption that 'the danger of persecution should generally outweigh all but the most egregious of adverse factors.'" *See Andriasian v. INS*, 180 F.3d 1033 (9th Cir.1999).

After IIRIRA, the Secretary of Homeland Security may in his or her discretion deny an asylum application if the non-citizen may be removed to a third country which has offered resettlement and "in which the alien's life or freedom would not be threatened on account of race, religion, nationality, membership in a particular social group, or political opinion." INA § 208(a)(2). The Secretary's determination with regard to such a safe third country is not subject to judicial review. *See* INA § 208(a)(3).

d. Right of Notice

The courts have differed over whether non-citizens must be informed of their right to apply for asylum. The court in *Nunez v. Boldin*, 537 F.Supp. 578 (S.D.Tex.1982) decided that the due process protection of non-citizens within the borders of the United States requires that citizens of El Salvador and Guatemala held at an INS detention facility be informed of their right to apply for asylum. The United States has "by treaty, statute, and regulations, manifested its intention of hearing the pleas of aliens who come to this country claiming a fear of being persecuted in their homelands." The court stated that although no regulation specifically requires immigration authorities to inform detainees of their right to apply for asylum, failure to do so may effectively render these treaties and statutes virtually nonexistent for the majority of non-citizens who would otherwise claim their benefits.

The court in *Jean v. Nelson*, 727 F.2d 957 (11th Cir.1984) took an opposing view. The court concluded that "too many asylum applications may only bury the truth by straining INS resources and preventing careful assessment of individual claims. If the volume of asylum claims rises significantly, the INS may feel compelled to rely more and more on group profiles and less on individual evidence and credibility." The court held that although non-citizens have a protected statutory and regulatory right to apply for asylum, the Constitution, the Refugee Act, and its regulations do not require immigration authorities to inform non-citizens of this right.

The decision in *Orantes–Hernandez v. Thornburgh*, 919 F.Supp 549 (9th Cir.1990) and the settlement in *American Baptist Churches v. Thornburgh*, 760 F.Supp. 796 (N.D.Cal.1991) imply that non-citizens must be notified of their right to apply for political asylum and their right to retain counsel at no cost to the government. In *Orantes–Hernandez*, the court held that the INS had to advise the Salvadorans seeking entry of their rights in English and Spanish. Immigration authorities must tell detainees that they are being detained for an immigration violation, that they will be given written notice of

their rights prior to deciding whether to return voluntarily to El Salvador, and that they will have to acknowledge that they received the written notice of their rights
(called an "*Orantes* advisal"). In 2007, a district court
refused to lift the injunction requiring immigration officials to provide notice to Salvadorans of their right to
apply for asylum. *Orantes–Hernandez v. Gonzales*, 504
F.Supp.2d 825 (C.D.Cal.2007). The court found that Customs and Border Patrol agents had complied inconsis-
tently with the terms of the *Orantes* injunction.

The written notice advises the non-citizen that he or
she has the privilege to be represented by counsel, the
right to a removal hearing, the right to apply for political
asylum, and the right to request a voluntary departure.
In addition, each detainee must be given a list of organizations that provide free legal services in the area. The
ABC settlement, discussed in greater detail below, reit-
erates these requirements. The privilege of counsel and
list of organizations have been codified at INA
§ 208(d)(4). Moreover, 8 C.F.R. §§ 1240.11(c) requires
the immigration judge presiding over a removal proceeding to advise the non-citizen that he or she may apply for
asylum in the U.S. if the non-citizen expresses a fear of
persecution upon returning to his or her country of
origin.

A non-citizen who has been found removable and requests a reopening of removal proceedings to apply for
asylum may be denied that opportunity if he or she has
not reasonably explained the failure to apply for asylum
prior to completion of the initial removal proceedings.
INS v. Abudu, 485 U.S. 94 (1988). Abudu, a citizen of
Ghana, had expressly declined to seek asylum during
removal proceedings. Upon motion to reopen, Abudu

alleged that a surprise visit from a former acquaintance, who had become a high official in the government of Ghana, was aimed at enticing Abudu to return to Ghana in order to force him to disclose the whereabouts of his brother and other enemies of the government. All the other facts upon which Abudu based his claim were available at the time of the removal hearing. The Supreme Court held that the Board of Immigration Appeals did not abuse its discretion in holding that Abudu had not reasonably explained his failure to request asylum during the initial removal proceedings as required by 8 C.F.R. § 1003.2. If Abudu had made a timely application for asylum, supported by the same factual allegations and evidence set forth in his motion to reopen, the immigration judge would have been required to grant him an evidentiary hearing. But an "alien who has already been found deportable has a much heavier burden when he first advances his request for asylum in a motion to reopen."

e. *Employment*

A non-citizen who has a pending application for asylum becomes eligible for employment authorization 180 days after filing the application. INA § 208(d)(2). The applicant must file an initial application for employment authorization (I–765) no earlier than 150 days after the date on which he or she submitted a complete asylum application. 8 C.F.R. § 208.7(a)(1). Non-citizens whose asylum applications have been recommended for approval may apply for employment authorization when so notified, even if before 150 days have passed. *Id.* The CIS is supposed to grant or deny the application for employment within 30 days from the date of filing of the Form

I–765, but as a practical matter it typically takes much longer.

If the non-citizen's application for asylum is granted, he or she will be eligible to apply for permanent residence after one year. If the asylum officer does not approve the asylum application, the officer must deny, refer, or dismiss the application as instructed in 8 C.F.R. § 208.14(c). If the non-citizen is maintaining valid non-immigrant status at the time his or her application is rejected, the non-citizen may continue in that status if it has not expired. 8 C.F.R. § 208.23.

f. Approval and Adjustment of Status

If the application for asylum is approved, asylum status is granted for an indefinite period. Employment authorization is automatically granted incident to status as an asylee. In addition, a spouse or children present in the United States at the time the application for asylum is approved may be granted asylum. See 8 C.F.R. § 208.21. Asylees may petition to bring their spouse or children not present in the United States at the time of asylum approval, using Form I–730. Asylees may also apply for a refugee travel document, using Form I–131, to obtain permission to travel abroad.

Asylum may be terminated under certain circumstances. An immigration judge or the BIA may reopen proceedings to terminate a grant of asylum. The immigration officer seeking to terminate the grant of asylum must establish by a preponderance of the evidence that conditions have changed in the asylee's country of origin, that the asylee was guilty of fraud in the application process, or that the asylee had committed an act that would have been grounds for denial. An immigration judge may terminate asylum at any time after the non-citizen has been provided a notice of intent to terminate. The termination may occur in conjunction with a removal proceeding. 8 C.F.R. § 208.24(e).

A non-citizen who has been granted asylum and who is physically present in the U.S. for one year may apply for adjustment of status to that of a permanent resident. 8 C.F.R. § 209.2. The asylee must generally meet the normal admission requirements of any immigrant with the exceptions that an asylee does not require labor certification, proof of self-sufficiency, or a valid visa. The acceptance of unauthorized employment by the asylee does not bar adjustment of status. A non-citizen may be permanently ineligible for any immigration benefits, however, if he or she knowingly files a frivolous application for asylum. The non-citizen also must continue to be a refugee within the meaning of INA § 101(a)(42) and must not have been firmly resettled in a foreign country. 8 C.F.R. § 209.2(a). Further, there must be a number available for the fiscal year from the admission allowance for refugees in general, as provided by INA § 207(a). Prior to 2005, there was an annual numerical limitation of 10,000 on the number of adjustments for asylees, but the REAL ID Act eliminated this limitation. 8 C.F.R. § 209.2(a); INA § 209(b).

The denial of an application for adjustment of status is without prejudice to the applicant's right to renew the application in removal proceedings. 8 C.F.R. § 209.2(f). If the application is granted, the date of admission as a permanent resident is recorded as one year prior to the date of application approval. INA § 209(b). The date on which the non-citizen becomes a permanent resident will determine when the non-citizen may apply for citizenship. The existence of a waiting list for asylee adjustment of status is significant since the asylee must frequently wait several years before actually acquiring permanent residence.

§ 10–2.5 Temporary Protected Status

Temporary Protected Status is a congressionally defined remedy that authorizes the Secretary of Homeland Security to provide temporary protection to nationals of countries experiencing civil upheaval or natural disasters. Previously, the Attorney General had provided temporary relief to nationals who could not return home due to country-wide chaos by granting voluntary departure for a limited period of time through an administrative program called Extended Voluntary Departure. Extended Voluntary Departure was devised by the executive branch to respond to changing world events; it was not, however, codified in the INA or any other statute. The 1990 Act amended the INA by replacing EVD with a similar program called "Temporary Protected Status" (TPS). INA § 244. Under the Homeland Security Act, administration of this program was transferred from the Attorney General to the Secretary of Homeland Security.

The 1990 Act specifically provided eligibility for Salvadorans who were in this country as of September 19, 1990, and applied for TPS between January 1 and June 30, 1991. Immigration Act of 1990, P.L. 101–649, § 303, 104 Stat. 4978, 5036. Salvadorans meeting § 303 of the 1990 Act requirements received protected status for eighteen months. The Secretary of Homeland Security possesses the discretion to make TPS designations except for the initial mandatory grant to Salvadorans, which was statutorily imposed. One of the three conditions must be met before the Secretary can exercise his discretion and grant TPS: (1) ongoing war or armed conflict within the state would pose a serious threat to a non-citizen if required to return to that country; (2) "substantial, but temporary disruption of living conditions" due to earthquake, flood, drought, epidemic, or other environmental disaster that has caused the foreign state to request TPS designation because it temporarily cannot adequately handle the return of its nationals; or (3) "extraordinary and temporary conditions" preventing the safe return of a country's nationals, so long as the national interest of the United States is not compromised by allowing their temporary stay. INA § 244(b)(1).

Soon after the 1990 Act, Kuwait, Liberia, and Lebanon received TPS designations. 56 Fed.Reg. 12745–02. Bosnia–Herzegovina (terminated August 2000), Burundi (extended until November 2004), Rwanda (terminated 1997), Sierra Leone (terminated March 2004), Somalia (extended until September 2011), and Sudan (extended until 2010) have also received TPS designation. Liberia was again designated for TPS in 2002 (extended until October 2005) because of fighting between the government and Liberians United for Reconciliation and Democracy. Each of the named countries receiving extended coverage has experienced civil war or armed conflict. Temporary Protected Status, however, may also be granted for other reasons, including environmental disasters.

In 1997, TPS was applied to Montserrat (termination effective February 2005) because of a devastating volcanic eruption and was the first example of granting this status to the victims of natural disaster. In 1999 Nicaragua and Honduras were also granted TPS as a result of severe flooding. Similarly, in an effort to assist El Salvador in recovering from two earthquakes in 2001, the Attorney General designated El Salvador for TPS benefits for a period of eighteen months. TPS has been extended for El Salvador, Nicaragua, and Honduras until 2010. TPS was granted to Haitians for a period of eighteen months after an earthquake in 2010.

Under TPS, the Secretary may designate a country or region as too unstable for aliens to return. For example, in 1998 the Attorney General extended TPS designation to a region of Yugoslavia—the province of Kosovo—to provide temporary relief to residents of Kosovo who were victims of the ethnic conflict in that province. Kosovo's TPS designation terminated in May 2000.

TPS may be granted for up to eighteen months, and the Secretary's decision to designate a country for TPS is not subject to judicial review. INA §§ 244(b)(2), 244(b)(5)(A). The Secretary must, however, establish an administrative procedure for the review of denials. INA § 244(b)(5)(B). At least sixty days prior to the end of the initial TPS period, the Secretary must review the conditions in the foreign state and determine whether the TPS designation should be terminated or extended. TPS designation may be extended for six, twelve, or eighteen months if the Secretary determines, after consultation with appropriate agencies of the government, that the conditions leading to the TPS designation are still met. INA § 244(b)(3).

The benefit of TPS is freedom from removal and authorization for employment during the effective period of protection. INA §§ 244(a)(1), (2). Also, non-citizens with TPS may not be detained on the basis of their immigration status. INA § 244(d)(4). The grant of TPS is similar to the grant of nonimmigrant status and a non-citizen granted TPS is considered as being in, and maintaining, lawful status. INA §§ 244(a)(5), 244(f). The non-citizen is restricted, however, in his or her ability to travel abroad and to receive welfare. INA § 244(f)(1)–(3). As soon as the non-citizen's TPS terminates, removal proceedings may begin.

A national of the country designated for TPS should file an application with the CIS district director having jurisdiction over the applicant's place of residence during the registration period established by the Secretary. 8 C.F.R. § 244.7. If the non-citizen has a pending removal proceeding before the immigration judge or Board of Immigration Appeals at the time of designation, the non-citizen will receive written notice of TPS and will be given an opportunity to apply for TPS unless he or she is determined to be ineligible. 8 C.F.R. § 244.7(a)(3).

To be eligible for TPS, an applicant must establish that he or she is a national of the designated foreign state; has been continuously physically present in the United States since the effective date of TPS designation; has continuously resided in the United States since a date designated by the Secretary; and is generally admissible as an immigrant under INA § 212(a). 8 C.F.R. § 244.2. Several of the inadmissibility provisions (*e.g.*, documentation requirements, limitations on foreign medical graduates, the need for a labor certificate, and the prohibition on becoming a public charge) do not apply to TPS or may be waived. Certain inadmissability provisions, however, including those covering criminal offenses, drug trafficking, matters relating to national security, and Nazi persecution may not be waived. 8 C.F.R. § 244.3. INA § 244(c)(2)(B) makes non-citizens who have been convicted of any felony or more than two misdemeanors in the United States ineligible for TPS.

To apply for TPS, the non-citizen must submit an I–821 Application for TPS, an I–765 work authorization form, two identification photos, and supporting evidence as to identity and nationality. Also, all applicants fourteen or older must be fingerprinted. 8 C.F.R. § 244.6. The applicant may be required to appear in person and present documentary evidence to establish his or her eligibility. 8 C.F.R. § 244.8.

§ 10–2.6   ABC Settlement and NACARA

a.   The ABC Settlement

In *American Baptist Church v. Thornburgh*, 760 F.Supp. 796 (N.D.Cal.1991) the INS and ABC reached a settlement in a class action suit against the Service for discriminatory handling of asylum cases involving Guatemalans and Salvadorans. Unless removal was based on criminal conduct or the proceedings were commenced after November 30, 1990, removal proceedings for noncitizens already present in the U.S. were stayed during the pendency of their *de novo* asylum adjudications; removal proceedings were also closed until the new adjudications were made. All members of the class were entitled to employment authorization in the meantime and the "non-frivolous" standard did not apply. A significant aspect of the settlement is that the government is barred from considering the following factors in making asylum determinations: (1) U.S. foreign policy as regards the applicant's country of origin, (2) border enforcement considerations, (3) U.S. support of the applicant's country of origin, and (4) the applicant's political or ideological beliefs. All Salvadorans and Guatemalans in detention were to be released, advised of their "*ABC* rights," and given the appropriate forms for complying with formal procedures. The TPS designation for El Salvador expired in 1992. As discussed above, in 2001, the Attorney General newly designated El Salvador to provide temporary relief from the earthquakes. Salvadorans who were "continuously physically present" in the U.S. since March 9, 2001, and "have continuously resided in" the U.S. since February 13, 2001, were eligible to apply for TPS as well as any Salvadoran who had already applied for "any other benefit or protection." *See also* § 2–3.2(d), *supra.*

b. NACARA

The Illegal Immigration Reform and Immigrant Responsibility Act of 1996 (IIRIRA) tightened standards for non-citizens seeking hardship relief from removal and imposed a limit on such relief of 4,000 each fiscal year. This change would have resulted in the possibility that thousands of Central Americans who were previously granted temporary protected status in the United States would now face removal. The Nicaraguan Adjustment and Central American Relief Act (NACARA) was enacted to avoid this possibility. Under NACARA, roughly 150,-000 Nicaraguans and 5,000 Cubans became eligible for adjustment of status without having to prove hardship, and approximately 200,000 Salvadorans, 50,000 Guatemalans and certain nationals of the former Soviet Union countries became eligible to apply for suspension of deportation under the more lenient, pre-IIRIRA rules. The pre-IIRIRA standard allows non-citizens who can show seven years of physical presence in the U.S., good moral character, and extreme hardship to be granted suspension of deportation and the ability to adjust to permanent resident status. These individuals are also exempt from the 4,000 annual cap imposed by IIRIRA.

CHAPTER 11

INTERNATIONAL LAW ISSUES RELATED TO IMMIGRATION

§ 11-1 FREEDOM OF MOVEMENT

§ 11-1.1 Freedom of Exit

The right of an individual to leave a nation was first mentioned in the Magna Carta of 1215, which stated that everyone had the right to leave England, subject to feudal obligations. In the following centuries, a common law writ of *Ne Exeat Regno* developed in England, conferring on the King the right to refuse exit to specific persons without special authorization. Everyone else enjoyed freedom of exit and even this royal prerogative gradually lost its importance. Blackstone stated that there was an absolute right to leave England, subject to an injunction to remain, but he also advocated the common law doctrine of perpetual allegiance, or citizenship.

In Medieval Germany, free departure was recognized as release from the feudal structure. Peasants and townspeople, who were "freemen," normally had the right to leave, but they had to pay a tribute for the privilege. Serfs, however, could not claim this right until they had bought themselves free from their bondage. In 1555 the Edict of Augsburg conferred the right to leave Germany for religious reasons. The Peace of Westphalia of 1648 also contained the right of departure. During the subsequent period, however, emigration from Germany was permitted only in exceptional situations.

416

The right to leave a nation was further recognized near the end of the Eighteenth Century. The U.S. Declaration of Independence and the Bill of Rights, and the French Declaration des Droits de l'Homme et du Citoyen of 1789 did not mention the right of exit, but were, of course, important foundations of human rights. The French Constitution of 1791 specifically proclaimed the right to leave a nation. By the middle of the nineteenth century, most European nations in practice allowed individuals to leave freely, though no generally accepted right to emigrate existed.

The right to leave a nation became more generally recognized after World War II, with the adoption of several international instruments. The Charter of the United Nations, which came into force on December 24, 1945, is the most prominent international document dealing with human rights. The Charter announces a duty of states to promote and respect human rights; it does not, however, specifically mention the right to leave. The Universal Declaration of Human Rights, adopted by the General Assembly on December 10, 1948, provides an authoritative interpretation of the human rights proclaimed by the Charter and states that "everyone has the right to leave any country, including his own. . . ." Article 12(2) of the International Covenant on Civil and Political Rights contains almost identical language that is binding on the more than 165 nations that have ratified the Covenant, including the United States. The Human Rights Committee's General Comment 15, interpreting the Covenant on Civil and Political Rights, states that non-citizens "have the right to liberty of movement and freedom of choice of residence; they shall be free to leave the country." The Fourth Protocol, Article 2(2), of the European Convention on Human Rights also contains nearly identical wording. Further, the right to leave is recognized in Article 22(2) of the American Convention on Human Rights and in Article 12(2) of the African Charter on Human and Peoples' Rights. These documents mention only the right to leave a nation, but one may infer that this right also includes the right to renounce one's citizenship.

The most recent international guarantee of the right to leave is Article 8 of the International Convention on the Protection of All Migrant Workers and Members of Their Families that protects the "freedom to leave any country" for all migrant workers and their families. This Migrant Workers convention entered into force on July 1, 2003. *See* § 11–5, *infra*.

§ 11–1.2   Right to Return

An individual may leave his or her home state, only to find that the home state will not allow his or her return. This problem may occur especially when an unpopular individual temporarily leaves the country to travel abroad. Article 13(2) of the Universal Declaration of Human Rights, Article 12(4) of the International Covenant on Civil and Political Rights, the Fourth Protocol to the European Convention on Human Rights, Article 22(5) of the American Convention on Human Rights, and Article 12(2) of the African Charter recognize the right of an individual to return to his or her home state. Moreover, the Human Rights Committee has broadly interpreted the right to return to "his own country" to give rights to stateless persons who have been resident in a particular state. Also, Article 8 of the International Convention on the Protection of All Migrant Workers calls for the freedom of migrants and their families to enter their country of origin. *See* § 11–3, *infra*.

§ 11–1.3 Right to Enter

There is no corresponding right to enter or reside in any nation of which the individual is not a citizen. *See, e.g., Boultif v. Switzerland*, 33 E.H.R.R. 50 (Eu.Ct.H.R.2001). The ability to deny entry to non-citizens is based on the theory of sovereignty. Both Blackstone and Vattel recognized the right of every nation to exclude non-citizens, or to place upon their entrance whatever restrictions the nation may want. Most nations place the greatest restrictions on immigration. Nations regularly admit non-citizens for a limited period if there is a treaty of commerce, establishment, and navigation between the non-citizen's home state and the admitting state. Parties to these treaties usually retain the right to exclude individuals who are deemed physically, medically, morally, or socially undesirable. The international human rights treaties do not grant individuals the right to enter any nation other than their own, but several provide protection from return to a dangerous situation. For example, the Convention and Protocol relating to the Status of Refugees protect a refugee from being expelled or returned to a country where his or her life or freedom will be threatened. The Convention Against Torture states and the Civil and Political Covenant and European Convention on Human Rights have been interpreted to provide that individuals may not be returned to a country where they are in danger of being tortured. *See* § 11–3.1, *infra*; chapter 10, *supra*.

§ 11–1.4 Right to Travel

No general international right to travel between nations exists. While an individual has a right to leave any nation, the individual does not have a right to enter another nation. Special travel rights are, however, given to stateless persons and to refugees. These groups will be considered in the sections below. Nations do, however, admit non-citizens more readily for temporary travel than for immigration, especially if the nation is a party to a treaty of commerce, establishment, and navigation. The Helsinki Accord, which is a European/North American regional agreement adopted in 1975 at the European Conference on Security and Cooperation in Europe (CSCE), provides for freer movement of individuals between the signatories. In particular, the agreement provides for freer movement on the basis of family ties, family reunification, proposed marriages, and personal or professional travel. In addition, further agreements in the CSCE context and changes in Eastern Europe and the former Soviet Union indicate a trend away from obstacles to free travel. In 1994, the CSCE changed its name to the Organization for Security and Cooperation in Europe (OSCE). The new name reflects the development of an administrative structure and increased activity.

European unification is another indicator of a trend toward freer travel. Under the European Union, citizens of member states have the right to travel to any other EU country upon the showing of a valid passport or identity card. This right of free travel may only be restricted for reasons of public order, public security, or public health. Family members of EU citizens share the same right of travel if they accompany the EU citizen. Spouses, children under twenty-one, dependent children over twenty-one, dependent parents, and dependent spouse's parents all qualify as family members. These family members generally travel freely regardless of nationality, but some nations require an entry visa. In addition to the freedom from special formalities, EU citizens and their families are free from any questions on the purpose of their travel and have channels at airports and seaports reserved for them to cross borders more rapidly. In addition, most of the EU nations (except Ireland and the U.K.) plus a number of other European countries (including Norway and Switzerland) have joined the Schengen Agreement, abolishing internal borders and allowing travel without the need to show passports for citizens of those 25 nations.

The United States allows freedom to travel among the states, but it has reserved the right to limit travel abroad. In *Haig v. Agee*, 453 U.S. 280 (1981), the Supreme Court upheld a regulation granting the Secretary of State broad discretion to revoke or withhold passports for reasons of national security or foreign policy. In so doing, the Court expressly limited the right to travel abroad, first announced by the Court in *Kent v. Dulles*, 357 U.S. 116 (1958). Chief Justice Burger reasoned in *Agee* that Congress had implicitly authorized passport denials and revocations in the Passport Act of 1926 by remaining inactive in the years during which that act has been construed. Under *Agee,* the Secretary of State can deny or revoke a passport only if he or she finds that "serious damage" has been done to U.S. foreign policy or national security.

The Universal Declaration of Human Rights (Art. 13(1)), the International Covenant on Civil and Political Rights (Art. 12(1)), the Fourth Protocol to the European Convention on Human Rights (Art. 2(1)), the American Convention on Human Rights (Art. 22(1)), and the African Charter (Art. 12(1)) do not guarantee travel between nations, but they do provide certain persons the freedom of movement within a state. For example, the Civil and

Political Covenant grants "the right to liberty of movement" to persons who are "lawfully within the territory of the state." The Convention and Protocol relating to the Status of Refugees as well as the Convention relating to the Status of Stateless Persons also provide for freer movement within a state for refugees and stateless persons. These last three instruments subject the right of free movement to any regulations generally applicable to non-citizens in the same circumstances.

§ 11–2 THE RIGHTS OF STATELESS PERSONS

Traditionally, states had full authority to determine who could be citizens. This authority led to dual nationalities for some, and statelessness for others. Statelessness also can occur through denationalization, voluntary renunciation of citizenship, or territorial transfer. In addition, citizenship can be lost because of a conflict of nationality laws. For example, statelessness can arise at birth when the state in which the child is born only recognizes the child as receiving the nationality of the parents, while the parent's home state recognizes only the nationality of the state where the child is born.

Stateless persons had no rights under traditional principles of international law, because they had no home state to protect them. Stateless persons were therefore totally at the mercy of the nation in which they lived.

The traditional law regarding stateless persons began to change after World War I. Little effort was made to address the issue before World War I because the problem of statelessness had not occurred on a large scale. Most of the progress, however, was made after World

War II in connection with two types of international instruments.

The first type of agreement gives rights to stateless persons. The leading instrument is the Convention relating to the Status of Stateless Persons. This treaty grants three types of rights. First, stateless persons are given rights at least as favorable as non-citizens in the particular nation where they live, for activities such as the acquisition of property. Second, stateless persons have the same rights as citizens in regard to government services such as elementary public education and public relief. Third, stateless persons are given special rights with respect to identity papers and travel documents for the purpose of traveling outside the host state.

The second type of instrument tries to prevent statelessness. Article 15 of the Universal Declaration of Human Rights says "1. Everyone has a right to a nationality. 2. No one shall be arbitrarily deprived of his nationality nor denied the right to change his nationality." Article 32 of the Convention relating to the Status of Stateless Persons provides that "the Contracting States shall as far as possible facilitate the assimilation and naturalization of stateless persons." The Convention on the Nationality of Married Women provides that a woman's nationality is not dependent on her husband's nationality. The Convention on the Rights of the Child provides that the children of stateless parents have a right to a name, to acquire nationality, and to attend school. The Convention on the Reduction of Statelessness similarly deals with the problem of statelessness at birth. A state may not deprive a person of his or her nationality under this Convention if the deprivation would render the person stateless. Further, this Convention provides that no person shall become stateless as a result of a transfer of territory. None of these instruments does much to gain citizenship for people who are already stateless. Granting these people the citizenship of the nation where they live may be the only adequate way to solve this problem. Most nations, however, have not gone that far.

In 1997 the International Law Commission adopted draft Articles on Nationality in Relation to the Succession of States, which *inter alia* attempt to prevent statelessness and assist in the determination of nationality for persons who live in countries that previously were part of such nations as the former Czechoslovakia, the Soviet Union, and Yugoslavia. In 1999, the Commission adopted the commentaries to the draft articles and decided to recommend the adoption of the declaration to the General Assembly. The draft Articles deal with general principles of nationality in relation to the succession of states and also specific categories of succession as to which model legislation is provided. The declaration reflects a trend towards assuring children born in a country of the nationality of that country if they would otherwise be stateless, that is, preferring the *jus soli* approach.

In 2005, the Inter–American Court of Human Rights relied on the principle of *jus soli* in *Case of the Girls Yean and Bosico v. Dominican Republic*, 2005 Inter-Am.Ct.H.R. (ser.C) No. 130 (Sept. 8, 2005) to determine that the Dominican Republic's birth registration and nationality laws were in violation of fundamental human rights. The Dominican Republic's discriminatory laws prevented two girls of Haitian descent who were born and resided in the Dominican Republic from attaining nationality, acquiring birth certificates and other identity documents, as well as attending school. The Inter–American Court of Human Rights ordered the Dominican Republic to develop new procedures to ensure that children born within the country, regardless of their parent's citizenship status, receive birth certificates and have the opportunity to attain citizenship and attend school. The decision affirmed that nations have a responsibility to develop laws and procedures that protect against racial discrimination and reduce the possibility of statelessness.

Following the efforts of international bodies, some states have taken action to prevent statelessness. For example, with the help of the United Nations High Commissioner for Refugees (UNHCR), Kyrgyzstan naturalized over 1500 Tajik refugees who fled from the Tajikistan Civil War during the 1990s. The UNHCR also has worked with the Ukraine, the Czech Republic, and several other countries to naturalize refugees and stateless persons residing within their borders.

Not all states have been as proactive in addressing the problem of statelessness. In 2002–03, the Committee on the Elimination of Racial Discrimination examined the conditions of several countries and recommended changes to ease the acquisition of citizenship process. For example, the Committee reported that it remained "concerned by the significantly high number of stateless persons residing in Estonia" and recommended "a thorough investigation into the possible barriers" in procedure and motivation to apply for citizenship. In 2004, the Committee issued General Recommendation No. 30 calling on states to ensure the non-discriminatory enjoyment of the right to nationality. The Committee recommended *inter alia* that states reduce statelessness, particularly among children, by encouraging parents to obtain citizenship; ease restrictions barring long-term or permanent residents from obtaining citizenship; and avoid collective expulsions of non-citizen groups and expulsions of individual non-citizens that would disproportionately interfere with the right to family life.

§ 11–3 THE RIGHTS OF REFUGEES

Refugees have problems concerning travel, social and political rights, as well as resettlement. In 1922 the High Commissioner for Russian Refugees, in conjunction with the League of Nations, created the Nansen passport. This document, which was a certificate of identity in the form of a passport, was intended to permit the bearer to travel abroad during the period of its validity, and, if specifically stated, to permit the bearer to return to the issuing country. The state where the refugee was located issued the passport, not the League of Nations.

The 1951 Convention relating to the Status of Refugees and the 1967 Protocol relating to the Status of Refugees define a refugee as:

Any person who owing to well-founded fear of being persecuted for reasons of race, religion, nationality, membership of a particular social group or political opinion, is outside the country of his nationality and is unable or, owing to such fear, is unwilling to avail himself of the protection of that country; or who, not having a nationality and being outside the country, of his former habitual residence is unable or, owing to such fear, is unwilling to return to it.

The Convention applies to persons affected by events in Europe occurring prior to January 1, 1951. The Protocol extends the protections of the Convention without the geographic and date limitations. For the 149 nations (including the U.S.) that are parties to either the Convention or the Protocol, those treaties establish the basic norm of *non-refoulement* that prohibits states from expelling or returning refugees to frontiers or territories where they would be threatened on account of race, religion, nationality, membership of a particular social group, or political opinion. The norm of *non-refoulement* was reiterated in 2001 when the International Law Commission adopted draft Articles on State Responsibility. Article 16 addresses those states that aid other states in committing internationally wrongful acts, including returning refugees to threatening situations. *See also* § 11–3.1, *infra.* These instruments also prohibit a state from expelling a refugee lawfully in its territory without fair procedures.

Article 13 of the Covenant on Civil and Political Rights similarly provides that unless national security requires otherwise, the expulsion of a non-citizen who is lawfully present is to be carried out in accordance with domestic law, and the non-citizen is to be allowed to have his or her reasons for expulsion reviewed by a competent authority. A General Comment of the Human Rights Committee in 1986 concerning Article 13 says that the rights of Article 13 also apply if the legality of a non-citizen's presence is in dispute. If a refugee is found to be inadmissible, he or she should be given an opportunity to find another country that will grant refuge. In views adopted by the Human Rights Committee in 1981 concerning *Maroufidou v. Sweden*, Comm. No. 58/1979, U.N. Doc. CCPR/C/12/D/1979 (Apr. 8, 1981), the Committee found that Sweden's expulsion of Anna Maroufidou had followed the requirements of Article 13. In views adopted in 1986 concerning *Hammel v. Madagascar*, however, the

Human Rights Committee found that Eric Hammel was expelled from Madagascar in violation of Article 13 because he did not have an opportunity to submit reasons against his expulsion or to have his case reviewed by a competent authority.

The European Court of Human Rights has also sought to protect the right of non-citizens in expulsion proceedings under Protocol 4 (Art. 4) and Protocol 7 (Art. 1) of the European Convention on Human Rights and Fundamental Freedoms that provide for procedural fairness and protection in the expulsion of non-citizens. The Court has established that Article 4 of Protocol 4 prohibits collective expulsion unless a reasonable and objective examination of each individual in the group is conducted. In *Conka v. Belgium*, 2002 WL 347196 (2002), the Court examined the case of a family of four that was collectively expelled after their asylum request was denied. The Court found a violation of Article 4 because "at no stage ... did the procedure afford sufficient guarantees demonstrating the personal circumstances of *each* of those concerned had been genuinely and *individually* taken into account."

The United States' obligations under the Protocol to protect refugees are not respected by the Illegal Immigration Reform and Immigrant Responsibility Act of 1996 (IIRIRA). The expedited removal process (IIRIRA § 302) is inconsistent with the international standards identified in Executive Committee Conclusions of the United Nations High Commissioner for Refugees (UNHCR). Executive Committee Conclusions are attained by consensus of the member states. In 1983, the UNHCR Executive Committee concluded that unless an asylum seeker's claims are "manifestly unfounded or abusive," full review of a negative decision should be available to unsuccessful applicants. Under IIRIRA § 302, however, asylum seekers are required to establish a "credible fear" before being allowed to present claims for asylum to an immigration judge. INA § 235(b)(1)(B)(iii). IIRIRA's requirement of a credible fear thus reduces opportunities for review.

Other examples of differences between IIRIRA and decisions of the UNHCR Executive Committee concern the detention of asylum seekers and the filing deadlines for asylum applications. In 1986, the UNHCR Executive Committee concluded that detention should be avoided. Under IIRIRA § 302, however, detention often occurs even when a non-citizen has established a "credible fear." INA § 235(b)(1)(B)(ii). For further discussion on the detention of asylum seekers, see § 11–4.2, *infra.* In 1977, the UNHCR Executive Committee concluded that the failure of asylum seekers to apply for asylum within a certain time period should not prevent the consideration of late applications. Under IIRIRA § 604, an asylum seeker must apply for asylum within a year of arrival unless the asylum seeker can show changed country conditions or extraordinary circumstances relating to the delay. INA § 235(a)(2)(B). IIRIRA's filing deadline removes the option of asylum for at least some of those persons whom the Protocol seeks to protect.

In a 1994 speech, the United Nations High Commissioner for Refugees, Sadako Ogata, linked the norm of *non-refoulement* with the rights to life and freedom from cruel, inhuman, or degrading treatment. Her statement echoes earlier statements by the Executive Committee of UNHCR that refusing admission to stowaway asylum-seekers could be cruel or degrading treatment and that treaty provisions are increasingly interpreted to protect against the expulsion of a person to a country where that person is at risk of being tortured or subjected to inhuman or cruel treatment or punishment.

The Refugee Convention of 1951 and the Protocol of 1967 give refugees certain travel rights. Article 26 of the Convention affords refugees the same right as other noncitizens, in the same circumstances, to travel within a state. Article 27 provides that states "shall issue identity papers to any refugee in the territory who does not possess a valid travel document." Furthermore, Article 28 provides that states shall issue travel documents to refugees lawfully staying in their territory for the purpose of traveling outside their territory.

The Refugee Convention of 1951 and 1967 Protocol also give rights to refugees almost identical to the rights given stateless persons in the Convention relating to the Status of Stateless Persons. Under the 1951 Convention, refugees have rights at least as great as other noncitizens in the same state in regard to such subjects as the acquisition of property. The Universal Declaration of Human Rights and the two International Covenants on Human Rights provide civil, political, economic, social, and cultural rights to all people, including refugees. The rights of people displaced by armed conflicts are also protected by the Fourth Geneva Convention of 1949, as extended by the two Additional Protocols of 1977.

The Organization of African Unity Convention Governing the Specific Aspects of Refugee Problems in Africa of 1969 broadens the definition and thus the protection of refugees to include as refugees:

> [E]very person who, owing to external aggression, occupation, foreign domination or events seriously disturbing public order in either part or the whole of his

country of origin or nationality, is compelled to leave
his place of habitual residence in order to seek refuge
in another place outside his country of origin or nationality.

A similarly broad definition of refugee was also accepted
by the Colloquium on the International Protection of
Refugees in Central America, Mexico, and Panama in its
Cartegena Declaration of 1984 to include persons who
have fled their country because their lives, safety, or
freedom have been threatened by generalized violence,
foreign aggression, internal conflicts, massive violations
of human rights, or other circumstances that have seriously disturbed public order.

There are several international organizations that protect and provide assistance to refugees. The United Nations High Commissioner for Refugees (UNHCR) provides "for the protection of refugees falling under the
competence of his [her] office." The UNHCR also helps
to house, feed, resettle, repatriate, and integrate refugees. The International Organization for Migration and
many voluntary agencies assist the UNHCR in these
tasks. The International Committee of the Red Cross and
the Red Cross/Red Crescent Societies around the world
also assist victims of armed conflicts.

At the start of 2009, there were 34.1 million persons
who were of concern to the UNHCR. This number has
doubled since 2004. Of the 34.1 million, there were 9
million refugees; 830,000 asylum seekers; 14.4 million
internally displaced; 2 million returned refugees and
internally displaced persons; and 9 million others of
concern (that is, who were in a refugee-like situation but
have not been formally recognized as refugees). The
UNHCR has been requested by the Secretary–General or

other U.N. organs to assist some, but not all, internally displaced persons. In part because of the relationship between external and internal displacement, the UNHCR has been involved with internally displaced in Central America, Africa, countries of the former Soviet Union and former Yugoslavia, and elsewhere. In 1994, UNHCR Executive Committee Conclusions emphasized the need for the international community to respond to the problem of internally displaced persons and the UNHCR has since increased its involvement with internally displaced, returnees, and persons threatened with displacement by armed conflict.

At the request of the U.N. Commission on Human Rights, a Special Representative of the Secretary–General on internally displaced persons was appointed in 1998. The U.N. Special Representative on internally displaced persons estimated that there were more than 16 million internally displaced in the world during 1994. By the end of 2001, the number rose to 25 million internally displaced persons spread over forty-seven countries. In 2008, the number stood at 14.4 million spread over twenty-three countries. The Special Representative reports regularly to the Human Rights Council as the successor to the Commission and raises consciousness about the treatment of the internally displaced, and has made efforts to develop guiding principles that address the needs of the internally displaced.

One area that has received an increasing amount of attention has been housing and property restitution for refugees and the internally displaced. According to a preliminary report to the United Nations Sub–Commission on the Promotion and Protection of Human Rights (now the United Nations Human Rights Council Advisory Committee), "this attention is due in large part to the unique role that housing and real property restitution play in securing the voluntary, safe and dignified return of refugees and other displaced persons to their homes and places of origin." In 2005 the Sub–Commission endorsed the Principles on Housing and Property Restitution for Refugees and Displaced Persons (also known as the Pinheiro Principles) to provide guidance in implementing housing and property restitution programs.

§ 11–3.1   Right Not to Be Returned, and Suffer Torture or Ill–Treatment

The Convention against Torture, which has 147 parties (including the U.S.), states that "No State Party shall expel, return ('refouler') or extradite a person to another State where there are substantial grounds for believing that he would be in danger of being subjected to torture." The presence of "a consistent pattern of gross, flagrant or mass violations of human rights" is to be considered in determining if substantial grounds are present. The Committee against Torture has applied Article 3 of the Convention against Torture to find an obligation not to expel a person to a country when that individual is personally at risk of being expelled or returned to a country to be tortured. In its General Comment No. 1, the Committee against Torture explained that "the risk of torture must be assessed on grounds that go beyond mere theory or suspicion, [h]owever, the risk does not have to meet the test of being highly probable." The norm of *non-refoulement* under the Convention against Torture does not require that the torture that an individual faces be for reasons of race, religion, nationality, membership of a particular social group or political opinion.

The Committee against Torture has considered several alleged violations of the Convention against Torture. In 2002, the Committee decided *Karoui v. Sweden*, 2002 WL 32093023 (2002) and found that removal of Karoui to Tunisia would violate Article 3 because of the pattern of detention, imprisonment, torture, and ill-treatment of persons accused of political opposition activities. Karoui had been tried *in absentia* in Tunisia and convicted for being a member of an outlaw organization. Other Committee decisions include *F.F.Z. v. Denmark*, 2002 WL 32093021 (2002) (no breach because expulsion of complainant would not have the "foreseeable consequence of exposing him to a real and personal risk of being arrested and tortured") and *Y.H.A. v. Australia*, 2000 WL 33541815 (2000) (no breach since complainant would not now face a risk of torture because of a new government). Although the U.S. is a party to the Convention against Torture, it does not recognize the authority of the Committee to consider individual complaints made against it under the Convention.

The Covenant on Civil and Political Rights has been interpreted even more broadly than the Convention against Torture to prohibit the sending back of a person to his or her country of origin where that person would be at risk of either torture or ill-treatment. Article 7 of the Covenant on Civil and Political Rights prohibits the subjection of anyone to "cruel, inhuman or degrading treatment or punishment." As with the Convention against Torture, the interpretation of the Covenant on Civil and Political Rights in the context of returning a person to his or her country of origin applies Article 7 even to persons who have committed serious offenses.

Cruel and inhuman treatment within the meaning of Article 7 of the Covenant can include capital punishment if the punishment is not carried out with a minimum of suffering. The Human Rights Committee in 1993 considered a communication concerning *Ng v. Canada*, Comm. No. 469/1991, U.N. Doc. CCPR/C/49/D/469/1991 (Jan. 7, 1994), and determined that the possibility that Charles Ng would be executed by gas asphyxiation if he were returned to California would make complying with a request for his extradition a violation of the Covenant. The same year, the Committee rejected a communication concerning *Kindler v. Canada*, Comm. No. 470/1991, U.N. Doc. CCPR/C/48/D/470/1991 (1993) holding that capital punishment is not always a violation of the Covenant and found that the potential execution of Joseph Kindler by lethal injection would not violate the Covenant. Similarly in *Cox v. Canada*, Comm. No. 539/1993, U.N. Doc. CCPR/C/52/D/539/1993 (1994), the Human Rights Committee in 1994 adopted the view that the confinement of Keith Cox on death row would not violate the Covenant, at least in part because of the possibility of appeal or pardon.

In 2008, Texas executed a Mexican national, José Medellin, despite a ruling by the International Court of Justice (ICJ) to reexamine Medellin's case. Mexico brought an action against the United States in the ICJ for violating the Vienna Convention on Consular Relations by failing to allow Mexican citizens like Medellin to consult with Mexican diplomats after being charged with a crime by U.S. authorities. The ICJ found in favor of Mexico and ordered the U.S. to reconsider Medellin's case. The U.S. Supreme Court, however, ruled that Texas did not need to comply with the IJC decision and Texas carried out Medellin's execution.

Article 3 of the European Convention for the Protection of Human Rights and Fundamental Freedoms states that a person shall not be "subjected to torture or to inhuman or degrading treatment or punishment." In 1989, the European Court of Human Rights, in *Soering v. United Kingdom*, 161 Eur. Ct. H.R. (ser. A) (1989), found that the extradition of Jens Soering to the U.S. would violate Article 3. In making this finding, the European Court held that it would inflict inhuman and degrading treatment on Soering if he were subjected to a prolonged detention on death row in Virginia. (Eventually, he was extradited to stand trial for murder under an assurance that he would not be sentenced to death.) In 1991, the European Court of Human Rights in *Vilvarajah v. United Kingdom*, 215 Eur. Ct. H.R. (ser. A) (1991), stated that the possibility of ill-treatment of Nadarajah Vilvarajah and others when they were returned to Sri Lanka did not violate Article 3 because there were not substantial grounds for believing that the applicants would be subject to a real risk. In 1996, the European Court, in *Chahal v. United Kingdom*, 23 Eur. H.R. Rep. 413 (1997), held that there was a real risk of Mr. Chahal being subjected to treatment contrary to Article 3 if he were to be returned to India. Chahal was a leading Sikh militant supporting the cause of separatism and was likely to be targeted by Punjab police and/or the security forces, irrespective of which part of India to which he returned. The Court gave little credence to assurances of the Indian government that Chahal would not be subjected to ill-treatment, because the government had been unable to curb human rights violations by the Punjab police and other security forces.

In 2009, the European Court of Justice in *Elgafaji v. Staatssecretaris van Justitie*, Case C-465/07 (Feb. 17, 2009), http://curia.europaeu, held that persons may be entitled to asylum if there is widespread and indiscriminate violence in their home countries, even if the applicants cannot demonstrate that they are the specific targets of violence. Under this ruling, a member state of the

European Union must consider whether the indiscriminate violence taking place in the asylum seeker's home country reaches such a high level that the asylum seeker will face a substantial risk of being the victim of violence if returned to his or her home country. In this case, the European Court of Justice found that the risk of indiscriminate violence an Iraqi couple would face if returned to Iraq warranted the granting of asylum even though the couple was not subject to specific threats.

Article 8 of the European Convention for the Protection of Human Rights and Fundamental Freedoms states that "everyone has the right to respect for his private and family life, his home and his correspondence and there shall be no interference by a public authority with the exercise of this right except such as is in accordance with the law and is necessary in a democratic society, in the interests of national security, public safety or the economic well-being of the country, for the prevention of disorder or crime, for the protection of health or morals, or for the protection of the rights and freedoms of others." In 1997, the European Court of Human Rights, in *Boujlifa v. France*, 1997-VI Eur. Ct. H.R. 2250 (1997), held that the deportation of a Moroccan national did not constitute a violation of Article 8. Mr. Boujlifa claimed that deportation would interfere with his private and family life. He had lived in France since he was five years old and received his education there; his parents and eight brothers and sisters lived in France; and he was living with a French woman. The Court noted that the offenses of armed robbery and robbery, for which Mr. Boujlifa's deportation was sought, constituted a particularly serious violation of security and of public order. Under the circumstances of this case, the requirements of public order outweighed the interference with Boujlifa's personal and family life. Hence, the Court found that deportation could not be regarded as disproportionate to the legitimate aims pursued.

In 2001, the European Court found a breach of Article 8 in *Boultif v. Switzerland*, 33 E.H.R.R. 50 (2001). The applicant, an Algerian citizen, moved to Switzerland in 1992 and married in 1993. He then committed a violent crime in 1994 and Switzerland refused to renew his residence permit. The Court balanced the applicant's right to respect for his family life and the prevention of disorder and crime and found "the interference with his family life was not proportionate to the aim pursued" because the applicant posed little future danger to public order and it would be "practically impossible for him to live with his family outside Switzerland."

The right to family life is also protected in the International Covenant on Civil and Political Rights (Art. 17), the Convention on the Protection of All Migrant Workers and Members of Their Families (Art. 13), the American Convention on Human Rights (Arts. 17 and 19), the African Charter on Human and Peoples' Rights (Art. 18), and the Convention on the Rights of the Child (Arts. 3, 9, 10 and 16).

§ 11–4 ASYLUM

§ 11–4.1 The Right to Grant Asylum

A nation may grant either asylum within its territory ("territorial asylum") or within its embassies, consular offices, military ships, or other such locations. The idea of asylum developed before the Middle Ages when churches granted a refuge in holy places where persons fleeing from danger could be free from seizure. As the power of governments grew, asylum in churches became less prevalent.

European governments began granting territorial asylum as the Reformation divided the continent. An increase in the granting of territorial asylum occurred in the Eighteenth Century. Legal writers in the eighteenth century began invoking asylum for those persons guilty of political crimes and for victims of religious persecution. Grotius went so far as to view asylum as both a state's right and duty. Most other writers, however, did not go as far as saying that states had a duty to grant political asylum. During and after the French Revolution, this notion was transformed into a juridical principle. The Revolution considered it a duty of countries to help the oppressed. The French Constitution of 1793 provided asylum for foreigners who were exiled from their home state in the cause of human rights and liberty.

The right to grant asylum is reflected in several international instruments. Article 14 of the Universal Declaration of Human Rights provides the right to "seek and enjoy" asylum. This right, however, "may not be invoked in the case of prosecutions genuinely arising from non-political crimes or from acts contrary to the purposes and principles of the United Nations." The U.N. General Assembly Resolution 2312 (XXII) on Territorial Asylum of 1967 reaffirmed the right to grant asylum contained in Article 14 of the Universal Declaration of Human Rights.

§ 11–4.2   The Right to Receive Asylum

While it is generally agreed that nations have the right to grant asylum, there is no similar agreement on the right of an individual to demand asylum. Article 14 of the Universal Declaration of Human Rights provides a "right to seek and to enjoy in other countries asylum from persecution." There is no right, however, to be granted asylum. An earlier draft provided for a right to "seek and be granted" asylum. This language was amended to make clear that states were not willing to accept an obligation to open their borders in advance to an unascertainable and possibly large number of refugees.

Although an individual may not have a right to asylum, the Convention and Protocol relating to the Status of Refugees forbid a nation from forcibly returning a refugee who is fleeing from a neighboring state. The admitting nation is then free to force the individual to go to another nation. This right is reflected in U.N. General Assembly Resolution 2312 (XXII) on Territorial Asylum of 1967. Article 3, paragraph 1, states that "no person referred to in Article 1, paragraph 1, shall be subjected to measures such as rejection at the frontier or, if he has already entered the territory in which he seeks asylum, expulsion or compulsory return to any state where he may be subjected to persecution." Paragraph 2 provides an exception in the case of national security, public safety, or massive influx of persons.

The UNHCR attempted in 1977 to establish a treaty on territorial asylum along the same lines as the Declaration on Territorial Asylum by convening a Conference of Plenipotentiaries in Geneva. The participating states, however, were unable to agree; the UNHCR adjourned the conference indefinitely because of the concern that the states would diminish the international protections for those persons who seek asylum.

The Executive Committee of the UNHCR in 1981 adopted non-binding recommendations regarding the protection of asylum seekers particularly in the context of massive movements of population. The Executive Committee recommended that asylum seekers be admitted to the state where they first seek entry, so that they may be afforded protection and assistance, even for a temporary period. The recommendations also state that asylum seekers should not be punished for illegal entry, should enjoy the rights established in the Universal Declaration of Human Rights, should be granted all the necessary facilities to enable them to obtain a satisfactory durable solution, etc.

Despite the various recommendations, the Convention on Refugees, the related Protocol, and national asylum procedures, there seems to be a growing recognition that these instruments do not establish a satisfactory legal framework for dealing with the recent large influxes of asylum seekers. The recommendations, the Convention, the Protocol, and the national procedures, which they inspired, are premised upon the need for an individual determination of eligibility for asylum. Massive population movements in which many claim asylum do not permit such individual determinations. Also, intended immigrants claim asylum in many countries knowing that the procedures for individual adjudication are so overloaded that they effectively will be able to remain indefinitely. Governments have begun to respond by detaining large numbers of asylum seekers and by developing expedited asylum procedures. Detention is acceptable in limited circumstances, but at no time may governments engage in arbitrary detention. *See, e.g., Conka v. Belgium*, 2002 WL 347196 (Eur.Ct.H.R.2002) (ruling that all individuals must be protected from arbitrary detention, but that states may arrest or detain noncitizens to prevent crimes or fleeing during the deportation or extradition process). The Standing Committee of the Executive Committee of the High Commissioner's

Programme on Detention defines detention as arbitrary if:

It is not in accordance with the law; if the law itself allows for arbitrary practices, or is enforced in an arbitrary way; when it is random or capricious or not accompanied by fair and efficient procedures for its review. It may also be arbitrary if it is disproportionate or indefinite.

Prohibitions on arbitrary detention are well established. The Human Rights Committee has stated that arbitrary detention violates Article 9 of the Civil and Political Covenant. In 1995, the Executive Committee of the UNHCR issued "Guidelines on Detention of Asylum–Seekers" and revised them in 1999 to further address the issue of arbitrary detention. These guidelines provide minimum standards for state detention practices and reiterate the exceptional situations that allow for detention that were originally set forth in the Executive Committee's "Conclusion on Detention of Refugees and Asylum–Seekers" of 1986.

The United States and several other states have not complied with the prohibitions and guidelines on detention. In 1999, a UNHCR study monitored detention practices in Asia, Africa, and the Americas, as well as Europe, and reported that the results "suggest no amelioration of the problem." Since 1999, the United States has shown no signs of correcting its detention practices. For example, the United States established Operation Liberty Shield in 2003, calling for denial of parole and detention of all arriving asylum applicants from thirty-four countries. Even though the Department of Homeland Security later limited detention to those asylum seekers without identity documents, several international bodies have stated that asylum seekers should not be detained for lack of identity papers.

While there is a need for a new structure to protect asylees and refugees worldwide, there is concern that such a structure may be less protective of the rights of asylum seekers than the present approach. Rather than seek a new legal structure, the UNHCR has used ad hoc approaches in which, for example, a prima facie determination of eligibility for asylum is made for whole groups at a time. Governments have also begun to provide temporary protected status and similarly restricted entry rather than refugee status as a way of dealing with major influxes. *See* § 10–2.5, *supra*. Nonetheless, there is little doubt that the problem of mass exodus and asylum represents a continuing challenge for both domestic and international legal systems.

§ 11–5 THE RIGHTS OF MIGRANT WORKERS

International Labor Organization (ILO) Conventions and recommendations generally protect the rights of all workers irrespective of citizenship. Several ILO conventions and recommendations, however, specifically protect migrant workers and their families. In 1949, the ILO promulgated Convention No. 97 concerning Migration for Employment and the related Recommendation No. 86 concerning Migration for Employment. These two instruments provide:

    1.   Safeguards against misleading information relating to emigration and immigration;

    2.   assurance of medical services for migrants;

3.   a prohibition against discrimination in regard to conditions of employment, trade union membership, social security, and taxes;

4.   a prohibition against returning a migrant to his or her country of origin after he or she was admitted on a permanent basis, but is no longer able to work by reason of illness; and

5.   similar protections for migrants.

The Migrant Workers (Supplementary Provisions) Convention of 1975 (No. 143) and the Migrant Workers Recommendations of 1975 (No. 151) supplement these legal protections by providing that governments should not only repeal discriminatory legislation, but also enact promotional legislation to guarantee equality of opportunity and treatment in respect of employment, occupation, social security, trade union and cultural rights, as well as individual and collective freedoms of migrant workers. The ILO also has adopted a convention supporting the rights of migrant workers to social security.

Forty-nine countries have ratified Convention No. 97, including Belgium, France, the Federal Republic of Germany, Italy, Netherlands, Portugal, Spain, and the United Kingdom. The United States is conspicuously absent from this list. Only twenty-three countries have, so far, ratified the supplementary Convention No. 143; of the countries just mentioned, only Italy and Portugal have ratified this instrument.

There is also a European Convention on the Legal Status of Migrant Workers. This convention came into force on 1 May 1983. As of 2010, it has been ratified by Albania, Belgium, France, Germany, Greece, Italy, Luxembourg, Moldova, Netherlands, Norway, Portugal, Spain, Sweden, Turkey, and Ukraine.

After eleven years of drafting, the U.N. General Assembly on December 18, 1990, adopted the International Convention on the Protection of the Rights of All Migrant Workers and Members of Their Families. A total of twenty parties were required and thus on July 1, 2003, the Convention came into force after ratification by the twentieth and twenty-first nations. The present 43 ratifying nations include Colombia, Egypt, Malawi, Morocco, Philippines, Seychelles, Sri Lanka, Uganda, and other source countries but not receiving countries. The Convention provides further protection for the rights of all migrant workers and their families, including frontier workers, seasonal workers, itinerant workers, and project-tied workers. The Convention does not apply to investors, international organization employees, foreign development staff, students, trainees, refugees, and stateless persons. Furthermore, Article 35 of the Convention provides that none of its provisions shall be interpreted to imply the regularization of undocumented migrant workers.

With regard to certain rights, the U.N. Convention is broader and more specific than the existing ILO instruments. Articles 43 and 45 of the U.N. Convention provide for equality of treatment for migrant workers and their families in access to educational institutions, vocational training, social and health services, and to cultural life. Furthermore, the migrant worker is guaranteed equality of treatment in access to co-operatives and self-management enterprises without change in migration status, and to housing. Further rights provided in the Convention include: the right to equality of treatment with nationals of the state concerned before courts and tribunals (Article 18); the prohibition of collective expulsion (Article 22); equal treatment with nationals as regards remuneration (Article 25); trade union rights and freedom of association (Articles 26 and 40); the facilitation of reunification of migrant workers with their families (Article 44); and the right to transfer earnings, particularly for the support of their families, to the country of origin (Article 47).

In accordance with the Convention, the Committee on the Protection of the Rights of All Migrant Workers and Members of Their Families was established to examine government reports submitted every five years on their laws and practices with regard to the rights recognized in the Convention. This Committee will also be authorized to consider complaints made by one state party concerning the laws and practices of another state party and will consider individual complaints if that individual's government declares that it is willing to authorize the Committee to receive such complaints.

§ 11–6 RIGHTS OF NON–CITIZENS

According to an International Organization for Migration 2009 report, the number of individuals residing in a country other than where they were born increased from 75 million to 200 million from 1975 to 2009. Many of these people face a reality different than the guarantees of the international instruments interpreted to protect non-citizen rights. This disparity has worsened as countries have increasingly violated non-citizens' rights in response to fears of terrorism.

International human rights law generally requires the equal treatment of citizens and non-citizens, but no widely ratified treaty specifically addresses the rights of non-citizens. Members of various international bodies have thus had to interpret the widely ratified treaties as including non-citizens and they have had to adopt declarations and recommendations for the treatment of non-citizens. In 1985, for example, the U.N. General Assembly adopted by consensus a declaration on the human rights of individuals who are not citizens of the country in which they live. The declaration covers all individuals who are not nationals of the state in which they are present. The declaration provides for the respect of fundamental human rights of non-citizens (Article 5—right to life; right to privacy; equality before the courts and tribunals; freedom of opinion and religion; and retention of language, culture, and tradition). Subject to certain national restrictions, non-citizens shall also be guaranteed the right to leave the country, to freedom of expression, to peaceful assembly, and to own property alone or collectively.

Articles 7 and 8 provide rights for non-citizens lawfully in the country. Article 7 prohibits individual or collective expulsion on discriminatory grounds. Article 8 provides for trade union rights as well as the right to safe and healthy working conditions and the right to medical care, social security, and education.

The rights of non-citizens are also set forth in the General Comment of the Human Rights Committee issued in 1986 to interpret the relevant provisions of the International Covenant on Civil and Political Rights. In general, the Comment and other human rights treaties protect the rights of all persons or "everyone" including non-citizens, but states may make distinctions between citizens and non-citizens if they serve a legitimate state objective and are proportional to the achievement of that objective.

In 2004, the Committee on the Elimination of Racial Discrimination (CERD) issued General Recommendation 30 to reiterate the responsibilities of states to protect the rights of non-citizens. CERD identified five areas of particular concern: protection against hate speech; access to citizenship; administration of justice; expulsion and deportation; and economic, social and cultural rights. CERD urged states to take stronger action to punish racially motivated violence against non-citizens, avoid arbitrary detention of non-citizens, and ensure that non-citizens have access to legal remedies for discrimination and violence directed against them.

One area of increasing concern for non-citizens is the use of unlawful and indefinite detentions by governments. In the aftermath of terrorist attacks in the United States, Spain, the United Kingdom, and elsewhere, many countries have used the threat of terrorism to indefinitely detain non-citizens. The U.S. detention of terrorism suspects at Guantánamo Bay, Cuba, is one particularly controversial case. In 2009, the United Kingdom House of Lords ruled in *A (FC) and Others v. Secretary of State for the Home Department*, 49 E.H.R.R. 29 (2009), that the UK government's detention of nine non-UK nationals suspected of terrorism violated the Article 5 protections of liberty and security of the European Convention on Human Rights. The House of Lords also relied upon other European human rights law and upon CERD's General Recommendation 30 in rendering its decision.

CHAPTER 12

CITIZENSHIP

§ 12–1 CONCEPTS OF CITIZENSHIP

§ 12–1.1 Citizenship and Alienage

Citizenship connotes membership in a political society to which a duty of permanent allegiance is implied. The United States Supreme Court in *United States v. Cruikshank*, 92 U.S. 542 (1875), stated:

Citizens are the members of the political community to which they belong. They are the people who compose the community, and who, in their associated capacity, have established or submitted themselves to the dominion of a government for the promotion of their general welfare and the protection of their individual as well as collective rights.

Alienage has the opposite meaning and signifies a condition of not belonging to the nation. The allegiance required of non-citizens is temporary and consists of willingness to comply with the nation's laws while residing in its territory.

The status of citizens in the United States carries with it all the rights and privileges embodied in the Constitution. Although non-citizens also enjoy certain constitutional protections, some provisions protect only "citizens," such as the Privileges and Immunities Clause of Article IV and the Fourteenth Amendment. Moreover, citizens have the right to vote and to hold office. *See*

§ 13–4.1, *infra*. While there are numerous grounds for removal of non-citizens, a citizen can only lose his or her right to live in the United States through voluntary expatriation or revocation of naturalization.

With the additional rights of citizenship come added responsibilities, such as the obligation to accept jury duty when called. 28 U.S.C.A. § 1861. In contrast, non-citizens are disqualified from serving on a jury, and a non-citizen's presence on a jury in a felony trial has served as ground to vacate the conviction

The connections one must have with the nation to be a citizen varies with the manner by which citizenship is acquired. Almost all persons born in the United States, for example, acquire citizenship automatically and cannot lose it involuntarily, even if they leave the United States immediately after birth and never return. Non-citizens seeking citizenship by naturalization, however, generally must reside in the United States for five years after having been granted permanent residence and demonstrate their good moral character, attachment to the United States, and English literacy, as well as their understanding of United States history and principles of government. INA § 316(a).

When the United States acquired outlying territorial possessions at the beginning of the twentieth century, native populations were not considered citizens, though their allegiance to the United States was expected. The Supreme Court held in the "Insular Cases" that these territories were not "incorporated" into the United States, and hence, local populations were to be accorded a reduced level of constitutional protection. *See Balzac v. Pörto Rico*, 258 U.S. 298 (1922). The degree of constitutional protection afforded to residents of U.S. Territories, as well as their citizenship status, is controlled by Congress. *See Torres v. Puerto Rico*, 439 U.S. 815 (1978).

This chapter examines the two major methods by which citizenship may be acquired—birth and naturalization. It describes the substantive requirements of naturalization and the procedures involved in seeking citizenship under the naturalization laws. The final section focuses on loss of nationality through either denaturalization or expatriation. As a preliminary matter, however, the discussion first considers the two rules for determining citizenship—the principles of *jus soli* and *jus sanguinis*.

§ 12–1.2   The Principles of Jus Soli and Jus Sanguinis

Citizenship at birth in the United States is conferred automatically—the person's volition plays no part. Such automatic acquisition of citizenship assures that each person will have a nationality in the United States. In light of experience such a result appears reasonable, as people have traditionally remained loyal and committed to the citizenship they acquire at birth. There exists no universal nationality rule, however. While some nations adhere to the principle of *jus soli*—citizenship by the place of one's birth, others embrace the principle of *jus sanguinis*—citizenship by descent, or literally, blood relationship. Moreover, a number of nations, including the United States and the United Kingdom, have adopted a combination of the two principles.

The principle of *jus soli* was a tenet of the common law of England. Although it has its roots in feudalism, it still serves well as a basic rule of citizenship in many parts of the world. *Jus sanguinis* was the rule of civil law countries in Europe which determined an individual's citizenship at birth by the citizenship of his or her parents. The concept of nationality based upon blood took hold in Europe during the French Revolution, which had created a spirit of patriotism and fraternity for the French as a distinct people, and this sort of nationalistic fervor eventually spread to other peoples of Europe.

Jus soli continued to establish the citizenship of people born in England even after feudalism no longer existed. The rule's primary advantage as the criterion for citizenship lay in the certainty it provided each person's political status. In the United Kingdom the principle of *jus soli* remains the basis of nationality law. Nonetheless, the development of the British Empire, resulting foreign trade, and travel led to statutory provisions which followed the approach of *jus sanguinis*—granting citizenship to children born abroad of British parents.

Similarly, in the United States the principle of *jus soli* generally was accepted as part and parcel of the common law inherited from England. *See United States v. Wong Kim Ark*, 169 U.S. 649 (1898). Hence, citizenship was conferred ordinarily upon the native born, although large groups of native-born persons—American Indians, people of African descent, and Asians—did not enjoy citizenship status for many years after the formation of the republic. *See Elk v. Wilkins*, 112 U.S. 94 (1884).

The principle of *jus soli* was codified in the Fourteenth Amendment of 1868. The principle of *jus sanguinis* in United States nationality law was first established by the Act of 1790, which provided that children born abroad of United States citizens who had resided in the United States "shall be considered as natural-born citizens." 1 Stat. 103. Every subsequent statute has precluded acquisition of United States citizenship by a child born abroad unless the citizen parent or parents have resided in the United States. *See* INA § 301.

§ 12–1.3   Dual Nationality

Because different countries have different rules for conferring citizenship, an individual can be a citizen of more than one nation. Individuals born of non-citizen parents in the United States ordinarily obtain U.S. citizenship at birth yet they also may be vested with the citizenship of their parents by the *jus sanguinis* laws of the foreign state. *See, e.g., Mandoli v. Acheson*, 344 U.S. 133 (1952). Likewise, children born abroad to U.S. citizen parents may acquire dual citizenship at birth.

Dual nationality can also arise through naturalization. U.S. citizens who obtain naturalization in another country will retain U.S. citizenship unless they formally relinquish it. INA § 349(a)(1). *See* § 12–3.3(d), *infra*. Similarly, since some countries do not consider the oath of allegiance required for naturalization in the United States to be an expatriating act, individuals may acquire U.S. citizenship without losing their prior citizenship. *See* § 12–2.2(b)(6), *infra*.

Dual nationality is not without problems. Citizenship normally implies allegiance to only one country, so dual citizens may face conflicts of loyalty. They may also be subject to multiple or inconsistent obligations, such as owing military service or taxes to more than one country. Diplomatic conflicts can arise if a dual citizen claims the protection of one country of citizenship when he or she faces legal difficulties in the other country. Foreign governments might be able to affect U.S. policies—at least inadvertently—through the votes of their dual nationals.

Hence, the U.S. government, although recognizing that it exists, officially discourages dual nationality.

The problems caused by dual nationality may become particularly serious in times of war, as the case of *Kawakita v. United States*, 343 U.S. 717 (1952) demonstrated. Tomoya Kawakita was born in the United States of Japanese parents and obtained dual citizenship by virtue of the nationality laws of each country. He lived in the United States until 1939, when at age seventeen he went to Japan and undertook studies at the Meiji University. After December 7, 1941, the United States and Japan were engaged in war but Kawakita remained in Japan to continue his studies. In March 1943, he registered in the Koseki, a family census register, after being told by the Japanese police that he must make a choice of citizenship. He never served in the armed forces of Japan. Rather, he obtained employment as an interpreter with the Oeyama Nickel Industry Co., Ltd., where he worked until Japan's surrender. He was hired to interpret communications between the Japanese and the prisoners of war who were assigned to work at the mine and in the factory of the company. During his employment he allegedly committed acts of brutality against United States prisoners.

In December 1945, Kawakita went to the United States consulate at Yokohama and applied for registration as a U.S. citizen, stating under oath that he was a citizen of the United States and had not done any acts amounting to expatriation. He obtained a passport and returned to the United States in 1946. Shortly thereafter he was recognized by one of the former prisoners of war; Kawakita was arrested, charged, and tried for treason.

At his trial Kawakita argued that he had terminated his United States citizenship in 1943 before the alleged acts of brutality, and thus could not be guilty of treason. The trial court submitted the issue as to whether he had expatriated himself to the jury, and charged that upon finding Kawakita had lost his citizenship prior to the time specified in the indictment, they must acquit him, since his duty of allegiance would have ceased with the termination of his United States citizenship. The jury found that Kawakita had not expatriated himself under any of the methods prescribed by Congress, and he was found guilty of treason and sentenced to death. The Ninth Circuit affirmed in 1951.

On writ of certiorari the United States Supreme Court (by a four-to-three majority) affirmed the conviction and death sentence, upholding the jury's findings of fact. The Court further stated: "He cannot turn (his United States citizenship) into a fair-weather citizenship, retaining it for possible contingent benefits but meanwhile playing the part of the traitor. An American citizen owes allegiance to the United States wherever he may reside." President Eisenhower later commuted Kawakita's death sentence to life imprisonment. In 1963 he obtained his release and returned to Japan.

Despite the potential problems of dual nationality, a growing number of countries recognize this status. In the 1990s, several Latin American countries, most notably Mexico, opted to permit dual nationality. Many European countries, including France, Ireland, Italy, and the United Kingdom, also recognize dual nationality.

The increasing acceptance of dual nationality reflects changes in the nature of immigration. Until the late twentieth century, difficulties in travel and communication forced most immigrants to make a total break from their country of origin. Today, however, immigration need not result in complete or permanent separation from one's home country. Immigrants may retain property and provide financial support to family in their homelands or remain involved with politics there. Some immigrants intend to resume residence in their country of origin in the future. Some fear the loss of property or inheritance rights that are only available to citizens of their home countries. Consequently, many immigrants may be reluctant to relinquish citizenship in their home countries even though they have acquired the benefits of U.S. citizenship. While the U.S. requires non-citizens to renounce their previous nationality in obtaining naturalization (INA § 337), the effect of this renunciation, and thus the availability of dual citizenship, depends upon the laws of the naturalized citizen's country of origin.

§ 12–2 METHODS OF OBTAINING CITIZENSHIP

§ 12–2.1 Citizenship at Birth

a. Birth Within the United States

There are four ways to obtain citizenship: by birth in the United States or its territories, by birth outside the U.S. to a U.S. parent, by naturalization, or by naturalization of a parent while a child is under eighteen years old.

All persons born in the United States and subject to its jurisdiction automatically acquire citizenship. INA § 301(a). This principle of common law was codified by the Fourteenth Amendment to the Constitution, adopted in 1868:

All persons born or naturalized in the United States, and subject to the jurisdiction thereof, are citizens of the United States and of the State wherein they reside.

The Citizenship Clause was intended to go further than the common law and included all African–Americans born in the United States. Before the amendment, African–Americans—whether slaves or free—had been denied the status of U.S. citizen. The Supreme Court in *Scott v. Sandford*, 60 U.S. 393 (1857) had declared that Dred Scott was not a "citizen" but a "Negro" of African descent, whose ancestors were slaves. He was thus barred from filing suit in U.S. District Court to obtain recognition of the freedom he had gained by entering and residing in free territory. The resulting Civil War led to the abolition of slavery. Because of the *Dred Scott* decision, however, proponents of the Fourteenth Amendment argued that while the Emancipation Proclamation had freed African–Americans, they could not become citizens without a constitutional amendment. The Fourteenth Amendment was thus adopted.

The Fourteenth Amendment also eliminated any doubt that persons born in the United States of non-citizen parents were citizens. Such a proposition was confirmed by the Court in *United States v. Wong Kim Ark*, 169 U.S. 649 (1898). Wong Kim Ark was born in San Francisco in 1873. His parents were native-born Chinese merchants who lived in this country as resident aliens. They left the United States in 1890 and returned to China permanently. Wong Kim Ark made a temporary visit to his parents in 1894, but upon return the following year to the United States, was not permitted to land at San Francisco. The government claimed Wong Kim Ark was not a U.S. citizen but a Chinese laborer, and was barred entrance under the Chinese Exclusion Act (22 Stat. 58). He challenged his exclusion in federal court, claiming citizenship under the Fourteenth Amendment. Justice Gray, in delivering the opinion of the United States Supreme Court, rejected the government's contention that the rule of *jus sanguinis*—citizenship by blood relationship—determined nationality in the United States. To the contrary, both the Fourteenth Amendment and the Civil Rights Act of 1866 (14 Stat. 27) had explicitly reaffirmed "the fundamental principle of citizenship by birth within the dominion." *Wong Kim Ark*. Hence, children born in this country were citizens without regard to the nationality of their parents. Wong Kim Ark won readmission to the United States.

The words "subject to the jurisdiction thereof" provide for exceptions to the general rule of *jus soli* or citizenship by birth within the dominion. For example, children born in the United States to the French Ambassador are subject to the jurisdiction of the French Republic, not that of the United States. The physical fact of birth in this country does not alone confer citizenship. *In re Thenault*, 47 F.Supp. 952 (D.D.C.1942).

A second, now defunct, exception concerning Native Americans is illustrated by the case of *Elk v. Wilkins*, 112 U.S. 94 (1884). John Elk was born a member of a Native American tribe. He severed his tribal relations and moved to Omaha, Nebraska. He asked to be registered and permitted to vote in local elections, but registrar Wilkins refused him, claiming Elk—as a Native American—was not a citizen of the United States and thus not qualified to vote. Elk claimed citizenship under the Fourteenth Amendment in his suit against the registrar. The Supreme Court held that the Fourteenth

Amendment failed to confer citizenship upon Elk, who was born subject to the jurisdiction of his tribe rather than that of the United States. His subsequent renunciation of his tribal allegiance was irrelevant. He could only become a U.S. citizen by being "naturalized in the United States."

The Citizenship Act of 1924, however, established the citizenship status of Native Americans born in the United States after its enactment. 43 Stat. 253. The Nationality Act of 1940 reconfirmed the citizenship of all Native Americans born in the U.S. 54 Stat. 1137. INA § 289 also recognizes the right of many "American Indians born in Canada" to cross the border of the United States. INA § 301(b) provides:

The following shall be nationals and citizens of the United States at birth:

(b) A person born in the United States to a member of an Indian, Eskimo, Aleutian, or other aboriginal tribe: *Provided,* that the granting of citizenship under this subsection shall not in any manner impair or otherwise affect the right of such person to tribal or other property.

By its proviso expressly excepting tribal property rights, Congress emphasized its intention to impose all other obligations of citizenship, or so found the Second Circuit in *Ex parte Green,* 123 F.2d 862 (2d Cir.1941). Accordingly, appellant Green, a member of the Onondaga Tribe, was a citizen within the meaning of § 3(a) of the Selective Service Act of 1940, and subject to military service.

Two additional exceptions to the general rule of *jus soli* merit mention. Children born on foreign public ships while such vessels sit in the territorial waters of the United States are not subject to U.S. jurisdiction and thus do not receive U.S. citizenship. *United States v. Wong Kim Ark*, 169 U.S. 649 (1898). Persons born in private vessels within the territorial sovereignty of the United States, however, acquire United States citizenship. Further, children born to non-citizen enemies in hostile occupation of United States territory would not be subject to United States jurisdiction and would not gain citizenship upon their birth.

Concerns over undocumented immigration have led some to challenge the validity and prudence of granting citizenship to children born in the United States to undocumented parents. These critics argue that the children of undocumented immigrants are not born "subject to the jurisdiction" of the government because the government has not consented to the presence of their parents inside the country. Legislation is frequently introduced in Congress to limit birthright citizenship to children born in the United States to at least one citizen or lawful permanent resident parent. The odds of Congress passing such legislation, and the chance of the courts sustaining the constitutionality of such a law, however, remain quite low.

b. *Birth in the Territories of the United States*

Near the end of the nineteenth century the United States began to acquire territories and possessions beyond its mainland. The issue of how and whether to grant United States citizenship to the peoples of these territories generated much debate. Congress has passed several statutes granting nationality to the residents of some but not all territories and possessions of the United States.

(1) *Hawaii*—The Hawaiian Islands became part of the United States on July 7, 1898, and persons born in Hawaii after that date are United States citizens. 30 Stat. 750. A person who was a citizen of the Republic of Hawaii on August 12, 1898, obtained United States citizenship as of April 30, 1900, the date Congress enacted a statute incorporating Hawaii into the Union as a territory. 31 Stat. 141. Hawaii became a state on August 21, 1959. 73 Stat. 4.

(2) *Alaska*—Russia owned Alaska until 1867 when it sold the territory to the United States. 15 Stat. 539. All persons born in Alaska after March 30, 1867, except noncitizen Native Americans, acquired United States citizenship. A Native American living or born in Alaska as of June 2, 1924, is a citizen of the United States. 43 Stat. 253. Alaska gained statehood on January 3, 1959. 72 Stat. 339.

(3) *Puerto Rico*—In 1899, the island of Puerto Rico was ceded to the United States by Spain in the treaty concluding the Spanish–American War. 30 Stat. 1154. Persons born in Puerto Rico from the date of cession to January 13, 1941, did not acquire citizenship at birth. With the Nationality Act of 1940, persons born there after January 13, 1941, and subject to the jurisdiction of the United States became U.S. citizens. 54 Stat. 1137. Persons born between April 11, 1899, and January 12, 1941, gained U.S. citizenship as of January 13, 1941, if they were residing in territory over which the United States exercised sovereignty.

(4) *Canal Zone and Panama*—The United States acquired the Canal Zone by treaty with Panama in 1904, to lease it in perpetuity. 33 Stat. 1234. By legislation first enacted in 1937 (50 Stat. 558), children born in the

Canal Zone after February 25, 1904, became U.S. citizens if either the father or mother was a U.S. citizen. INA § 303(a). A child born in the Republic of Panama also received U.S. citizenship if either parent was a citizen employed by the United States, by the Panama Railroad Company, or by its successor in title. INA § 303(b).

In 1979, Congress ratified a treaty to return sovereignty over the Canal Zone to Panama. 93 Stat. 452. Citizenship acquired under the statute prior to the transfer is unaffected; but since the Canal Zone no longer constitutes U.S. territory, children born to United States citizens in the region are subject to the general rules applicable to children born outside the United States.

(5) *Virgin Islands*—The United States purchased the Virgin Islands from Denmark pursuant to an Act of January 25, 1917. 39 Stat. 1706. The Act of 1952, 66 Stat. 237, grants citizenship to all persons born in the Virgin Islands after January 17, 1917, and to any former Danish citizens who (1) did not declare an intent to preserve their Danish citizenship as provided under the treaty of purchase or (2) had subsequently renounced the declaration. INA § 306(a)(1). Several other categories of Virgin Island residents also became U.S. citizens after 1917.

(6) *Guam*—The island of Guam was acquired from Spain in settlement of the Spanish–American War. Persons living in Guam on April 11, 1899, and their children born on or after that date were declared citizens of the United States as of August 1, 1950, if on this date they were residing in Guam or in other territory over which the United States exercises sovereignty and had taken no steps to retain or acquire a different nationality. All persons born in Guam on or after April 11, 1899, are

citizens of the United States as of the date of their birth, provided that if they were born before August 1, 1950, they had taken no steps to retain or acquire a different nationality. INA § 307.

(7) *American Samoa and Swains Island*—Persons born in the "outlying possessions" of the United States are nationals, but not citizens, of the United States at birth. INA § 308. As such, they owe allegiance to the United States, but receive none of the privileges of citizenship. Currently the only outlying possessions of the United States are American Samoa and Swains Island in the South Pacific. INA § 101(a)(29).

(8) *The Philippines*—The United States acquired the Philippines as a result of the Spanish–American War. Filipinos never collectively obtained the status of U.S. citizens, instead being designated "non-citizen nationals." INA § 308. In 1946, the Philippines obtained independence; Filipinos thus acquired a new nationality and the status of non-citizens in regard to the United States. 61 Stat. 1174.

c. Birth Outside the United States

Individuals born abroad of United States citizen parents can acquire United States citizenship. This acquired form of citizenship is controlled by statute, rather than by the Constitution or the Fourteenth Amendment. Each statute dating from the original 1790 Act has required the citizen parent or parents to have lived in the United States prior to the child's birth. 1 Stat. 103. This limitation prevents citizenship by descent for individuals whose parents have never lived in the U.S. and thus have relatively little contact with the country and, accordingly, prevents the creation of a large external community of

U.S. citizens with little knowledge or experience of the United States. The statutes conferring citizenship by *jus sanguinis* (blood relationship) underwent substantive changes in 1934, 1940, and 1952. Hence, whether an individual obtained U.S. citizenship at birth depends upon the statute in force at the time that person was born. *See* 66 Interp.Rel. 444 (containing a reprinted chart illustrating the rules that apply to legitimate and illegitimate children born at various time periods).

(1) PERSONS BORN ABROAD BEFORE MAY 24, 1934

The first Congress exercised its constitutionally granted power to "establish an Uniform Rule of Naturalization" by enacting the Act of March 26, 1790, which provided: "And the children of citizens of the United States, that may be born beyond sea, or out of the limits of the United States, shall be considered as natural born citizens: *Provided*, That the right of citizenship shall not descend to persons whose fathers have never been resident in the United States." 1 Stat. 103. This provision, with minor phrasing changes and with the same emphasis on paternal residence, was retained by three subsequently enacted naturalization statutes. 1 Stat. 415; 2 Stat. 155; 10 Stat. 604. In 1994, Congress granted citizenship retroactively to children born before 1934 whose citizen mothers resided in the United States before the child's birth. INA § 301(h).

(2) BIRTH ABROAD BETWEEN MAY 24, 1934, AND JANUARY 12, 1941

The Act of May 24, 1934, extended acquired citizenship to persons whose *mothers* were citizens and past residents of the United States. 48 Stat. 797. In addition, the Act imposed new requirements for retention of citizenship. The Act required that a child reside in the United States for the five years immediately preceding his or her eighteenth birthday and take an oath of citizenship within six months of attaining the age of twenty-one. 48 Stat. 797. The Nationality Act of 1940 retroactively changed the residence requirement to five years between the ages of thirteen and twenty-one and abolished the oath. 54 Stat. 1139.

(3) BIRTH ABROAD BETWEEN JANUARY 13, 1941, AND DECEMBER 23, 1952

The Nationality Act of 1940 conferred citizenship at birth to children of parents who were both United States citizens, or of which one was a citizen and the other a national, as long as a citizen parent had previously resided in the United States or its outlying possessions. 54 Stat. 1138. If only one parent was a citizen and the other a non-citizen, the citizen parent was required to have resided previously in the United States or its outlying possessions for ten years, at least five of which were after attaining the age of sixteen. A 1946 amendment changed the residence requirement to five years after the age of twelve for persons who served honorably in the armed forces during World War II. 60 Stat. 721. Moreover, a child could lose citizenship by failure to take up residence in the United States or its outlying possessions for a period or periods totaling five years between the ages of thirteen and twenty-one. This residency requirement did not apply to a child born abroad whose U.S. citizen parent was, at the time of the child's birth, residing abroad solely or principally in the employment of the United States government, certain U.S. organizations having their principal place of business in the United States, or an international agency in which the

United States participates. Persons born between January 13, 1941, and December 23, 1952, are covered by the provisions of the 1940 Act.

(4) PERSONS BORN ABROAD AFTER DECEMBER 23, 1952

Under the Immigration and Nationality Act of 1952, 66 Stat. 163, where both parents of a foreign-born child are United States citizens, the child inherits citizenship in the same manner as provided by the 1940 Act. If one parent is a citizen and the other a U.S. "national" (*see, e.g.,* § 12–2.1.b(7)), the citizen parent must have been physically present in the United States or its outlying possessions for one year prior to the child's birth. INA § 301(d). If one parent is a citizen and the other a noncitizen, the 1952 statute provided that the citizen parent must have been physically present in the United States or its outlying possessions for a period of ten years, at least five of which were after attaining the age of fourteen. INA § 301(g). In 1986 this physical presence requirement was reduced to five years, at least two of which were after attaining the age of fourteen. The physical presence requirement is satisfied by presence in the United States for any reason; unlike the 1940 Act, the INA does not require the citizen parent to have had his or her primary dwelling in the United States.

(5) AMENDMENTS TO THE 1952 ACT

(i) *Exemption for Foreign Service.* In 1966, Congress passed an amendment to § 301(g) of the 1952 Act, 80 Stat. 1322, attaching a proviso which allowed periods of overseas service in the armed forces, in the employment of the United States government, or in the employment of an international organization of which the United States is a member, as counting towards satisfaction of the ten year physical presence requirement. INA § 301(g). Congress retained this provision when it reduced the physical residence requirement to five years in 1986. In addition, any period during which the citizen parent was physically present abroad as an unmarried dependent of a person in such service counts towards satisfying the requirement.

The amendment was designed specifically to alleviate the hardship of the children of parents in foreign civilian service who, if they were to marry a foreign national, were precluded by law from transmitting their United States citizenship to their foreign-born children because they lacked the requisite years of physical presence in the United States. As the State Department wrote in its letter to then Vice–President Humphrey requesting the legislation:

> It is not uncommon for the children of a foreign service officer to spend most of their youthful years abroad accompanying the parents from one assignment to another. The proposed amendment, in effect, would treat the time spent abroad in such cases as constructive physical presence in the United States for the purpose of transmitting U.S. citizenship.

(ii) *Elimination of Retention Requirement for Children Born Abroad.* Until 1972, INA § 301(b) required that the citizen child born abroad of parents, one of whom was a citizen and the other a non-citizen, had to reside in the United States for five consecutive years after attaining the age of fourteen but before reaching age twenty-eight. Congress decided in 1972 that the intent of the law could be met by a lesser period of residence, "thereby alleviating the hardship that is often caused by the separation of children or young adults from their families and the attendant financial burden imposed by such separation." Therefore, Congress reduced the residence requirement to two years of physical presence in the United States for a continuous period between the ages of fourteen and twenty-eight, further providing that absence of less than sixty days in the aggregate would not break the continuity of such physical presence. Further, the legislation provided that these residence requirements would not apply in the case of a child whose non-citizen parent was naturalized while the child was under age eighteen.

Despite the liberalized residence requirement of the 1972 amendment, 693 citizens lost their citizenship between 1972 and 1977 for failure to comply. This unhappy result prompted Congress in 1978 to eliminate altogether the residence requirement for children born of one citizen parent and one non-citizen parent. In its report accompanying the bill, the House Judiciary Committee stated, "The Committee believes that section 301(b) of the Immigration and Nationality Act currently creates an inconsistency in our citizenship laws, in that this is the only class of United States citizens who are subject to any residence requirement in order to retain their citizenship."

The Judiciary Committee felt that repeal of § 301(b) would best redress the inequity. While some members of Congress expressed concern that repeal of § 301(b) would create the possibility of "generations of citizens residing with little or no connection with the United States," such fears were groundless. Until 1986, § 301(g) continued to provide that in order for United States citizens to transmit citizenship to children born abroad of a citizen parent and a non-citizen parent, the citizen parent must have resided in the United States for ten years at least five of which were after attaining the age of fourteen. In 1986, this residency requirement was reduced to five years, at least two of which were after attaining the age of fourteen.

(6) CHILDREN BORN OUT OF WEDLOCK

INA § 309 governs the acquisition of citizenship by children born out of wedlock outside the United States. A child born out of wedlock abroad acquires citizenship at birth if his or her mother is a U.S. citizen who resided in the United States for one year prior to the child's birth. INA § 309(c). Such a child can, however, only acquire citizenship through a U.S. citizen father if the father agrees to provide financial support for the child until the child's eighteenth birthday and acknowledges paternity by one of three specified methods before the child attains the age of eighteen. INA § 309(a).

Children born out of wedlock to U.S. citizen fathers prior to January 13, 1941, acquired citizenship if legitimated under the laws of the father's place of residence at any age. Children born out of wedlock between January 13, 1941, and December 23, 1952, could acquire citizenship through their U.S. citizen fathers only if they were legitimated before the age of twenty-one and the father met the physical presence requirements then in force (see § 12–2.1(c), supra). INA § 301(b). Children born out of wedlock to citizen mothers before 1952 acquired citizenship at birth provided only that the mother previously resided for any length of time in the United States. INA § 301(h); 54 Stat. 1140.

Nguyen v. INS, 533 U.S. 53 (2001) challenged the constitutionality of imposing additional requirements on fathers who wish to transmit their citizenship to their children born out of wedlock. Tuan Anh Nguyen was born in Vietnam but was raised by his U.S. citizen father in the United States. The INS initiated deportation proceedings against him after he pleaded guilty to sexual assault at the age of twenty-two. While an appeal was pending, Nguyen's father obtained a court order establishing his paternity. Nonetheless, the Board of Immigration Appeals found that Nguyen was not a citizen because his father had failed to establish paternity before Nguyen attained the age of eighteen. In affirming the decision, the Supreme Court found that the Act does not violate equal protection because its requirements are substantially related to the important government interest of assuring that there is a genuine connection between the father, the child, and the United States.

§ 12–2.2   Citizenship by Naturalization

a.   *Historical Development*

Naturalization is the principal process by which persons not acquiring citizenship at birth may obtain citizen status. The power to confer citizenship in this manner derives from Article I, section 8 of the Constitution which authorized Congress "to establish an uniform Rule of Naturalization." Since the initial naturalization statute of 1790, 1 Stat. 103, Congress has exclusively exercised the power to establish the conditions upon which non-citizens might be naturalized. *See Collet v. Collet*, 2 U.S. 294 (1792).

In the original statute of 1790 Congress prescribed that a "free white alien" who had resided in the United States for two years might be naturalized in a court proceeding, provided he or she was of good moral character and took an oath to support the Constitution. 1 Stat.

103. The Act of 1795 lengthened the residency requirement to five years and enacted additional conditions that
the applicant for naturalization declare formal intent to
seek citizenship three years before actual admission; that
the applicant renounce any former allegiance and swear
allegiance to the United States; that the applicant satisfy
the court that he or she "has behaved as a man [sic] of
good moral character, attached to the principles of the
Constitution of the United States, and [is] well disposed
to the good order and happiness of the same." 1 Stat.
414.

An unfortunate period (1798–1802) of hysteria against
foreigners produced the Alien and Sedition Acts and
much more restrictive naturalization requirements (residence requirement increased to fourteen years, declaration of intent period increased to five years). 1 Stat. 566.
The hysteria soon dissipated, however, and Congress
enacted the more lenient provisions of the 1795 Act in
the Act of April 14, 1802. 2 Stat. 153. The substantive
provisions of 1795 closely resemble the general requirements of the present law, notwithstanding several refine-
ments discussed *infra*.

Congress established substantive requirements for naturalization in the first years of the republic, but failed to
provide uniform procedures and administration until
passage of the Naturalization Act of 1906. 34 Stat. 596.
The statute vested responsibility for administrative supervision of naturalization in the Bureau of Immigration
and Naturalization within the U.S. Department of Commerce and Labor; it prescribed uniform naturalization
forms; required that each petitioner for naturalization
obtain an official certificate of lawful admission and
attach it to the petition for naturalization; required

uniform naturalization fees; established time limitations for the courts to hear and grant petitions (minimum of ninety days after filing, no hearings permitted within thirty days of a general election); and finally, required that each petition be supported by two citizen witnesses who would testify to the petitioner's qualifications for citizenship.

Subsequent procedural revisions included permitting heretofore excluded "alien enemies" to petition for naturalization and the establishment of court-appointed naturalization examiners who would hear the evidence in naturalization cases and recommend dispositions to the federal courts. 44 Stat. 709. Congress added several substantive revisions in the Nationality Act of 1940. 54 Stat. 1137. Most significantly, the Act eased racial restrictions on naturalization. Persons from races indigenous to the Western Hemisphere became eligible for naturalization. Up until that time only white persons and persons of African nativity or descent had been eligible. 1 Stat. 414; 16 Stat. 254. In 1943 Congress added Chinese immigrants as a fourth class of eligible persons, (57 Stat. 600) while at the same time repealing the Chinese Exclusion Act (22 Stat. 58) which had specifically prohibited naturalization of Chinese persons.

The Immigration and Nationality Act of 1952 provided comprehensive codification of the law governing citizenship. 66 Stat. 163. Among the most significant changes enacted by the 1952 law was elimination of all racial and gender qualifications for naturalization. The statute finally ended the blatantly racist formulations of previous naturalization provisions. INA § 311. The statute did, however, preclude naturalization (1) of persons belonging to certain subversive groups (INA § 313), (2) of persons who had sought relief from United States military service on the ground of their alienage (INA § 315) or who had deserted from the armed forces during wartime (INA § 314), and (3) of non-citizens against whom a deportation proceeding or order was outstanding. INA § 318. Congress also enacted provisions to facilitate naturalization of non-citizens who had actively served in the armed forces during World War I, World War II, the Korean hostilities, the Vietnam Conflict, or later conflicts. INA § 329.

The 1990 Act and the 1991 Act made the INS the sole decision maker in naturalization cases. The Homeland Security Act, in 2002, transferred this responsibility to the U.S. Citizenship and Immigration Services, without changing the substantive requirements for naturalization. While the federal courts no longer adjudicate naturalization applications, they continue to administer the oath of allegiance for many naturalized citizens.

The number of people seeking naturalization increased dramatically in the 1990s, for a variety of reasons. Many permanent residents were encouraged to apply for citizenship because of concern that they would be denied education, health benefits, and participation in other governmental programs or would be subject to removal from the U.S. for committing relatively minor criminal offenses known as "aggravated felonies." *See* § 1–9, *supra*. During the 1970s and 1980s, the average number of naturalizations per year was just under 200,000. The number of applications for naturalization rose dramatically during the 1990s, peaking at 1.4 million in 1997. There were 730,000 applications in 2006, 1.3 million in 2007, and 526,000 in 2008. The applications for naturalization rose sharply in 2007 in anticipation of an increase of the application fees. Demand for naturalization is expected to remain relatively high as immigrants continue to seek the benefits of U.S. citizenship.

b. *Requirements of Naturalization*

(1) RESIDENCE AND PHYSICAL PRESENCE

Section 316(a) of the Immigration and Nationality Act requires that, except as otherwise provided, no person shall become a U.S. citizen by being naturalized unless: (1) the person has resided continuously in the United States for five years as a lawfully admitted permanent resident, (2) during the five years immediately prior to filing the petition for naturalization he or she has been physically present in the United States for at least half of the time, and (3) the person has resided within the district in which he or she filed the petition for at least three months. Applicants must reside continuously within the United States from the date of the petition up to the time of admission to citizenship, although short visits outside the U.S. are acceptable. INA § 316. The purpose of the residency requirements is to create a reasonable period of "probation" that will enable candidates to discard their foreign attachments, to learn the principles of the U.S. system of government, and to develop an identification with the national community.

To comply with the statute a legal residence is necessary; a valid statutory residence prior to naturalization cannot be founded on an illegal entry into the country. Congress has defined "residence" under the 1952 Act to mean "the place of general abode ... [a person's] principal, actual dwelling place in fact, without regard to intent." INA § 101(a)(33). The question of residence thus turns on a determination of where an applicant has held the status of lawful permanent resident.

An applicant for citizenship need not show that he or she stayed at the claimed residence each day of the five-year statutory period. Temporary absences from the place of abode—even from the United States—do not alone break the continuity of an applicant's residence. Absence from the United States for less than six months during the statutory period does not affect continuous residence, while an absence of more than six months but less than one year presumptively breaks the continuity. INA § 316(b). The applicant can overcome the presumption by "establish[ing] ... that he did not in fact abandon his residence in the United States during such period." *Id.* An absence from the United States for one year or more will as a matter of law break the continuity of residence; the applicant will be required to complete a new period of residence after returning to the United States. *Id.*

As an exception to the physical residency requirement, persons who expect to be away from the United States for a year or more in service of the United States government, a recognized U.S. research institution, a U.S. corporation engaged in foreign trade and commerce, a public international organization of which the United States is a member by treaty or statute, or a religious organization, may apply for permission to be absent without breaking their residence for purposes of naturalization. Before seeking such exception with Form N–470, applicants must continuously reside in the United States—following lawful admission—for one year or more. INA §§ 316(b), 317. Applicants must establish that their absence from the United States for such period is in service of the government, for the purpose of conducting scientific research, for the purpose of developing trade or commerce necessary to protect property rights in a foreign country, in the employ of a public international organization, or for the purpose of performing qualifying religious functions. INA §§ 316(b)(1), 317. A 1981 amendment provides that dependent unmarried sons and daughters of a person who qualifies for benefits under this provision are also entitled to such benefits during the period for which they were residing abroad as dependent members of the person's household. INA § 316(b).

In most cases, however, the exception to the one-year limitation on absences from the U.S. does not exempt qualifying individuals from the requirement of being physically present in the United States for half of the five-year period. Persons employed abroad by the U.S. government (INA § 316(c)) or a qualifying religious organization (INA § 317) are considered both resident and physically present in the U.S. for the purpose of naturalization. Likewise, service aboard a vessel owned and operated by the United States government or a vessel whose "home port" is in the United States is deemed residence *and* physical presence in the U.S. INA § 330. In all other cases, applicants for naturalization must satisfy the physical presence requirements. INA § 316(c).

Where a non-citizen's absence from the United States is involuntary, courts have excused the absence for the purpose of residence and physical presence requirements. In the case of *In re Yarina*, 73 F.Supp. 688 (N.D.Ohio 1947), a Czech immigrant who had spent his entire childhood in the United States, was employed by a U.S. company at Wake Island, a United States territory in the South Pacific. In December 1941, the Japanese captured the island and took petitioner Yarina and many others prisoner. He remained a captive in a Japanese prisoner of war camp until September 1945. He filed his petition for naturalization in the year following his liberation and return to the United States. The court held that the provision depriving a non-citizen of the right to naturalization in case of absence from the United States for a year or more during the statutory period preceding the application contemplated a voluntary departure from this country. Since the forces of the enemy transported Yarina from Wake Island to the prison camp, petitioner "never left his residence in the United States within the purview of the statute." He was thus granted naturalization.

Nonetheless, if a petitioner departs the United States voluntarily but is prevented from returning by events beyond his or her control, the absence is unexcused. Mary Holzer, an Israeli national, was a lawfully admitted permanent resident alien who left the United States to visit Israel in October 1952. She cited financial reasons for her inability to return to the United States within the one-year period. The court found that her extended absence barred the petition for naturalization, stating "the rule applies even where the absence from the United States beyond the statutory period was involuntary." *Petition of Holzer*, 143 F.Supp. 153 (S.D.N.Y.1956). The court applied the same reasoning in the case of *In re Naturalization of Vafaei–Makhsoos*, 597 F.Supp. 499 (D.Minn.1984). Petitioner, a lawful permanent resident in the United States, while visiting Iran during the hostage crisis of 1979–81, was prevented by the U.S. government's travel restrictions from returning to the U.S. for more than a year. Because he left the country voluntarily, the petitioner's absence did not provide an exception to the one-year-absence rule which broke the continuity of residence for the purposes of naturalization.

(2) AGE

To apply for naturalization an applicant generally must have attained the age of eighteen years. INA § 334(b). The Child Citizenship Act of 2000, 114 Stat. 1631, provides that children under age eighteen acquire citizenship automatically if they reside in the United States as lawful permanent residents in the legal custody of a parent who is a citizen by birth or naturalization. INA § 320. Consequently, most children acquire citizenship when their parents are naturalized and no separate application or proceeding is required. In some circumstances, U.S. citizens may also apply for naturalization on behalf of their children residing outside the United States. INA § 322. *See* § 12–2.2(c)(3), *infra*.

(3) LITERACY AND EDUCATIONAL REQUIREMENTS

Unless unable to do so because of a physical or developmental disability or mental impairment, applicants for naturalization must be able to speak and understand simple English, as well as read and write it. INA § 312(a)(1), (b)(1). During their naturalization interview, applicants must both read and write one sentence in English. Persons who are over fifty years of age and have lived in the United States as lawful permanent residents for at least twenty years as of the date they file their application are exempt from this requirement, as are persons over the age of fifty-five who have lived in the United States as lawful permanent residents for at least fifteen years. INA § 312(b)(2). The Hmong Veterans' Naturalization Act of 2000 provides a limited exemption for members of Laotian guerilla forces who supported the

United States during the Vietnam War, their spouses, and their widows or widowers. *See* § 12–2.2(c)(5), *infra*.

Section 312 further requires "a knowledge and understanding of the fundamentals of the history, and of the principles and form of government, of the United States." INA § 312(a)(2). The U.S. Citizenship and Immigration Service (CIS) examiners administer examinations to applicants on American civics and history as part of the naturalization interview. Applicants must answer six out of ten questions correctly in order to pass the examination. Study questions are available on the CIS website. Persons with a qualifying disability are exempt from this requirement. INA § 312(b)(1). Applicants who are exempt from the literacy requirement because of their age must still satisfy the civics requirement. The CIS must, however, give special consideration to persons over sixty-five years of age who have lived in the United States for at least twenty years and to persons covered by the Hmong Veterans Naturalization Act. INA § 312(b)(2)–(3); *see* § 12–2.2(c)(5), *infra*. An interpreter or sign language may be used during the examination if the applicant is exempt from the literacy requirement or if needed to test technical or complex subjects. 8 C.F.R. § 312.2(c)(2). Since questions are selected at random by computer, however, applicants may not have the opportunity for translation of complex questions. Applicants who fail either the civics or English tests have the opportunity to retake the examination between 60 and 90 days from the date of their initial interview. 8 C.F.R. § 312.5.

The power of Congress to establish literacy requirements has withstood constitutional challenge. In *Trujillo–Hernandez v. Farrell*, 503 F.2d 954 (5th Cir.1974), petitioner brought a class action, attacking the statute on equal protection grounds. The Fifth Circuit held that a direct attack on Congress' exercise of its naturalization power was foreclosed and nonjusticiable, as such power was part of the foreign relations responsibilities committed to Congress.

(4) GOOD MORAL CHARACTER

"Applicants for naturalization must show that, during the five-year period before filing and up until the final hearing of the naturalization petition, they have been and still are of good moral character. . . ." INA § 316(a). Although only five years of good moral character is required by statute, the CIS has discretion to consider applicants' earlier behavior in its determination. 8 C.F.R. § 316.10. Applicants who qualify for reduced residence requirements must establish good moral character for the required period of residence or for a reasonable time. The burden of establishing good moral character falls upon the petitioner, as an applicant must prove his or her eligibility for citizenship in every respect. *Berenyi v. INS*, 385 U.S. 630 (1967).

Courts have struggled with the issue of what constitutes good moral character. Judge Learned Hand stated that it is a "test, incapable of exact definition; the best we can do is to improvise the response that the 'ordinary' man or woman would make, if the question were put whether the conduct was consistent with a 'good moral character'." *Posusta v. United States*, 285 F.2d 533 (2d Cir.1961). Prior to 1952, no attempt had been made to define good moral character by statute. Then, in the 1952 Act, Congress chose to define by enumerated exclusions what would *preclude* a finding of good moral character. 66 Stat. 166. Under the current version of the

INA, a person will not be considered of good moral character if he or she was at any time during the five-year period:

(1) a habitual drunkard;

(2) a person convicted of or admitting to a crime of moral turpitude; a person involved with prostitution, smuggling of a person, or drug trafficking, except for a single conviction involving possession of no more than 30 grams of marijuana; a polygamist; or a non-citizen who was previously removed;

(3) one whose income is principally from illegal gambling activities;

(4) a person who had been convicted of two or more gambling offenses committed during this period;

(5) one who has given false testimony for the purpose of obtaining any benefits under the Act; or

(6) a person who had been convicted and jailed for 180 days or more, regardless of whether the offense was committed within this period.

INA § 101(f). Furthermore, a conviction *at any time* for an aggravated felony precludes a finding that a person has good moral character. *Id.*

Applicants may also be found to lack good moral character for reasons other than those listed in the INA. Immigration regulations list additional acts that will preclude a finding of good moral character, absent extenuating circumstances. These acts include failure to support dependents and committing unlawful acts other than those listed in § 101 that adversely reflect upon the person's character. 8 C.F.R. § 316.10(b)(3). The fact that an applicant has been on probation, parole, or suspended sentence during the statutory period does not preclude a finding of good moral character, but the application will not be approved until the probation, parole, or suspended sentence has been completed. 8 C.F.R. § 316.10(c)(1).

(i) *Adultery*. Until 1981, the list of acts that bar a finding of good moral character included adultery. This provision of the INA created great controversy as immigration authorities struggled to define what constitutes adultery and what extenuating circumstances might excuse it. While the law remained in effect, immigration authorities took the position that anyone who had committed adultery would be ineligible for immigration benefits. *See In re Pitzoff*, 10 I. & N. Dec. 35, Interim Decision (BIA) 1237 (BIA 1962). The federal courts, however, did not always take such a strict view. In *Moon Ho Kim v. INS*, 514 F.2d 179 (D.C. Cir.1975), the D.C. Circuit held that the definition of "adultery," as the term is used in the act, is "extramarital intercourse which tends to destroy an existing, viable marriage, and which would represent a threat to public morality." In addition, the existence of extenuating circumstances were generally deemed relevant in determining whether a non-citizen had established good moral character despite the commission of adultery. Hence, in *Wadman v. INS*, 329 F.2d 812 (9th Cir.1964), petitioner's isolated acts of sexual intercourse with another, after his wife had willfully and permanently abandoned him, did not preclude him from establishing good moral character.

Congress ultimately repealed the adultery provision in 1981. 95 Stat. 1611. It stated its rationale for repeal in the report accompanying the legislation:

With respect to adultery, the Committee believes that the Immigration Service should not be required to inquire into the sex lives of applicants for naturalization. Such questions clearly represent an invasion of privacy. Furthermore, in testimony before the 96th Congress witnesses concurred in the view that the adultery bar was merely "window dressing" in the law; INS estimated that "7 out of 10 persons today who would admit to that conduct would fall within one or more of the judicial interpretations which excuse that conduct for purposes of naturalization."

Despite the repeal of the adultery provision, the CIS may still find that a person who has committed adultery lacks good moral character under its discretionary power. Immigration regulations continue to list adultery "that tends to destroy an existing marriage" as an act that precludes good moral character (8 C.F.R. § 316.10), but it is unclear whether this regulation is actively enforced.

(ii) *Criminal Activity*. In its original form, INA § 101 barred a finding of good moral character if a person had been convicted at any time of the crime of murder. 66 Stat. 166. In 1990, this provision was changed to any aggravated felony. INA § 101(f)(8). Since 1990, Congress has extended the definition of "aggravated felony" several times, most notably in 1996, in the Antiterrorism and Effective Death Penalty and Illegal Immigration Reform and Immigrant Responsibility Acts. *See* AEDPA § 441(e) and IIRIRA § 321. In its current form, the INA definition of "aggravated felony" includes murder, rape, sexual abuse of a minor, drug trafficking, offenses related to prostitution and child pornography, and theft offenses or crimes of violence carrying a sentence of at least one year. INA § 101(a)(43).

In determining whether a particular crime is an aggravated felony, federal law, not state law, controls. *See In* re Small, 23 I. & N. Dec. 448, Interim Decision (BIA) 3476 (BIA 2002). Consequently, convictions for relatively minor offenses may bar naturalization and can even render a person removable. In the case of In re Small, the BIA held that sexual abuse of a minor, although categorized as a misdemeanor under the applicable state law, was an aggravated felony within the meaning of the INA definition. Similarly, in United States v. Pacheco, 225 F.3d 148 (2d Cir.2000), the Court of Appeals found that a misdemeanor theft charge for which the defendant received a one-year suspended sentence constituted an aggravated felony. Pacheco, who had lived in the U.S. as a lawful permanent resident for twenty years, was removed following his convictions for stealing a ten-dollar video game and for assaulting his wife. The court noted that, under INA § 101(a)(48), the suspension of a sentence does not change the classification of the underlying crime as an aggravated felony.

The inclusion of drug trafficking crimes within the definition of aggravated felony has been the source of some controversy in recent years. The INA follows the definition of "drug trafficking" in 18 U.S.C.A. § 924(c), which includes possession, as well as the sale and distribution of controlled substances. See 18 U.S.C.A. § 924(c); 21 U.S.C.A. § 801 et seq. In the case of In re of K.V.D., 22 I. & N. Dec. 1163, Interim Decision (BIA) 3422 (BIA 1999), the BIA held that state law drug convictions would be considered aggravated felonies if the crimes were analogous to those punishable as felonies under federal law. The Board overruled that decision in the case of In re Yanez–Garcia, 23 I. & N. Dec. 390, Interim Decision (BIA) 3473 (BIA 2002) and decided instead to defer to the federal circuit courts of appeals as to whether a particular state crime constitutes a felony drug trafficking offense. The Supreme Court determined in *Lopez v. Gonzales*, 549 U.S. 47 (2006) that a state felony conviction for drug possession does not qualify as an aggravated felony for drug trafficking because drug possession under federal law is punishable only as a misdemeanor.

Considerable controversy also arose regarding whether convictions for driving under the influence of drugs or alcohol (DUI) constitute aggravated felonies. In the case of *In re of Puente*, 22 I. & N. Dec. 1006, Interim Decision (BIA) 3412 (BIA 1999), the Board held that driving under the influence was a crime of violence, and thus would be considered an aggravated felony when punishable by a sentence of one year or more. After four of the circuit courts disagreed, the BIA reconsidered this decision and decided that DUI convictions cannot be considered aggravated felonies. *In re Ramos*, 23 I. & N. Dec. 336, Interim Decision (BIA) 3468 (BIA 2002). In *Leocal v. Ashcroft*, 540 U.S. 1176 (2004), the Supreme Court held unanimously that driving while intoxicated does not constitute a crime of violence, and, therefore, is not an aggravated felony.

Since seemingly minor convictions can be a bar to naturalization and even expose an individual to the threat of removal, a non-citizen who has been convicted of one of these crimes should consider carefully whether to seek naturalization. Often these crimes only come to the attention of immigration authorities because of the non-citizen takes some action, such as applying for citizenship.

Even crimes that do not rise to the level of an "aggravated felony" can serve as a bar to naturalization. *See* INA § 101(f)(3–7). An applicant who admits to committing a "crime of moral turpitude" or a controlled substance violation will be found not to possess good moral character even if never charged, indicted, arrested or convicted of the crime. 8 C.F.R. § 316.10(b)(2)(iv). See § 8–1.2(b), *supra*, for a discussion of what constitutes a "crime of moral turpitude."

INA § 316(e) provides that, in determining whether the person applying for naturalization is of good moral character, "the [CIS] shall not be limited to the applicant's conduct during the five years preceding the filing of the application, but may take into consideration ... the applicant's conduct and acts at any time prior to that period." The Second Circuit in *Tieri v. INS*, 457 F.2d 391 (2d Cir.1972) held that in evaluating petitioner's application for naturalization in 1966, the district court properly considered evidence of the petitioner's six arrests between 1922 and 1959, two of which resulted in convictions of robbery and bookmaking. The Second Circuit concluded that "petitioner persistently attempted to obscure any past conduct which he feared might prove suspicious or embarrassing to his cause, and that, accordingly, the district court was not mistaken in discerning a pattern of deception in the whole mosaic of petitioner's testimony." Convictions outside the statutory period should not be a bar to naturalization, however, if the applicant can prove that he or she has been rehabilitated. In *Gatcliffe v. Reno*, 23 F.Supp.2d 581 (D.V.I.1998), the court found that the INS had improperly denied naturalization to a man who had committed two offenses more than seven years before applying for citizenship. The plaintiff produced numerous character witnesses to establish that he had rehabilitated himself and was a person of good moral character throughout the statutory period.

(iii) *False Testimony*. The Third Circuit held that INA § 101(f)(6), regarding the giving of false testimony for the purpose of obtaining benefits under the act, is mandatory in its terms and not subject to a distinction between material and immaterial matters. *In re Haniatakis*, 376 F.2d 728 (3d Cir.1967). Haniatakis falsely stated on her naturalization application that she was unmarried for fear that her naturalization would be delayed for five more years if the INS knew of her marriage to another non-citizen. The petitioner also misrepresented her prior places of residence.

The INS declared that her marriage to another non-citizen would not have affected her application. The district court concluded that the false testimony did not affirmatively demonstrate the absence of good moral character because the misrepresentations were immaterial and the facts concealed would not have been a barrier to her naturalization. In reversing the judgment of the district court, the Third Circuit reasoned that naturalization is denied whenever false testimony is given for a practical reason, and that one who gives false testimony to deceive the government is unworthy of citizenship. A false answer which appears immaterial may nonetheless cut off a line of inquiry which might have revealed facts material to the applicant's eligibility for citizenship. The court distinguished *Chaunt v. United States*, 364 U.S. 350 (1960), in which the Supreme Court refused to denaturalize a citizen who had twenty years before failed to reveal on his naturalization application that he had previously been arrested. The provision of the act involved in *Chaunt*, INA § 340(a), specifically required that the fact concealed be "material." The government in *Chaunt* was attempting to deny the privileges of citizenship to one who had already been granted them.

False testimony may not preclude a finding of good moral character, however, if the applicant did not make the false statement with the subjective intent of obtaining naturalization benefits. In *Chan v. INS*, 2001 WL 521706 (E.D.N.Y.2001), the court granted Chan's application for naturalization despite the fact that he denied a previous arrest and gave conflicting statements regarding his marital status. The court found that the misrepresentations were a result of the applicant's limited English skills and misunderstanding of the U.S. legal system.

(5) ATTACHMENT TO CONSTITUTIONAL PRINCIPLES

Applicants must show that they are "attached to the principles of the Constitution of the United States, and well disposed to the good order and happiness of the United States." INA § 316(a). The purpose behind this requirement is the admission to citizenship of only those persons who are in general accord with the basic principles of the community. *Petition of Sittler*, 197 F.Supp. 278 (S.D.N.Y.1961). Courts have defined attachment to the Constitution as a belief in representative democracy, a commitment to the ideals embodied in the Bill of Rights, and a willingness to accept the basic social premise that political change only be effected in an orderly manner. Similarly, a favorable disposition to the good order and happiness of the United States has been characterized as a belief in the political processes of the United States, a general satisfaction with life in the United States, and a hope for future progress and prosperity. Nonetheless, attachment to Constitutional principles and a favorable disposition to the good order of the United States are not considered incompatible with a desire to change the U.S. form of government within the limits of the Constitution.

Whether applicants for citizenship are attached to the principles of the Constitution depends on their state of mind, which must be determined on the basis of their conduct and expressions over a period of time. The CIS cannot safely base its judgment on isolated statements of the applicant. Hence, the federal court in the case of *In re Kullman*, 87 F.Supp. 1001 (W.D.Mo.1949) found that petitioner's isolated statement made before the United States' involvement in World War II expressing sympathy for the German people and praise for Adolf Hitler would not deny him citizenship, in light of his thirty-seven years of law-abiding residence in the United States and his aid to U.S. armed forces during World War I.

Although the general requirement of attachment to the Constitution allows discretion in evaluating a case on its own facts, several statutes enacted in 1952 specifically and automatically preclude naturalization of certain persons. Individuals belonging to the Communist Party or other totalitarian groups (INA § 101(a)(37)), and persons who advocate the overthrow of the United States government by force or violence or other unconstitutional means may not obtain naturalization. INA § 313(a)(4). Applicants are not disqualified, however, if they can show that membership in the proscribed organization is or was involuntary. INA § 313(d). Moreover, if the applicants can establish that such membership or affiliation terminated before they attained sixteen years of age, or such membership or affiliation was by operation of law or for purposes of obtaining employment, food, or other essentials, they may still qualify for naturalization. In *Grzymala–Siedlecki v. United States*, 285 F.2d 836 (5th Cir.1961), therefore, petitioner's enrollment in the Polish Naval Academy, which automatically conferred Communist Party membership, did not disqualify him from naturalization where the college education was necessary to the applicant's earning a livelihood in Poland.

A few courts have added another exception to the disqualification for Communist membership. Such membership or affiliation does not disqualify an applicant unless it was a "meaningful association." The Supreme Court has held, in the context of removal proceedings, that a "meaningful association" signifies at minimum "[an] awareness of the Party's political aspect." *Rowoldt v. Perfetto*, 355 U.S. 115 (1957). The federal district court of Puerto Rico applied the same analysis in the case of *In re Pruna*, 286 F.Supp. 861 (D.P.R.1968) holding that where petitioner's membership in an organization supporting Fidel Castro's revolution in Cuba in 1958 resulted from a belief that the organization's objective was to restore to the Cuban people a representative democracy, and where he was unaware that the organization was connected with the Communist Party, his participation did not constitute a "meaningful association" with a subversive group. His membership thus did not preclude him from naturalization.

Applicants may escape the preclusion statute if more than ten years have passed since they were members of the subversive organization. INA § 313(c). A 1999 amendment grants a further exemption to past members of the Communist Party who have made a contribution to the national security of the United States. INA § 314(e). This section does not require the applicant to have been free from Communist Party involvement for any particular length of time.

Section 314 of the INA permanently precludes the naturalization of anyone who, during the time that the U.S. "has been or shall be at war," deserts the U.S.

armed forces or leaves the country with the intent of avoiding the military draft, and is convicted of that offense by a court-martial or a court of competent jurisdiction. INA § 314. The provision also specifically prohibits such people from ever holding an official position of the United States. Uncertainty remains whether the term "at war" includes hostilities lacking a formal declaration of war—such as the Korean, Vietnam, and Persian Gulf conflicts. The Immigration Service has stated that the Korean conflict constituted a "time of war" within the meaning of the 1940 version of this provision. To the date of this writing, no reported judicial determinations exist.

INA § 315(a) provides that non-citizens who seek or obtain exemption from service in the U.S. armed forces on the ground that they are not citizens become permanently ineligible for citizenship, unless they had served in the military of a country that has a treaty with the U.S. INA § 315(a). Selective Service records are conclusive on the issue of whether a non-citizen secured the exemption because of alienage. INA § 315(b). Simple failure to register for the Selective Service is not a bar to naturalization, but a knowing and willful failure to register may be a ground for finding that the applicant lacks good moral character. Hence, men between the ages of eighteen and twenty-six should register before seeking naturalization.

(6) Oath of Allegiance to the United States

Related to the requirement that applicants be attached to the Constitution of the United States, they also must take an oath in open court, renouncing allegiance to their previous countries of citizenship and affirming allegiance to the United States. Section 337(a) of the INA requires that the applicants pledge (1) to support and bear true faith and allegiance to the Constitution of the United States; (2) to renounce all allegiance to any foreign state or sovereign; (3) to support and defend the Constitution and laws of the United States against all enemies, foreign and domestic; and (4) to bear arms on behalf of the United States when required by law, or to perform noncombatant service in the armed forces, or to perform civilian work of national importance when required by law. INA § 337. The CIS may, however, waive the oath requirement for children or for applicants who are unable to understand the oath because of a physical or developmental disability or mental impairment. INA § 337(a).

If applicants can show by clear and convincing evidence that they are opposed to the bearing of arms, they may revise the pledge to perform only noncombatant services in the armed forces. Similarly, applicants who can show by the same standard of proof that they oppose any type of service in the armed forces by reason of "religious training and belief" may pledge merely to perform important civilian work. INA § 337(a).

The present statute was designed to codify judicial decisions relieving conscientious objectors of naturalization requirements to bear arms. The moral stand taken by conscientious objectors frequently resulted in the denial of their naturalization petitions between the world wars—a result the Supreme Court affirmed in *United States v. Schwimmer*, 279 U.S. 644 (1929) and *United States v. Macintosh*, 283 U.S. 605 (1931). In the 1946 case of *Girouard v. United States*, 328 U.S. 61 (1946), however, the Court overruled these prior cases and held that religious objection to bearing arms was not of itself incompatible with allegiance to the United States. Congress adopted the Supreme Court's holding by enacting the statute currently in effect.

Congress followed *United States v. Seeger*, 380 U.S. 163 (1965), a later Supreme Court decision on conscientious objection to military service, in defining the phrase "religious training and belief" as "an individual's belief in a relation to a Supreme Being involving duties superior to those arising from any human relation, but does not include essentially political, sociological, or philosophical views or a merely personal moral code...." INA § 337(a). The Supreme Court has construed this language in *Seeger* to apply to persons who, while not believing in a personalized God, possess a sincere and meaningful belief which occupies in the life of the believer a place "parallel" to that filled by the God of persons who clearly qualify for the exemption. Hence, the applicant need not found a claim of conscientious objector status upon the precepts of an organized religion or a belief in a Supreme Being. *In re Weitzman*, 426 F.2d 439 (8th Cir.1970).

In *Petition for Naturalization of Kassas*, 788 F.Supp. 993 (M.D.Tenn.1992), the petitioner, who was a native of Syria, expressed reservations based on his Islamic faith, about bearing arms on behalf of the U.S. against persons of the Islamic faith or a predominantly Islamic country. The court held that the petitioner is not eligible for an exemption from swearing to bear arms on behalf of the U.S. because he is opposed only to some but not all war.

Although applicants for naturalization are required to renounce allegiance to any foreign state, some countries do not recognize the oath as an effective renunciation of citizenship. Hence, a naturalized citizen may retain dual nationality in his or her country of origin. Immigration regulations require, however, that the applicant take the oath without any mental reservations. 8 C.F.R. § 337.1. At least one court has held that taking the oath without a genuine intent to renounce one's former citizenship constitutes fraud. *United States v. Wurzenberger*, 56 F.Supp. 381 (D.Conn.1944).

c.   *Relaxed Requirements for Particular Persons*

Although the naturalization requirements discussed in the preceding subsections apply to most applicants for citizenship, Congress has chosen for various policy reasons to relax the requirements with respect to particular persons. The most significant special classes are: persons serving in the armed forces, spouses of United States citizens, and minor children of U.S. citizens.

(1) PERSONS SERVING IN THE ARMED FORCES

A lawful permanent resident who has served honorably in the armed forces of the United States for periods totaling three years may apply for naturalization without meeting the standard residence and physical presence requirements, provided such application is filed while the applicant is still in the service or within six months of discharge. INA § 328(a). If the applicant's service was continuous, a certificate of honorable service establishes compliance with the requirements of good moral character. INA § 328(e). Where the service was not continuous, the applicant must establish good moral character by the standards applicable to other naturalization applicants. INA § 328(c).

The statute further provides that a non-citizen whose service in the armed forces terminated more than six months prior to filing of the application is not exempted from the standard residence and physical presence requirements. INA § 328(d). Nonetheless, the period of time served in the military, if within five years immediately preceding the date of filing, shall constitute residence and physical presence for the purpose of meeting the standard requirements.

Another statute provides even broader exemptions for non-citizens who have actively and honorably served in the armed forces for at least one day during periods of hostilities—from World War I to the war in Afghanistan or during any periods which the President designates involving armed conflict with a hostile foreign force. INA § 329. Such persons may be naturalized without having been lawfully admitted to the United States if they enlisted or re-enlisted in the United States or specified territories. INA § 329(a). Applicants who were not within these territories when they enlisted must subsequently obtain lawful admission to qualify under the provision.

An applicant seeking naturalization through active duty service in the armed forces is exempt from the standard age requirement, the generally prescribed residence and physical presence requirements, and the provision precluding the naturalization of persons subject to an outstanding deportation order. INA § 329(b). Although no period of residence is required, a person who served on active duty must demonstrate good moral character for one year prior to his or her application for naturalization. 8 C.F.R. § 329.2(d). Citizenship granted under this provision may be revoked if the individual subsequently receives a dishonorable discharge. INA § 329(c).

Non-citizens who die while on active duty for the U.S. armed forces during periods of hostilities can receive posthumous citizenship under INA § 329A. The person's survivors must apply for this honor within two years of his or her death. INA § 329A(c). Originally, citizenship obtained posthumously did not confer any benefits on the citizen's surviving spouse or children. In 2003, Congress amended the INA to allow for the survivors of those granted posthumous citizenship after September 11, 2001, to receive the benefits of the deceased's citizenship.

(2) SPOUSES OF UNITED STATES CITIZENS

Section 319 of the Immigration and Nationality Act relaxes the naturalization requirements for spouses of United States citizens. This section also applies to persons who obtain lawful permanent resident status under the special provisions for spouses and children battered by U.S. citizens. *See* § 5–5.1(c), *supra*. The applicant spouse must have resided continuously in the United States for three years—instead of five—immediately before filing the petition for naturalization. INA § 319(a). The residence must follow lawful admission, and the applicant must live "in marital union" with the citizen spouse throughout this period, unless he or she is a victim of domestic violence. Short periods of separation where the couple does not intend permanent dissolution of the marriage do not violate the marital union requirement. For example, in *Petition of Omar*, 151 F.Supp. 763 (S.D.N.Y.1957) the court ordered a separation of petitioner from his citizen spouse for two weeks as a "cooling off" period, following the petitioner's arrest (at his wife's request) for allegedly striking her. The judicially enforced separation did not preclude compliance with the statute. Further, at least one court has held that this requirement is satisfied where a couple separates before the non-citizen spouse is naturalized, so long as they were living in marital union when the non-citizen applied for naturalization and are still legally married when naturalization is granted. *Ali v. Smith,* 39 F.Supp.2d 1254 (W.D.Wash.1999).

Although a short separation, such as the two weeks involved in *Omar,* will not operate to destroy the marital union for purposes of the statute, an extended estrangement produces a different result. The rationale behind § 319(a), said the federal court in *Petition of Kostas,* 169 F.Supp. 77 (D.Del.1958), was "the congressional expectation that a non-citizen spouse who lived in close association with a citizen spouse for three years would more speedily absorb the basic concepts of citizenship than one not so situated." In *Kostas* the facts showed an "uneasy union marked by frequent separations of substantial duration," to the extent that it appeared the couple spent more time apart than together during the three-year statutory period. On that record the court determined that petitioner fell far short of the "marital union" requirement.

The statute does not relieve the spouse applicant of the burden of establishing good moral character and attachment to the principles of the Constitution.

If the citizen spouse is an employee of the United States government, a U.S. firm engaged in foreign commerce, a recognized U.S. institution of research, a public international organization in which the United States participates by treaty or statute, or the citizen performs qualified religious functions abroad, and is regularly stationed abroad in such activity, the applying spouse may be naturalized without any prior residence in the United States. The applying spouse, however, must declare to the CIS in good faith an intention to take up residence in the United States immediately upon the termination of such employment abroad of the citizen spouse. INA § 319(b). The applicant also must comply with all other requirements for naturalization.

Further, when a U.S. citizen dies while serving honorably in the armed forces, his or her non-citizen spouse may be naturalized without any prior residence or physical presence in the United States. INA § 319(d).

(3) CHILDREN OF CITIZENS AND DERIVATIVE CITIZENSHIP

The Child Citizenship Act of 2000 modified the procedures for naturalizing the children of U.S. citizens. The Act was intended to make it easier for parents to naturalize children adopted from overseas and to ensure that children of U.S. citizens are not deprived of citizenship because their parents failed to take the necessary steps to naturalize them. Under the provisions of the Act, a child born outside of the United States automatically acquires U.S. citizenship if, while the child is under the age of eighteen, at least one parent of a child is a U.S. citizen, whether by birth or by naturalization, and the child is residing in the United States as a lawful permanent resident in the custody of the citizen parent. INA § 320(a). No application is required. Consequently, children born outside the United States to non-citizens derive citizenship by operation of law when their parents are naturalized. Children born to or adopted by a U.S. citizen overseas acquire citizenship as soon as they are admitted to the United States as a lawful permanent resident in the custody of their citizen parents. INA § 320(b).

U.S. citizens may also apply for naturalization of their biological or adopted children residing outside the United

States. INA § 322(a). Parents must file Form N–600 for biological children or Form N–643 for adopted children. 8 C.F.R. § 322.2. Prior to filing the application, U.S. citizen parents must have been physically present in the United States for five years, at least two of which were after attaining the age of fourteen. If a U.S. citizen parent has not lived in the United States for five years, the physical presence requirement can be satisfied by one of the children's grandparents, if they are U.S. citizens. The child must lawfully enter the United States and appear before an immigration officer for an interview. INA § 322(a)(4). If the application is approved, the child must take the oath of allegiance, unless it is waived pursuant to INA § 337 because the child cannot understand its meaning. INA § 322(b).

The foregoing provisions apply only to children under the age of eighteen on February 27, 2001, the effective date of the Child Citizenship Act. Prior to that date, children residing in the United States as lawful permanent residents acquired citizenship automatically only if their non-citizen parents were naturalized while the children were under age eighteen. INA § 321 (repealed 2001). Under the former version of INA § 322, U.S. citizens could also apply for naturalization on behalf of their natural or adopted children. Children who did not acquire citizenship by one of these means may still apply for citizenship on their own behalf after attaining the age of eighteen.

(4) Persons With Disabilities

The availability of naturalization for persons with disabilities became a pressing issue in the 1990s after the Personal Responsibility and Work Opportunity Reconciliation Act ended Social Security Disability (SSI) payments to non-citizens. Congress has since reinstated SSI benefits for lawful permanent residents who were receiving them prior to 1996. INA § 402(a)(2)(E). Several provisions remain in place to address the special needs of disabled applicants for naturalization.

Since 1994, applicants with physical or developmental disabilities or mental impairments have been exempt from the literacy and civics requirements for citizenship. *See* § 12–2.2(b)(3), *supra*. To qualify for this exemption, the applicant must have a medically determinable disability that has lasted or is expected to last for at least twelve months. 8 C.F.R. § 312.2(b). This exemption does not apply to anyone whose impairment is directly attributable to the illegal use of drugs. To qualify for the exemption, the applicant must submit a Medical Certification (Form N–648), completed by a licensed doctor, which explains how the applicant's disability renders him or her unable to comply with the requirements. Other accommodations available to disabled applicants include off-site testing, interviews, and oath ceremonies.

Despite the exemption from the literacy and civics requirements, until 2000, disabled applicants were still required to take the oath of allegiance. In *Galvez–Letona v. Kirkpatrick*, 54 F.Supp.2d 1218 (D.Utah 1999), a district court held that this requirement must be waived for an applicant who was unable to understand the oath because of a developmental disability. The applicant was a twenty-six-year-old man with severe Down Syndrome who had a mental age of eighteen months. He met all of the requirements for citizenship except that he was unable to demonstrate understanding of the oath of allegiance or a willingness to take the oath. The court found that failure to waive the oath in this circumstance violated the Rehabilitation Act, which prohibits federal agencies from discriminating on the basis of a disability. The following year, Congress amended INA § 337(a) to provide a waiver of the oath requirement for anyone who is unable to understand it or communicate his or her understanding because of a physical or developmental disability.

(5) HMONG VETERANS

The Hmong Veterans' Naturalization Act of 2000 temporarily exempts Hmong veterans, their spouses, and their widows or widowers from the literacy requirements of INA § 312. 114 Stat. 316. The Act also requires the CIS to give qualified Hmong applicants special consideration with regard to the civics requirements of INA § 312. Congress enacted this exemption in recognition of the critical support Hmong guerilla forces provided to the United States during the Vietnam War. The literacy and civics requirements have been a barrier to naturalization for many Hmong refugees who had limited access to education in their homeland. The exemption applies to any person admitted as a refugee from Laos who served in a guerilla force that supported the United States during the Vietnam War, as well as anyone who was the spouse of a qualified veteran on the day when the veteran applied for refugee status, or the surviving spouse of a Hmong veteran who died in Southeast Asia. 114 Stat. 316, 1810. Applicants must provide proof of their service in a qualifying guerilla unit. The Hmong Veterans Act originally made this exemption available for a period of eighteen months; Congress later extended the exemption to three years. 115 Stat. 765. Hence, Hmong veterans and their spouses must have applied by May 2003 and widows and widowers must have applied by November

2003. The exemption is further limited to the first 45,000 applicants.

d. *Naturalization Procedures*

(1) JURISDICTION TO NATURALIZE

Exclusive authority to naturalize is conferred upon the Secretary of Homeland Security. INA § 310(a). Prior to the 1990 Act, the federal court decided whether a petitioner had complied with statutory conditions for citizenship. An INS designated examiner recommended whether naturalization should be granted, but the court could decide regardless of the INS recommendation. The 1990 Act temporarily shifted both the decision on naturalization and the principal responsibility for administration of the oath of allegiance to the INS. The 1990 Act authorized the federal district court to review *de novo* denials of naturalization and to adjudicate naturalization applications if the immigration agency fails to issue a decision within 120 days after a hearing. INA §§ 210(d), 336(b). The 1991 Technical Amendments returned principal responsibility for administration of oaths to the federal district courts. Title I of the Technical Amendments Act gives the courts forty-five days to administer the oath of naturalization, after which an applicant can choose to have the oath administered by the CIS. This compromise gives the courts an important role in naturalization, without creating backlogs due to crowded court dockets. INA § 310 *et seq.* State courts of record are also authorized, but not required, to aid in the administration of oaths of allegiance.

(2) APPLICATION

Applicants for naturalization first must file an application to enable the U.S. Citizenship and Immigration

Services (CIS) to conduct an investigation of the applicant's qualifications. INA § 334(a). This application may be submitted up to ninety days before the applicant becomes eligible for citizenship. 8 C.F.R. § 334.2. The application (Form N–400) consists of several pages wherein the applicant must provide background information regarding family history, periods of residence in the United States, criminal record, affiliations, and other factors that may affect eligibility for citizenship. All applicants must submit three color photographs and a copy of their Permanent Resident Card with their application. Some applicants may be required to submit additional documents, depending on their particular circumstances. All applicants must also be fingerprinted at an authorized fingerprinting center.

After receiving the application, the CIS checks criminal records and performs a background check on the addresses where the applicant has lived and worked for the preceding five years. 8 C.F.R. § 335.1. In *Price v. INS*, 962 F.2d 836 (9th Cir.1992), the Ninth Circuit approved the immigration service's broad authority to make inquiries as long as they are related in some way to the naturalization requirements. U.K. citizen Price was denied naturalization because he refused to list on his application all the organizations with which he had ever been affiliated. The Court found that the identity of the organizations with which a petitioner is associated might be relevant to one or more requirements of citizenship.

The applicant may not withdraw his or her application without the consent of the CIS. INA § 335(e). The CIS may, however, deny the application if the applicant fails to prosecute it. An individual should exercise caution in filing an application if he or she thinks that it could reveal grounds for the applicant's removal. In this situation it would probably be better not to apply for naturalization and thus avoid bringing the case to the attention of the immigration authorities.

An applicant may also file a formal declaration of intention to naturalize, but such a declaration is no longer mandatory. INA § 334(f).

(3) EXAMINATION

Before being naturalized, applicants must appear before a naturalization examiner. INA § 335(b). The examiner may also subpoena witnesses who can testify as to the applicants' qualifications for citizenship. If an applicant fails to appear at the examination and does not provide a reason for this failure within thirty days, the application may be administratively closed. 8 C.F.R. § 335.6. Each applicant and witness is interrogated separately; the applicant's attorney or representative may be present during the questioning if he or she has filed a notice of appearance. The proceeding may be videotaped or tape-recorded; the hearing is not formal and rules of evidence do not apply. The record of the examination is admissible in any subsequent hearing under INA § 336(a).

Applicants should answer all questions asked during the interview honestly, even if they are afraid that the answers might be detrimental to their case. Applicants who give false testimony risk having their application for citizenship denied, even if the concealed information would not in itself have been a bar to naturalization. *See* § 12–2.2(b)(4), *supra*; § 12–3.2(c)(1), *infra*.

After the examination, the examiner must make a determination within 120 days. INA § 336(b). If the examiner determines that the application lacks any necessary qualifications, he or she advises the applicant of that determination. An applicant is not bound, however, by the examiner's findings, and may as a matter of right file a request for a hearing before an immigration officer and then may seek *de novo* review by the federal district court. INA §§ 310(c), 336.

(4) HEARING ON DENIAL OF APPLICATION

If the application is initially denied, a new hearing takes place before another immigration officer. INA § 336(a). The applicant's attorney may take an active part in this hearing, present evidence, subpoena witnesses, make objections, and conduct cross-examination of the government's witnesses. The hearing is supposed to be scheduled within 180 days after a request is filed; it is tape-recorded or videotaped for purposes of judicial review. Upon consideration of the testimony and review of all documents properly submitted in support or opposition, the immigration officer decides whether the application for naturalization should be granted or denied. If the immigration officer fails to decide the matter within 120 days after the examination, the federal district court may determine the naturalization or remand the matter to the CIS with instructions. INA § 336(b).

(5) ADMINISTRATION OF OATH AND JUDICIAL REVIEW

If the examiner approves the naturalization, the applicant will be granted citizenship at a hearing in open court after taking the oath of allegiance to the United States. INA § 337. If the applicant fails to appear for more than one oath ceremony, he or she will be deemed to have abandoned the application for naturalization. 8 C.F.R. § 337.10. The CIS must, however, provide for expedited administration of the oath if the applicant's age, disability, or other special circumstances preclude appearance at a public ceremony. INA § 337(c). As provided under the technical amendments to the 1990 Act, if the court cannot administer the oath within forty-five days, the applicant may choose to have the oath administered by the CIS.

If the CIS denies the application, the applicant can seek judicial review in federal district court. Upon request by the applicant, the court can consider all issues *de novo*. If the CIS does not act upon the application within 120 days, the applicant can request a hearing in federal district court. These procedures have been designed and modified to expedite the naturalization process, which, given the benefits that naturalization confers, is significant to the applicant.

(6) CERTIFICATE OF NATURALIZATION

Upon granting citizenship to an individual, the CIS issues a certificate of naturalization. INA § 338. The certificate itself does not convey citizenship, but simply serves as evidence that the CIS has granted citizenship. The statute prescribes the information that the naturalization certificate will contain, including the number of the petition and the certificate; date of naturalization; the name, signature, place of residence, signed photograph, and personal description of the naturalized person (including age, sex, marital status, and country of former nationality); and a statement that the CIS has found the application in full compliance with the requirements of the naturalization laws and has ordered that the applicant be admitted to citizenship. INA § 338.

Minor clerical errors do not affect the evidentiary value of the certificate nor do informalities in the certificate—such as the misspelling of names or the misnaming of the applicant. *Brassert v. Biddle*, 148 F.2d 134 (2d Cir.1945).

The date on the certificate of naturalization is determined by the date of the oath. If the oath is waived, the date is the day on which the application is granted. If the court administers the oath, it may also grant a name change.

A naturalization order is subject to *direct* attack in independent denaturalization proceedings as prescribed by Congress. INA § 340(a). Revocation of naturalization is discussed below.

GENERAL RULES OF NATURALIZATION

SECTION INA	STATE RESIDENCE (at time of filing) Sec. 101(a)(33)	LPR² STATUS REQUIRED	LENGTH OF STATUS REQUIRED	PHYSICAL PRESENCE (Months in U.S.)	GOOD MORAL CHARACTER	ENGLISH LITERACY (Sec. 312)	GOVERN-MENT TEST (Sec. 312)	OATH OF ALLEGIANCE (Sec. 337)	OTHER REQUIREMENTS
316¹	3 Months in state or CIS District where filed	YES	5 Years	30/60 Aggregate	5 yrs. +	YES unless exempt³	YES unless exempt⁴	YES, unless exempt	None
319(a)	3 Months in state or CIS District where filed	YES	3 Years	18/36 Aggregate	3 yrs. +	YES, unless exempt³	YES, unless exempt⁴	YES, unless exempt	Married to same USC⁵ for 3 yrs. and living in marital union
319(b)	N.P.*****	YES	N.P.⁶	N.P.⁶	N.P.⁶	YES, unless exempt³	YES, unless exempt⁴	YES, unless exempt	Married to USC⁵ (N.P.) & living in marital union & USC spouse to be employed abroad 1 yr. with US gov't or corp., etc. appl. will join
320	N.P.*****	YES	N.P.⁶	N.P.⁶	N.P.⁶	NO	NO	NO	Biological or adopted child of U.S. citizen, under 18 years old, in custody of citizen parent
322	N.P.*****	NO	N.P.⁶	N.P.⁶	N.P.⁶	NO	NO	Yes, unless waived by Attorney General	Biological or adopted child under 18 yrs. old residing outside the U.S.
328	N.P.*****	YES	N.P.⁶	N.P.⁶	5 yrs (good character presumed during honorable service)	YES unless exempt³	YES unless exempt⁴	YES, unless exempt	3 years honorable active military less than 6 mo. since discharged
329	N.P.*****	YES — But not if enlisted or inducted in US	N.P.⁶	N.P.⁶	1 year	YES unless exempt³	YES unless exempt⁴	YES, unless exempt	1 day honorable active service during certain periods of hostilities

1 In 2003, 91% of all naturalizations were under INA § 316
2 LPR = Lawful permanent resident
3 Test Exemptions: 15 years in the U.S./over 55 years old, 20 years in the U.S./over 50 years old
4 Test Exemptions: Mental or physical disability, or 15 years in the U.S./over 65 years old and disability
5 USC = United States Citizen
6 N.P. = No particular time period

§ 12–3   LOSS OF NATIONALITY

§ 12–3.1   Introduction

There are two ways by which a citizen may lose citizenship: denaturalization and expatriation. Denaturalization involves the judicial revocation of the naturalization order based on a finding that the naturalization was illegally or fraudulently procured. INA § 340(a). Obviously, denaturalization applies only to naturalized citizens. Expatriation, however, applies to both naturalized and all other citizens, and does not assume a defect in the original acquisition of citizenship. Rather, expatriation results from certain actions enumerated in INA § 349 by which citizens voluntarily relinquished their citizenship.

§ 12–3.2   Denaturalization

a.   *Congress' Power to Denaturalize*

The authority of Congress to provide for cancellation of wrongfully procured naturalization certificates is derived from the constitutional power of Congress to establish a uniform rule of naturalization under Article I, § 8, and the "Necessary and Proper" clause.

The Supreme Court in *Costello v. United States*, 365 U.S. 265 (1961) sustained the constitutionality of the 1952 version of the denaturalization statute with respect to Congress' powers to cancel certificates procured "by concealment of a material fact or by willful misrepresentation." But while the power of Congress to prescribe grounds for revoking naturalization has been repeatedly upheld, the Supreme Court has stricken those provisions it deemed arbitrary or discriminatory. Hence, in *Schneider v. Rusk*, 377 U.S. 163 (1964) the Court invalidated the provision prescribing loss of nationality by a naturalized citizen who resided in a foreign state for three years or more. Native-born citizens faced no such punishment. Justice Douglas wrote:

This statute proceeds on the impermissible assumption that naturalized citizens as a class are less reliable and bear less allegiance to this country than do the native born. This is an assumption that is impossible for us to make. Moreover, while the Fifth Amendment contains no equal protection clause, it does forbid discrimination that is "so unjustifiable as to be violative of due process."

The court thus held that the provision discriminated against naturalized citizens in violation of due process, creating a "second-class citizenship" without a rational justification.

b. *Denaturalization Procedures*

(1) JUDICIAL PROCEEDINGS

The revocation statute empowers United States district attorneys, upon an affidavit showing good cause, to institute proceedings in equity to cancel the naturalization certificate. INA § 340(a). The original naturalization order has no *res judicata* effect against this independent attack by the United States, *Johannessen v. United States*, 225 U.S. 227 (1912), in contrast to the immunity it enjoys from collateral attack. *Tutun v. United States*, 270 U.S. 568 (1926).

(2) ADMINISTRATIVE DENATURALIZATION

The revocation statute also reserves to immigration authorities the power to reopen or vacate naturalization orders. INA § 340(h). In accordance with this provision, the INS in 1996 instituted a procedure known as "administrative denaturalization." This procedure, which the Service was later enjoined from using, enabled INS district directors to revoke a person's citizenship if they had "clear, convincing, and unequivocal evidence" that the INS granted the person's application by mistake or the person concealed or misrepresented a material fact. 8 C.F.R. § 340.1(a). Immigration regulations required the district director to serve the naturalized citizen with notice of intent to reopen the naturalization proceedings. If the citizen did not request a hearing within sixty days, his or her citizenship was revoked. 8 C.F.R. § 340.1(b). An individual whose citizenship was revoked could appeal to the INS Office of Examinations, Administrative Appeals Unit and could seek judicial review of an adverse decision from that agency. 8 C.F.R. § 340.1(e).

A group of naturalized citizens who were served with notices of intent to revoke their naturalization challenged this regulation in *Gorbach v. Reno*, 219 F.3d 1087 (9th Cir.2000). The Ninth Circuit, sitting *en banc,* held that the Attorney General lacked the authority to revoke citizenship administratively. The court subsequently issued a permanent injunction preventing the INS from enforcing the administrative denaturalization procedure.

c. Grounds for Denaturalization

(1) CONCEALMENT OF MATERIAL FACT OR WILLFUL MISREPRESENTATION

Naturalization may be revoked if the certificate of naturalization was "procured by concealment of a material fact or by willful misrepresentation" or was "illegally procured." INA § 340(a). Fraud and illegal procurement as grounds for denaturalization date back to the original 1906 statute. 34 Stat. 596. The introduction of the phrase "concealment of a material fact by willful misrepresentation" was intended to assure that both "extrinsic fraud" (outside of the proceedings—like concealment of witnesses) and "intrinsic fraud" (perjured testimony) would serve as grounds for denaturalization. *Costello v. United States*, 365 U.S. 265 (1961).

Clearly, facts suppressed or concealed in a naturalization proceeding are "material" if disclosure of those facts alone would justify denial of citizenship. But the scope of materiality also includes concealed facts which, if disclosed, would have led to the investigation and discovery of other facts bearing on the applicant's eligibility for naturalization. In *Chaunt v. United States*, 364 U.S. 350 (1960), the Supreme Court considered the materiality of Chaunt's failure to disclose three prior arrests for petty offenses in his naturalization application. The government argued that the arrests were material because, if disclosed, the Immigration Service would have investigated and *might* have discovered that Chaunt was (as one witness testified) an active member of the Communist Party. The Court established a two-part test for materiality, by which it concluded on the facts before it that "the government failed to show by 'clear, unequivocal, and convincing' evidence *either* (1) that facts were suppressed which, if known, would have warranted denial of citizenship, or (2) that their disclosure *might* have been useful in an investigation *possibly* leading to the discovery of other facts *warranting* denial of citizenship." (emphasis added).

Confusion has ensued as to the second part of the *Chaunt* test—that "disclosure might have been useful in an investigation possibly leading to the discovery of other facts warranting denial of citizenship." The Ninth Circuit in *United States v. Rossi*, 299 F.2d 650 (9th Cir. 1962) held that a concealed or suppressed fact is material only "if disclosure of the true facts would have justified a refusal to issue a visa." The Sixth Circuit, however, took a different view in *Kassab v. INS*, 364 F.2d 806 (6th Cir.1966), holding it sufficient if the suppressed fact, if revealed, "*might* have led to further action and the discovery of facts which would have justified the refusal of the visa." (emphasis in original).

The Southern District Court of Florida in *United States v. Fedorenko*, 455 F.Supp. 893 (S.D.Fla.1978) ruled that the government must *prove the existence* of the facts which would have warranted denial of naturalization, although it need only show that an investigation leading to discovery of these facts *possibly* would have taken place. The court found the government had failed to establish that the defendant had voluntarily served as a guard and committed atrocities at a German death camp while a prisoner of war during World War II, which the government contended it might have discovered through investigation, had the defendant disclosed on his visa application that he had resided at the particular concentration camp. The Fifth Circuit reversed, stating that the government need only prove "that disclosure of the true facts would have [prompted] an inquiry that might have uncovered other factors warranting denial of citizenship." The government would not be burdened with the overwhelming task of conducting an investigation into the past, discovering ultimate facts warranting disqualification, and proving those facts in court by clear and convincing evidence.

The Supreme Court affirmed the Fifth Circuit, but on other grounds, not addressing the materiality question. The Tenth Circuit, however, in *United States v. Sheshtawy*, 714 F.2d 1038 (10th Cir.1983), adopted Justice Blackmun's views expressed in his concurring opinion to the *Fedorenko* case. The court concluded that the *Chaunt* test "requires that the government demonstrate the existence of actual disqualifying facts—facts that themselves would have warranted denial of petitioner's citizenship." Since the government had not claimed to have established facts that would have warranted denial of citizenship, it had not met the rigorous *Chaunt* test, and revocation of naturalization under INA § 340(a) was not justified.

In *Kungys v. United States*, 485 U.S. 759 (1988), the Supreme Court attempted to clarify the *Chaunt* holding. The Court held that the test of whether concealments or misrepresentations are "material" under INA § 340(a) is whether they can be shown by clear, unequivocal, and convincing evidence to have been predictably capable of affecting the naturalization decision, *i.e.*, to have "had a natural tendency to influence the decisions of the INS." Of the seven other participating justices, four joined this part of Justice Scalia's opinion.

Kungys was admitted to the United States for permanent residence in 1948 and became a naturalized citizen in 1954. In 1982 the United States commenced denaturalization proceedings. The government alleged that Kungys had participated in executing over 2,000 Lithuanians, most of them Jewish, in Kedainiai, Lithuania, between July and August 1941. The government also demonstrated that, in his visa application and in his naturalization petition, Kungys misrepresented his date and place of birth, as well as his occupation and residence during World War II.

In determining whether Kungys' misrepresentations met the Court's new standard of materiality, the Court held that § 340(a) is limited to falsehoods or deceptions in the naturalization proceedings and not misrepresentations made in the visa process, because it is the former falsehoods which "procure" the naturalization. The Court concluded that Kungys' misrepresentations of the date and place of his birth in his naturalization petition were not material. There was no suggestion that the facts were themselves relevant to Kungys' qualifications for citizenship. Likewise, there was no showing that the true date and place of birth would have disclosed other facts relevant to his qualifications and would have resulted either in outright denial or an investigation resulting in denial of the naturalization application. Hence, the government failed to establish clearly, unequivocally, and convincingly that Kungys' misrepresentations had a natural tendency to influence the decision of the INS. Only two justices joined Justice Scalia in this part of the opinion.

As an alternative basis for upholding denaturalization, the government argued that Kungys' naturalization had been "illegally procured" because, at the time of his naturalization, he lacked the good moral character required under INA § 316(a). (Illegal procurement of naturalization is discussed further in the following section of this chapter.) In the government's view, Kungys' misrepresentations, whether material or not, constituted false testimony given for the purpose of obtaining benefits in both the visa and naturalization proceedings, which indicates a lack of good moral character under INA § 101(f)(6).

The Court decided in favor of the government on this issue, holding that § 101(f)(6) does not contain a materiality requirement for false testimony for the purposes of determining whether naturalization was "illegally procured" because of a lack of good moral character. In the Court's view, lack of good moral character is present to some degree whenever there is subjective intent to deceive, no matter how immaterial the deception. The Court pointed out, however, that "testimony" is limited to oral statements made under oath and that the false testimony provisions do not apply to "concealments." Section 101(f)(6) applies to only those misrepresentations made with the subjective intent of obtaining immigration benefits, and this intent must be proven by clear, unequivocal, and convincing evidence. The Court concluded that it would be "relatively rare that the Government will be able to prove that a misrepresentation that does not have the natural tendency to influence the decision regarding immigration or naturalization benefits was nonetheless made with subjective intent of obtaining those benefits." A majority of the justices joined this part of the opinion.

Although a majority of the justices agreed that § 101(f)(6) contains no materiality requirement, only three of the justices concurred in Justice Scalia's opinion holding that denaturalization could not be affirmed under that provision. The question whether Kungys' misrepresentations constituted false testimony for the purpose of obtaining immigration or naturalization benefits cannot be answered without first resolving two issues: (1) whether Kungys' misrepresentations constituted "testimony" and (2) whether in making the misrepresentations, Kungys possessed the subjective intent to obtain immigration or naturalization benefits. The latter question is one of fact to be resolved by the trier of fact. Since the case had to be remanded in any event, the Court chose not to resolve the former question of law.

Five separate opinions were filed in the *Kungys* case and there was no clear majority holding on many of the issues presented in the majority opinion. Hence, *Kungys* did little to dispel the uncertainty about the *Chaunt* standard of materiality. The Court revisited the issue of materiality in 1995, in *United States v. Gaudin*, 515 U.S. 506 (1995), where it held that materiality in a criminal prosecution is a question of law and fact to be submitted to the jury. The Court distinguished its *Kungys* holding, however, on the basis that since there is no right to a jury in denaturalization proceedings, the court may decide whether a false statement is material.

On remand, Kungys entered a consent judgment with the Department of Justice in which the government revoked his citizenship but agreed not to deport him. 65 Interp.Rel. 1287. Consequently, Kungys was able to remain in the United States as a lawful permanent resident.

In addition to being material, a misrepresentation must be intentional. Hence, where the defendant in *Maisenberg v. United States*, 356 U.S. 670 (1958) had answered "no" to a question on her preliminary application for naturalization asking whether she belonged to or was associated with any organization which teaches or advocates anarchy or overthrow of the existing government, she did not conceal a material fact or commit willful misrepresentation. Although she was at the time a member of the Communist Party, the question was ambiguous and she could reasonably have interpreted it as relating solely to anarchy, and not as calling for disclosure of membership in nonanarchistic organizations advocating violent overthrow of the government. Moreover, applicants do not "conceal" a material fact, within the meaning of the statute, if they merely fail to *volunteer* facts which might have a bearing on eligibility. In *Cufari v. United States*, 217 F.2d 404 (1st Cir.1954) the First Circuit held that a naturalized citizen could not be denaturalized for failing to disclose his criminal record at the time of naturalization, unless the government could prove that he had been asked during the proceedings whether he had a criminal record and that he had answered in the negative.

Specific concealments and misrepresentations which courts have found sufficient to warrant denaturalization include: deliberate suppression of criminal records where there is a duty to disclose (*United States v. Oddo*, 314 F.2d 115 (2d Cir.1963))—unlike the situation in *Cufari*; knowingly making false statements concerning marital or family status (*United States v. D'Agostino*, 338 F.2d 490 (2d Cir.1964)); and deliberate misstatement concerning an applicant's fulfillment of the residence requirements. *Rosenberg v. United States*, 60 F.2d 475 (3d Cir.1932).

(2) Illegal Procurement of Naturalization

Illegal procurement provides an independent ground for revoking naturalization. That phrase has been held to convey something wider in scope than fraud and is not restricted to intentional deception. It has encompassed naturalizations procured when prescribed requirements—for example, attachment to the principles of the Constitution or lack of good moral character—had no existence in fact. *United States v. Ginsberg*, 243 U.S. 472 (1917). In *Kungys v. United States*, 485 U.S. 759 (1988), the Supreme Court held that false testimony given for the purpose of obtaining benefits in a naturalization proceeding indicates a lack of good moral character under INA § 101(f)(6) and may render the naturalization "illegally procured," even though the misrepresentations may not have been material. This case is discussed in more detail in the immediately preceding section. The term also connotes affirmative misconduct by the applicant to induce the court or governmental agents to act in a manner not authorized by law; it encompasses the granting of certificates upon an error of law, for example, as to jurisdiction or procedural irregularities such as denying the government the opportunity to question the applicant in open court or to introduce evidence.

To justify denaturalization, however, the error must be substantial. Hence, clerical mistakes in connection with the issuance of a naturalization certificate will not constitute grounds for revocation and errors of judgment in granting citizenship against the preponderance of the evidence are better corrected on appeal in the original naturalization proceeding than in an action to revoke naturalization.

Illegal procurement of naturalization is also subject to criminal penalties under 18 U.S.C.A. § 1425. When a person is convicted under this statute, his or her naturalization is automatically revoked. INA § 341.

(3) RESIDENCE IN FOREIGN COUNTRY WITHIN ONE YEAR AFTER NATURALIZATION

Prior to 1994, § 340 provided that if a naturalized citizen takes up permanent residence in a foreign country within one year after naturalization, it would be considered prima facie evidence of a lack of intention to establish permanent residence in the United States at the time of the application for citizenship. INA § 340(d) (repealed 1994). The Technical Corrections Act of 1994 repealed this provision as to anyone who obtained citizenship on or after October 25, 1994. 108 Stat. 4305.

(4) OTHER GROUNDS FOR DENATURALIZATION

The denaturalization statute provides two additional grounds for revoking naturalization: (1) Refusal on the part of the naturalized citizen, within ten years following naturalization, to testify as a witness before a congressional committee concerning his or her subversive activities, will be a ground for revocation of naturalization, if such refusal resulted in a conviction for contempt. INA § 340(a). The refusal to testify establishes as a matter of law that naturalization was procured by concealment of a material fact or by willful misrepresentation and the naturalized citizen is not granted an opportunity within this provision to present countervailing evidence. (2) If within five years of naturalization a naturalized citizen becomes a member of any of the proscribed subversive organizations, of which membership would have precluded naturalization in the first place, it shall constitute prima facie evidence that such person was not attached to the principles of the Constitution at the time of naturalization. INA § 340(c). In the absence of countervailing evidence it will be sufficient to revoke the person's citizenship as having been obtained by concealment of a material fact or by willful misrepresentation. Neither ground has been invoked in any naturalization proceeding to date and the constitutionality of these provisions may be in doubt because of the discrimination they impose on naturalized citizens. *Cf. Schneider v. Rusk*, 377 U.S. 163 (1964).

d. *Effect on Spouses or Children*

A person who claims citizenship based on the naturalization of a parent or spouse will lose his or her citizenship if the parent or spouse's citizenship is revoked due to concealment of a material fact. INA § 340(d). If the parent's or spouse's naturalization is revoked for any other reason, those claiming derivative citizenship will not lose their citizenship unless they reside outside the United States at the time of revocation.

§ 12–3.3   Expatriation

a.   Introduction

Expatriation provides the second means for loss of nationality, to which both naturalized and all other citizens are subject. INA § 349(a). The term is defined as the *voluntary* act of abandoning one's country and becoming the citizen or subject of another. Under current Supreme Court jurisprudence, the specific intent of the alleged expatriate to renounce citizenship must accompany the expatriating act, in order to constitute relinquishment of citizenship. In 1986, Congress amended INA § 349(a) to conform to the rulings of the Supreme Court, by providing that individuals will lose their U.S. citizenship only by "voluntarily performing any of the following acts with the intention of relinquishing United States nationality."

b.   Development of the Law of Expatriation

The Constitution makes no mention of expatriation. Courts were reluctant in the early days of the United States to acknowledge expatriation of a citizen without express consent of the government. The right of a citizen to voluntary expatriation notwithstanding lack of the sovereign's consent was first recognized by Congress in 1868. 15 Stat. 223. The 1868 Act proclaimed that "the right of expatriation is a natural and inherent right of all people, indispensable to the enjoyment of the rights of life, liberty and the pursuit of happiness." Although intended to protect naturalized United States citizens from claims of allegiance by their former sovereigns, the Attorney General construed the statute to permit U.S. citizens to abandon their citizenship. 14 Ops. Att'y Gen. 295. Also in 1868 the United States initiated a series of treaties—named the Bancroft Treaties for George Bancroft, a United States diplomat who negotiated the first of these treaties with the North German Confederation (15 Stat. 615)—which provided that each country would regard as citizens of the other, those of its own subjects who became naturalized by the other.

Although the right of expatriation was thus established, Congress did not first define the manner by which a citizen may lose citizenship until the Expatriation Act of 1907. 34 Stat. 1228. The statute defined three means of expatriation: U.S. citizens were deemed expatriated if they naturalized in any foreign state in conformity with its laws or took the oath of allegiance to any foreign state, female citizens who married non-citizens assumed the nationality of their husbands, and naturalized citizens returning to their country of origin and living there for two years were also presumed to have effected expatriation. 34 Stat. 1228. Marriage to a foreigner ceased to be an expatriating act in 1922. 42 Stat. 1022. Expatriating naturalized citizens who return to their country of origin was held to be unconstitutional in 1964. *Schneider v. Rusk*, 377 U.S. 163 (1964). As to the present status of those who naturalize in a foreign state, see § 12–3.3(d), *infra*.

The Nationality Act of 1940 expanded the grounds for expatriation to include service in the military or government of a foreign state, voting in a political election in a foreign state, formal renunciation of United States citizenship, court martial conviction and discharge from the armed services for desertion in wartime, conviction for treason against the United States, and failure for nationals born abroad to take up permanent residence in the United States before attaining sixteen years of age. 54 Stat. 1137. In addition, the Act modified the provisions for expatriation of naturalized citizens. They could then be expatriated for three years continuous residence in the state of their birth or for five years continuous residence in any other foreign state. Many of these provisions reflected the trying economic times and the security consciousness resulting from the onset of World War II. The Immigration and Nationality Act of 1952 essentially re-enacted the expatriation provisions of the 1940 statute, with some minor additions. INA § 349 (examined in sections 12–3.3(c)–(d), *infra*).

c. *The Power of Congress to Prescribe Grounds for Expatriation*

The 1907 statute prescribed specific methods of expatriation. 34 Stat. 1228. Certain provisions appeared to mandate loss of nationality without regard to intent, most notably, marriage of a female citizen to a noncitizen. In *MacKenzie v. Hare*, 239 U.S. 299 (1915), the petitioner challenged this provision, which withdrew her citizenship upon her marriage to a British national. She argued that expatriation required not merely the act of marrying a foreign national, but a subjective intent to "permanently reside elsewhere [and] to throw off the former allegiance, and become a citizen or subject of a foreign power." The Court determined that Mrs. Mac-Kenzie had voluntarily relinquished her citizenship because her marriage was voluntary, and she had notice of the consequences.

The Court further held that Congress had authority to prescribe grounds for expatriation, based on powers "implied, necessary or incidental" to its expressed power over nationality and foreign relations. The Court viewed the law in controversy as a reasonable exercise of government power for the prevention of potential international controversies arising out of dual nationality.

Subsequent cases over the next forty years reinforced an "objective intent" standard for determining relinquishment of citizenship. In *Savorgnan v. United States*, 338 U.S. 491 (1950), the petitioner was a native-born U.S. citizen who was engaged to an Italian government official. To obtain royal approval of her marriage, she was informed she would have to become naturalized as an Italian citizen, recite an oath of allegiance to Italy, and sign a document renouncing her United States citizenship. She believed her signing was only a technical requirement, and she asserted that she never intended to renounce her United States citizenship. The Court held that under the statute one who obtained citizenship in a foreign country loses United States citizenship, regardless of subjective intent:

> [T]he acts upon which the statutes expressly condition the consent of our Government to the expatriation of its citizens are stated objectively. There is no suggestion in the statutory language that the effect of the specified overt acts, when voluntarily done, is conditioned upon the undisclosed intent of the person doing them.

The Supreme Court's attitude, heretofore one of deference to Congress regarding laws of expatriation, began to change in 1958. In *Perez v. Brownell*, 356 U.S. 44 (1958), the Court upheld the constitutionality of the provision (54 Stat. 1137) prescribing loss of nationality for voting in a foreign political election. Justice Frankfurter, speaking for the majority, ruled that a "rational nexus" existed between the congressional power to regulate foreign affairs and the withdrawal of citizenship for voting in a foreign election. The power of Congress to terminate citizenship did not depend on consent of the citizen but the voluntary performance of the expatriating act. The holding thus reaffirmed the power of Congress to prescribe acts which would constitute loss of nationality, but the Court was closely divided, five justices to four. Chief Justice Warren wrote a vigorous dissent, maintaining that Congress did not have the power to take away the "most basic right" of citizenship. Congress could only acquiesce in the wishes of citizens to abandon their nationality.

On the same day, March 31, 1958, the Court for the first time held an expatriation provision unconstitutional; Chief Justice Warren wrote the plurality opinion in another five-to-four decision, *Trop v. Dulles*, 356 U.S. 86 (1958). The suit challenged § 401(g) of the Nationality Act of 1940, which provided for expatriation upon conviction by court martial and dishonorable discharge for desertion in time of war. 54 Stat. 1137. Private Trop, serving abroad in the United States army, escaped from a stockade where he had been confined for disciplinary reasons. He turned himself in several hours later, but for his offense he was court martialed and convicted of desertion, sentenced to three years of hard labor, and dishonorably discharged. Chief Justice Warren concluded that § 401(g) was a penal statute, violative of the Eighth Amendment's prohibition against cruel and unusual punishment, as it stripped the individual of any nationality, leaving him stateless. (In 1978 Congress repealed the statute. 92 Stat. 1046.)

A second expatriation provision was invalidated in *Kennedy v. Mendoza–Martinez*, 372 U.S. 144 (1963). The challenged statute provided loss of citizenship for those persons who had left the United States in time of war to evade military service. 58 Stat. 746. In 1942, Mendoza–Martinez (a native born U.S. citizen with dual Mexican nationality) went to Mexico, as he admitted, solely for the purpose of evading service in the U.S. armed forces. He further conceded that he remained there for that purpose until November 1946, when he voluntarily returned to the United States. In 1947, he pleaded guilty to and was convicted of, evasion of his service obligation, and sentenced to imprisonment of a year and one day. He served his sentence and upon his release lived undisturbed until 1953 when, after a lapse of five years, he was arrested and subjected to deportation proceedings. The government asserted that Mendoza–Martinez was deportable as he had expatriated himself by committing the act specified in the provision. Justice Goldberg wrote for the majority, holding that the statute's automatic deprivation of nationality for the offense of evading military service was an unconstitutional punishment, in violation of rights to due process and trial by jury.

In 1964, the Court again limited the power of Congress to expatriate in *Schneider v. Rusk*, 377 U.S. 163 (1964). It decided that the statute expatriating naturalized citizens for three years continuous residence in the state of their former nationality was an invalid discrimination against naturalized citizens.

In *Trop*, *Mendoza–Martinez*, and *Schneider*, the Court utilized an *ad hoc* approach for restricting congressional power to expatriate, by invalidating several provisions as violative of specific constitutional rights. The issue of the requisite intent for finding a voluntary relinquishment of citizenship had not been addressed since *Perez v. Brownell*, *supra*. In *Afroyim v. Rusk*, 387 U.S. 253 (1967), the Supreme Court overruled its 1958 decision in *Perez*, holding that Congress had no general power, express or implied, to expatriate without the citizen's assent. Afroyim was a naturalized U.S. citizen who went to Israel and while in that country voted in an Israeli election. The State Department subsequently refused to renew his passport, asserting Afroyim's loss of citizenship under § 401(e) of the Nationality Act of 1940. 54 Stat. 1137. Afroyim contended that neither the Fourteenth Amendment nor any other provision of the Constitution allowed Congress to extinguish his citizenship without his voluntary renunciation. Writing for the majority, Justice Black agreed, and held that the Fourteenth Amendment "can most reasonably be read as defining a citizenship which a citizen keeps unless he voluntarily relinquishes it. Once acquired, this Fourteenth Amendment citizenship was not to be shifted, canceled, or diluted at the will of the Federal Government, the States or any other governmental unit."

The expansive language of Justice Black's majority opinion caused speculation as to its meaning. Some reasoned that *Afroyim* had invalidated all expatriation statutes, leaving the decision as to one's nationality at all times with the individual. With the right of citizenship judicially defined as absolute, it was not necessary for the allegedly expatriated individual to do more than assert a claim to citizenship in order to recover it. Others believed that *Afroyim* had reinstated a subjective intent test, which required for expatriation a finding that not only did the citizen commit the expatriating act, but he or she did so with the specific intent of relinquishing citizenship.

The Court's next opportunity to consider the scope and vitality of the *Afroyim* holding occurred in *Rogers v. Bellei*, 401 U.S. 815 (1971). Bellei acquired citizenship by birth outside the United States to a U.S. citizen mother and Italian father. He lived abroad, although he visited the United States several times on a United States passport. He was warned shortly before his twenty-third birthday that the statute conferring his citizenship required him to remain in the United States for five years in order to preserve his citizenship. Bellei left the United States one year later and was notified that he had lost his citizenship. He sought to enjoin the statute, claiming it was violative of due process, and constituted cruel and unusual punishment. The district court ruled the statute unconstitutional, citing *Afroyim* and *Schneider*. The Supreme Court reversed in another five-to-four decision, holding that Bellei's citizenship acquired upon birth abroad was not constitutionally conferred, nor was it protected under the Fourteenth Amendment, which referred in its first sentence to "persons born or naturalized *in the United States.*" (emphasis added). As a mere creation of statute his citizenship was subject to congressional restrictions, and it was perfectly reasonable for Congress to impose a "condition subsequent" to the grant of citizenship. In dissent, Justice Black saw no distinction between the various forms of citizenship which justified the second class treatment afforded citizens born abroad. "I cannot accept the Court's conclusion that the Fourteenth Amendment protects the citizenship of some Americans and not others." (Congress has since repealed the statute at issue in *Bellei*. 92 Stat. 1046.)

The Supreme Court's 1980 pronouncement on the issue of congressional power to expatriate, *Vance v. Terrazas*, 444 U.S. 252 (1980), went in two directions. Terrazas was born in the United States of Mexican parents, thus acquiring dual nationality. He obtained a certificate of Mexican nationality while in Mexico in 1970, which included renunciation of all other nationalities. He claimed it was not his intent to relinquish U.S. citizenship. On the one hand, the Court unanimously reaffirmed the basic holding of *Afroyim*—that expatriation required a showing of specific intent to relinquish citizenship voluntarily, in addition to proof that the expatriating act itself was committed voluntarily. The specific intent could be expressed in words or fairly inferred from proven conduct. On the other hand, the Court upheld a statute providing that the government must prove merely by "a preponderance of the evidence" that citizenship was voluntarily relinquished. The Court of Appeals had declared the statute unconstitutional, believing a "clear and convincing" standard of proof was required. In reversing, Justice White stated "[We do not] agree with the Court of Appeals that, because under *Afroyim* Congress is constitutionally devoid of power to impose expatriation on a citizen, it is also without power to prescribe the evidentiary standard to govern expatriation proceedings." The "preponderance of the evidence" standard was held to apply, for both the government's burden of proving voluntary relinquishment, and for the citizen's burden of rebutting the presumption that the expatriating act, which the government proved to have been committed, was voluntary.

The case of Rabbi Meir Kahane illustrates the difference between an intent-based and an allegiance-based approach to expatriation. Kahane was a U.S. citizen at birth. He moved to Israel where he became active in politics and was elected to the Israeli Parliament. Kahane, aware of the fact that accepting an office under a foreign government was an expatriating act listed in INA § 349(a)(4), communicated on several occasions with the State Department that he did not intend to give up his U.S. citizenship. The State Department nonetheless claimed that Kahane committed the expatriating act by shifting his allegiance to Israel. The court rejected this argument because an actor who contemporaneously with the expatriating act declares his intent to stay a U.S. citizen automatically preserves his citizenship. *Kahane v. Shultz*, 653 F.Supp. 1486 (E.D.N.Y.1987).

One year later, the Israeli Parliament passed a law providing that its members could only be Israeli citizens. Kahane executed a formal oath of renunciation of his U.S. citizenship to remain eligible for a seat in the Parliament. After Kahane's party was barred, on different grounds, from running in the elections, Kahane tried to revoke his renunciation of U.S. citizenship claiming that the Israeli law compelled his act. The court ruled against Kahane, who remained expatriated, although he was permitted to visit the United States and was eventually assassinated in New York City. *Kahane v. Secretary of State*, 700 F.Supp. 1162 (D.D.C.1988).

d. *Methods of Expatriation*

(1) Obtaining Naturalization in a Foreign State

Subject to the constitutional and statutory requirement of voluntariness, INA § 349 provides that citizens may lose their nationality by obtaining naturalization in a foreign state, either upon personal application or that of a parent or duly authorized agent, after having obtained the age of eighteen years. For further clarification, see § 12–3.3(d)(5), *infra*.

(2) Oath of Allegiance to a Foreign State

Citizens who take an oath or other formal declaration of allegiance to a foreign state after attaining the age of eighteen are expatriated under the current statute. INA § 349(a)(2). Under *Vance v. Terrazas*, 444 U.S. 252 (1980) the courts will inquire if the person taking the oath actually intended to abandon United States citizenship. If the oath is taken in circumstances indicating lack of voluntariness, such as military conscription, the requisite intent to transfer allegiance may not be found. *Riccio v. Dulles*, 116 F.Supp. 680 (D.D.C.1953).

(3) Military Service in a Foreign State

Citizens who enter the armed forces of a foreign country are expatriated if such armed forces are engaged in hostilities against the United States or if the citizens serve as commissioned or noncommissioned officers. INA § 349(a)(3). Again, the requirement that the expatriating act be done with the intention of relinquishing United States nationality applies to service in foreign armed forces. INA § 349(a).

(4) Foreign Government Employment

Employment in the government of a foreign state coupled with (as a condition of employment) acquisition of nationality in or declaration of allegiance to the foreign state will serve as grounds for expatriation. INA § 349(a)(4). This broad language has, however, been restricted by the courts. For example, in *Kenji Kamada v. Dulles*, 145 F.Supp. 457 (N.D.Cal.1956) petitioner had taught public school in Japan during and after World War II, for which the United States government claimed she was expatriated. A federal district court disagreed, focusing not only on the voluntariness question but upon the nature of the government service. Teaching school, reasoned the district judge, was not the type of foreign government employment envisioned by the act; rather, the law was intended to encompass service to a foreign government the performance of which required absolute allegiance to the foreign government. Teaching, as such, did not come within this category.

(5) Formal Renunciation of Nationality

Making a formal renunciation of nationality before a diplomatic or consular officer of the United States in a foreign country will lead to expatriation, if performed in a manner prescribed by the Secretary of State. INA § 349(a)(5). Informal renunciations of citizenship are ineffective, however, as are other methods not meeting the State Department regulations. *Vance v. Terrazas*, 444 U.S. 252 (1980).

Davis v. District Director, 481 F.Supp. 1178 (D.D.C. 1979) is, perhaps, the most dramatic case in which a citizen's renunciation was held to be effective. In 1948 Davis, a native-born citizen, voluntarily signed an oath of renunciation before the U.S. Consul in Paris, on the form provided by the Consul. Davis indicated at the time that he wanted to become "a citizen of the world." He set up a "World Service Authority" and issued himself a passport. The Immigration Service refused to permit Davis to enter the U.S. in 1977 on the ground that he was not a U.S. citizen and lacked a visa to enter as a non-citizen.

Even though Davis failed to obtain another citizenship when he renounced his U.S. citizenship, the federal district court sustained the Immigration Service's decision to exclude Davis from this country.

If renunciation occurs in the United States, it must be in writing and during time of war to take effect. INA § 349(a)(6). The Attorney General is empowered to promulgate procedures for accepting such a renunciation. The current statute has not been invoked, although a prior version was used to expatriate several citizens of Japanese descent during World War II.

(6) ACTS OF TREASON AND SUBVERSION

A citizen will lose his or her nationality, if convicted of committing any act of treason against the United States, of attempting to overthrow the government of the United States, or of conspiring to incite insurrection against the government. INA § 349(a)(7). The constitutionality of this provision has not been tested in the courts.

(7) REPEALED EXPATRIATION PROVISIONS; BURDEN OF PROOF; AND AGE OF MATURITY

Several expatriation provisions have been repealed as a result of Supreme Court decisions declaring them unconstitutional. Specifically, they are: (1) residence abroad by a naturalized citizen in excess of three years (in the country of former nationality) or five years (in another foreign state), declared unconstitutional by *Schneider v. Rusk*, 377 U.S. 163 (1964); (2) voting in a foreign political election, declared invalid by *Afroyim v. Rusk*, 387 U.S. 253 (1967); (3) desertion from the United States armed forces in time of war, struck down in *Trop v. Dulles*, 356 U.S. 86 (1958); and (4) departing from the United States to avoid military service, declared unconstitutional by *Kennedy v. Mendoza–Martinez*, 372 U.S. 144 (1963).

Regarding the burden of proof, the statute places the initial burden on the proponent of expatriation, requiring proof by a "preponderance of the evidence" that the expatriating act occurred. INA § 349(c). The act shall be presumed to have been done voluntarily, but such presumption may be rebutted upon a showing by a preponderance of the evidence that the act was not committed voluntarily. The Supreme Court upheld the constitutionality of this provision in *Vance v. Terrazas*, 444 U.S. 252 (1980).

A second general restriction applicable to most expatriating acts is the requirement that the citizen (at the time of the act) must have attained the age of legal maturity. The statute sets the age of maturity at eighteen years for performance of several expatriating acts—obtaining foreign naturalization, oath of foreign allegiance, military service in a foreign state, renunciation of nationality, and employment in a foreign government. INA § 351(b).

In 1990, the State Department issued new and more lenient evidentiary standards applicable to expatriation cases. The new evidentiary standards are based upon the presumption that United States citizens intend to retain U.S. citizenship when they (1) obtain naturalization in a foreign state, (2) subscribe to routine declarations of allegiance to a foreign state, or (3) accept non-policy level employment with a foreign government. Based on this presumption, U.S. citizens who naturalize in a foreign state, take a routine oath of allegiance, or accept foreign government employment, are not required to state their intent to retain U.S. citizenship. The intent to retain United States citizenship is not presumed when individuals: (1) renounce U.S. citizenship before a consular officer, (2) take employment at a policy level in a foreign government, (3) are convicted of treason, or (4) perform a potentially expatriating act under the statute accompanied by conduct which is inconsistent with retention of United States citizenship to such an extent that it compels a conclusion that they intended to relinquish U.S. citizenship. These new standards are subject to change and reflect only evidential presumptions. Citizens who do a potentially expatriating act may still be well advised to record their intent to remain U.S. citizens, if that is the case.

(8) EXPATRIATING TO AVOID TAXATION

Some very wealthy individuals leave the United States and renounce their U.S. citizenship to avoid paying U.S. income taxes. In 1996, Congress passed two laws intended to curtail the use of expatriation as a tax-sheltering device. While these laws do not change the procedural requirements for expatriation, they do alter the potential consequences of renouncing citizenship for some individuals. The first law, contained in the Health Insurance Portability and Accountability Act of 1996, provides that individuals who renounce citizenship to avoid taxes remain taxable for ten years after their expatriation. 110 Stat. 2093. The same Act creates a presumption that if a person whose annual income tax is over $100,000 renounces citizenship, he or she does so to avoid paying taxes. The Illegal Immigration Reform and Immigrant Responsibility Act further provided that former citizens who renounced U.S. citizenship to avoid taxation are not admissible to the U.S. INA § 212(a)(10)(E). Consequently, some wealthy expatriates could inadvertently lose their right to enter the U.S. by renouncing their citizenship.

CHAPTER 13

THE RIGHTS OF NON–CITIZENS IN THE UNITED STATES

§ 13–1 INTRODUCTION

As the Supreme Court has said, non-citizens comprise a "heterogeneous multitude of persons with a wide-ranging variety of ties to this country." *Mathews v. Diaz*, 426 U.S. 67 (1976). While non-citizens may claim many of the protections offered by the Constitution, they do not enjoy all of the privileges of citizenship, nor are all non-citizens treated alike. In general, the rights of non-citizens depend upon their legal status and the duration of their residence in the United States; persons who have a greater affinity for the U.S. based on extended residence are generally granted more rights than those individuals who do not have such an affinity.

Persons seeking to be admitted to this country have virtually no rights recognizable under United States law. The judiciary is very reluctant to interfere with Congress's authority over immigration matters. As a result, Congress and immigration officials lawfully exercise a great deal of discretion in establishing and applying immigration law; they control the hopeful immigrant's application for admission. Far from having any right to be admitted to this country, an individual is granted admission exclusively on the terms prescribed by Congress. In determining who shall be admitted, Congress has the authority to discriminate with impunity; it has done so on the basis of national origin and race, and currently employs a system of priorities that excludes, among others, persons with undesirable political beliefs, moral character, and mental or physical disability. INA § 212(a). Special preference is granted to certain relatives of U.S. residents, and to persons possessing work skills needed in the U.S. economy. INA §§ 201, 203. The Supreme Court has unwaveringly held that the decisions to exclude or expel certain non-citizens are within the exclusive province of Congress. *Chae Chan Ping v. United States*, 130 U.S. 581 (1889); *Fiallo v. Bell*, 430 U.S. 787 (1977).

Non-citizens who are admitted, however, can claim certain general protections under the Constitution. Almost all constitutional guarantees of individual freedom are extended by terms to "persons," without regard to citizenship. The right to hold federal elective office is reserved for citizens, as is the entitlement to the "privileges and immunities of citizens." Non-citizens admitted to the U.S. appear to be guaranteed the rights secured by the Bill of Rights including the freedoms of speech, association, religion, and the press; the rights to be free from unreasonable searches and seizures as well as self-incrimination; and other criminal procedure protections.

This chapter sets forth the rights enjoyed by non-citizens once they reside in or are admitted to the United States, the limitations imposed on those rights, and their theoretical rationale. The first section briefly reminds the student of immigration law about the often hostile social reality faced by immigrants to this country. The second section concentrates on official discrimination against non-citizens. Third, specific rights and liabilities are discussed with regard to use of the courts, welfare, employment, education, military service, payment of taxes, property ownership, and other areas of concern to non-citizens living in the United States.

§ 13–2 THE EXPERIENCE OF BEING A NON–CITIZEN IN THE UNITED STATES

Despite legal guarantees of equal treatment and the image of the Statue of Liberty welcoming distressed immigrants, permanent residents have experienced difficulties with adjustment and assimilation. Official hostility, expressed in immigration law and other restrictive legislation, has been especially flagrant in periods of war, racial animosity, and high unemployment. At various times, some academics theorized that certain racial and ethnic groups were unfit or unacceptable for "Americanization." Many U.S. citizens readily adopted such justifications for their own prejudice. Thousands of immigrants, historically poor, were faced with social stigma, language barriers, unfamiliar customs, and a complete lack of political representation.

Some improvement in official and popular thought has been won since the great waves of immigration occurred in the nineteenth and early twentieth centuries. Immigrants to the United States today still, however, encounter discrimination sanctioned by state and federal governments as well as the racial and ethnic prejudice of many U.S. citizens. The aftermath of the September 11, 2001, attacks demonstrated the persistent prejudice against non-citizens, particularly persons from Middle–Eastern and Muslim backgrounds, who were subjected to heightened scrutiny by government officials. While some immigrants were subject to overt discrimination and even attacked by U.S. citizens, many U.S. citizens showed sympathy for these immigrants and an appreciation of the cultural diversity they bring to the United States. Recognition of the immigrant's difficult experience in adjusting to life in the United States is essential to an understanding of the full impact of U.S. law and policy.

§ 13–3   DISCRIMINATION ON THE BASIS OF ALIENAGE

§ 13–3.1   Introduction

For purposes of immigration and other laws affecting non-citizens, four broad classes of non-citizens can be identified: (1) persons seeking admission to the United States; (2) persons admitted as immigrants or lawful permanent residents; (3) persons admitted as nonimmigrants or temporary visitors; and (4) undocumented persons or "illegal aliens" who are present in the country without the official knowledge or permission of the federal government.

Most of the law involving discrimination on the basis of alienage has developed in cases concerning lawful permanent residents. These individuals are most like citizens of the United States: they have established residence in this country; they pay taxes, are subject to military service, contribute to the economic and cultural life of their communities, and generally have a stake in the country that a nonimmigrant cannot ordinarily claim. Lawful permanent residents are entitled to some protection under the equal protection guarantees of the Fifth and Fourteenth Amendments.

Courts have provided less protection to individuals who are less like citizens. In *Plyler v. Doe*, 457 U.S. 202

(1982), however, the United States Supreme Court decided that even undocumented non-citizens are entitled to equal protection—at least in so far as the children of undocumented non-citizens have the right to attend public schools.

This section will discuss the historical and modern treatment of discrimination against non-citizens. Because of the distinct governmental interests involved and because of markedly different judicial treatment, state and federal discrimination will be considered separately.

§ 13–3.2   State Discrimination

a.   Historical Treatment: Before Graham v. Richardson

In 1886 the Supreme Court declared in *Yick Wo v. Hopkins*, 118 U.S. 356 (1886) that the guarantees of the Fourteenth Amendment extended universally to all persons within the territorial jurisdiction of the United States, without regard to race, color, or nationality. *Yick Wo* invalidated a San Francisco ordinance that city officials enforced in a way that effectively prohibited Chinese residents from operating laundry facilities while allowing white citizens under similar circumstances to own laundries. In *Yick Wo*, the Court definitively established that non-citizens must be treated on a basis equal to citizens and that the state had no authority to restrict arbitrarily a non-citizen's "life, or the means of living, or any material right essential to the enjoyment of life. . . ."

For many years, however, the strictures of *Yick Wo* were not followed and the Supreme Court applied an extremely lax standard of review in alienage discrimination cases, upholding even severe restrictions on lawful permanent residents. Only in recent years has the non-citizen enjoyed a degree of the protection guaranteed by the Equal Protection Clause of the Fourteenth Amendment so clearly enunciated in *Yick Wo.*

Throughout the late nineteenth and early twentieth centuries, when massive immigration to the United States took place, states imposed a wide variety of restrictions on the activities of lawful permanent residents. Most of these discriminatory measures easily withstood equal protection challenges. Several theories justified state discrimination:

(1) If a public resource or "special public interest" was involved, public monies could properly be reserved for citizens and withheld from non-citizens. On this ground, the Court in 1915 upheld New York's exclusion of non-citizens from employment on public works and other public employment. *Heim v. McCall*, 239 U.S. 175 (1915).

(2) If the resource in question was viewed as "common property" of the citizens of the state, non-citizens could be prohibited from enjoying it. Therefore, Pennsylvania could limit permission to hunt wildlife and carry firearms to citizens (*Patsone v. Pennsylvania*, 232 U.S. 138 (1914)), and Virginia could reserve for its citizens the right to plant oysters in a streambed within its boundaries. *McCready v. Virginia*, 94 U.S. 391 (1876).

(3) If the limitation constituted a valid exercise of police power, the non-citizen could be barred from activities routinely allowed citizens, including certain forms of private employment. Such reasoning perhaps was stretched the furthest in *Clarke v. Deckebach*, 274 U.S. 392 (1927), in which the Court upheld the requirement of citizenship for licensing of pool hall operators as a valid exercise of police power. The Court's rationale was that pool halls often attracted criminals and other undesirable people and that non-citizens were less familiar

with U.S. laws and customs than native-born or natural-ized citizens. The Court held that it was in the interest of the public welfare to limit pool hall operators' licenses to citizens.

(4) If the particular benefit was characterized as a "privilege" not a "right," it could be withheld from the non-citizen who was not entitled to the privileges and immunities guaranteed to citizens by the Constitution. On this ground and because of the states' traditionally broad power over the regulation of property ownership, the Court approved prohibitions against the inheritance and ownership of land by non-citizens in the absence of a treaty to the contrary. *Hauenstein v. Lynham*, 100 U.S. 483 (1879); *Terrace v. Thompson*, 263 U.S. 197 (1923). It was not until 1948 that doubt was cast on the validity of such restrictions on property rights. *Oyama v. California*, 332 U.S. 633 (1948).

In this tradition, the Court gave short shrift to most permanent residents' claims under the Equal Protection Clause. The standard of review was not very severe, indicating the Court's unwillingness to interfere with the judgments of local governments. The ordinance was af-firmed where "the possibility of a rational basis for the legislative judgment" was not "preclud[ed]," and where the Court had "no such knowledge of local conditions . . . to say it is wrong." *Clarke v. Deckebach*, 274 U.S. 392 (1927).

Despite this deference to state discriminatory actions, the Court in *Truax v. Raich*, 239 U.S. 33 (1915) struck down an Arizona law which required private employers of more than five persons to employ at least 80% "quali-fied electors or native-born citizens." Noting that the discrimination in *Truax* was imposed on private enterprise, reaching broadly across all industries, the Court found no special public interest or public resource involved that could justify the restriction. The Court held that the discrimination was "an end in itself" and inimical to the Fourteenth Amendment's guarantee of personal freedom and opportunity. Significantly, the Court also found that the state's attempt to deny non-citizens the opportunity to work collided with the federal government's exclusive power to permit non-citizens to enter and reside in the United States. The Court reasoned that the privilege of living in the U.S., granted by Congress, would be destroyed if the state could severely restrict employment solely on the basis of alienage and that the privilege to reside here carried with it "the right to work for a living in the common occupations of the community." Arizona's attempt virtually to take away from lawful permanent residents the opportunity to earn a livelihood impinged on the authority of Congress over immigration.

Truax v. Raich, 239 U.S. 33 (1915) was a significant decision because it laid the foundation for the Court's later repudiation of the line of cases in which state discriminatory actions had been almost routinely upheld. It was not until 1948, however, that a non-citizen was again successful in an equal protection challenge. In *Takahashi v. Fish and Game Commission*, 334 U.S. 410 (1948), the Supreme Court considered a California statute which forbade the granting of commercial fishing licenses to persons "ineligible to citizenship." Federal law at that time provided that Japanese nationals were ineligible for United States citizenship. The Court quoted extensively from *Truax*, rejecting California's assertion that because the state owned the fish off the coast as trustee for its citizens, it had a "special public interest" in conserving fish for the benefit of its citizens. In holding that this ground was inadequate for discriminating against Japanese residents, the Court implicitly overruled its earlier line of cases. Justice Murphy's concurring opinion in *Takahashi* argued vigorously that California's action was racially motivated; he cited impressive historical evidence and claimed that the statute was invalid for that reason. The majority, however, did not address the race question. *Takahashi* represented a departure from traditional equal protection analysis in alienage discrimination cases. In refusing to approve a state's citizenship requirement in a case that involved public interests as strong as many in earlier cases, the Court signaled that it would more carefully review such discrimination in the future.

b. *Modern Treatment*

Takahashi made clear that states would not be allowed to discriminate casually on the basis of alienage: "the power of a state to apply its laws exclusively to its non-citizen inhabitants as a class is confined within narrow limits." Such language suggested that non-citizens should be protected more diligently than the traditional rational basis standard of review demanded. Finally, in 1971, the Supreme Court explicitly held in *Graham v. Richardson*, 403 U.S. 365 (1971) that non-citizens as a group constitute a "discrete and insular minority" deserving of heightened judicial protection, and that alienage is a "suspect classification" prompting strict scrutiny of state discrimination under the Equal Protection Clause.

Graham involved the denial of state welfare benefits to non-citizens. The state argued that the receipt of welfare benefits was a privilege, a share in the state's wealth, which could properly be reserved for members of the body politic. In rejecting this assertion, the Court laid to rest the special public interest doctrine and the right-privilege distinction that had justified many earlier restrictions on non-citizens. As it had in *Truax* and *Takahashi*, the Court also objected to the statute as an impermissible state interference with the exclusive federal power to regulate immigration. *See* § 2–2.2, *supra*.

For several years following *Graham*, the Court analyzed cases of alienage discrimination by using the same equal protection mode that it had developed in racial discrimination and other cases: if a personal fundamental interest is at stake or if a suspect class is found, state laws almost invariably fall when submitted to strict judicial scrutiny. To sustain its burden, the state must show that its purpose or interest justifying the classification is "substantial" and that the classification is " 'necessary . . . to the accomplishment' of its purpose or the safeguarding of its interest." *Application of Griffiths*, 413 U.S. 717 (1973). Many state restrictions on non-citizens were overturned by the lower courts.

Following this approach, the Supreme Court in *Sugarman v. Dougall*, 413 U.S. 634 (1973) struck down a New York statute that barred all non-citizens from competitive civil service employment. The state asserted that its interest in assuring the loyalty of its employees who implement government policy justified the bar. While recognizing a state's interest in limiting government participation to those persons who are within the "basic conception of a political community," and the state's authority to define that political community, the Court found that the statute swept far too broadly. Within New York's statutory framework, menial competitive civil service positions were subject to the citizenship requirement while other elective and high appointive offices were not. The Court declared that despite a valid state interest, the means employed were too imprecisely drawn to survive strict scrutiny.

Sugarman did recognize a state's prerogative to define a class of positions requiring citizenship in some situations: the power of the state to define the political community applied to persons holding state elective or important non-elective legislative and judicial positions, that is, for officers who participate directly in the formulation, execution, or review of broad public policy perform functions that go to the heart of representative government.

Decided the same day as *Sugarman*, the Court in *Application of Griffiths* invalidated a Connecticut law that limited to U.S. citizens licenses to practice law. The Court rejected the state's argument that because lawyers are officers of the Court, the state must be assured of undivided allegiance by requiring citizenship. Furthermore, in spite of their access to courts and their traditional leadership role in government, the Court found that a lawyer is not "so close to the core of the political process as to make him a formulator of government policy." In so ruling, the Court appeared to confine narrowly the reaches of the political function exception mentioned in *Sugarman*.

In similar fashion, the Court struck down a Puerto Rican statute that denied engineering licenses to nearly all non-citizens in *Examining Board v. Flores de Otero*, 426 U.S. 572 (1976), and a New York statute that denied higher education financial assistance to certain lawful permanent residents in *Nyquist v. Mauclet*, 432 U.S. 1 (1977). In *Mauclet* the Court held that a suspect class existed, even though non-citizens were eligible for assistance if they applied for citizenship or filed statements of intent to become citizens. New York's stated interest in encouraging naturalization was held, first, to be related insufficiently to preservation of the political community and, second, an interference with the federal government's power over immigration and naturalization, since only the national government was properly concerned with encouraging naturalization. Furthermore, the Court found that while the state has a legitimate interest in enhancing the educational level of the electorate, allowing non-citizens to participate in financial aid programs would not defeat that goal. By way of *dicta*, the Court explained that the political function exception to which the Court had alluded in *Sugarman* was very narrow, limited to the states' historical or constitutional powers to define such characteristics as the qualifications of voters or of government officers who directly participate in the formulation, execution, or review of broad public policy.

Despite the purported narrowness of the "political function" exception extracted from *Sugarman*, the Court has retreated from its suspect classification-strict scrutiny approach to alienage cases. In 1978 the Court read "political function" expansively in *Foley v. Connelie*, 435 U.S. 291 (1978) to uphold a New York statute that allows only citizens to compete for the job of state trooper. In a clear withdrawal from the Court's previous position, Chief Justice Burger's majority opinion cited his own dissenting opinion in *Mauclet* to pronounce that not every statutory restriction on non-citizens demands strict scrutiny. The Court theorized that as only citizens are entitled to participate in the political process, the right to govern thereby could be properly reserved to citizens; as

states have the authority to delimit the political community, a state could permissibly exclude non-citizens from
positions relating to "the right of the people to be
governed by their citizen peers." If the position under
review involves discretionary decision-making or execution of policy, "which substantially affects members of
the political community," a lesser standard of review
would be proper. The Court then held that police officers
have considerable discretionary powers, exercise a high
degree of judgment in executing state policy, and affect
the public significantly. Therefore, the state may assume
that citizens are "more familiar with and sympathetic to
American traditions," which presumably the Court found
important if citizens were to submit to such police powers as arrest, search, and seizure.

In *Ambach v. Norwick*, 441 U.S. 68 (1979), the political function exception was also used as the basis for upholding New York's denial of permanent certification as
public school teachers to any non-citizen unless that
person declared an intention to become a citizen. The
State Commissioner of Education was authorized to cer-
tify non-citizens provisionally only in certain narrowly
prescribed situations. The Court first emphasized the
importance of education in preparing students for participation as citizens, in preserving societal values, and
instilling civic virtues. Second, the Court held that the
role of teachers was critical in developing students' attitudes toward government and the political process. In
order to place a teacher within the governmental function principle, the Court cited a teacher's discretion over
communication of course material and position as a role
model. The Court then held that (1) the state has a
valid interest in furthering its educational goals and (2)
in pursuit of that interest, it could rationally conclude

that non-citizens or permanent residents who did not want to become citizens were inappropriate candidates for teachers. Strong dissenting opinions in both *Foley* and *Norwick* protested the Court's opinions as unjustified departures from equal protection precedents and as an unwarranted expansion of the *Sugarman dicta.*

In 1982, the Supreme Court upheld a California statute that limits positions classified as "peace officers" to citizens. Plaintiffs were lawful permanent residents seeking employment as deputy probation officers, positions within the statutory classification of "peace officers." The district court twice had held the statute unconstitutional both on its face and as applied, the latter decision rendered after consideration in light of *Foley.* In *Cabell v. Chavez–Salido,* 454 U.S. 432 (1982), a five-to-four majority read *Sugarman, Foley,* and *Norwick* to require strict review of state restrictions on lawful permanent residents only where a non-citizen's *economic interests* were affected; here the restriction served a political function and a far less stringent standard of review was appropriate. The Court set out a two-step evaluation process to determine the character of the restriction. First, the specificity of the classification would be considered; substantial under—or over—inclusiveness would tend to negate the claim that the classification is intended to serve a political function. Second, even if "sufficiently tailored," the classification as applied must affect only persons who "perform functions that go to the heart of representative government." The Court would look at the extent of discretionary decision-making or policy implementation that affects members of the political community.

The statutory scheme in *Chavez–Salido* defined about seventy positions as peace officers, including toll service employees, cemetery sextons, and livestock identification inspectors. The Court found, however, that such over-inclusiveness is not fatal: "the classifications used need not be precise; there need only be a *substantial fit*" to support the state's claim that an important government function is involved. The Court held that nearly all peace officers shared a law enforcement function primarily because they had the power to arrest and must undergo training for arrests and the use of firearms. Such an exercise of the sovereign's "coercive police powers" could be limited to members of the political community under *Foley.*

In considering the statute as applied, the Court characterized the work of a probation officer as involving a great deal of discretion, because their decisions must be made in the first instance without supervision. Alluding to the "educational function" of probation officers, the Court also asserted that the position symbolized the state's sovereign power and the political community's control over the juvenile offender.

In a forceful dissent, Justice Blackmun asserted that the majority distorted *Sugarman* by employing a weak standard of review and by approving a mere "substantial fit" between the classification and justifications asserted by the state. The dissenters would have found the statute to be fatally under—and over—inclusive as it limited to citizens some jobs which were not even rationally related to the political community, while in other areas failed to bar non-citizens from jobs which arguably encompassed a political function. After setting out compelling statutory inconsistencies that allow non-citizens to play integral roles in the criminal justice system and noting that probation officers' discretion is limited by judicial supervision and by statute, the dissent concluded that the state discrimination "stems solely from state parochialism and hostility toward foreigners who have come to this country lawfully." By abolishing a strict standard of review, Justice Blackmun stated, "*Sugarman*'s exception swallows *Sugarman*'s rule."

The Supreme Court, however, returned to its suspect classification-strict scrutiny approach to alienage cases in *Bernal v. Fainter*, 467 U.S. 216 (1984). By a vote of eight-to-one, the Court struck down as a violation of the Equal Protection Clause a Texas statute requiring a notary public to be a U.S. citizen. Applying strict scrutiny, the Court found no legitimate political function to support a citizenship requirement. Because the functions of a notary public are primarily clerical and ministerial, the position is not one "such that the office holder would necessarily exercise broad discretionary power over the formulation or execution of public policies importantly affecting the citizen population, power of a sort that a self-governing community could properly entrust only to full-fledged members of that community." In contrast to the state troopers in *Foley*, notaries public do not routinely exercise the state's monopoly of "legitimate coercive force," nor do they "exercise the wide discretion typically enjoyed by public school teachers" as in *Norwick*.

Another exception to the strict scrutiny standard applied to state discrimination against non-citizens may exist where Congress authorizes the discrimination. As discussed in § 13–3.3, *infra*, Congress has far greater latitude to discriminate against non-citizens than state governments. Some commentators have suggested that Congress could authorize the states to discriminate. In *Graham*, Arizona argued that its residency requirement for permanent residents to receive state welfare benefits had been authorized by federal law. The Court rejected this argument, finding that Congress had not affirmatively authorized such eligibility restrictions. In *dicta*, the Court further stated that Congress cannot authorize the states to violate the Equal Protection Clause, and that a federal law permitting states to adopt divergent citizenship requirements for welfare benefits would contravene the Constitutional mandate to establish a "uniform rule of naturalization." *Graham v. Richardson*, 403 U.S. 365 (1971).

Despite this strong statement from the Court, in 1996 Congress enacted the Personal Responsibility and Work Opportunity Reconciliation Act (Welfare Act), which explicitly authorizes states to discriminate against non-citizens in the provision of welfare benefits. The Welfare Act made most non-citizens, including lawful permanent residents, ineligible for federally-funded welfare benefits for at least five years after entering the United States (*see* § 13–4.4, *infra*). The Act authorizes, but does not require, states to provide state-funded benefits to non-citizens who are barred from receiving federal benefits and to determine the eligibility requirements for such benefits. Since passage of the Welfare Act, some states have continued to provide some state-funded welfare benefits to non-citizens, but many states either restrict eligibility for these benefits to certain classes of non-citizens or provide fewer benefits to non-citizens than to citizens. While such restrictions were found to violate equal protection in *Graham*, some state courts have upheld these laws, finding that the strict scrutiny standard does not apply because of the Congressional authorization.

In *Cid v. South Dakota Department of Social Services*, 598 N.W.2d 887 (S.D.1999), the South Dakota Supreme Court upheld that state's denial of state-funded welfare benefits to permanent residents. The court found that since the state law was consistent with national immigration policy, the preemption concern expressed in *Takahashi* and *Graham* did not exist, and heightened scrutiny was unnecessary. Similarly, in *Doe v. Commissioner of Transitional Assistance*, 773 N.E.2d 404 (Mass.2002), the Massachusetts Supreme Court upheld a state statute requiring non-citizens to have resided in the state for six months to be eligible for the state's TANF (Temporary Assistance for Needy Families) program. The court held that since the state created the program specifically for non-citizens who were ineligible for federal benefits and it did not apply to citizens, the state had not discriminated on the basis of alienage. Since the state had acted to help non-citizens, the court found heightened scrutiny unnecessary.

At least one federal appellate court has adopted the view presented by the Massachusetts Supreme Court in *Doe*. In *Soskin v. Reinertson*, 353 F.3d 1242 (10th Cir. 2004), the Tenth Circuit upheld a Colorado statute that denied Medicaid coverage to any non-citizen not deemed a "qualified alien" under the Welfare Act. The court determined that Congress essentially created two welfare systems in the Welfare Act, one for citizens and another for non-citizens. Furthermore, the court reasoned, Congress left the decision to provide coverage to certain classes of non-citizens to the discretion of the states. The court concluded that when states discriminate "within the aliens-only program against one class of aliens as compared to other classes of aliens,'' this discrimination is based on non-suspect classifications and subject only to rational-basis review.

Other courts have continued to adhere to the strict scrutiny doctrine established in *Graham*. For example, the Maryland Court of Appeals in *Ehrlich v. Perez*, 908 A.2d 1220 (Md. 2006) found that because Congress has allowed states to develop their own individualized policies regarding state-funded medical assistance programs, courts, under *Graham*, must apply strict scrutiny to those policies that discriminate on the basis of alienage.

In *Aliessa v. Novello*, 754 N.E.2d 1085 (N.Y.2001), the New York Court of Appeals invalidated a statute that denied Medicaid assistance to most non-citizens. The court cited the Supreme Court's statement in *Graham* that Congress cannot authorize state discrimination, and applied strict scrutiny to the statute. The New York Court of Appeals, in *Khrapunskiy v. Doar*, 909 N.E.2d 70 (N.Y.2009), however, failed to apply its holding from *Aliessa* to review a state statute that terminated benefits for certain elderly, blind, and disabled permanent residents. New York amended its social services law to exclude individuals from state disability benefits who became ineligible for federal benefits under the Welfare Act. The court held that the permanent residents could not challenge the statute on equal protection grounds ''because the State did not create a program of benefits which excluded [permanent residents].''

In 2010, the Arizona legislature passed the Support Our Law Enforcement and Safe Neighborhoods Act, which mandates state and local officials to verify the immigration status of anyone with whom they come in contact. One week later, the legislature passed an amendment, which limited investigation of status to a "lawful stop, detention or arrest." The act also makes it a state misdemeanor when an alien is not able to produce registration documents. Legal challenges, including one by the federal government, raised extensive questions about the power of states to supplement what they see as a broken federal immigration system.

Although the Supreme Court has never repudiated it's holding in *Graham* that classifications on the basis of alienage are suspect, the political function doctrine and the theory of Congressional authorization have confused the analysis of such cases. Commentators have suggested several alternative theories that would provide a more consistent approach to alienage discrimination. In cases involving a political function, the Court could have maintained its strict scrutiny review of alienage restrictions by finding a compelling state interest that justified the classification, if precisely drawn. The significance of citizenship in the political process cannot be dismissed: in certain situations the public or political character of the position in question may justify the requirement. In that way, the Court would have remained consistent with *Graham* and its progeny.

c. *Alternative Theories to Graham*

Alternatively, the Supreme Court could have straightforwardly re-evaluated the suspect classification rubric and concluded that non-citizens, indeed, do not require the judicial vigilance evident in racial classifications. Significantly, alienage is not an immutable characteristic, nor is it always evident. Certainly important state and federal interests are connected with citizenship that in some cases may warrant different treatment. But non-citizens comprise a class that is in many ways prototypic of a discrete and insular minority group which needs judicial protection against a political process which is often oblivious or hostile to its interests. Historically, non-citizens have been discriminated against, socially stigmatized, and ostracized, though arguably their experience has not been as severe as that of racial minorities. Deprived of political rights, non-citizens have no representative voice and thus need the protection of courts which must protect minority and under-represented interests. In any case, it undermines the integrity of the suspect classification approach to equal protection to hold that alienage is suspect for some purposes, but not for others.

Other commentators suggest that equal protection analysis is inappropriate in this area; that those cases that strike down state restrictions under the Equal Protection Clause are expounding an unarticulated preemption theory. In each case, the Court either specifically indicated or consistently could have indicated, that the state provision in question interfered with the federal government's exclusive authority over immigration and naturalization. *Truax* and *Takahashi* expressly held that a state's restriction on the non-citizen's opportunity to earn a living conflicted with congressional power to set the terms and conditions of continued residence. Under this preemption theory, state laws that are expressly authorized by Congress, or are at least consistent with federal policy, should withstand challenge. The Court applied this reasoning in *De Canas v. Bica*, 424 U.S. 351 (1976), when it upheld a California statute prohibiting the employment of undocumented workers as consistent with federal policy. This theory raises the question, however, of whether there are limits to Congress' power to authorize discrimination: could Congress, for example, authorize states to restrict non-citizens' access to certain non-political jobs?

A clearly articulated approach to state restrictions on non-citizens is needed to assure minimally uniform treatment. Lawful permanent residents at least are entitled to consistently reasoned judgments when challenging discrimination under a Constitution that promises equal treatment to all persons.

§ 13–3.3 Federal Discrimination

a. *Introduction*

In contrast to state discrimination, actions by the federal government that classify individuals on the basis of alienage touch upon policies and interests traditionally immune from searching judicial review. This section will examine the deferential judicial approach to alienage discrimination by the federal government and the special federal interests grounded in congressional power over immigration that are asserted in its defense.

b. *Judicial Deference to the Political Branches: Special Federal Interests*

The Court has long held that immigration and naturalization, like foreign policy generally, encompass an area over which Congress maintains almost plenary power and the judiciary has a very limited responsibility. *E.g.*, *Fong Yue Ting v. United States*, 149 U.S. 698 (1893). Immigration matters raise complex and sensitive questions of national policy, calling for informed political judgments. This country's treatment of prospective immigrants or temporary foreign visitors is intertwined with U.S. foreign policy. It may be a factor in treaty negotiations, contribute to this country's influence abroad, and influence how other governments treat U.S. citizens traveling abroad. Sometimes, national security matters may be implicated. The Supreme Court considers itself an inappropriate forum, and judges inexpert, for the weighing of policy choices presumably made by Congress in setting immigration and naturalization priorities.

In fact, in reviewing immigration legislation, the Court has stopped just short of applying the political question doctrine that is grounded in the separation of government powers and in effect would render nonjusticiable any challenges to congressional authority in this area. Historically, the Court has thus upheld discrimination on any basis Congress may choose in deciding what groups shall be admitted to this country and under what terms. Constitutional challenges to such admission and removal laws repeatedly have failed.

Although the Court has admitted to misgivings about the extent of congressional plenary power and its own virtual abdication of review, the strength of long-standing precedent has thus far prevented any effective reconsideration: As Justice Frankfurter explained:

In light of the expansion of the concept of substantive Due Process as a limitation upon all powers of Congress, even the war power, ... much can be said for the view, were we writing on a clean slate, that the Due Process Clause qualifies the scope of political distinction heretofore recognized as belonging to Congress in regulating the entry and deportation of aliens.... But the slate is not clean. As to the extent of the power of Congress under review, there is not merely "a page of history," ... but a whole volume.

Policies pertaining to the entry of aliens and their right to remain here are peculiarly concerned with the political conduct of government. In the enforcement of these policies, the Executive Branch of the Government must respect the procedural safeguards of Due Process. . . . But that the formulation of these policies is entrusted exclusively to Congress has become about as firmly embedded in the legislative and judicial tissues of our body politic as any aspect of our government. *Galvan v. Press*, 347 U.S. 522 (1954).

Quoting the above passage, the Court declined again to expand the scope of judicial review in *Fiallo v. Bell*, 430 U.S. 787 (1977), a case in which substantive constitutional rights of U.S. citizens and lawful permanent residents were compromised by provisions of the Immigration and Nationality Act. In *Fiallo*, the statutes in question granted special preference immigration status to non-citizens qualified as "children" or "parents" of U.S. citizens or lawful permanent residents. The INA's definition of "child" excluded illegitimate children whose claim to preferential status was based on their relationship with their natural fathers, while including those who claimed through their mothers. Further, a natural father was ineligible to claim a preference status for his illegitimate child, while a natural mother was eligible.

Plaintiffs were natural fathers and their illegitimate children who sought to be reunited under the special preference provisions, claiming, among other things, that the INA discriminated against them on the basis of gender, marital status, and illegitimacy. Despite the statute's clear detrimental impact on the rights of citizens and lawful permanent residents, the Court refused to expand the scope of judicial review of immigration matters. In rather parrot-like fashion the Court reiterated that it had a limited role to play in such policy decisions, and applied an extremely lax minimum rationality standard of review to uphold the restrictions. (The Immigration Reform and Control Act of 1986 amended INA § 101(b)(1) to allow an illegitimate child to claim preferential status through its natural father "if the father has or had a bona fide parent-child relationship with" the child. INA § 101(b)(1)(D)). The Court had an opportunity to reconsider its approach in *Nguyen v. INS*, 533 U.S. 53 (2001), where it upheld a provision of the INA that applies different requirements for men and women to transmit their U.S. citizenship to their children born out of wedlock. Because the Court found that the statute survived heightened scrutiny, however, it did not address the question of whether Congress was due special deference because of its power over immigration.

The federal government regulates the lives of non-citizens in a myriad of ways, however, other than directly through its immigration and naturalization policies. Historically, federal, like state restrictions on the activities of lawful permanent residents have been substantial and severe. Because congressional power is viewed as broadly encompassing "regula[tion] of the relationship between the United States and our alien visitors," *Mathews v. Diaz*, 426 U.S. 67 (1976), those justifications for deferring to Congress and the Executive on matters of immigration, foreign policy, national security, etc. have apparently been extended to any federal actions that affect non-citizens. Consequently, the guarantee of equal protection of the law inferred from the Due Process Clause of the Fifth Amendment has had little meaning for lawful permanent residents.

c. *Protection Under the Fifth Amendment*

The Court's treatment of federal discrimination on the basis of alienage departs sharply from equal protection jurisprudence in the areas of discrimination on the basis of race, national origin, and religion. Classification on these bases is immediately suspect, invokes strict judicial scrutiny, and virtually never survives an equal protection challenge. The federal government has been required to abide by similar standards under the Fifth Amendment as have the states under the Fourteenth Amendment.

Where the classification is on the basis of alienage, however, the Court has declared that the equal protection component of the Fifth Amendment is not co-extensive with that of the Fourteenth although the analysis is much the same:

Not only does the language of the two Amendments differ, but more importantly, there may be overriding national interests which justify selective federal legislation that would be unacceptable for an individual State. *Hampton v. Mow Sun Wong*, 426 U.S. 88 (1976) (fn. omitted).

Only where the federal government acts very much like a state, must it adhere to standards applicable to the states:

[W]hen a federal rule is applicable to only a limited territory, such as the District of Columbia, or an insular possession, and when there is no special national interest involved, the Due Process Clause has been construed as having the same significance as the Equal Protection Clause. *Hampton v. Mow Sun Wong* (fn. omitted).

Therefore, stepping outside its precedent in *Graham v. Richardson*, 403 U.S. 365 (1971), the state discrimination case in which non-citizens' "discrete and insular minority" status prompted "heightened judicial solicitude," the Supreme Court has refused to scrutinize closely nationwide federal actions that burden non-citizens. Two leading cases (*Hampton* and *Diaz*), neither directly involving immigration or naturalization, firmly establish the Court's refusal to restrain the federal government in any area relating to non-citizens. Unfortunately, the Court's deference to Congress overshadows the significant deprivation of individual rights involved in those cases.

In *Hampton v. Mow Sun Wong*, 426 U.S. 88 (1976), the Supreme Court considered a U.S. Civil Service Commission regulation that excluded non-citizens from employment in the competitive federal civil service. The lawful permanent resident plaintiffs argued that they had been deprived of equal protection of the laws. On that ground the Ninth Circuit invalidated the regulation; the Supreme Court relied on rather narrow due process grounds to affirm the lower court.

In *Hampton* the Supreme Court first refused to use the same approach for federal as for state discrimination: "the paramount federal power over immigration and naturalization forecloses a simple extension of the holding in *Sugarman v. Dougall*, 413 U.S. 634 (1973), in which New York's bar of non-citizen employment in state competitive civil service was held to be a violation of the Equal Protection Clause of the 14th Amendment." The Court did concede, however, that some judicial interference may be proper, noting that plenary federal power does not allow *any* agent of the federal government to discriminate between non-citizens and citizens. Writing for the Court, Justice Stevens recited the disabilities suffered by non-citizens due to lack of political rights and unfamiliarity with language and customs, holding that the inability to be employed by the federal civil service was a deprivation of a liberty interest which entitled the plaintiff non-citizens to due process of law. The Court set out the standard under which the deprivation was reviewable:

> When the Federal Government asserts an overriding national interest as justification for a discriminatory rule which would violate the Equal Protection Clause if adopted by a State, Due Process requires that there be a legitimate basis for presuming that the rule was actually intended to serve that interest. If the agency which promulgates the rule has direct responsibility for fostering or protecting that interest, it may reasonably be presumed that the asserted interest was the actual predicate for the rule. That presumption would, of course, be fortified by an appropriate statement of reasons identifying the relevant interest. Alternatively, if the rule were expressly mandated by the Congress or the President, we might presume that any interest which might rationally be served by the rule did in fact give rise to its adoption.

Applying such presumptions, the Court found that the Civil Service Commission was not authorized or required by Congress or the President to promulgate the citizenship requirement. Although legitimate national interests could be asserted, only the interest in administrative convenience was within the concern of the Civil Service Commission. In the absence of specified reasons, the Court was unwilling to presume that the Commission was attempting to further national interests outside of its responsibility. Therefore, the regulation as promulgated deprived plaintiffs of due process. The Court strongly suggested, however, that had the President or Congress expressly adopted the rule or had the agency done so with justifications that were within its scope of concern, the rule would not have been invalid.

Indeed, within three months of the Court's decision in *Hampton*, President Ford issued an Executive Order that in effect restored the invalidated Commission rule barring non-citizens from competitive civil service. 5 C.F.R. § 7.3. He did not specify, as the Court had implied was important, the national interests to be furthered by this rule. The Ninth Circuit later held the new Executive Order to be constitutional in *Mow Sun Wong v. Campbell*, 626 F.2d 739 (9th Cir.1980); the Supreme Court denied certiorari. The Court of Appeals found the order to be within the President's constitutional and statutory authority. Under the standards set forth in *Hampton v. Mow Sun Wong*, 426 U.S. 88 (1976), the national interest in creating an incentive for non-citizens to be naturalized was sufficient to justify the rule.

The Supreme Court did not hesitate to decide plaintiff's equal protection claim in *Mathews v. Diaz*, 426 U.S. 67 (1976), which was issued the same day as the Court's decision in *Hampton*. *Diaz* challenged the constitutionality of a statute limiting eligibility for certain Medicare benefits to citizens and lawful permanent residents who have resided in the United States for at least five years. A unanimous Court held that such a classification was constitutional because it was not "wholly irrational." The Court invoked both the plenary power of Congress over immigration and naturalization as well as the political question doctrine to justify such an extremely lax standard of review:

Any rule of constitutional law that would inhibit the flexibility of the political branches of government to respond to changing world conditions should be adopted only with the greatest caution. The reasons that preclude judicial review of political questions also dictate a narrow standard of review of decisions made by the Congress or the President in the area of immigration and naturalization.

Although the Court conceded that the five year residency requirement is longer than necessary to protect the fiscal integrity of the program and that unnecessary hardship is incurred by some persons, the Court found that the restriction reasonably insured that those qualified for the benefits have a greater affinity with the United States; accordingly, the classification was not "wholly irrational." The Court did not state why affinity with the United States is somehow significant in relation to Medicare; nor did it examine how well the classification furthered that end. The *Diaz* court distinguished *Graham v. Richardson*, 403 U.S. 365 (1971), which had invalidated a similar restriction on state welfare benefits on the ground that a state's relationship with non-citizens differs substantially from that of the federal government.

The message from *Diaz* and *Hampton* appears clear: virtually no federal limitation on non-citizens would fail under the Fifth Amendment. Under the minimum rationality standard of *Diaz* no real evaluation of the asserted government interest nor the necessity of the means employed to further that interest would be undertaken. Although *Hampton* spoke in terms of an "overriding national interest," that case in effect requires only that an administrative agency, which is not officially concerned with national interests involving non-citizens, must spell out its reasons for imposing a restriction based on alienage. Where Congress or the President acts, or presumably the Citizenship and Immigration Services, virtually any national interest would sustain the restriction against an equal protection challenge.

Following *Diaz* and *Hampton*, equal protection challenges to federal legislation concerning lawful permanent residents have failed in such diverse areas as employment in federal non-competitive civil service, eligibility for farm operating loans, licensure as commercial radio operators, and eligibility for certain Social Security benefits. In most cases plaintiffs were long time lawful permanent residents qualified in every way for the benefit in question except for their alienage. Courts usually applied minimum rational basis review, resulting in ready acceptance of the government interest asserted. Rational basis review of alienage classifications has survived in spite of the Supreme Court's holding in *Adarand v. Pena*, 515 U.S. 200 (1995) that the federal government must be held to the same standard of review as state governments in racial discrimination challenges. In *Adarand*, the Court suggested that a less exacting standard would apply in areas like immigration where Congress is due special deference.

Federal courts have applied the rational basis standard to the 1996 Welfare Act, uniformly upholding the denial of federal benefits to most non-citizens. *See, e.g., Aleman v. Glickman*, 217 F.3d 1191 (9th Cir.2000); *Rodriguez ex rel. Rodriguez v. United States*, 169 F.3d 1342 (11th Cir.1999); *City of Chicago v. Shalala*, 189 F.3d 598 (7th Cir.1999). In the only successful challenge to that Act, the Second Circuit invalidated a provision that denied automatic Medicaid eligibility to children born in the United States to non-citizen mothers; the court found strict scrutiny applicable because of the statute's detrimental effect on the children, who are citizens by virtue of their birth in the U.S. *Lewis v. Thompson*, 252 F.3d 567 (2d Cir.2001).

One lower court has read *Hampton* as requiring an intermediate standard of review, at least where a liberty interest is involved and the statute in question is not directly related to the admission, exclusion, or expulsion of non-citizens. *Yuen v. IRS*, 649 F.2d 163 (2d Cir.1981). In that case, however, the government nonetheless prevailed. In 2002, a district court applied strict scrutiny in reviewing a law that required airport security screeners employed by the federal government to be U.S. citizens. *Gebin v. Mineta*, 231 F.Supp.2d 971 (C.D. Cal.2002). The court found that Congress was not entitled to any special deference because the law prohibited the employment of U.S. non-citizen nationals (such as U.S. nationals from American Samoa) as well as other non-citizens. Hence, the discrimination fell outside Congress' immigration and naturalization power. The court denied the government's motion to dismiss the case and issued an injunction barring enforcement of the citizenship requirement. In response to the injunction, Congress amended the disputed provision to allow U.S. nationals to qualify for airport security positions. The Ninth Circuit vacated the district court injunction in light of this statutory change allowing for the employment of U.S. nationals.

d. *Implications of the Current Approach*

Non-citizens can expect to be afforded more judicial protection when the state discriminates against them than when the federal government does so. This discrepancy may be entirely defensible in immigration or other areas that directly involve questions of foreign policy and where refined political judgments are crucial to maintaining consistency and strength as an international power. Unquestionably, the national government requires a degree of flexibility that a state does not in order to pursue the international affairs of the country.

Important national interests, however, should not obscure the impact of discrimination on the individual rights of non-citizens who have been lawfully admitted and have taken up permanent residence here. The Supreme Court has mechanically extended its deference to congressional plenary power and its restraint in the face of the political question implications of immigration to all other areas of federal control over non-citizens. This unfounded extrapolation subordinates constitutional rights to the interests of the national government regardless of the substantive area involved or the relative importance of the governmental interest asserted.

Rational basis review may be particularly misplaced in cases of alienage discrimination. Professor Rosberg in his article, *The Protection of Aliens from Discriminatory Treatment by the National Government*, argues that non-citizens are in as much need of protection from state-sponsored discrimination as are members of the more traditional suspect classifications. Like other groups given suspect classification status, non-citizens have suffered a history of discriminatory treatment. Although alienage is not an immutable characteristic, as is race, before a non-citizen fulfills the five-year residency requirement to acquire citizenship, his or her status is inescapable. Political powerlessness, however, is the non-citizen's most obvious and significant debilitating condition. While other protected minorities may have seriously weakened political voices, a non-citizen has no voice or vote. The suspect classification doctrine is at least partially based on the understanding that judicial vigilance is necessary because the political process does not adequately represent the interests of oppressed groups. In Rosberg's words:

> Where a group is systematically shut out of the political process, ... and is denied an opportunity to form alliances with any other group, it may well lose on every issue. At that point the proper functioning of the majoritarian political process is very much in question. In such case, the Court begins to fear that the injury to the members of the disadvantaged class, far from being an unintended by-product of the state's effort to serve a legitimate interest, was in fact the very purpose of the classification. And the likelihood increases that the classification was based on a stereotypical and erroneous view of the characteristics of the members of the group.

It would seem that the suspect classification rubric fits perfectly the particular needs of non-citizens for extra protection. In fact, the applicability of the political question doctrine is ironic: The Court's refusal to interfere with any congressional judgment regarding non-citizens assumes that debate and political reflection are essential. Yet the political powerlessness of non-citizens guarantees a one-sided debate.

Of course, broad use of the suspect classification doctrine and strict scrutiny would make it very difficult for the federal government to carry out any legitimate immigration or foreign policy objectives with the use of alienage classifications. The Court's fear of imposing constitutional rigidity in an area in which flexibility is important would be justified. While adherence to strict scrutiny may hamstring the federal government, the current rational basis review virtually ignores the legitimate interests of lawful permanent residents.

Unfortunately, the strict/rational dichotomy causes an all or nothing situation; the Court should explore alternative methods of analysis in which asserted government interests and the means employed to further them are balanced against the severity of the burden on lawful permanent residents. At least three approaches provide for such balancing. First, within equal protection analysis, an intermediate standard of review could be applied. *See Reed v. Reed*, 404 U.S. 71 (1971). Less severe than strict scrutiny, intermediate judicial review would nonetheless substitute more exacting justification than the weak rational basis standard.

Second, analysis under the Due Process Clause affords another alternative. The Court already has been innovative in this area. In *Hampton v. Mow Sun Wong*, 426 U.S. 88 (1976), the Court looked at the process of decision-making to declare invalid an administrative rule that discriminated against non-citizens. While in that case, the Court's intervention proved very short-lived, a more aggressive track could similarly examine the process of congressional decision-making.

To alleviate the concern that questions of national policy as to non-citizens must be left to Congress, the Court could first determine whether such issues are raised by the particular classification. If so, the Court could examine the statute and legislative history to assess whether Congress indeed considered the national interest that is to be served by the alienage classification. Such an approach would necessarily abandon any presumption that Congress made an informed policy judgment simply because the legislation relates to non-citizens. At the least, this approach would force the political branches to evaluate and justify discrimination against lawful permanent residents. Depending on the vigor of the Court's review, it could succeed in weeding out arbitrary and very harmful discrimination that contributes little or nothing to U.S. immigration or foreign policies.

Third, focusing on fairness to the individual, cases of alienage discrimination by the federal government could be reviewed under the conclusive presumption doctrine. In essence, that doctrine requires that if an individual is disadvantaged by a classification which is premised on a congressional presumption, for a particular purpose, the individual must be given an opportunity to prove that the presumption is untrue. A restriction which *conclusively presumes* a characteristic or fact without allowing rebuttal would be a deprivation of due process. On the one hand, this approach to alienage discrimination cases would avoid the rigidity of an equal protection holding because even if struck down, a restriction could be reinstituted with a provision allowing for a rebuttable presumption. On the other hand, substantive review of congressional presumptions would assure greater protection of individual rights. Only some similar type of analysis that recognizes and investigates competing interests will result in fairness to both the individual non-citizen and the federal government.

The real question that the federal government, including both the political and judicial branches, needs to answer is whether fairness is a goal in its treatment of non-citizens. The rationales advanced by the Court for its hands-off approach do not justify the poor treatment lawful permanent residents sometimes suffer. Less laudable reasons probably explain it.

At the least, much legislation appears to be the effect of stereotypic thinking about foreigners, unwarranted assumptions about loyalty and the importance of "affinity" to the United States, and in some situations outright racial prejudice. The Court has ignored or avoided any significant curtailment of this abuse although such bases for law-making are repugnant.

Hundreds of lawful classifications are embodied in the immigration laws that set preferences for admittance and establish conditions under which a non-citizen may remain in this country. In characterizing all legislation that burdens non-citizens after they have been admitted as part of an ongoing scheme with foreign policy overtones, the government may simply extend the prejudices expressed in the immigration laws. The U.S. government apparently prefers affluent immigrants who will not need Medicare; immigrants who will seek only private or state civil service employment, while refraining from federal employment; who will not request government farm loans, but who will nonetheless pay taxes, contribute to the community, and if necessary, serve in the military. A prospective immigrant could not know the true terms of entry without checking all federal legislation for restrictions as to citizenship.

In any case, unprincipled discrimination against non-citizens creates an image of the United States in the eyes of the world as being hypocritical and unfair. If, indeed, treatment of non-citizens is a crucial element in foreign relations, then the government has the opportunity to improve its international image by treating non-citizens fairly.

§ 13–3.4   Conclusion

Historically, non-citizens have experienced discrimination after immigration to this country. While technically the law guarantees treatment equal to that of citizens, such has never been the case. As waves of immigrants came to the United States to escape economic and political difficulties in their native countries, social stigma and official discrimination have been commonplace. While significant steps were taken during the early and middle 1970s to halt discrimination by states on the basis of alienage, the Supreme Court has since retreated from its briefly active role in that area.

Vis-a-vis the federal government, non-citizens have never been found to be deserving of significant protection and apparently can be disadvantaged with little or no justification.

§ 13–4   OTHER RIGHTS AND DUTIES OF NON–CITIZENS

§ 13–4.1   Right to Vote

The Constitution reserves the right to vote for citizens only, and no state presently allows non-citizens to vote in elections. Throughout much of the nineteenth and part of the twentieth century, however, non-citizens were able to vote in many states. Arkansas was the last state to end alien suffrage in 1928. The progressive disenfranchising of non-citizens in the early part of the twentieth century was due primarily to increased hostility to and distrust for foreigners. Anti-alien sentiment was fueled in part by the assassination of President McKinley, the large influx of immigrants who did not have Anglo–Saxon origins, and the outbreak of World War I.

When an opportunity arose for the Supreme Court to decide whether a state could deny non-citizens the right to vote, the Court declined to hear the case for failure to present a substantial federal question. *Skafte v. Rorex*, 430 U.S. 961 (1977). (The Colorado Supreme Court had sustained a Colorado statute that denied non-citizens the right to vote in school elections.) While the Supreme Court has stated that citizenship is a permissible criterion for determining who may vote, the Court has not explained the basis for requiring voters to be citizens. *See, e.g., Sugarman v. Dougall*, 413 U.S. 634 (1973). Many arguments have been suggested to preserve the citizenship requirement. Voting is seen by many as the quintessential right of citizenship. Others claim that non-citizens are unable to vote intelligently in elections because of unfamiliarity with U.S. institutions and values. Still others argue that non-citizens may be incapable of voting responsibly because they lack loyalty, due to strong ties with their native country.

Although non-citizens are a protected class in the eyes of the Supreme Court, it is unlikely that the Court would acknowledge a right to vote. But as a suspect class, non-citizens are provided some degree of protection in the courts without being held to the political responsibilities which accompany participation in the political processes.

§ 13–4.2   Capacity to Use the Courts

Early English common law decisions barred all aliens from the courts. By 1698, England allowed resident aliens—even from enemy nations—to proceed in court, and the United States adopted a similar rule. The Supreme Court held, in *Ex parte Kawato*, 317 U.S. 69 (1942), that lawful permanent residents have a full capacity to sue and be sued in United States courts.

This principle may not apply to nonresident aliens. In state courts, nonresidents will usually be allowed to sue only where it is necessary to avoid injustice or to serve the interests of international comity. In federal courts, nonresidents can sue if there is subject matter jurisdiction.

a.   *Federal Question Jurisdiction*

Any non-citizen may bring suit in federal court if the non-citizen can claim federal question jurisdiction. This jurisdiction specifically covers cases where the non-citizen's constitutional, treaty, or federal statutory rights have been violated. 28 U.S.C.A. § 1331.

b.   *Federal Diversity Jurisdiction*

Non-citizens may sue or be sued in federal court based on diversity of citizenship, but the Constitution limits such suits to those between U.S. citizens and subjects of a foreign state. U.S. Const. Art. III, § 2. Hence, a non-citizen may not sue another non-citizen based on diversity jurisdiction, even if a U.S. citizen is party to the suit. 28 U.S.C.A. § 1332. A non-citizen may sue a citizen, however, even if the non-citizen resides in the same state as the citizen. Hence, the non-citizen has greater jurisdictional rights in this respect than a similarly situated citizen would have. *Breedlove v. Nicolet*, 32 U.S. 413 (1833). Stateless non-citizens, though, can never meet diversity jurisdiction requirements, because they are not subjects of a foreign state.

c. Alien Tort Claims Act

Other statutes contain their own grant of federal jurisdiction. The Alien Tort Claims Act (ATCA), also known
as the Alien Tort Statute (ATS), provides U.S. district
courts with jurisdiction for "any civil action by an alien
for a tort only, committed in violation of the law of
nations or a treaty of the United States." 28 U.S.C.A.
§ 1350.

In *Sosa v. Alvarez–Machain*, 542 U.S. 692 (2004), the
Court limited the claims available under § 1350. In 1990,
the U.S. Drug Enforcement Administration (DEA) directed the kidnapping of Dr. Alvarez–Machain, a Mexican
doctor suspected of assisting the murder of a DEA agent
in Mexico. The kidnappers forcibly brought Alvarez–
Machain to the United States to stand trial for murder.
The Supreme Court rejected a claim that the U.S.-Mexico
extradition treaty barred such kidnapping. *United States
v. Alvarez–Machain*, 504 U.S. 655 (1992). Dr. Alvarez
escaped prosecution when the district court dismissed his
case for lack of sufficient evidence. He then filed a suit
under § 1350 against persons responsible for his kidnapping. The Supreme Court, however, held that Alvarez's
"arbitrary arrest" did not violate any norm of international law sufficient for a claim under the ATCA. The
ATCA, the Court held, does not allow claims for "violations of any international law norm with less definite
content and acceptance among civilized nations than the
historical paradigms familiar when § 1350 was enacted."
When the ATCA was adopted in 1789, it authorized
actions for certain torts in violation of the law of nations,
such as violation of safe conducts, infringement of the
rights of ambassadors, and piracy.

Nonetheless, the Supreme Court in *Sosa v. Alvarez–Machain*, 542 U.S. 692 (2004) endorsed the use of the ATCA as initiated in *Filartiga v. Peña–Irala*, 630 F.2d 876 (2d Cir.1980) and continued in the case of *In re Estate of Marcos Human Rights Litigation*, 25 F.3d 1467 (9th Cir.1994).

The Second Circuit in *Filartiga v. Peña–Irala*, 630 F.2d 876 (2d Cir.1980), permitted the Paraguayan relatives of a Paraguayan youth who had been tortured to death in Paraguay by a police officer acting under the authority of the Paraguayan government to maintain an action in federal district court against the Paraguayan police officer, who was visiting the United States. The court found that "the torturer has become—like the pirate and slave trader before him—*hostis humani generis*, an enemy of all mankind." Accordingly, torture was held to violate the law of nations under the ATCA. The Court of Appeals did not, however, decide the difficult issues related to choice of laws to be applied and as to the doctrine of *forum non conveniens*. The trial court on remand applied Paraguayan law and awarded damages. *Filartiga v. Peña–Irala*, 577 F.Supp. 860 (E.D.N.Y.1984).

In the case of *In re Estate of Ferdinand E. Marcos Human Rights Litigation*, 25 F.3d 1467 (9th Cir.1994), the court allowed a non-citizen to sue the former head of Philippine military intelligence for the torture and wrongful death of her son in the Philippines. The court found subject matter jurisdiction not only under the *Filartiga* interpretation of 28 U.S.C.A. § 1350, but also on the basis of the Torture Victim Protection Act. In *Marcos Human Rights Litigation*, 94 F.3d 539 (9th Cir. 1996) the court affirmed awards of 800 million dollars in compensatory damages plus 1.2 billion dollars in exemplary damages, but the plaintiffs have not yet been able to collect any of those funds.

The ATCA has also been used to sue companies for their complicity in human rights abuses. In *Wiwa v. Royal Dutch Petroleum Co.*, 226 F.3d 88 (2d Cir.2000), the Second Circuit allowed the plaintiffs to bring claims against Royal Dutch Co. (also known as Shell) for encouraging and aiding the Nigerian government in attacking leaders of the Ogoni people in Nigeria who opposed Royal Dutch oil developments in their region. Royal Dutch eventually reached a settlement agreement with the plaintiffs. The Ninth Circuit in *Doe v. Unocal*, 248 F.3d 915 (9th Cir.2001) allowed ATCA claims to proceed against the Unocal Corporation. The plaintiffs claimed Unocal participated in the forced labor, murder, and rape of villagers during the construction of a gas pipeline through Myanmar. This case also ended in a settlement agreement.

d. Sovereign Immunity

The Federal Tort Claims Act (FTCA) authorizes suits against the United States which sovereign immunity would otherwise bar. 28 U.S.C.A. §§ 1346(b), 2674. Claims arising in a foreign country are, however, exempt from coverage under the FTCA. 28 U.S.C.A. § 2680(k). In *Sosa v. Alvarez–Machain*, 542 U.S. 692 (2004), the Supreme Court found that the arbitrary arrest of Alvarez–Machain arose in Mexico. Hence, sovereign immunity barred Alvarez–Machain's FTCA claims against the U.S. DEA agents in California who ordered his kidnapping. The Court rejected the "headquarters doctrine" in which a claim does not "arise in" a foreign country when acts or omissions within the United States have their effect in another country. Seven justices held that an

FTCA claim arises in the place where the injury occurs. The remaining justices said a claim arises in the place of the "last act."

Sovereign immunity does not extend, however, to government officials sued in their individual capacities. The U.S. Supreme Court ruled in *Samantar v. Yousuf*, 130 S.Ct. 2278 (2010) that an ATCA suit by victims of torture, rape, and mass executions against a Somali general was not barred by the FSIA. In *Jama v. INS*, 22 F.Supp.2d 353 (D.N.J.1998), the court dismissed an ATCA action against the INS brought by asylum seekers who were ill-treated at an INS detention facility, but allowed the suit to proceed against individual INS officials and the private contractor who operated the facility.

While the Foreign Sovereign Immunities Act of 1976 (FSIA) protects governments from suits arising out of their public acts, the FSIA can also provide jurisdiction for suits arising out of a foreign government's commercial acts. 28 U.S.C.A. § 1602 *et seq.* In *Verlinden B.V. v. Central Bank of Nigeria*, 461 U.S. 480 (1983), the Supreme Court allowed a Dutch corporation to sue an instrumentality of Nigeria over a contract dispute. If an exception to sovereign immunity specified under 28 U.S.C.A. §§ 1605–07 applies, a federal district court may exercise subject matter jurisdiction under § 1330(a).

In *Republic of Austria v. Altmann*, 541 U.S. 677 (2004), the Court held that the FSIA applies to conduct before the statute's 1976 enactment. Altmann escaped from Austria after it was annexed by Nazi Germany in 1938 and she became a U.S. citizen in 1945. Altmann was an heir of a wealthy uncle whose property was confiscated by the Nazis. In 1998, journalists discovered evidence that Altmann was entitled to six Klimt paintings—once owned by her uncle—located in the Austrian Gallery. Altmann sued in the U.S. to recover the paintings under the FSIA exception for expropriation in violation of international law. The Supreme Court rejected Austria's sovereign immunity defense and allowed Altmann to sue, because the FSIA applies retroactively.

Any non-citizen also may sue the U.S. in the Court of Federal Claims if U.S. citizens are granted reciprocal rights by the non-citizen's country and subject matter jurisdiction would otherwise exist. 28 U.S.C.A. § 2502.

e.   *Enemy Aliens and Enemy Combatants*

During times of war, persons who are citizens or nationals of enemy nations face substantial restrictions on their access to U.S. courts. Resident "enemy aliens" have full access to all courts. *Ex parte Kawato*, 317 U.S. 69 (1942). Nonresident "enemy aliens," in contrast, may have limited access. In *Rasul v. Bush*, 542 U.S. 466 (2004), the Supreme Court allowed twelve Kuwaiti citizens and two Australian citizens captured in Afghanistan to challenge their detention at the Guantánamo Bay Naval Base in Cuba. The Court, however, based its decision on the *habeas corpus* statute, 28 U.S.C.A. § 2241, rather than constitutional grounds. In *Johnson v. Eisentrager*, 339 U.S. 763 (1950), the Court found no constitutional right of access for enemy aliens who have never been in the U.S., were captured outside U.S. territory in a theater of war, were held in military custody outside of U.S. territory, were tried and convicted outside of U.S. territory by the military for offenses committed outside of U.S. territory, and were imprisoned outside of U.S. territory at all times.

The Court in *Boumediene v. Bush*, 553 U.S. 723 (2008) held that the privilege of habeas corpus applied to enemy combatants held in Guantánamo Bay, Cuba. Examining the factors established in *Eisentrager*, the Court found that although the U.S. does not have *de jure* sovereignty over Guantánamo Bay, it does exercise effective control over the territory. Given the government's level of control over Guantánamo Bay, the Court concluded that the government cannot deny the privilege of habeas corpus to enemy combatants detained at the military base without Congress fulfilling the requirements of the Suspension Clause.

§ 13–4.3   Education

A non-citizen's right to education depends both on the status of the non-citizen in the U.S. and on the level of education sought. While permanent residents may attend schools on the same basis as U.S. citizens, other non-citizens must apply for nonimmigrant student status to study in the U.S. *See* chapter 7, *supra*. Nonetheless, the Supreme Court has rendered decisions delineating the limits of a state's power in relation to non-citizens and education.

The first of these decisions, *Plyler v. Doe*, 457 U.S. 202 (1982), considered the right of undocumented non-citizen children to receive elementary education. The Court noted that undocumented non-citizens do not constitute a "suspect class," so that any statute on this subject would not be subject to strict scrutiny. The Court then described the unique and lifelong effect that elementary education has on a person. The Court feared that denying these children an education might create a nearly permanent underclass of undocumented non-citizens who probably would remain in the U.S. for the rest of their lives. Furthermore, any statute that discriminated against the undocumented non-citizen children would punish them for the acts of their parents, since the children had no choice in coming to the U.S. Accordingly, the Court held that any state statute which created special burdens for undocumented non-citizen children to receive an elementary education would be voided unless it could be shown that the statute furthered some substantial state interest. No such interest was found in the *Plyler* case.

The second decision of the Supreme Court on non-citizens and education was *Toll v. Moreno*, 458 U.S. 1 (1982). This case concerned the right of the children of non-citizens who are international organization employees (G–4 nonimmigrants) domiciled in a state to pay the lower in-state tuition rate at the state university. The Court noted that G–4 nonimmigrants were a special group of non-citizens to which Congress had granted the right of acquiring domicile in the U.S. If the state then required the children of a domiciled G–4 nonimmigrant to pay a higher out-of-state tuition, the state would be creating a burden on them not contemplated by Congress. The Court held that the imposition of such a burden would be impermissible, since it would frustrate the federal policy. Although the case only dealt with G–4 nonimmigrants, presumably other classes of nonimmigrants would also be covered by this decision if they, too, were not required to maintain their domicile outside the U.S. Hence, the reasoning of *Toll* might extend to the children of holders of a few other nonimmigrant visas, such as H and L visa holders.

In November 1994 California voters passed Proposition 187 to prohibit public schools in that state from admitting undocumented non-citizen children to attend school. Each school was supposed to verify the immigration status of every student as well as his or her parents or guardians. The school was also to report to the INS the immigration status of any student, parent, or guardian suspected to be out of status. The court in *League of United Latin American Citizens v. Wilson*, 997 F.Supp. 1244 (C.D.Cal.1997), relying upon *Plyler v. Doe*, rejected the provisions of Proposition 187 that limited the right of undocumented non-citizen children to attend public schools. Rather than appealing the decision, California governor Gray Davis submitted the proposition to binding arbitration in 1999, which effectively upheld the court's decision.

The trial court also found that provisions in Proposition 187 limiting undocumented non-citizens' access to post-secondary education were preempted by the Illegal Immigration Reform and Immigrant Responsibility Act of 1996 (IIRIRA). That Act provides that undocumented non-citizens may not receive state resident college tuition benefits or other post-secondary education benefits unless the state makes those benefits available to all U.S. citizens and nationals without regard to residence. 8 U.S.C.A. § 1623. In a dramatic change of policy, the California Assembly in 2001 enacted a law that grants resident tuition to certain undocumented students. In accordance with § 1623, the law makes resident tuition rates available to any student who attended high school in California for three years or more and graduated from a California high school, regardless of where that student resides. Undocumented students are further required to apply for legal immigration status. It is unlikely, however, that undocumented students will qualify for a visa.

§ 13–4.4   Eligibility for Federal Benefit Programs

Non-citizens' eligibility for federal benefit programs is largely determined by their status in the United States. Under the Personal Responsibility and Work Opportunity Reconciliation Act of 1996 (Welfare Act), non-citizens are either "qualified" or "unqualified." "Qualified" non-citizens include lawful permanent residents, refugees, asylees, immigration parolees, persons granted Temporary Protected Status, and a few other categories of non-citizens. 8 U.S.C.A. § 1641. All other non-citizens, including nonimmigrants as well as undocumented non-citizens, are "unqualified." Before 1996, lawful permanent residents and non-citizens "permanently residing in the U.S. under color of law" (PRUCOLs) were generally eligible for benefits. The classification "permanently residing under color of law" was liberally construed to mean any non-citizen permitted to remain in the U.S. indefinitely. *Holley v. Lavine*, 553 F.2d 845 (2d Cir.1977). The Welfare Act, however, makes all unqualified non-citizens ineligible for most federal benefits and limits eligibility for qualified non-citizens. The restrictions in the Welfare Act and the related public discussion have encouraged many permanent residents to become U.S. citizens. *See* § 12–2.2, *supra*.

"Unqualified" non-citizens are ineligible for all federal public benefits except for emergency medical assistance, disaster relief, and a few other exempt services. The federal benefits withheld from unqualified non-citizens include welfare, disability insurance, public housing, food stamps, unemployment benefits, and grants for post-secondary education. 8 U.S.C.A. § 1611.

"Qualified" non-citizens, with some significant exceptions, are also ineligible for federal benefits such as food

stamps and Supplemental Security Income (SSI). 8
U.S.C.A. § 1612. Lawful permanent residents become
eligible for these benefits only if they have worked forty
"qualifying quarters." Asylees and refugees, however,
may receive food stamps and SSI for the first seven years
after they are admitted to the United States. Veterans
and persons on active duty with the U.S. Armed Forces
are also eligible for these benefits. Non-citizens who were
receiving SSI on August 22, 1996, and non-citizens who
were residing in the U.S. on that date and subsequently
qualified for SSI because of blindness or disability are
also eligible to receive SSI benefits.

The Welfare Act further bars lawful permanent residents who entered the U.S. on or after August 22, 1996,
from receiving any means-tested federal benefit for five
years after entering the U.S. 8 U.S.C.A. § 1613. Persons
in this group remain eligible, however, for emergency
medical assistance, disaster relief, some programs for
school children, and a few other benefits.

Even non-citizens who are qualified may also find
limitations in a number of lesser used programs. These
programs include loans for farm purchases (7 C.F.R.
§ 1822), housing financial assistance (42 U.S.C.A.
§ 1436a), student financial aid, or student eligibility for
state resident tuition. *See Nyquist v. Mauclet*, 432 U.S. 1
(1977). These programs are usually limited to lawful
permanent residents, but other restrictions may exist,
and they may change from time to time-particularly in
regard to state welfare programs.

The Welfare Act also states that "federal means-tested
programs" are to use the income and resources of the
sponsor of the non-citizen in addition to the income of
the non-citizen to determine eligibility for benefits. 8

U.S.C.A. § 1631. Unless the non-citizens are refugees or asylees, this sponsor-to-non-citizen deeming rule may keep most non-citizens ineligible for federal benefits until they naturalize or have forty "qualifying quarters." After IIRIRA, the federal government, a state government, or any other entity that provides means-tested public benefits may enforce an affidavit of support against the non-citizen's sponsor. INA § 213A(A)(1)(B). See § 5–5.1(d), *supra*, discussing affidavits of support.

Many welfare programs, including Medicaid, Temporary Assistance for Needy Families (TANF—formerly Aid to Families with Dependent Children), and social services block grants, are funded jointly by state and federal governments. States must provide these benefits to permanent residents who have worked forty qualifying quarters, veterans, people on active military duty, refugees, and asylees admitted to the U.S. within the past seven years. 8 U.S.C.A. § 1612(b). Qualified non-citizens admitted to the U.S. after August 22, 1996, are ineligible for these programs for five years. Apart from these specific requirements, the Welfare Act gives states the option to grant or withhold these benefits from "qualified" non-citizens. Despite this invitation to withhold benefits from immigrants, nearly all states have continued providing Medicaid and TANF to persons who entered the U.S. before August 22, 1996.

The Welfare Act allows, but does not require, states to provide state-funded benefits to unqualified non-citizens and to non-citizens who are otherwise ineligible for federal benefits. The Act required states that wish to provide such benefits to pass laws after August 22, 1996, affirmatively establishing non-citizens' eligibility for these programs. 8 U.S.C.A. § 1621(d). Many states have created TANF and food stamp substitutes for non-citizens, and some states also provide medical assistance or other general assistance benefits. States that provide such benefits generally limit eligibility, however, by providing assistance only to particularly needy groups of people or by imposing residence requirements.

The federal courts have uniformly upheld restrictions on federally-funded benefits against constitutional challenges. *See* § 13–3.3, *supra*. The response to state restrictions on welfare has been more mixed, with some state courts finding that such restrictions violate equal protection, while others have held that Congressional authorization makes such restrictions permissible. *See* § 13–3.2, *supra*.

The largest category of federal benefits is authorized under the Social Security Act. Old Age, Survivors and Disability Insurance (OASDI) is available to persons who hold social security numbers for work purposes. In order to obtain a social security number for work purposes, a person must be a citizen, lawful permanent resident, or a non-citizen who, under authority of law, is permitted to work in the U.S. 20 C.F.R. § 422.104. Not all non-citizens who are permitted to work in the U.S. are "qualified aliens" and not all lawful permanent residents will have worked at least forty "qualifying quarters." Where the non-citizen already holds a social security number, the non-citizen will be eligible to receive OASDI, assuming other qualifications are met.

Coverage with OASDI can be suspended, however, regardless of the non-citizen's status, if the non-citizen leaves the U.S. for more than six months. 42 U.S.C.A. § 402(t). Coverage can also be suspended if the non-citizen is removed for certain reasons, or if the non-citizen is not lawfully present in the United States. 42 U.S.C.A. § 402(n), (y). This suspension is not a violation of due process. *Flemming v. Nestor*, 363 U.S. 603 (1960). These conditions for OASDI also apply to hospital insurance benefits. 42 U.S.C.A. § 426. For the uninsured non-citizen, Medicare is available, but this coverage is restricted to lawful permanent residents who have resided in the U.S. for five or more years. 42 C.F.R. § 405.205. The Supreme Court unanimously upheld this restriction as within the authority of Congress in *Mathews v. Diaz*, 426 U.S. 67 (1976). In 2010, Congress passed a health care reform law that greatly expanded health insurance coverage. Those eligible for benefits under the law include United States citizens and lawful permanent residents. The health care reform law, however, excludes undocumented immigrants from participating in health insurance exchanges, even if an undocumented immigrant is willing to purchase insurance with his or her own funds. The health care reform law also left in place the five year waiting period for lawful permanent residents to be eligible for Medicare.

If the non-citizen leaves the U.S. and then tries to re-enter, the INS may refuse to admit the non-citizen as one likely to become a public charge, based on the non-citizen's previous welfare history. There also may be an adverse effect if the non-citizen applies for an adjustment of status to permanent resident. Further, in the extreme, a non-citizen who becomes a public charge within five years after entry may be removed, unless the causes arise after entry. INA § 237(a)(5).

Temporary residents who receive benefits for which they are not qualified, either through agency inadvertence or "grandfathering," will not necessarily be denied permanent residency. The INS applies two tests to determine whether a non-citizen legalized under the 1986 Immigration Reform and Control Act (IRCA) is not admissible as "likely to become a public charge." 8 C.F.R. § 245a.3(g)(4). The first test examines the non-citizen's current earnings, job history, skills, education, and past receipt of welfare. The second test, deemed the "special rule," considers only whether the non-citizen has maintained a consistent job history without receiving public cash assistance. Formerly undocumented non-citizens who were legalized under IRCA are disqualified for a period of five years after the date of legalization from receiving "programs of financial assistance furnished under Federal law ... as such programs are identified by the Attorney General." INA § 245A(h)(1). This five year waiting period does not necessarily apply to Cubans and Haitians, or non-citizens who are aged, blind, or disabled. INA § 245A(h)(2).

Refugees, as defined by INA § 207(c)(2), may qualify for Refugee Assistance, a program through which the federal government makes grants to, and contracts with, public or private nonprofit agencies for initial resettlement of refugees in the United States. INA § 412. The goals of the program are to (i) make available sufficient resources for employment training and placement in order to achieve economic self-sufficiency among refugees as quickly as possible, (ii) provide refugees with the opportunity to acquire sufficient English language training to enable them to be resettled effectively as quickly as possible, (iii) insure that cash assistance is made available to refugees in such a manner as not to discourage their economic self-sufficiency, and (iv) insure that women have the same opportunity as men to participate in training and instruction. INA § 412(a)(1)(A). Through the Refugee Medical Assistance program, refugees who do not qualify for Medicaid may receive free health care.

§ 13–4.5 Freedom of Speech

The Supreme Court decided in *Schneider v. New Jersey*, 308 U.S. 147 (1939) that non-citizens present in the U.S. are entitled to the same right of freedom of speech as any citizen. Nonetheless, any non-citizen may be removed for engaging in terrorism or in any activity a purpose of which is the overthrow of the U.S. government by force or other unconstitutional means. INA § 237(a)(4). A non-citizen's statements could also be used to attack the non-citizen's good moral character or attachment to the principles of the Constitution, which are both required for naturalization. INA § 313.

Under former INA § 241, non-citizens could be deported for, among other things, advocating world communism or the establishment of a totalitarian dictatorship in the United States, or for affiliating with any organization that advocates communism or the establishment of a totalitarian dictatorship. One federal district court declared these provisions unconstitutional on their face as being "substantially overbroad," but the U.S. Court of Appeals reversed for lack of standing and ripeness. *American–Arab Anti–Discrimination Committee v. Thornburgh*, 940 F.2d 445 (9th Cir.1991). The district court reasoned that the provisions are applicable to both constitutionally permissible and impermissible activities. The statutes prohibited a range of conduct, including the teaching of organizational viewpoints, advocacy of imminent lawless violence, and even a non-citizen's wearing of an organization's button. The district court noted that lawful permanent residents have First Amendment rights generally and these rights cannot be infringed despite the plenary power of Congress over immigration matters. The 1990 Act modified INA § 241 (currently § 237) considerably, restricting its application in this respect to a non-citizen's activities after entry and removing the offending provisions.

This case continued when the INS instituted further deportation proceedings under the terrorist activity provision of the 1990 Act, because the seven Palestinians and one Kenyan were members of the Popular Front for the Liberation of Palestine. The non-citizens again filed suit claiming that the INS had singled them out for selective enforcement of the immigration laws in retaliation for their constitutionally protected associational activity. The district court enjoined deportation of those non-citizens with visas and the Court of Appeals affirmed. In *Reno v. American–Arab Anti–Discrimination Committee*, 525 U.S. 471 (1999), the Supreme Court reversed, finding that under INA § 242(g), enacted in 1996 as part of IIRIRA, federal courts no longer had jurisdiction to review the INS decision to commence proceedings against non-citizens. Consequently, the Court found that non-citizens have no constitutional right to challenge the selective enforcement of immigration laws.

An unadmitted nonresident alien has no right of free speech in the U.S. The Supreme Court stated in *Kleindienst v. Mandel*, 408 U.S. 753 (1972), that non-citizens could be excluded for views held or opinions expressed because non-citizens have no constitutional right of entry to the U.S. Additionally, the Court held that U.S. citizens have no right to have non-citizens enter the country so that ideas may be exchanged. The plenary power of Congress to control admission of non-citizens overrides a citizen's right to receive information under the First Amendment.

§ 13–4.6 Non–Citizen's Rights and National Security

While admitted non-citizens generally are entitled to the constitutional protections of due process and freedom from unreasonable search and seizure (*see Kwong Hai Chew v. Colding*, 344 U.S. 590 (1953)), in times of crisis the government has been willing to infringe on these rights in the interest of national security. Following the September 11, 2001, attacks, the U.S. government carried out extensive investigations that targeted thousands of non-citizens, primarily from Arab and Muslim backgrounds. The government used its immigration powers to question and detain non-citizens thought to have information about terrorism, in some cases holding them for months without formal charges. Many of the detainees were eventually removed on grounds unrelated to terrorism, but the EOIR nonetheless authorized closure of removal hearings in these "special interest" cases. Even non-citizens who were not suspected of terrorist connections were subjected to heightened government scrutiny, as the INS targeted individuals from Arab and Muslim backgrounds for enforcement of other immigration laws.

a. *Questioning of Non–Citizens and Selective Enforcement of Immigration Laws*

From November 2001 through March 2002, the Department of Justice interviewed approximately 8,000 men between the ages of eighteen and thirty-three, primarily from Muslim and Arab backgrounds, who were present in the United States on nonimmigrant visas. The interviews were primarily intended to find people with information about terrorist activities, but the questioners were also instructed to report to immigration officers any interviewee whom they suspected of violating immigration laws. In similar circumstances, the D.C. Circuit in 1979 upheld a special registration rule applied to Iranian students during the Iran hostage crisis. *Narenji v. Civiletti*, 617 F.2d 745 (D.C. Cir.1979). Although the rule differentiated on the basis of national origin, the court applied only rational basis scrutiny, deferring to the Attorney General's power over immigration, and the President's power over foreign affairs.

In addition to conducting the interviews, the Department of Justice has targeted Muslim and Arab noncitizens for selective enforcement of immigration laws. In February 2002, the Department announced its "Absconder Apprehension Initiative," designed to locate and arrest individuals who have remained in the U.S. although subject to a final removal order. Some 300,000 such people are currently believed to be in the U.S. The INS began entering the names of these individuals in the FBI's National Crime Information Center database, to which state and local law enforcement officers have access. The INS has also begun efforts to locate and apprehend these individuals, starting with persons from the Middle East. In late 2002, the INS instituted new registration requirements for nonimmigrants, again targeting mainly people from Arab and Muslim countries, as well as other "state sponsors of terrorism." *See* § 8–2.2(c), *supra*. Some individuals were detained for alleged immigration violations after attempting to register at CIS offices; many of them were placed in removal proceedings.

As the Supreme Court held in *Reno v. American–Arab Anti–Discrimination Committee*, 525 U.S. 471 (1999), non-citizens have no constitutional right to challenge the selective enforcement of immigration laws. In that case, the Court also stated that because law enforcement priorities are often established on the basis of sensitive foreign-policy concerns, the government "should not have to disclose its 'real' reasons for deeming nationals of a particular country a special threat."

b. Detentions

In fall 2001, the Department of Justice rounded up and detained approximately 1,200 non-citizens suspected of having connections to the September 11th attacks. Ultimately, none of the detainees were found to have terrorist connections, but the vast majority were held or removed because of immigration violations. A small number who had not committed any immigration violation were held on material witness warrants.

Under an administrative rule promulgated in September 2001, immigration officials are permitted to hold non-citizens in custody without charge for "a reasonable period of time" in emergency situations. *See* 8 C.F.R. § 287. Hundreds of the people detained during this period were held without any charges for weeks or, in a few cases, months, while the INS and FBI investigated their cases.

Further, the INS refused to release information about the individuals held in these "special interest" cases. Several public interest groups sued the Department of Justice under the Freedom of Information Act to obtain the names of the detainees, the nature of the charges filed against them, and information on the circumstances of their arrest or detention. *See, e.g., Center for Nat'l Sec. Studies v. Department of Justice*, 331 F.3d 918 (D.D.C. 2003). The government argued that release of this information would enable terrorist groups to monitor its investigations and deter cooperation by the detainees. The District Court ordered the Department of Justice to disclose the names of the detainees, except those persons who requested in writing that their names not be released. For security reasons, the court did not require the government to release information about the dates and location of arrest and detention for security reasons. A few days after the ruling, the court stayed its order pending an appeal. the D.C. Circuit reversed.

In 2003, the Inspector General of the Department of Justice admitted in a pair of reports that the government detained many non-citizens for unreasonably long periods of time and that many of these non-citizens suffered from a pattern of abuse by detention officials. Several detainees have brought civil suits against the government for unlawful detention and abuse. In *Ashcroft v. Iqbal*, 129 S.Ct. 1937 (2009), the Supreme Court held in a 5–4 decision that the complaint of Iqbal, a former detainee, failed to plead sufficient facts to state a claim. Iqbal alleged that he was subjected to various forms of physical and psychological abuse including prolonged periods of solitary confinement, repeated and unwarranted cavity searches, and frequent beatings. The Court dismissed Iqbal's claim for failing to allege sufficient facts indicating that government officials knew of, condoned, and willfully and maliciously agreed to subject Iqbal to harsh conditions of confinement as a matter of policy, solely on account of his religion, race, and/or national origin.

c. *Secret Hearings*

In general, removal hearings, like judicial proceedings, are open to the public and the press, except for cases involving spousal abuse or child abuse. In 2001, Chief Immigration Judge Michael Creppy directed immigration courts to close hearings of "special interest" cases involving non-citizens suspected of having information about the September 11th attacks. Further, immigration courts were not to list these cases on courtroom calendars or in the immigration courts' automated telephone information service. In support of the closure, the government argued that terrorists might use information revealed in such hearings to formulate future actions against the U.S., that they might try to disrupt the hearings, and that non-citizens in such hearings would more readily cooperate with the government if the hearings are closed.

Media groups in two states brought suits against the government, arguing that closure of such hearings violates their First Amendment rights. In *Detroit Free Press v. Ashcroft*, 303 F.3d 681 (6th Cir.2002), the Court of Appeals ordered the hearings to be opened unless an immigration judge makes an individualized finding that a specific case should be closed for security reasons. The Third Circuit, however, in *North Jersey Media Group, Inc. v. Ashcroft*, 308 F.3d 198 (3d Cir.2002), upheld the Creppy directive and the Supreme Court denied certiorari.

§ 13–4.7 Labor Laws

Non-citizens may only work in the United States if they are lawful permanent residents, asylees, or refugees, or they have a nonimmigrant status that permits employment. *See* chapter 6, *supra*. The INA imposes penalties on non-citizens who work without authorization and on employers who knowingly hire unauthorized workers. *See* § 14–2.6, *infra*. Many non-citizens who are not authorized to work find employment in spite of these laws, which raises the question of what protections, if any, unauthorized workers have against employer misconduct.

In *Sure–Tan, Inc. v. NLRB*, 467 U.S. 883 (1984), the Supreme Court found that undocumented workers who had been reported to immigration activities in retaliation for union activities could bring an action against their employer under the National Labor Relations Act (NLRA). The Court found, however, that the usual remedy in such cases, reinstatement with backpay, was not available to the workers because they had voluntarily departed to Mexico and were barred from re-entering the United States; they would have had to violate the law to collect the remedy to which they were entitled. When *Sure–Tan* was decided, there were no laws prohibiting employers from hiring undocumented workers or preventing undocumented non-citizens from seeking employment. Then, in 1986, Congress passed the Immigration Reform and Control Act (IRCA), which made these actions illegal for the first time.

In 2002, the Court again considered the remedies available to undocumented workers under the NLRA. In *Hoffman Plastic Compounds, Inc. v. NLRB*, 535 U.S. 137 (2002), the Court held that an undocumented worker who had been fired in retaliation for union organizing activities was not entitled to backpay. The employee in *Hoffman* had used fraudulent documents to obtain his job and the company did not learn of his immigration status until the hearing on his claim. Unlike the *Sure–*

Tan plaintiffs, the employee had remained in the United States. The National Labor Relations Board had previously determined that the employee was entitled to backpay for the period from his termination to the date the employer learned about his unlawful status, reasoning that, but for the wrongful termination, he would have continued at the job until that time. The Court found, however, that awarding backpay to an undocumented worker for years of work not performed, in a job that he obtained by criminal fraud, would contravene federal immigration policy, and it denied the backpay award. Since *Hoffman*, several lower courts have considered the issue of whether the Supreme Court's ruling applies to claims under other federal labor laws, such as wage claims under the Fair Labor Standards Act (FLSA) or discrimination claims under the Americans with Disabilities Act (ADA) and Title VII of the Civil Rights Act. Before *Hoffman*, the Eleventh Circuit, in *Patel v. Quality Inn South*, 846 F.2d 700 (11th Cir.1988), found that undocumented workers could recover for unpaid wages under the FLSA, even though their employment was illegal after enactment of the IRCA. That court reasoned that denying undocumented workers protection under the FLSA would undermine federal immigration policy by giving employers an incentive to hire such workers at less than the minimum wage. Further, the court found that allowing a cause of action under the FLSA was not likely to encourage illegal immigration, as it is not the protections of U.S. labor laws, but rather the possibility of finding work at any wage that draws immigrants. Applying the same reasoning, several lower courts have upheld claims under the FLSA and ADA since *Hoffman*. *See, e.g., Lopez v. Superflex*, 2002 WL 1941484 (S.D.N.Y. 2002) (denying summary judgment for defendant in ADA suit despite plaintiff's refusal to admit to immigration status); *Singh v. Jutla*, 214 F.Supp.2d 1056 (N.D.Cal. 2002) (denying motion to dismiss FLSA suit for unpaid wages where employer knowingly hired undocumented worker); *Flores v. Albertsons, Inc.*, 2002 WL 1163623 (C.D.Cal.2002) (denying defendant's motion to compel discovery of plaintiff's immigration status in FLSA suit and finding plaintiffs entitled to backpay for work performed). In these cases, the courts have distinguished between backpay claims for work not performed, such as the claim denied by the Court in *Hoffman*, and claims for unpaid wages for work performed, finding that undocumented workers may be entitled to pay for work performed.

The *Hoffman* decision has also affected undocumented non-citizens' eligibility for workers' compensation. Workers' compensation laws differ from state to state, but in general, these funds are paid by employers to compensate workers for the loss of earning power attributable to an on-the job injury. The issue of whether undocumented employees are entitled to workers' compensation has divided state courts. In some cases, employers have been able to avoid paying compensation to injured workers when they learned that the workers were undocumented. In such cases, the courts found, the workers' loss of wages was due to their inability to work legally, and not to their injuries. *See, e.g., Sanchez v. Eagle Alloy, Inc.*, 658 N.W.2d 510 (Mich.Ct.App.2003); *Reinforced Earth Co. v. Workers Compensation Appeal Board*, 810 A.2d 99 (Pa.2002). Other courts, however, have ruled in favor of an undocumented worker seeking workers' compensation. These courts have held that their states, regardless of an employee's immigration status, have a strong public policy in protecting wages. *See, e.g., Coma Corp. v.*

Kansas Department of Labor, 154 P.3d 1080 (Kan. 2007); *Design Kitchen and Baths v. Lagos*, 882 A.2d 817 (Md.Ct. App.2005). In *Affordable Housing Foundation v. Silva*, 469 F.3d 219 (2d Cir.2006), the Second Circuit ruled that IRCA did not preempt a state law that explicitly allowed for non-citizens to collect monetary damages for workplace injuries. Additionally, some courts have allowed undocumented non-citizens to recover medical expenses from their employers in tort actions. *See Hernandez v. GPSDC*, 2006 WL 563308 (S.D.N.Y.2006)

Title VII of the Civil Rights Act of 1964 protects employees from discrimination in the workplace on account of race, national origin, gender, and religion. After *Hoffman*, the U.S. Equal Employment Opportunity Commission affirmed its commitment to preserving the protections of Title VII for employees regardless of their immigration status. In light of *Hoffman*, employers sought to discover the citizenship status of employees raising Title VII claims. Courts have precluded such inquiries in order to avoid discouraging employees from bringing claims and to further public interest in abolishing workplace discrimination. *Rivera v. NIBCO, Inc.*, 364 F.3d 1057 (9th Cir.2004).

§ 13–4.8 Driver's Licenses

For many non-citizens, a driver's license is a necessity, without which they would not be able to get to work or school or carry out many other everyday activities. Since September 11, 2001, however, many state governments have proposed or enacted laws that restrict non-citizens' access to driver's licenses. Proponents of such laws argue that driver's licenses facilitated the activities of the terrorists responsible for the September 11th attacks, and that linking driver's licenses to immigration status will enable state and local law enforcement officers making routine traffic stops to identify persons who are in the country illegally. Opponents of the laws argue that state driver's license agencies lack the expertise required to determine a non-citizen's immigration status and the authority to enforce immigration laws, that the laws will jeopardize highway safety by encouraging non-citizens to drive without licenses, and that many non-citizens will be subjected to great inconvenience without adequate justification.

In 2005, Congress sought to end the driver's license debate in passing the REAL ID Act. Under the Act, states have until 2013 to begin issuing driver's licenses that meet certain security requirements. Licenses that fail to meet these new requirements will not be accepted as valid forms of identification for federal purposes, including air travel. As part of the Act's requirements, states may only issue driver's licenses to applicants who can prove their citizenship or lawful presence in the country. The Act also requires applicants to have a social security number. Since the Social Security Administration will only issue an SSN to people who are eligible to work in the United States or need the number to obtain state or federal benefits, this requirement may be a significant obstacle for many nonimmigrants. Although government leaders in several states have criticized these new restrictions, most states have begun inquiring into the citizenship and immigration status of driver's license applicants.

§ 13–4.9   Military Service

The United States currently has a Selective Service registration requirement, 50 U.S.C.A.App. § 453, even though there is no longer any military draft, 50

U.S.C.A.App. § 467. This registration requirement applies to all males between the ages of eighteen and twenty-six who reside in the U.S. except for lawfully admitted nonimmigrants (50 U.S.C.A.App. § 453), and non-citizens who have resided in the U.S. less than one year, 50 U.S.C.A.App. § 455(a)(1)(3). The U.S. also has treaties with a number of other countries granting exemption from military service on a reciprocal basis. A lawful permanent resident from one of these countries may apply for a classification of exemption from the Selective Service. 32 C.F.R. § 1630.42. If the non-citizen is granted the exemption based on alienage, however, the non-citizen is barred from becoming a citizen, unless the non-citizen is covered by a treaty. INA § 315. Any non-citizen permanently ineligible for citizenship is inadmissible. INA § 212(a)(8)(A). Therefore, a lawful permanent resident who obtains an exemption from military service and then leaves the U.S. may be excluded from re-entering. A non-citizen in this category may apply to the Attorney General for an authorization for admission, but such authorizations are discretionary. INA § 212(c). Non-citizens who have departed the U.S. in order to avoid military service are also inadmissible. INA § 212(a)(8)(B).

A non-citizen who does enter military service will receive the benefit of reduced residency requirements when applying for naturalization. INA § 328(a). If the service is during a time of hostilities, additional benefits are granted, including waiver of any age and residency requirement. INA § 329(b). Following September 11, 2001, President George W. Bush issued Executive Order 13269 declaring that the United States is engaged in a time of hostilities. As of the time of this writing, the executive order remains in effect. Non-citizens serving in the military after September 11, 2001, therefore, are eligible for the naturalization benefits of § 329. *See* § 12–2.2(c), *supra*. Non-citizens in the military are ineligible to become commissioned officers and if the non-citizen deserts the service, he or she is permanently barred from naturalization. INA § 314. Non-citizens killed while serving in a military conflict may be eligible for posthumous citizenship. *See* § 12–2.2(c), *supra*.

§ 13–4.10   Right to Own Land

Land ownership laws in the United States originally developed from English land laws. England prohibited non-citizens from owning land because all land grants required an oath of loyalty to the King; that oath conflicted with the non-citizen's allegiance to another sovereign. That prohibition, however, inhibited territorial expansion and was even a subject of complaint in the Declaration of Independence. Yet, after the U.S. gained independence, the common law restrictions against non-citizen ownership remained intact; states relaxed them slowly over the next century as the needs of territorial growth and foreign investment dictated. By the end of the 1800s, however, when unlimited territorial expansion was no longer possible, both state and federal legislatures began re-establishing restrictions on non-citizen landholding. Many federal enactments from this era are still in effect, although few of the state restrictions are.

Non-citizen land ownership law is primarily a state concern, and there are only three principal areas of federal restriction. First, the federal government has been concerned in time of war when enemy non-citizens hold land; second, the federal government is concerned with safeguarding of natural resources for citizens or permanent residents; third, the federal government has an interest in seeing that foreigners are treated equitably and in a manner consistent with national policies regarding immigration and foreign affairs.

As to the *first* area of federal concern, the Trading with the Enemy Act, 50 U.S.C.A.App. § 1, empowers the government to control land transactions during times of *declared* war. The Foreign Assets Control Regulations limit land transactions for non-citizens of certain listed countries, such as Cuba and the Democratic People's Republic of Korea at present. The International Emergency Economic Powers Act, 50 U.S.C.A. § 1701, grants the President broad authority to control non-citizen property during a time of declared national emergency. President Carter used this authority during the Iranian hostage crisis to freeze all Iranian assets, including land. Similarly, President Bush froze Iraqi and Kuwaiti assets in 1991 after Iraq invaded Kuwait. Following the September 11, 2001, attacks, President George W. Bush froze the assets of certain suspected terrorists.

Second, federal laws restrict non-citizen exploitation of agricultural, grazing, mineral, or timberland. Foreigners are required to notify the Department of Agriculture if they own agricultural land. 7 U.S.C.A. § 3501. The Taylor Grazing Act, 43 U.S.C.A. § 315b, restricts grazing rights on public lands to citizens or immigrants who have applied for citizenship. The Mining Law of 1882 and the Mineral Lands Leasing Act of 1920, 41 Stat. 437, create restrictions on non-citizen ownership of mineral rights, including petroleum. 30 U.S.C.A. § 181. More recent laws restrict non-citizen development of offshore oil deposits and geothermal resources. In addition, the Forest Service places some restrictions on standing timber sales to non-citizens, using a national preference system.

The *third* area of federal concern is founded upon constitutional protections and treaty rights. The Equal Protection Clause of the Fourteenth Amendment invalidates state laws that forbid lawful permanent residents from owning land. Furthermore, in *Zschernig v. Miller*, 389 U.S. 429 (1968), the Supreme Court relied on the constitutional grant of the foreign affairs power to the federal government to invalidate state laws that restrict inheritance by nationals of totalitarian countries. The reasoning of this decision conceivably could be used to void any state restriction on non-citizen investment as an infringement on the federal foreign affairs power. Also, if the federal government has granted another nation's citizens land ownership rights by treaty, the state cannot abridge these rights, since treaties are part of the "supreme law of the land."

In state law, there is a wide diversity of statutes that control non-citizen land ownership. All states permit lawful permanent residents who have applied for citizenship to purchase and inherit land, but the uniformity ends there. A few states prohibit nonresident alien ownership; a few others limit the duration of land ownership; and some place acreage limits on ownership in order to inhibit non-citizens from owning agricultural land. Some states have restricted ownership by "enemies" in times of war. Other states limit land ownership to those who are eligible for citizenship. Minor restrictions abound: For example, South Carolina restricts ownership to one-half million acres; other states will not sell state-owned property or mineral rights to non-citizens. States generally do not restrict inheritance of land by non-citizens, except that some states insist upon reciprocity by the foreign country, permitting inheritance by U.S. citizens and receipt of the land by the heir. A few states require that the land inherited by a non-citizen be sold within a statutory period after inheritance. About a dozen states also place restrictions on non-citizen corporate landholding.

In general, the practitioner must examine the laws of each state with regard to both the type of land transaction and the identity of the non-citizen individual or corporation involved. These laws must also be examined for constitutionality, because non-citizen land ownership or usage is still an unsettled area of law.

§ 13–4.11   Federal Taxation of Non–Citizens

The liability of a non-citizen in the United States to pay taxes will depend on the non-citizen's status as a resident or a nonresident. This status for tax purposes is determined by the Internal Revenue Code (26 U.S.C.A. § 1 *et seq.*) and not by the Immigration and Naturalization Act. Under 26 U.S.C.A. § 7701(b)(1)(A), non-citizens are treated as U.S. residents with respect to any calendar year in which they are (1) lawful permanent residents, (2) meet a "substantial presence test," or (3) elect to be taxed as residents. With certain exceptions for teachers, students, commuters from Canada and Mexico, and individuals claiming treaty exemptions, a non-citizen will meet the substantial presence test and be considered a U.S. resident for federal income tax purposes if the non-citizen (1) is physically present in the U.S. on at least 31 days during the current year, and (2) the sum of the days physically present in the U.S. totals at least 183 days within the last three years, with each day present in the current taxable year counting as a full day, each day in the first preceding year as one-third of a day, and each day in the second preceding year as one-sixth of a day. To meet the substantial presence test, the non-citizen must also not have a tax home in a foreign country, and, unless holding a green card, not have a closer connection to a foreign country than to the United States. If a non-citizen holds a green card, he or she will automatically be considered a United States resident for federal income tax purposes, regardless of the number of days present in the United States.

Non-citizens who are considered resident in the United States for tax purposes are generally taxed in the same way as U.S. citizens. A resident is thus taxed on income derived from all sources, including sources outside the U.S., and this income is subject to the graduated tax rates that apply to U.S. citizens. An individual who was a resident for the entire tax year may also claim the same deductions allowed for U.S. citizens. 26 C.F.R. § 1.871–1. Certain tax laws, however, have a greater impact on lawful permanent residents than on citizens; examples include: (1) a taxpayer may claim as a dependent only a citizen, national, or resident of the United States, a resident of Canada or Mexico, or a child adopted by and living with the U.S. citizen or national taxpayer (26 U.S.C.A. § 152(b)(3); 26 C.F.R. § 1.152–2(a)(2)); (2) a qualified individual may elect to exclude from gross income up to $80,000 of income earned in a foreign country and a limited amount based on housing costs paid or incurred because of foreign employment (26 U.S.C.A. § 911); and (3) a tax credit or deduction may be taken for certain foreign tax paid (26 U.S.C.A. § 901; 26 C.F.R. §§ 1.901–1, 1.901–2).

The situation of a nonresident alien is considerably more complicated. If the individual is engaged in a U.S. trade or business (which includes attending school or participating in an exchange program as an F, J, M, or Q nonimmigrant), all business or wage income from U.S. sources, with a few exceptions, is taxed at the graduated rates applicable to U.S. citizens and residents. 26 U.S.C.A. §§ 871, 872. Other income not effectively connected with a trade or business in the United States, such as dividends, interest, annuities, or the income from the sale of a capital asset, is taxed at either a flat 30% rate, or a lower rate if a separate treaty exists with the non-citizen's country. 26 C.F.R. § 1.871–8.

Nonresident aliens engaged in a trade or business in the United States may be able to exclude certain U.S. income from their effectively connected gross income. Excludable income includes certain interest income from U.S. sources that is not connected with a trade or business; income from personal services performed in the United States as an employee of a foreign corporation provided the foreign corporation does not have an office or permanent establishment in the U.S. and if the noncitizen was present in the U.S. for no more than ninety days and the total pay for the services is not more than $3,000; income received by students with F, J, or Q status from foreign employers; annuities received in compensation for personal services; and income that is exempt from tax by treaty.

In general, deductions for nonresident aliens are allowed only if they are effectively connected with a trade or business. The following deductions, however, are allowed whether or not the nonresident's income was effectively connected with a U.S. trade or business: (1) deductions for casualty and theft losses on property located within the U.S.; (2) deductions for charitable contributions; and (3) deductions for personal exemptions. 26 U.S.C.A. § 873. Nonresident aliens who receive income effectively connected with their U.S. trade or business may make certain itemized deductions, including state and local income taxes, charitable contributions to U.S. organizations, casualty and theft losses on property located in the U.S., moving expenses, and miscellaneous deductions.

Nonresident aliens may also claim credits against U.S. income tax liability for certain taxes paid, including certain foreign income taxes paid. With limited exceptions, nonresident aliens engaged in a trade or business in the U.S. are allowed only one personal exemption. A fuller discussion, complete with examples, is available in Publication 519, U.S. Tax Guide for Aliens, from the local office of the Internal Revenue Service (IRS) or online at the IRS website. This guide includes an updated list of tax treaties in effect.

In order to ensure that all taxes owed are paid, the departing non-citizen is required to obtain a Certificate of Compliance from the IRS. Also known as a Sailing Permit or Exit Permit, this document shows that either the taxes have been paid or an adequate bond has been posted to cover taxes owed. Diplomats, certain employees of foreign governments and international organizations, non-citizens present in the U.S. for a short term with no taxable income, commuting residents of Canada or Mexico, and some students or trainees do not have to obtain a Sailing Permit before departing. 26 C.F.R. § 1.6851–2(a)(2).

In 1996, Congress imposed new tax penalties on citizens who renounce their citizenship and long-term permanent residents who depart the U.S. to avoid paying taxes. *See* 26 U.S.C.A. § 877. Under this "expatriation tax" provision, expatriates and former permanent residents may be taxed on U.S. source income in the same manner as nonresident aliens, for ten years following their expatriation or departure. A tax avoidance motive is presumed when the expatriate or former resident has an income in excess of $100,000 or a net worth of $500,000 or more, but exceptions apply if the individual leaves the U.S. to live in a country where he or she, or his or her parent or spouse, was born. In addition, persons who renounce their citizenship to avoid paying taxes are inadmissible. INA § 212(a)(10)(E).

A non-citizen who has obtained a social security number for work purposes also will pay social security taxes for work performed in the U.S. 26 U.S.C.A. § 3101. The United States has bilateral social security agreements with many foreign countries to coordinate social security coverage and generally to make sure that social security taxes are paid only to one country. Agreements are in effect with Australia, Austria, Belgium, Canada, Chile, Finland, France, Germany, Greece, Ireland, Italy, South Korea, Luxembourg, Netherlands, Norway, Portugal, Spain, Sweden, Switzerland, and the United Kingdom. Under these agreements, non-citizens are generally subject to social security tax only in the country where they are working.

Residents, like U.S. citizens, are subject to gift tax no matter where the gift property is situated and whether it is tangible or intangible property. Expatriates and former residents who are subject to the expatriation tax are also subject to a tax on gifts. 26 U.S.C.A. § 2501(a); 26 C.F.R. § 25.2501–1(a). Nonresident aliens are generally liable for gift tax only with respect to gifts of real property or tangible personal property situated in the U.S. when the non-citizen made the gift. 26 U.S.C.A.

§§ 2501(a), 2511(a). The annual exclusion for present interest gifts between spouses is limited to $100,000 ($133,000, in 2009, as adjusted for inflation) when the recipient spouse is not a U.S. citizen (present interest gifts to a citizen spouse are excludable in their entirety). 26 U.S.C.A. §§ 2503, 2523(a), 2523(i). Federal estate taxes are also applied to non-citizens and citizens on a similar basis, with a separate rate table for estates of nonresidents. 26 U.S.C.A. § 2101. A marital deduction, however, is not allowed for bequests made to a surviving spouse who is not a U.S. citizen. 26 U.S.C.A. § 2056(d). Estates of nonresident non-citizens are entitled to a credit against their federal estate tax liability; however, the amount of this credit is only $13,000, which is much lower than the unified credit allowed to citizens and resident non-citizens, and permits the estate of a nonresident non-citizen to transfer only $60,000 worth of property free of estate tax. 26 U.S.C.A. § 2102(c). The United States has bilateral estate tax and gift tax treaties in effect with more than fifteen countries. These treaties contain provisions designed to prevent double taxation that may aid a nonresident non-citizen in reducing that taxpayer's U.S. federal estate and gift tax liability. In addition to federal estate taxes, estates of citizens and non-citizen residents often are required to pay state estate taxes or inheritance taxes, which vary from state to state.

CHAPTER 14

CRIMINAL ASPECTS OF IMMIGRATION

§ 14–1 INTRODUCTION

In addition to the harsh consequence of removal, non-citizens may incur criminal penalties for misconduct related to immigration. Such criminal sanctions are found under both the Immigration and Nationality Act and portions of the U.S. Criminal Code. This chapter describes immigration-related conduct that may result in criminal penalties for both citizens and non-citizens, including unlawful entry, bringing non-citizens into the U.S. without inspection, transporting or concealing a non-citizen who entered unlawfully, encouraging non-citizens to enter unlawfully, misrepresentation or fraud in obtaining immigration status, failure to comply with removal regulations, and employment of unauthorized workers. The chapter also discusses the immigration consequences of a non-citizen's criminal activity, including denial of asylum, inadmissibility, and removal.

Criminal prosecutions have become a signification part of immigration law. Criminal prosecutions for immigration offenses rose dramatically from 17,100 prosecutions in 2000 to 91,899 prosecutions in 2009. Moreover, prosecutions for immigration offenses accounted for fifty-four percent of all federal criminal cases in 2009. The vast majority of these prosecutions are for unlawful entry or reentry, and roughly ninety percent of immigration cases are brought in the five federal districts located along the United States–Mexico border. While at one time individuals usually faced just the possibility of removal for such immigration offenses, it is now the case these violations will result in both criminal prosecution and removal. Those persons convicted for unlawful entry or reentry serve an average sentence of less than six months before facing removal. The consequence of a conviction is significant as criminal conduct constitutes a ground for inadmissibility that could prevent an individual from lawfully immigrating at a later time.

Although the George W. Bush administration instituted the practice of vigorously prosecuting immigration cases, the strategy has continued under President Obama. Proponents of increased prosecutions argue that the practice acts as a deterrent that has helped lower unlawful immigration, while critics maintain that prosecuting and jailing persons who will ultimately be removed is a waste of resources.

§ 14–2 CRIMINAL PROVISIONS RELATED TO IMMIGRATION

§ 14–2.1 Unlawful Entry

a. Entry at Improper Time or Place; Evading Inspection; Misrepresentation

Unlawful entry into the United States became a criminal offense in 1929. 45 Stat. 1551. Today, INA § 275 penalizes all non-citizens who enter or attempt to enter this country improperly—at any time or place other than as designated by immigration officials—by eluding examination or inspection or by being responsible for a willfully false or misleading representation or the willful concealment of a material fact. The majority of criminal immigration prosecutions are for unlawful entry under INA § 275. A non-citizen who enters the country unlawfully can be fined or imprisoned not more than six months, or both, for a first offense in violation of § 275. For a subsequent conviction the prison sentence increases to a maximum of two years. Persons caught entering or attempting to enter the U.S. unlawfully may also be subject to a civil penalty of $50 to $250. INA § 275(b). Section 275 also establishes criminal penalties for marriage fraud and for establishing a commercial enterprise for the purpose of evading immigration laws. INA § 275(c), (d). This section and other provisions of the INA instruct judges to determine the criminal fine or sentence according to the federal sentencing guidelines found in Title 18 of the United States Code.

To accommodate the vast number of prosecutions under INA § 275, judges in federal courts in districts along the Mexican border began taking pleas en masse. The district court for the District of Arizona, for instance, took 25,000 guilty pleas for unlawful entry during a twelve-month period, often hearing forty to fifty defendants accept guilty pleas simultaneously. The Ninth Circuit in *United States v. Roblero–Solis*, 588 F.3d 692 (9th Cir. 2009) rejected this practice of receiving guilty pleas en masse as a violation of Rule 11 of the Federal Rules of Criminal Procedure because no judge could accurately hear fifty guilty pleas at once. The court, however, upheld the convictions, finding that none of the defendants could show a reasonable probability that, but for the en masse pleading, they would not have pleaded guilty.

To incur a felony sentence under this provision, the non-citizen must have previously been *convicted* of unlawful entry. Mere proof that the non-citizen entered the country unlawfully is insufficient. *United States v. Arambula–Alvarado*, 677 F.2d 51 (9th Cir.1982). Prosecution under the misdemeanor provision of § 275 has become more frequent. Criminal charges are also often used as a threat by immigration officers to get non-citizens to accept prompt removal.

b. *Re-entry After Removal*

Under INA § 276, a non-citizen who has been denied admission or removed, or who departed the U.S. while removal proceedings were pending, and who thereafter re-enters, attempts to re-enter, or is found in the United States without permission, is guilty of a felony. The penalty for this felony is imprisonment up to two years, a fine determined under Title 18, or both. The section authorizes longer sentences for non-citizens who were removed after being convicted of an "aggravated felony" or misdemeanor drug offense, or who have previously been denied admission on national security grounds. INA § 276(b).

The sentence enhancement provision in § 276 raises many of the same questions regarding the definition of "aggravated felony" as does the removal ground for aggravated felonies. *See* § 8–2.2, *supra*. For example, in *United States v. Christopher*, 239 F.3d 1191 (11th Cir. 2001), a non-citizen who received a one-year sentence for shoplifting, was removed, and subsequently re-entered the United States, was convicted under § 276 and sentenced to more than six years in prison because his shoplifting conviction constituted an "aggravated felony."

Theoretically, an individual who re-enters the United States without permission after removal is subject to criminal penalties under both § 275 and § 276. In *United States v. Ortiz–Martinez*, 557 F.2d 214 (9th Cir.1977), however, the Ninth Circuit held that since one act of re-entering is involved, a person convicted of violating both statutes cannot be subjected to consecutive terms of imprisonment.

Specific intent to re-enter the country illegally is not required for a conviction under § 276. Hence, the government need not prove that the non-citizen knew he or she was not entitled to re-enter the United States without permission of the Attorney General. *Pena–Cabanillas v. United States*, 394 F.2d 785 (9th Cir.1968); *United States v. Hernandez*, 693 F.2d 996 (10th Cir.1982). In *United States v. Anton*, 683 F.2d 1011 (7th Cir.1982), however, the Seventh Circuit held that a non-citizen's reasonable belief that he or she had the consent of the Attorney General to re-enter the country constitutes a viable mistake-of-law defense to a § 276 charge.

A non-citizen prosecuted for unlawful entry after removal may be able to challenge collaterally the validity of the underlying removal order. In *United States v. Mendoza–Lopez*, 481 U.S. 828 (1987), the Supreme Court held that although the language of § 276 does not require the removal to have been lawful and there is no evidence that Congress intended to permit a challenge to the validity of the prior removal order, "[i]f the statute envisions that a court may impose a criminal penalty for re-entry after *any* deportation, regardless of how violative of the rights of the alien the deportation proceeding may have been, the statute does not comport with the constitutional requirement of due process." The Court further held that where the removal (formerly deportation) proceeding effectively eliminates the right of the non-citizen to obtain judicial review, that review must be made available in any subsequent proceeding in which the result of the removal proceeding is used to establish an element of a criminal offense.

A majority of the Courts of Appeals have interpreted *Mendoza–Lopez* narrowly, holding that in a collateral challenge, the non-citizen must show that the underlying removal order was fundamentally unfair, such that the procedural deficiencies caused the non-citizen prejudice. *See, e.g., United States v. Lopez–Vasquez*, 227 F.3d 476 (5th Cir.2000). Congress partially codified these decisions in a 1996 amendment to § 276. The statute now states that a non-citizen charged with a violation of § 276 may not challenge the validity of the prior removal order unless he or she has exhausted all administrative remedies providing relief from the order, the removal proceeding denied the non-citizen effective judicial review, and the entry of the removal order was fundamentally unfair. INA § 276(d).

c. *Removal Consequences of Unlawful Entry*

Besides the criminal penalties imposed by INA §§ 275 and 276, a non-citizen who enters or re-enters the United States unlawfully may also be subject to removal. The non-citizen's guilty plea to a § 275 or § 276 charge will establish unlawful entry or re-entry for purposes of removal under § 237(a)(2). *See, e.g., Marroquin–Manriquez v. INS*, 699 F.2d 129 (3d Cir.1983). The Fifth Circuit in *Garcia–Trigo v. United States*, 671 F.2d 147 (5th Cir. 1982) held that the non-citizen need not be informed of the collateral immigration consequences of a conviction under § 275.

Although removal, rather than criminal penalties, is more often imposed in cases of unlawful entry, a non-citizen who is subject to removal under § 237(a)(1)(B) may also be subject to criminal prosecution. During the removal proceeding, once the government has established that the respondent is a non-citizen, the respondent has the burden of proof to show the time, place, and manner of his or her entry into the United States. If this burden is not sustained, the individual will be presumed to be in the U.S. in violation of law and thereby subject to criminal prosecution. INA § 291. Generally, since a removal hearing is not a criminal proceeding, there is no presumption of innocence, and therefore, no abridgement of the non-citizen's Fifth Amendment rights in requiring him or her to demonstrate the time, place, and manner of entry into the United States. *Chavez–Raya v. INS*, 519 F.2d 397 (7th Cir.1975); *Cabral–Avila v. INS*, 589 F.2d 957 (9th Cir.1978).

Because of potential criminal liability for unlawful entry under § 275 or § 276, however, the right to remain silent is available in removal proceedings under § 237(a)(1)(B). In *Cabral–Avila* the Ninth Circuit held that the non-citizen's decision to remain silent during removal proceedings was an appropriate exercise of his Fifth Amendment privilege. Nonetheless, silence did not shield the non-citizen from the adverse inference that he or she was in the U.S. illegally, nor did it satisfy the duty to rebut the government's prima facie case.

§ 14–2.2   Crimes Related to Facilitating a Non–Citizens' Unlawful Entry or Continued Unlawful Presence in the United States

a.   *Bringing Non–Citizens into the United States*

The INA contains two sections that impose criminal penalties on persons who unlawfully participate in bringing non-citizens into the U.S. The first, INA § 274(a)(1)(A), applies to any person who helps bring or attempts to bring a non-citizen into the country without inspection (*i.e.*, by crossing the border somewhere other than an official port of entry), even if the non-citizen had received prior official authorization to enter or reside in the United States. Unlike the related removal ground (*see* INA § 237(a)(1)(E)), this section does not provide an exemption when the person aiding the illegal entry is related to the non-citizen. The penalties imposed for this violation include a fine under Title 18, imprisonment up to ten years, or both, for each non-citizen in respect to whom the violation occurred. INA § 274(a)(1)(B). If the violation causes serious bodily injury to any person, the penalty may be increased to twenty years imprisonment; if the violation causes the death of any person, the maximum penalty is life imprisonment.

The second section, INA § 274(a)(2), applies to any person who, knowing or in reckless disregard of the fact that a non-citizen has not received prior official authorization to enter or reside in the United States, brings or attempts to bring that individual into the country, whether at an official port of entry or not. The penalties under this section include a fine under Title 18, imprisonment up to one year, or both, for each transaction constituting a violation of this section, regardless of the number of non-citizens involved. If the non-citizen is not immediately brought to an immigration officer for inspection, the penalty may be increased to as long as ten years imprisonment. If the offense was committed for commercial or financial gain, or if the offender brought a non-citizen into the United States with reason to believe that the non-citizen would commit an offense punishable by more than one year in prison, the penalty is at least three and not more than ten years imprisonment. For the offender's third or subsequent offense, the penalty is five to fifteen years imprisonment. A 2000 amendment also provides for the forfeiture of any vessel, vehicle, or aircraft used in violating this section, as well as forfeiture of the gross proceeds of the violation. INA § 274(b)(1).

Under § 274(a), penalties are to be imposed regardless of any further official action that may later be taken with respect to the non-citizen. No consideration is given to the manner in which the offender brought or attempted to bring the non-citizen into the United States. Under § 274(a)(1)(A)(v), conspiring to bring a non-citizen into the country illegally is a violation of the statute even if the plan does not succeed and the non-citizen never enters the United States. *See also* § 14–2.4, *infra.*

It is interesting to note that the 1986 amendments to INA § 274(a)(1)(A) were expressly intended to correct "shortcomings and ambiguities" identified in *United States v. Anaya*, 509 F.Supp. 289 (S.D.Fla.1980) and *United States v. Zayas–Morales*, 685 F.2d 1272 (11th Cir.1982). In those cases, the defendants had made no effort to land undocumented Cubans surreptitiously or evasively, but instead brought them directly to immigration officers in Key West, Florida, to apply for asylum. According to House Report No. 99–682(I), the Immigration Reform and Control Act of 1986 closed a perceived "gap" in the law that allowed smugglers to bring in large numbers of undocumented migrants, so long as the migrants immediately applied for asylum. Therefore, an individual may be charged and convicted under INA § 274(a)(1)(A) even if he or she is merely bringing an undocumented non-citizen to the border for purposes of applying for asylum.

Problems may arise in a criminal prosecution under § 274(a)(1)(A) or (a)(2) if, before trial, the government removes the non-citizen witnesses who allegedly were brought into the U.S. unlawfully. The defendant may claim that his or her Sixth Amendment right to call defense witnesses has been violated by the removal of these witnesses. In *United States v. Valenzuela–Bernal*, 458 U.S. 858 (1982), the Supreme Court held that to show a denial of due process through the removal of non-citizen witnesses, the defendant must show that the testimony of the removed witnesses would have been material and favorable to his or her defense in ways not merely cumulative to the testimony of available witnesses.

b. *Transporting a Non–Citizen Within the United States*

INA § 274(a)(1)(A)(ii) imposes a criminal penalty on any person who, knowing or in reckless disregard of the fact that a non-citizen has entered or remains in the United States in violation of the law, transports or attempts to transport the non-citizen within the United States, in furtherance of such violation of the law. To support a conviction for this offense, the government must prove that (1) the defendant transported or attempted to transport a non-citizen within the United States; (2) the non-citizen was in the United States in violation of the law; (3) the defendant knew the non-citizen was in the United States in violation of the law or acted in reckless disregard of this fact; and (4) the defendant acted willfully in furtherance of the non-citizen's violation of the law. The penalty for violating this section is a fine under Title 18, imprisonment for up to five years, or both. If the violation was committed for commercial advantage or private financial gain, the penalty may be increased to ten years imprisonment. If the violation results in the serious injury or death of any person, the penalty may be increased to twenty years or life imprisonment. INA § 274(a)(1)(B).

The mere transportation of a person known to be unlawfully present in the country is not a violation of this provision. The transportation must be "in furtherance of [the alien's] violation of law." The statute does not delineate the specific circumstances under which transportation of a non-citizen will constitute transportation "in furtherance of such violation of law." In *United States v. Moreno*, 561 F.2d 1321 (9th Cir.1977), the Ninth Circuit held that "there must be a direct or substantial relationship between [the] transportation and its furtherance of the [non-citizen's] presence in the United States." *Moreno* involved the transportation of undocumented workers by a foreman of a reforestation company who was required to transport employees from one job site to another. The court concluded that "his transportation of aliens was only incidentally connected with the furtherance of the violation of the law, if at all," and was thus "too attenuated" to come within the boundaries of the statute.

Other courts have looked to such factors as the defendant's relationship to the non-citizens and reason for transporting them, the distance and duration of the trip, and the defendant's role in organizing the trip, to determine whether the transportation was in furtherance of the non-citizen's unlawful presence. *See United States v. Barajas–Chavez*, 162 F.3d 1285 (10th Cir.1999). In *Barajas–Chavez*, the court found that the defendant, himself an undocumented non-citizen, had violated § 274 by planning a trip to bring several relatives and friends from Phoenix to Denver to seek employment, which, if successful, would have enabled them to remain in the United States unlawfully. In *United States v. Aguilar*, 883 F.2d 662 (9th Cir.1989) the court sustained the conviction of several individuals who had helped Arizona churches give sanctuary to Central Americans. The court found that the possibility that the non-citizens could obtain legal status by applying for asylum did not mean that they resided lawfully in the U.S. prior to their asylum application. In contrast, the Fifth Circuit held, in *United States v. Merkt*, 764 F.2d 266 (5th Cir.1985), that the defendant did not violate the statute by bringing a non-citizen to an INS office, since helping a non-citizen obtain legal status is, by definition, not in furtherance of the non-citizen's illegal presence in the U.S.

While a mistake of fact may constitute a valid defense to the crime of unlawfully transporting a non-citizen, a mistake of law will not. In *Merkt*, the defendant's belief that the non-citizens' genuine qualifications for political asylum entitled them to legal status even though they had not yet filed an asylum claim was held to be based on a mistake of law and therefore did not constitute a defense.

c. *Concealing, Harboring, or Shielding a Non–Citizen*

Under INA § 274(a)(1)(A)(iii), criminal penalties are imposed upon any person who, knowing or in reckless disregard of the fact that a non-citizen has "come to, entered, or remains in the United States in violation of law," conceals, harbors, or attempts to conceal or harbor the non-citizen in any place, including buildings or vehicles. A violation will subject the defendant to a fine under Title 18, imprisonment up to five years, or both, for each non-citizen in respect to whom the violation occurred. The penalty increases if the violation is committed for commercial or financial gain, or if a person is killed or seriously injured as a result of the violation.

Because INA § 274 is aimed at preventing undocumented non-citizens from remaining in the United States, not just preventing them from entering, the harboring need not be directly connected with the non-citizen's illegal entry to be prohibited. The activity need only substantially facilitate the person's continued unlawful presence in the United States. *United States v. Lopez*, 521 F.2d 437 (2d Cir.1975); *United States v. Cantu*, 555 F.2d 1327 (5th Cir.1977).

Prosecutions under this section typically involve cases where the defendant has provided housing and employment for many non-citizens, usually for financial gain. *See, e.g., United States v. Zheng*, 306 F.3d 1080 (11th Cir.2002). INA § 274(a) previously contained a clause providing "[t]hat for the purposes of this section, employment (including the usual and normal practices incident to employment) shall not be deemed to constitute harboring." The 1986 amendment to INA § 274(a) eliminated this exception; hence, an employer who actively assists an undocumented employee to avoid detection by immigration authorities may be prosecuted under § 274, rather than under § 274A, which covers unlawful employment.

d. Inducing a Non–Citizen to Enter

Under INA § 274(a)(1)(A)(iv), it is a crime to encourage or induce a non-citizen to come to, enter, or reside in the United States, knowing that such action is in violation of the law. The penalties for this crime are the same as those for harboring a non-citizen.

The defendant in *United States v. Hanna*, 639 F.2d 194 (5th Cir.1981) petitioned for a rehearing of his conviction under this section, claiming that he did not violate the statute because his passengers were paroled into the United States. The Fifth Circuit denied the rehearing, holding that parole "is simply a device through which needless confinement is avoided while administrative proceedings are conducted" and that parole "was never intended to affect an alien's status...." The court held that "[i]t would be a misuse of the parole concept to conclude that one who physically transports into the United States persons not otherwise entitled to come in cannot be guilty under [INA § 274(a)(1)(A)] if the United States grants parole to those brought in while it determines whether they should be given asylum."

The act of inducement or encouragement need not have been committed in the United States. For example, the Ninth Circuit in *United States v. Castillo–Felix*, 539 F.2d 9 (9th Cir.1976) upheld the defendant's conviction under this section for meeting a Mexican citizen in Mexico, giving her a false passport, and promising her employment if she reached the United States. The court reasoned that acts of inducement committed outside the United States may constitute crimes since such acts "have no purpose unless they are intended to facilitate the unlawful entry of an alien or his continued illegal presence in the United States." The effect of the inducement—the illegal entry—is felt in the United States, so "in terms of the regulation of immigration, it is unimportant where acts constituting the crime occur."

e. Aiding or Assisting a Subversive Non–Citizen to Enter the U.S.

Any person who knowingly aids or assists any criminal or subversive non-citizen inadmissible to enter the United States under INA § 212(a)(2) (because of an aggravated felony) or INA § 212(a)(3) (because of security or related grounds), or who connives or conspires with any person to permit any such non-citizen to enter the United States, can be fined under Title 18, or imprisoned not more than ten years, or both. INA § 277.

f. Importing a Non–Citizen for an Immoral Purpose

Under INA § 278, it is a felony offense to import, directly or indirectly, any non-citizen for prostitution or for any other immoral purpose. Attempts to import a non-citizen for such purposes are also covered by the statute. Similarly, it is an offense to hold a non-citizen for any such purpose or to "keep, maintain, control, support, employ, or harbor in any house or other place, for the purpose of prostitution or for any other immoral purpose" a non-citizen in pursuance of such illegal importation. Persons convicted of this offense may be punished by a fine under Title 18, imprisonment up to ten years, or both.

g. Immigration Consequences of Bringing In, Transporting, or Harboring Non–Citizens

In addition to the criminal penalties described above, bringing in, transporting, or harboring undocumented non-citizens can have immigration consequences for non-citizens who commit these acts. "Alien smuggling" is a ground of inadmissibility under INA § 212(a)(6)(E). An exception to this ground of inadmissibility is available, however, if the person the non-citizen helped to enter the United States was a close relative. Further, violations of

§ 274 are considered "aggravated felonies" under INA § 101(a)(43)(N). Consequently, a non-citizen who is convicted of one of these offenses will be subject to removal and can be permanently barred from the United States. *See* § 8–2.2, *supra*.

h.   Related Civil Penalties

Several sections of the INA provide civil penalties for certain acts related to bringing in non-citizens. For example, INA § 271 imposes a duty upon every person who brings a non-citizen to or provides the means for a non-citizen to come to the United States, "including the owners, masters, officers, and agents of vessels, aircraft, transportation lines or international bridges or toll roads," to prevent the unauthorized landing of non-citizens. Violators are subject to a $3,000 fine. Transportation lines must obtain a contract with immigration authorities to bring non-citizens into the United States from foreign territory. INA § 233(a); 8 C.F.R. § 233.1. Carriers who have such contracts are exempt from penalties under § 271. An owner or operator of a railroad line, international bridge, or toll road may also escape liability by establishing that it acted diligently and reasonably to prevent unauthorized landings, even though such a landing occurred. INA § 271(c)(1). Any owner or operator of a railroad line, international bridge, or toll road may request that the Attorney General inspect any facility or method used at a point of entry to the United States to comply with this provision. If the Attorney General has approved the facility or method, proof that the individual has diligently maintained the approved facility or used the approved method is prima facie evidence that the individual acted diligently and reasonably to fulfill the duty to prevent unauthorized landings. INA § 271(c).

The INA contains several other provisions that impose civil fines upon carriers. INA § 234 provides a $2,000 penalty for failure of an aircraft to land at a designated port of entry or for violating regulations related to such ports of entry. The failure or refusal of a transportation line to receive and remove an inadmissible non-citizen or to pay removal expenses, as ordered by the Attorney General, will subject the carrier to a $2,000 penalty for each violation under IIRIRA § 307(a); INA § 243. The failure to remove a stowaway subjects a carrier to a $5,000 penalty. IIRIRA § 307(a); INA § 243. A civil penalty also is imposed upon persons, including transportation lines and other vessel operators, who bring in non-citizens who do not have valid passports and unexpired visas, if a visa is required, or who fail to detain or remove a stowaway or removable crewmember. The penalty consists of a $3,000 fine per non-citizen, and in the case of a non-citizen who is not admitted or permitted to land temporarily, an additional amount equal to that amount paid by the non-citizen for his transportation from the initial point of departure. This additional amount paid is then returned to the non-citizen. Any amounts paid as a penalty for bringing in a non-citizen without an unexpired visa may be refunded if the Attorney General is convinced that the violator did not know, and could not have discovered by the exercise of reasonable diligence, that the individual transported was a non-citizen and that a visa was required. INA § 273.

§ 14–2.3 Failure to Comply With Registration Requirements

Although rarely enforced until 2002, INA § 262 provides that every non-citizen who remains in the United

States for thirty days or more must be registered and fingerprinted. Any person who "willfully fails or refuses" to register may be fined up to $1,000, imprisoned up to six months, or both. INA § 266(a). INA § 264 requires the immigration authorities to issue an "alien registration receipt card" to all arriving non-citizens, and requires non-citizens to carry this card at all times. Failure to comply with this requirement can result in a fine of $100, imprisonment for up to thirty days, or both. INA § 264(e).

These registration requirements have been part of immigration law since the Alien Registration Act of 1940, 54 Stat. 670, but for many decades they were not enforced. The INS routinely waived the fingerprinting requirements, and nonimmigrants received no registration card other than the Form I–94 Arrival–Departure record. (Permanent residents receive a Permanent Resident Card after admission to the U.S.) In 2002, however, the immigration authorities, acting under the authority of § 262(a), implemented special registration requirements for nonimmigrants from certain countries, principally in the Middle East. These requirements were intended to improve the ability of immigration authorities to monitor nonimmigrants whom it believes "present a heightened risk of involvement in terrorist or criminal activity." 67 Fed.Reg. 40581–01. Nonimmigrants subject to the special registration procedure (as identified by notices in the Federal Register) are fingerprinted and photographed upon arrival in the United States. If they remain in the U.S., they must report to an immigration office thirty days after arrival and annually thereafter to confirm compliance with the terms of their admission. At that time, the nonimmigrant must provide proof of residence, and employment or registration at an approved school.

Nonimmigrants subject to this rule must also report to an immigration officer when departing from the U.S. and are only allowed to depart from certain ports. Failure to comply with these requirements may result in the nonimmigrant being inadmissible in the future. 8 C.F.R. § 264.1. Some nonimmigrants already in the United States have been fingerprinted and photographed through "call-in registration" procedures.

The special registration requirements only apply to a small group of nonimmigrants. Under another provision, however, all non-citizens present in the United States, including permanent residents, must report changes of address to immigration authorities within ten days of such a change. INA § 265(a). Like the registration requirement, the change of address reporting requirement remained unenforced for several decades. When they published the special registration requirement, the immigration authorities announced their intention to begin enforcing the change of address requirement against all non-citizens. *See* 67 Fed.Reg. 40581–01. Failure to comply with this requirement may result in a misdemeanor conviction and a fine of $200, imprisonment for not more than thirty days, or both. A violation of this section also constitutes a ground of removal under INA § 237(a)(3).

A non-citizen who files an application for registration containing statements known by the applicant to be false or who registers or attempts to register through fraud is guilty of a misdemeanor. Upon conviction, such person may be fined up to $1,000, imprisoned up to six months, or both. INA § 266(c). Conviction will also render the non-citizen removable under INA § 237(a)(3). Other statutes dealing with conspiracy to defraud the United States also may penalize fraud or falsification in registration. *See* § 14–2.4, *infra*. Counterfeiting a certificate of alien registration or an alien registration receipt card is an offense punishable by a fine of up to $5,000, imprisonment up to five years, or both. INA § 266(d). Persons who manufacture and sell counterfeit cards also are punishable under 18 U.S.C.A. § 1426.

§ 14–2.4 Misrepresentation, False Statements, Fraud, and Conspiracy

a. Perjury

Several statutes apply to perjury in immigration proceedings. These statutes overlap to some extent, and depending on the situation, a prosecution can be brought under any of them.

The perjury provision of the Immigration and Nationality Act is contained in INA § 287(b). This statute empowers immigration officers and employees to administer oaths, and imposes criminal penalties on anyone who knowingly makes a false statement after taking an oath administered by an immigration officer.

18 U.S.C.A. § 1621 is the general perjury provision of the United States Code. It defines the crime of perjury as stating or subscribing as true a material matter which the declarant does not believe to be true, after taking an oath before a tribunal or government officer. The penalty for perjury is a fine or imprisonment up to five years, or both.

A third statute related to perjury in immigration proceedings is 22 U.S.C.A. § 4221. This statute authorizes certain embassy officials and consular officers to administer oaths, and directs that any person who "willfully and corruptly" commits perjury or "by any means procure[s] any person to commit perjury" before such officers may be prosecuted in any United States district court in the same manner as if the offense had been committed in the United States.

The fact that false statements made under oath may constitute perjury does not preclude prosecution under other applicable statutes. Because of the demanding requirements for proof of perjury, prosecutors often proceed under other statutes whose requirements are less stringent, such as laws dealing with false statements, fraud, misuse of documents, or conspiracy. *See* §§ 14–2.4(c)–(e), *infra*.

b.   False Claim to Citizenship

Under 18 U.S.C.A. § 911, persons who falsely and willfully represent themselves to be United States citizens may be fined and imprisoned for not more than three years. The misrepresentation of citizenship must be willful, in addition to being false. The Ninth Circuit in *Chow Bing Kew v. United States*, 248 F.2d 466 (9th Cir.1957) held that "willfully" means only that the misrepresentation was made voluntarily and deliberately and, therefore, the prosecution need not show that the misrepresentation was made for a fraudulent purpose. In reaching this conclusion, the court pointed out that § 911 was an amendment to a prior statute (35 Stat. 1088, 1103) which, in contrast, specifically required a fraudulent purpose. *See also De Pratu v. United States*, 171 F.2d 75 (9th Cir.1948); *United States v. Franklin*, 188 F.2d 182 (7th Cir.1951).

The statute reaches misrepresentations of citizenship in many contexts, including statements made to unions, in voting, in applying for a U.S. passport, in an immigration or naturalization proceeding, in a selective service questionnaire, in applying for a license, and in responding to questions of arresting police officers. Under some circumstances, the false representation of citizenship may constitute perjury. *See* § 14–2.4(a), *infra.* The false citizenship claim also may be punishable under 18 U.S.C.A. § 1001, which deals with false statements made to government officers, or under 18 U.S.C.A. § 1546, concerning fraud and misuse of visas and other documents. *See* §§ 14–2.4(c), (d), *infra.*

c.   *False or Fraudulent Statements and Representations*

18 U.S.C.A. § 1001 establishes a broad foundation for criminal penalties against false statements and misrepresentations in general. The statute makes it a crime to falsify or conceal a material fact, make a materially false or fraudulent statement, or use a false or fraudulent document, in "any matter within the jurisdiction of the executive, legislative, or judicial branch of the Government of the United States." The penalty for violating § 1001 is a fine or imprisonment of up to five years. This section applies to false statements and misrepresentations made to immigration and consular officers in a broad variety of immigration contexts. False statements made in applying for naturalization are specifically punishable under 18 U.S.C.A. § 1425. False statements made in applying for or use of a passport are punishable under 18 U.S.C.A. § 1542.

d.   *Fraud and Misuse of Visas, Permits, and Other Documents*

18 U.S.C.A. § 1546 criminalizes a wide variety of acts involving misuse of a visa, permit, or other document required for entry into the United States or as evidence of authorized stay or employment in the United States.

Offenses that are punishable under § 1546 include forging immigration visas or other entry documents; unauthorized possession of copies of immigration documents or the materials used to make such documents; selling or offering to sell a visa; making false statements in an application for immigration benefits; or using a false identification document to satisfy the requirements of the employment verification system.

Persons who violate any of the first five offenses in § 1546 may be fined in accordance with Title 18, imprisoned for up to ten years, or both. If the offense was committed to facilitate a drug trafficking crime, the maximum term of imprisonment increases to twenty years; it increases to twenty-five years if the offense was committed to facilitate an act of international terrorism. A person who uses false identification for employment verification is subject to a fine, imprisonment for up to five years, or both. Similarly, 18 U.S.C.A. §§ 1543 and 1544 provide for a fine and/or imprisonment for up to ten years (longer if the offense was committed to further a drug trafficking offense or act of terrorism), for forgery or misuse of a passport.

In addition to facing possible criminal penalties, a noncitizen who arrives in the United States with fraudulent documents is inadmissible and will be subject to expedited removal unless he or she indicates an intention to apply for asylum. *See* INA § 235(b). Expedited removal is discussed in § 9–2.3, *supra*.

e. Conspiracy

The general conspiracy statute, 18 U.S.C.A. § 371, provides yet another means of penalizing false statements, misrepresentations, and other fraud in immigration matters. This statute provides:

> If two or more persons conspire either to commit any offense against the United States, or to defraud the United States, or any agency thereof in any manner or for any purpose, and one or more of such persons do any act to effect the object of the conspiracy, each shall be fined under this title or imprisoned not more than five years, or both.

If, however, the conspired offense is a misdemeanor only, the punishment for the conspiracy must not exceed the maximum punishment provided for the misdemeanor. 18 U.S.C.A. § 371.

An individual may be convicted under both 18 U.S.C.A. § 371 and the statute relating to the substantive offense. *Pereira v. United States*, 347 U.S. 1 (1954). Showing participation in a conspiracy is often easier than proving a substantive crime. INA § 274 (a)(1)(A)(v) makes it a crime to conspire to bring in or harbor certain non-citizens. For that crime, a conspiracy can be shown under both the INA and 18 U.S.C.A. § 371.

f. Marriage Fraud

The Immigration Marriage Fraud Amendments of 1986 intended to deter non-citizens from seeking immigration benefits through a fraudulent marriage to a U.S. citizen or permanent resident. Those amendments, for example, impose a two-year residency requirement on non-citizen spouses before they may obtain unconditional permanent resident status on the basis of a "qualifying marriage" to a U.S. citizen or permanent resident. The Fraud Amendments also provide a criminal penalty for marriage fraud. INA § 275(c) states, "[a]n individual who knowingly enters into a marriage for the purpose of evading any provision of the immigration laws shall be imprisoned for not more than five years, or fined not more than $250,000, or both." The statute applies to the U.S. citizen or permanent resident and also to the non-resident involved in the fraudulent marriage. See § 5–2.1, *supra*, for a discussion of the Immigration Marriage Fraud Amendments of 1986.

§ 14–2.5 Failure to Comply With Removal Proceedings

a. *Failure to Comply With Supervision Regulations*

The Attorney General has a period of ninety days from the date of a non-citizen's final removal order within which to effect that person's departure from the United States. INA § 241(a)(1)(A). The removable non-citizen can be detained during this ninety-day period. INA § 241(a)(2). If removal cannot be arranged within that period, the non-citizen may be released subject to supervision. INA § 241(a)(3). The conditions of supervision include periodic reporting; submission, if necessary, to medical and psychiatric examination; testimony as to the non-citizen's "nationality, circumstances, habits, associations, and activities" and other such information as the Attorney General deems proper; as well as conformity to other written restrictions. Any non-citizen who willfully fails to comply with these requirements may be fined up to $1,000, imprisoned for up to one year, or both. INA § 243(b).

b. *Failure to Depart*

INA § 243(a) penalizes non-citizens who willfully fail or refuse to depart the United States within ninety days of the date of a final order of removal, or who willfully fail or refuse to apply in good faith for travel documents, connive or conspire to hamper their departure, or willfully fail or refuse to present themselves for removal at the time and place required in a removal order. The penalty for failure to depart is a fine under Title 18, imprisonment for up to four years, or both. INA § 243(a)(1). A non-citizen does not violate the statute, however, by taking any proper steps to secure cancellation of removal or other relief. INA § 243(2).

If the non-citizen who fails to depart is removable under INA §§ 237(a)(1)(E), (2), (3), or (4), he or she may be imprisoned for up to ten years. These sections prescribe removal for national security offenses, certain criminal convictions, and drug addiction.

Before a removable non-citizen can be convicted of a willful failure to depart, the country willing to receive the person must be identified. *Heikkinen v. United States*, 355 U.S. 273 (1958). The defendant in *Heikkinen* had been convicted for willful failure to depart. Because the government had not shown that any country would have admitted the defendant, the Supreme Court reversed, holding the evidence insufficient to support conviction.

§ 14–2.6   Employment of Undocumented Workers

The Immigration Reform and Control Act (IRCA) of 1986 was enacted as a response to growing concern that the United States had lost control over the influx of undocumented non-citizens to the country. IRCA attempted to control immigration by creating sanctions for the employment of unauthorized workers.

IRCA makes it unlawful for any person or entity to hire, recruit, or refer for a fee for employment in the United States, a non-citizen, knowing that the non-citizen is unauthorized with respect to such employment, or to hire any individual without complying with the employment verification system established under INA § 274A(b). INA § 274A(a)(1). It is also unlawful for a person or entity to continue employing a non-citizen, knowing that the employee is or has become unauthorized. INA § 274A(a)(2).

In addition to civil fines, which increase with multiple offenses, IRCA imposes criminal penalties upon persons and entities engaging in a "pattern or practice of violations." These penalties include a fine of up to $3,000 for each undocumented worker, imprisonment for up to six months, or both. INA § 274A(f)(1). The term "pattern or practice" means "regular, repeated and intentional activities, but does not include isolated, sporadic or accidental acts." *United States v. Mayton*, 335 F.2d 153 (5th Cir. 1964); *International Brotherhood of Teamsters v. United States*, 431 U.S. 324 (1977); *United States v. International Association of Iron Workers Local No. 1*, 438 F.2d 679 (7th Cir.1971). These interpretations were incorporated expressly into the legislative history accompanying the Immigration Reform and Control Act of 1986 by House Report No. 99–682(I).

Although IRCA imposes no penalties upon unauthorized non-citizens merely for working illegally, unauthorized non-citizens seeking employment in the United States must attest under penalty of perjury that he or she is a citizen or national of the U.S.; a permanent resident; or otherwise authorized to be hired, recruited, or referred for employment. INA § 274A(b)(2). Similarly, the employer must attest under penalty of perjury that it has verified that the individual is not an unauthorized non-citizen by examining documents that establish employment authorization and the identity of the individual.

The employer sanctions do not apply to individuals who were hired, recruited, or referred before November 6, 1986. An employer also may establish an affirmative defense to an allegation of unlawful employment by showing that it has complied in good faith with the requirements of the employment verification system. INA § 274A(a)(3). Although the employer sanctions do not apply to continuing employment of a non-citizen who was hired before November 6, 1986, the felony provisions of INA § 274, which penalize the concealing, harboring, or shielding of undocumented non-citizens, may still apply. IRCA § 112(a) removed from INA § 274 an earlier clause providing that employment does not constitute harboring. The removal from INA § 274 of the so-called "Texas Proviso" was a considerable departure from prior law, which had excepted mere employment from conduct constituting a harboring offense. *See* § 13–4.7, *supra* (discussing labor laws).

§ 14–3 IMMIGRATION CONSEQUENCES OF CRIMINAL ACTIVITY

A non-citizen convicted of a crime generally will suffer the penalties prescribed by statute. A criminal conviction, however, may have a direct effect on the individual's immigration status as well. The effect of the conviction may be felt almost immediately, as when conviction of the crime constitutes a ground for removal, or the impact of the conviction may not occur for several years, as when conviction of the crime precludes the showing of good moral character necessary for naturalization. In this context, it is important to note that the removal provisions of the INA frequently apply retroactively, such that a person may become removable for a past crime if Congress makes that crime a ground of removal. In *Padilla v. Kentucky*, 130 S.Ct. 1473 (2010), the Supreme Court acknowledged that immigration law has dramatically increased the consequences of a criminal conviction for a non-citizen. Accordingly, the Court held that non-citizens may raise Sixth Amendment ineffectiveness of counsel claims if their attorneys fail to advise them of the immigration consequences of accepting a guilty plea. *Id.*

§ 14–3.1   Ineligibility for Admission

A person seeking to enter the United States may be ineligible for admission because of prior criminal activity. INA § 212 provides several categories of crimes that make the perpetrator inadmissible. These inadmissibility grounds apply equally to non-citizens who seek entry to the United States for the first time, to persons who, after residing in the United States for a period of time, seek re-entry after a temporary departure (although some exceptions apply for permanent residents—*see* § 8–1.1(b), *supra*), and the persons seeking adjustment of status.

The grounds of inadmissibility include (1) being convicted of, or admitting to the commission of a "crime of moral turpitude"; (2) being convicted of two or more offenses of any type for which the aggregate sentence was five or more years; (3) trafficking in controlled substances; (4) coming to the U.S. to engage in prostitution; (5) previously departing from the U.S. as a condition of receiving immunity from prosecution; (6) engaging in severe violations of religious freedom as an official in a foreign government; (7) engaging in or benefiting from trafficking in persons; and (8) laundering money. *See* INA § 212(a)(2). Waivers are available for some of these grounds. *See, e.g.*, INA § 212(h). In addition to these crimes, membership in or support for a terrorist organization is also a ground of inadmissibility. INA § 212(a)(3).

The "crime of moral turpitude" is perhaps the most difficult ground of inadmissibility to define. Some of the specific crimes that have been found to involve moral turpitude include murder, rape, robbery, kidnapping, voluntary manslaughter, theft, spousal abuse, and any crime involving fraud (such as passing bad checks). Designating a crime as one involving moral turpitude is often, but not always, based on the intent element of the crime. Consequently, whether a particular criminal act has immigration consequences will depend on the statute under which the perpetrator is charged.

See § 8–1.2, *supra*, for further discussion of the grounds of inadmissibility.

§ 14–3.2 Removal

Removal also may be a direct result of a non-citizen's involvement in criminal activity. INA § 237 lists several grounds for removal related to criminal activity. For a discussion of these grounds, see § 8–2.2, *supra*.

Among the criminal grounds of removal are aggravated felonies. The definition of "aggravated felony" includes rape, sexual abuse of a minor, money laundering, crimes of violence for which the term of imprisonment is at least one year, theft, burglary, kidnapping, child pornography,

Racketeering Influenced and Corrupt Organizations (RICO) offenses, running a prostitution business, transporting people for the purpose of prostitution, fraud offenses where the loss exceeds $10,000, forgery, obstruction of justice, and other crimes. INA § 101(a)(43). As with crimes of moral turpitude, these offenses range from very serious crimes to relatively minor ones. The consequences of being convicted of an aggravated felony are severe. In addition to being subject to removal, noncitizens convicted of such offenses are permanently barred from re-entering the U.S. and may be sentenced for up to twenty years in prison if they re-enter illegally. INA §§ 212(a)(9)(i)(A), 276(b). Persons convicted of aggravated felonies are subject to mandatory detention, can be removed, and are ineligible for most forms of relief from removal. INA §§ 236, 238, 240A, 240B. *See* § 8–2.2(b), *supra*. The Supreme Court in *Carachuri–Rosendo v. Holder*, 130 S.Ct. 2577 (2010) concluded that the state definition of the crime for which an immigrant is convicted must correspond to a federal definition in order for an aggravated felony to be found. The government may not consider any circumstances of the crime beyond the definition.

Many states require defense attorneys to advise noncitizen defendants as to the immigration consequences of pleading guilty to a crime. *See, e.g., People v. Soriano*, 240 Cal.Rptr. 328 (Cal.App.1987). Some courts have allowed the withdrawal of a guilty plea upon a showing of ineffective assistance of counsel, for failure to research or explain the immigration consequences of the plea. *See, e.g., State v. Lopez*, 379 N.W.2d 633 (Minn.App.1986) and *People v. Pozo*, 746 P.2d 523 (Colo.1987). The majority rule, however, is that an attorney's failure to advise a client of the immigration consequences of a guilty plea does not constitute ineffective assistance of counsel. *See, e.g., State v. McFadden*, 884 P.2d 1303 (Utah 1994).

§ 14–3.3   Failure to Establish Good Moral Character

Conviction of a crime may prevent a non-citizen from establishing good moral character, which is a statutory prerequisite to a number of immigration benefits. These benefits include naturalization (INA § 316), voluntary departure (INA § 240B), cancellation of removal (INA § 240A), and registry (INA § 249). A petitioner for naturalization or voluntary departure must establish good moral character during the five years prior to application. A person seeking cancellation of removal must show good moral character during the previous ten years, unless he or she is a battered spouse or child, in which case only three years of good moral character are required. INA § 240A(b). An applicant for registry need only show that he or she is presently of good moral character. INA § 249(c). For a discussion of what constitutes "good moral character," see § 12–2.2(b)(4), *supra*.

§ 14–3.4   Denial of Asylum

Another possible consequence of a non-citizen's criminal activity is denial of that person's application for asylum or termination of asylum status. An immigration judge or asylum officer must deny a request for asylum if it is determined that the applicant has been convicted of an aggravated felony or who, "[h]aving been convicted by a final judgment of a particularly serious crime in the United States, constitutes a danger to the community of the United States." Further, even if the asylum seeker has not been convicted of a crime, asylum will be denied if there are reasons to believe that he or she has committed a serious nonpolitical crime or otherwise poses a danger to the security of the United States. INA § 208(b)(2). Restriction on removal (formerly "withholding of removal") also must be denied for such reasons. INA § 241(b)(3)(B)(iv).

Similarly, once granted asylum, a person's asylum status will be terminated if he or she becomes a danger to the United States as described in § 208(b)(2). INA § 208(c)(2). Asylum status also will be terminated if there is a showing of fraud in the asylee's application, such that he or she was not eligible for asylum at the time it was granted. 8 C.F.R. § 208.24. Once an individual's asylum status is terminated, that person, unless eligible for other immigration benefits, will be subject to removal proceedings.

A person who has been denied asylum or whose asylum has been terminated may be able to avoid removal or even extradition under the Convention Against Torture. The Convention prohibits the removal of a person to a country if there are substantial grounds for believing that he or she would be subject to torture there. Individuals who are granted relief under the Convention Against Torture do not thereby obtain a regular immigration status, but they may not be removed to the country where they would be subject to torture. *See* 8 C.F.R. § 208.17; *see also* chapter 10, *supra*.

CHAPTER 15

ETHICAL DIMENSIONS OF IMMIGRATION PRACTICE

Immigration lawyers are confronted by ethical issues more often than the majority of other practitioners. The non-citizen clients of the immigration lawyer are often suspicious about the fairness of United States laws and administrative practices and are usually unfamiliar with them. Some non-citizens may try to suggest or pursue courses of conduct from their culture that might be inappropriate or, perhaps, unethical for a lawyer in the United States. In addition, immigration lawyers are frequently confronted with issues of dual representation. Hence, the student of immigration law should be aware of the ethical dimensions of an immigration practice.

This chapter analyzes three typical ethical problems encountered by the immigration lawyer from the perspective of the Model Rules of Professional Conduct and the relevant provisions of the Code of Federal Regulations. The three problems deal with common situations faced by immigration lawyers:

Problem 1: The non-citizen is in violation of his or her immigration status, or has fraudulently married to gain permanent resident status. Must the lawyer report his or her client to the immigration authorities?

Problem 2: A non-citizen consults the lawyer about admission to the United States. The client is qualified for

a student visa, but in discussing the non-citizen's ultimate objectives, the lawyer learns that the client may
want eventually to become an immigrant and a United
States citizen. If the non-citizen has a present intent to
immigrate to the United States, he or she would be
ineligible for the student visa. What should the lawyer
tell the client?

Problem 3: An immigration lawyer is paid by a company to obtain a visa for an employee or potential employee. In the course of the representation the lawyer learns
facts—such as the employee's career plans—which may
be adverse to the new employer's interest. What should
the lawyer do? Can he or she tell the employer? Whom
does the lawyer actually represent?

While each problem will be examined in some detail,
this chapter does not attempt to provide definitive answers but merely raises the ethical issues. Several standards address these issues.

This chapter discusses two sources of ethical constraint
on the immigration lawyer. The first source is the Model
Rules adopted by the American Bar Association (ABA) in
1983. The Model Rules have now been adopted by forty-
nine states and the District of Columbia, either completely or with modifications. California is the only state that
maintains a set of rules for professional conduct not
based on the Model Rules.

The second source derives from the regulations governing the conduct of lawyers who appear before the Department of Homeland Security. In 1996, the Code of Federal
Regulations listed fifteen nonexclusive reasons for sus-
pending or disbarring the immigration lawyer, some of
which overlap the Model Rules and some of which are
unique to immigration practice. 8 C.F.R. § 292.3. In

2000, the grounds for suspension or disbarment were moved to 8 C.F.R. § 1003.102. 65 Fed.Reg. 39513–01. In 2008, the Executive Office for Immigration Review added more grounds for disciplining an immigration lawyer. Many of these additional grounds are similar to grounds for attorney sanction under the Model Rules, such as failing to provide competent representation or failing to maintain communication with a client. 8 C.F.R. § 1003.102(*o*) and (r). The 2008 additions also provide a ground for disciplining any attorney that "engages in conduct that is prejudicial to the administration of justice or undermines the integrity of the adjudicative process." 8 C.F.R. § 1001.102(n). 8 C.F.R. § 292.3 lists the general rules and procedure for disciplining a practitioner.

§ 15–1 MUST THE LAWYER REPORT HIS OR HER CLIENT TO THE IM-MIGRATION AUTHORITIES?

Problem 1: The non-citizen is in violation of his or her immigration status, or has fraudulently married to gain permanent resident status. Must the lawyer report his or her client to the immigration authorities?

A situation that frequently confronts the immigration lawyer is when the attorney becomes aware, through discussions with the client, independent investigation, or other outside sources, that the client is not observing his or her visa conditions. For example, a student-client with an F–1 visa accepts employment outside the educational institution without the requisite permission. See chapter 7, *supra*, for a discussion of F–1 visas. Under these circumstances, what is the lawyer's obligation to (a) report the client's violation of immigration status to the immigration authorities and/or (b) advise the client as to the possible consequences of accepting employment?

Similarly, an immigration attorney is occasionally confronted with a non-citizen who marries a U.S. citizen for the purpose of acquiring permanent resident status. Congressional studies indicate that about 8% of marriages between foreign nationals and U.S. citizens are fraudulent. *See* 8 U.S.C.A. § 1375. What if the attorney becomes suspicious that his or her client is involved in a sham marriage solely to attain permanent resident status? Does the attorney have an obligation to report his or her client's fraudulent marriage to the immigration authorities? Would disclosure violate lawyer-client confidentiality requirements?

§ 15–1.1   Reporting the Client's Activities

Under the provisions of the Model Rules, the lawyer appears to face competing mandates concerning whether to report the client. On the one hand, the Model Rules require the attorney not to reveal a confidence except in a limited number of circumstances. Model Rules of Professional Conduct Rule 1.6 (2010). In addition, Rule 1.6 prohibits any use of the confidence that disadvantages the client. In the F–1 student example, the information about the student's employment is a client confidence or secret because it was obtained in the course of representing the client. Similarly, information regarding a client's fraudulent marriage received in the course of representing that client is also a client confidence or secret. In the former case, if the attorney informed the immigration authorities of the client's employment, the client could be deprived of the student visa and possibly removed. Likewise, if the attorney informed the immigration authorities of his or her client's fraudulent marriage, that client could be denied resident status, prosecuted, fined, removed, and/or subject to a bar for readmission. Hence, it appears the lawyer cannot disclose the information to the immigration authorities without violating the Model Rules.

On the other hand, the Model Rules and the applicable C.F.R. provision, however, prohibit the lawyer from making false statements to the immigration authorities. According to the Model Rules, the lawyer shall not "knowingly ... make a false statement of material fact or law to a third person." Model Rules of Professional Conduct Rule 4.1(a)(2010). The Code of Federal Regulations contains similar language. 8 C.F.R. § 1003.102. On certain applications, the lawyer is required by law to reveal information about his or her client. If the lawyer knowingly makes a false statement on these forms, he or she is subject to substantial penalties. *See, e.g., United States v. Lew*, 875 F.2d 219 (9th Cir.1989) (immigration attorney convicted of making false statements to Department of Labor).

Attorneys who knowingly make false statements can also be criminally liable for their unethical conduct. In *United States v. Maniego*, the court affirmed the conviction of a lawyer whom a jury found to have knowingly prepared immigration documents that were based on fraudulent marriages in violation of 18 U.S.C.A. §§ 371 and 1546. *United States v. Maniego*, 710 F.2d 24 (2d Cir. 1983). Similarly in *United States v. Zalman*, the court affirmed the conviction of a lawyer who failed to disclose a fraudulent marriage in violation of 18 U.S.C.A. § 1001. *United States v. Zalman*, 870 F.2d 1047 (6th Cir.1989). An attorney that makes a material representation that he or she later discovers to be false must take "appropriate remedial measures''. 8 C.F.R. § 1003.102(c); *see also Matter of Shah*, 24 I. & N. Dec. 282, Interim Decision (BIA) 3580 (BIA 2007) (disciplining an attorney for failing to correct information in a Labor Condition Application he later learned to be false).

In such circumstances, a lawyer faces either violating the mandate regarding client confidences or violating the mandate regarding false statements. The Model Rules provide no clear answer. This immigration lawyer's dilemma, however, is not without resolution. A minority of states, such as Minnesota, provide that a lawyer's duty to the tribunal always trumps her duty to preserve the client's confidence. Minnesota Rules of Professional Conduct 3.3[10](2005). The Model Rules suggest that the lawyer is charged with preserving client confidences only within the bounds of the law. Hence, while a lawyer cannot volunteer information about the client's activities to the immigration authorities, he or she must advise the client to answer truthfully. The lawyer does not impermissibly violate a client confidence when he or she proceeds with an application at a client's request and truthfully answers a direct question because to make a false statement would violate the law.

§ 15–1.2   Advising the Client

Under the circumstances of this problem the Model Rules apparently require the lawyer to discuss the probable consequences of the client's actions with the client. Rule 2.1 of the Model Rules requires the lawyer to render candid advice in his or her role as advisor to the client. In a comment to the rules, the Committee notes:

> [W]hen a lawyer knows that a client proposes a course of action that is likely to result in substantial adverse

legal consequences to the client, the lawyer's duty to the client ... may require that the lawyer offer advice....

In the case of the F–1 student, the client may suffer such adverse consequences as loss of visa and removal. If the client later qualifies for an immigrant visa, the client, at a minimum, may be required to pursue immigrant status outside the United States.

The client may not have realized the adverse consequences of his or her decision to accept employment at the time it was made. Therefore, the lawyer's obligation to his or her client is to inform the client of the negative consequences of violating the visa conditions. The strength of the obligation may depend on whether the lawyer learns of the student's employment before or after the work commences. If the lawyer learns of the student's intention before the employment begins, the duty to act is stronger because the lawyer can prevent the adverse consequences by rendering the correct legal advice. If the lawyer learns afterwards, the duty to act is not as great because the legal consequences (loss of visa, removal, and ineligibility to adjust status in the United States) would have already become applicable. Nonetheless, a lawyer might advise the client against continued employment because the immigration authorities might take more severe enforcement action against a client who has been illegally employed for a longer period. Upon fulfilling this duty to inform a client, the lawyer should withdraw from representation of a client who persists in presenting an untruthful application for immigration benefits.

§ 15–2   SHOULD THE LAWYER TELL THE CLIENT ABOUT A FIXED INTENT TO IMMIGRATE?

Problem 2: A non-citizen consults the lawyer about admission to the United States. The client is qualified for a student visa, but in discussing the non-citizen's ultimate objectives, the lawyer learns that the client may want eventually to become an immigrant and a United States citizen. If the non-citizen has a present intent to immigrate to the United States, he or she would be ineligible for the student visa. What should the lawyer tell the client?

Different sorts of ethical problems are raised in advising the client regarding his or her fixed intent to immigrate to the United States. The problem arises when a client, otherwise eligible for a nonimmigrant visa, for example an F–1 student visa, informs the lawyer that he or she wants to immigrate to the United States. The client would be ineligible for the F–1 visa and certain other nonimmigrant visas, however, if he or she has a present intent to immigrate. What should the lawyer tell the client to do? If the lawyer tells the client not to form a present intent to immigrate, would the lawyer be assisting the client in perpetrating a fraud?

The Model Rules have sections dealing with client fraud and the lawyer's duty. Rule 1.2(d) of the Model Rules refers most directly to this situation: "[a] lawyer shall not counsel a client to engage, or assist a client, in conduct that the lawyer knows is criminal or fraudulent...." *See also* the similar language in 8 C.F.R. § 1003.102. These provisions, however, do not resolve whether the client commits a fraud in declaring that he or she has no present intent to immigrate. It is not clear that the lawyer would assist the client in committing a fraud or in preserving false evidence by discussing the effect of the client's intent on his or her immigration status. The situation is made more complex because only the client knows his or her own intent. An attorney, however, can advise the client as to the consequences of pursuing a specific course of conduct, which is separate from the question of the client's intent. The key is for the lawyer to convey that information before the client describes his intent in detail, which could foreclose the lawyer from assisting the client further.

Other sections of the Model Rules imply that the lawyer has an obligation to discuss the probable consequences of alternate courses of action with the client. Rule 1.2 of the Model Rules prohibits the lawyer from assisting the client in fraudulent conduct, but "a lawyer may discuss the legal consequences of any proposed course of conduct with a client and may counsel or assist a client to make a good faith effort to determine the validity, scope, meaning or application of the law." Model Rule 1.2(d). In this situation, the lawyer is not urging the client to adopt one course of action over another. Rather, he or she is merely discussing the client's two legal alternatives—to form a present intent to become an immigrant or a nonimmigrant—and the legal effects of each. The lawyer explains the consequences and the client makes the decision about his or her present intent. Such advice does not appear to be the kind of fraud contemplated by the Model Rules.

In addition, one might draw inferences from the drafting history of the Model Rules. In an earlier discussion draft of the Model Rules, Rule 2.3(a)(2) declared that a lawyer could not give advice that he or she "could reasonably foresee would ... aid the client in contriving false testimony." No counterpart to this draft Rule 2.3 appears in the Model Rules adopted in 1983. From this omission one could infer (1) that the drafting committee did not consider this advice an ethical violation, (2) that in a criminal law context this draft provision would be inappropriate, or (3) possibly that Rule 1.2 already covered this situation. In any case, even if draft Rule 2.3(a)(2) had appeared in the final version, the lawyer's advice would be unethical only in the unlikely event that it aided the client in contriving false testimony. Hence, the immigration lawyer probably can explain the consequences of the client's present intent to immigrate or his or her eligibility for a nonimmigrant visa without ethical violation, so long as the lawyer does not suggest which course of action the client should actually adopt.

The 1990 Act addressed this dilemma to an extent by recognizing the "dual intent" of many non-citizens seeking nonimmigrant visa status under the H and L categories. *See* §§ 6–8, 6–12, *infra.* Under the 1990 Act, a temporary worker with an H visa or a transferee with an L visa is not precluded from eventually seeking an adjustment of his or her status to that of a permanent resident. The problem still exists, however, with regard to several other nonimmigrant statuses, such as B, F, and J.

§ 15–3 WHOM DOES THE LAWYER REPRESENT?

Problem 3: An immigration lawyer is paid by a company to obtain a visa for an employee or potential employee. In the course of the representation the lawyer learns facts—such as the employee's career plans—which may be adverse to the new employer's interest. What should the lawyer do? Can he or she tell the employer? Whom does the lawyer actually represent?

The third problem concerns the lawyer who is retained by an employer to secure the proper work authorization for a present or prospective non-citizen employee. For example, consider an engineering company that hires the lawyer to obtain an L–1 visa for a non-citizen engineer. Although the company retained the lawyer, the lawyer is viewed as being in a dual representation situation. The non-citizen employee becomes a client during the petition process because the process usually requires the lawyer to obtain confidential information from the non-citizen employee and the lawyer may be asked to give legal advice regarding the non-citizen employee's visa eligibility. The lawyer is now in a dual representation because he or she is seen as representing two co-clients in a single matter. Dual representation also results when the non-citizen employee retains the lawyer. When the firm agrees to help the non-citizen employee by filing the petition through the lawyer, the firm agrees to representation by the lawyer.

Lawyers in dual representation must take special care from the outset since two ethical concerns are raised. First, the lawyer must consider whether the interests of each client can be represented without conflict. The Model Rules state in Rule 1.7 that:

> [A] lawyer shall not represent a client if the representation involves a concurrent conflict of interest. A concurrent conflict of interest exists if: (1) the representation of one client will be directly adverse to another client; or (2) there is a significant risk that the representation of one or more clients will be materially

limited by the lawyer's responsibilities to another client, a former client or a third person or by a personal interest of the lawyer.

In most cases the interests of the non-citizen employee and the company will coincide in that the company needs the skills of the individual and the non-citizen employee wants to work for the company in the United States. Nonetheless, in representing both the company and the non-citizen employee, the company's interest could end up being directly adverse to the non-citizen's interest. For example, the possibility exists that in discussing the non-citizen's ultimate career goals, the lawyer learns that the non-citizen plans eventually to open his or her own engineering firm. The non-citizen's interest is adverse to the employer's interest. In addition, the lawyer now faces a separate conflict of interest. Client confidences are protected under the Model Rules. Rule 1.6 of the Model Rules provides that the "lawyer shall not reveal information relating to the representation of a client" except in a limited number of circumstances such as to prevent the commission of a very serious crime.

It appears that the lawyer cannot reveal the non-citizen's statement to the employer, but at the same time the lawyer has a duty to keep the employer informed. Model Rule 1.4 states that "[a] lawyer shall ... (3) keep the client reasonably informed about the status of the matter."

These potential conflicts of interest and confidentiality problems are not insurmountable. Rule 1.7 allows a lawyer to represent clients with conflicting interests if the lawyer reasonably believes that the representation of each client will not adversely affect the relationship with the other and that each client consents to the arrangement after consultation. According to the Comment to Rule 1.7, the lawyer should consider "the likelihood that a difference in interests will eventuate and, if it does, whether it will materially interfere with the lawyer's independent professional judgment in considering alternatives or foreclose courses of action that reasonably should be pursued on behalf of the client." The lawyer also should consider whether each client is willing to accommodate the other interest involved. Because of their common interest in allowing the employee to work for the employer, each may be willing to accommodate the other's interests.

With full disclosure of the potential for conflict and the consent of the parties to the lawyer's role in representing them both, the lawyer can represent the non-citizen and the employer, sharing relevant information between the two. Hence, dual representation is ethically possible, but lawyers must take the proper action from the *beginning*. Before representation, lawyers need to obtain consent from both clients after full disclosure. Lawyers should also seek consent to limit the scope of representation. Model Rule 1.2(c) states "[a] lawyer may limit the scope of the representation if the limitation is reasonable under the circumstances and the client gives informed consent." For example, the lawyer and the two clients could agree that the scope of representation for the non-citizen employee is limited to obtaining the visa and that the lawyer will not disclose confidential information given by either the employer or the employee unless required by law. The lawyer would need to explain to the non-citizen employee that he or she would be reviewing some information pertinent to the petition process, such as prevailing wage determinations, to which the non-citizen employee will not be privy.

As stated above, the lawyer will have to make adequate disclosure to both clients to obtain effective consent. Model Rule 1.6, pertaining to confidentiality of information, states that "[a] lawyer shall not reveal information relating to the representation of a client unless the client gives informed consent. . . ." Similarly, Model Rule 1.7, concerning conflicts of interest, states that "[n]otwithstanding the existence of a concurrent conflict of interest . . . a lawyer may represent a client if . . . (4) each affected client gives informed consent, confirmed in writing." The level of disclosure required will vary, but enough information should be provided to allow each client to make an informed decision on whether to continue with representation. Model Rule 1.0(e) defines "informed consent" as "the agreement by a person to a proposed course of conduct after the lawyer has communicated adequate information and explanation about the material risks of and reasonably available alternatives to the proposed course of conduct."

Certain disclosures particularly relevant to the employer-employee hypothetical include: (1) potential problems during the application process, (2) specific conflicts of interest that may arise, including disclosures that must be made to the immigration authorities, (3) full or limited waivers of confidentiality, and (4) ethical constraints of dual representation and why the lawyer is obtaining written consent. Disclosure and written consent can be accomplished on a single consent form. This form should be drafted with care and tailored to each client's circumstances. The form should also be explained to each client before signing.

In the event a conflict of interest or confidentiality issue arises without the lawyer obtaining written consent at the start of dual representation, the lawyer will likely be forced to withdraw. The lawyer must withdraw from representing both clients in that matter if the lawyer cannot use independent judgment on each client or cannot assure each client that his or her confidences will not be breached. Alternatively, the lawyer may attempt to obtain consent when the conflict arises, but the duties of loyalty and confidentiality will often make this nearly impossible.

CHAPTER 16

CONCLUSION

The immigration laws and administrative structure and procedures described in this Nutshell have changed significantly in the twenty-six years since the publication of the first edition. Beyond landmark legislation like IRCA (1986), the 1990 Act, AEDPA (1996), IIRIRA (1996), and the Homeland Security Act (2002), the immigration authorities and the judiciary continually revise and clarify the regulations that form the foundation for practicing immigration law. After September 11, 2001, the threat of terrorism stimulated efforts to increase border security and tighten visa and admission procedures. These security concerns have led to increases in funding and staffing for the Department of Homeland Security and agencies the Department oversees: the Border Patrol, Immigration and Customs Enforcement, and Citizenship and Immigration Services. As a result, immigration authorities are apprehending, detaining, prosecuting, and removing undocumented immigrants at unprecedented rates. Many delays and frustrations remain, however, for persons seeking visas to enter the United States or obtain citizenship.

Congress and the Administration have undertaken reforms to modernize immigration procedures, to resolve at least partially the very difficult problems created by the hundreds of thousands—if not millions—of non-citizens who wish to live in the United States, and to decide which non-citizens should be allowed to immigrate. Many elected representatives, immigration officials, and lawyers recognize that new reforms are necessary to improve the current immigration system, but the debate over immigration reform has proven to be contentious and polarizing. Nonetheless, immigration concerns will continue to persist. Population analysts have noted that the U.S. may suffer a severe shortage of workers in coming decades and that immigration will be an important way of supplying workers for the U.S. economy. During periods of high unemployment and economic distress, however, immigration becomes particularly unpopular and the long-term needs of the U.S. economy may be ignored.

Hence, students should be aware that the target at which they are shooting is, indeed, moving and will require continued attention.

It seems appropriate to conclude this Nutshell by making a general observation about the nature of immigration law practice. Faced with all the detailed requirements for visas and other immigration remedies about which this volume says so much, some advocates, including attorneys, and their clients devote most of their attention to gathering the minimum information necessary to fulfill the various requirements. Unfortunately, some lawyers and almost all unrepresented non-citizens do not view the immigration process as an appropriate place for intelligent advocacy. This tendency has been addressed by groups such as the American Immigration Lawyers Association (AILA) which, through seminars and publications, has sought to raise the level of expertise in the practice of immigration law.

Ultimately, it is the duty of immigration lawyers to muster the relevant facts in such a way as to convince immigration officers that the lawyers' clients should receive the appropriate immigration status. One should never forget when submitting an application that one has the power to establish the record on which the client's case will be won or lost. In addition, lawyers should remember that immigration officers are administrative decision-makers who ought to receive the same sort of attention and polite, effective advocacy as judges. Certainly, immigration laws and the multitude of immigration forms about which the student has read are not invitations to forget all the advocacy skills used in other contexts.

CHAPTER 17

BIBLIOGRAPHY

This chapter suggests some principal references for research in immigration law. Items which are starred (*) might be found in the core immigration law library of an immigration practitioner or serious student.

§ 17–1 LAWS AND REGULATIONS

8 U.S.C.—Aliens and Nationality (Codification of the Immigration and Nationality Act, Pub. L. 414, ch. 477, 66 Stat. 163, June 27, 1952; and its subsequent amendments. This is the basic source of immigration law).*

The U.S. Code (incorporating all the Public Laws listed in this section) is available at http://www.gpoaccess.gov/uscode. Westlaw has a database of immigration-related statutes at FIM–USCA; LexisNexis has a similar database at Area of Law—By Topic > Immigration > Find Statutes & Regulations > USCS—Immigration—Titles 8, 18, 29 and 42.

22 U.S.C.—Foreign Affairs (Laws regulating the activities of U.S. consulates).*

8 C.F.R.—(Regulations governing immigration procedures).*

The Code of Federal Regulations (including all regulations listed in this section) is available at http:// www.gpoaccess.gov/ecfr.

20 C.F.R.—(Labor Department regulations, including alien labor certification).*

22 C.F.R.—(Foreign relations regulations giving procedures and guidelines to U.S. consulates for issuing visas and passports).*

Agency Interpretations of Immigration Policy: Cables, Memos, and Liaison Minutes (Randy P. Auerbach ed., Washington, DC: American Immigration Lawyers Assoc., 2007).

Antiterrorism and Effective Death Penalty Act of 1996, Pub. L. 104–132, 110 Stat. 1214, Apr. 24, 1996.*

Bender's Immigration Regulations Service (New York, NY: Matthew Bender, 1994–) (2 vols. looseleaf updated bimonthly).

Bender's Immigration and Nationality Act Pamphlet (New York, NY: Matthew Bender, 1987–) (Immigration and Nationality Act, issued annually).

Scott M. Borene, *Global Immigration Guide: Crossing Borders for Business* (Washington, DC: American Immigration Lawyers Assoc., 2002).

Enhanced Border Security and Visa Entry Reform Act of 2002, Pub. L. 107–173, 116 Stat. 543, May 14, 2002.*

Extradition Laws and Treaties, United States (Igor I. Kavass & Adolf Sprudzs, comps., Buffalo, NY: W.S. Hein, 1980–2007) (4 vols. looseleaf).

Federal Immigration Laws and Regulations (St. Paul, MN: West Group, 1993–) (1 vol. containing the basic statutes and regulations, issued annually).*

Federal Register (daily newspaper-like publication that updates the C.F.R. and publishes proposed rules, regulations, and notices from federal administrative agencies).

The *Federal Register* is available online at http://www.gpoaccess.gov/fr/index.html.

Homeland Security Act of 2002, Pub. L. 107–296, 116 Stat. 2135, Nov. 25, 2002.*

Illegal Immigration Reform and Immigration Responsibility Act of 1996, Pub. L. 104–208, Div. C, 110 Stat. 3009, Sept. 30, 1996.*

Immigration Act of 1990, Pub. L. 101–649, 104 Stat. 4978, Nov. 29, 1990.*

Immigration Act of 1990 (New York, NY: Matthew Bender, 1991) (special supplement to *Immigration Law and Procedures* which contains the text of the 1990 Act with explanation and analysis by Charles Gordon and Stanley Mailman).

The Immigration Marriage Fraud Amendments of 1986, Pub. L. 99–639, 100 Stat. 3537, Nov. 10, 1986.

Immigration and Nationality Act (Washington, DC: American Immigration Lawyers Assoc., annual softbound volume).

Immigration and Nationality Laws of the United States: Selected Statutes, Regulations, and Forms: As Amended to ... (T. Alexander Aleinikoff et al., St. Paul, MN: West Group, 1997–) (issued annually).*

Immigration Law Service (Anna Marie Gallagher ed., St. Paul, Minn.: Thomson West, 2004–) (multivolume looseleaf service with statutes, regulations, and instructions; updated quarterly).

Immigration Reform and Control Act of 1986, Pub. L. 99–603, 100 Stat. 3359, Nov. 6, 1986.

Personal Responsibility and Work Opportunity Reconciliation Act, Pub. L. 104–193, 110 Stat. 2105, Aug. 22, 1996

United States Department of Labor, Office of Administrative Law Judges, Immigration Collection, http://www.oalj.dol.gov/libina.htm.

Contains selected labor-related immigration statutes and regulations.

United States Department of State, *Foreign Affairs Manual* (vol. 9 contains State Department interpretations and regulations on immigration and citizenship) (reproduced in *Immigration Law Service, supra, and Immigration Law and Procedure, infra*; available at http://www.state.gov/m/a/dir/regs/fam/).*

Uniting and Strengthening America by Providing Appropriate Tools Required to Intercept and Obstruct Terrorism (USA PATRIOT ACT) Act of 2001, Pub. L. 107–56, 115 Stat. 280, Oct. 26, 2001.

§ 17–2   CASES AND DECISIONS

Bender's Immigration Case Reporter (New York, NY: Matthew Bender & Co., 1993–) (contains selected court cases and administrative agency decisions, updated monthly; formerly *Immigration Law and Procedure Reporter*).

BIA Index Decisions Reporter (Washington, DC: American Immigration Lawyers Assoc., 1986–1995) (4 issues/year; annual from 1986–89).

Federal Immigration Law Reporter (Washington, DC: Washington Service Bureau, 1983–1990) (contains selected court cases and administrative agency decisions).

Hein's Interim Decision Service (Buffalo, NY: W.S. Hein & Co., 1984–) (begins with #2951, Dec. 12, 1983) (contains all opinions and orders of the Att'y. General, Bd. of Immigration Appeals, and Comm. of Immigration and Naturalization Service).

Immigration Labor Certification Reporter (New York, NY: Matthew Bender & Co., 1981–1985) (contains selected court cases and administrative agency decisions).

Immigration Law and Procedure Reporter (New York, NY: Matthew Bender & Co., 1985–1993) (contains selected court cases and administrative agency decisions) (now *Bender's Immigration Case Reporter*).

LexisNexis: Area of Law—By Topic > Immigration (federal immigration statutes, court cases, administrative decisions, regulations, and treatises). Area of Law—By Topic > Immigration > Find Cases > Federal Immigration Cases; Area of Law—By Topic > Immigration > Find Cases > Federal Immigration Cases and Agency Decisions

The Michigan/Melbourne Refugee Caselaw Site (http://www.refugeecaselaw.org)

Summaries and text (in vernacular) of selected cases on asylum and refugee law from numerous asylum countries.

United States Board of Immigration Appeals, *Administrative Decisions Under Immigration and Nationality Laws* (23 vols., Washington, DC: U.S. Government Printing Office, 1940–)*(http://www.justice.gov/eoir/vll/intdec/lib_indecitnet.html (vols. 8–present)).

United States Board of Immigration Appeals, *Interim Decisions* (Washington, DC: U.S. Government Printing

Office, irregular; ceased 2000; continued online at http://www.usdoj.gov/eoir/vll/intdec/lib_indecitnet. html).

United States Department of Labor, Office of Administrative Law Judges, *Decisions of the Office of Administrative Law Judges and Office of Administrative Appeals* (Washington, DC: U.S. Government Printing Office, 1987–1993) (contains decisions concerning labor certification; see United States Department of Labor, Immigration Collection, *infra*).

United States Department of Labor, Office of Administrative Law Judges, Immigration Collection

Contains the full text of recent BALCA en banc decisions, Digest of BALCA PERM Decisions, and various other immigration-related DOL decisions.

United States Supreme Court (Cornell) (http://supct.law. cornell.edu/supct)

Access to Supreme Court decisions. Keyword searching is available.

Westlaw: combined federal immigration court cases (IM–CS) and combined administrative decisions (FIM–ADMIN).

§ 17–3 HISTORY

Edward P. Hutchinson, *Legislative History of American Immigration Policy, 1798–1965* (Philadelphia, PA: University of Pennsylvania Press, 1981).

IIRAIRA: Selected Legislative History of the Illegal Immigration Reform and Immigrant Responsibility Act of 1996 (Washington, DC: American Immigration Lawyers Assoc., 1997).

Nancy C. Montwieler, *The Immigration Reform Law of 1986: Analysis, Text, Legislative History* (Washington, DC: Bureau of National Affairs, 1987).

Edward E. Proper, *Colonial Immigration Laws* (New York, NY: AMS Press, Inc., 1967).

Selected Legislative History of the Immigration Act of 1990 (Washington, DC: American Immigration Lawyers Assoc., 1991) (including text of the 1990 Act).

Selected Legislative History of the Immigration Reform and Control Act of 1986 (Washington, DC: American Immigration Lawyers Assoc., 1987).

Oscar Trelles & James Bailey, *Immigration and Nationality Acts: Legislative Histories and Related Documents* (multivolume set with index; Buffalo, NY: W.S. Hein Co., 1979).

Voices from Ellis Island: An Oral History of American Immigration (Frederick, MD: University Publications of America, 1989).

Peter H. Wang, *Legislating Normalcy: The Immigration Act of 1924* (San Francisco, CA: R & E Research Associates, 1975).

§ 17–4 BOOKS, TREATISES, AND DIGESTS

Immigration & Nationality Law Handbook (Randy P. Auerbach ed., Washington, DC: American Immigration Lawyers Assoc., 1996–(vol. 1 Immigration Basics; vol. 2 Advanced Practice; issued annually)).

The AILA U.S. Consular Posts Handbook (Seymour Rosenberg ed., 13th ed., Washington, DC: American Immigration Lawyers Assoc., 2002) (now the *Visa Processing Guide and Consular Posts Handbook, infra*).

Grace E. Akers, *Navigating the Fundamentals of Immigration Law: Guidance and Tips for Successful Practice* (Washington, DC: American Immigration Lawyers Assoc., 2007–, issued annually).

Thomas Alexander Aleinikoff et al., *Immigration and Citizenship Process and Policy* (6th ed., St. Paul, MN: West Group, 2008).

Deborah E. Anker, *The Law of Asylum in the United States* (3d ed., Washington, DC: American Immigration Lawyers Assoc., 1999 and 2002 Supplement) (now published by the Refugee Law Center).

Annual Immigration and Naturalization Institute (New York, NY: Practising Law Institute, 1968–, annual).

Basic Immigration Law (New York, NY: Practising Law Institute, 1989–, annual).

M. Cherif Bassiouni, *International Extradition: United States Law & Practice* (5th ed., Dobbs Ferry, NY: Oceana, 2007).

Richard A. Boswell, *Essentials of Immigration Law* (Washington, DC: American Immigration Lawyers Assoc., 2009.)

Richard A. Boswell, *Immigration and Nationality Law: Cases and Materials* (4th ed., Durham, NC: Carolina Academic Press, 2010).

John L. Cable, *Decisive Decisions of United States Citizenship* (Charlottesville, VA: Michie Co., 1967).

David Carliner, *The Rights of Aliens and Refugees: The Basic ACLU Guide to Alien and Refugee Rights* (2d ed., Carbondale, IL: Southern Illinois University Press, 1990).

Robert C. Divine, *Immigration Practice* (Huntington, NY: Juris Publishing Co., 1997–, issued annually).

Diana Elles, *International Provisions Protecting the Human Rights of Non–Citizens*, U.N. Doc. E/CN.4/Sub.2/392/Rev.1 (1980).

Federal Procedural Forms, Lawyers Edition (Rochester, NY: Lawyers Co-operative Pub. Co., 1975–) (contains sample immigration law forms and includes references to statutes, court rules, administrative regulations, cases, law review articles, legal encyclopedia sections, and ALR annotations related to the subject matter of the forms).

Austin T. Fragomen et al., *Immigration Employment Compliance Handbook* (St. Paul, MN: West Group, 1999–, issued annually).

Austin T. Fragomen & Steven C. Bell, *H–1B Handbook* (St. Paul, MN: West Group, 1995–, issued annually).

Austin T. Fragomen & Steven C. Bell, *Immigration Fundamentals: A Guide to Law and Practice* (4th ed., New York, NY: Practising Law Institute, 1996–) (looseleaf).

Austin T. Fragomen et al., *Immigration Legislation Handbook* (St. Paul, MN: West Group, 1997–, issued annually).

Austin T. Fragomen et al., *State Immigration Compliance Handbook* (St. Paul, MN: Thomson/West, 2009–, issued annually).

Anna Marie Gallagher & Maria Baldini–Potermin, *Immigration Trial Handbook* (St. Paul: Thomson/West, c2008–).

Regina Germain, *AILA's Asylum Primer* (6th ed. Washington, DC: American Immigration Lawyers Assoc., 2010).

Guy S. Goodwin–Gill & Jane McAdam, *The Refugee in International Law* (3d ed., New York, NY: Oxford Univ. Press, 2007).

Charles Gordon & Stanley Mailman, *Immigration Law and Procedure* (2d rev. ed., New York, NY: Matthew Bender, 1988–) (formerly C. Gordon & S. Rosenfield) (multivolume looseleaf with case references, statutes, regulations, instructions, etc.).* [Also on LexisNexis].

Hurst Hannum, *The Right to Leave and Return in International Law and Practice* (Dordrecht, Neth.: Martinus Nijhoff Publishers, 1987).

Bill Ong Hing, *Handling Immigration Cases* (2d ed., New York, NY: Aspen Publishers, 1995, with 2000 supp.) (2 vols.).

Sarah B. Ignatius & Elisabeth S. Stickney, *Immigration Law and the Family* (New York, NY: Thomson West, 1995–, looseleaf, updated annually).

Dan Kesselbrenner & Lory D. Rosenberg, *Immigration Law and Crimes* (St. Paul, Minn.: West Group, 2002–).

Ira J. Kurzban, *Kurzban's Immigration Law Sourcebook* (12th ed., Washington, DC: American Immigration Lawyers Assoc., 2010, published every two years).*

Daniel Levy & Nat'l Immigration Project of the Nat'l Lawyers Guild, *U.S. Citizenship and Naturalization Handbook* (St. Paul, MN: West Group, 1999–, annual softcover volume).

A Legal Guide for INS Detainees: Petitioning for Release from Indefinite Detention (Washington, DC: American Bar Association, 2002).

Stephen H. Legomsky & Cristina M. Rodríguez, *Immigration and Refugee Law and Policy* (5th ed., Westbury, NY: Foundation Press, Inc., 2009, 2010 Update).

Richard Lillich, *The Human Rights of Aliens in Contemporary International Law* (Manchester, U.K.: Manchester University Press, 1984).

Charles M. Miller et al., *Immigration Law in the Workplace* (Austin TX: Aspen Publishers, 2009–).

Karen Musalo, Jennifer Moore & Richard A. Boswell, *Refugee Law and Policy: A Comparative and International Approach* (3d ed. Durham, NC: Carolina Academic Press, 2007).

National Lawyers Guild, *Immigration Law and Defense* (3d ed., New York, NY: Clark Boardman Callaghan, 1988–) (2 vols. looseleaf, updated semi-annually).

Pravinchandra J. Patel, *Patel's Citations of Administrative Decisions Under Immigration and Nationality Laws* (annual, New York, NY: Legal Research Bureau, 1982–).

Pravinchandra J. Patel, *Patel's Immigration Law Digest: Decisions from 1940* (Rochester, NY: Lawyers Co-operative Pub. Co., 1982–1998) (2 vols. looseleaf).

Juan Perea, *Immigrants Out!: The New Nativism and the Anti-Immigrant Impulse in the United States* (New York, NY: New York University Press, 1997).

Records of the Immigration and Naturalization Service (Alan M. Kraut, ed., Bethesda, MD: United Publications of America, 1991–1997) (microfilm).

Michael A. Scaperlanda, *Immigration Law: A Primer* (Washington, D.C.: Federal Judicial Center, 2009) (http://purl.access.gpo.gov/GPO/LPS121690).

Gerald Seipp, *Asylum Case Law Sourcebook* (9th ed. St. Paul, MN: West Group, 2009).

Shepard's Immigration and Naturalization Citations (Colorado Springs, CO: Shepard's/McGraw–Hill, 2d. ed. 1991–) (also on LexisNexis).

Gregory H. Siskind et al., *J Visa Guidebook* (2 vols., New York, NY: Matthew Bender & Co., 2010, annual editions).

Richard D. Steel, *Steel on Immigration Law 2d* (St. Paul, MN.: West Group, 2002–) (multi-volume looseleaf set).

United Nations High Commissioner For Refugees, *Collection of International Instruments & Other Legal Texts Concerning Refugees and Other Displaced Persons* (2007) (4 vols., vol. 1 International Instruments: UNHCR, Refugees and Asylum, Statelessness, Internally Displaced Persons, Migrants, Human Rights; vol. 2 International Instruments: International Humanitarian Law, International Criminal Law, International Maritime and Aviation Law, Miscellaneous; vol. 3 Regional Instruments: Africa, Middle East, Asia, Americas; vol. 4 Regional Instruments: Europe.)

Available at http://www.unhcr.org/455c460b2.html.

United Nations High Commissioner for Refugees, *Conclusions on the International Protection of Refugees*, HCR/IP/2/Eng/Rev.1994 (1994) (no new volume has been issued since 1998).

Available at http://www.unhcr.org.

United Nations High Commissioner for Refugees, *Handbook on Procedures and Criteria for Determining Refugee Status*, U.N. Doc. HCR/IP/4/Eng/Rev.2 (1992). (The Handbook is available in English, French, and Spanish at http://www.unhcr.org.)

United Nations High Commissioner for Refugees, *United Nations Resolutions and Decisions relating to the Office of the United Nations High Commissioner for Refugees*, U.N. Doc. HCR/INF.49/Add.4 (1993). (This publication has been discontinued since all of the documents are available on REFWORLD, *infra*.)

U.S. Citizenship & Immigration Services, *A Guide to Naturalization*, http://www.uscis.gov/files/article/M–476.pdf

General guide to naturalization, 58 pages.

United States Department of Labor, *Dictionary of Occupational Titles* (4th ed. rev., Washington, DC: U.S. G.P.O., 1991) (available at: http://www.oalj.dol.gov/libdot.htm). *

United States Department of Labor, Office of Administrative Law Judges, Immigration Collection, The Judges' Benchbook: Alien Labor Certification (2d ed. with supplements) (http://www.oalj.dol.gov/libina.htm).

United States Immigration Commission, *Reports* (Washington, DC: U.S. Government Printing Office, 1911) (41 vols.). *Visa Processing Guide and Consular Posts Handbook* (Washington, DC: American Immigration Lawyers Assoc., 2005–, annual).

David Weissbrodt, *The Human Rights of Non–Citizens* (Oxford, U.K.: Oxford Univ. Press, 2008).

David Weissbrodt, *The Rights of Non–Citizens*, U.N. Doc E/CN4/Sub.2/2003/23 (2003). Available at http://www.unhchr.ch.

§ 17–5 PERIODICALS

For articles about immigration law, policy, and procedure, the *Index to Legal Periodicals or Current Law*

Index (LegalTrac) should be consulted under the following headings: Emigration & Immigration; Deportation, Citizens & Citizenship; and Aliens. The following periodicals are of continuing interest in the area of immigration.

Annual Immigration and Naturalization Institute (New York, NY: Practicing Law Institute, 1967–).

Georgetown Immigration Law Journal (Washington, DC: Georgetown University Law Center, 1985–) (4 issues/year).

Immigration Briefings (Washington, DC: Federal Publications, 1988–) (monthly).

Immigration Business News & Comment (St. Paul, MN: West Group, 1999–) (biweekly; formerly *Immigration Law Report.*)

Immigration Law Advisory (Rochester, NY: Lawyers Cooperative Pub. Co.; Bancroft Whitney Pub. Co.; 1985–) (published 8 times per year as part of the Immigration Law Service).

Immigration Law Report (New York, NY: Clark Boardman Co., 1981–1999) (11 issues/year) (Continued by *Immigration Business News & Comment*).

Immigration and Nationality Law Review (Buffalo, NY: W.S. Hein & Co., 1977–) (annual).

INS Reporter (Washington, DC: Immigration and Naturalization Service, 1976–1989) (includes administrative decisions, C.F.R. changes, and statistics) (4 issues/year).

International Journal of Refugee Law (Oxford, U.K.: Oxford Univ. Press, 1989–) (4 issues/year).

International Migration Review (New York, NY: Center for Migration Studies, 1966–) (4 issues/year).

Interpreter Releases (New York, NY: American Council for Nationalities Service, 1924–) (weekly; good for articles and analysis of new rules and decisions).*

Journal of Refugee Studies (Oxford, U.K.: Oxford Univ. Press, 1988–) (4 issues/year).

Refugee Abstracts (Geneva, Switz.: Centre for Documentation for Refugees, UNHCR, 1982–1993) (4 issues/year).

Refugees (Geneva, Switz.: Office of the United Nation's High Commissioner for Refugees, 1984–) (monthly) (online at http://www.unhcr.org).

Siskind's Immigration Bulletin (http://www.visalaw.com/bulletin.html).

Provides access to the Immigration Bulletin through an index and keyword searching. Free email subscription also available.

Transnational Immigration Law Reporter (Palo Alto, CA: Immigration Common Law Exchange Society, 1979–1985) (covers international immigration problems) (monthly).

United States Immigration and Naturalization Service, Annual Report (Washington, DC: Immigration and Naturalization Service, 1946/47–2002).

Visa Bulletin (Washington, DC: U.S. Dept. of State, Bureau of Consular Affairs, 1968–) (lists availability of visas by country) (monthly) (available on the State Department website at http://travel.state.gov/visa/bulletin/bulletin_1360.html).*

§ 17–6   COUNTRY REPORTS

Listed below are the principal country materials for use with applications for political asylum. For further information, see David Weissbrodt, Fionnuala Ní Aoláin, Mary Rumsey, Marci Hoffman, and Joan Fitzpatrick, *Selected International Human Rights Instruments and Bibliography for Research on International Human Right Law* 722 (4th ed. 2009).

Amnesty International Report (London, U.K.: Amnesty International Publications, 1962–, annual) (from 1994–, available at http://www.amnesty.org/).*

Canadian Immigration and Refugee Board, National Documentation Packages (http://www.irb.gc.ca/eng/resrec/ndpcnd/Pages/index.aspx).

Country Reports on Human Rights Practices (Washington, DC: U.S. Government Printing Office, 1977–, annual) (reports for 2000 and later are on the current State Department Web site at http://www.state.gov/g/drl/rls/hrrpt; earlier reports are on the archived State Department Web site at http://www.state.gov/www/global/human_rights/hrp_reports_mainhp.html).

Critique: Review of the Department of State's Country Reports on Human Rights Practices for ... (New York, NY: Lawyers Committee for Human Rights & formerly Human Rights Watch, 1983–1996, annual).

Human Rights Watch, *World Report* (New York, NY: Human Rights Watch, 1990–, annual) (summaries available on the Human Rights Watch Web site at http://www.hrw.org).

International Religious Freedom Report (Washington, D.C.: U.S. Dep't of State), (http://www.state.gov/g/drl/rls/irf/).

Country Reports on Terrorism (formerly *Patterns of Global Terrorism*) (Washington, D.C.: U.S. Dep't of State), (http://www.state.gov/s/ct/rls/crt/).

Victims of Trafficking and Violence Protection Act of 2000: Trafficking in Persons Report (Washington, D.C.: U.S. Dep't of State), (http://www.state.gov/g/tip/rls/tiprpt/).

§ 17-7   BIBLIOGRAPHIES AND RESEARCH GUIDES

T.J. BeMent, *AILA's Guide to Technology & Legal Research for the Immigration Lawyer*, 3rd Edition (Washington, DC: American Immigration Lawyers Assoc., 2003).

Leah F. Chanin, Immigration Law, *in Specialized Legal Research*, Chapter 8 (Boston, MA: Little, Brown and Co., 1987–).

Claire M. Germain, Immigration Law, *in Germain's Transnational Law Research: A Guide for Attorneys* (Ardsley-on-Hudson, NY: Transnational Juris Pubs., 1991–).

Georgetown Law Library, CALS Asylum Case Research, (http://www.ll.georgetown.edu/guides/CALSAsylumLaw ResearchGuide.cfm).

Daniel J. Jacobs, *Immigration Reform and Control Act of 1986 and the Illegal Alien: A Selective Bibliography*, 50 Record 246 (1995).

Donatella Luca, *The 1951 Convention Relating to the Status of Refugees: A Selected Bibliography*, 3 International Journal of Refugee Law 633 (1991).

Elisa Mason, *Guide to Country Research for Refugee Status Determination* (2002) (http://www.llrx.com/features/rsd2.htm).

§ 17–8 ELECTRONIC SOURCES

Subscription–Based Sources

AILALink (Washington, DC: American Immigration Lawyers Assoc., frequent updates) (full-text immigration library including statutes, BIA decisions, and secondary sources).

IRIS (Immigration Resource and Information Service) CD–ROM (St. Paul, MN: West Group, quarterly updates) (full-text immigration library including statutes, BIA decisions, and secondary sources).

LEXIS Legal > Area of Law—By Topic > Immigration (federal immigration statutes, court cases, administrative decisions, regulations, and treatises).

LEXIS Legal > Legislation & Politics—U.S. & U.K. > U.S. Congress (federal bills, bill tracking, Congressional Record, legislative histories, and other information related to Congress).

WESTLAW (federal immigration statutes, court cases, administrative decisions, regulations, and other materials).

Web Sites

American Civil Liberties Union, Immigrants' Rights (http://www.aclu.org/immigrants-rights). ACLU immigration materials and information on immigration and civil liberties.

American Immigration Lawyers Association (http://www.aila.org).

Background information on immigration and this organization. Provides information about legislation, AILA's publications, and links to other relevant sites.

Immigration and Refugee Board of Canada (http://www.cisr.gc.ca).

This site has country of origin research information, other information on immigration and refugee issues in Canada, and links to other Canadian immigration information.

REFWORLD

REFWORLD is a collection of databases developed by the UNHCR Centre for Documentation and Research (CDR). REFWORLD contains authoritative information on refugees including current country reports, legal and policy-related documents and literature references. REFWORLD is available at http://www.unhcr.org/cgi-bin/texis/vtx/refworld/rwmain.

Thomas Legislative Information (http://thomas.loc.gov/home/thomas.html).

Provides timely access to pending legislation, status of bills, and recent enactments, legislative history; prepared by the Library of Congress.

Transactional Records Access Clearinghouse (http://trac.syr.edu)

Provides statistics relating to immigration detention and prosecutions

United States Citizenship and Immigration Services (US-CIS) [within the Department of Homeland Security (DHS)]. (http://www.uscis.gov/portal/site/uscis*).

BCIS processes all immigrant and non-immigrant benefits provided to visitors to the United States, including family-based petitions, employment-based petitions, asylum and refugee processing, naturalization, and document issuance and renewal.

United States Department of Homeland Security (DHS). (http://www.dhs.gov/index.shtm*).

Within DHS, the Directorate of Border and Transportation Security has responsibility for border security and the enforcement of immigration laws. BTS has absorbed the INS's Border Patrol agents and investigators, agents from the U.S. Customs Service, Transportation Security Administration and other enforcement personnel.

United States Department of State, Visa Services (http://travel.state.gov/visa/visa_1750.html*).

Information and notices on visas, the text of immigration legislation, and a variety of visa publications.

U.S. Department of State, Treaty Traders and Treaty Investors (http://travel.state.gov/visa/temp/types/types_1273.html).

Information on special visas for non-citizens coming to the U.S. in connection with substantial trade or investments.

University of Minnesota Human Rights Library (http://www1.umn.edu/humanrts).

This site provides access to the full text of the most important human rights instruments and documents related to human rights. Documents from various international human rights organizations are available in full text. An extensive collection of human rights related links are also available.

INDEX

References are to Pages

ADJUSTMENT OF STATUS
See also Citizenship; Citizenship and Immigration Services (CIS), U.S.; Crimes; Legalization; Naturalization; Nonimmigrant Visas; Proof

Asylum, 408–10
Legalization, 24–27
Marriage, 227
Nonimmigrant to immigrant, 179–81, 227, 247
Relief from removal, 343–45
Refugees, 330
Unauthorized employment, bar to adjustment, 227, 247, 409
Visa waiver program, 193

ADOPTED CHILD
See Child

ADULTERY
See Good Moral Character

AFGHANISTAN (AFGHAN), 162

AFRICA, 2, 367, 430
African Charter on Human and Peoples' Rights, 418

AFRICAN-AMERICAN, 10

AGGRAVATED FELONY
See also Asylum; Bond; Citizenship; Crimes; Crimes of Moral Turpitude; Detention; Good Moral Character; Illegal Immigration Reform and Immigrant Responsibility Act (IIRIRA)

Asylum precluded, 398
Defending an accused, 288–89

†